INFORMATION TECHNOLOGY LAW

INFORMATION TECHNOLOGY LAW

Fifth Edition

IAN J. LLOYD

Professor of Information Technology Law and Director of the Center of Law, Computers and Technology, University of Strathclyde, Glasgow

OXFORD
UNIVERSITY PRESS

OXFORD

UNIVERSITY PRESS

Great Clarendon Street, Oxford OX2 6DP

Oxford University Press is a department of the University of Oxford.
It furthers the University's objective of excellence in research, scholarship,
and education by publishing worldwide in

Oxford New York

Auckland Cape Town Dar es Salaam Hong Kong Karachi
Kuala Lumpur Madrid Melbourne Mexico City Nairobi
New Delhi Shanghai Taipei Toronto

With offices in

Argentina Austria Brazil Chile Czech Republic France Greece
Guatemala Hungary Italy Japan Poland Portugal Singapore
South Korea Switzerland Thailand Turkey Ukraine Vietnam

Oxford is a registered trade mark of Oxford University Press
in the UK and in certain other countries

Published in the United States
by Oxford University Press Inc., New York

First edition 1993
Second edition 1997
Third edition 2000
Fourth edition 2004
Fifth edition 2008

British Library Cataloguing in Publication Data

Data available

Library of Congress Cataloging in Publication Data

Data available

Typeset by Newgen Imaging Systems (P) Ltd., Chennai, India
Printed in Great Britain
on acid-free paper by
Ashford Colour Press Ltd, Gosport, Hampshire

ISBN 978-0-19-929977-5

1 3 5 7 9 10 8 6 4 2

Preface

Opinions appear to vary whether the ancient Chinese invocation that a party should live in interesting times ought to be classed as a blessing or a curse. Anyone working in the field of information technology law may have similarly ambivalent feelings regarding their own lot. Whilst in most areas changes in the law occur at a slow and measured pace, scarcely a day goes by without some new technological development raising new issues to challenge accepted legal wisdom. Yesterday's knowledge readily becomes tomorrow's unanswered question. The plus side is that life is seldom boring, and increasingly there is the sense that information technology law is relevant to the issues which are troubling people and governments today. When half of the population can feel threatened by the loss of two CDs by the Department of Work and Pensions, it is clear that data protection legislation has moved from being what the author has described in previous editions as an 'unwanted and isolated statute' to something which no public or private sector organisation is likely to take lightly ever again.

This book is now in its fifth edition and is approaching twenty years of existence. So much has changed in most areas and one lesson I have learned is that prophecy is a difficult art. I do suspect that recent developments may signal something of a sea change in individuals' and the law's reaction to information. As mentioned above, data protection is no longer a Cinderella subject, and the passage of the Fraud Act 2006 should bring about an effective end to the conceptually interesting but legally sterile question of whether a machine can be the victim of deception. The *Gowers Report*, commissioned by the Treasury, makes a number of eminently sensible suggestions for updating of the principles and practices of the intellectual property system.

There is much to be frightened of in the future, and it is notable that Privacy International in their 2007 national privacy ranking survey places the United Kingdom (or at least England and Wales) in the category of surveillance society (for reasons which are not totally clear to a Scottish-based author, Scotland scores slightly better). There does seem to be something intellectually dishonest about the introduction of a system of voluntary ID cards that can work only if they become compulsory on at least a de facto basis. The hope may be that the dawning awareness of the importance of personal information might permeate even the most authoritarian recesses of government. Freedom is a multifaceted topic and no reasonable person would argue against freedom encompassing the ability to live life free from crime or terrorism.

Any book is the product of more than a single author, something of which copyright law perhaps takes insufficient account. At the end of the process of completing a new edition, it is a pleasant task to make some small recognition towards the people who have contributed so generously towards the work. At the academic level, I would like to thank Catherine Colston and Konstantinos Komaitis, who share IT law teaching at Strathclyde University. Thanks also to Richard Susskind, Steve Saxby, and Andreas Wiebe for their help and support over the years and to Christopher Millard for taking time out of an impossibly busy life to read and comment upon the data protection chapters. I would like to give a special word of thanks to the book's commissioning editor at Oxford University Press, Ruth Ballantyne, for encouragement and help at times when I doubted that the work would ever be completed. Finally, not just thanks but love to Thomas, the best little boy in the world, and to James, who selflessly made sure that I had the opportunity to at least think about ideas for the book whilst trying to persuade him that 1, 2, 3, and 4 o'clock in the morning were times for sleep rather than for games. Unfortunately, he is proving a slow learner in this respect—or more likely I am a bad teacher. And Moira, I love you very much.

Ian Lloyd
2008

Outline contents

PART I PRIVACY AND DATA PROTECTION

PART II COMPUTER-RELATED CRIME

Detailed Contents

List of Figures

List of Tables

Table of Cases

Table of Statutes

Table of Statutory Instruments

Table of European Legislation

Regulations

Table of Conventions and Other Enactments

PART I

PRIVACY AND DATA PROTECTION

1

Privacy, technology, and surveillance

Introduction

Today, much is written and spoken about the increasing level of surveillance which permeates almost all aspects of our lives, with the consequential dimunition of personal privacy. The Information Commissioner, who is responsible for the enforcement of the United Kingdom's data protection and freedom of information legislation, warned in 2004 against the dangers of 'sleepwalking into a surveillance society'.[1] Introducing the report, *A Surveillance Society*,[2] commissioned by his Office and published in November 2006, the Information Commissioner went further:

> Today I fear that we are in fact waking up to a surveillance society that is already all around us. Surveillance activities can be well-intentioned and bring benefits. They may be necessary or desirable—for example to fight terrorism and serious crime, to improve entitlement and access to public and private services, and to improve health-care. But unseen, uncontrolled or excessive surveillance can foster a climate of suspicion and undermine trust. As ever more information is collected, shared and used, it intrudes into our private space and leads to decisions which directly influence people's lives. Mistakes can also easily be made with serious consequences—false matches and other cases of mistaken identity, inaccurate facts or inferences, suspicions taken as reality, and breaches of security.[3]

Concern at these privacy implications of information technology was expressed by Lord Hoffmann when delivering his judgment in the House of Lords in the case of *R v Brown*:

> My Lords, one of the less welcome consequences of the information technology revolution has been the ease with which it has become possible to invade the privacy of the individual. No longer is it necessary to peep through keyholes or listen under the

---

[1] <http://news.bbc.co.uk/1/hi/uk_politics/6260153.stm>

[2] <http://www.ico.gov.uk/upload/documents/library/data_protection/practical_application/surveillance_society_full_report_2006.pdf>

[3] <http://www.ico.gov.uk/upload/documents/pressreleases/2006/waking_up_to_a_surveillance_society.pdf>

eaves. Instead, more reliable information can be obtained in greater comfort and safety by using the concealed surveillance camera, the telephoto lens, the hidden microphone and the telephone bug. No longer is it necessary to open letters, pry into files or conduct elaborate inquiries to discover the intimate details of a person's business or financial affairs, his health, family, leisure interests or dealings with central or local government. Vast amounts of information about everyone are stored on computers, capable of instant transmission anywhere in the world and accessible at the touch of a keyboard. The right to keep oneself to oneself, to tell other people that certain things are none of their business, is under technological threat.[4]

The potential dangers were further considered by Lord Browne-Wilkinson VC in *Marcel v Metropolitan Police Commissioner*.[5] Documents belonging to the plaintiff had been seized by the police in the course of a criminal investigation. Civil proceedings were also current in respect of the same incidents, and a subpoena was served on behalf of one of the parties to this litigation seeking disclosure of some of these documents. Holding that the subpoena should be set aside, the judge expressed concern that:

> ...if the information obtained by the police, the Inland Revenue, the social security offices, the health service and other agencies were to be gathered together in one file, the freedom of the individual would be gravely at risk. The dossier of private information is the badge of the totalitarian state.[6]

As indicated in the above passage, an appropriate balance between privacy—classically expressed in terms of the right to be left alone—and surveillance—representing the wish to discover information about another, is difficult to define. Although initially appearing as opposites, privacy and surveillance are linked almost as if they were conjoined twins.

A wide range of surveys of public opinion evidence strong support for the protection of privacy. Although many of these derive from the United States, in the United Kingdom, the Information Commissioner has commissioned annual surveys of public opinion. In the annual report for 2000, the then Commissioner noted:

> Respondents were read a list of issues and asked to say how important they think each is. The proportion who thought that protecting peoples' rights to personal privacy was very important increased but not significantly from 73% to 75%. In terms of people's hierarchy of priorities the issue remains extremely important. Again only Crime Prevention and Improving Standards of Education are thought to be more important issues by the public.

Subsequent surveys have adopted a different formulation, more closely linked to the Information Commissioner's remit, by asking for respondents' views concerning

---

[4] [1996] 1 All ER 545 at 555–56.

[5] [1992] Ch. 225.

[6] [1992] Ch. 225 at 240. This quotation is also of considerable relevance to the emerging practice of data matching, which is considered more fully below.

Table 1.1 Concerns with issues of social importance

Concerned	2004	2005	2006
Preventing crime	85%	88%	93%
The National Health Service	78%	83%	90%
Equal rights for everyone	69%	81%	85%
Protecting people's personal information	70%	83%	83%
National security	71%	78%	82%
Improving standards in education	76%	84%	81%
Protecting freedom of speech	67%	80%	81%
Environmental issues	66%	74%	77%
Unemployment	50%	70%	72%
Access to information held by public authorities	48%	66%	68%

the importance of protecting personal information. The answers, however, have remained fairly constant. Table 1.1 contains the results from the 2006 survey.[7]

Whilst it would be an exceptional person who placed no value upon privacy, significant difficulties have to be overcome in the attempt to give the concept a concrete legal meaning. First, it is undoubtedly the case that different people and societies have widely varying interpretations as to which matters are private and which reasonably belong in the public arena. Millions of (mainly) younger people place details of their lives on social networking websites such as 'MySpace'[8] or 'Facebook'.[9] In many cases, the level of detail exposed appears excessive to those of an older generation.[10] Celebrities may court and value a greater degree of attention than the average person would find tolerable, although as cases such as *Campbell v MGN*[11] and *Douglas v Hello*[12] illustrate, even celebrities draw distinctions between public and private life. Those living in close-knit communities may accept that their every action will be known to and commented upon by others. City-dwellers may expect much more in the way of freedom from observation but this may carry with it the spectre of the lack of interest and concern.

At a societal level, the United Kingdom is noted for attaching great value to privacy in respect of dealings with the tax system. In Sweden, by way of contrast, information about tax returns is a matter of public record. This is reported to have produced problems for the authorities at the time when the pop group Abba was at the height of its fame. Many thousands of fans discovered that they could readily obtain copies of their

---

[7] <http://www.ico.gov.uk/upload/documents/library/corporate/research_and_reports/2006_annual_tracking_report_individuals_final.pdf>
[8] <http://www.myspace.com/>
[9] <http://www.facebook.com/>
[10] See, for example, <http://nymag.com/news/features/27341/>
[11] [2005] UKHL 61.
[12] [2007] UKHL 21.

idols' tax returns (which included a photograph). Dealing with the demand for copies is claimed to have brought the system close to meltdown. Even in the age of freedom of information legislation, it is difficult to envisage such a scenario being acceptable to the average British citizen. As perhaps an anecdote, however, whilst traditional forms of publication of financial information caused little stir, the emergence of a website, 'Ratsit.se', pushed even Swedish notions of openness to their limits when it started publishing financial details obtained from the national tax authority on its website, from where they could be accessed by anyone free of charge. The service proved popular, with about 50,000 searches being made each day. Many, it appears, were made by individuals curious to know details about their friends and neighbours. Whilst most might have hesitated to make a personal visit or request to the tax authorities for the data, the anonymity associated with web searches proved attractive. Numerous complaints were made to the Swedish data protection authorities. The tax authorities indicated to the website owners that, whilst Swedish freedom of information law obliged them to supply tax data, it did not require that it be supplied in electronic form. Provision of the data in paper form would have involved a massive effort to convert documents into electronic formats. Faced with this prospect, the site was reorganised. From June 2007, access could be obtained only upon payment of a fee and in line with the principles applying in respect of Swedish credit reference agencies, the subject would be informed of the fact that a request had been made and of the identity of the requesting party.

Whilst surveillance is often seen as involving the surreptitious and unwelcome collection of personal data, this is not always the case. Although individuals may claim to value privacy, they frequently appear to do little to protect themselves. Hundreds of thousands of individuals have applied for supermarket 'loyalty cards'. Such cards provide an invaluable point of linkage between details of individual transactions and the more generic stock management computer systems which have long been a feature of retail life. The seller now knows not only what has been bought but also who has bought it, when, in conjunction with what other products, and what form of payment has been tendered. Analysis of the information will reveal much about the individual's habits and lifestyle which may be used as the basis for direct marketing, targeted at the individual customer.[13] Again, many thousands of individuals respond to lifestyle questionnaires which may be delivered either as a mailshot or accompanying a magazine. In return for the chance to win what are often low-value prizes, respondents freely disclose all manner of items of personal information.[14]

Privacy and the law

The classical legal definition of privacy is attributed to a United States judge, Judge Cooley, who opined that it consists of 'the right to be let alone'. A considerable number

---

[13] For an excellent collection of links to materials on this topic see <http://www.amadorbooks.com/nocardsg.htm>

[14] See, for example, <https://www.homeofresearch.com/Index.aspx>

of other definitions have been formulated over the years. A number of these were cited in the Report of the Committee on Privacy.[15] The essential component, at least for the purposes of the present book, may be stated in terms that an individual has the right to control the extent to which personal information is disseminated to other people.

This notion, which is often referred to as involving 'informational privacy', has two main components. The first concerns the right to live life free from the attentions of others, effectively to avoid being watched. This perhaps is the essence of privacy as a human condition or state. Once a third party has information, the second element comes into play, with the individual seeking to control the use to which that information is put and, in particular, its range of dissemination.

The post-Second World War expansion of rights to privacy

Notions of a right to privacy have formed a feature of many domestic laws for decades and even centuries. Generally, however, rights to privacy would be rooted in a number of other legal concepts. In the United States, for example, the right of privacy has been seen as emerging from a range of constitutionally guaranteed protections. As was stated by Mr Justice Douglas in the case of *Griswold v Connecticut*:

> Various guarantees create zones of privacy. The right of association contained in the penumbra of the First Amendment is one, as we have seen. The Third Amendment in its prohibition against the quartering of soldiers 'in any house' in time of peace without the consent of the owner is another facet of that privacy. The Fourth Amendment explicitly affirms the 'right of the people to be secure in their persons, houses, papers, and effects, against unreasonable searches and seizures.' The Fifth Amendment in its Self-Incrimination Clause enables the citizen to create a zone of privacy which government may not force him to surrender to his detriment. The Ninth Amendment provides: 'The enumeration in the Constitution, of certain rights, shall not be construed to deny or disparage others retained by the people.'[16]

This expansive basis for the right to privacy has resulted in the doctrine being held applicable to an extensive range of situations, including forming the basis of the seminal Supreme Court ruling in the case of *Roe v Wade*,[17] which established a constitutional right to abortion.

In the aftermath of the Second World War, the concept of human rights began to be recognised at an international level. In 1948, the General Assembly of the United Nations adopted the Universal Declaration of Human Rights. This proclaimed in Article 12 that:

> No one shall be subjected to arbitrary interference with his privacy, family, home or correspondence, nor to attacks upon his honour and reputation. Everyone has the right to the protection of the law against such interference or attacks.

---

[15] Available from <http://itlaw.law.strath.ac.uk/readingqxq/infosec/commitee.html>
[16] (1965) 381 United States 479 at 484.
[17] 410 United States 113.

Although influential, the Universal Declaration has no binding legal force. Such an instrument was not long delayed. In 1949, the Council of Europe was established by international treaty. Its stated goals include the negotiation of agreements with the aim of securing 'the maintenance and further realisation of human rights and fundamental freedoms'.[18] One of the first actions undertaken within the Council was the negotiation of the Convention for the 'Protection of Fundamental Rights and Fundamental Freedoms' (European Convention on Human Rights, ECHR). The ECHR was opened for signature in November 1950 and entered into force in September 1953. As the Preamble to the ECHR states, the signatory states reaffirmed:

> ...their profound belief in those fundamental freedoms which are the foundation of justice and peace in the world and are best maintained on the one hand by an effective political democracy and on the other by a common understanding and observance of the human rights upon which they depend...

Of the many rights conferred by the ECHR, Article 8 is of particular relevance in the present context. This provides that:

1. Everyone has the right to respect for his private and family life, his home, and his correspondence.

2. There shall be no interference by a public authority with the exercise of this right except such as is in accordance with the law and is necessary in a democratic society in the interests of national security, public safety or the economic well-being of the country, for the prevention of disorder or crime, for the protection of health or morals, or for the protection of the rights and freedoms of others.

Although the second paragraph of Article 8 is couched in terms relating to interference by public authority, the jurisprudence of the ECHR has established that the obligation imposed upon Member States is to ensure that private and family life is protected by law against intrusions by any person or agency, whether within the public or the private sector. In the case of *Hatton v United Kingdom*,[19] the court referred to the existence of 'a positive duty on the State to take reasonable and appropriate measures to secure the applicants' rights under Article 8 § 1 of the Convention'.

The term, 'private life', is not defined further in the Convention. As with the United States concept of privacy, the term has been broadly interpreted by the ECHR, which was established to supervise the state's compliance with the Convention's requirements. In one important respect, the Convention right goes beyond the United States notion of privacy. In the United States, a critical distinction exists between activities taking place on private property and those in public (or semi-) public places. The European notion of private life is less tied to physical objects, and may protect

---

[18] Statute of Council of Europe, Article 1.
[19] (Application No. 36022/97) (2003) 15 BHRC 259.

individuals in respect of their activities in the public arena. In the case of *Halford v United Kingdom*,[20] the ECHR held that the protection of Article 8 extended to telephone conversations made by the applicant from her office phone. When her employers monitored the calls in the course of disciplinary proceedings against the applicant, the court ruled that there had been a breach of Article 8.

The recent case of *Copland v United Kingdom*[21] is also of considerable significance. Here, the applicant was employed at a college in Wales. The college's Deputy Principal formed a suspicion about her relationship with another individual and believed that the applicant was misusing college facilities for personal purposes. Although there was no direct monitoring of the content of calls, the communications records of both outgoing and incoming telephone calls were analysed. Monitoring and analysis extended also to Internet usage in the form of the locations of the websites viewed, together with the dates and duration of browsing activities. Details of the addresses of email messages were subjected to a similar process.[22] Arguing that there had been no breach of the applicant's rights under Article 8, the United Kingdom government claimed that:

> Although there had been some monitoring of the applicant's telephone calls, e-mails and internet usage prior to November 1999, this did not extend to the interception of telephone calls or the analysis of the content of websites visited by her. The monitoring thus amounted to nothing more than the analysis of automatically generated information to determine whether College facilities had been used for personal purposes which, of itself, did not constitute a failure to respect private life or correspondence.[23]

This contention was rejected by the court which, referring to its previous decision in *Halford*, held that email messages should be regarded in the same manner as telephone calls. Although in this case there was no monitoring of the content of either telephone calls or emails, the data recorded, it was held, constituted an 'integral element of the communications'.[24] In the absence of any warning having been given to the applicant of the possibility of monitoring, the conduct constituted a breach of Article 8.

In addition to expanding the scope of private life beyond the limits of private property, the jurisprudence of the ECHR has shown that the enforcement of the right to respect for private life imposes positive obligations encompassing the grant of access to at least some forms of personal data. In the case of *Gaskin v United Kingdom*,[25] the complainant, whose childhood had been spent in the care of Liverpool City Council, sought access in adulthood to a wide range of social work and medical records compiled during these years. At the time the request was made, the Data Protection Act

---

[20] 1997, 3 BHRC 31.

[21] [2007] ECHR 62617/00.

[22] At the time (around 1998–9) that the activities occurred, United Kingdom law made no provision regarding such conduct. The Telecommunications (Lawful Business Practice Regulations) 2000 made under the authority of the Regulation of Investigatory Powers Act 2000 would now apply to this form of activity.

[23] Para. 32.

[24] Para. 43.

[25] (1990) 12 EHRR 36.

1984 provided a right of subject access only in respect of data held in electronic format. Although the Council took significant steps to assist the complainant—in particular by seeking the consent of all those responsible for creating records to their disclosure—access was denied, save where positive consent was obtained.[26] Recognising that the grant of access to records containing personal data was an integral part of the requirements of Article 8, the court held that the United Kingdom was in breach of its obligations by failing to establish an appropriate mechanism for determining the extent to which access should be granted.

As demonstrated in *Gaskin*,[27] although the breadth of Article 8 rights offers benefits for individuals, it also suffers from an inevitable lack of precision, especially in situations where conflict arises between competing claims. Building on the general principles, a trend emerged within Western Europe during the last third of the twentieth century for the introduction of data protection laws concerned specifically with the issues arising from the processing of personal data. One of the major concerns was that the capability of the computer to store, process, and disseminate information posed significant threats to the individual's ability to control the extent to which personal information was disseminated and the uses to which it might be put.

A linkage has frequently been drawn between the general right to privacy and the notion of informational privacy. This is clearly seen, both in the Council of Europe Convention on the Automated Processing of Personal Data, and more recently and extensively in the text of the EC Directive 'On the Protection of Individuals with Regard to the Processing of Personal Data and on the Free Movement of Such Data',[28] which makes no fewer than fourteen references to the noun 'privacy'. Article 1 of the Directive is explicit:

1. In accordance with this Directive, Member States shall protect the fundamental rights and freedoms of natural persons, and in particular their right to privacy with respect to the processing of personal data.

The scope of these measures will be discussed in more detail in the following chapters.

Privacy and surveillance

One of the main ways in which privacy can be threatened is by the act of placing an individual under surveillance. Surveillance can take a variety of forms. Physical surveillance is as old-established as society. At an official level, it might involve placing individuals suspected of criminal conduct under surveillance, whilst at the private level, reference can be made to the nosy neighbour looking at life through the corner

---

[26] In some cases, consent was refused but in a majority of cases, the original author either could not be traced or failed to respond to the request. Effectively, silence was regarded as constituting refusal.

[27] *Gaskin v United Kingdom* (1990) 12 EHRR 36.

[28] Directive 95/46/EC, OJ 1995 L 281/31 (the Data Protection Directive).

of a set of lace curtains. In some instances, the success of surveillance may depend on its existence being unknown to its target. In other cases, the fact that conduct may be watched is itself used as an instrument for social control. As George Orwell described in his novel *1984*, the mere fact that people were aware that their activities might be subject to monitoring by the authorities would cause them to modify their behaviour, regardless of whether they were being watched or not.

Forms of surveillance

In 1971, Alan Westin in his seminal work, *Information Technology in a Democracy*,[29] identified three forms of surveillance:

physical;

psychological; and

data.

At that time, it may be suggested, clear distinctions could be drawn between the three categories.

Physical surveillance, as the name suggests, involves the act of watching or listening to the actions of an individual. Such surveillance, even making use of technology, has tended to be an expensive undertaking capable of being applied only to a limited number of individuals. In investigations subsequent to the 7 July 2005 bombings in London, it emerged that at least one of the bombers had come to the notice of the security services but had not been placed under surveillance. An intelligence source was reported as suggesting that MI5 considered that at the time of the London bombings in 2005, there were in the region of 800 Al Qaeda suspects, a figure which subsequently rose by a further 200. Whilst the security services tried to keep as many people under surveillance as possible, this was an extremely labour-intensive process, with the source suggesting that keeping a person under surveillance for twenty-four hours a day would require a team of between twenty and forty watchers. At the lower estimate, this would require MI5 to have 20,000 operatives. At the time in question, the total staff to cover all aspects of its work was in the region of 2,000.[30] Obviously—and as illustrated by the failure to monitor the actual bombers more closely—only a small proportion of identified suspects could be subjected to physical surveillance.

Examples of *psychological surveillance* include forms of interrogation or the use of personality tests, as favoured by some employers. Once again, logistical and cost constraints have served to limit the use of these techniques. The end product of any form of surveillance is data or information.

---

[29] Unir Microfilms Int., 1971.

[30] <http://scotland on sunday.scotsman.com/index.cfm?id=720032006.> The Intelligence and Security Committee made the same point in their report on the bombings (available from http://www.cabinetoffice. gov.uk/publications/reports/intelligence/isc_7july_report.pdf) although the precise numbers cited above were omitted for reasons of national security.

With both physical and psychological surveillance, an active role is played by the watcher. *Data surveillance* involves a different, more passive, approach. Every action of an individual reveals something about the person. Very few actions do not involve individuals in giving out a measure of information about themselves. This may occur directly, for example, in filling out a form, or indirectly, as when goods or services are purchased. The essence of data surveillance lies in the collection and retention of these items of information.

With the ability to digitise any form of information, boundaries between the various forms of surveillance are disappearing with the application of information technology linking surveillance techniques into a near seamless web of surveillance. Developments in data processing suggest that the distinction between informational and physical privacy is becoming more and more flimsy. The reach of systems of physical surveillance has been increased enormously by the involvement of the computer to digitise and process the information received.

Examples and consequences of data surveillance

As far back as 1972, in considering the threats to privacy resulting from computerised data processing, the Committee on Privacy identified the prospect that:

> Because the data are stored, processed and often transmitted in a form which is not directly intelligible, few people may know what is in the records or what is happening to them.[31]

In an information-based society, extensive details concerning the most trivial actions undertaken are recorded. In the context of e-commerce, an online bookshop will know, at least once customers have bought goods and accepted the presence of cookies on their computers, the title of every book which is examined and the nature of catalogue searches made. This can be linked to name and address details.

Perhaps the most noticeable and extensive surveillance tool is the closed circuit television camera (CCTV). It is a rare high street or even shop which does not have one or more cameras. It is estimated that there are in the region of 4.2 million CCTVs in the United Kingdom. With a population approaching 60 million, that equates to roughly one camera for every fourteen inhabitants of the country. Two million motorists are fined each year as a result of being caught by speed cameras. In general, it is estimated that the average person can expect to be 'caught' on camera around 300 times a day.[32]

Traditionally, CCTV systems have relied upon images being viewed and assessed by human operators. In at least some instances this is no longer the case. A nationwide system of Automatic Number Plate Recognition cameras is being installed on the United Kingdom's roads, scheduled for completion in 2008, by which time about 50 million number plates will be recorded each day[33] and compare against records

---

[31] *Report of the Committee on Privacy*, Cmnd 5012 (1972), at para. 130.
[32] <http://news.bbc.co.uk/1/hi/uk/6108496.stm>
[33] <http://www.telegraph.co.uk/news/main.jhtml?xml=/news/2006/11/02/nspy202.xml>

maintained by the Driver and Vehicle Licensing Agency and motor insurance companies to identify vehicles which are not taxed or insured. The system will also link with police databases to flag the appearance of any vehicle recorded as being of interest to the police.[34]

Even in the physical environment, trials are being conducted with image-recognition systems linked to CCTV cameras,[35] which can monitor the movements of specific individuals. One of the most extensive systems has been installed in the London Borough of Newham.[36] Here it has been reported that images from 150 cameras are compared against a database of around 100 known offenders maintained by the Council. If a targeted individual was identified by the system, the police would automatically be informed. The system, known as 'Mandrake', is claimed to be sufficiently sophisticated to defeat attempts to conceal identity by such tactics as wearing glasses or make-up, or even growing a beard. An accuracy rate of 75 per cent is claimed for the system,[37] although other sources have cast doubt on this figure.[38] The downside, of course, is that 25 per cent of those recorded on the system are innocent people who will be viewed with suspicion because of a false identification. In more recent developments, it has been reported that CCTV systems are being tested which use advanced monitoring techniques to assess the movements and actions of individuals within their range, with the aim of identifying behavioural patterns which might be regarded as suspicious. An example might be of a person who remains on an underground station platform for a considerable period of time, allowing a number of trains to arrive and depart without attempting to board it.[39]

Surveillance devices in the workplace allow employers to monitor the activities and efficiency of individuals. At a potentially extreme level, the United States Patent Office has published an application from Microsoft for a system which will monitor an employee's heart rate, body temperature, blood pressure, and movement. It is claimed that the system will automatically detect signs of stress or illness. Even the Internet and World Wide Web (WWW), which are often touted as the last refuge of individualism, might equally accurately be described as a surveillance system par excellence. An individual browsing the Web leaves electronic trails wherever he or she passes. A software program can transmit a tracer known as a 'cookie'[40] from a website to the

---

[34] Details of the system and its possible uses are given in a document, 'ANPR Strategy for the Police Service 2005–8', produced by the Association of Chief Police Officers and available from <www.acpo.police. uk/asp/policies/Data/anpr_strat_2005-08_march05_12x04x05.doc>

[35] As was reported in the *Independent*, 12 January 2004, more than 4 million CCTV cameras are in use in the United Kingdom. At a ratio of 1 camera to 15 people, this, it is claimed, makes the United Kingdom the 'most-watched nation in the world'.

[36] <http://www.bbc.co.uk/londonlive/news/july/cctv_170701.shtml>

[37] *Daily Mail*, 15 October 1998.

[38] The *Guardian* has published claims that the system had never identified a suspected individual. See <http://www.guardian.co.uk/Archive/Article/0,4273,4432506,00.html>

[39] <http://rinf.com/alt-news/contributions/mick-meaney/20-of-uk-cctv-could-judge-your-behaviour-within-3-years/614/>

[40] For information about the nature of these devices see <http://www.cookiecentral.com/faq.htm>

user's computer. Cookies can take a variety of forms and may retain details relating to the user's actions, either for the duration of a visit to a site or for a specified and potentially unlimited period of time.[41]

In terms of goods themselves, the ubiquitous barcode which facilitates identification of the product and its price at the checkout may be replaced by radio frequency identification tags (RFID). RFID tags, which are essentially a form of microchip, are capable of transmitting information, both prior to and after the point of sale. This would, for example, enable the movement of the object to be tracked, both in the store and also externally. One possibility which has been canvassed is that future generations of banknotes will have RFID tags embedded in them in order to enable movements of cash to be tracked with a view to countering money laundering. In respect of motor cars, the European Commission has launched a programme designed to specify standards for electronic vehicle identification (EVI). The programme, it is stated, aims to develop:

> an *electronic, unique identifier for motor vehicles*, which would enable a wealth of applications, many of them of crucial importance for the public authorities to combat congestion, unsafe traffic behaviour and vehicle crime on the European roads. It is clear that such an identifier as well as the communication means to remotely read it should be standardised and *interoperable* all over Europe.[42]

In the United Kingdom, it has been reported in a similar context that plans are being drawn up to fit all cars with a microchip which will monitor driving behaviour and automatically report a range of traffic offences, including speeding, road-tax evasion, and illegal parking.[43]

Examples of thickening information threads and trails are legion. Barely ten years ago, the only records compiled by United Kingdom telephone companies regarding telephone usage concerned the number of units (an amalgam of the time of day when a call is made, its duration, and its identification as local, long distance or international). Today, it is near universal practice to present users with itemised bills. These may provide considerable assistance to the person (or company) responsible for paying the bill in monitoring and controlling usage but they do also provide useful marketing information to the service provider, as well as raising issues concerning the privacy of other persons who might make use of the facility. Recent research conducted on behalf of BT illustrates well the issues involved. It is reported that 15,000 calls an hour are made from work phones to sex or chat telephone lines.[44] With mobile phones, even more data is recorded, with location data enabling the movements of the phone to be tracked with ever greater precision. Again, the widespread use of cash-dispensing

---

[41] A Report on Privacy on the Internet has been prepared for the European Commission Working Party on Data Protection and gives some interesting insights into the topic. The report is available from <http://www.europa.eu.int/comm/internal_market/privacy/docs/wpdocs/2000/wp37en.pdf>

[42] <http://europa.eu.int/comm/transport/road/roadsafety/its/evi/index_en.htm> (emphasis in original).

[43] *Sunday Times*, 24 August 2003.

[44] Cited on Ceefax (an electronic information service broadcast by the BBC), 21 July 2003.

machines allows the withdrawals of bank customers to be tracked on a real-time basis, both nationally and internationally.

There is no doubt that the world we inhabit today has changed and is changing at considerable speed. As well as being a commodity in its own right, data is the motor and fuel which drives the information society. A database with no data is a poor creature indeed and with the development of more and more sophisticated search-engine technologies, the value of a database lies increasingly in the amount of data held rather than the thought which lies behind the selection and organisation of material. The Internet and its use in academic life provides a very apposite example. There is no doubt that it provides teachers and students with access to a massively increased range of data. An author trying to track down a missing citation need often require only to submit a few words to a search engine such as 'Google' to be presented with the answer in seconds. More, however, does not always mean better. Excessive use of electronic resources will cause traditional research skills to atrophy, the availability of 100 electronic articles saying the same thing adds little to the reader's understanding of a topic—even making the charitable assumption that the articles are accurate in what they say. The tendency is to seek to find the answer before one has understood the question.

Similar issues arise in the wider world. Information is replacing knowledge and the change in terminology also indicates reliance on a more mechanistic- and statistical-based view of the world. An example can be seen in the increasing use of DNA technology for crime detection purposes. In the United Kingdom, aided by a policy of taking and retaining samples from everyone charged and convicted of even the most minor offence, the national police DNA database now contains over 2 million entries. This tool, as with most forms of scientific evidence, is based upon calculations of probability. Recent high-profile cases in the United Kingdom have shown up some of the failings of such an approach and, in particular, that technology is only as effective as those using it. The consequences for those wrongly identified and convicted on the basis of the misunderstanding of statistics has been profound and tragic.

Although we may challenge the efficacy of some of the models, there is no doubt that the underlying principles of data protection matter more today than ever before. With developments in data processing and other forms of technology, there is the potential for every movement we make to be tracked and recorded. There is a well-established tradition of providing for necessary exceptions from the strict application of data protection principles in the context of national security and crime prevention and detection. These have been applied in the context of specific investigations and with the attempt made to secure a reasonable balance between the interests of the state and of individuals. With a move towards reliance upon databases, whether of DNA samples or other forms of information, there has been a significant shift in the nature of policing, from the attempt to find evidence linking an individual with an offence, to one where an individual is sought whose profile fits that of a suspected offender. In many cases, such an approach is justified but, as will be discussed in the final section of this chapter, the perceived and accepted need to defeat terrorism is leading to the removal of some data protection safeguards, with little being put in place to replace these. As with all aspects of design, unless components are included at an early stage, it is more difficult and expensive to incorporate them at a later stage.

Many of the recorded instances of the misuse of information have occurred, not as part of the original design, but as a by-product of the fact that the information is available. The story has been told of how the elaborate population registers maintained by the Dutch authorities prior to the Second World War (no doubt with the best possible motives) were used by the invading Germans to facilitate the deportation of thousands of people.[45] In this case, as in any similar case, it is clear that it was not the information per se that harmed individuals, but rather the use that was made of it. In this sense, information is a tool, but a very flexible tool; and whenever personal information is stored, the subject is to some extent 'a hostage to fortune'. Information which is freely supplied today, and which reflects no discredit in the existing social climate, may be looked upon very differently should circumstances change. It may, of course, be questioned how far any legal safeguards may be effective in the situation of an external invasion or unconstitutional usurpation of power. In discussions on this point in Sweden it has been suggested that:

> Under a threat of occupation there may be reason to remove or destroy computer installations and various registers in order to prevent the installations or important information from falling into enemy hands. An enemy may, for example, wish to acquire population registers and other records which can assist his war effort. There may be reason to revise the plans as to which data processing systems should be destroyed or removed in a war situation.[46]

Whilst such plans and procedures might appear to afford protection against the possibility of outside intervention, it must be recognised that, in the past, the use of personal information as a weapon against individuals has not been the exclusive province of totalitarian states. Again, during the Second World War, the United States government used information supposedly supplied in confidence during the Census to track down and intern citizens of Japanese ancestry.[47] More recently, it has been reported that the United States Selective Service system purchased a list of 167,000 names of boys who had responded to a promotion organised by a chain of ice-cream parlours offering a free ice cream on the occasion of their eighteenth birthday. This list of names, addresses, and dates of birth was used in order to track down those who had failed to register for military service.[48] Such practices illustrate, first, the ubiquitous nature of personal information; and, second, that no clear dividing line can be drawn between public- and private-sector users, as information obtained within one sector may well be transferred to the other.

---

[45] F. W. Hondius, *Emerging Data Protection in Europe* (Amsterdam, 1975).
[46] *Transnational Data Report*, vol. 1, no. 5 (1978), p. 17.
[47] W. Petersen, *Japanese Americans* (New York, 1971).
[48] *Transnational Data Report*, vol. 10, no. 4 (1987), p. 25.

At a slightly less serious level, it was reported in the United Kingdom that information supplied in the course of the 1971 Census describing the previous occupations of respondents was passed on to health authorities, who used it to contact retired nurses with a view to discovering why they left the profession and to encourage them to consider returning to work.[49] Whilst it may be argued that no harm was caused to the individuals concerned by the use to which this information was put, it provides further evidence of the ubiquitous nature of information, and of the ease with which information supplied for one purpose can be put to another use.

Informational privacy after September 11, 2001

Great and tragic events invariably carry a lasting legacy and aftershocks from the events of September 11, 2001 continue to reverberate around the globe. The perception, true or false, that the Internet and forms of electronic communications are linked with the spread of global terrorism has impacted significantly on governmental attitudes to many of the issues discussed in this chapter and, indeed, throughout the whole of the field of information technology law. Of particular relevance to the present discussion is the extent to which changes have been made—and are being made—to the delicate balance between personal privacy and the interests of the government and also, of course, of society at large, in preventing the commission of terrorist offences. Many of the legislative responses to the threat of global terrorism, especially those within the United Kingdom, have been enacted with great speed, driven by perceived necessity but also carrying with them the risk of creating a chasm between those whose primary interest is in law enforcement and individuals and bodies concerned with the protection and promotion of individual rights and freedoms. Creative tension between different interest groups is inevitable and can produce benefits when there is a degree of acceptance that each group is acting in good faith. When creation turns to destruction, everyone loses and in many respects the present debate between civil libertarian lobbyists and governments has become sterile. Possible consequences are that individuals may lose some of the major elements of the protection introduced and developed over the past decades, whilst governments risk losing popular legitimacy if they are seen as being unconcerned with and threatening towards the rights of citizens.

Many significant legislative moves have been made in order to enhance the powers of law enforcement and national security agencies in the aftermath of September 11. Most of the aspects, such as increased powers of arrest and detention, are outside the scope of this book. For present purposes, the most important changes relate to increased rights of access to personal data.

The starting point of the analysis should be the EC Directive on Privacy and Electronic Communications.[50] As originally drafted, this Directive provides individuals with extensive guarantees of privacy in respect of data pertaining to their electronic

---

[49] D. Madgwick and T. Smythe, *The Invasion of Privacy* (London, 1974).
[50] Directive 2002/58/EC, OJ 2002 L 201–37.

communications. At a very late stage in the legislative process, however, and following the events of September 11, an amendment was accepted by the European Parliament permitting EU Member States to 'adopt legislative measures providing for the retention of data for a limited period justified on the grounds laid down in this paragraph'.[51] The grounds referred to include the safeguarding of 'national security ... defence, public security, and the prevention, investigation, detection and prosecution of criminal offences or of unauthorised use of the electronic communication system'. Even prior to the entry into force of the Directive, this power has been extensively used within the United Kingdom.

Initial legislative provisions date back to the Regulation of Investigatory Powers Act 2000, which empower a senior police office to require a communications provider to disclose any communications data in its possession where this is considered necessary in the interests of national security, the prevention or detection of crime, or a number of other situations.[52] The term 'communications data' is defined broadly to include traffic and location data, although, as has been stated by the Home Office:

> It is important to identify what communications data does include but equally important to be clear about what it does *not* include. The term communications data in the Act does not include the content of any communication.[53]

The Regulation of Investigatory Powers Act 2000 did not require that providers retain data, although concerns had been expressed that mobile-phone operators were retaining customer records for a period of months and in some cases years.[54] The conformity of this practice with the requirements of the Data Protection Act 1998 that:

> Personal data processed for any purpose or purposes shall not be kept for longer than is necessary for that purpose or those purposes...[55]

had been doubted. The passage of the Anti-Terrorism, Crime and Security Act 2001, which was rushed through Parliament in a matter of weeks, provided a legal basis for the retention of data. The Act conferred power on the Secretary of State to draw up a code of practice specifying periods of time during which communications providers would be required to retain communications data.[56] Although the Secretary of State was granted legislative power, it was envisaged that a voluntary code would be agreed between government and the communications industry. To date, however, negotiations have not produced agreement with industry concerns centring in large part on the cost implications of retaining large amounts of data. The leading service provider, AOL, for example, has estimated that it would require 36,000 CDs in order to store one year's supply of communications data relating to its customers with set-up costs of £30m and annual running costs of the same amount.

---

[51] Article 15.

[52] Section 22.

[53] Consultation Paper on a Code of Practice for Voluntary Retention of Communications Data (March 2003).

[54] See, for example, 'Liberties fear over mobile phone details', *Guardian*, 27 October 2001, reporting that the mobile network, Virgin, has retained all data from the establishment of its network in 1999.

[55] Schedule 1, fifth data protection principle.

[56] Section 102.

Initial proposals by the government for the establishment of a code of practice received heavy criticism, both in terms of the period of time within which data might require to be retained and the range of government agencies which might be granted access to this data. An initial draft code was withdrawn in July 2002 and a further draft was published in March 2003.[57] This restricted the range of agencies which might seek access to data but retains the requirement that data be retained for a period of twelve months.

Conclusions

Almost sixty years ago, the world was recovering from the trauma of global conflict. The negotiation of the Universal Declaration and the European Convention on Human Rights was regarded as a major legislative component of the road to recovery. The enhancement of individual rights was seen as the best response to the trauma of global terror. Today, the view appears to be that rights need to be restricted in order to defeat terror. Whilst it may, of course, be argued that a closer parallel is with the enactment of emergency legislation in time of war, the present situation is perhaps more akin to the image portrayed in George Orwell's novel *1984*, where a condition of perpetual and undeclared war existed between three power blocks, with shifting alliances and battles generally fought far from home but used as justification for repressive domestic policies.

Few issues in the field admit of easy answers. Any attempt to strike a balance between competing interests is difficult, especially in a fast-changing environment. Most would agree that law enforcement agencies should be provided with the best possible tools to enable them to perform their vital tasks. Data can constitute an extremely valuable investigative tool but the whole premise of data protection legislation over the decades has been that the potential for misuse is considerable. At least within a United Kingdom context, the main problem is perhaps a lack of awareness. If data were nuclear particles or perhaps even genetically modified foodstuffs, people would be aware of and respectful of the dangers involved in their use and transportation. The danger today is that data flows are invisible and when society becomes aware of the potential for misuse, it may be too late to put this technological genie back in the bottle.

Suggestions for further reading

Information Commissioner's Office (2006, and follow up document, May 2007), *A Surveillance Society* (Wilmslow).

WESTIN, A. (1971), *Information Technology in a Democracy* (Cambridge, MA).

---

[57] Available from <http://www.homeoffice.gov.uk/docs/consult.pdf>

2

The emergence of data protection

Introduction

As indicated in the previous chapter, a variety of concerns about the potential use and misuse of computers spawned a growing call for legislative intervention. Two general approaches can be identified. The first—as applied within the United States and perhaps the majority of countries in the world—adopts a sectoral approach, with a range of privacy protection statutes being enacted to regulate specific forms of information handling, generally regardless of whether data is processed by computer or manually. Examples from the United States include the Fair Credit Reporting Act 1970, which gives a right of access to information held by credit reference agencies, and the Privacy Act 1974, giving a right of access to certain records held by public agencies and placing restrictions on the use to which data may be put by these agencies. A considerable number of more sector-specific statutes also exist at both federal and state level.

On occasion, these statutes have been adopted in response to a specific instance involving the misuse of data. Thus, the Video Privacy Protection Act 1970 was enacted following an incident when the publication of video rental records indicating a penchant for pornographic films proved extremely damaging to the subject—a judge who had been nominated for appointment to the Supreme Court.[1] The Act prohibits the disclosure of identifiable rental information, except with the consent of the individual or in closely defined situations such as where required by a warrant issued to a law enforcement agency. As one commentator has suggested, 'the United States has a tendency to kneejerk reactions to issues which results in inconsistent, overlapping, situation-specific legislation'.[2]

A different approach has prevailed within Europe, where the tendency has been to enact omnibus data protection statutes regulating all (or almost all) instances where personal data is processed by computer. In terms of matters of substance, there is perhaps little difference between the privacy protection and data protection models. The major divergence exists at the level of enforcement. It has been commented that:

---

[1] <http://www.epic.org/privacy/vppa/>
[2] Clarke (2001), *Beyond the OECD Guidelines: Privacy Protection for the 21st Century*, available from <http://www.anu.edu.au/people/Roger.Clarke/DV/PP21C.html>

data protection rules only contribute to the protection of individuals if they are followed in practice. It is therefore necessary to consider not only the content of rules applicable to personal data transferred to a third country, but also the system in place to ensure the effectiveness of such rules. In Europe, the tendency historically has been for data protection rules to be embodied in law, which has provided the possibility for non-compliance to be sanctioned and for individuals to be given a right to redress. Furthermore such laws have generally included additional procedural mechanisms, such as the establishment of supervisory authorities with monitoring and complaint investigation functions. These procedural aspects are reflected in Directive 95/46/EC, with its provisions on liabilities, sanctions, remedies, supervisory authorities and notification. Outside the Community it is less common to find such procedural means for ensuring compliance with data protection rules.[3]

The first data protection statute was enacted in the German state of Hesse[4] in 1970, with the initial national statute being the Swedish Data Protection Act 1973. The fact that data protection laws were first introduced in these two countries may not be entirely a matter of coincidence, and also illustrates what might be classed as the positive and negative aspects of the system. In the case of Germany, there had been experience of totalitarian regimes and of the ease with which personal data might be misused. In seeking to place limits on the ability of public and private sector bodies to process personal data, the law can be seen as acting primarily in a defensive or negative manner. The Swedish situation was rather different. There was no background of totalitarianism, but, as referred to in the previous chapter, there was a more than two-century long tradition of freedom of information, under which almost any item of official information was considered to be in the public domain. By conferring rights on individuals to access information held on any computer, data protection could be seen as extending some of the concepts of freedom of information into the private sector.

International data protection initiatives

Although the first data protection laws were enacted on a national basis, even prior to these interventions, pressure had been exerted for international action in the field. In many respects, a comparison can be drawn with the first form of electronic data transfer made possible by the electric telegraph around the middle of the nineteenth century. Initially based on national networks, governments resisted international connection largely because of fears that messages against the national interest might be transmitted without the possibility for interception in transit. Within a very few years, international transfer agreements were adopted, firstly, on a unilateral basis, then between regional groupings, and, finally, from 1865, under the auspices of the International Telegraph Convention and Union, which formed the world's first

---

[3] Transfers of Personal Data to Third Countries: Applying Articles 25 and 26 of the EU Data Protection Directive; Article 29 Working Party, available from <http://ec.europa.eu/justice_home/fsj/privacy/docs/wpdocs/1998/wp12_en.pdf>

[4] The capital city of Hesse is Wiesbaden but its largest city is Frankfurt.

international organisation and laid the basis for the free transfer of data on a global basis.

The first national data protection statutes tended to have stringent provisions relating to the export of personal data. The Swedish Data Act of 1973 provided that:

> If there is reason to assume that personal data will be used for automatic data processing abroad, the data may be disclosed only after permission from the Data Inspection Board. Such permission may be given only if it may be assumed that the disclosure of the data will not involve undue encroachment upon personal privacy.[5]

Whilst such an approach might be justified in order to protect the interests of individuals, the 1970s also marked the period where developments in computers and communications technology rendered feasible a massive expansion in multinational organisations. Although these had existed for many years, activities tended to be restricted to activities such as car production, where assembly plants in different companies operated largely as independent freedoms. The year 1971 marked the opening of the first McDonald's restaurant in Europe.[6] The essence of this and similar businesses in the service sector is uniformity of product and identity across the globe. Such activities required the application of computer systems able to communicate across national boundaries.

It was quickly recognised that international solutions were required in order to reconcile the interests of individual privacy with commercial interests. It was accepted that impossible burdens could be placed upon multinational enterprises should they be required to comply with differing standards in every country in which they acquired, stored, processed, or even transferred data. This indeed remains a problematic issue, even following the adoption of the European Unions Data Protection Directive in 1995, which sought to harmonise national data protection laws.

From the late 1960s, a range of international agencies have been active in the field of data and privacy protection. At the initial stages, the most prominent actors were the Council of Europe and the Organization for Economic Cooperation and Development (OECD). The following sections will consider the major activities carried out under the auspices of these organisations. Brief attention will also be paid to work conducted under the auspices of the UN. During the 1990s, much of the focus—at least so far as relates to the impact upon the United Kingdom—switched to work within the EU and the slow progress towards the adoption of the Data Protection Directive.[7]

The Council of Europe

In 1968, the Parliamentary Assembly of the Council of Europe addressed a request to the Committee of Ministers that they consider the extent to which the provisions of the European Convention on Human Rights safeguarded the individual against the abuse

---

[5] Section 11.

[6] In Zaandam near Amsterdam in the Netherlands.

[7] Directive 95/46/EC.

of modern technology. The Assembly noted particular concern at the fact that the European Convention, together with its UN predecessor, the Universal Declaration of Human Rights, had been devised before the development and widespread application of the computer.

Whilst identifying the dangers of computer abuse, the Assembly's report also drew attention to a paradox which remains largely unresolved to this day. Data protection seeks to give an individual a greater measure of control over personal information and to place controls over the dissemination of this information. This approach may conflict with another individual's claim to be allowed access to information under the European Convention on Human Rights. Here it is provided that: [e]veryone has the right to freedom of expression. This shall include freedom to hold opinions and to receive and impart information and ideas without interference by public authority and regardless of frontiers.'[8] The conflict is well illustrated in cases such as *Campbell v Mirror Group Newspapars*[9] and *Douglas v Hello*,[10] where celebrities clashed with newspapers and magazines over the publication of photographs and stories about them. In both cases, the disputes went to the House of Lords, which delivered judgment for the complainants by slender 3:2 majorities.

Acting upon the Assembly's report, two separate resolutions were adopted by the Committee of Ministers, dealing with the private and the public sectors. The differences between the two sets of recommendations are comparatively minor, and for both sectors it was recommended that national laws should ensure that:

1. The information stored should be accurate and kept up to date. In general, information relating to the intimate private life of persons or information which might lead to unfair discrimination, should not be recorded or, if recorded, should not be disseminated.

2. The information should be appropriate and relevant with regard to the purpose for which it has been stored.

3. The information should not be obtained by fraudulent or unfair means.

4. Rules should be laid down or specify the periods beyond which certain categories of information should no longer be kept or used.

5. Without appropriate authorisation, information should not be used for purposes other than those for which it has been stored, nor communicated to third parties.

6. As a general rule, the person concerned should have the right to know the information stored about him, the purpose for which it has been recorded, and particulars of each release of this information.

---

[8] Article 10.

[9] [2004] UKHL 22 on appeal from [2002] EWCA Civ 1373 and [2002] EWHC 499 (QB).

[10] [2007] UKHL 21 on appeal from [2005] EWCA Civ 106 and [2005] EWCA Civ 595, [2005] EWCA Civ 861.

7. Every care should be taken to correct inaccurate information and to erase obsolete information or information obtained in an unlawful way.

8. Precautions should be taken against any abuse or misuse of information. Electronic data banks should be equipped with security systems which bar access to the data held by them to persons not entitled to obtain such information, and which provide for the detection of misdirections of information, whether intentional or not.

9. Access to the information should be confined to persons who have a valid reason to know it. The operating staff of electronic data banks should be bound by rules of conduct aimed at preventing the misuse of data and, in particular, by rules of professional secrecy.

10. Statistical data should be released only in aggregate form and in such a way that it is impossible to link the information to a particular person.[11]

To a very considerable extent, these principles remain at the heart of data protection laws to this day, although, as is the case with other general statements of good practice such as the Ten Commandments, the message needs continually to be redefined, both in the context of specific activities and in the light of changes in society and technology.

The initial Council of Europe resolutions did not attempt to prescribe the means by which Member States should give effect to the principles contained therein. As more and more European countries enacted data protection legislation, so too did the problems resulting from the international trade of information—frequently referred to as transborder data flows—become more acute. In an effort to minimise restrictions on the free flow of information, and in the hope of preventing major discrepancies between the national data protection laws, the Council of Europe moved beyond its earlier recommendations to sponsor the Convention for the Protection of Individuals with Regard to the Automatic Processing of Personal Data (hereafter, 'the Convention'). The Convention was opened for signature in January 1981 and was to enter into force when it was ratified by five Member States of the Council of Europe. This did not occur until October 1985. The Convention has been amended by an additional protocol, 'regarding supervisory agencies and transborder data flows', which was opened for signature in October 2001 and entered into force in July 2004. At the time of writing, 38 countries have ratified the Convention and 16 the additional protocol which strengthens the original provisions in the areas referred to. Although the Convention is open for signature by countries who are not members of the Council of Europe, to date, no non-Member State has done so.[12] The view has been expressed by several United States commentators that the provisions of the Convention were motivated more by considerations of commercial expediency and economic protectionism than by a genuine concern for

---

[11] Resolution (73)22.

[12] This may be contrasted with the Council of Europe's Convention on Cybercrime (discussed below), which has been signed by Canada, Costa Rica, Japan, Mexico, and South Africa, and signed and ratified by the United States.

individual privacy. In the course of a meeting of the Committee of Experts, the United States observer contrasted the sectoral approach adopted in that country with the omnibus data protection legislation envisaged under the Convention, and concluded that:

> ...the draft convention appears to regulate a function, that is, it appears to regulate automated or electronic data processing and what the automated data processing industry may do with records about individuals. To our mind the draft convention is, in essence, a scheme for the regulation of computer communications technology as it may be applied to personal data record-keeping. The establishment and exercise of individual rights and the privacy of the individual seem to be treated in a secondary fashion...I would note particularly that the word 'privacy' is rarely mentioned in the Convention and is not included in its title.[13]

This criticism is perhaps unfounded. The Convention is rooted in the European Convention of Human Rights and, indeed, in a number of states such as Spain and Germany, data protection has the status of a fundamental human right. Article 8 of the European Union's Charter of Fundamental Rights provides that 'Everyone has the right to the protection of personal data concerning him or her.' At present, the Charter does not have legal effect, but implementation of the EU Reform Treaty as successor to the ill-fated EU Constitution would give the Charter legal effect, although the United Kingdom has secured an opt-out from this provision.

In its Preamble, the Convention reaffirms the Council of Europe's commitment to freedom of information regardless of frontiers, and proceeds to prohibit the erection of national barriers to information flow on the pretext of protecting individual privacy.[14] This prohibition extends, however, only where the information is to be transferred to another signatory state. Impliedly, therefore, the Convention permits the imposition of sanctions against any non-signatory state, especially one whose domestic law contains inadequate provision regulating the computerised processing of personal data.[15] A recalcitrant state could effectively be placed in data quarantine. The standards required of domestic laws are laid down in Chapter 2 of the Convention, and its requirements will be considered in detail when considering the substantive aspects of data protection.

In addition to the Convention itself, the Council of Europe has adopted a substantial number of recommendations concerning the interpretation and application of the Convention principles in particular sectors, and in respect of particular forms of processing. The list below gives details of these instruments:[16]

Recommendation No R(2002) 9 on the protection of personal data collected and processed for insurance purposes (18 September 2002)

---

[13] Text of United States Department of State telegram, quoted in *Transnational Data Report*, vol. 1, no. 7 (1978), p. 22.

[14] Article 12(2).

[15] The additional protocol referred to above was drafted to bring the Convention into line with the EU's Data Protection Directive. It provides that data may be transferred to an external state only if that state guarantees an adequate level of protection. These issues will be considered in more detail in Chapter 8 below.

[16] The text of all these instruments can be obtained from <http://www.coe.int/T/E/Legal_affairs/Legal_co-operation/Data_protection/Documents/International_legal_instruments/2CM.asp>

Recommendation No R(99) 5 for the protection of privacy on the Internet (23 February 1999)

Recommendation No R(97) 18 on the protection of personal data collected and processed for statistical purposes (30 September 1997)

Recommendation No R(97) 5 on the protection of medical data (13 February 1997)

Recommendation No R(95) 4 on the protection of personal data in the area of telecommunication services, with particular reference to telephone services (7 February 1995)

Recommendation No R(91) 10 on the communication to third parties of personal data held by public bodies (9 September 1991)

Recommendation No R(90) 19 on the protection of personal data used for payment and other operations (13 September 1990)

Recommendation No R(89) 2 on the protection of personal data used for employment purposes (18 January 1989)

Recommendation No R(87) 15 regulating the use of personal data in the police sector (17 September 1987)

Recommendation No R(86) 1 on the protection of personal data for social security purposes

Recommendation No R(85) 20 on the protection of personal data used for the purposes of direct marketing (25 October 1985)

Recommendation No R(81) 1 on regulations for automated medical data banks (23 January 1981)

Recommendation No R(2002) 9 on the protection of personal data collected and processed for insurance purposes (18 September 2002)

Although some of the Recommendations are now somewhat dated and have no legal force, they provide useful guidance on how general statements of good practice might be applied in the context of concrete applications.

The Organization for Economic Cooperation and Development (OECD)

The second international agency which has been active in the field of data—or to use its preferred terminology, privacy protection—is the Organization for Economic Cooperation and Development (OECD). The OECD was established by international convention in 1960. Article 1 of the Convention sets out the aims of the organisation as being:

to promote policies designed:

(a) to achieve the highest sustainable economic growth and employment and a rising standard of living in Member countries, while maintaining financial stability, and thus to contribute to the development of the world economy;

(b) to contribute to sound economic expansion in Member as well as non-member countries in the process of economic development; and

(c) to contribute to the expansion of world trade on a multilateral, non-discrimina-
tory basis in accordance with international obligations.

Article 2 provides that in pursuit of these aims states are to:

(d) pursue their efforts to reduce or abolish obstacles to the exchange of goods and
services and current payments and maintain and extend the liberalisation of
capital movements.

The OECD currently has thirty members: Australia, Austria, Belgium, Canada, the
Czech Republic, Denmark, Finland, France, Germany, Greece, Hungary, Iceland,
Ireland, Italy, Japan, Korea, Luxembourg, Mexico, the Netherlands, New Zealand,
Norway, Poland, Portugal, the Slovak Republic, Spain, Sweden, Switzerland, Turkey,
the United Kingdom, and the United States.

Unlike other international organisations, the OECD functions as something of a
Members Club, with states wishing to join being required to satisfy the existing members as to their suitability. Discussions regarding possible membership are ongoing
with a number of countries, including Russia and China, and cooperative agreements
are in force with about seventy countries.[17] A Council consisting of representatives of
all the Member States is 'the body from which all acts of the organization derive'.[18]

The OECD's work in the field began in 1969 when a group of experts was appointed
to analyse 'different aspects of the privacy issue, e.g. in relation to digital information,
public administration, transborder data flows, and policy implications in general'.[19]
A further group was established in 1978 under Mr Justice Kirby, then Chairman of the
Australian Law Commission. The United States representatives also played a prominent
role in the group's activities and the resulting product in the form of a Recommendation
to Member States concerning Guidelines on the Protection of Privacy and Transborder
Data Flows was endorsed by the OECD Council in September 1980.

It was part of the group's remit that its 'work was to be carried out in close co-operation with the Council of Europe and the European Community'.[20] Although covering
much the same ground as the Convention, the Guidelines can perhaps be seen as a
common law-based approach to the issues, as opposed to the Convention which was
drafted very much in line with the civil law tradition. It has been suggested that:

> In the final result, although substantially similar in core principles, the Convention
> and the Guidelines could be analogised, albeit in a rough fashion, to the civil and
> common law approaches, respectively. Common law systems proceed pragmatically,
> formulating the rules of legal behaviour as they acquire experience, while the civil law
> tradition tends to rely upon codification of rules in advance of action.[21]

Whilst the Convention is a legally binding instrument, the Guidelines, as the terminology indicates, have no legal force.

---

[17] <http://www.oecd.org/pages/0,3417,en_36734052_36761800_1_1_1_1_1,00.html>
[18] Article 7.
[19] <http://www.oecd.org/document/18/0,3343,en_2649_34255_1815186_1_1_1_1,00.html>
[20] Ibid.
[21] L. Kirsch, 1 *Legal Issues of European Integration* (1982), 21 at 45.

A further Declaration on Transborder Data Flows was adopted by the OECD in April 1985. This made reference to the fact that:

> Flows of computerised data and information are an important consequence of technological advances and are playing an increasing role in national economies. With the growing economic interdependence of Member countries, these flows acquire an international dimension.

It also indicated its signatories' intention to:

1. *Promote* access to data and information and related services, and avoid the creation of unjustified barriers to the international exchange of data and information.

2. *Seek* transparency in regulations and policies relating to information, computer and communications services affecting transborder data flows.

3. *Develop* common approaches for dealing with issues related to transborder data flows and, when appropriate, develop harmonized solutions.

4. *Consider* possible implications for other countries when dealing with issues related to transborder data flows.

It is clear from these objectives that commercial and trading interests provide at least as significant a force for action as do concerns for individual rights. Although the Declaration commits its member countries to conduct further work relating to specific types of transborder data flows, especially those accompanying international trade, marketed computer services, and computerised information services and intra-corporate data flows, no further measures have been adopted.

In addition to its work in producing legal texts, the OECD has also sponsored the development of what is referred to as a privacy generator. This online package is intended to be used by website developers and others to incorporate procedures and safeguards to ensure that sites operate in conformity with the principles laid down in the Guidelines.[22]

The UN

On 20 February 1990, the United Nations' Economic and Social Council agreed to the Guidelines Concerning Computerised Personal Data Files.[23] These identify ten principles which, it is stated, represent the 'minimum guarantees that should be provided in national legislation'. The principles follow what might be regarded as the standard model, but there are two features of these Guidelines which justify mention at this point. First, they make provision for the application of the principles by international agencies,[24] bodies which might fall outside of national laws. Second, the UN Guidelines provide the option for the extension of the principles, both to

---

[22] http://cs3-hq.oecd.org/scripts/pwv3/pwhome.htm.>
[23] Available from <http://www.unhchr.ch/html/menu3/b/71.htm>
[24] Part B.

manual files and to files held concerning legal persons.[25] In line with the Convention's approach, the UN Guidelines envisage the establishment of a supervisory agency providing that:

> the law of every country shall designate the authority which, in accordance with its domestic legal system, is to be responsible for supervising observance of the principles set forth above. This authority shall offer guarantees of impartiality, independence vis-à-vis persons or agencies responsible for processing and establishing data, and technical competence. In the event of violation of the provisions of the national law implementing the aforementioned principles, criminal or other penalties should be envisaged together with the appropriate individual remedies.[26]

The Asia-Pacific Privacy Charter initiative

At a rather less formal level than has occurred within Europe, considerable work has been done by a range of countries in the Asia-Pacific region who have established the Asia-Pacific Privacy Charter Council. Hosted at the Cyberspace Law and Policy Centre of the University of New South Wales, the Council is described as a 'regional expert group' which aims to:

> develop independent standards for privacy protection in the region in order to influence the enactment of privacy laws in the region, and the adoption of regional privacy agreements, in accordance with those standards.[27]

The Council's work draws heavily on the APEC Privacy Framework drawn up by the Asia Pacific Economic Cooperation organisation, the Preamble to which recognises the need for APEC economies to provide adequate protection for personal data in order to give individuals the confidence necessary to participate in electronic commerce, behaviour which almost of necessity requires the transfer of significant amounts of pesonal data.[28] Although still at a relatively early stage of development, the work provides further recognition of the global nature of privacy issues and the relationship between the development of electronic commerce and the effective protection of individuals' data.

Data protection in the United Kingdom

As with many inventions, the United Kingdom could claim credit for some pioneering developments in the field of data protection, failed to develop these, and subsequently had to act in response to external pressures. Whilst it is not intended to present an exhaustive survey of the historical development of data protection legislation in general, and the background to the United Kingdom Data Protection Act 1998 in

---

[25] Para. 10.
[26] Para. 8.
[27] <http://www.bakercyberlawcentre.org/appcc/members.htm>
[28] <http://www.bakercyberlawcentre.org/ipp/apec_privacy_framework/index.html>

particular, many of the aspects of the current legislation can be understood only in terms of their historical context. In particular, the lack of either of the historical motivations of the Germans or Swedes (or indeed of many of the European states which adopted data protection laws in the 1970s) has resulted in a situation whereby the concept has been seen as somewhat isolated. This chapter will essay an account of the major factors prompting both the introduction and the format of legislation.

The Report of the Committee on Privacy

As far back as 1969, a Data Surveillance Bill was introduced in the House of Commons by Kenneth Baker MP. If matters had been different, the United Kingdom would have possessed the world's first data protection law but, in common with most private member's initiatives, this failed to make significant progress. In the following Parliamentary session, a further Private Member's Bill was introduced by Brian Walden MP. This sought to establish a statutory right to privacy. In a manner which has not changed through a range of governments over the past thirty-four years, ministers expressed reluctance to establish what would necessarily be a rather vague right. An agreement was made with the Bill's sponsor that in return for its withdrawal, the government would establish the Committee on Privacy.[29] Chaired by Sir Kenneth Younger, the Committee was established in 1970 with a remit to:

> ...consider whether legislation is needed to give further protection to the individual citizen and to commercial and industrial interests against intrusions into privacy by private persons or by companies and to make recommendations.

In its report, the Committee devoted a chapter to the implications of the computer. After receiving evidence as to the nature and scale of processing activities, it concluded that '[w]e cannot on the evidence before us conclude that the computer as used in the private sector is at present a threat to privacy'.[30] Despite this, the Committee identified the computer's capacity to store and process large amounts of personal information, to develop personal profiles, and to allow remote access to databases as factors causing legitimate public concern.

The Committee's report was published in July 1972. Its contents and recommendations were debated in the House of Commons one year later, in July 1973. Speaking in this debate, the Home Secretary studiously avoided expressing any views on the Younger proposals on computers, but announced the publication for later that year, of a White Paper describing computer practices in the public sector and outlining the government's response to the Younger recommendations.[31] In fact, setting a precedent which was to become depressingly familiar, the White Paper, entitled *Computers and Privacy*, was not published until some two-and-a-half years later, in December 1975.[32] As indicated, the White Paper's coverage extended into the public sector, with a supplement detailing the extent of government computer usage.

---

[29] Cmnd 5012, 1972.   [30] Cmnd 5012, para. 619.
[31] 859 HC Official Report (5th series), col. 1956, 13 July 1973.   [32] Cmnd 6353.

Whilst the White Paper reiterated the finding of the Younger Committee that there was little concrete evidence of computer abuse, its conclusion was rather different. The potential dangers were considered so substantial that:

> In the Government's view the time has come when those who use computers to handle personal information can no longer remain the sole judges of whether their own systems adequately safeguard privacy.[33]

Accordingly, it was announced that a Data Protection Committee was to be established, with a remit to make detailed recommendations as to the scope and extent of data protection legislation and as to the form of supervisory mechanism which should be introduced.

The Committee on Data Protection

With hindsight, the publication of the 1975 White Paper can be seen as marking a high-water point in governmental enthusiasm for the concept of data protection. This enthusiasm was certainly matched by that of the Data Protection Committee, which, under the chairmanship of Sir Norman Lindop, presented its voluminous report in June 1978.[34] This remains the most comprehensive and detailed survey of the impact of data processing activities upon the rights and liberties of the individual conducted in the United Kingdom.

The Lindop Committee's report was published towards the end of 1978. In early 1979, a general election saw a change of government, with the arrival of a Conservative Party pledged to reduce bureaucracy. Particularly, given the lack of any evidence of misuse of personal data or tradition of freedom of information, data protection was initially regarded as an unnecessary and unwanted expense and it appeared that little action would be taken. International developments were to bring about a change of mind, however. During the 1970s, the lack of data protection law could be seen as a factor which would make the United Kingdom attractive to companies wishing to establish a European data processing centre. Unlike the situation in other countries, no formal or procedural requirements would limit the nature of the processing which could be conducted. As communications technologies developed to facilitate the international transfer of data, the possibility that national controls might be evaded was not lost on countries possessing data protection laws. Controls over the export of data were introduced. In commending the first Data Protection Bill to the House of Commons, the then Home Secretary commented that it was designed 'to meet public concern, to bring us into step with Europe and to protect our international, commercial and trading interests'.[35] Whilst undoubtedly civil libertarian concerns are fundamental to the concept of data protection, it is significant that these represented only one out of five interests identified and that, at least numerically, commercial and trading factors assumed greater significance. In a manner akin to a stereotype of the British Establishment's way of proceeding, a significant catalyst for action was a letter sent to *The Times* newspaper

---

[33] Cmnd 6353, para. 30.   [34] Cmnd 7341.
[35] HC Official Report (6th series), col. 562, 11 April 1983.

by a number of leading industrialists lamenting the fact that the lack of data protection legislation was beginning to impact adversely upon overseas trade by causing the United Kingdom to be regarded as an 'offshore data haven'. Although concern was expressed that old-fashioned economic protectionism might lie behind any sanctions ostensibly imposed on data protection grounds, the clear conclusion was that data protection legislation was needed in the nation's commercial interest.[36]

The validity of this observation is demonstrated by several well-documented instances in which British companies had been prevented from carrying out data processing or related activities on behalf of Swedish companies, owing to the Swedish authorities' concern at the lack of legislative safeguards.[37] Commercial interests and lobbying succeeded where civil libertarian concerns had failed, and, in March 1981, the Home Secretary announced that: 'The Government has decided in principle to introduce legislation for this purpose when an opportunity occurs.'[38]

Following a further round of consultations, a further White Paper was published in April 1982.[39] By this time, the Lindop Report was reduced to the status of 'very helpful background information'. A Data Protection Bill based on the provisions of the White Paper was introduced in the House of Lords in November 1982. It successfully passed through that House, but fell at the committee stage in the House of Commons when Parliament was dissolved prior to the 1983 general election. An amended Bill was speedily introduced by the incoming government, receiving the Royal Assent on 12 July of the Orwellian year, 1984.

The Data Protection Act 1984

Given that the Data Protection Act 1984 was replaced in its entirety by the Data Protection Act 1998, detailed consideration of its contents is unnecessary. Many of its provisions do, of course, remain applicable under the current regime and decisions made by the courts and the Data Protection Tribunal, which was established as an appellate body, continue to be cited as valid precedent. A few general comments concerning the 1984 Act and a brief assessment of its impact may be helpful in providing initial comment on the impact and relevance of data protection within a United Kingdom context.

As indicated above, the legislation was not introduced out of any genuine enthusiasm by the (Conservative) government of the day. Time after time, *Hansard* reports comments from ministers to the effect that the legislation was being introduced for commercial reasons in order to enable the United Kingdom to ratify the Council of Europe Convention. This was to be done at the most minimal level. On every occasion where the Convention prescribed minimal standards but left the way open for signatories

---

[36] *The Times*, 3 March 1980.

[37] See, for example, J. Bing in J. Bing and K.S. Selmer (eds), *A Decade of Computers and Law* (Oslo, 1980), pp. 70–1, describing the loss of contracts involving the processing of financial and medical data because of these concerns.

[38] HC Official Report (6th series), col. 161, 19 March 1981.

[39] Cmnd 8539.

to provide additional protection in national legislation, the United Kingdom Data Protection Act 1984 remained conspicuously silent. Moving ahead some 15 years to the introduction of the Data Protection Act 1998, *Hansard* reports on the debates are replete with comments from (Labour) ministers to the effect that the legislation was being introduced reluctantly in order to comply at a minimal level with European requirements, this time in the form of European Directive 95/46. It is tempting to suggest that the Conservative ministers of the 1980s could have succeeded in an action alleging breach of copyright in their speeches.

Lack of governmental commitment has been a factor which bedevils data protection to this day. A decision that the concept should not impose any financial burdens on the taxpayer led to the introduction of an outdated and bureaucratic system of registration, whereby anyone involved in processing personal data was obliged to register details of their activities and pay a fee. Failure to do so constituted a criminal offence. Beyond providing the supervisory agency's only significant source of revenue, it is difficult to identify any significant benefits arising from the concept. The financial straitjacket imposed in the Data Protection Act 1984 continues under the Data Protection Act 1998, with the consequence that, whilst terminology changes from registration to notification, the requirement to pay what is effectively a tax associated with computer ownership remains.

Recent events such as the attempt by police forces to blame data protection requirements for the failure to pass on information which may have prevented the Soham murders[40] suggests that data protection retains a role as a scapegoat for organisational failings. Given, as was discussed in Chapter 1, the increasing role and importance of information in our everyday lives, it is disappointing and perhaps even dangerous that there should continue to be such limited understanding of what data protection is and is not about.

The EU Directive and the Data Protection Act 1998

Until the early 1990s, the EU had played a peripheral role in the data protection arena. This could be ascribed to two main causes. First, the limited nature of the legislative competencies conferred by the establishing treaties gave rise to doubts as to whether, and to what extent, the EU was empowered to act in this field. Although the increasing importance of information as a commodity within the Single Market has provided a basis for European action, the exclusion of matters coming within the ambit of national security and, to a partial extent criminal and taxation policy, has served to limit the scope of the EU's intervention.

A second factor influencing work in this field had been a reluctance on the part of the Commission to duplicate work being conducted under the auspices of the Council of Europe and in 1981, the Commission addressed a Recommendation to Member

---

[40] This case concerned the murder in Cambridgeshire of two schoolgirls by a person who had been employed by a caretaker at their school. Subsequent to his conviction, it transpired that allegations concerning his behaviour towards young women had been made to the police in a different location some time previously but that these had not been passed on, allegedly, but almost certainly wrongly, because of concerns that this could contravene the data protection principles.

States that they sign and ratify the Convention.[41] By 1990, the Convention had been signed by all the Member States, but ratified only by six.[42] As will be described, the Convention establishes minimal standards but affords considerable discretion to signatories. A number of Member States, such as Germany and Sweden, had enacted laws which were considerably in advance of the Convention's minimum standards, whilst others, such as the United Kingdom, had openly indicated an intention to do the bare minimum necessary to satisfy obligations under that instrument. By 1990, Commission concern at the effect that discrepancies in the Member States' laws and regulations might have on inter-community trade resulted in proposals being brought forward for a Directive 'On the Protection of Individuals with Regard to the Processing of Personal Data and on the Free Movement of Such Data'.[43] The EU legislation, it was stated, would 'give substance to and amplify'[44] the provisions of the Convention. The objective of the proposal was stated to be to harmonise the data protection laws of the Member States at a 'high level'.[45] This approach was necessary because the Directive was adopted under the authority of Article 100A of the Treaty of Rome. This provides that the Community's law-making bodies may:

> adopt the measures for the approximation of the provisions laid down by law, regulation or administrative action in Member States which have as their object the establishing and functioning of the internal market.

Reliance upon Article 100A has the further significant consequence in that any harmonising measures introduced under its authority have to secure 'a high level of protection'. Effectively, therefore, the Directive has to secure a level of protection equivalent to the highest currently available in the Member States. It is unclear how effective the Directive has been in this regard, with complaints being aired from countries such as Germany that implementation might dilute their existing regimes, especially in respect of transborder data flows. For the United Kingdom, implementation of the Directive required significant change to the Data Protection Act 1984, as well as its expansion. A Consultation Paper was published by the Home Office in March 1996, seeking views on the implementation of the Directive and indicating a preference for a minimalist approach to law reform:

> Over-elaborate data protection threatens competitiveness, and does not necessarily bring additional benefits for individuals. *It follows that the Government intends to go no further in implementing the Directive than is absolutely necessary to satisfy the United Kingdom's obligations in European law. It will consider whether any additional changes to the current data protection regime are needed so as to ensure that it does not go beyond what is required by the Directive and the Council of Europe Convention.*[46]

The Commission's proposal for a general Directive in the area of data protection was accompanied by a further proposal for a Directive 'Concerning the Protection of Personal Data and Privacy in the Context of Public Digital Telecommunications

---

[41] OJ 1981 L 246/31.   [42] Denmark, France, Germany, Luxembourg, Spain, and the United Kingdom.
[43] OJ 1990 C 277/03.   [44] OJ 1990 C 277/03, para. 22.
[45] OJ 1990 C 277/03, Preamble, para. 7.   [46] Para. 1.2 (emphasis in original).

Networks'.[47] Following a five-year journey through the EU's legislative processes, the Data Protection Directive was adopted on 24 October 1995,[48] with a requirement that it be implemented within the Member States by 24 October 1998. The Telecoms Directive—which for a while appeared to have been dropped from the legislative agenda—resurfaced, to be adopted in December 1997.[49] It also required to be implemented by October 1998. The Telecoms Data Protection Directive proved to be a somewhat shortlived measure. In conjunction with a much broader reform of the European telecommunications regulatory regime, the Directive was replaced in 2002 by the Directive 'Concerning the Processing of Personal Data and the Protection of Privacy in the Electronic Communications Sector'.[50] This was required to be implemented in the Member States by 31 October 2003. The provisions of the communications Directive will be discussed in more detail in Chapter 7.

In January 1998 a Data Protection Bill was introduced in the House of Lords. Its progress through Parliament was relatively uncontroversial, with only one division being required throughout its parliamentary passage.[51] The major feature of the Bill's progress was the very large number of amendments tabled by the government —more than 200 in total. The Act received the Royal Assent on 16 July, although its entry into force was delayed pending the drafting of what proved to be seventeen items of secondary legislation and it was not until 1 March 2000 that the new legislation entered into force. In its failure timeously to implement the Data Protection Directive,[52] the United Kingdom was joined by a majority of the Member States. Legal action was raised by the Commission against Denmark, France, Germany, Ireland, Luxembourg, and the Netherlands, alleging a continuing failure to implement the Directive, although in the case of every state except Luxembourg, the belated implementation of the Directive resulted in the legal proceedings being abandoned.[53]

The Data Protection Act 1998 and its relationship with the Directive

As an initial comment, it may be noted that the Data Protection Act 1998 is considerably larger than the 1984 legislation. The Data Protection Act 1984 has 43 Sections and 6 Schedules; the 1998 statute has 75 Sections and 16 Schedules. To an extent greater than its 1984 precursor, the Act provides only a framework, with significant matters remaining to be determined by statutory instruments. Although this approach will

---

[47] OJ 1990 C 277/12.

[48] Directive 95/46/EC, OJ 1995 L 281/31.

[49] Directive 97/66/EC Concerning the Protection of Personal Data and Privacy in the Context of Public Digital Telecommunications Networks, OJ 1998 L 24.

[50] Directive 2002/58/EC, OJ 2002 L 201/37 (Privacy and Electronic Communications Directive).

[51] This was in relation to proposals in the Bill to provide ministers with wideranging powers to exempt processing activities from the subject access provisions. The House of Lords voted to remove these powers from the Bill. A more closely defined provision was introduced in the House of Commons.

[52] Directive 95/46/EC.

[53] For current information on the status of implementation, see <http://europa.eu.int/comm/internal_market/en/media/dataprot/law/impl.htm>

allow easier modification and updating of the legislation than was possible with the 1984 Act, significant issues relating to the identification of those data controllers who may be exempted from the notification requirement are not covered in the Act.

Given that the Data Protection Act 1998 is intended to implement a European Directive,[54] account has to be taken of the provisions of the latter. In *Campbell v MGN Ltd*,[55] Lord Phillips of Worth Matravers MR stated that:

> In interpreting the Act it is appropriate to look to the Directive for assistance. The Act should, if possible, be interpreted in a manner that is consistent with the Directive. Furthermore, because the Act has, in large measure, adopted the wording of the Directive, it is not appropriate to look for the precision in the use of language that is usually to be expected from the parliamentary draftsman. A purposive approach to making sense of the provisions is called for.

The European Court of Justice has also held in *Österreichischer Rundfunk*[56] that at least some of the provisions of the Directive are sufficiently precise to be relied upon directly by individuals within the Member States.

The Data Protection Act 1998 extends significantly the area of the application of the legislation, including regulating some systems of manual records. In the accompanying Explanatory and Financial Memorandum, it is estimated that compliance with the new regime will result in start-up costs to private sector data-users of some £836 million, with recurring costs of £630 million. The start-up costs for the public and voluntary sectors are estimated at £194 million and £120 million. respectively, with recurring costs of £75 million and £37 million. These figures are in addition to the costs incurred in complying with the present data protection regime, although no evidence has been published as to the scale of the present costs. The Home Office Regulatory Appraisal and Compliance Cost Assessment makes it clear that estimates are based upon a very small sample of users. Only four large and three small manufacturers were surveyed, for example, and although much publicity has been given to headline figures of £1 billion cost arising from implementation, the assessment document itself highlights the need to approach these estimates with caution. The Commissioner has also questioned the accuracy of the financial calculations,[57] suggesting that this may have resulted from misunderstandings as to the nature of the Data Protection Directive's[58] requirements.

To date, it does not appear that data protection has had a significant impact on public consciousness. To justify costs of some £20 for every inhabitant of the United Kingdom, it is to be hoped that the new legislation—perhaps coupled with other leg-islative initiatives in the field of human rights and freedom of information—will pro-vide the basis for enhanced public awareness of the crucial importance of information in modern society, and the need to secure an appropriate balance between those who hold and use data and those who may be affected by such activities.

---

[54] Directive 95/46/EC.
[55] [2002] EWCA Civ 1373, [2003] QB 633 at [96].
[56] Joined Cases C–465/00, C–138/01 and C–139/01 [2003] ECR I–4989.
[57] Press Release, 28 January 1998.
[58] Directive 95/46/EC.

Conclusions

Although a right of access to information held by credit reference agencies had been available since 1976 under the provisions of the Consumer Credit Act 1974, the Data Protection Act 1984 has been seen as a somewhat isolated measure. In particular, the lack of anything approaching a right to privacy has deprived the legislation of solid legal foundations, whilst criticism has been voiced by the Registrar that inadequate account has been taken of data protection issues in formulating other statutes, such as those concerned with the community charge or poll tax, which involve the obtaining and use of personal data.[59]

The situation in 2008 is significantly different, and the Data Protection Act 1998 should be seen as one of a trilogy of measures operating in the same general field. The Human Rights Act 1998 incorporates the European Convention on Human Rights into domestic law. The provisions of Articles 8 and 10 are of particular relevance to data protection. Article 8 provides that 'everyone has the right to respect for his private and family life, his home and his correspondence'. Any interference with such rights by a public authority must be sanctioned by law and be:

> ...necessary in a democratic society in the interests of national security, public safety or the economic well being of the country, for the prevention of disorder or crime, for the protection of health or morals, or for the protection of the rights and freedoms of others.[60]

In its jurisprudence, the European Court of Human Rights has interpreted Article 8 liberally to include rights of access to personal data. Indeed, following the decision of the court in the case of *Gaskin v United Kingdom*,[61] changes were required to be made to statutory provisions relating to subject access.

Perhaps the most controversial aspect of the interface between the Human Rights Act 1998 and the Data Protection 1998 concerns the activities of the media. Article 10 of the European Convention on Human Rights guarantees the right to freedom of expression. Once again, this may be subject to derogation on conditions similar to those applying to respect for private and family life. Clearly, media activities, especially in the field of investigative journalism, may conflict with Article 8 rights. Both the Data Protection 1998 and the Human Rights Act 1998 contain provisions and procedures for seeking to resolve such conflicts. Rather surprisingly, these differ in certain respects with the former statute's provisions, receiving a considerably warmer reception from media representatives than those found in the human rights legislation.[62]

A further area where the Data Protection Act 1998 has to relate with other measures is connected with the introduction of freedom of information legislation. A White Paper, *Your Right to Know*, was published in December 1997,[63] and a Bill was introduced in

---

[59] See the *Fourth Annual Report of the Data Protection Registrar* (1989).
[60] Article 10(2).
[61] (1990) 12 EHRR 36.
[62] See Chapter 9.
[63] Cm. 3818.

Parliament in 1999, receiving Royal Assent in 2000 but not entering into force until January 2005.[64] There is a clear overlap between the two concepts and the Information Commissioner has responsibility in respect of both statutes. In other countries which have freedom of information legislation, it has been estimated that some 80 per cent of requests relate to the inquirer's own personal data. In respect of this issue, freedom of information legislation may well supplement rights under the Data Protection 1998 by extending these to a wider range of manual records, but, with proposals for significant variations in access rights and exceptions thereto, the prospect arises of what the House of Commons Select Committee on Public Administration described as a 'confusing and messy patchwork of different provisions under which one may obtain access to one's own file'.[65] Even more significantly, however, there will be the potential for conflict between the aims and objectives of the statutes where personal data relates to a party other than the inquirer. Here, whilst freedom of information may give priority to openness and accessibility, data protection seeks to protect individual privacy and confidentiality.

In many respects, it might have been desirable had reform to the Data Protection Act proceeded in parallel with the freedom of information legislation. The Select Committee, whilst welcoming the prospect of freedom of information legislation, commented critically on the possibility for overlap and conflict between the two systems. It also noted the fact that the Data Protection Registrar had not been consulted prior to the publication of the White Paper.[66] It is perhaps ironic that whilst the prospect of the European Directives adopted was used to justify much needed reform of the United Kingdom system during the first half of the 1990s, the desire to comply with the timetable for its implementation resulted in the 1998 Act being brought forward in isolation rather than as part of a comprehensive and coherent strategy governing access to information. To compound the irony, of course, the delay in formulating necessary items of secondary legislation meant that the United Kingdom ultimately failed to meet the European deadline.

Suggestions for further reading

APEC Privacy Framework drawn up by the Asia Pacific Economic Cooperation Organisation (2003), available at <http://www.nacpec.org/docs/APECS_Privacy Framework.pdf> and <http://www.worldlii.org/int/other/PrivLRes/2003/1.html>.

CLARKE, R. (2000), Beyond the OECD Guidelines: Privacy Protection for the 21st Century, available from <http://www.anu.edu.au/people/Roger.Clarke/DV/PP21C.html>.

Explanatory Report to the Council of Europe Convention on the Automated Processing of Personal Data (1981), available from <http://conventions.coe.int/treaty/en/Reports/Html/108.htm>.

---

[64] Separate legislation applies within Scotland.
[65] Third Report from the Select Committee on Public Administration (HC Paper 398/1 (1997–98)), para. 17.
[66] Ibid., para. 21.

3

The scope of data protection

Introduction

Dictionaries and definitions seldom make compelling reading but in law, an understanding of basic concepts is key to an understanding of a topic. Prior to considering more substantive aspects of data protection, this chapter will consider in some detail the core concepts which define the scope of data protection legislation. A number of definitional terms are closely linked to form a knot which is almost Gordian in its complexity. Any attempt to describe and analyse them is hindered by the fact that appreciation of the scope of one term presupposes to some extent understanding of others. In the absence of a sufficiently sharp sword, the following precis may serve as an introduction. The italicised terms will be subjected to more detailed comment analysis in the remainder of the chapter:

> The legislation applies where *personal data* (including *sensitive personal data*) *relating to an identifiable individual* (*data subject*) is subjected to certain forms of *processing*. The nature and extent of the processing will be determined by a *data controller,* although the actual processing may be carried out by a *data processor* operating under an outsourcing or similar contract with the data controller.

The apparent simplicity of the terms is unfortunately misleading and there has been and remains debate and uncertainty, both as to the scope of the concepts per se and as to the extent to which the United Kingdom's legislation adequately implements the provisions of the Directive. Decisions of the courts also have to be taken into account, with the leading authorities being the decision of the English Court of Appeal in *Durant v Financial Services Authority*[1] and the judgment of the European Court of Justice in the case of *Bodil Lindqvist*.[2]

Key definitions

Personal data

The Data Protection Directive defines personal data as including 'any information relating to an identified or identifiable natural person (data subject)',[3] whilst the Data

---

[1] [2003] EWCA Civ 1746.   [2] C101/01.
[3] Article 2(a).

Protection Act refers to 'data which relate to a living individual'.[4] The Act expands on the definition providing that the term extends 'to any expression of opinion about the individual and any indication of the intentions of the data controller or any other person in respect of the individual'. This represents a perhaps unfortunate legacy from the original United Kingdom Data Protection Act 1984 which included a widely criticised distinction between statements of opinion—which were classed as personal data—and statements of intention—which were not. The argument put forward by the government of the day was that statements of intention were personal to the data holder rather than to the subject. This is certainly arguable, but the point applies with equal if not greater validity with regard to statements of opinion. Even the then Data Protection Registrar was moved to comment to the effect that he found the distinction unclear and the provision in the Data Protection Act 1998 should perhaps be seen as a measure to remove what had generally been considered an unsatisfactory distinction, rather than a conscious effort to limit the scope of the definition of personal data.

As can be seen, there is some terminolgical difference between the two definitions and some debate on whether the United Kingdom definition is excessively restrictive. One issue is whether the legislation should apply to data relating to deceased individuals. A minority of Member States have, indeed, chosen to extend their national laws to this category of data. Even accepting the validity of the United Kingdom's interpretation of the concept of a 'natural person', there may be circumstances in which data concerning a deceased person may also have implications for living individuals. Certain diseases such as haemophilia are heriditary in nature. The son of a woman suffering from the disease in its active form will always inherit the condition. Data indicating the mother's condition will therefore convey information about the medical condition of any male children, even in the event that she is dead. Again, some EU Member States apply at least elements of the legislation to data relating to legal persons. The United Kingdom does not, although it should be noted that legal persons do acquire some protection under the provisions of the Directive 'Concerning the Processing of Personal Data and the Protection of Privacy in the Electronic Communications Sector (Directive on Privacy and Electronic Communications)'. The provisions of this Directive and its implementation in the United Kingdom will be discussed in Chapter 7 below.

Although in its early stages data protection laws tended to apply almost exclusively to textual information, developments in technology mean that almost any form of recorded information is likely to come within the ambit of the legislation. In the event that an individual interacts with an automated telephone service by speaking a series of numbers or words to allow a call to be directed to the appropriate department, those recorded words will class as personal data. Again, CCTV or similar camera systems generally fall within the scope of the legislation in respect of the video images recorded.

Much attention is paid today to the collection and use of biometric data. Although the term does not have a precise definition, it is generally regarded as encompassing two

---

[4] Section 1(1).

categories of data. The first relates to the physiological characteristic relating to aspects of physical identity. This category would include items such as finger prints and, perhaps relating to more advanced forms of technology, face and iris recognition. A second category of biometric data relates to what are referred to as behavioural characteristics. As the name suggests, this concerns the manner in which a person acts. A simple and long-established example would relate to the manner in which a person signs his or her name. More technologically advanced versions relate to the use of software to monitor the manner in which a particular individual uses a computer keyboard in terms of the speed, accuracy, and force with which keys are depressed.

Biometric data, which forms a cornerstone of modern passports and the proposals for a national identity card scheme, is clearly an aspect of personal data. Data may be objective or subjective and, indeed, true or false. In an Opinion on the concept of personal data,[5] the Article 29 Working Party, which was established as an advisory body under the Data Protection Directive and is composed of national data protection authorities,[6] suggested that:

> As a result of a neuro-psychiatric test conducted on a girl in the context of a court proceeding about her custody, a drawing made by her representing her family is submitted. The drawing provides information about the girl's mood and what she feels about different members of her family. As such, it could be considered as being 'personal data'. The drawing will indeed reveal information relating to the child (her state of health from a psychiatric point of view) and also about e.g. her father's or mother's behaviour. As a result, the parents in that case may be able to exert their right of access on this specific piece of information.

As indicated in the above example, personal data may relate to more than one person, a topic which will be considered in more detail below.

Sensitive data

Any form of information, however insignificant, may be classed as personal data. The extent to which certain forms of data can be classed as especially sensitive and deserving of special protection has long been a contentious issue. During the passage of the Data Protection Act 1984, the attempt to identify sensitive data was compared, somewhat scornfully, by government ministers with the quest for the unicorn. Both were considered mythical creatures. In the case of personal data, the context in which data was held or used was considered far more important than the data itself. A list of names and addresses, for example, would not normally be considered sensitive, but this view might change if it referred to the movements of prominent persons and was in the hands of a terrorist organisation. Whilst this view is not without merit, it does seek to transform the exceptional into the norm. Almost invariably, data protection statutes have recognised that there are certain categories of information which would generally be regarded as possessing a degree of sensitivity and in respect of which,

---

[5] Available from <http://ec.europa.eu/justice_home/fsj/privacy/docs/wpdocs/2007/wp136_en.pdf>
[6] Described more fully below.

substantial numbers of data subjects might wish to be assured that dissemination would be limited and controlled.

As enacted, the Data Protection Act 1984 provided that regulations might be made to strengthen the data protection principles in respect of data relating to racial origin, political opinions, religious or other beliefs, physical or mental health, sexual life, or criminal convictions.[7] This power was never exercised. The Data Protection Act 1998 brings the treatment of sensitive data into the heart of the legislation and subjects its processing to more extensive requirements than is the case with other forms of data. Sensitive data is now defined as encompassing any data relating to:

(a) the racial or ethnic origin of the data subject;

(b) his political opinions;

(c) his religious beliefs or other beliefs of a similar nature;

(d) whether he is a member of a trade union;

(e) his physical or mental health or condition;

(f) his sexual life;

(g) the commission or alleged commission by him of any offence; or

(h) any proceedings for any offence committed or alleged to have been committed by him, the disposal of such proceedings, or the sentence of the court in such proceedings.[8]

With the exception of substituting the term 'other beliefs of a similar nature' for the Directive's 'philosophical beliefs', the Act's terminology mirrors that of the Directive.

This definition is considerably wider than the 1984 Act and undoubtedly reflects diverse attitudes towards issues across the Member States of the European Union. Research conducted for the Information Commissioner in 2006[9] sought views on the extent to which respondents regarded specific types of information as being sensitive. The results are set out in Table 3.1. Interestingly, financial data, which attracted the highest response rate, is not included in the statutory list of sensitive data.

In addition to covering a wide range of categories of information, the scope of particular categories has been broadly interpreted by the courts. In *Bodil Lindqvist*,[10] the European Court of Justice was asked to give a preliminary ruling in response to a number of questions posed by the Swedish courts. Mrs Lindqvist had been convicted of breaches of the Swedish data protection law in respect of her work as a catechist in the Swedish Lutheran Church and preparation of a number of www pages which contained information about Mrs Lindqvist and eighteen of her parish colleagues, including brief details of the nature of their work and hobbies. It appears that much of the information

---

[7] Section 2(3).

[8] Section 2.

[9] *2006 Annual Tracking Report*, available from <http://www.ico.gov.uk/upload/documents/library/corporate/research_and_reports/2006_annual_tracking_report_individuals_final.pdf>

[10] Case 101/01, [2004] QB 1014.

Table 3.1 Attitudes towards sensitivity of types of data

	Percentage
Financial data	88.0
Health information	72.0
Personal contact details	68.0
Sexual life information	67.0
Biometric information	63.0
Genetic information	63.0
Criminal records	58.0
Clickstream data	43.0
Political opinions	42.0
Education qualification	42.0
Data concerning race or ethnic origin	41.0
Employment history	41.0
Membership of political party/organisation	38.0
Religious or philosophical beliefs	37.0
Trade-union membership	33.0

was presented in what was intended to be a light-hearted manner. One particular item of information which was the cause of specific investigation was the indication that a named person had injured her foot and as a consequence was able to work only on a part-time basis. Data concerning the subject's health life? Mrs Lindqvist was prosecuted by the Swedish authorities on a number of charges, including one of processing sensitive personal data without having secured authorisation from the data protection authorities. The European Court of Justice was asked to rule on the question of whether the reference to the foot injury of Mrs Lindqvist's colleague constituted sensitive data relating to health. The court's reply was succinct and emphatic:

> In the light of the purpose of the Directive, the expression data concerning health used in Article 8(1) thereof must be given a wide interpretation so as to include information concerning all aspects, both physical and mental, of the health of an individual.

In some respects, the decision in *Bodil Lindqvist* illustrates the difficulties surrounding the concept of sensitive data. Once included in a list of sensitive data, it is almost impossible to say that a reference to illness or injury is not included, but as indicated above context is perhaps more important than content. A reference to the fact that an athlete was unable to compete in a race because of a broken leg, for example, does not seem to be possessed of a sufficient degree of sensitivity to justify the imposition of additional controls.

Relating to the data subject

In *Bodil Lindqvist*, there was no doubt that the information about the foot injury related to the individual concerned. In other cases the situation may be more complex. In the example of the child's drawing cited above, the data contained might relate in varying degrees to the child and to other family members. Neither the Directive nor the Act provide any definition when data relates to an individual but the point was discussed extensively in the case of *Durant v Financial Services Authority*,[11] and more recently has been considered in an Opinion of the Article 29 Working Party and in Guidance produced by the United Kingdom's Information Commissioner.

In *Durant*, the appellant had been involved in a protracted dispute with Barclays Bank. This had resulted in unsuccessful litigation in 1993 and a continuing course of complaints to the industry regulatory body, the Financial Services Authority (FSA). The present case arose from a request from the appellant for access to a range of records under the ambit of the subject access provisions of the Data Protection Act 1998. Although some information was supplied, access to other records was provided only in partial form through the concealment or redaction of information which it was considered related to third parties. Other records were withheld on the grounds either that the information contained therein did not constitute personal data relating to the appellant, or—as will be discussed below, in the case of a number of records which were maintained in manual filing systems—that the system was not covered by the Data Protection Act.

Although there was no doubt that much, if not all, of the data in question had been generated following complaints from the appellant, the critical issue was whether it related to him. Counsel for Durant argued that the term 'relate to' should be interpreted broadly to encompass any data which might be generated following a search of a database made by reference to an individual's name. Thus, for example, a document describing the action which had been taken in response to a complaint from the appellant would be classed as personal data by virtue merely of the fact that his name would appear within the text. Counsel for the respondent advocated a more restrictive approach, making reference to the *Shorter Oxford English Dictionary*, which contained two definitions of the term, a broad reference to having 'some connection with, be connected to' and a more restrictive notion that there should be reference to or concern with a subject, 'implying, in this context, a more or less direct connection with an individual'.

This more restrictive interpretation was adopted by the Court of Appeal. The purpose of the subject access provisions in the legislation was, it was stated, to enable the data subject to verify that processing did not infringe his or her rights of privacy and to exercise any available remedies in the event this was considered not to be the case. The purpose of the legislation was not, it was held, to give an automatic right of access to information purely by virtue of the fact that he might be named in a record or have

---

[11] [2003] EWCA Civ 1746.

some interest in the matters covered. In particular, it was stated, subject access was not intended:

> to assist him, for example, to obtain discovery of documents that may assist him in litigation or complaints against third parties.

Giving effect to this principle was that the mere fact that a search of a computer's contents by reference to a data subject's name revealed a number of documents did not mean that these documents necessarily constituted personal data relating to the subject. A more sophisticated analysis was required:

> It seems to me that there are two notions that may be of assistance. The first is whether the information is biographical in a significant sense, that is, going beyond the recording of the putative data subject's involvement in a matter or an event that has no personal connotations, a life event in respect of which his privacy could not be said to be compromised. The second is one of focus. The information should have the putative data subject as its focus rather than some other person with whom he may have been involved or some transaction or event in which he may have figured or have had an interest, for example, as in this case, an investigation into some other person's or body's conduct that he may have instigated. In short, it is information that affects his privacy, whether in his personal or family life, business or professional capacity.[12]

This approach adopts, it is suggested, an overly restrictive view of the rationale of data protection laws. Whilst determining the legality of data processing and correcting errors certainly constitute important elements, equally important is the ability to become aware of what data is held. Much of the Data Protection Directive[13] and the Data Protection Act 1998's requirements relating to the factors legitimising data processing stress the importance of the data subject being aware of what is happening with regard to personal data. As was stated by the German Constitutional Court in the 1980s:

> The possibilities of inspection and of gaining influence have increased to a degree hitherto unknown and may influence the individual's behaviour by the psychological pressure exerted by public interest...if someone cannot predict with sufficient certainty which information about himself in certain areas is known to his social milieu, and cannot estimate sufficiently the knowledge of parties to whom communication may possibly be made, he is crucially inhibited in his freedom to plan or to decide freely and without being subject to any pressure/influence.[14]

These factors support the adoption of an expansive definition of the scope of personal data. In a case such as *Durant*, it may well be that personal data in the form of an individual's name or other identifying data makes a peripheral appearance in a record. Rather than arguing that the appearance of the data does not come within the scope of the Act, it might be preferable to focus upon the extent of the information which might be supplied. Whilst the court was clearly concerned that the data

---

[12] *Durant v Financial Services Authority* [2003] EWCA Civ 1746 at paras 27–8.
[13] Directive 95/46/EC.
[14] 'The Census Decision', *Human Rights Law Journal* 5 (1984), 94.

protection legislation was being invoked in the present case in the attempt to obtain discovery of documents and data that could not be obtained through other legal channels, it might have been preferable to have laid greater stress on the limited nature of the information which would be classed as personal data.

The Information Commissioner has recently noted that 'the Court of Appeal was widely understood to have adopted a rather narrower interpretation of personal data...than most practitioners and experts had followed previously'.[15] The Article 29 Working Party's Opinion provides extensive guidance when data relates to an individual. Referring to its previous work in relation to RFID chip technology, it affirms that '*data relates to an individual if it refers to the identity, characteristics or behaviour of an individual or if such information is used to determine or influence the way in which that person is treated or evaluated*'.[16]

The Opinion identifies three elements which may indicate that data relates to a particular individual. These are referred to as content, purpose, and result elements. The distinction between the elements may be complex on occasion but the Working Party stress that only one element needs to be present in order to justify a finding that data relates to a particular individual. The content element will be satisfied when information is about an individual. A medical or personnel record, for example, will fall within this category. The purpose element applies when the data is intended to be used to determine the manner in which an individual is treated. Data may, for example, be recorded by an employer of the websites accessed from workplace computers. The purpose may be to take disiplinary action against employees who violate Internet usage policies. Finally, a result element applies when the use of data, even though not collected originally for that purpose, is likely to have even a minor impact upon an individual's rights and interests. Guidance produced by the United Kingdom's Information Commissioner emphasises similar criteria, suggesting that:

> Data which identifies an individual, even without a name associated with it, may be personal data where it is processed to learn or record something about that individual, or where the processing of that information has an impact upon that individual.

Issues of identification

The premise underlying data protection legislation is that the processing of data relating to individuals constitutes a threat to the subject's rights and freedoms. If an individual cannot be identified from the manner in which data is collected, processed, or used, there can be no significant threat to privacy and no justification for the application of legislative controls. The Data Protection Directive provides that:

> an identifiable person is one who can be identified directly or indirectly, in particular by reference to an identification number or to one or more factors specific to his physical, psychological, mental, economic, cultural or social identity.[17]

---

[15] Data Protection Technical Guidance. Determining what is personal data.
[16] Working Party Document No. WP 105: 'Working document on data protection issues related to RFID technology', adopted on 19 January 2005, p. 8.
[17] Directive 95/46/EC, Article 2(a).

Also relevant are the provisions of Recital 26 to the Directive. This states that:

> Whereas the principles of protection must apply to any information concerning an identified or identifiable person; whereas, to determine whether a person is identifiable, account should be taken of all the means likely reasonably to be used either by the controller or by any other person to identify the said person.

The United Kingdom's Data Protection Act 1998 provides that personal data:

> ...means data which relates to a living individual who can be identified—
>
> (a) from those data; or
>
> (b) from those data and other information which is in the possession of, or is likely to come into the possession of, the data controller.

It will be recognised that the Directive and the Act differ in that the Act restricts its application to information which is or is likely to come into the possession of the data controller. The Directive's application is open-ended, applying whenever anyone might be able to identify an individual. A recent example might illustrate a difference between the two approaches. In 2006, AOL placed on the Internet data relating to search requests made by millions of its subscribers. Although no names were published, in at least some cases it proved possible to identify individuals following analysis of their search history. One case concerned a user allocated the identifying number 4417749. This user had conducted searches on a range of topics, including medical conditions relating to humans and animals, landscape gardening, persons with a particular surname (Arnold), and house sales in a particular area of the United States. Taking this data, researchers focused on a particular individual, Thelma Arnold, who, when read in a list of the searches, confirmed that they had been made by her.[18]

Under the United Kingdom approach, it is likely that the data would not have been considered personal data at the point it was compiled by AOL because that organisation would not have possessed the necessary additional information to identify users.[19] Under the Directive's criteria, the material would probably have been classed as personal data, as AOL would have been required to consider the possibility that third parties could perform the task of identification. It is likely that if its disclosure and decoding were to be carried out in the United Kingdom (or any other state of the European Economic Area (EEA)) the person identifying individuals would be classed as a data controller in his or her own right and subject to the same obligations to comply with data protection law. Matters would be much less satisfactory were the decoder to be located outside of the EEA and, of course, dissemination of information via the Internet is global in its nature.

The AOL example undoubtedly represents an extreme case but the issue of identifiability may frequently be an issue. Once again, the Article 29 Opinion on the concept of

---

[18] <http://www.iht.com/articles/2006/08/09/business/aol.php>

[19] Given that AOL operates on a subscription service it may be that the company would have possessed the necessary data. The example might be more accurate in the event that it applied to an organisation such as Google, which does not require users to give their names. Indeed, one of the reasons why Google refused to comply with a United States government request for access to search data was because of concerns that individuals might be identified. See <http://news.bbc.co.uk/1/hi/technology/4630694.stm>

personal data identifies a wide range of potential situations and provides extensive guidance. Linking data to a name is an obvious form of identification, although especially in the case of a common name such as Smith or McDonald this may not be sufficient. Use of an identification number may aid identification. In other cases, an individual may be identifiable indirectly. The example might be posited of a CCTV operator instructing an undercover police officer to detain the person wearing a Glasgow Rangers' football shirt and carrying a can of lager sitting slumped in the doorway of 27 Hoops Street, Glasgow. No name is given but the individual is readily identifiable. Again, Internet Service Providers (ISPs) and possibly employers may maintain records of Internet use associated with particular computers and from these to the individuals behind the computers. Identification may not always be possible; the Working Party posit the example of computers used in an Internet café, but stress that so long as identification is possible in some cases, all processing will be covered by the legislation.

The concept of processing

Much of what has been said above is predicated on the notion that data is processed. It is now appropriate to consider what forms of activity can be classed as constituting processing. The Directive provides here that processing includes:

> any operation or set of operations which is performed upon personal data, whether or not by automatic means, such as collection, recording, organization, storage, adaptation or alteration, retrieval, consultation, use, disclosure by transmission, dissemination or otherwise making available, alignment or combination, blocking, erasure or destruction.[20]

The Act's definition differs slighty in terminology, largely because of the need to make separate provision for the treatement of non-automated or manual processing. It provides that:

> ...'processing', in relation to information or data, means obtaining, recording or holding the information or data or carrying out any operation or set of operations on the information or data, including—
>
> (a) organisation, adaptation or alteration of the information or data;
>
> (b) retrieval, consultation or use of the information or data;
>
> (c) disclosure of the information or data by transmission, dissemination or otherwise making available; or
>
> (d) alignment, combination, blocking, erasure or destruction of the information or data.[21]

Linked to this is a definition of the word data:

> (a) is being processed by means of equipment operating automatically in response to instructions given for that purpose;

---

[20] Article 2(b).   [21] Section 1(1).

(b) is recorded with the intention that it should be processed by means of such equipment; or

(c) is recorded as part of a relevant filing system or with the intention that it should form part of a relevant filing system.[22]

The term 'relevant filing system' is designed to extend the legislation to certain forms of manual filing systems and will be considered separately below. It will be noted that the scope of the definition is extremely broad. It might be suggested, with little element of exaggeration, that whilst the act of dreaming about data will not constitute processing, any further activities will bring a party within the scope of the legislation.

Although not yet at issue before a United Kingdom court, the question of what acts constitute processing was raised before the European Court in *Bodil Lindqvist*.[23] An initial issue concerned the question of whether the mention of a person on a web page constituted processing of personal data as defined in the Data Protection Directive.[24] Two issues arose in this context: first, whether the data on Mrs Linqvist's web page included personal data. The court's reply was unequivocal:

> The term undoubtedly covers the name of a person in conjunction with his telephone coordinates or information about his working conditions or hobbies.[25]

Equally clear and unsurprising was the court's determination that processing had taken place. The Swedish government argued for a broad approach, suggesting that 'as soon as personal data are processed by computer, whether using a word-processing programme or in order to put them on an Internet page, they have been the subject of processing'. Although Counsel for Mrs Lindqvist argued that something more was needed beyond compilation of what was effectively a word-processed document and that only metatags and other technical means used to assist with the compilation of indexes and retrieval of information would suffice, the court agreed with the Swedish government's submission:

> According to the definition in Article 2(b) of Directive 95/46, the term processing of such data used in Article 3(1) covers any operation or set of operations which is performed upon personal data, whether or not by automatic means.[26]

Although all forms of processing are potentially covered by the Data Protection Directive,[27] the most stringent controls apply in the case of processing by automatic means. It is arguable that any use of a computer to create a document comes within the scope of this criterion, as there is no direct physical link between the author pressing a key and a letter or symbol appearing on the screen. The act of loading a page onto

---

[22] Article 12.
[23] Case 101/01, [2004] QB 1014.
[24] Directive 95/46/EC.
[25] Case 101/01, [2004] QB 1014, para. 24.
[26] Case 101/01, para. 25.
[27] Directive 95/46/EC.

a web server involved a number of operations, some at least of which are performed automatically.

Non-automated filing systems

Under the Data Protection Act 1984, access was strictly limited to data which had been the subject of some form of automated processing. The Data Protection Directive[28] required an extension to certain forms of manual records. Article 2 of the Directive provides that its scope is to extend to any 'personal data filing system' defined in terms of:

> any structured set of personal data which are accessible according to specific criteria, whether centralised, decentralised or dispersed on a functional or geographical basis.

By omitting any reference to automated processing the effect is clearly to encompass manual recordkeeping systems. Whilst, reflecting the ease with which modern retrieval systems can perform full text searches of vast collections of data in accordance with criteria determined by a user, every automated system is covered by the legislation, not every manual system is to be included. Recital 15 of the Data Protection Directive[29] explains that:

> Whereas the processing of such data is covered by this Directive only if it is automated or if the data processed are contained or are intended to be contained in a filing system structured according to specific criteria relating to individuals, so as to permit easy access to the personal data in question; ...

Recital 27 continues the story:

> Whereas the protection of individuals must apply as much to automatic processing of data as to manual processing; whereas the scope of this protection must not in effect depend on the techniques used, otherwise this would create a serious risk of circumvention; whereas nonetheless, as regards manual processing, this Directive covers only filing systems, not unstructured files; whereas, in particular, the content of a filing system must be structured according to specific criteria relating to individuals allowing easy access to the personal data; whereas, in line with the definition in Article 2(c), the different criteria for determining the constituents of a structured set of personal data, and different criteria governing access to such a set, may be laid down by each Member State; whereas files or sets of files as well as their cover pages, which are not structured according to specific criteria, shall under no circumstances fall within the scope of the Directive.

This provision clearly leaves considerable scope for EU Member States to determine the extent to which manual records should be brought within the scope of their implementing legislation. As indicated above, the Data Protection Act 1998 utilises

---

[28] Directive 95/46/EC.   [29] Directive 95/46/EC.

the concept of a 'relevant filing system' as the vehicle for this endeavour. The statutory definition is somewhat complex, in large part because the legislation seeks to coexist with a range of earlier statutes which had provided for a right of access to certain medical, educational, social work, and credit reference files. In its essential element, however, it provides that:

> 'relevant filing system' means any set of information relating to individuals to the extent that, although the information is not processed by means of equipment operating automatically in response to instructions given for that purpose, the set is structured, either by reference to individuals or by reference to criteria relating to individuals, in such a way that specific information relating to a particular individual is readily accessible.[30]

The extension to some forms of manual records has been the cause of considerable controversy, largely concerning the potential costs of organisations of complying with requests for subject access. It should be noted, however, that the Consumer Credit Act 1974 and the Access to Health Records Act 1990 have long provided for access to credit and medical records, irrespective of the format in which these are stored. More recently, the Freedom of Information Act 2000 has provided very extensive rights of access to public sector information and as the Information Commissioner has commented:

> Experience elsewhere indicates that in practice, in many cases, information provided in response to Freedom of Information requests will relate to the individual making the request.[31]

In determining what manual records will be covered, the question of when information should be considered 'readily accessible' is of critical importance. In the discussion of the extent of the provision in Parliament, it was suggested that it would not be sufficient that information about an individual should be located in a single place, for example, a manila folder containing all of an employee's work records. In order for the records to be covered, it would additionally be required that the information within the folder should be held in a structured format so that individual items might readily be extracted. Speaking during the Bill's Report stage in the House of Lords, Lord Williams stated that:

> Our intentions are clear. We do not wish the definition to apply to miscellaneous collections of paper about individuals, even if the collections are assembled in files with the individual's name or other unique identifier on the front, if specific data about the individual cannot be readily extracted from that collection. An example might be a personnel file with my name on the front. Let us assume that the file contains every piece of paper or other document about me which the personnel section has collected over the course of my career and those papers are held in the file in date order with no means of readily identifying specific information about me except by looking at

---

[30] Section 1(1).   [31] Our Answers 1998, para. 3.8

every document. The Government's clear intention is that such files should not be caught.[32]

The then Data Protection Registrar, however, commented that:

> It has...been put to us that 'particular information' refers to information of a very specific nature. On this analysis information held in a file relating to an immigration application would arguably be covered as all the information in the file will, or should, be directly pertinent to that application. However, it has been argued that information held in a normal personnel file will not be 'particular information' as there will be a range of information concerning such matters as sickness absence, performance, pay, next of kin. We find this distinction unconvincing. The range of information in a personnel file may be wide because there is a wide range of information relevant to an individual's employment. Nevertheless, the information is 'particular' in that it is all information held for, and relevant to, employment.[33]

Some answers (but at least as many questions) to the issues raised can be found in the Court of Appeal decision in *Durant v Financial Services Authority*.[34] In addition to the issue discussed above of whether data is classed as personal in its nature, the court gave extensive consideration to the appellant's claim for access to a range of manual records. As described in the judgment, these took a variety of forms and demonstrated differing levels of structure and organisation. In some cases, documents were located in a folder under Mr Michael Durant's name but in other instances the name on the file was that of the bank against which complaints had been made—whether by Mr Durant or by other persons. It was accepted by the FSA that all of these files contained some information which related to the appellant. The degree and level of identification varied, with some files identifying him 'by reference to specific dividers within the file'. Files also contained a range of documents, including copies of telephone attendance notes and:

> a report of forensic examination of documents, transcripts of judgments, handwritten notes, internal memoranda, correspondence with Barclays Bank, correspondence with other individuals and correspondence between the FSA and him.[35]

Again taking account of the issue of whether data might be regarded as personal, the court considered the extent to which the records in question could be considered to constitute a relevant file. Again, reference was made to the Act's intention being to protect the privacy of the data subject rather than that of documents. As had been described above, it would be a relatively simple task to identify documents but a more complex one to determine whether a document constituted personal data. Consideration was given to the magnitude of the task which a data controller might be faced with in seeking to respond to a request for subject access. The responsibility

---

[32] 587 HL Official Report (5th series), col. 467, 16 March 1998.
[33] Briefing Note, 29 January 1998.
[34] [2003] EWCA Civ 1746.
[35] *Durant v Financial Services Authority* [2003] EWCA Civ 1746 at para. 17.

for the task, it was held, would often fall on administrators who might not have a specialised knowledge of the subject area or documents involved. In order for the extent of access to be manageable, the obligations could only be applied in respect of manual systems:

> that enable identification of relevant information with a minimum of time and costs, through clear referencing mechanisms within any filing system potentially containing personal data the subject of a request for information. Anything less, which, for example, requires the searcher to leaf through files to see what and whether information qualifying as personal data of the person who has made the request is to be found there, would bear no resemblance to a computerised search.[36]

It is not clear whether this conclusion is necessarily supported by the reality of modern databases. A Google-type search, for example across an organisation's electronic filing systems, might identify a large number of documents in which an applicant's name appeared—as indeed was at issue in the *Durant* case. Whilst certainly there could be no obligation on a data controller to read, or request an administrator to read, every piece of paper in the organisation, the level of structure and organisation required seems excessive.

It is often stated that hard cases make bad laws. It may also be the case that bad cases make hard laws. These is no doubt that the judges in *Durant*[37] were extremely wary of what was regarded as an attempt to invoke the provisions of the Data Protection Act 1998 for purposes beyond those envisaged by the legislature. It might be noted that in many cases, data of the kind sought by Durant could have been obtained under the Freedom of Information Act 2000, although this legislation was not in force at the time his litigation commenced. Given that the Financial Services Authority had identified the material relating to Durant's case in the context of the data protection proceedings, it might be difficult to refuse any future freedom of information request on the basis that the information would be excessively difficult to collect. Perhaps the most intractable problem facing the courts in a case such as this is that there is the clear signal, not least from the Data Protection Directive,[38] that the legislation is concerned with the protection of the right to privacy, yet, as discussed extensively elsewhere, this remains something which is not explicitly protected in the United Kingdom. The content of the right to privacy has long evaded precise definition. The classic formulation, however, refers to the right 'to be left alone', whilst references to the concept of informational privacy lay stress on the more proactive ability to control the storage and dissemination of personal data. If the right to exercise at least a measure of control over the collection and use of personal data is to have any meaning, knowledge of the nature and extent of the information which is held must be a necessary concomitant. In adopting a restrictive view of the scope of relevant filing systems, the court in *Durant* pays insufficient regard to the concept of informational privacy.

---

[36] Ibid. at para. 45.
[37] *Durant v Financial Services Authority* [2003] EWCA Civ 1746.
[38] Directive 95/46/EC.

Data protection actors

Data controllers

Data controllers are subject to the most extensive forms of control under the Data Protection Act and Directive. The Directive provides that:

> 'controller' shall mean the natural or legal person, public authority, agency or any other body which alone or jointly with others determines the purposes and means of the processing of personal data; where the purposes and means of processing are determined by national or Community laws or regulations, the controller or the specific criteria for his nomination may be designated by national or Community law.[39]

The Data Protection Act provides that a party will be classed as a data controller when it:

> …(either alone or jointly or in common with other persons) determines the purposes for which and the manner in which personal data are, or are to be processed.[40]

In the case where data are processed only for purposes required by statute, for example the compilation of an electoral roll, the agency charged with conducting the work will be classed as the data controller.

The key element of the above definitions relates, with the exception of the performance of statutory functions, to the ability to determine the nature and extent of the processing which is to be carried out. It is quite possible for persons to be classed as data controllers even though they do not own a computer. An example might concern the owner of a small business who records details of transactions on pieces of paper which are stored in the archetypal shoebox. Once a year, the shoebox may be collected by an accountant, who transfers the data to computer in order to prepare a set of accounts. Assuming that some of the data in the accounts relate to individual creditors and debtors, all the criteria necessary for the application of the legislation will be satisfied and, doubtless much to their surprise, the business person will be classed as a data controller. In such a situation, the accountant will also be so regarded, the Divisional Court confirming in *Data Protection Registrar v Griffin*,[41] a case brought under the Data Protection Act 1984, that anyone who processed data on behalf of clients would be regarded as a data user when he or she possessed any control or discretion concerning the manner in which the processing was carried out.

A similar result is postulated in the Recitals to the Data Protection Directive:

> …where a message containing personal data is transmitted by means of a telecommunications or electronic mail service, the sole purpose of which is the transmission of such messages, the controller in respect of the personal data contained in the message will normally be considered to be the person from whom the message originates, rather than the person offering the transmission services; whereas, nevertheless, those

[39] Article 2(d).   [40] Section 1(1).
[41] *The Times*, 5 March 1993.

offering such services will normally be considered controllers in respect of the process-ing of the additional personal data necessary for the operation of the service.[42]

Data processors

As in the example given above, some data controllers may seek to have processing carried out on their behalf by a third party. This was perhaps more prevalent in the early days of computing than is the case today, although one aspect which remains sig-nificant is where undertakings make arrangements as part of a disaster recovery plan, to obtain access to external processing facilities in the event of some interruption to service. Mirroring once again the terminology of the Data Protection Directive,[43] the Data Protection Act 1998 utilises the term 'data processor' which encompasses:

> ...any person (other than an employee of the data controller) who processes the data on behalf of the data controller.[44]

The phrase in brackets was included to avoid the possibility that employees engaged in processing in the course of their employment might be regarded as data processors. Given the expanded definition of processing adopted in the 1998 Act, it will be the case that anyone who collects data for the processor—perhaps by conducting market research surveys—will be classed as a processor.

Although a wide range of persons may be classed as data processors, the require-ments imposed on them are limited. Data processors will not be subject to the notification requirements,[45] whilst, in respect of the requirement to maintain appropri-ate security (now found in the seventh principle), the onus is placed upon the data con-troller for whom processing is conducted. The controller is responsible for selecting a processor who can provide satisfactory guarantees regarding security.[46] A written con-tract must also be entered into obliging the processor to act only on instructions from the controller in respect of the processing carried out, and also to comply with the requirements of the seventh principle.[47] Further, it is only the data controller who may be liable to compensate data subjects for losses arising from processing.[48]

Data subjects

A data subject is 'an individual who is the subject of personal data'.[49] It would be a unique individual who is not to be classed as a data subject—many times over. In contrast to

---

[42] Directive 95/46/EC, Recital 41.
[43] Directive 95/46/EC.
[44] Section 1(1).
[45] Section 17, which provides for notification, refers only to this obligation being imposed upon data controllers.
[46] Schedule 1, Pt 2, para. 11.
[47] Schedule 1, Pt 2, para. 12.
[48] Section 13.
[49] Section 1(1). Section 1(4) contains the equivalent provision in the Data Protection Act 1984.

the situation with data controllers and processors, where the focus is very much on the obligations imposed under the legislation, for data subjects, the purpose of the statute is to confer rights. The most important right for data subjects is undoubtedly that of obtaining access to data held by controllers and of securing the correction of any errors contained therein.

Jurisdictional issues

The Data Protection Act 1984 'applies to all data users who control the contents and use of personal data from within the United Kingdom'.[50] In part, this approach was necessary in order to comply with the Council of Europe's provisions regarding mutual assistance. In the situation where data is processed in the United Kingdom relating to, for example, French or German data subjects, the Data Protection Act will apply, with the main issue being the identification of the data user. The question of whether an undertaking can be considered resident in the United Kingdom is one which arises in a number of contexts and which may produce different results. As the Commissioner has commented, a company could be regarded as resident in the United Kingdom for the purpose of the Data Protection Act but not for taxation purposes. In the event that the company is not considered resident, it may be that it will be represented in the United Kingdom by a 'servant or agent' who will be classed as a data user for this purpose. It may also be the case that the undertaking which carries out the processing may be regarded as a computer bureau for the purpose of the legislation.

Similar problems arise when data relating to United Kingdom data subjects is processed abroad. In many instances, the data will remain under the legal control of the United Kingdom-based user, who will therefore be subject to the legislation. The view has been taken by the Commissioner that jurisdiction will be claimed even where all aspects of the processing are carried out abroad but where it is intended that the data will be used in the United Kingdom—regardless of the form in which it is imported. The correctness of this interpretation has not been tested before the courts or the Information Tribunal.

In the Data Protection Directive,[51] it is provided that EU Member States are to apply national laws where processing 'is carried out in the context of the activities of an establishment of the controller on the territory of the Member State'. Such a formulation may lead to extra-territorial application of national laws. Article 28(6) provides further that:

> Each supervisory authority is competent, whatever the national law applying to the processing in question, to exercise, on the territory of its own Member State, the powers conferred on it (to investigate suspected violations of the law and to intervene by legal or administrative measures to terminate breaches). Each authority may be requested to exercise its powers by an authority of another Member State.

[50] Section 39.   [51] Directive 95/46/EC.

There is potential for overlapping jurisdiction in the situation where multinational undertakings process personal data in a variety of Member States. In its Consultation Paper, the Home Office asserts that:

> While some of the provisions relating to geographical extent are clear enough, others are obscure and potentially ambiguous. There is, therefore, the potential for inconsistent approaches being adopted in different Member States. The danger is that this could make it possible for the national law of *more* than one Member State to apply to a single processing operation, or for *no* Member State's law so to apply.[52]

The multiple jurisdiction situation would appear to be an inevitable consequence of the free movement of data within the EU. Given that a major purpose of the Data Protection Directive[53] is to harmonise the laws of the Member States, such a result should not be excessively burdensome for data users and, indeed, corresponds to the UK Commissioner's interpretation of the existing situation under domestic law. It is difficult to envisage that a reasonable interpretation of the Directive's terms could produce a situation where no national law applied. In implementing the Directive's provisions, the Data Protection Act 1998 will apply where:

(a) the data controller is established in the United Kingdom and the data are processed in the context of that establishment; or

(b) the data controller is established neither in the United Kingdom nor in any other EEA state but uses equipment in the United Kingdom for processing the data otherwise than for the purposes of transit through the United Kingdom.[54]

An example of the latter situation might be where equipment forming part of a computer network, perhaps involving an ISP, is located in the United Kingdom but managed from the United States.

The question of establishment is defined more precisely than under the Data Protection Act 1984. The criteria adopted are that the controller satisfies one of the following criteria:

1. The controller is an individual who is ordinarily resident in the United Kingdom.

2. The controller is a body incorporated under United Kingdom law.

3. The controller is a partnership or unincorporated association subject to United Kingdom law.

4. The controller is a person maintaining an office, branch agency, or regular practice in the United Kingdom.[55]

For multinational companies, it is the case that they will be regarded as established in every country in which they operate. The geographical location of any data

---

[52] 'Data Protection: The Government's Proposals' (1997), para. 2.27.
[53] Directive 95/46/EC.
[54] Section 5(1).
[55] Data Protection Act 1998, s 5(3).

processing operation will not be relevant. A company established, for example, in France, Germany, and the United Kingdom will need to comply with the national laws of each of these states. The effect will be that the Data Protection Commissioner would be obliged to assist any inquiries made by the German supervisory authority regarding processing relating to German citizens carried out in the United Kingdom and to apply German law in determining the legality of this processing. The Data Protection Act 1998 provides that an Order may be made by the Secretary of State relating to the manner in which these functions might be exercised.[56]

Conclusions

Given the expanded nature of some of its basic definitions, there is little doubt that the Data Protection Act 1998 governs a greater range of activities than was the case under the Data Protection Act 1984. In addition to legal changes, developments in technology, such as permitting the automatic identification of individuals whose images are captured on video camera or, indeed, car number-plates, will mean that many of these forms of surveillance will also be governed by the legislation. The scope of the legislation has begun to be examined by the courts. In *Bodil Lindqvist*,[57] the European Court adopted an expansive view of the scope of the legislation. In *Durant v Financial Services Authority*,[58] the Court of Appeal took a rather more restrictive approach. It may well be that further decisions of the European Court will be necessary in order to provide a comprehensive and consistent approach to the scope of the Data Protection Directive[59] across the EU Member States.

It is clearly the task of the courts to apply legislative provisions at issue before them. The courts have perhaps been ill served by the legislature, which has promulgated laws that are rather imprecise. In *Campbell v MGN*,[60] Lord Phillips of Worth Matravers MR said:

> In interpreting the Act it is appropriate to look to the Directive [Data Protection Directive[61]] for assistance. The Act [Data Protection Act 1998] should, if possible, be interpreted in a manner that is consistent with the Directive. Furthermore, because the Act has, in large measure, adopted the wording of the Directive, it is not appropriate to look for the precision in the use of language that is usually to be expected from the parliamentary draftsman. A purposive approach to making sense of the provisions is called for.[62]

---

[56] Section 51(3). The Data Protection (Functions of Designated Authority) Order 2000, SI 2000/186, makes provisions for the Commissioner to cooperate with, and seek the cooperation of, other Member State supervisory authorities in such matters. This provision is discussed in more detail below.

[57] Case 101/01, [2004] QB 1014.

[58] [2003] EWCA Civ 1746.

[59] Directive 95/46/EC.

[60] [2002] EWCA Civ 1373, [2003] QB 633.

[61] Directive 95/46/EC.

[62] [2002] EWCA Civ 1373, [2003] QB 633 at [96].

Even the most purposive form of interpretation cannot and should not provide an excuse for unfettered judicial decision-making. Beyond issues of ambiguity and lack of precision in the drafting of the legislation, the Directive and the Act are to a considerable extent surviving dinosaurs from the age when computers were mainly freestanding machines, used almost exclusively by businesses and large organisations but with limited networking capabilities. The world has moved on and, whilst the European Court was undoubtedly correct in determining that the development of a web page constituted processing as defined in the legislation, it is difficult to see that this, and a myriad of other pages maintained by individuals effectively by way of a hobby, constitute a sufficiently serious threat to the rights and freedoms of other individuals to justify the imposition of criminal sanctions. As will be discussed in Chapter 6, the legislation does not apply where processing is for social or domestic purposes. The problem, which arises also in the context of copyright infringement, is that what used to be clearcut distinctions, not least in terms of the scale of activities possible, are no longer applicable. The old models are broken but the form of their replacements has yet to be resolved in a satisfactory manner.

Suggestions for further reading

Article 29 Working Party Opinion No. 4/2007 on the Concept of Personal Data (2007).

Information Commissioner's Office(1989), *Legal Guidance on the Data Protection Act.*

4

Supervisory agencies

Introduction

The notion that a specialised agency should be established with responsibility for action in the field of data protection is one which is common to virtually all European systems and marks a major point of divergence from the approach adopted in the United States. One leading authority, Professor Spiros Simitis, former Data Protection Commissioner for the German State or Lander of Hesse, has suggested that:

> data protection presupposes...the establishment of an independent control authority. Experience confirms what was already stated in the earliest debates: It is not enough to trace a mandatory framework for data processing. The legislator must also secure the monitoring of the processing conditions. Neither the participation of the data subject nor any of the traditional means of control guarantees, however, adequate supervision. Even if the data subject is entrusted with a series of rights he remains an outsider, deprived of the necessary information permitting him to analyze and evaluate the activities of the various public and private agencies.[1]

From an American standpoint, however, it has been suggested that the:

> United States approach towards privacy protection is designed to put the individual in the centre of the action, to let him have a large voice in decisions as to what information will be collected, used and disseminated about him. The Europeans take a paternalistic approach choosing to vest enforcement in bureaucracy.[2]

Both positions have elements of validity. There is no doubt that supervisory agencies are better placed than individuals to take an overview of processing activities. However, the agencies have to straddle—sometimes uncomfortably—a wide range of roles ranging from consumer ombudsman, through law enforcer, to acting. This has been notable in the United Kingdom in recent years, as a protaganist in the ongoing debate as to the future development of the law in fields such as identity cards and data sharing, where the interests of law enforcement potentially clash with informational privacy. As will be discussed further below, however, issues largely associated with finance have served to make the United Kingdom's supervisory regime more burdensome for data controllers, with a limited concomitant benefit for individuals.

---

[1] Simitis (1985), at 11–12.
[2] L. Hummer in 'Transnational Data Regulation, The Realities' Online Conferences (1979).

The establishment of a specific supervisory agency was not originally a requirement of the Council of Europe Convention, which requires signatories merely to 'designate one or more authorities' who will, at the request of another designated authority, furnish information on national laws and administrative practices, provide factual information related to specified automated files, and undertake any investigations related to the request in conformity with national legal provisions.[3] When the Data Protection Act 1984 was being prepared, it was indeed suggested that the supervisory function might be carried out by the Home Office. Ultimately, however, the decision was taken to establish an independent Data Protection Registrar, an approach which was common to all European states enacting data protection laws, with the exception of Luxembourg. The Data Protection Directive is more prescriptive, requiring the establishment of an independent supervisory authority (or authorities).[4] It specifies in Recital 62 that the establishment of independent supervisory authorities is an essential component of the protection of individuals with regard to the processing of personal data, and provides under Article 28 that:

> Each Member State shall provide that one or more public authorities are responsible for monitoring the application within its territory of the provisions adopted by the Member States pursuant to this Directive. These authorities shall act with complete independence in exercising the functions entrusted to them.

Amendments to the Council of Europe Convention now make similar provision.[5] It should also be noted that the Treaty of Amsterdam—which made significant changes to the treaties establishing the EU—provides that independent supervisory agencies are to be established in respect of the Community institutions. Article 286 of the amended Treaty provides that:

1. From 1 January 1999, Community acts on the protection of individuals with regard to the processing of personal data and the free movement of such data shall apply to the institutions and bodies set up by, or on the basis of, this Treaty.

2. Before the date referred to in paragraph 1, the Council, acting in accordance with the procedure referred to in Article 251, shall establish an independent supervisory body responsible for monitoring the application of such Community acts to Community institutions and bodies and shall adopt any other relevant provisions as appropriate.

Action was not taken until the end of 2000, when Regulation 45/2001 on the protection of individuals with regard to the processing of personal data by the Community institutions and bodies and on the free movement of such data[6] was adopted, entering into force at the end of January 2001. The Regulation provides for the appointment of a European Data Protection Supervisor[7] and contains provisions, equivalent in scope to those contained in the Data Protection and Electronic Communications Privacy Directives which will apply to processing carried out by the European institutions. A

---

[3] Article 13(2).   [4] Article 28.
[5] Article 1 of the Additional Protocol.
[6] *Official Journal* (2001) L8/1.   [7] Article 1.

further two years were to elapse before Decision 2004/55[8] announced the appointment of Peter Hustinx as the first Supervisor, with Mr Joaquim Delgada as his assistant. Both were appointed for five-year terms.

In the majority of Member States, a single supervisory agency has been established. In Germany, however, responsibility is divided between twenty different federal and state agencies, with separate agencies for the public and the private sectors. One of the key decisions which needs to be made concerns the structure of the regulatory agency. Many options are available but the key choice lies perhaps between the appointment of a single regulator, albeit supported by what may be a substantial staff, or vesting authority in a multi-membered commission or authority. The relative merits of single and multiple regulators have been ventilated in many other areas. A single regulator may well be able to bring a more focused and consistent approach to regulation, although much will obviously depend upon the personality and abilities of the post holder. With a collegiate body there is more potential for internal dissent, but it is also likely that a wider range of interests and expertise may be represented, with the consequence that decisions, when reached, may carry greater weight.

In part, the choice of whether to appoint a single regulator or a commission is influenced by national traditions. Historically, the United Kingdom has favoured the appointment of a single official. Examples include the Information Commissioner, the Director General of Fair Trading, and the regulators for the privatised gas, electricity, and railway industries. More recently, however, the Communications Act 2003 provided for the establishment of the Office of Communications (OFCOM) as a multi-membered regulatory body to take over the functions of five individual regulators in the media and telecommunications sector.

As indicated above, the Directive lays stress on the need for supervisory agencies to be independent. Although independence is a key component of the regulatory structure, it has been described by the International Telecommunications Union—in the context of telecommunications regulation—as a 'complex and widely misunderstood concept'.[9] Independence cannot mean that the supervisory agency has complete freedom to act but rather that there is to be a separation between the agency and those whose activities it supervises. This is a matter which is easy to stipulate but harder to achieve in real life. Particular problems arise in respect of public sector data-processing, especially given that the supervisory authorities tend to be funded directly or indirectly from the public purse.

Key functions of supervisory agencies

In addition to requiring the establishment of an independent agency or agencies, the Data Protection Directive also prescribes the basic powers to be vested in these agencies. These agencies are to be afforded:

[8] *Official Journal* (2004) L 012/47.
[9] Trends in Telecommunication Reform, Effective Regulation ITU 1992.

- investigative powers, such as powers of access to data forming the subject-matter of processing operations and powers to collect all the information necessary for the performance of its supervisory duties;

- effective powers of intervention, such as, for example, that of delivering opinions before processing operations are carried out, in accordance with Article 20, and ensuring appropriate publication of such opinions, of ordering the blocking, erasure, or destruction of data, of imposing a temporary or definitive ban on processing, of warning or admonishing the controller, or that of referring the matter to national parliaments or other political institutions; and

- the power to engage in legal proceedings where the national provisions adopted pursuant to this directive have been violated or to bring these violations to the attention of the judicial authorities[10]

It is further provided that:

Each supervisory authority shall hear claims lodged by any person, or by an association representing that person, concerning the protection of his rights and freedoms in regard to the processing of personal data. The person concerned shall be informed of the outcome of the claim.[11]

The Information Commissioner and Tribunal

Under the United Kingdom's Data Protection Act 1984, the office of Data Protection Registrar was created. In addition to the Registrar, the Act provided for the establishment of a Data Protection Tribunal. The sole function of the Data Protection Tribunal was to hear appeals brought by data users or computer bureaux against decisions taken by the Registrar which directly affect them. The Tribunal could uphold the Registrar's original ruling, reverse it, or, where the Registrar's act involved the exercise of a discretion, substitute its own ruling.

The first Data Protection Registrar, Mr Eric Howe, was appointed in 1984, and after serving two terms of office was replaced in 1994 by Mrs Elizabeth France, who served until 2003, when she became Telecommunications Ombudsman. The current holder is Richard Thomas, whose term of office runs to June 2009. In her *Twelfth Annual Report*, published in 1996, the then Registrar indicated concern that the title of Registrar placed undue emphasis on one (rather bureaucratic) aspect of her role and suggested that with the introduction of a new Data Protection Act there should be a change in nomenclature so that her office should be described as Privacy Protection Commissioner. This request was accepted in part, although the Data Protection Act 1998, in common with the 1984 Act, eschewed any mention of the word 'privacy'. From the date of the 1998 Act's entry into force, it provided that the 'Data Protection Registrar...shall continue in existence by the name of the Data Protection Commissioner.'[12] With the enactment

---

[10] Article 28(3).   [11] Article 28(4).
[12] Schedule 5.

of the Freedom of Information Act 2000, the Commissioner also became responsible for the operation of that legislation. Recognising this fact, there has been a further change in the nomenclature to Information Commissioner.[13] At the same time, the Tribunal was renamed as the Information Tribunal, reflecting additional responsibilities placed on it under the Freedom of Information Act.

The Data Protection Act 1998 specifies the terms and conditions under which the Commissioner is to be appointed. This is to be for a fixed term, not exceeding five years. Within this period, the Commissioner might be removed from office only following a resolution passed by both Houses of Parliament, a status equivalent to that of High Court judges. One change made from the Data Protection Act 1984 is the provision that a Commissioner may only serve for two terms, save where special circumstances make a continuation of appointment 'desirable in the public interest'.[14] Under the 1984 Act, there was no limit on the number of terms which an individual could serve. Concern has been expressed in the past that the government's role in deciding whether to continue an appointment might deter the supervisory agency from investigating public sector data processing. One incident has been reported in Germany, where a state Data Protection Commissioner's appointment was not continued shortly after the individual concerned had been involved in a well-publicised disagreement concerning governmental data-processing practices. Although the matter is not likely to be of significance in the near future, it might be considered unfortunate that the default has effectively been switched from the assumption that the Commissioner might continue in the post for more than two terms, to the assumption that this will not be the case.

The Information Commissioner's Office is a substantial one. Separate offices, each headed by an Assistant Commissioner have been established for Scotland, Wales, and Northern Ireland. In total, some 262 staff are employed. Inevitably, the operation of such a substantial organisation requires considerable resources and in 2006–7, operating costs were in the region of £17.3 million. The issue of how the supervisory agency's work should be funded has been at the core of many of the debates about the format of the legislation. Although the Data Protection Act 1998 makes provision for public funds to be used to meet the Commissioner's expenses, it is the intention that the office should be largely self-financing. This decision drives many others concerning the scope of the Act and the obligations imposed upon data users. Although the Office's functions in respect of freedom of information legislation are funded by a government grant of about £5.5 million, the only other significant source of income is from the fees payable by data controllers in connection with the Act's registration procedures. In 2006–7 these raised some £10.2 million.[15] Clearly, maximisation of the numbers of those classed as data controllers will have a similar effect upon the income

---

[13] Introduced by s 18 of the Freedom of Information Act 2000.

[14] Data Protection Act 1998, Schedule 5, para. 2.

[15] All data taken from the Information Commissioner's *Annual Report for 2006-7*. Available from <http://www.ico.gov.uk/upload/documents/library/corporate/detailed_specialist_guides/annual_report_2007.pdf>

of the Commissioner, whilst any significant reduction in the numbers of those liable to register would have significant implications, either for the financial burdens imposed on those remaining subject to a registration requirement or for the Commissioner's income stream.

Initially, this chapter will focus on the establishment and maintenance of the Data Protection Register and the obligations imposed on data controllers. Attention will then be paid to the investigative and enforcement powers conferred on the Commissioner, before concluding with an account of the remaining powers and duties imposed on the Commissioner.

Regulation of data controllers

A feature of many of the early data protection statutes was the imposition of a system of licensing of data users. Although terminology in the field is somewhat inconsistent, the procedure might be analogised to the obtaining of a licence for the possession of a gun or the driving of a motor vehicle, with the onus being placed on the applicant to demonstrate fitness to receive the award. With the massive increase in the number of computers since the 1970s, the impossibility of exercising effective control in this manner has been widely recognised. An initial step, which was implemented in the Data Protection Act 1984, saw the introduction of a system of registration of data users. Registration continues to require those wishing to process personal data to seek authorisation and retains qualitative criteria, but switches the onus to the supervisory agency to indicate the cause of an application being rejected. Failure to apply for registration would constitute an offence punishable by a fine. Applications might be rejected on three grounds. First, that, in the Registrar's opinion, 'the particulars proposed for registration . . . will not give sufficient information as to the matters to which they relate'.[16] An application may also be refused if the Registrar was satisfied that the applicant is likely to contravene any of the data protection principles,[17] and, finally, if the Registrar 'considered that the information available to him is insufficient to satisfy him that the applicant is unlikely to contravene any of those principles'.[18]

In the fourteen years that the registration system operated, very few applications were formally refused. Thirty-two applications were refused in the year 1994–95, 31 in 1995–96, and none in subsequent years.[19] Even at the 'higher' levels, this translated into a refusal rate of one in every 2,650 applications.

From registration to notification

The effectiveness of the registration process adopted in the Data Protection Act 1984 was criticised from the outset. More recent statutes, such as the German Data Protection Act 1990, moved away from the requirements of universal registration by exempting large numbers of data controllers from any procedural requirements. Even

---

[16] Section 7(2)(a).   [17] Section 7(2)(b).
[18] Section 7(2)(c).   [19] *Fifteenth Report of the Data Protection Registrar* (1999), ch. 5.

where users remain subject to a requirement to record details of their processing, systems of declaration or notification have been adopted. Notification, as the terminology suggests, involves the controller giving information about the nature of processing activities but does not give the supervisory agency any power of rejection—although concerns about the activities notified might serve to trigger further enforcement actions. The Data Protection Directive follows this model. It initially provides that:

> Member States shall provide that the controller or his representative, if any, must notify the supervisory agency…before carrying out [processing of personal data].[20]

Having established the principle of notification, the Data Protection Directive[21] continues to provide that simplification or exemption from notification may be offered:

> …for categories of processing operations which are unlikely, taking account of the data to be processed, to affect adversely the rights and freedoms of data subjects.

This was subject to conditions being imposed on the kinds of data to be processed, the persons to whom it is to be disclosed, and the length of time the data are to be stored. A range of other possible exemptions are identified in the Directive, some of which are adopted in the Data Protection Act 1998.[22]

Implementing the Directive, the Data Protection Act 1998 imposes a general requirement to notify details of processing:

> Subject to the following provisions of this section, personal data must not be processed unless an entry in respect of the data controller is included in the Register maintained by the Commissioner.[23]

Breach of this provision constitutes an offence.[24] Unlike the situation under the Data Protection Act 1984, where liability was strict, a defence of 'due diligence' is available to data controllers.[25] This may be justified on account of the wider range of exceptions potentially available from notification and the fact that controllers, under the mistaken impression that they are so exempt, will, nonetheless, be required to comply with the substantive requirements of the legislation.

When initial consultations on the implementation of the Data Protection Directive began, the then Data Protection Registrar was—as discussed further below—an advocate of the view that the powers to grant exemption should be used widely to remove thousands of data controllers from the bureaucratic burdens associated with the registration/notification process. Such an approach would find support in a significant difference between the approach of the Data Protection Act 1984 and that of the Directive and the Data Protection Act 1998 towards the effect of exemption. Exemption under the 1984 Act removed a data user from any obligation to comply with the legislation, whilst exemption under the 1998 Act is—with two exceptions (relating to processing solely for the purposes of an individual's 'personal, family or household affairs'[26]

---

[20] Directive 95/46/EC, Article 18(1).   [21] Directive 95/46/EC.
[22] Article 18(2).   [23] Section 17(1).   [24] S 21(1).   [25] S 20(3).   [26] Section 36.

and processing for the purposes of national security[27])—only from the requirement to notify details of processing. In all other cases, controllers who are exempt from the requirement to notify will remain subject to the substantive provisions of the legislation, with the requirements, for example, that data be processed fairly and that subject-access requests be acceded to.

Exemptions from the requirement to notify

Under the Data Protection Act 1984, the list of categories of exempt processing was defined exhaustively in the statute.[28] The 1998 Act adopts a more flexible approach. It provides that:

> If it appears to the Secretary of State that processing of a particular description is unlikely to prejudice the rights and freedoms of data subjects, notification regulations may provide [for exemption from the requirement to notify].[29]

The Information Commissioner is to play a significant role in the drafting of the regulations, the Act providing that the Commissioner is 'as soon as practicable after the passing' of the Act, to submit 'proposals as to the provisions to be included in the first notification regulations'.[30] The Commissioner is charged with the duty of keeping the working of the regulations under review and may submit further proposals to the Secretary of State.[31] The Secretary of State may also require the Commissioner to consider specific topics and make proposals.[32] Although the regulatory power remains with the Secretary of State, there is a statutory duty to consider proposals made by the Commissioner and, more generally, to consult with the Commissioner before making use of any regulatory power conferred under the legislation.[33]

In initial consultation exercises concerning the extent of exemptions, the Registrar advocated that extensive use should be made of this provision in order to exclude 'potentially hundreds of thousands of data controllers from notification'. Subsequent events saw a substantial withdrawal from this position. In part, this can be traced to definitional problems. In proposals submitted in 1999, the Registrar commented:

> We consider it important that exemptions from notification must not have the effect of increasing administrative costs either for data controllers or for the Commissioner. This means that if there are to be exemptions, boundaries between the exempt and the non-exempt should be clear. It also means that in exempting certain processing operations, the objective should be to exempt certain categories of data controller as a whole. There is little point in creating exemptions for certain processing operations if, by and large, data controllers still have to notify because other common processing operations are not exempt.
>
> Accepting this in principle is easy; the difficulty is in the detail. It is not simply a question of saying that certain types of business, categorised, for example, by the number of employees or by turnover are exempt. The exemptions have to be formulated

---

27 S 28.   28 Sections 32 and 33.   29 Section 17(3).   30 Section 25(1).
31 Section 25(2).   32 Section 25(3).   33 Section 67(3).

in terms which satisfy Article 18.2 of Directive 95/46/EC [which requires that] *'the purposes of the processing, the data or categories of data undergoing processing, the category or categories of data subject, the recipients or categories of recipient to whom the data are to be disclosed and the length of time the data are to be stored'* all have to be specified.[34]

It was concluded that no data controllers, other than those processing for social or domestic purposes, should be exempted from the requirement to notify. As will be discussed, however, a number of purpose-related exemptions do apply.

Definitional problems apart, pragmatic considerations undoubtedly also served to limit the numbers of those exempted from the requirement to notify details of processing. As stated above, the fees obtained from those submitting applications for registration/notification constitute virtually the only source of income for the Registrar/Commissioner. The Data Protection Act 1998 provides that, in fixing the level of fees, 'the Secretary of State shall have regard to the desirability of securing that the fees payable to the Commissioner are sufficient to offset the costs of running the Commissioner and Tribunal's statutory activities'.[35] A significant reduction in the level of those requiring to notify would inevitably increase the level of fees for those remaining subject to the requirement.

The scope of the exemptions

The Data Protection (Notification and Notification Fees) Regulations 2000[36] (the 'Notification Regulations') provide for a limited number of data controllers to be exempted from the notification requirement. The exemptions can be placed in two categories, the first relating to particular forms of processing and the second to specific categories of data controller. Especially in respect of the first category, it should be noted that whilst some forms of processing need not be notified, in the (likely) event that a controller engages in additional and notifiable forms of processing, a choice will be given, either to notify everything or to include an indication in the Register entry to the effect that:

This data controller also processes personal data which is exempt from Notification.

The purpose of this is to put data subjects on notice that the entry on the Register will not give a complete picture of the controller's activities. Whilst the same argument could also have been advanced under the 1984 regime, the more limited scope of exemption warrants a change from previous practice.

---

[34] Proposals for Notification Regulations (1999).

[35] Section 26(2). It was indicated in Parliament that the cumulative deficit on the Registrar's activities since 1986 is some £4.5 million. The Act further provides that account may be taken of the amount of any outstanding deficit when fixing fees. The Act contains a further provision allowing different levels of fees to be charged to different categories of controller (s 26(1)).

[36] SI 2000/188.

Exempt forms of processing

The Notification Regulations[37] provide for exemption in respect of three forms of processing, involving what has been referred to by the Commissioner as 'core business activities'.[38] It is stressed, however, that the conditions attached to the exemptions are, in common with similar provisions found in the Data Protection Act 1984, likely to ensure that they are of value only to small businesses. In addition to the purpose-related exemptions, a further exemption applies in respect of certain forms of processing conducted by non-profit-making organisations.

Staff administration

Although the concept of staff administration sounds relatively broad, the scope of the exemption is much more narrowly circumscribed. The activity of staff administration is defined as involving the purposes of:

> Appointments or removals, pay, discipline, superannuation, work management or other personnel matters.[39]

Data held may relate to past, present, or potential employees, or to 'any person, the processing of whose personal data is necessary for the exempt purposes'. This latter category might include, for example, the processing of data relating to the partner of an employee who will be entitled to pension or other benefits in the event of the employee's death. The data may consist of names, addressees, and other identifiers, as well as information relating to:

(i)   qualifications, work experience or pay; or

(ii) other matters, the processing of which is necessary for the exempt purposes.

Two further requirements will also need to be satisfied for an exemption to be available. First, the data must not be disclosed to third parties, except with the consent of the data subject, or where this is necessary for the exempt purposes. An example within the latter category would concern the transfer of data to the Inland Revenue for the purpose of operating the system of PAYE. Second, the data must not be retained for longer than is necessary for the exempt purposes. In most cases, this might be taken to mean that data may not be retained once an employee has left employment.[40]

The word 'necessary' has been quoted on several occasions in the previous paragraphs and is used extensively throughout the provisions relating to exemption. A *Concise Oxford Dictionary* definition of the adjective 'necessary' refers to concepts such as:

> Unavoidable, indispensable, enforced, that which cannot be left out or done without.

---

[37] SI 2000/188.

[38] *Notification Exemptions: A Self Assessment Guide*, available from <http://www.dpr.gov.uk/notify/self/index.html.>

[39] SI 2000/188, Schedule, para. 2.

[40] SI 2000/188, Schedule, para. 2(d).

The restrictions imposed by these definitions should be borne in mind when considering all of the exemptions. An employer might, quite reasonably, seek to maintain a record of employees' next of kin. This will be of obvious benefit in the event of an accident or illness occurring at work. It is more arguable, however, whether the holding of such data is essential for staff administration purposes.

Advertising, marketing, and public relations

This exemption applies when processing is:

> For the purpose of advertising or marketing the data controller's business, activity, goods or services and promoting public relations in respect of that business or activity or those goods or services.[41]

Whilst the purpose is broad, the exemption is subject to limitations largely similar to those described above in relation to the nature of the data that may be processed, the range of disclosure, and period of retention. The exemption applies only in respect of the marketing of the controller's own goods or services.

Accounts and records

This exemption is couched in terms very similar to those applying under the Data Protection Act 1984. Exemption is offered in respect of processing conducted:

> ...for the purposes of keeping accounts relating to any business or other activity carried on by the data controller, or deciding whether to accept any person as a customer or supplier, or keeping records of purchases, sales or other transactions for the purpose of ensuring that the requisite payments and deliveries are made or services provided by or to the data controller in respect of those transactions, or for the purpose of making financial or management forecasts to assist him in the conduct of any such business or activity.[42]

Data must be limited to personal identifiers, together with information about the financial standing of the data subject and any other information necessary to conduct the exempt processing.

The exemption is somewhat broader than that previously provided for under the Data Protection Act 1984, but, once again, the requirement to show that data must necessarily be processed will constitute a significant limitation.

Non-profit-making organisations

Under the Data Protection Act 1984, exemption was offered in respect of the activities of 'unincorporated members clubs'. This proved to be a difficult concept to define and the Notification Regulations provide for exemption for non-profit-making organisations. The concept is undoubtedly broader than applying under the 1984 Act but, as

---

[41] SI 2000/188, Schedule, para. 3(a).
[42] SI 2000/188, Schedule, para. 4(1)(a).

with the other exceptions discussed above, only a limited range of activities will be covered. Processing is exempt in so far as it:

(a) is carried out by a data controller which is a body or association which is not established or conducted for profit; and

(b) is for the purposes of establishing or maintaining membership of or support for the body or association, or providing or administering activities for individuals who are either members of the body or association or have regular contact with it.[43]

The data processed may relate only to limited categories of individuals, principally present, past, or prospective members of the organisation and be limited to identifiers, together with such information as is necessary for the purposes of the organisation, for example data relating to subscription records. In common with the other exemptions, the data may be disclosed to third parties only with the consent of the data subject or where this is necessary for the exempt purpose.

Independent data protection supervisors

Under the German data protection law, it is common practice for data controllers to appoint 'in-house' data protection supervisors. Provided that such supervisors possess sufficient independence, this will exempt the controller from the requirement to notify the Federal Data Protection Commissioner. The Data Protection Directive also sanctions the adoption of such an approach,[44] and the Data Protection Act 1998 provides that the Secretary of State may make an order enabling controllers to appoint a data protection supervisor who will 'monitor in an independent manner the data controller's compliance' with the legislation. Any order will also specify the extent to which such action will exempt the controller from the notification requirement.[45]

In debate on this provision, the United Kingdom government pointed out that when such an option had been outlined in the consultation exercise preceding the introduction of the legislation, it had received some expressions of interest but little active support. It was indicated that, given the workload involved in implementing the new legislation, the making of any enabling regulations would not be seen as a priority issue.[46] Nearly ten years later, there is still no sign of any enabling regulations. In a paper published in 2007, *Sharing Personal Information—A New Approach*, the Information Commissioner's Office indicated that a code of practice would be developed which would make provision for in-house data protection supervisors.[47] A draft

---

[43] SI 2000/188, Schedule, para. 5.
[44] Directive 95/46/EC, Article 18(2).
[45] Section 23.
[46] HC Official Report, SC D (Data Protection Bill), cols 165–66, 19 May 1998.
[47] <http://www.ico.gov.uk/upload/documents/library/data_protection/practical_application/sharing_personal_info_in_public_sector_new_approach.pdf>

code was published in August 2007 which made no reference to this possibility.[48] Quite apart from the notiification aspect, it does appear that the appointment of internal data protection supervisors might be a practical way of providing reassurance to the public that data protection interests will be taken fully into account in the development of data sharing.

Optional notification

Although it might appear logical for a data controller to seek to benefit from any exemption which might be on offer, the reality may be more complex. Where details of processing are held on the Register, the controller is under no further obligation to inform data subjects as to these matters. A controller whose details do not appear is required to supply the information otherwise required at registration within twenty-one days of receiving a request from any person. Failure to reply timeously will constitute an offence.[49] Responding to a single request may be as burdensome as making notification to the Registrar. Given the nature of this obligation, it is perhaps not surprising that the Data Protection Act 1998 provides that a normally exempt data controller may voluntarily notify details of processing activities.[50]

Information to be supplied on notification

The Data Protection Act 1998 specifies the information which must be supplied to the Commissioner.[51] Referred to as the 'registrable particulars', this encompasses:

- the controller's name and address together with that of any nominated representative
- a description of the personal data to be processed and the categories of data subject to whom it relates
- a description of the purposes for which the data will be processed
- a description of the intended recipients or categories of recipient of the data
- in the event any additional processing is being carried out under the terms of an exemption from the notification requirement, a statement to this effect
- details of any countries outside the EEA to which it is intended that the data may be transferred. Controllers have the option either of specifying particular countries or indicating that 'worldwide' transfers are envisaged.[52]

---

[48] <http://www.ico.gov.uk/upload/documents/library/data_protection/practical_application/ico_information_sharing_framework_draft_1008.pdf>

[49] Data Protection Act 1998, s 24.

[50] Section 18.

[51] Section 16(1).

[52] Notification Handbook, available from <http://www.ico.gov.uk/upload/documents/library/data_protection/detailed_specialist_guides/notification_handbook_final.pdf>

The above information will be made publicly available in the form of the Data Protection Register. This was originally established under the 1984 Act with the 1998 Act continuing an obligation upon the Commissioner to:

(a) maintain a register of persons who have given notification under Section 18, and

(b) make an entry in the register in pursuance of each notification received by him under that section from a person in respect of whom no entry as data controller was for the time being included in the register.

In addition to the information which will appear on the Register, controllers are required to provide:

...a general description of measures to be taken for the purpose of complying with the seventh data protection principle.[53]

The seventh principle relates to the requirement to maintain appropriate data security measures. The Commissioner has identified four matters which need to be addressed:

- a statement of information security policy;
- control of physical security (restrictions on access to sites and equipment);
- controls on access to information (anti-hacking measures such as the use of passwords and encryption);
- a business continuity plan (disaster recovery).

Specific reference and endorsement is made to BS 7799, the British Standard on Information Security Management, and to the certification scheme 'c:cure' associated with it.[54] It should be stressed that this information—which might be of use to potential hackers—will not appear on the publicly accessible register.

Notification procedures

Notifications may be made in two ways. A copy of the notification form can be accessed over the Internet and completed online.[55] Users are guided on a step-by-step basis through the form but, in a reversion to more old-fashioned technology, there is no provision for the completed form to be submitted electronically; instead, the controller is required to print out the completed form and post it to the Commissioner. An alternative approach is to make contact by telephone. After giving details of the nature of the organisation and the forms of processing conducted, a form will be completed

---

[53] Section 18(2)(b).

[54] Data Protection Commissioner, *Notification Handbook* (2000), para. 3.2.3, available from <http://www.dpr.gov.uk/notihand.doc>

[55] <http://www.dpr.gov.uk/notify/1.html>

and posted to the controller who may then make any necessary changes before returning it to the Commissioner.

In cases where a notification form is transmitted by recorded post, it will become
valid from the day after posting. In other cases, it will be valid from the date it is
received by the Commissioner.[56] Once made, notification will be valid indefinitely
(subject to an obligation to notify changes in any of the registered particulars),[57] subject to payment of an annual fee. This fee may be collected by automatic mechanisms
such as direct debit.

Under the Data Protection Act 1984, the fee for registration rose in stages to stand
at £75 by the end of the regime. The notification fee is £35.[58] Whilst as a headline figure
this marks a reduction, the reduced period of validity means that most data controllers
will be faced with an increase of £30 over a three-year period.

Preliminary assessments

In most cases, once notification of processing is submitted, processing operations may
commence. Certain forms of processing may, however, be subject to additional controls. The Data Protection Directive obliges Member States to:

> Determine the processing operations likely to present specific risks to the rights and
> freedoms of data subjects and shall check that these processing operations are exam-
> ined prior to the start thereof.[59]

As implemented in the Data Protection Act 1998, regulatory power is conferred on
the Secretary of State to determine categories of processing, referred to as 'assessable
processing', which appear particularly likely:

(a) to cause substantial damage or substantial distress to data subjects; or

(b) otherwise significantly to prejudice the rights and freedoms of data subjects.[60]

To date, no order has been made specifying the form of processing which will be subject to preliminary assessment. It has been indicated that few forms of processing will
be covered by such regulations. In Parliament, specific reference was made to activities
involving data matching, genetic data, and private investigations.[61]

Where processing comes within the ambit of such regulations, the controller may
not commence activities until an assessment of its compliance with the data protection
principles has been made by the Commissioner. The timetable for the Commissioner
to act is a tight one. When receiving notification from any data controller, the
Commissioner is to consider whether any of the processing activities described involve

---

[56] SI 2000/188, Reg. 8.
[57] SI 2000/188, Reg. 12.
[58] SI 2000/188, Reg. 7.
[59] Directive 95/46/EC, Article 20.
[60] Section 22(1).
[61] HC Official Report, SC D (Data Protection Bill), cols 160–61, 19 May 1998.

assessable processing[62] and, if so, whether the processing is likely to comply with the requirements of the statute. Such notice is to be given within 10 days from receipt of the notification. The Commissioner is then required to give notice of his or her opinion to the controller within 28 days from the date of receipt of notification, which period might, in special circumstances, be extended by a further 14 days.[63] Processing must not be carried on during this period. In the event the Commissioner's assessment is that the processing would be unacceptable, there would not appear to be any mechanism to prevent the controller continuing with the plans, although it might be expected that an enforcement notice would be served in short order should this occur.

The Data Protection Register

The Data Protection Act requires the Commissioner to:

(a) provide facilities for making the information contained in the entries in the register available for inspection (in visible and legible form) by members of the public at all reasonable hours and free of charge; and

(b) may provide such other facilities for making the information contained in those entries available to the public free of charge as he considers appropriate.

Continuing the practice established under the 1984 Act, the Register can be accessed over the Internet.[64]

It is unclear, however, how valuable the information contained on the Register may be to the average data subject. The Information Commissioner's Annual Report for 2007 indicates that the Register held over 287,000 entries. In one respect, the size of the Register makes browsing a daunting task for data subjects. The Register can only be searched by reference to the name of a data controller or a registration number. Unless a subject knows that an organisation is likely to hold information about them, the Register will be of very little assistance in a quest to discover who might hold personal information. If a data subject knows of an organisation there may be little need to consult the Register, other perhaps than to confirm contact details for making a request for a copy of the information held.

Although the figure of 287,000 entries may seem large, it is perhaps the case that after more than twenty years of data protection legislation, many data controllers have failed to comply with the notification requirements. On a point of comparison, Jersey which has a population of around 87,000 and a Data Protection law almost identical to that applying in the United Kingdom has around 3,500 entries on its Data Protection Register. A similar ratio of entries to population would give the United Kingdom a register with almost 2.5 million entries. It is relevant to note that the heavy dependence of Jersey's economy on the financial services sector, with its voracious appetite

---

[62] Data Protection Act 1998, s 18(2).
[63] Section 18(3).
[64] <http://www.esd.informationcommissioner.gov.uk/esd/search.asp>

for personal data, may result in a proportionately higher number of data controllers; nonetheless it does appear that non-notification is a fact of data protection life in the United Kingdom. As indicated above, failure to notify does constitute a criminal offence.[65] In 2006–7, however, only ten organisations were convicted on this basis, with a maximum fine of £350, with £500 costs.[66]

Enforcement of the legislation

Having established a Register of those processing personal data, the ongoing task for the supervisory agency is to seek to ensure that controllers remain within the scope of their entries on the Register and that in general, processing complies with the substantive requirements of the legislation. The nature of these requirements, principally in the form of the data protection principles, will be considered in Chapter 7. Failures on the part of controllers may constitute an offence and will also expose them to a range of sanctions made available to the Commissioner.

Powers of entry and inspection

Section 50 of and Schedule 9 to the Data Protection Act 1998 provide that the Commissioner may approach a circuit judge (or in Scotland, a sheriff) seeking a warrant to enter and search any premises. The warrant will be granted if the judge is satisfied that a data controller is in breach of one or more of the principles or has committed an offence under the Act, and that evidence to that effect is to be found at the address specified. The warrant will empower the Commissioner or his or her staff to:

> Inspect, examine, operate and test any equipment found there which is intended to be used for the processing of personal data and to inspect or seize any document or other material found there.[67]

Procedures for the award of the warrant are similar to those found in the Data Protection Act 1984, although one significant loophole has been closed. Under the earlier Act, if the Registrar had sought entry to premises and had been granted admission only for the occupier to refuse to cooperate further with inquiries, it was not subsequently possible in England to obtain a search warrant. The Data Protection Act 1998 now provides that a warrant may be sought in the situation where:

> Although entry to the premises was granted, the occupier unreasonably refused to comply with a request by the Commissioner or any of the Commissioner's officers or staff to [perform any of the acts which might be permitted in the execution of a search warrant].[68]

Apart from delaying action, there will be little benefit to a data controller in exercising evasionary tactics of the kind identified.

---

[65] Section 17. [66] *Annual Report 2006–7*, pp. 56–7.
[67] Schedule 9, para. 1(3). [68] Schedule 9, para. 2(1)(b)(ii).

Information notices

Although the Data Protection Act 1984 empowered the Registrar to seek and execute search warrants in the event a breach of the principles was suspected,[69] that statute conferred no general investigative power and placed data users under no obligation to cooperate with any inquiries made by the Registrar. The Data Protection Act 1998 stops short of providing a general investigative power, but confers a new power on the Commissioner to serve an 'information notice', requiring the supply within a specified time of specified information relating to the matter under investigation.[70] An appeal against service of an information notice will lie to the Data Protection Tribunal and, save in exceptional circumstances, this act will suspend the operation of the notice.[71] Failure to comply with an information notice will constitute an offence, as will the reckless or intentional provision of false information in response to an information notice.[72]

An information notice may be served either on the Commissioner's own initiative, when he or she considers that information is reasonably required in order to determine 'whether the data controller has complied or is complying with the data protection principles',[73] or following a complaint from a data subject. In this latter respect, the Data Protection Act 1998 provides that any person may contact the Commissioner seeking an assessment whether it is likely that personal data has been or is being processed lawfully.[74] The Commissioner is obliged to consider the request and determine an appropriate response taking into account, inter alia, whether the data subject could have obtained the information by means of a request for subject access.[75]

Although the information notice does constitute a new weapon in the Commissioner's armoury, it may be queried as to how useful the power will be in practice. The notice may be served when the Commissioner reasonably requires information to determine whether the principles are being observed, rather than the requirement for service of an enforcement notice that the Commissioner be satisfied that a breach has occurred. Beyond this, however, the appeal procedures are identical. Whilst it may be expected that many controllers will be happy to respond to an information notice in order to clarify what might be a misunderstanding of the nature of their processing activities, the possibility for appeals may persuade less scrupulous controllers to prevaricate in their response. Even if the Information Tribunal ultimately upholds the information notice and the Commissioner obtains information indicating that a breach of the principles has occurred, no action can be taken until an enforcement notice, with its own appeal procedures, has been served.

Enforcement notices

The Data Protection Act 1998 retains the 1984 Act's concept of enforcement notices.[76] Under these, the Commissioner may serve notice on data controllers where he or she

---

[69] Section 16.   [70] Section 43(1).   [71] Section 43(4)–(5).   [72] Section 47.
[73] Section 43(1).   [74] Section 42(1).   [75] Section 42(7).   [76] Section 40.

is satisfied that a breach of one or more of the data protection principles has occurred. The notice will identify the act or omission complained of and specify the steps that require to be taken to put matters right. Failure to comply with an enforcement notice constitutes an offence.[77] As with all other forms of notice served by the Commissioner, the recipient data controller may appeal to the Information Tribunal. Save in exceptional circumstances, the lodging of an appeal will suspend the operation of the notice.

Experience under the Data Protection Act 1984 indicated that a period of years might elapse between the initial moves to serve an enforcement notice and the completion of appeal proceedings. To date, there has been no appeal from a Tribunal decision to the courts, a step which would extend the length of the process even further. Little can be done to speed up the process itself, but one of the problems identified under the previous regime was that the passage of time might render all or part of the terms of an enforcement notice of dubious relevance. The Data Protection Act 1998 establishes a more flexible approach, providing that the Commissioner may, if he or she considers that all of its provisions need not be complied with in order to ensure compliance with the principles, vary or cancel an enforcement notice.[78] The recipient controller may also make written request to the Commissioner for variation or cancellation on the ground that a change of circumstances means that compliance with its terms is not necessary to secure compliance with the principles.[79] In order to avoid the possibility of a double appeal, such a request may only be made after the time available for submitting an appeal to the Tribunal has elapsed.

Undertakings

Although the concept does not have any statutory recognition, the Commissioner has placed considerable reliance upon obtaining formal undertakings from organisations whose processing activities it is considered might contravene the data protection legislation.

Assessment of processing

Another new power conferred under the Data Protection Act 1998 enables the Commissioner, with the consent of the data controller involved, to assess any processing 'for the following of good practice and shall inform the data controller of the results of the assessment'.[80] Such action may provide a data controller with reassurance concerning the legality of current or proposed processing, thereby minimising the possibility that more formal enforcement measures, such as service of an enforcement or information notice, will be taken at some stage in the future.

---

[77] Section 47.   [78] Section 41(1).
[79] Section 41(2).   [80] Section 51(7).

Audits

Linked in many respects to the making of assessements of processing is the concept that the Information Commissioner should be able to conduct an audit of an organisation's processing activities. Under the present legislation, as was stated above, the Commissioner may act only with the consent of the controller or where there is evidence of breach sufficient to justify service of an information notice. It is perhaps doubtful whether this approach complies with the provisions of the Data Protection Directive, which requires that national supervisory agencies be granted:

> investigative powers such as powers of access to data forming the subject-matter of processing operations and powers to collect all the information necessary for the performance of its supervisory duties.

For a number of years, successive Commissioners have lobbied to be granted audit powers. In evidence before the House of Commons Justice Committee in December 2007,[81] the Commissioner lamented what he described as a 'bizarre situation' where, unlike almost all other national data protection authorities 'and, indeed, many other United Kingdom regulatory authorities such as those concerned with Health and Safety and the Financial Services sector, the Information Commissioner had no general power of audit.

Some developments have taken place in the aftermath of the loss of child benefit data, with the Prime Minister announcing that the Information Commissioner would be enabled to perform spot checks on public sector controllers. This would be sanctioned as a matter of administrative direction rather than as a legal requirement, although it has been suggested that more general audit powers may be conferred on the Commissioner in the forthcoming Government of Britain Bill.

General powers and duties of the Information Commissioner

Disseminating information

The remaining powers of the Commissioner follow in large part those established under the Data Protection Act 1984. The Commissioner is to disseminate information giving guidance about good practice under the Data Protection Act 1998.[82] Good practice is defined as:

> Such practice in the processing of personal data as appears to the Commissioner to be desirable having regard to the interests of data subjects and others and includes (but is not limited to) compliance with the requirements of this Act.[83]

Under the 1984 Act, a wide range of material was published, perhaps most notably the series of Guidelines giving information about the Registrar's interpretation of the

---

[81] Protection of Personal Data: First Report of Session 2007–8, 17 December 2007.
[82] Section 51(1).   [83] Section 51(9).

legislation. Members of the Registrar's office were also frequent speakers at conferences. It is likely that these activities will continue. The 1998 Act does give a new power to the Commissioner to levy fees for any matters concerned with the exercise of her powers.[84] It was indicated in Parliament that income from publications and presentations might account for 10 per cent of the Commissioner's income.[85]

Codes of practice

Provision relating to codes of practice was inserted into the Data Protection Act 1984 at a late stage during its parliamentary passage by a somewhat reluctant government, which pointed to the nebulous legal status of these documents. Under the 1984 regime, the Registrar's role is limited to encouraging 'trade associations or other bodies' to prepare and disseminate codes of practice.[86] The decision of the Data Protection Tribunal in the case of *Innovations (Mail Order) Ltd v Data Protection Registrar*[87] lends support to this view. Here, the Tribunal held that the appellant was in breach of the data protection principle relating to the fair obtaining of data, even though its conduct complied with a relevant industry code of practice.

In spite of doubts concerning their legal status, a considerable number of codes were adopted under the Data Protection Act 1984. The Data Protection Directive also envisages a substantial role for both national and Community codes, providing that:

1. The Member States and the Commission shall encourage the drawing up of codes of conduct intended to contribute to the proper implementation of the national provisions adopted by the Member States pursuant to this Directive, taking account of the specific features of the various sectors.

2. Member States shall make provision for trade associations and other bodies representing other categories of controllers which have drawn up draft national codes or which have the intention of amending or extending existing national codes to be able to submit them to the opinion of the national authority.

3. Member States shall make provision for this authority to ascertain, among other things, whether the drafts submitted to it are in accordance with the national provisions adopted pursuant to this directive. If it sees fit, the authority shall seek the views of data subjects or their representatives.

4. Draft Community codes, and amendments or extensions to existing Community codes, may be submitted to the Working Party referred to in Article 29. This Working Party shall determine, among other things, whether the drafts submitted to it are in accordance with the national provisions adopted pursuant to this Directive. If it sees fit, the authority shall seek the views of data subjects or their

---

[84] Section 51(8).
[85] HC Official Report, SC D (Data Protection Bill), col. 253, 2 June 1998.
[86] Section 36(4).
[87] Case DA/92 31/49/1.

representatives. The Commission may ensure appropriate publicity for the codes which have been approved by the Working Party.[88]

The major novelty for the United Kingdom is the provision in the Directive that supervisory agencies should take a view on the conformity of a draft code with statutory requirements. This is coming close to giving an unelected agency law-making powers—a practice which has been traditionally resisted in the United Kingdom.

The Data Protection Act 1998 establishes two roles for the Commissioner in respect of codes of practice. Acting either on his or her own initiative or under the direction of the Secretary of State, and after consulting with relevant trade associations and representatives of data subjects, the Commissioner may 'prepare and disseminate codes of practice for guidance as to good practice'.[89] Any code of practice prepared following directions from the Secretary of State is to be laid before Parliament, either in its own right or as part of another report by the Commissioner to Parliament.[90]

As with the procedure under the Data Protection Act 1984, the Commissioner is also under a duty to encourage the adoption and dissemination of codes by relevant trade associations. Additionally, however, it is provided that:

> …where any trade association submits a code of practice to him for his consideration, consider the code and, after such consultation with data subjects or persons representing data subjects as appears to him to be appropriate, notify the trade association whether in his opinion the code promotes the following of good practice.[91]

In many respects, this provision formalises practice under the 1984 Act, where many of the codes adopted contain a foreword from the Registrar indicating her views on the appropriateness of the code.

International cooperation

As was the case under the Data Protection Act 1984, the Commissioner is the United Kingdom agency responsible for liaison with other data protection agencies under the auspices of the Council of Europe Convention.[92] The Commissioner is also responsible for working with the various Committees and Working Parties established at EU level[93] by the Data Protection Directive.[94] Such bodies have a particularly important role to play in determining whether third countries provide an adequate level of protection for personal data. The Commissioner is charged with the duty of disseminating information about any such findings and seeking to implement these within the United Kingdom.[95]

---

[88] Directive 95/46/EC, Article 27.

[89] Section 51(3).

[90] Section 52(3).

[91] Data Protection Act 1998, s 51(4)(b).

[92] The Data Protection (Functions of Designated Authority) Order 2000, SI 2000/186.

[93] Data Protection Act 1998, s 54(1).

[94] Directive 95/46/EC.

[95] Data Protection Act 1998, s 51(6).

The Data Protection Directive[96] also contains provisions requiring national supervisory agencies to cooperate with each other. In particular, '[e]ach authority may be requested to exercise its powers by an authority of another Member State'. The Data Protection Act 1998 provides that the Secretary of State may make an order relating to such tasks and specifying, in particular, the approach to be taken when a request for assistance relates to processing which is exempt under the United Kingdom legislation but is included in the national law of the requesting state.[97] The Data Protection (International Co-operation) Order 2000[98] makes appropriate provision. Article 5 applies in the situation where processing is taking place in the United Kingdom but where the provisions of s 5 would normally exclude jurisdiction—principally where the controller is not established in the United Kingdom. Where the processing is subject to the jurisdiction of a supervisory authority from another Member State, the Commissioner may, in responding to a request for assistance from that authority, act as if the processing were subject to the 1998 Act. Article 6 of the Order provides that the Commissioner may make a similar request for assistance to another supervisory authority in respect of processing subject to United Kingdom jurisdiction which is being carried out in another Member State.

Professional secrecy

In addition to providing that powers be conferred on supervisory agencies, the Data Protection Directive also requires that:

> Member States shall provide that members and staff of the supervisory authority, even after their employment has ended, are to be subject to a duty of professional secrecy with regard to confidential information to which they have access.[99]

The Data Protection Act 1998's interpretation of this provision was the cause of a degree of controversy, and, indeed, was criticised by the then Commissioner as likely to impede the effective performance of her duties. It is provided that an offence will be committed where information obtained in the course of employment and relating to an 'identified or identifiable individuals or business' is disclosed by past or present Commissioners or members of staff without lawful authority.[100] The term 'lawful authority' is defined as requiring the consent of the individual, the availability of statutory authority, necessity for the performance of functions under the Act, compliance with Community obligations or in the course of legal proceedings. Finally, and most significantly, it is provided that 'having regard to the rights and freedoms or legitimate interests of any person, the disclosure is necessary in the public interest'.[101]

Although it is clearly reasonable that confidential information relating to a data controller should not be disclosed, the effect of this provision might be, for example, to prevent the Commissioner from publicising the fact that data controllers have been served with enforcement notices. It was indicated in Parliament that the government has 'found

---

[96] Directive 95/46/EC.   [97] Section 54(2).   [98] SI 2000/190.
[99] Directive 95/46/EC, Article 28(7).   [100] Section 59(1).   [101] Section 59(2).

it difficult to get the provision right' and that the issue might be revisited in the context of freedom of information legislation.[102] The format finally adopted is less restrictive than that originally proposed, which would have empowered disclosure only when 'necessary for reasons of substantial public interest', but it remains unclear how extensively it might be interpreted. One possible compromise was suggested in Parliament, that notification regulations may require controllers to include information regarding enforcement notices (or other notices) as part of their entry on the Register.[103]

The Information Tribunal

Reference has been made above to the appellate role of this body. The Tribunal was established under the Data Protection Act 1984 and little change is made to its make-up.[104] The Tribunal's membership consists of a Chairman and a number of Deputy Chairmen.[105] These appointees are to be barristers, advocates, or solicitors of at least seven years' standing.[106] Additionally, a number of other members may be appointed by the Secretary of State representing the interests of data users and of data subjects.[107] A panel of three members will be convened to hear particular appeals.

Under the Data Protection Act 1984, the Tribunal's sole function was to hear appeals brought by data users (or computer bureaux) against decisions by the Registrar adverse to their interests. The only notable change introduced by the Data Protection Act 1998 is that in very limited cases concerned with the application of the exemption for data processed for national security purposes, a data subject will, for the first time, have the right to bring a case before the Tribunal.[108] The procedures to be followed before the Tribunal are specified in detail in the Data Protection Tribunal (Enforcement Appeals) Rules 2000.[109] More specialised rules are prescribed for proceedings involving national security. Here, the provisions of the Data Protection Tribunal (National Security Appeals) Rules 2000[110] will apply. The Tribunal may uphold the Registrar's original ruling, reverse it, or, where the Registrar's act involves the exercise of a discretion, substitute its own ruling.[111] Tribunal decisions may be appealed on a point of law to the High Court or to the Court of Session.[112]

Other supervisory agencies

Although not part of the formal data protection structure, brief reference should be made to the fact that many data controllers may be subject to other forms of regulation and that a failure to comply with data protection requirements may result in sanctions being imposed by these regulators. Perhaps the best example can be taken

---

[102] 316 HC Official Report (6th series), cols 603–4, 2 July 1998.
[103] 316 HC Official Report (6th series), col. 602, 2 July 1998.
[104] Section 6 and Schedule 5, Pt 2.
[105] The number of deputy chairmen is to be determined at the discretion of the Lord Chancellor.
[106] Section 3(4).   [107] Section 3(5).   [108] Section 28.   [109] SI 2000/189.
[110] SI 2000/206.   [111] Section 14(3)–(4).   [112] Section 14(5).

from the financial services regulator where the responsible regulator, the Financial Services Authority, imposed a fine of £1.26 million pounds on the insurance company Norwich Union Life in December 2007 for a failure to maintain adequate security in respect of customers' personal data. As the Financial Services Authority's press release stated, weaknesses in Norwich Union's systems allowed fraudsters to access the data and commit instances of identity fraud. In addition to accessing confidential data, the criminals were also able to request the surrender of seventy-four insurance policies and receive payments totalling some £3.3 million pounds. Previously, a fine of almost £1 million pounds was imposed on the Nationwide Building Society following the loss of personal data as a consequence of the theft of a laptop computer from a Nationwide employee's home.

Although the penalties might not be as substantial, it might be expected that other regulators such as those in the medical and legal fields would adopt a similar approach in respect of unduly lax data processing practices.

Conclusions

Throughout the currency of the Data Protection Act 1984, the Data Protection Registrars proved vigilant in pursuing the interests of the data subjects. The Data Protection Tribunal also demonstrated a determination to interpret the data protection principles in an expansive and subject-friendly fashion. This element of the supervisory authority's work will be considered in Chapter 7 in more detail. The new provisions do confer additional powers upon the Data Protection Commissioner and, as such, are to be welcomed. Less satisfactory, perhaps, is the fact that financial factors appear to have dictated the continuance of a system of near-universal notification. Although much has been done to make the system as user-friendly as possible, it is difficult to avoid the conclusion that notification and the associated fee represents nothing more than a tax on computer owners.

As indicated at the beginning of this chapter, the notion that supervisory authorities are to be independent is integral to the Data Protection Directive's approach.[113] Successive Registrars and Commissioners have shown a willingness to become involved in debate on the role of data protection in modern society. Given the developments subsequent to September 11, 2001, attention has increasingly focused on activities within the public sector. In evidence before the House of Commons Home Affairs Committee, the Information Commissioner recently expressed strong reservations concerning the privacy implications of Home Office proposals for the introduction of identity cards. This in turn produced comments from a Home Office spokesperson, suggesting that the Commissioner was engaging in 'grandstanding'.

Many of the legislative responses to the threat of global terrorism, especially those within the United Kingdom, have been enacted with great speed, driven by perceived necessity but also carrying with them the risk of creating a chasm between those

---

[113] Directive 95/46/EC.

whose primary interest is in law enforcement and individuals and bodies concerned with the protection and promotion of individual rights and freedoms. Creative tension between different interest groups is inevitable and when there is a degree of acceptance that each group is acting in good faith, can produce benefits. When creation turns to destruction, everyone loses and in many respects the present debate between civil libertarian lobbyists and government has become sterile. Possible consequences are that individuals may lose some of the major elements of protection introduced and developed over the past decades, whilst governments risk losing popular legitimacy if they are seen as unconcerned with and threatening towards the rights of citizens. For data protection supervisory authorities, the danger is that as the debate focuses increasingly on public-sector processing, independence may become equated with impotence.

Suggestions for further reading

SIMITIS, S. (1985), 'Data Protection—Experiences and Tendencies', *Law/Technology* 3 (1985), pp. 1–31.

5

The data protection principles

Introduction

Whilst notions of the form of supervision of data users have changed significantly over the years, the substantive requirements of acceptable processing practice have remained more stable. The formulation of general statements of acceptable processing practice has been a feature of data protection legislation from the earliest days. The role of such principles may fairly be analogised to that of the Ten Commandments; both establish general formulations of good conduct, but require to be interpreted and expanded in the context of specific activities and circumstances. Article 6 of the Data Protection Directive prescribes five 'principles relating to data quality', requiring Member States to ensure that personal data is:

    (a) processed fairly and lawfully;

    (b) collected for specified, explicit and legitimate purposes and not further processed in a way incompatible with those purposes;

    (c) adequate, relevant and not excessive in relation to the purposes for which they are collected and/or further processed;

    (d) accurate and where necessary, kept up to date; every reasonable step must be taken to ensure that data which are inaccurate or incomplete, having regard to the purposes for which they were collected or for which they are further processed, are erased or rectified; and

    (e) kept in a form which permits identification of data subjects for no longer than is necessary for the purposes for which the data were collected or for which they are further processed.

Under the United Kingdom's Data Protection Act 1984, a set of eight data protection principles was laid down. The 1998 Act continued this approach in implementing the Directive with Schedule 1 requiring that:

    1. Personal data shall be processed fairly and lawfully and, in particular, shall not be processed unless—

        (a) at least one of the conditions in Schedule 2 is met; and

        (b) in the case of sensitive personal data, at least one of the conditions in Schedule 3 is also met.

2. Personal data shall be obtained only for one or more specified and lawful purposes, and shall not be further processed in any manner incompatible with that purpose or those purposes.

3. Personal data shall be adequate, relevant and not excessive in relation to the purpose or purposes for which they are processed.

4. Personal data shall be accurate and, where necessary, kept up to date.

5. Personal data processed for any purpose or purposes shall not be kept for longer than is necessary for that purpose or those purposes.

6. Personal data shall be processed in accordance with the rights of data subjects under this Act.

7. Appropriate technical and organisational measures shall be taken against unauthorised or unlawful processing of personal data and against accidental loss or destruction of, or damage to, personal data.

8. Personal data shall not be transferred to a country or territory outside the European Economic Area unless that country or territory ensures an adequate level of protection for the rights and freedoms of data subjects in relation to the processing of personal data.[1]

The scope of the United Kingdom principles is broader than those adopted under Article 6 but the additional topics covered, namely the rights of data subjects, the maintenance of adequate security, and controls over transborder data flows, are dealt with elsewhere in the Directive. The data protection principles span the whole continium of data processing, from the stage when data is first acquired, perhaps using pen and paper, to the time when it is permanently and irretrievably destroyed. A formula frequently used to justify data protection legislation is to the effect that there should be no processing whose very existence is a secret. More expansively, the principles seek to ensure that data subjects are aware who processes data about them and for what purposes; they should feel confident that it will be kept in secure conditions and that they will be able to verify the accurancy and relevance of the data held.

As with all general statements, almost all of the principles require expansion in the context of particular forms of activity. Detailed guidance concerning the application of the principles can be taken from a variety of sources. No fewer than four Schedules to the Data Protection Act 1998 expand upon the interpretation of the principles, something which has prompted an expression of concern from the Commission as possibly restricting the scope of the provisions beyond the level required by the Directive,[2] whilst provisions in the body of the statute make additional provisions, often in the form of providing exceptions from or restrictions to their applications giving priority to other interests, for example, the prevention or detection of crime. As with other statutes, further guidance on issues of interpretation will become available

---

[1] Schedule 1.

[2] Analysis and impact study on the implementation of Directive 95/46 in Member States, available from <http://ec.europa.eu/justice_home/fsj/privacy/lawreport/index_en.htm>

through decisions of the courts and the Information Tribunal resolving actual cases. It is perhaps surprising that in almost eight years of the Act's application, only two cases have reached the stage of a Tribunal determination. A number of decisions made under the Data Protection Act 1984 will remain of some relevance, although changes—especially in the definition of processing—may limit their continuing relevance. Finally, a significant role is envisaged for sector-specific codes of practice, with the 1998 Act providing for these to receive an enhanced legal status compared with their 1984 forbears.

For the purposes of the present work, the sixth and the eighth principles dealing with the rights of the data subject and controls over transborder data flows, respectively, will be considered separately. Focusing on the remaining principles, this chapter will consider to what extent and under what conditions a data controller may lawfully process personal data. Use may take a variety of forms and will include disclosure of data to a third party. Finally, this chapter will consider the operation of the seventh data protection principle, requiring that users adopt appropriate security measures.

Fair and lawful processing

The Act's first data protection requires that data be processed 'fairly and lawfully'. The Directive's principles are to the same effect. The first principle imposes three cumulative obligations on data controllers. They are required to process data:

- fairly;
- lawfully; and
- in accordance with at least one of the specific Schedule 2 or 3 conditions.

Failure in any respect may place the controller in breach of the legislation. Processing might be fair and lawful but if it does not come within one of the Schedule 2 or 3 conditions will be in breach of the Data Protection Act. Again, as will be described below, processing may be lawful but considered to be unfair.

Fair processing

The notion of fair processing is perhaps ill-suited to detailed definition. Although the Directive refers to the concept of fairness both in its Recitals and Articles, all of the requirements imposed are in the form of legal requirements. The Act makes rather more extensive reference to fairness in the context of the manner in which data is obtained but even here, any breach of the provision will render processing unlawful.

Two aspects of fair processing are relevant. First, reference is made in the legislation to some specific requirements with regard to the manner in which information is obtained; and, second, a number of actions brought by the Commissioner and decisions of the Information Tribunal illustrate how the concept may be applied in respect of particular forms of processing.

In Part II of Schedule 1 of the Data Protection Act, guidance is given concerning the interpretation of a number of the Data Protection Principles. Here, it is provided that in determining where personal data are processed fairly:

> ...regard shall be had to the method by which it was obtained, including in particular whether any person from whom it was obtained was deceived or misled as to the purpose or purposes for which it is to be held, used or disclosed.[3]

Surreptitious and deceptive collection of personal data, perhaps in the form of a photograph, would contravene this requirement but would also be likely to constitute a breach of the data subject's rights under Article 8 of the European Convention on Human Rights.

It is not enough that the data subject is not misled as to the purpose for which the data is to be used. In order for processing to be lawful it is necessary that information be given to the data subject about the purposes for which processing will be carried out. Two situations are specified in the Act and the Directive, the first applying where the data is collected directly from the data subject, perhaps through the completion of a form, and the second where data is obtained from some other source.

Information obtained from the data subject

Where data is obtained from the data subject, it is provided that information must be given to or 'made readily available' to the data subject. This formulation differs from that used in the Directive, which requires that information be provided to the subject 'except where he already has it'.[4] It is not clear whether the United Kingdom's approach fully implements the Directive. If a website, for example, provides a prominent link to its data protection policy giving the necessary details, it could be argued that the information is 'readily available', but unless and until the data subject follows the link it cannot be argued that 'he already has it'.

In terms of the information required to be submitted, the Act requires details as to the identity of the controller or that of a nominated representative for cases where the controller is not established in the EEA,[5] the purposes for which the data are intended to be used, and any intended recipients of the data. The subject must be supplied with:

> ...any further information which is necessary, having regard to the specific circumstances in which the data are or are to be processed, to enable processing in respect of the data subject to be fair.[6]

This requirement is not specified further in the Act. The Data Protection Directive, however, states that subjects must also be informed, whether providing answers to any questions is voluntary or compulsory and as to the possible consequences of a failure to reply.[7] Notice must also be given of the right of subject access.

---

[3] Schedule 1, Pt II, para. 1. [4] Article 10.
[5] Section 5(2) [6] Schedule 1, Pt II, para. 2(3).
[7] Directive 95/46/EC, Article 10(c).

The Act does not specify when the information is required to be given to the data subject. In a case brought under the 1984 legislation, *Innovations (Mail Order) v Data Protection Registrar*,[8] the Data Protection Tribunal ruled that the requirements must be met at the time the data was collected from the data subject. The Commissioner has expressed the view that the same approach would be followed under the 1998 Act.[9]

Information not obtained from the data subject

In many instances, information may not be obtained from a source other than the data subject. An example might be in the situation where a medical practitioner compiles an assessment of a patient's medical condition and passes this on to a third party, such as a potential employer. In such a situation the Act provides for notification—similar in scope and extent to that described above—to be given to the data subject by the third party.[10] Specific provision is made for the time at which notification is to be made, although this is somewhat complex, with a range of possible scenarios:

If the data is processed by the recipient data controller, notification must be made at that time.

If data is disclosed to a third party, notification must be given at that time.

If it is subsequently determined that data is unlikely to be disclosed, notification must be made at that time.

In any other situation, notification must be given within a reasonable period.[11]

Given the fact that the statutory definition of processing includes the acts of 'obtaining, recording or holding'[12] the data, it is difficult to envisage how any time other than that at which the data is obtained would constitute the moment at which notification may be required.

In some cases, it might be that data concerning particular subjects makes only a peripheral and individually insignificant appearance in a collection of data. An example might be the individual voters listed in the edited version of the Electoral Register, which may be purchased by a data controller. The Act provides that notification need not be given where it would involve a 'disproportionate effort'.[13] No definition is given as to what might constitute 'disproportionate effort'. The Information Commissioner has expressed the view that this will be a question of fact to be determined in each individual case. A balancing act will require to be performed between the costs and workload implications for the controller and the possible prejudicial effect of the data

---

[8] Case DA/92, available from <http://www.informationtribunal.gov.uk/Documents/decisions/innovations.pdf>

[9] *Legal Guidance*, para. 3.1.7.7. Available at <http://www.ico.gov.uk/upload/documents/library/data_protection/detailed_specialist_guides/data_protection_act_legal_guidance.pdf>

[10] Schedule 1, Pt 2, para. 2(1)(b).

[11] Schedule 1, Pt 2, para. 2(2).

[12] S1(1).

[13] Schedule 1, Pt 2, para. 3(2)(a).

for the interests of the subject. One specific factor identified as being of relevance would be the extent to which the subject may already know about the processing of the personal data. In the example given above, although the issue of disproportionate effect may not arise, the data subject would be likely to be well aware that the results of his medical examination would be forwarded to the potential employer as part of the process of determining whether an offer of employment would be made.

General notions of unfairness

Where perhaps notions of fairness continue to play a valid role is where conduct is perhaps not against the specific provisions of the law but is considered to be unfair. An example of the situation which may arise can be seen in the enforcement notice served by the Commissioner in August 2006 against the operators of a website company B4U.com The website promoted itself as providing facilities for tracking the location of individuals using the Electoral Roll. As the enforcement notice[14] states:

> This website offers 'people searching' facilities and claims to contain 'over 45 million records from the United Kingdom Electoral Roll'. The website further claims that those records are 'from the 2001 roll'. These search facilities are offered free of charge and require no subscription or registration. Users need only enter the surname and rough location of the person they wish to trace for the system to return a list of electoral register entries that match the search criteria.[15]

Use of the Electoral Roll for commercial and other non-voting purposes had long been a cause of controversy. Under the terms of the Representation of the People (Amendment) Regulations 1990,[16] Electoral Registration Officers were obliged to supply copies of the register for their area upon request. Prior to the introduction of these regulations, the officers were required to supply copies of the Register only where these were readily available. The consequence was a massive increase in the usage of data from the Electoral Rolls for direct marketing and similar purposes. Following the report of a working group, the Home Secretary reported to Parliament concerns that:

> As the law stands, anyone may buy a copy of the electoral register for any purpose. The Home Office and electoral administrators receive more complaints about that than any other subject. People are unhappy about the large amount of unsolicited mail—junk mail—from companies that have obtained their details from the electoral register.
>
> Perhaps more worryingly, the advent of powerful CD-Roms compiled from the electoral register, which allow for searching by name, means for example that abusive spouses can trace their former partners with considerable ease using a single CD-Rom. People who feel threatened in that way may simply not dare to register.
>
> All of that, together with the requirements of the European Union data protection directive,[17] which was signed and agreed by the previous Administration and,

---

[14] Available from <http://www.ico.gov.uk/upload/documents/library/corporate/notices/b4u_enforcement_notice_130706.pdf>

[15] Para. 3.   [16] SI 1990/520.

[17] Directive 95/46/EC.

generally, of the right to privacy, led the working party to conclude that it was wrong that people should be under a statutory obligation to provide their details for electoral registration purposes and then have no say about whether that information could be used for other unrelated purposes.[18]

Section 9 of the Representation of the People Act 2000 made provision for regulations to be made to establish two versions of the Electoral Register. As implemented in the Representation of the People (England and Wales) (Amendment) Regulations 2002,[19] voters will be given information regarding the purposes for which data contained in the register might be used and given the opportunity to opt out of having their data disclosed. Registration officers will then be charged with producing two registers. The full register will contain details of all persons eligible to vote, which will be restricted to electoral purposes and a number of closely defined applications. Although this is available for public consultation it is provided in Regulation 6 that:

> A person who inspects the full register and makes a copy of it or records any particulars included in it otherwise than by means of hand-written notes shall be guilty of an offence.

An edited copy excluding the details of those who have opted out will also be produced, which may be supplied[20] and used for commercial purposes.[21]

By 2005, around 30 per cent of voters had exercised their right to opt out of the commercially available Electoral Register. Such a level would diminish the value of the resource. The data held on the B4U.com website was taken from the 2001 Electoral Roll, the last created before the 2002 Regulations. The use to which the data was put was lawful under the law as it stood at the time that the Electoral Roll was drawn up. However, the Information Commissioner determined that the use of the data in 2006 constituted unfair processing. The enforcement notice concluded that:

1. The Commissioner considers that it is inherently unfair for individuals to be compelled to provide personal information on penalty of a criminal conviction only for that information to be subsequently disclosed to commercial organisations without any express restrictions on its use.

2. Given that individuals now have a right to request that they are excluded from the edited register, it is unfair to undermine the express wishes of those who have exercised that right and the 2002 Regulations by continuing to make the relevant data available on the data controller's website.

3. The Commissioner considers that the processing of the relevant data by the data controller is unfair given that a significant proportion of the individuals whose

---

[18] 357 HC Official Report (6th series), col. 168, 30 November 1999.

[19] SI 2002/1871.

[20] When supplied in electronic format, the charge will be £20 plus an additional £1.50 for each thousand names on the register (Reg. 110).

[21] Section 9.

details are contained in the relevant data will have subsequently exercised their right not to have those details included in the edited electoral register.

Accordingly, the website owner was ordered to cease making the data available on its website.[22]

The case can perhaps be seen as a borderline one and it is perhaps unfortunate that the Information Tribunal was not called upon to deliver a determination. If data was from registers ten years old, could processing still be classed as unfair? Or twenty years old? Data controllers should be able to assess whether their processing will comply with the requirements of the legislation and at least in this area, it is submitted, the state of the law is insufficiently precise.

Although electoral registers may represent the most extensive record of their kind, similar issues have arisen with other forms of records which are required to be made available to the public. Concern has been expressed on a number of occasions at the use made of lists of company shareholders, particularly in the case of privatised undertakings which might have several hundred-thousand shareholders. It may be argued that the purpose of making details of shareholders publicly available is to allow identification of the owners of a limited liability company. Use of this information for the purposes of compiling mailing lists for direct marketing purposes raises different issues, although it is difficult to see how prohibitions might be enforced against the use of publicly available information for such purposes.[23]

A further aspect of the fair processing requirement was at issue in a number of cases brought before the Data Protection Tribunal under the provisions of the 1984 Act. At issue was the conduct of the then four leading credit reference agencies: CCN, Credit and Data Marketing Services, Equifax, and Infolink, each of which was the recipient of an enforcement notice served by the Registrar.

Although the details of their operations vary, each of the credit reference agencies referred to above holds a core of data culled from public sources. Infolink, for example, is reported as holding:

- electoral registration information in the form of the collected electoral rolls for the United Kingdom;
- the Scottish Valuation Roll;
- County Court Judgments from courts in England and Wales, Northern Ireland, and the Channel Islands;
- Scottish Court Decrees;
- bankruptcy information obtained from court records and other public sources, such as the London, Belfast and Edinburgh *Gazette*;

---

[22] When checked in September 2007, the site posted a notice claiming that its systems were being upgraded and providing a link to a 'sister site' selling electrical goods.

[23] In the recent conversion process of the Halifax Building Society, members were encouraged to place their new shareholding in a nominee account administered by the Society. One advantage claimed for this was that the shareholder's name and address would not appear on publicly available registers.

- bills of Sale;

- postal address information—taken from a listing of all addresses and postcodes produced and made available by the Post Office.

In addition to this publicly available information, each agency holds information supplied by its subscribers reporting instances of bad debts and maintains records of searches made. An indication of the scale of the agencies' operations can be taken from the report of the Tribunal in the *Credit and Data Marketing* appeal, which indicated that this agency conducted in excess of 5 million searches per year, whilst Infolink conducted some 30 million searches.

The information held by the credit reference agencies and extracted in connection with a particular application for credit might be used in a variety of ways. The established method of operation would be for the agency to supply the information generated to its client, the potential creditor, leaving the determination whether to extend credit facilities entirely to the recipient. All of the credit reference agencies involved in the Tribunal actions operated on this basis. In a number of cases, the agencies also offered more extensive facilities. Instead of supplying a client with raw data, the client's own acceptance criteria might be applied. These might operate at a fairly simple level so as, for example, to reject all applicants who were not home owners. If searches revealed this fact, a recommendation that the application be rejected would be transmitted to the client.

The critical point concerning the agencies' operations, and the aspect to which exception was taken by the Registrar, is that in all cases, searches were conducted by reference to an address rather than a name. Although at first sight the practice might seem illogical, it was based upon a number of factors. Names constitute a rather inefficient means of identification. A glance at any telephone directory will show that most surnames appear more than once. Even full names are unlikely to be unique and most recipients of 'junk mail' will be aware of the many and various permutations of names and initials that may appear on envelopes. By contrast, addresses tend to be represented in a reasonably static format and, especially with the use of postcodes, the possibility of duplication is limited. However, the consequence of processing by reference to address would inevitably be that a search resulting from an application for credit by one individual, would retrieve information about previous residents at the address given and as to members of family or others who shared the address with the applicant.

The extraction of third-party data in making decisions about an individual applicant was considered by the Registrar to constitute unfair processing of personal data and, as such, contravened the first data protection principle. After discussions with the credit industry failed to provide an acceptable solution, enforcement notices were served on the four major agencies in August 1990. The terms of these notices were virtually identical, requiring the recipients to ensure that:

> …personal data relating to the financial status of individuals ceases to be processed by reference to the current or previous address or addresses of the subject of the search whereby there is extracted in addition to information about the subject of the search

any information about any other individual who has been recorded as residing at any time at the same or similar current or previous address as the subject of the search.[24]

Appeals were lodged by all the agencies with the Data Protection Tribunal which considered evidence submitted on behalf of the appellant, arguing that depriving them of third-party information would render their operations less effective. The consequence would be either an increase in bad debts or the denial of credit to persons who might otherwise have been accepted. It might even be that certain creditors would cease to operate in the consumer field.

The Tribunal accepted that the operation of credit reference agencies provided benefits. It noted that the Data Protection Act 1984 essayed no definition of the word 'fairly' but held that the prime purpose of the legislation was to protect the rights of the individual. Whilst the interests of the credit industry should not be ignored, primacy must be given to the interests of the individual applicant. On this basis it was considered:

> ...unfair for a credit reference agency, requested by its customers to supply information by reference to a named individual, so to program the extraction of information as to search for information about all persons associated with a given address or addresses notwithstanding that they may have no links with the individual [who is] the subject of the inquiry or may have no financial relationship with that individual.[25]

It was also argued that much of the information held, for example, judgments from county courts, was public information. It was in the public interest that such data should be readily available. Whilst not disputing this argument, the Tribunal pointed out that they were concerned with a much narrower issue: whether the extraction of this information in connection with a search relating to an unconnected individual could be considered fair. The answer to this must be in the negative.

In all of the credit reference agency decisions, the Tribunal accepted that a breach of the first data protection principle had occurred, sufficient to justify the Registrar in serving an enforcement notice. In all the cases, however, the Tribunal considered that the terms of the notice were excessively broad. Although the unrestricted use of third-party information was considered objectionable, the Tribunal did accept that information relating to members of the applicant's immediate family or to persons with whom the applicant shared property might be relevant to a decision concerning the grant of credit. To this extent, the terms of the Registrar's enforcement notice would be varied to permit the extraction of third-party information in a restricted set of circumstances.

The most recent case concerned with the issue of fair processing is *Johnson v Medical Defence Union*.[26] The facts of this case have been described above in the context of the issue of whether the Medical Defence Union's activities constituted processing. By

---

[24] At para. 18.
[25] <http://www.informationtribunal.gov.uk/Documents/decisions/infolink.pdf> at para. 53.
[26] [2007] EWCA Civ 262.

a majority decision, the Court of Appeal held that they did not. Some consideration was also given to the matter of whether, should this view be wrong, any processing was unfair. The case centred upon whether the use of a risk assessment policy by the Medical Defence Union could be considered unfair. The scheme took account of the volume of incidents reported involving a particular member and it was an integral element that limited regard was taken of the outcome of such cases. The view was taken that if a doctor had a significant history of complaints brought against him in the past, this would be a reliable indicator that the trend would continue, regardless of whether the previous complaints had proved to be unfounded. The prediction would be that the Medical Defence Union would be required to incur continuing expenditure in representing the doctor in the future.

Although there was disagreement between the judges on whether processing had taken place, there was unanimity on the issue of fairness. At trial, having taken account of the decision of the Data Protection Tribunal in the case of *CCN Systems v Data Protection Registrar*,[27] discussed above, Mr Justice Rimer concluded that:

> there is in principle nothing relevantly unfair about the MDU's risk assessment policy or about the way in which it processed information in applying that policy.... the policy is directed at risk management—at preserving the MDU funds against a risk of claims, and the incurring of costs, *in the future*. The MDU experience is that a risk of that nature cannot be measured simply by awaiting the happening of a statistically significant number of occurrences that do in fact cause a drain on its funds.[28]

Such a situation could be distinguished from that applying in the credit reference agency cases, where there was only the most tenuous statistical correlation between data about a third party and the likelihood that an applicant would default on a credit agreement. In the present case:

> it is not open to this court to hold that the MDU's risk assessment policy was unfair;...and that its operation involved...no unfair processing for the purposes of the first data protection principle.[29]

This conclusion was unanimously upheld by the Court of Appeal. It may be noted that had the risk assessement processes been carried out completely automatically the complainant would have had the right to object under the provisions of Section 12 of the Act. This is discussed in more detail below. By providing for some degree of human intervention, the Medical Defence Union processes fell outside the scope of Section 12 and although the result may have been perceived as unfair by one data subject, the evidence presented to the court satisfied it that the process was based upon rational criteria and sought to produce results which were fair to the totality of the data subjects who made up the membership of the Medical Defence Union, and were also compatible with its legitimate and necessary goal of managing its level of exposure to risk.

[27] Available from <http://www.informationtribunal.gov.uk/Documents/decisions/cnn_systems.pdf>
[28] [2006] EWHC 321 (Ch) at para. 122.
[29] Ibid., at para. 124.

Lawful processing

As with the requirement of fairness, neither the Act nor the Directive provide any definition when conduct will be lawful. In the decision of the House of Lords in *R v R*, a case concerned with marital rape, the concept of unlawful conduct was defined by Lord Keith as relating to 'something which is contrary to some law or enactment or is done without lawful justification or excuse'.[30] In *Legal Guidance on the Act*,[31] the Information Commissioner indicated that:

This means that a data controller must comply with all relevant rules of law whether derived from statute or common law, relating to the purpose and ways in which the data controller processes personal data.

A number of particular areas were identified as being of particlar relevance:

(a) Confidentiality arising from the relationship of the data controller with the data subject.

(b) The ultra vires rule and the rule relating to the excess of delegated powers, under which the data controller may only act within the limits of its legal powers.

(c) Legitimate expectation, that is, the expectation of the individual as to how the data controller will use the information relating to him.

(d) Article 8 of the European Convention on Human Rights (the right to respect for private and family life, home, and correspondence).

Many of these topics are dealt with in the Data Protection Act itself, although, again, there is evidence of collision between concepts of fairness and lawfulness.

Specific factors legitimising processing

In addition to imposing a general requirement that data be processed fairly and lawfully, the Act places the onus on the data controller to evidence specific justification for processing. In the case of general data, processing will be permitted only where the controller can demonstrate compliance with one of a list of conditions laid down in Schedule 2. For sensitive data, Schedule 3 provides a more restrictive set of qualifying conditions. In both Schedules, the list of legitimising factors begins with the notion of subject consent.

Subject consent

It is a fundamental tenet of contract law that silence cannot constitute acceptance of an offer. Silence, however, can take a variety of forms. Many supermarket transactions may be carried out without the exchange of a single word, let alone one possessing legal

---

[30] [1992] 1 AC 599.
[31] Available from <http://www.ico.gov.uk/upload/documents/library/data_protection/detailed_specialist_guides/data_protection_act_legal_guidance.pdf>

significance. Silence coupled with conduct indicating a wish to contract can establish a valid contract.

Over the years, there has been extensive debate on how a data subject may validly give consent to the processing of personal data. Anyone who has entered into almost any form of mail order or online transaction will be familiar with the basic techniques which are used. Typically, as was described in the context of the *Innovations* and *Linguaphone* Tribunal cases discussed below, a note of the data controller's processing intentions will be given on an order form or similar document. Under what is referred to as an 'opt out' procedure, the data subject will be told that the specified forms of processing will take place unless notice of objection is received. This would normally require that the subject places a mark in an 'opt out' box. The alternative approach, referred to as 'opting in', is again to give notice of the desired forms of processing but also to ask the data subject to indicate that they are content for this to take place. Typically, data controllers have sought to maximise the use of the former technique, as it is well accepted that this will maximise the number of persons whose data may be processed. In many cases, data subjects may not read the notice or may be unaware of the full implications of what is being proposed. A typical formulation might be along the lines, 'We would like to share your data with other carefully selected companies whose goods or services we consider may be of interest to you.' A rough translation might be along the lines, 'We will sell your details to anyone who pays us money'! Whilst data subject apathy may help controllers on an opt-out basis, the reverse will be the case where subjects are asked to opt in.

Schedule 2 to the Data Protection Act 1998 provides that processing will be lawful when 'the data subject has given his consent to the processing'. Schedule 3 requires that the subject gives 'explicit consent'. Neither phrase is defined in the Act. The Data Protection Directive is a little more helpful, providing that:

> ...the data subject's consent shall mean any freely given specific and informed indication of his wishes by which the data subject signifies his agreement to personal data relating to him being processed.[32]

In the context of consent to the processing of data, the Directive requires that consent be given unambiguously. This term is not defined. As interpreted in the United Kingdom, it is generally seen as being compatible with either an opt-out or opt-in approach, with the basic requirement being that the data subject is able readily to give an indication of his wishes. Albeit in a different context, the Article 29 Working Party appears to suggest that an opt in approach may be needed. In an 'Opinion on unsolicited communications for marketing purposes.'[33] it considered the requirement in the Privacy and Electronic Communications Directive that prior consent be obtained before commercial emails are sent to data subjects. It concluded that:

> Implied consent to receive such mails is not compatible with the definition of consent of Directive 95/46/EC and in particular with the requirement of consent being the

---

[32] Directive 95/46/EC, Article 2(h).

[33] Opinion 5/2004, available from <http://ec.europa.eu/justice_home/fsj/privacy/docs/wpdocs/2004/wp90_en.pdf>

indication of someone's wishes, including where this would be done 'unless opposition is made' (opt-out). Similarly, pre-ticked boxes, e.g., on websites are not compatible with the definition of the Directive either.

At least pending any court decision either in the United Kingdom or before the European Court of Justice, it appears that an 'opt out' approach will be accepted in the United Kingdom. A key criteria in determining the acceptability of the technique concerns the clarity of the notification. In *Linguaphone Institute v Data Protection Registrar*,[34] a case brought before the Tribunal under the 1984 Act, the appellant included in its advertisements a notice to the effect that:

(Please) tick here if you do not wish Linguaphone to make your details available to other companies who may wish to mail you offers of goods or services.

In holding that there was a breach of the data protection principles, the Tribunal expressed concern that:

...the opt-out box appears in minute print at the bottom of the order form. In the Tribunal's view the position, size of print and wording of the opt-out box does not amount to a sufficient indication that the company intends or may wish to hold, use or disclose that personal data provided at the time of enquiry for the purpose of trading in personal data.

Beyond giving information to the data subject, the controller must afford a reasonable opportunity for the subject to express consent (or the lack of it). This was at issue in another case brought before the Data Protection Tribunal under the 1984 Act, *Innovations v Data Protection Registrar*.[35] In this case, the appellant was in the business of mail order sales. Custom was solicited in a variety of ways, including the distribution of catalogues and the placing of advertisements in various media, including newspapers, radio, and television. The appellant's catalogues gave customers notice of this possibility and its order forms offered customers the opportunity to exclude use of their data for broking purposes. Some adverts, especially those appearing on radio or television, did not make mention of the possibility, and in the event that catalogue orders were placed by telephone, no mention would be made of this secondary purpose. An acknowledgement of an order would, however, be sent and this would convey the message:

For your information. As a service to our customers we occasionally make our customer lists available to carefully screened companies whose products or services we feel may interest you. If you do not wish to receive such mailings please send an exact copy of your address label to...

The Registrar took the view that notification of the intended use came too late in the contractual process and served an enforcement notice alleging a breach of the first data protection principle, which, as formulated under the 1984 Act, required that data be obtained fairly and lawfully.

---

[34] Case DA/94 31/49/1.
[35] *Innovations (Mail Order) Ltd v Data Protection Registrar* Case DA/92 31/49/1.

A number of arguments were put forward by the applicant as justifying their practices. It was suggested that, at the time of placing an order, customers would be concerned primarily with obtaining the goods and that a notice along the lines referred to above would have limited impact. Where orders were made by telephone, giving specific notice would increase the length of the call, thereby increasing costs for both the supplier and the customer. It was also pointed out that the details would not be used for list-broking purposes until thirty days from the date the acknowledgement order was sent. This, it was suggested, allowed ample time for the customer to opt out. It was also pointed out that the appellant's practices were in conformity with an industry code of practice and the Council of Europe's Recommendation on the protection of personal data used for the purposes of direct marketing.[36]

Notwithstanding these factors, the Tribunal upheld the Registrar's ruling. Although Codes of Practice and Recommendations might constitute useful guidance, the task for the Tribunal was to interpret the law. Use of the data for list-broking purposes, it was held, was not a purpose which would be obvious to the data subjects involved. Fair obtaining required that the subject be told of the non-obvious purpose before the data was obtained. Whilst a later notification might 'be a commendable way of providing a further warning', it could not stand by itself. Where prior notification might not be practicable, the Tribunal ruled that 'the obligation to obtain the data subject's positive consent for the non-obvious use of their data falls upon the data user'.[37]

Duration of consent

Consent is not a permanent condition. It is open to a data subject to withdraw consent at any time. This point is not specified directly in either the Data Protection Act or the Directive. Article 9 of the Directive on Privacy and Electronic Communications,[38] which refers specifically to the processing of personal data in the electronic communications sector,[39] provides that:

> Users or subscribers shall be given the possibility to withdraw their consent for the processing of location data other than traffic data at any time.

There is no doubt that whilst the withdrawal of consent cannot have retrospective effect, it would serve to render unlawful any future processing which is dependent upon this head of authority.

Other factors legitimising processing

Although the concept of consent has been a high-profile aspect of the new regime, it constitutes only one of a number of grounds, capable of legitimising processing. For

---

[36] Recommendation 85/20   [37] Para. 31.
[38] Directive 2002/58/EC, *Official Journal* (2002) L201/37.
[39] The provisions of this Directive are discussed in Chapter 7 below.

both general and sensitive data, a range of grounds are specified which may allow processing to take place without the subject's consent being obtained.[40]

General data

Necessity for concluding or performing a contract with the data subject

Processing may lawfully take place when this is necessary, either for entering into or performing a contract with the subject. Some stress should be placed on the adjective 'necessary'. This frequently appears in instruments such as the European Convention on Human Rights, and the jurisprudence of the European Court of Human Rights—which has been approved by the European Court of Justice—has adopted an interpretation requiring that the practice in question be close to essential for the specified purpose.[41] Clearly, information about a data subject's income may be necessary for a lender to determine whether to grant a loan and information as to address will be vital for a mail order sale, but controllers should take care not to require more information than is strictly necessary for the purpose.

Necessity for the controller to comply with a legal obligation

Similar comments apply to this requirement. A controller may, for example, require information to ensure that credit facilities are not extended to those under the age of eighteen. It would be reasonable for such a controller to require applicants to give an indication that they are over eighteen years of age.

Necessity to protect the vital interests of the data subject

It is easy to envisage situations where the interests of the data subject may require that data be processed in situations where it is not practicable to obtain consent. The limitation to the subject's 'vital interests' might mean, in practice, that the data is likely to be of a kind considered sensitive. The Information Commissioner has indicated support for this view. The only significant exception might be in respect of information relating to a data subject's financial affairs. As was noted earlier, public opinion surveys conducted for the Commissioner indicate that protection of financial data was ranked higher by most respondents than the protection of many of the categories of data designated as sensitive. Processing designed to guard against the dangers of identity theft, for example, might be seen as coming within the scope of this provision, although, as will be discussed below, the first data protection principle does not apply where processing is conducted in connection with the prevention or detection of crime and where compliance with the principle would prejudice the attainment of those purposes.[42]

---

[40] As will be discussed below, a data subject has the right to object to processing in limited circumstances.

[41] See, for example, the case of *Barthold v Germany* (1985) 7 EHRR 383.

[42] Section 29.

Necessity for the administration of justice, etc.

Data may be processed lawfully when this is necessary for a range of specified public sector purposes. In addition to the administration of justice, processing may be carried out when necessary for the exercise of statutory functions, for example in compiling registers of data controllers, in the exercise of governmental functions, or any other functions of a public nature exercised in the public interest. This might include, for example, the operation of systems of educational scholarships.

Legitimate interests of the controller

This final justification for processing is perhaps the most extensive. It sanctions processing where this is:

> ...necessary for the purposes of legitimate interests pursued by the data controller or by the third party or parties to whom the data are disclosed, except where the processing is unwarranted in any particular case by reason of prejudice to the rights and freedoms or legitimate interests of data subjects.

It is provided that regulations may be made to specify the circumstances in which this provision may or may not be applied.[43] To date, no regulations have been made.

Although many situations might be identified in which it will be useful for a data controller to hold information, the restrictions associated with the adjective 'necessary' must constantly be borne in mind. It would, for example, be useful for an employer to record details of employees' next of kin in the event of accident or illness at work. This would not, however, be essential for the normal purposes of employment, and subject consent would be required. In general, data controllers might be well advised not to place too much reliance upon this ground. In the example cited, it might be assumed that it would be a reasonably straightforward matter to obtain the details from an employee at the stage employment commences under the consent heading (although it might well be the next of kin who should be consenting). Even if consent is not forthcoming, the matter can be handled in a relatively simple manner by, for example, inserting a note to the effect that contact details have been refused. Matters become more complicated when a controller has to overcome an initial failure to seek consent by subsequent actions. The likelihood is that only a small percentage of subjects will respond to a request for retrospective consent, with the low response rate being due as much to indifference as to opposition.

Sensitive data

Subject consent

As with general data, the first ground specified as legitimising processing of sensitive personal data is the fact that the subject has given consent. In this case, the requirement

---

43 Schedule 2, para. 6.

is that consent be 'explicit'. Although the term is not defined in either Act or Directive the *Concise Oxford Dictionary* definition refers to it being:

> not implied merely but distinctly: plain in language: outspoken: clear: unreserved.

Although the definition is perhaps not incompatible with an opt-out approach to consent, more may be required of the data controller to ensure that the subject is aware of what is proposed to be done with the data. The Information Commissioner has suggested that:

> The consent of the data subject should be absolutely clear. In appropriate cases it should cover the specific detail of the processing, the particular type of data to be processed (or even the specific information), the purposes of the processing and any special aspects of the processing which may affect the individual, for example disclosures which may be made of the data.[44]

Beyond the grant of explicit consent to the processing, the Act provides for a range of other grounds legitimising processing. This list has been supplemented by a number of items of secondary legislation.

Employment-related processing

> The processing is necessary for the purposes of exercising or performing any right or obligation which is conferred or imposed by law on the data controller in connection with employment.[45]

It is further provided that the Secretary of State may either exclude the application of this provision in certain cases or impose additional conditions. It may be noted that, in respect of the processing of employment-related data, the Data Protection Directive requires the provision of 'adequate safeguards'.[46] Unless it can be assumed that existing employment law provides adequate safeguards for the data subject, United Kingdom law will not comply with the Directive unless and until the regulations are made.

Vital interests

> Processing is necessary to protect the vital interests of the data subject or of another person where the data subject is incapable of giving consent or where the controller cannot reasonably be expected to obtain consent.[47]

Examples of such situations might be where medical data relating to the subject requires to be processed in order to treat the subject who is unconscious in hospital. Again, processing may be justified where the subject is a carrier of an infectious disease and where the data is needed to provide treatment to a third party. It is further provided that processing may take place when this is:

> necessary to protect the vital interests of a third party and the subject unreasonably withholds consent.[48]

---

[44] *Legal Guidance*, para. 3.1.5.   [45] Data Protection Act 1998, Schedule 3, para. 2.
[46] Directive 95/46/EC, Article 8(2)(b).   [47] Data Protection Act 1998, Schedule 3, para. 3(a).
[48] Schedule 3, para. 3(b).

This situation may well be similar to that discussed above, but with the distinction that the subject has been identified by the controller. An example might be where the subject suffers from an infectious disease but refuses to consent to the disclosure of a list of persons who might have come into contact with the subject and who might require to be contacted to receive treatment.

Processing by specified bodies

The processing is carried out in the course of legitimate activities by a non-profit-making body or association existing for political, philosophical, religious or trade union purposes. In such cases, appropriate safeguards must be provided for the rights and freedoms of data subjects, the data must relate only to members of the association or those in regular contact with it and does not involve disclosure of the data to third parties without the consent of the data subject.[49]

Given the extension of the definition of processing to include the collection of data, this definition may have some unanticipated consequences. It was conceded in Parliament that political canvassing would be covered if the intention were to transfer returns onto a computer system. A similar situation would apply where religious organisations sought to obtain converts through door-to-door visits. For political data, it was indicated that special regulations might be made.[50]

Information in the public domain

The information contained in the personal data has been made public as a result of steps deliberately taken by the data subject.[51]

It is significant to note in this context that it will not suffice that the information has come into the public domain; this must have occurred through the deliberate actions of the subject. There is clearly a relationship between this provision and the statutory provisions discussed below relating to the activities of the media.

Legal proceedings and the administration of justice

The processing is necessary for the purpose of or in connection with legal proceedings (including prospective proceedings), for obtaining legal advice or to establish, exercise or defend legal rights.[52]

This provision was criticised in Parliament as being excessively broad. Certainly, the provision relating to 'prospective proceedings' appears somewhat opaque.

The processing is necessary for the administration of justice, for the exercise of statutory or governmental functions. Once again, the Secretary of State may exclude the application of this provision in certain situations or require that additional conditions be satisfied.[53]

---

[49] Data Protection Act 1998, Schedule 3, para. 4.
[50] 315 HC Official Report (6th series), col. 613, 2 July 1998.
[51] Data Protection Act 1998, Schedule 3, para. 5.   [52] Ibid., Schedule 3, para. 6.
[53] Ibid., Schedule 3, para. 7.

An obvious example of such a situation would be the maintenance of criminal records. It may be noted that the Data Protection Directive provides that 'a complete register of criminal convictions may be kept only under the control of official authority'.[54]

Processing for medical purposes

The processing is necessary for medical purposes and is undertaken by a health professional or by a person owing an equivalent duty of confidentiality.[55]

The term 'medical purposes' is defined broadly to include 'preventative medicine, medical diagnosis, medical research, the provision of care and treatment and the management of healthcare services'.[56] It should be stressed that in this case, as with all the exceptions described in the present section, the effect is essentially to free the controller from the requirement to seek explicit consent to processing. The processing must be carried out in accordance with the data protection principles and other requirements of the Act.

Ethnic monitoring

The processing relates to data indicating racial or ethnic origin but is carried out in order to monitor compliance with equal opportunities legislation. Appropriate safeguards must also be taken for the rights and freedoms of data subjects.[57]

Once again, it is provided that the Secretary of State may define more precisely the activities coming within the scope of this provision. Care will certainly require to be taken to ensure that information supplied for this purpose, for example by an applicant for employment, is used only for monitoring purposes and retained, at least in a form which can identify the subject, for no longer than is necessary.

Order of the Secretary of State

The processing occurs in circumstances specified by the Secretary of State.[58]

This provision confers a wideranging power on the Secretary of State to extend the range of exemptions. The Data Protection Directive requires that additional exemptions must be justified by 'reasons of substantial public interest',[59] and must be notified to the Commission.[60]

The regulatory power has been exercised with the making of the Data Protection (Processing of Sensitive Personal Data) Order 2000.[61] This provides no fewer than ten additional grounds justifying the processing of sensitive personal data.

---

[54] Directive 95/46/EC, Article 8(5).
[55] Data Protection Act 1998, Schedule 3, para. 8.
[56] Directive 95/46/EC, Article 8(5).
[57] Data Protection Act 1998, Schedule 3, para. 9.
[58] Ibid., Schedule 3, para. 10.   [59] Directive 95/46/EC, Article 8(4).
[60] Ibid., Article 8(6).   [61] SI 2000/417.

The first two grounds relate to processing for the purposes 'of the prevention or detection of any unlawful act' and the discharge of any functions intended to secure the public against:

(i) dishonesty, malpractice or other seriously improper conduct by, or the unfitness or incompetence of, any person; or

(ii) mismanagement in the administration of, or failures in services provided by any body or association.

In all cases, it is a requirement that the processing must necessarily be carried out without the explicit consent of the data subject.

A third ground might be seen as a form of whistle-blower's charter. It legitimises the disclosure of data relating to crime, dishonesty, or seriously improper conduct or mismanagement when this is with a view to the publication of the information and where the party making the disclosure reasonably believes that the publication will be in the public interest.

Processing may be carried out without explicit subject consent when this is in the public interest in connection with the provision of counselling, support, or other services. The exemption here is not an open-ended one, with the controller being required to demonstrate that it is impracticable, unreasonable, or undesirable to seek to obtain subject consent.

With developments in DNA research and increased awareness of the role of genetic factors in influencing life expectancy, data of this kind is of potential value to insurance companies. A person applying for insurance cover might be required to supply details relating to the health of parents, grandparents, or siblings. In the event that these persons remain alive, the processing of this data might contravene the requirements of the Data Protection Act 1998. The regulations legitimise this form of processing subject to three conditions: that it is not reasonable to obtain explicit consent; that the controller does not have actual knowledge that consent has been withheld; and that the processing is not used as the basis for decisions which will affect the data subjects concerned.

Processing for insurance purposes also benefits from a further transitional exemption covering activities which were underway prior to the commencement of the Data Protection Act 1998. Under the previous regime, the need for consent was less strict and it is provided that, save where there is actual knowledge that the data subject does not consent to processing, this may continue when it is necessary for the purpose and where it is not reasonable to expect the controller to seek explicit consent (or where the processing must necessarily be conducted without consent).

Two further exemptions serve to permit the continuance of activities which are generally considered desirable but which might otherwise contravene the data protection principles. Many employers may, whether required by law or otherwise, seek to process information to monitor the operation of policies relating to equal opportunities with the view to promoting such equality. It is provided that processing may take place where this is not used to support decisions affecting a particular subject and where the processing is not likely to cause substantial damage or distress to the data subject or to any other person.

One matter which attracted considerable discussion when the Data Protection Act 1998 was before Parliament was the realisation that the restrictions on the processing of sensitive data would serve to restrict the ability of political parties to conduct activities such as the canvassing of voters where this would involve maintaining a record of likely voting intentions. The regulations seek to avoid this prospect by providing that information relating to political opinions may be processed by persons or organisations registered under the Registration of Political Parties Act 1998 to the extent that this is not likely to cause substantial damage or distress. It is further provided that data subjects may give written notice that their personal data is not to be processed for such purpose. The Data Protection (Processing of Sensitive Personal Data) (Elected Representatives) Order 2002[62] makes further provisions regarding the use of such data by elected representatives.

A further exemption applies where data is processed for research purposes. This will apply where the processing is in the substantial public interest, for example as part of a medical research project; will not result in action being taken with regard to the particular data subject without explicit consent; and is not likely to cause substantial damage or distress.

The final exemption is the shortest of all, but carries significant implications. Sensitive data may be processed where this is:

> ... necessary for the exercise of any functions conferred on a constable by any rule of law.[63]

Given the extensive powers conferred on constables under the common law, this provision might serve to justify many forms of processing.

Exceptions to the first data protection principle

Law enforcement and revenue-gathering purposes

A significant exception to the operation of the first principle applies where data is acquired for the purposes of the prevention or detection of crime, the apprehension or prosecution of offenders, or the assessment or collection of any tax or duty and where compliance with the principle would be prejudicial to the attainment of the purpose in question. In such cases, the Commissioner may not take any action against the data user involved, alleging a breach of the principle where its application would be likely to prejudice the activity in question (s 29(1)). The rationale behind the exception lies in the recognition that law enforcement agencies might reasonably acquire information in ways which might normally be regarded as unfair, for example as the result of over-hearing—or even eavesdropping on—a conversation. It might, however, be considered

---

[62] SI 2002/2905.   [63] Data Protection Act 1998, Schedule 3, para. 10.

unfortunate that the Commissioner should not be given the power to define the concept of fairness in the light of the particular situation of the user involved rather than by providing a near-complete exception from the requirement to act fairly. It may also be noted that the restriction upon the Commissioner's ability to act exists even where the data has been acquired unlawfully, although here it may be difficult to sustain the argument that observance of the law would prejudice the prevention or detection of crime, the apprehension or prosecution of offenders, or the assessment or collection of any tax or duty.

Unlawful obtaining of personal data

The second data protection principle requires that:

> Personal data shall be obtained only for one or more specified and lawful purposes and shall not be processed further in any manner incompatible with that purpose or those purposes.

Given the breadth of the definition of processing—which refers specifically to the obtaining of data—it is difficult to identify a real need for the second data protection principle. Indeed, much the same comment could be made regarding most of the remaining principles which refer to specific aspects of processing. In interpreting the second principle, the Act provides that the purposes for which data are to be processed may be specified either by the giving of notice to the data subject or in a notification given to the Commissioner. It is to be noted, however, that notification by itself will not satisfy the requirements of the first data protection principle.

The more significant element of the second principle concerns what might be regarded as ongoing processing activities. Data may be obtained for one purpose with due notification given to the data subject but changes in circumstance or technical developments may make other forms of activity attractive to the controller. The Commissioner has indicated that a strict view will be taken in determining whether any future forms of processing—whether carried out by the controller or by a third party to whom the data are disclosed—are compatible with those originally notified to the Commissioner or to the data subject.[64]

During recent years, considerable publicity has been attached to the activities of private investigators and investigative journalists, who, through various forms of subterfuge or bribery, were able to secure access to personal information held by a data user. Stella Rimington, the former head of MI5, for example, has been quoted as claiming that upon her appointment to MI5, *The Sunday Times* had employed a private investigator who had been able to discover where she lived, how much money she had in her bank account, the shops she regularly patronised, her (ex-directory) phone number, and the telephone numbers that she most frequently called.[65]

---

[64] *Legal Guidance*, para. 3.2.
[65] *Herald* (formerly *Glasgow Herald*), 17 October 1996.

In the situation where the investigator obtained direct access to data held on a computer, it would be likely that an offence would be committed under the Computer Misuse Act 1990. In many instances, however, the information would be obtained, either through bribing an employee of the data user or by misleading the user as to identity and entitlement to access the data. In these situations, the investigator would normally commit to offence. To remedy this situation, Section 55 of the Data Protection Act 1998 provides that an offence will be committed by a person who 'knowingly or recklessly, without the consent of the data controller' seeks to obtain or disclose personal data or procure its disclosure to a third party. An exception is provided where the data is obtained in connection with the prevention or detection of crime or in pursuance of a court order. A further offence is committed by a person who sells or offers to sell data obtained in contravention of this provision. Both convictions are punishable by a fine of up to £5,000 in the Magistrates Court and to a potentially unlimited amount in the Crown Court.

In spite of the prohibition, there is extensive evidence that the trade in unlawfully acquired personal information is continuing. Taking action against those involved in the practice was identified as a priority in the Information Commissioner's Regulatory Stategy published in 2005 and between 2002 and 2007 28 prosecutions have been brought, with a maximum fine of £4,200 being imposed in a case in 2006. This figure was made up of fourteen fines of £300 each, imposed in respect of a number of offences, and the Commissioner expressed disappointment at the generally low level of punishments imposed by the courts.[66] A report published by the Information Commissioner in May 2006 entitled *What Price Privacy?* provides extensive evidence of the techniques and tactics used. Based on information obtained in the course of one investigation into the activities of one private investigator, the report presents a list of the sums charged for obtaining items of personal data; these included £17.50 for checking addresses on the Electoral Roll, £65–£75 for obtaining an ex-directory telephone number, £500 for a criminal records check, and £750 for obtaining data relating to a mobile telephone account. As stated in a follow-up report, *What Price Privacy Now?*[67] published in December 2006:

> Suppliers use two main methods to obtain the information they want: through corruption, or more usually by some form of deception, generally known as 'blagging'. Bloggers pretend to be someone they are not in order to wheedle out the information they are seeking. They are prepared to make several telephone calls to get it. Each call they make takes them a little further towards their goal: obtaining information illegally which they then sell for a specified price.[68]

The Information Commissioner argued for an extension of the penalties provided for the offence to include a maximum term of imprisonment on conviction in the

---

[66] Foreword in *What Price Privacy?*

[67] Available from <http://www.ico.gov.uk/upload/documents/library/corporate/research_and_reports/what_price_privacy_now.pdf>

[68] Ibid., p. 5.

Magistrates Court and two years before the Crown Court. Following a consultation exercise conducted by the Department of Constitutional Affairs in the second half of 2006, it was announced in February 2007 that the government had decided to accept the Commissioner's proposals and that legislation to this end would be brought forward when parliamentary time permitted.

Issues of adequacy and relevance

The third data protection principle of the Data Protection Act 1998 requires that data shall be 'adequate, relevant and not excessive in relation to the purpose or purposes for which they are processed'. The Data Protection Directive[69] uses the same term. No further guidance is available in either instrument concerning the application of these requirements. The principle is, however, identically worded to that in the Data Protection Act 1984. This has been at issue before the Data Protection Tribunal in the course of proceedings brought against a number of Community Charge Registration Officers.[70]

The Community Charge or 'poll tax' proved one of the most controversial forms of taxation introduced in recent times. Although much of the publicity generated concerned its financial aspects, the implementation of the requirement that registers be established of those liable to pay the tax attracted the attention of the Data Protection Registrar, who took issue with the processing proposals indicated by a number of local authorities: Harrow Borough Council,[71] Runnymede Borough Council,[72] Rhondda Borough Council,[73] and South Northamptonshire District Council.[74] Ultimately, registration was refused on the basis that the Registrar was satisfied that the applicants were likely to contravene the fourth data protection principle. Appeals against these decisions were brought before the Data Protection Tribunal.

Under the terms of the Local Government Finance Act 1988, charging authorities were required to compile and maintain a Community Charge Register.[75] It was specifically provided that the register should include details of the name and address of every person liable to pay the Community Charge. The Community Charge was payable by everyone over the age of eighteen. In some cases, local authorities, including Rhondda Borough Council, requested the date of birth of every member of the household, regardless of whether they were over eighteen or not. Dates of birth are clearly items of personal data.

Objecting to this form of processing the Data Protection Registrar, although accepting that a record would need to be held of those who would reach the age of eighteen

---

[69] Directive 95/46/EC.

[70] The officers involved represented Runnymede Borough Council, South Northamptonshire District Council, Harrow Borough Council, and Rhondda Borough Council.

[71] Case DA/90 24/49/5.

[72] Case DA/90 24/49/3.

[73] Case DA/90 24/49/2.

[74] Case DA/90 24/49/4.

[75] Section 6.

and become liable to pay the charge during the course of a tax year, took the view that the date of birth was irrelevant in the case of those who were already of an age to pay the tax. The appellant argued that many inhabitants of the Rhondda shared surnames and forenames. The addition of a note of date of birth would limit the possibility that an individual might escape inclusion on the register because his or her identity was confused with some other person of the same name. It was also argued that the inclusion of the information would assist the Registration Officer in the efficient performance of his or her duties.

These arguments were rejected by the Tribunal. It heard evidence that, nationally, fewer than 1 per cent of households contained persons who shared the same surname and forename. Although it accepted that the figure might be higher in the Rhondda, it did not consider that this justified the appellant's actions. The Tribunal concluded that:

> We find that the information the appellant wishes to hold on database concerning individuals exceeds substantially the minimum amount of information which is required in order for him to fulfil the purpose for which he has sought registration ... to fulfil his duty to compile and maintain the Community Charges Register.

Similar issues were involved in the case of the other councils. Each of the appellants held, or proposed to hold, details of the type of property occupied by each subject. Again, information of this type would be classed as personal data and the Registrar raised objection on the ground that its inclusion was, or would be likely to constitute, a breach of the fourth data protection principle. In the case of Harrow and Runnymede Borough Councils, action took the form of a refusal to accept an application for registration. In the case of South Northamptonshire District Council, whose application for registration had previously been accepted, an enforcement notice was served.

In terms of the status of the information relating to type of property, the Tribunal held that whilst there might be justification for holding some information additional to that required under the Local Government Finance Act 1988, the wish to record details of type of property in every case was excessive. The Tribunal endorsed the advice given to data users by the Registrar,[76] to the effect that they should seek to identify the minimum amount of personal data which is required in order to enable them to fulfil their purpose. Where additional data might be required in certain cases, these should again be identified and the further information sought or held only in those cases.

The application of the third (and also the fifth) data protection principles has recently been discussed before the Information Tribunal in the case of *The Chief Constables of West Yorkshire, South Yorkshire and North Wales Police and the Information Commissioner.*[77] At issue in this case were the data retention practices of a number

---

[76] Information Commissioner's Office, Guideline Booklet No. 4, *The Data Protection Principles* (Wilmslow, 1998).

[77] Available from <http://www.informationtribunal.gov.uk/Documents/decisions/north_wales_police.pdf>

of police forces in respect of three individuals. In each case, the individual had been convicted of criminal offences: in one case, a single offence in 1979; in the second, five offences relating to the taking of motor vehicles, the last conviction also being in 1979; and in the case of the third data subject, five offences ending with a conviction for theft in 1969. In each case, the primary cause for complaint was that the information had been disclosed for purposes unconnected with the operation of the criminal record system. In one case, in connection with a complaint made by the data subject in respect of the conduct of a police officer; in another, to the United States immigration authorities in respect of a visa application; and in the third, in connection with an application for employment. Following the receipt of complaints from the data subjects, the Information Commissioner exercised his powers under Section 42 of the Act to conduct an assessment of the legitimacy of the processing of the personal data. After extensive correspondence with the police authorities in question, the Commissioner served each with an enforcement notice alleging breaches of the third and fifth data protection principles. The authorities appealed to the Information Triibunal.

In all the cases, data had been retained on the police national computers and it was accepted that it was held in accordance with the latest version of 'Weeding Rules', which had been the subject of discussion, if not agreement, between the Information Commissioner (and his predecessors) and the Association of Chief Police Officers. In essence, these provide for details of relatively minor offences to be retained for 30 years and more serious offences for a period of 100 years—a period designed to ensure that the data is retained for the lifetime of the offender. It was accepted by the Tribunal that:

> the Weeding Rules in their present form and edition demonstrate that there is some incontestable value in retaining conviction data dependent largely upon the nature of the offence. The Weeding Rules represent a considered exchange between the parties, i.e. the Commissioner on the one hand and ACPO on the other which has in the result forged some form of generalised understanding that after a given data, certain offences should be removed from the PNC. However, the Tribunal finds equally that the Weeding Rules do not and could not conceivably represent an unqualified and rigid code.[78]

The Tribunal drew a distinction between retention and disclosure of the data. Accepting the benefit for policing purposes of retention of data, even at the level of maintaining links to fingerprint and DNA samples, it amended the Commissioner's ruling to require that within six months the appellants:

> ...procure that the Conviction Data relating to (the complainant data subjects) currently held on the PNC database be retained on the PNC subject to the retention rules of any current ACPO Code of Practice or any equivalent thereof and not be open to inspection other than by the data controller or by any other data controller who is or represents a chief officer of police.[79]

---

[78] Para. 206.   [79] At para. 218.

The case provides useful evidence of the fact that where data are processed for a range of purposes, some may continue to be fair and lawful for longer than others. The case is also significant in its advocation of the use of technical measures in the form of modifications of the structure of the PNC to achieve data protection goals.

Accuracy and timeousness of data

The fourth data protection principle requires that: 'personal data shall be accurate and, where necessary, kept up to date'. Data is regarded as being inaccurate when it is 'incorrect or misleading as to any matter of fact'.[80] In the event that personal data is inaccurate, a data subject may be entitled to seek its rectification and, in certain cases, compensation for any resultant damage or distress.[81]

Rather like beauty, accuracy may frequently lie in the eye of the beholder. Although many instances are reported of inaccurate data (for example, it has been suggested that data on the Police National Computer was subject to an 86 per cent error rate),[82] the question of whether data is accurate will not always be susceptible of a straightforward answer. In cases where data relates simply to an issue of fact, objective verification may be possible. A record reading 'Joe Bloggs is 75' will be inaccurate if Joe Bloggs is aged only 25. In some cases, however, a record may repeat information supplied by a third party. The statement may be in the format: 'Fred Smith informs us that Joe Bloggs has defaulted on three loan agreements.' If it is assumed that Joe Bloggs is in reality a person of the utmost financial probity, can it be said that the statement is false? In determining this issue, the fourth data protection principle is interpreted as follows:

> The fourth principle is not to be regarded as being contravened by reason of any inaccuracy in personal data which accurately record information obtained by the data controller from the data subject or a third party in a case where—
>
> (a) having regard to the purpose or purposes for which the data were obtained and further processed, the data controller has taken reasonable steps to ensure the accuracy of the data; and
>
> (b) if the data subject has notified the data controller of the data subject's view that the data are inaccurate, the data indicate that fact.[83]

These requirements are cumulative.

The second element of this principle requires that necessary updating of information shall be carried out. The Data Protection Act 1998 does not expand on this requirement, but it would appear that the question of whether updating is required will be dependent upon the nature of the data and the purpose to which it will be put. If the data is merely a record of a transaction between the data user and the data

---

[80] Data Protection Act 1998, s 70(2).

[81] Ibid., ss 13–14.

[82] 'Errors Rife in Police Data Files', *Computer Weekly*, 27 April 2000, p. 5.

[83] Data Protection Act 1998, Schedule 1, Pt II, para. 7. These provisions are substantially similar to those applying to the data subject's claim to compensation for or rectification of inaccurate data.

subject, no updating would be either necessary or justified. Where the information is being used as the basis for continuing decisions and actions, regular updating may be essential. Thus, where information is to be used for assessing an employee's suitability for promotion, an indication of periods of absence would require to be supplemented by any explanations which might subsequently have been provided.

Duration of record keeping

Linked to the issue of the topicality of data are the provisions of the fifth principle, which require that data should be retained for no longer than is necessary for the attainment of the purpose for which it is held. The Data Protection Directive contains an equivalent provision.[84] Neither instrument expands on this provision. In many cases, data users will be under an obligation to maintain data for a specified period of time, for example, solicitor–client data. In more general terms, there would appear justification for retaining data until the expiry of any limitation period for possible legal action. Save in the situation where data is maintained as a matter of historical record (Data Protection Act 1998, Schedule 8, Part IV), the fifth data protection principle would appear to require that users operate some form of policy for monitoring their data holdings and removing items which are no longer of value or relevance to their activities.

Data security

Under the terms of the seventh data protection principle data, controllers and the operators of computer bureaux are obliged to ensure that:

> Appropriate technical and organisational measures shall be taken against unauthorised or unlawful processing of personal data and against accidental loss or destruction of, or damage to, personal data.

Additionally, controllers will be responsible for ensuring that any data processors contracted by them comply with the requirements of the principle.

The comparable requirement in the Data Protection Directive is that, taking account of the state of the art and making an assessment of costs and risks involved:

> ...the controller must implement appropriate technical and organizational measures to protect personal data against accidental or unlawful destruction or accidental loss, alteration, unauthorized disclosure or access, in particular where the processing involves the transmission of data over a network.[85]

The Registrar has identified a considerable number of matters which are relevant to data security. Account might be taken of the physical security of premises, of any security

---

[84] Directive 95/46/EC, Article 6(1)(e).
[85] Directive 95/46/EC, Article 17(1).

measures incorporated into computer systems, for example password requirements, and of the level of training and supervision of employees. Account can also be taken of the manner in which data and equipment are disposed of. A number of instances have been reported of the purchasers of second-hand computers discovering that data belonging to the original owner remained in the machine's memory. Such lapses might constitute a breach of the principle, as might any deficiency in respect of the disposal of printouts of computer-generated data.[86] In 1992, the EC adopted a 'Decision in the field of the security of information systems'.[87] This is concerned, essentially, to establish the basis for Community action and in its Action Line IV calls, inter alia, for the '(d)evelopment of specifications, standardization, evaluation and certification in respect of the security of information systems'. Such measures might be of significant value in the field of data protection, although the diversity of processing activities might defeat any simple form of classification.

In November 1997, the Registrar published a Consultation Paper on information security in the context of the need to comply with the relevant provisions of the Data Protection Directive.[88] This suggested that data controllers would be required to undertake a risk-based approach in determining the relevant standard of security. Specific reference was made to BS 7799, which contains both a Code of Practice and a Specification for Information Security Management. In Parliament, however, the government rejected an amendment which would have recast the interpretative provisions attached to the principle to make specific reference to 'the risks associated with processing'[89] on the basis that as a:

> [g]eneral principle of law...it is usually necessary to prove a degree of damage. The words 'damage' and 'harm' can be taken together. There are not many actions before the courts that are based simply on the prospect of their being a problem.[90]

It might be considered, however, that such an approach smacks of closing the stable door after the horse has bolted.

Codes of practice

One of the most notable features of the data protection principles is their generality. Given the range of applications across which they have to be applied and the multitude of users subjected to regulation, it is difficult to envisage any other approach. In its report, the Lindop Committee advocated that statements of general principle should be supplemented by around fifty statutory codes of practice.[91]

---

[86] Information Commissioner's Office, Guideline Booklet No. 4.
[87] OJ 1992 L 123/19.
[88] Directive 95/46/EC.
[89] HC Official Report, SC D (Data Protection Bill), col. 304, 4 June 1998.
[90] Ibid., col. 305, 4 June 1998.
[91] Cmnd 7341 (1978), para. 13.26.

As originally introduced, the Data Protection Bill contained no reference to codes of practice. At a late stage in its parliamentary passage, an amendment was accepted which imposes a duty upon the Registrar:

> ...where he considers it appropriate to do so, to encourage trade associations or other bodies representing data users to prepare and to disseminate to their members, codes of practice for guidance in complying with the data protection principles.[92]

In common with many of the duties imposed upon the Registrar, this requirement is formulated in such a manner as to afford considerable discretion to the Registrar. In the years subsequent to the passage of the Data Protection Act 1998, a considerable number of codes have been produced giving guidance as to the interpretation of the principles within specific areas of activity.

In law, such codes possess only evidentiary value. Many of the codes contain a statement from the Registrar to the effect that:

> Observance of this code does not constitute an assurance that I will accept in all cases and without qualification that data users have complied with the Act [Data Protection Act 1998]. However, in considering relevant complaints it is my intention to give careful regard to whether the data user concerned has been complying with his code of practice and will take such compliance as a positive factor in his favour.

Not all the codes have received the Registrar's unqualified blessing. That produced by the Committee of Vice-Chancellors and Principals contained advice as to a method by which students might legally be prevented from obtaining access to their examination marks. This prompted the comment that:

> I note the comments made...about examination marks. Whilst the procedure envisaged in this section is not wrong in law, it is likely to give rise to difficulties and I find it disappointing that it should appear in an otherwise positive document.

The issue of the status of codes of practice was discussed in the Tribunal decision of *Innovations v Data Protection Registrar*.[93] The substantive issues concerned with the question of whether the appellant's information-gathering practices conformed with the requirement of the first data protection principle that data be obtained fairly has been considered earlier. It was also argued on behalf of the appellant that its practices conformed with a code of practice adopted by a relevant trade association, the Advertising Association. The strength of this argument was undoubtedly weakened by the fact that in a foreword to the code, the Registrar had intimated that the Association's view of what was necessary to ensure fair obtaining of data 'differs from my own', and also by the fact that the Council of the Advertising Standards Association and another trade association, the Direct Marketing Association, had adopted rules requiring prior notification to data subjects as part of their codes of conduct.

---

[92] Data Protection Act 1984, s36(4).
[93] Case DA/92 31/49/1.

Codes under the Data Protection Directive

The Data Protection Directive envisages a substantial role for codes of practice to operate at both a national and a Community level. The Preamble recognises that:

> Member States and the Commission in their respective spheres of competence, must encourage the trade associations and other representative organizations concerned to draw up codes of conduct so as to facilitate the operation of this Directive, taking account of the specific circumstances of the processing carried out in certain sectors, and respecting the national provisions adopted for its implementation.[94]

This much merely restates present practice under the Data Protection Act 1998. In implementing the provision, however, Article 27 of the Data Protection Directive[95] provides that draft codes are to be submitted to the national supervisory authority, which is to ascertain 'whether the drafts submitted to it are in accordance with the national provisions adopted pursuant to this Directive'. In making this determination, the authority may seek the views of data users or their representatives. This would appear to mark a significant advance on the present situation, where, although as cited above, the Registrar may express the view that the terms of a code do not comply with the requirements of the legislation, there is no precedent for a positive assertion that the code does comply. Such a development would also go at least part of the way to meeting the suggestion of the Registrar in his 1989 review of the working of the legislation that upon receipt of the Registrar's endorsement, the provisions of a code should have a status equivalent to the Highway Code, i.e. that although breach of its provisions would not itself constitute an offence, this could be taken into account in determining whether any provision of the legislation had been violated.

Provision is also made for the establishment of Community codes. These may be referred to a Working Party established under the Directive with the remit to examine the conformity of national implementing measures with the Directive's requirements; to advise on the level of data protection applying in third countries; to advise the Commission on any amendments to the Data Protection Directive; and 'to give an opinion on codes at Community level'.[96] The Working Party may also seek out the views of data subjects or their representatives before determining whether the draft is in accordance with national implementing provisions. In this event, the 'Commission may ensure appropriate publicity for the code'. Given the requirement that the Directive be implemented in all of the Member States, it is not clear what the role for Community codes will be.

Conclusions

The data protection principles remain pivotal to the operation of the Data Protection Act 1998. As has been discussed, it is perhaps doubtful whether any changes of

---

[94] Directive 95/46/EC, Recital 61.   [95] Directive 95/46/EC.
[96] Directive 95/46/EC, Article 29.

substance have been made from the situation existing under the Data Protection Act 1984. It appears that there is to be an enhanced role for codes of practice and, given the nebulous nature of the principles themselves, this is to be welcomed. Given the extent to which all aspects of our lives are affected by the processing of personal information, there is vital need that effective and transparent control regimes should be established. The decisions of the Data Protection Tribunal in cases brought under the 1984 Act demonstrated a desire to interpret the provisions in a liberal and subject-friendly fashion. It is to be hoped that this will continue to be the case under the new regime.

Suggestions for further reading

Information Commissioner's Office (2006, 2007), *What Price Privacy?* and *What Price Privacy Now?* (Wilmslow).

6

Individual rights and remedies

Introduction

The previous chapters have focused on the measures taken in data protection law to ensure that processing is conducted taking due account of the interests of data subjects. In large part, these impose obligations upon data controllers, for example to provide information as to the purposes of any processing and empower supervisory agencies to take action against any controllers who it is considered are engaging in unfair or unlawful processing. Additionally, the legislation confers a number of rights which may be invoked directly by data subjects and also a number of remedies which may be sought by them in the event that processing is considered to be unfair or unlawful. The Data Protection Act 1998 provides in the sixth data protection principle that 'Personal data shall be processed in accordance with the rights of data subjects under this Act.' Part II of the Act is entitled 'Rights of Data Subjects and Others' and provides for rights of access, the right to receive certain items of information and rights either total or qualified to object to certain forms of processing of their personal data.

Subject access

The concept of subject access is the aspect of data protection which may impact most directly on individuals. The Data Protection Directive requires that:

Member States shall guarantee every data subject the right to obtain from the controller:

(a) without constraint at reasonable intervals and without excessive delay or expense:

- confirmation as to whether or not data relating to him are being processed and information at least as to the purposes of the processing, the categories of data concerned, and the recipients or categories of recipients to whom the data are disclosed,

- communication to him in an intelligible form of the data undergoing processing and of any available information as to their source,

- knowledge of the logic involved in any automatic processing of data concerning him at least in the case of the automated decisions referred to in Article 15 (1).

In implementing this provision, the Act requires that a data controller respond to requests which are made in writing,[1] which contain sufficient information to allow for identification of the data subject and which enclose any fee required by the controller.[2] A maximum fee of £10 may be required before the controller responds to an access request.[3] In terms of the information which is to be provided, it is now stated that:

Subject to the following provisions of this Section and to Sections 8 and 9, an individual is entitled—

(a) to be informed by any data controller whether personal data of which that individual is the data subject are being processed by or on behalf of that data controller;

(b) if that is the case, to be given by the data controller a description of—

(i)   the personal data of which that individual is the data subject;

(ii) the purposes for which they are being or are to be processed; and

(iii) the recipients or classes of recipients to whom they are or may be disclosed;

(c) to have communicated to him in an intelligible form—

(i) the information constituting any personal data of which that individual is the data subject; and

(ii) any information available to the data controller as to the source of those data.

(d) where the processing by automatic means of personal data of which that individual is the data subject for the purpose of evaluating matters relating to him such as, for example, his performance at work, his creditworthiness, his reliability or his conduct, has constituted or is likely to constitute the sole basis for any decision significantly affecting him, to be informed by the data controller of the logic involved in that decision-taking.[4]

A request in respect of one of the items of information referred to above is to be taken as extending to most of the other items.[5] A request to be informed, therefore, whether personal data is held is to be taken as extending to a request for the information itself and for the further information specified relating to purposes, etc. The provision relating to information regarding the logic of processing is treated somewhat differently. The extent of the information to be supplied under this heading

---

[1] Section 64 of the Act provides in respect of the access procedures and a variety of other procedures under the Act that the requirement for writing may be satisfied where a notice is transmitted by electronic means, received in legible form and is capable of being used for subsequent reference. An email message would seem to satisfy these requirements, although it may be difficult for such a message to supply payment of the access fee.

[2] Section 7.

[3] The Data Protection (Subject Access) (Fees and Miscellaneous Provisions) Regulations 2000, SI 2000/191, Reg. 3.

[4] Section 7(2).

[5] Section 7(2), implemented by the Data Subject (Subject Access) (Fees and Miscellaneous Provisions) Regulations 2000. SI 2000 No. 191.

was the subject of considerable debate in the House of Lords, where concerns were expressed that the controller might be required to supply information which constituted valuable intellectual property.[6] It is provided that the obligation is not to extend to any information which 'constitutes a trade secret' (s 8(5)), but, as was pointed out in Parliament, this concept is an ill-defined one. The Data Protection (Subject Access) (Fees and Miscellaneous Provisions) Regulations 2000 provide that specific request must be made for receipt of this information.[7]

The traditional approach towards subject access has been to require that a written copy of data be supplied. The Act imposes the requirement that the copy be supplied in 'intelligible form'.[8] With developments in processing technology, it is possible that data may take the form of audio or video clips, and although the provision of written copies may be expected to remain the norm, expansion of the definition is clearly desirable. In terms of the material to be provided, it was stated by the Court of Appeal in *Durant v Financial Services Authority* that:

> The intention of the Directive, faithfully reproduced in the Act [Data Protection Act 1998], is to enable an individual to obtain from a data controller's filing system, whether computerised or manual, his personal data, that is, information about himself. It is not an entitlement to be provided with original or copy documents as such, but, as Section 7(1)(c)(i) and 8(2) provide, with information constituting personal data in intelligible and permanent form. This may be in documentary form prepared for the purpose and/or where it is convenient in the form of copies of original documents.[9]

It is further provided that, although the copy of the information is normally to be provided in permanent form, this requirement may be waived with the consent of the subject or in a case where the supply of such a copy would be either impossible or involve a disproportionate effort.[10] No indication is given of what might constitute a disproportionate effort but the Commissioner has indicated that decisions will have to be made in the light of the circumstances of each case. A significant factor will be the cost implications to the controller of responding to the request. The information supplied must be that which was held at the time the access request was received, except where any subsequent changes 'would have been made regardless of the receipt of the request'.[11]

The concept of subject access was pioneered in the United Kingdom by the Consumer Credit Act 1974, which provided that individuals should be entitled to obtain a copy of information held by a credit reference agency.[12] The 1974 Act's

---

[6] 586 HL Official Report (5th series), cols CWH 43–45, 23 February 1998.

[7] SI 2000/191, Reg. 2. Rather strangely, it is also provided that a request for information about the logic employed in processing will not automatically be taken as extending to the other items of information in s 7.

[8] Section 7(1)(c).

[9] [2003] EWCA Civ 1746 at [26].

[10] Section 8(2).

[11] Section 8(6).

[12] Section 158.

procedures were unaffected by the Data Protection Act 1984. Given that the majority of the complaints received by the Data Protection Registrar over the years related to the credit sector, the retention of two separate regimes might be considered illogical. The Data Protection Act 1998 merges the provisions for access to data held by credit reference agencies, which had previously been regulated under the Consumer Credit Act 1974. Provision is made for different fee levels to be fixed by the Secretary of State, and the Data Protection (Subject Access) (Fees and Miscellaneous Provisions) Regulations 2000[13] provides that a fee of £2 will be payable in respect of access to such records.[14] One issue concerning the change did cause discussion in Parliament.[15] Under the 1974 Act, a modified access procedure applies where the subject is a business person.[16] Effectively, this limits the amount of information supplied so that, for example, the applicant would not receive information about adverse credit reports which had been provided by bankers or suppliers. Where the business constitutes a sole trader or partnership, the general access provisions of the Data Protection Act 1998 will replace the specialised provisions. Concern was expressed that the consequence might be that third parties would be reluctant to supply such information in the knowledge that it could be obtained, with the consequence being that small businesses might find it more difficult to obtain credit. Whilst giving an undertaking to keep the matter under review, the government indicated that it was not convinced that the concerns were justified, and a proposal to amend the Bill to retain the current procedures was rejected.[17]

Access timetable

Valid requests for access must be satisfied within 40 days.[18] Where data is held by a credit reference agency, the current shorter time limit of seven days is to apply.[19] The information supplied must generally be that held at the date of receipt of the access request. Account may be taken, however, of any amendments or deletions made subsequently where these would have been made 'regardless of the receipt of the request'.[20] Having satisfied an access request from a data subject, a controller is not obliged to comply with a subsequent identical or similar request until a reasonable interval has elapsed.[21] In making his or her determination, account is to be taken of the nature of the data, the purpose of the processing, and the frequency with which amendments are made.

---

[13] SI 2000 No. 191.
[14] Regulation 4.
[15] Section 9.
[16] Section 160.
[17] 316 HC Official Report (6th series), cols 578–79, 2 July 1998.
[18] Data Protection Act 1998, s 7(10).
[19] Data Protection (Subject Access) (Fees and Miscellaneous Provisions) Regulations 2000, SI 2000/191, Reg. 4.
[20] Data Protection Act 1998, s 8(6).
[21] Section 8(3).

Exceptions to the subject access provisions

In certain situations, the individual's interest in obtaining access to personal data has to be restricted, either in the subject's own interests or as a result of giving priority to other competing claims. Access to medical data provides an example of the first situation, where it is provided that an access request may be refused where it is considered that this might be prejudicial to the enquiring subject's physical or mental health, whilst restrictions on access to data held for the purpose of crime prevention or detection illustrate how the subject's desire to know what information is held might reasonably be subjugated to the requirements of the data controller or those of society at large.

The Data Protection Directive provides that Member States may provide for exemptions from subject access when this constitutes a necessary measure to safeguard:

(a) national security;

(b) defence;

(c) public security;

(d) the prevention, investigation, detection and prosecution of criminal offences, or of breaches of ethics for regulated professions;

(e) an important economic or financial interest of a Member State or of the EU, including monetary, budgetary and taxation matters;

(f) a monitoring, inspection or regulatory function connected, even occasionally, with the exercise of official authority in cases referred to in (c), (d) and (e); or

(g) the protection of the data subject or of the rights and freedoms of others.[22]

In respect of the various provisions to be discussed below, a variety of approaches exist. Where data is held for national security purposes, total exemption is offered from all aspects of the legislation. In the case of data held for historical, research, or statistical purposes, the exemption relates only to subject access and the related supply of information relating to source, processing purpose, and intended disclosures as defined in the s 7 of the Data Protection Act 1998. In other cases, however, the exemption is stated as applying also in respect of the requirements of the first data protection principle relating to the fair and lawful processing of personal data. Although in many cases, the application of the exemption is limited to instances where it is necessary to avoid prejudicing the purpose for which the data is being processed, its linkage with subject access does mean that provisions which purport to protect data subjects may, in reality, work to their disadvantage.

Prior to considering the circumstances under which a user may legally deny a subject's access request, mention should be made of a problem that may arise whenever the user determines that all or part of a request for access falls within the scope of an exception. Under the Data Protection Act 1998's definitions, personal data is classed

---

[22] Directive 95/46/EC, Article 13(1).

as data to which the subject is entitled to have access. Where an exception is properly relied upon, it may be accepted that it is as undesirable from the user's standpoint to inform the subject that they hold data which they are not willing to disclose as it would be to divulge the information. In the event that a subject suspects that personal data has not been supplied pursuant to a request for access, action may be raised before the courts.[23] An alternative course of action will be to make a complaint to the Commissioner. In the event the Commissioner takes action, the onus will be on the user to justify their action. However, dependent upon the circumstances and the nature of the data, it may be that a subject who receives the reply that no relevant personal data is held may accept this at face value and will make no attempt to pursue the matter before the courts or with the Commissioner.

Third-party data

In some cases, as has been discussed above, the linkage of data relating to a third party with mention of a data subject may lead to the conclusion that a record does not constitute personal data relating to the data subject. In other cases, there can be no doubt that a record does constitute personal data but that this relates to more than one individual. It may be that data relates to some form of joint activity; transactions, for example, in connection with the operation of a joint bank account. In this situation, where one subject submits an access request, there is unlikely to be a serious issue concerning the identity of the other subject or subjects, but there may be a case for deleting items of data such as cheque or cash-machine withdrawals made under the signature or against the PIN of the other account holder. In a second situation, the data may relate to the inquiring subject but emanate from a third party. An example might see a social work record recounting an allegation from a named third party that a subject is behaving in a violent manner to other persons. The record could state that 'Fred Smith has reported that Joe Bloggs is mistreating his wife and children.' There is clearly personal data about Joe Bloggs here and it may be desirable to allow the subject to see and possibly refute the allegation of violence. The record also contains personal data relating to Fred Smith as the source of the data. It is likely to be extremely unwelcome to this person if the fact of his report is disclosed to Joe Bloggs. How the balance is to be struck has been a continuing cause of difficulty.

Under the Data Protection Act 1984, a data user was under no obligation to supply information relating to a third party—including the fact that the third party had been the source of information relating to the data subject. No obligation, however, was imposed on the data user to inquire whether the third party would be willing for the information to be transmitted to the subject.[24] A significant change to the extent of access rights required came as a consequence of the decision of the European Court of Human Rights in the case of *Gaskin v United Kingdom*.[25] The applicant in this case had spent much of his childhood in local authority care. In adulthood, he claimed that he

---

[23] Data Protection Act 1998, s 7(9).
[24] Section 21(4)(a).   [25] (1990) 12 EHRR 36.

had been the subject of ill-treatment and instituted legal proceedings against the local authority. As part of these proceedings, he sought discovery of all documents held by the authority relating to his case. Many of the documents had been compiled by third parties, such as doctors and social workers. Acting in excess of the statutory obligations imposed upon them, the authority contacted the third parties, seeking their approval to disclosure. Whilst the majority agreed to disclosure of the data, a number of parties refused consent and the authority took the view that this was determinative of the issue. Under United Kingdom law as it stood this was determinative of the issue, but proceedings were raised before the European Court of Human Rights alleging that the failure of the United Kingdom legislation to provide the applicant with a right of access to the data constituted a breach of its obligations under Article 8 of the European Convention on Human Rights requiring respect for private and family life. The European Court of Human Rights held that, whilst the applicant did not have an unqualified right of access to data, the failure to provide an independent review in the event that a third party refused consent constituted a breach of his rights:

> The Court considers…that under such a system the interests of the individual seeking access to records relating to his private and family life must be secured when a contributor to the records either is not available or improperly refuses consent. Such a system is only in conformity with the principle of proportionality if it provides that an independent authority finally decides whether access has to be granted in cases where a contributor fails to answer or withholds consent. No such procedure was available to the applicant in the present case.[26]

In seeking to bring United Kingdom law into conformity with the European Convention on Human Rights, the Data Protection Act 1998 now provides that:

> Where a data controller cannot comply with the request (for information) without disclosing information relating to another individual who can be identified from that information, he is not obliged to comply with the request unless—
>
> (a) the other individual has consented to the disclosure of the information to the person making the request, or
>
> (b) it is reasonable in all the circumstances to comply with the request without the consent of the other individual.[27]

In determining whether it is reasonable for a controller to provide access without the third party's consent the Act provides that account is to be taken in particular of:

> (a) any duty of confidentiality owed to the other individual,
>
> (b) any steps taken by the data controller with a view to seeking the consent of the other individual,
>
> (c) whether the other individual is capable of giving consent, and
>
> (d) any express refusal of consent by the other individual.[28]

---

[26] (1990) 12 EHRR 36 at 50.   [27] Section 7(4).   [28] Section 7(6).

It is further provided that 'reference to information relating to another individual includes a reference to information identifying that individual as the source of the information sought by the request'. The provision, however, 'is not to be construed as excusing a data controller from communicating so much of the information sought by the request as can be communicated without disclosing the identity of the other individual concerned, whether by the omission of names or other identifying particulars or otherwise'.[29]

The application of these provisions was at issue in the case of *Durant v Financial Services Authority*.[30] The background to this case has been described above (p. 119). Although some information was supplied, access to other records was provided only in partial form through the concealment or redaction of information which it was considered related to third parties. The complainant sought access to the names of this person. It appears that the data controller sought the views of the individual who 'had understandably withheld his or her consent because Mr Durant had abused him or her over the telephone'.

One issue which does not appear to have been discussed before the court concerned the status of the individual who it appears was an employee of the Financial Services Authority. The Data Protection Act provides that the term 'third party' does not include any person 'authorised to process data for the data controller'.[31] Employees would undoubtedly fall into this category,[32] although the court in *Durant* made extensive reference to data relating to third parties. However, Section 7(5)–(6)refers to data relating to 'another individual' and does not use the term 'third party'. Although, as discussed previously, there may be a question of whether the identity of an employee dealing with a data subject forms part of that subject's personal data, it would appear a strange result if a data controller could reject or respond only in part to an access request on the ground that data related to a member of staff.

Although in this particular case, the data controller had sought consent for disclosure of the data, the court continued to give guidance as to the nature of the consideration that the statute required to be given by a data controller when faced with such an access request. The general criterion, it was stated was 'whether it is reasonable to *comply* with the request for information notwithstanding that it may disclose information about another, not whether it is reasonable to *refuse* to comply'. The distinction it was stated:

> may be of importance, depending on who is challenging the data controller's decision, to the meaning of 'reasonable' in this context and to the court's role in examining it. The circumstances going to the reasonableness of such a decision, as I have just noted, include, but are not confined to, those set out in Section 7(6) [of the Data Protection Act 1998], and none of them is determinative. It is important to note that Section 7(4) leaves the data controller with a choice whether to seek consent; it does not oblige him to do so before deciding whether to disclose the personal data sought or, by redaction, to disclose only part of it. However, whether he has sought such consent and, if

---

[29] Section 7(5).   [30] [2003] EWCA Civ 1746.   [31] Section 70(1).
[32] Information Commissioner's Office, *Legal Guidance*.

he has done so, it has been refused, are among the circumstances mentioned in the non-exhaustive list in Section 7(6) going to the reasonableness of any decision under Section 7(4)(b) to disclose, without consent.

It is difficult to conceive of many situations where a data controller should decline to seek the third party's consent and then refuse an access request on the ground that the data would identify a third party. Such a result would conflict sharply with the principles laid down in *Gaskin*. In the event that the third party—as in the present case—was asked to consent, refused, and the controller determined not to diclose the data to the enquiring data subject, the courts, it was held, should be reluctant to routinely:

'second-guess' decisions of data controllers, who may be employees of bodies large or small, public or private or be self-employed. To so interpret the legislation would encourage litigation and appellate challenge by way of full rehearing on the merits and, in that manner, impose disproportionate burdens on them and their employers in their discharge of their many responsibilities under the Act [Data Protection Act 1998].

It continued:

the right to privacy and other legitimate interests of individuals identified in or identifiable from a data subject's personal data are highly relevant to, but not determinative of, the issue of reasonableness of a decision whether to disclose personal data containing information about someone else where that person's consent has not been sought. The data controller and, if necessary, a court on an application under Section 7(9), should also be entitled to ask what, if any, legitimate interest the data subject has in disclosure of the identity of another individual named in or identifiable from personal data to which he is otherwise entitled...
...Much will depend, on the one hand, on the criticality of the third party information forming part of the data subject's personal data to the legitimate protection of his privacy, and, on the other, to the existence or otherwise of any obligation of confidence to the third party or any other sensitivity of the third party disclosure sought. Where the third party is a recipient or one of a class of recipients who might act on the data to the data subject's disadvantage...his right to protect his privacy may weigh heavily and obligations of confidence to the third party(ies) may be non-existent or of less weight. Equally, where the third party is the source of the information, the data subject may have a strong case for his identification if he needs to take action to correct some damaging inaccuracy, though here countervailing considerations of an obligation of confidentiality to the source or some other sensitivity may have to be weighed in the balance.

A final issue concerns the question of when a third party is to be considered identifiable. A controller is obliged to supply as much information as is possible without disclosing the third party's identity. In particular, it is stated, this might involve the omission of names or other identifying particulars. Account is to be taken of:

any information which in the reasonable belief of the data controller, is likely to be in, or to come into, the possession of the data subject making the request.[33]

---

[33] Data Protection Act 1998, s 7(5).

In the *Durant* case, this task was relatively straightforward. The data subject did not know the identity of the employee he had been dealing with and a motive behind the access request was to obtain this information. This requirement may cause some difficulties for data controllers. In a case such as *Gaskin*,[34] for example, it may be a very difficult task for a data controller to assess whether the inquiring data subject would have, after the passage of many years, any recollection of the identity of particular doctors or social workers who had been responsible for submitting reports.

National security

Under the Data Protection Act 1984, information held for the purpose of national security was totally exempted from the legislation.[35] Given the increasing involvement of national security agencies such as MI5 in crime-related functions, such as operations against suspected drug dealers, the division between national security and criminal functions is frequently blurred. This has led the Registrar to express concern that exemptions have been claimed on an organisational rather than a task-related basis.[36] Although no changes were required to the 1984 Act in this regard, national security falling outwith the ambit of Community law-making competence, the Data Protection Act 1998 does contain significant new provisions. As under the 1984 Act, a certificate may be issued by a minister of the Crown indicating that personal data is held for the purpose of national security.[37] Under the 1984 Act, such a certificate was not open to challenge. It is now provided, however, that it may be challenged before the Information Tribunal by any person 'directly affected'. This may include a data subject who for the first and only time is given a right to initiate proceedings before the Tribunal. Applying 'the principles applied by the court on an application for judicial review', the Tribunal may quash the certificate if it considers that the minister did not have 'reasonable grounds' for issuing it.[38] Detailed provision for the procedures to be followed in the Tribunal are now found in the Information Tribunal (National Security Appeals) Rules 2005.[39]

With the introduction of the new right of appeal, a number of cases were brought before the Information Tribunal. In the first case, *Norman Baker v Secretary of State for the Home Department*,[40] the claimant, a Liberal Democrat MP, had sought access to records which he believed were held about him by the security services. This prompted a response:

> Under the Data Protection Act 1998 the Security Service intends to notify the Data Protection Commissioner that it processes data for three purposes. These are: staff

---

[34] *Gaskin v United Kingdom* (1990) 12 EHRR 36.
[35] Section 27.
[36] See, for example, *Sunday Times*, 1 February 1998.
[37] Section 28(2).
[38] Section 28(5).
[39] SI 2005 No. 13.
[40] [2001] UKHRR 1275.

administration, building security CCTV and commercial agreements. The Security Service has checked its records and holds no data about you in any of these categories.

Any other personal data held by the Security Service is exempt from the notification and subject access provisions of the Data Protection Act 1998 on the ground that such exemption is required for the purpose of safeguarding national security, as provided for in Section 28(1) of the Act. Thus, if it were to be the case that the Service held any data regarding you other than for the purposes set out in paragraph 2 above, the Data Protection Act would not confer a right of access. There is therefore no data to which you are entitled to have access under the Act, but you should not assume from this letter that any such data is held about you.

I would point out that a right of appeal exists under Section 28 of the Act. The Section provides that the exemption described above can be confirmed by a certificate signed by a Minister of the Crown who is a member of the Cabinet, or by the Attorney General. A certificate relating to the work of the Security Service was signed by the Home Secretary on 22 July. Any person directly affected by the issuing of the certificate may appeal…[41]

Such an appeal was brought and provided the opportunity for the first sitting of the National Security Appeals Panel of the Information Tribunal. The appellant argued before the Tribunal that he had been given information that the security services had collected information in connection with his past activities in support of an ecological group. Although his involvement with the organisation had now ceased, he indicated that he had been informed that the file remained in existence.

The Tribunal reviewed the certificate which had been issued by the Secretary of State. This, it was stated, 'can fairly be described as a blanket exemption for "any personal data that is processed by the Security Service" in the performance of its statutory functions'.[42]

By exempting the Security Service from the duty under Section 7(1)(a) of the Act [Data Protection Act 1998] to inform the individual making the request whether or not his personal data are being processed, the Certificate authorises the non-committal reply which was given to Mr Baker. This means that both the Certificate and the response gave effect to the policy which is known colloquially as 'neither confirm nor deny' and by the acronym 'NCND'. We have no doubt that they were intended to do so.[43]

The certificate at issue in the present case was typical of all certificates issued in response to requests for access under the Data Protection Act 1998. The case for applying this policy was that a reply indicating that information was held but was not being made available to an applicant could of itself compromise the national security interests for which the information had been collected.

Although such a policy raises major issues relating to access to national security data, the issue before the Tribunal was a more limited one, namely to determine

41 [2001] UKHRR 1275 at [14].
42 [2001] UKHRR 1275 at [25].
43 [2001] UKHRR 1275 at [30].

whether the Secretary of State had acted reasonably in formulating a certificate which left the decision of whether and to what extent a request for access should be granted entirely to the security services. As was stated:

> if the NCND response is permitted in all cases then the practical result is that the Service is not obliged to consider each request on its individual merits. That follows if the NCND reply is invariably justified, and we were furnished with no evidence that individual consideration is given to the possible consequences of making a positive response to every request.[44]

The question for the Tribunal was whether such a blanket policy was acceptable or whether the legislation imposed an obligation to give consideration to the individual circumstances of each application.

Discussion of whether the Secretary of State had reasonable grounds for issuing the certificate focused on the question of whether his action constituted a proportionate response to the need to balance the interests of individual rights and state security. After reviewing the principles appropriate to an action for judicial review, the Tribunal recognised that different situations called for different approaches:

> Where the context is national security judges and tribunals should supervise with the lightest touch appropriate; there is no area (foreign affairs apart) where judges have traditionally deferred more to the executive view than that of national security; and for good and sufficient reason. They have no special expertise; and the material upon which they can make decisions is perforce limited. That the touch should be the lightest in comparative terms does not, of course, assist in weighing up how light that should be in absolute terms.[45]

Even on this basis, however, the Tribunal was of the view that the certificate should be quashed. A blanket exemption, as provided for by the certificate, was wider than was necessary to preserve national security. It was clear from the evidence that there were cases where information held by the security services could be disclosed without prejudicing national security and no evidence that the task of sifting these cases from others where the established 'neither confirm nor deny' response would impose unreasonable burdens upon the security service. The decision in the *Baker* case[46] was not concerned in any respect with the merits of a decision that access should not be granted. It provides authority for the proposition that each request must be considered on its merits.

In two further cases brought before the National security Appeals Panel, *Hitchens v Secretary of State for the Home Department* and *Gosling v Secretary of State for the Home Department*,[47] the attempt was made to challenge the merits of decisions to

---

[44] [2001] UKHRR 1275 at [32].

[45] [2001] UKHRR 1275 at [76].

[46] [2001] UKHRR 1275.

[47] The transcript of these decisions can be obtained from the Department of Constitutional Affairs website at <http://www.dca.gov.uk/foi/inftrib.htm>

refuse to supply information which the appellants believed was held by the security services concerning their past activities. In the former case, the period covered was some thirty years previously when the claimant, who had become a somewhat right-wing newspaper columnist, was a member of an extreme Marxist group at York University. Whilst he accepted that the security services would have been justified to take an interest in his youthful activities he argued:

> My aim is purely to know what, if anything, is in these records, mainly because I feel I am entitled to know the details of such records as a matter of natural justice. Since I am no longer a revolutionary Marxist, and the politics of this country have been utterly transformed in the intervening period, and it is most unlikely that any individual mentioned in these files still holds a sensitive position of any kind, I can see no argument for withholding these files from me. I would, if asked, be quite happy to co-operate with the Security Service to ensure that no sensitive information was accidentally disclosed. Their response, however, is simple blank refusal…covered by the meaningless and hard-to-justify claim that this is 'safeguarding national security'. I think the Security Service needs to do better than this to justify secrecy over files almost 30 years old concerning my own youthful follies and their attempts to monitor them.

Following the panel's decision in *Baker*, the format of the ministerial certificate had been amended to make it incumbent upon the security service to give individual consideration to each request for access. The focus of argument in this case was on the merits of the individual decision. Here, the Panel was referred to the Investigatory Powers Tribunal, which was established under s 65 of the Regulation of Investigatory Powers Act 2000 to deal with a wide range of complaints that may be made about the exercise of powers under the Act. This tribunal, it was held, had jurisdiction to deal with complaints of the kind brought by the appellant. Furthermore:

> we believe that the Investigatory Powers Tribunal is the body best placed to determine any specific complaint that the Service has applied the provisos to the certificate in a manner that is manifestly unjustified. That Tribunal is presided over by a distinguished senior judge and has the appropriate expertise to investigate a complaint of this nature.[48]

On this basis, the appeal was rejected.

Whilst it is encouraging that another method of appeal should be available to individuals, the result appears indicative of a somewhat confused and confusing approach towards information policy. Whilst it may well be the case that the structure of the Investigatory Powers Tribunal makes it better equipped to deal with arguments on the merits of a particular access request, the question arises as to what is the continuing function of the National Security Appeals Panel. Having quashed the first version of the ministerial certificate in *Baker*, the terms of the revised version were accepted in *Hitchens*. Short of further changes in format, it is difficult to identify any circumstances in which an appeal to the panel would serve any useful purpose.

---

[48] [2001] UKHRR 1275 at [56].

Data held for policing and revenue-gathering purposes

The Data Protection Act 1998 provides an exception from the subject access provisions where personal data is processed in connection with:

(a) the prevention or detection of crime;

(b) the apprehension or prosecution of offenders; or

(c) the collection or assessment of any tax or duty

to the extent that the grant of access would be prejudicial to the attainment of the purpose in question.[49]

The determination of whether access would be prejudicial to any of the above purposes requires to be made in the context of an individual request for access. In the event that a denial of access is challenged before the Commissioner, the onus will be on the data user to demonstrate a likelihood of prejudice in the circumstances of the particular case. The criteria to be invoked was discussed before the High Court in *Lord v Secretary of State*,[50] an action in which a prisoner was seeking access to reports produced in the course of a prison review to determine whether his status should be reduced from that of a high risk (category A) inmate. For the authorities it was argued, inter alia, that disclosure would be likely to prejudice the interests of crime prevention. Considering the approach to be adopted Mr Justice Mumby commented:

> I accept that 'likely' in Section 29(1) does not mean more probable than not. But on the other hand, it must connote a significantly greater degree of probability than merely 'more than fanciful'. A 'real risk' is not enough. I cannot accept that the important rights intended to be conferred by Section 7 are intended to be set at nought by something which measures up only to the minimal requirement of being real, tangible or identifiable rather than merely fanciful. Something much more significant and weighty than that is required. After all, the Directive, to which I must have regard in interpreting Section 29(1), permits restrictions on the data subject's right of access to information about himself only (to quote the language of Recital (43)) 'in so far as they are *necessary* to safeguard' or (to quote the language of Article 13(1)) 'constitute a *necessary* measure to safeguard' the prevention and detection of crime [emphasis added]. The test of necessity is a strict one.[51] ... 'likely' in Section 29(1) connotes a degree of probability where there is a very significant and weighty chance of prejudice to the identified public interests. The degree of risk must be such that there 'may very well' be prejudice to those interests, even if the risk falls short of being more probable than not.

Consideration was also given to the extent to which the decision of whether data should be disclosed should be made solely by reference to the circumstances of the particular applicant. Whilst recognising that:

> this does not mean that one can simply ignore the consequential effect that disclosure in the particular case may have in others.[52]

---

[49] Section 28(1).   [50] [2003] EWHC 2073 (Admin).
[51] At paras 99–100.   [52] At para. 122.

It was held that a blanket policy of non-disclosure failed to satisfy the test and an order was made that the data should be released to the claimant.

A further exception is provided which operates at a higher level of generality. This provides that subject access will not be permitted where personal data is processed by a government department, local authority, or other authority administering housing benefit or council tax benefit as part of a system of risk assessment relating to the assessment of collection of tax or duty, the prevention or detection of crime, or the apprehension or prosecution of offenders and:

> ... where the offence concerned involves any unlawful claim for payment out of, or any unlawful application of, public funds

and where exemption is required in the interests of the operation of the system.[53]

By referring to the operation of the system, the provision obviates the need to show that allowing a particular data subject access would have prejudicial effects. It was explained on behalf of the government that the provision was intended primarily to benefit the Inland Revenue. An example might be that:

> ... the Inland Revenue's recently introduced self-assessment system uses a range of indicators to identify individual tax returns which justify further inquiries. Subsection 4 will allow an exemption to be made for withholding this critical risk assessment information from data subjects. If it was not withheld, tax experts, if not the individuals concerned, could soon start to compare cases and deduce the revenue's criteria for further inquiry.[54]

It is to be noted that the exemption relates only to the subject access provision and not to the requirements of the first data protection principle that data be obtained and processed fairly and lawfully.

Health data

The Data Protection Act 1984 established the general principle that access should be provided to medical and social work data. The Access to Personal Files Act 1987 and Access to Health Records Act 1990 extended these rights to manual files with procedures which are now gathered under the umbrella of the Data Protection Act 1998. The 1998 Act confers power on the Secretary of State to make regulations exempting or modifying the subject information provisions in respect of health data.[55] Such an approach is envisaged by the Data Protection Directive which states in Recital 42:

> Member States may, in the interest of the data subject or so as to protect the rights and freedoms of others, restrict rights of access and information; whereas they may, for example, specify that access to medical data may be obtained only through a health professional.

---

[53] Data Protection Act 1998, s 29(4).
[54] 586 HL Official Report (5th series), col. 505, 16 March 1998.
[55] Section 30(1).

Article 11 provides that measures may be taken to 'restrict the scope' of access rights on a range of grounds including 'the protection of the data subject or of the rights and freedoms of others'. The United Kingdom legislation perhaps stretches the concept of 'restrict' to its limits by providing for access to be excluded. The Data Protection (Subject Access Modification) (Health) Order 2000[56] provides for exemption when, in the opinion of a relevant health professional, the grant of access would 'cause serious harm to the physical or mental health or condition of the data subject or any other person'.

In cases where the data controller concerned is not a health professional, any decision to grant or refuse access may be made only after consultation with an 'appropriate health professional'. This term is defined as:

(a) the health professional who is currently or was most recently responsible for the clinical care of the data subject in connection with the matters to which the information which is the subject of the request relates; or

(b) where there is more than one such health professional, the health professional who is the most suitable to advise on the matters to which the information which is the subject of the request relates.[57]

A request for access may not be denied on the ground that disclosure would identify a health professional as being responsible for the compilation of a record, except where it can be shown that serious harm is likely to be caused to the physical or mental health or condition of the health professional. This is perhaps likely to apply only in the situation where there are grounds for suspecting that the data subject might be liable to attack or harass the health professional identified.

Special provision is made for the situation where access is sought, typically by a parent or guardian, on behalf of a child or a person suffering mental incapacity. In such a case, it is provided that data are exempted from the access rights where it has been:

(a) provided by the data subject in the expectation that it would not be disclosed to the person making the request;

(b) obtained as a result of any examination or investigation to which the data subject consented in the expectation that the information would not be disclosed; or

(c) which the data subject has expressly indicated should not be so disclosed.[58]

By providing that access may be denied only to the extent that this would cause 'serious harm' to the health of the data subject, the Order[59] must be seen as establishing a strong presumption in favour of access. Whilst recognising that circumstances—particularly those connected with psychiatric illness—may exist in which the supply of a copy of a medical record may not be in the best interests of the patient, it may be doubted whether the procedures adopted under the Order are, in themselves, likely to prove any less harmful. In common with the situations arising under other exemptions, a health professional may respond to a request for access with the statement that

---

[56] SI 2000/413.   [57] SI 2000/413, Reg. 2.   [58] SI 2000/413, Reg. 5(3).   [59] SI 2000/413.

no relevant personal data is held. To an extent perhaps greater than with the other exceptions, the data subject is likely to be aware of the fact that data is held. The failure to supply data may well be a source of distress in itself, whilst discovery of the fact that the data has been withheld for fear that access would cause serious harm to the patient's health would, in itself, appear inimical to his or her health interests.

Education and social work data

The basic format of the exemptions in respect of these categories of data is similar to that applying to health records. The relevant statutory instruments are the Data Protection (Subject Access Modification) (Education) Order 2000[60] and the Data Protection (Subject Access Modification) (Social Work) Order 2000.[61] In both cases, access may be denied in situations where its grant 'would be likely to cause serious harm to the physical or mental health or condition of the data subject or any other person'. Unlike the situation with health records, however, there is no requirement that the decision of whether to grant or refuse access should be made by a person possessing appropriate qualifications.

In both sectors, it is provided that a request for access may not be refused on the basis that the data would identify a third party where this would refer to an employee of the data controller responsible for producing a record in the course of employment, again subject to an exception where it can be shown that the grant of access would be likely to result in serious harm to the individuals concerned.

In the case of both categories of records—but especially in the case of educational records—there is a possibility that access may be sought by a third party acting on behalf of a data subject. In addition to the general ground for refusing access, it is provided in the case of educational records that access may be denied in respect of information indicating that the child is or may be at risk of child abuse, where the grant of access would not be in the best interests of the child. In respect of social work records, the criteria are identical to those described above concerning health data.

Regulatory activity

A broad range of statutory agencies engaged in regulatory tasks are provided with exemptions from the subject information provisions to the extent that compliance with these would prejudice the attainment of their purpose.[62] A number of agencies are specifically identified in the Data Protection Act 1998, namely the Parliamentary, Health Service, Local Government, and Northern Irish Assembly and Complaints Ombudsmen. Exemption is also offered to the Director General of Fair Trading in respect of the discharge of functions in the fields of consumer protection and competition policy. In addition to named agencies, exemption is also offered to those performing 'relevant functions' which are designed to protect against specified risks. The term 'relevant functions' is defined to encompass functions conferred by statute, performed

[60] SI 2000/414.   [61] SI 2000/415.   [62] Section 31.

by the Crown, ministers, or government departments, or 'any other function' which is of a 'public nature and is exercised in the public interest'. The activities involved relate to protection against loss due to 'dishonesty, malpractice or other seriously improper conduct' within the financial services, corporate and professional sectors, or through the conduct of discharged or undischarged bankrupts. Also exempted are functions concerned with the supervision of charities and the protection of health and safety, both for workers and for third parties who might be affected by particular activities.

Research, history, and statistics

Exemption for data of this description continues the approach adopted in the Data Protection Act 1998. Where data are 'not processed to support measures or decisions with regard to particular individuals' and where the processing is not likely to cause substantial damage or distress to any data subject, exemption is offered from the subject access provisions subject to the further condition that the results of processing are not made available in a form permitting identification of data subjects.[63]

Information required to be made available to the public

In many instances, personal data will be contained in some document which is made available to the public. An example would be the electoral roll, copies of which may be supplied in electronic format. In the situation where the data made available is the only data held concerning the data subject, there would be little value for the subject in exercising a right of access. Such an exemption previously applied under the Data Protection Act 1984 and continues under the Data Protection Act 1998, however, again, with the additional benefit to the data controller that there will be exemption from the first data protection principle.[64]

Miscellaneous exceptions

Schedule 7 to the Data Protection Act 1998 contains a substantial list of additional exceptions, which list may be supplemented by regulations made by the Secretary of State.[65] As described in the following paragraphs, the extent of the individual exemptions varies, ranging from the application of modified access procedures, through to exemption from access, and to exemption from the fair processing requirement.

Confidential references

In many cases under the Data Protection Act 1984, such references would have been excluded from scrutiny under provisions referring to the processing of data purely in order to create the text of a document (the word processing exemption).[66] This exemption is not retained in the Data Protection Act 1998 and the expanded definition of

---

[63] Section 33.   [64] Section 34.
[65] Section 38(1).   [66] Section 1(8).

processing in the 1998 Act will bring such documents within its scope. It is provided that the subject access provisions will not apply to references given in connection with the data subject's education, employment, or appointment to any office, as well as to the provision of any services by the data subject.[67]

Armed forces

The subject information provisions will not apply where their application would be likely to prejudice the combat effectiveness of the armed forces.[68] This is a new provision and it is difficult to identify situations in which it is likely to apply.

Judicial appointments and honours

Under the Data Protection Act 1984, information held for the first of these purposes was exempted from the subject access provisions.[69] The Data Protection Act 1998 extends the scope of the exemption to data processed in connection with the 'conferring by the Crown of any honour'. Such data are exempt from the subject information provisions, regardless of any issue of prejudice.[70]

Crown employment and Crown and ministerial appointments

Regulatory power is conferred on the Secretary of State to exempt data processed for the purpose of assessing a person's suitability for specified appointments. The Data Protection (Crown Appointments) Order 2000[71] provides that this is to apply in respect of the appointment of senior religious figures in the Church of England and a range of other dignitaries, including the Poet Laureate and the Astronomer Royal.

Management forecasts

Personal data processed for this (undefined) purpose benefit from an exemption to the subject information provisions, where compliance would prejudice the attainment of the purpose.[72] Under the Data Protection Act 1984, a data user was not required to give access to information indicating intentions held towards the data subject. Such information might frequently be held in records maintained for career-planning purposes and these may benefit from this provision.

Corporate finance

Extensive provisions are made for exemptions under this heading. The exemption will apply to data processed by 'relevant persons' concerned with the underwriting of share issues or the provision of advice on capital structure, industrial strategy, and acquisitions

---

[67] Schedule 7, para. 1.
[68] Data Protection Act 1998, Schedule 7, para. 2.
[69] Section 31.
[70] Schedule 7, para. 3.
[71] SI 2000/416.
[72] Data Protection Act 1998, Schedule 7, para. 4.

and mergers, and will apply when the application of the subject information provisions could affect the price of any shares or other instruments. In the situation this criterion is not satisfied, it is further provided that exemption may be granted 'for the purpose of safeguarding an important economic or financial interest of the United Kingdom'. It is provided that the Secretary of State may specify in more detail the circumstances and situations in which this latter exemption is to apply and this power is exercised in the Data Protection (Corporate Finance Exception) Order 2000.[73] This specifies that account is to be taken of the 'inevitable prejudicial effect' on:

(a) the orderly functioning of financial markets; or

(b) the efficient allocation of capital within the economy,

through granting access to data which might affect the decision of any person on whether or how to act within the financial markets or in respect of the conduct of any business activity.

Negotiations

Data processed in relation to negotiations between the controller and subject which record the intentions of the controller are exempt from the subject information provisions where compliance with these would be likely to prejudice those negotiations.[74] An example of such a situation might concern data relating to an employer's business strategy in a situation where an employee who has been identified as critical to the success of the business is seeking to negotiate a pay rise.

Examination marks and examination scripts

The Data Protection Act 1984 made special provision allowing examination authorities to delay responding to requests for access beyond the normal forty-day period.[75] This was considered necessary for large-scale examinations, such as the GCSE, where a period of months might elapse between examination and publication of the results. This approach continues in the Data Protection Act 1998.[76] One point which should be noted is that where an examination authority relies upon the extended time limits upon receipt of an access request, its response must provide information as to the data held at the time of receipt of the request, at the time the request is complied with, and any further data which was held at any intervening stage. An inquiring subject will, therefore, receive details of any changes made to exam marks during the various stages of the assessment process.

A novel exemption from the subject access provision relates to the materials produced by students during the examination process.[77] Under the Data Protection

---

[73] SI 2000/184.
[74] Data Protection Act 1998, Schedule 7, para. 7.
[75] Section 35.
[76] Schedule 7, para. 8.
[77] Schedule 7, para. 9.

Act 1984, it is unlikely that these would have been covered by the legislation. With the extension to some forms of manual records and the deletion of the text processing exemption, the Data Protection Act 1998 may well govern such materials.

Information about human embryos

The Data Protection Act 1998 provides an exemption from the subject information provisions in respect of information indicating that an individual was born following IVF treatment. The Data Protection Act 1984 made a similar provision with regard to the subject access right.[78] An alternative access procedure involving prior counselling is, however, provided under the Human Fertilisation and Embryology Act 1990.[79] These provisions are continued by the Data Protection (Miscellaneous Subject Access Exemptions) Order 2000.[80]

Legal professional privilege

Data are exempt from the subject information provisions where they consist of information in respect of which a claim to legal professional privilege (or client–lawyer confidentiality in Scotland) could be maintained in legal proceedings.[81] This provision replaces an equivalent exemption under the Data Protection Act 1984,[82] but once again with an extension from subject access to the subject information provisions.

Self-incrimination

Data controllers need not supply information in response to a request for access when the provision of the information would indicate that an offence might have been committed (other than under the Data Protection Act 1998), thereby exposing them to the risk of criminal prosecution. Any information supplied pursuant to a request for access is not admissible in any proceedings for an offence under the 1998 Act.[83]

Matters arising subsequent to an access request

Denial of access

If the subject's request is not satisfied, an action seeking access may be raised before the court. Here, it is provided that the court may order the grant of access, except where it considers that it would be unreasonable to do so 'because of the frequency with which

---

[78] Section 35A.
[79] Section 31.
[80] SI 2000/419.
[81] Data Protection Act 1998; Schedule 7, para. 10.
[82] Section 31(2).
[83] Schedule 7, para. 11.

the applicant has made requests to the data user...or for any other reason'.[84] Use of the word 'may' in the statute implies that the court possesses a measure of discretion on whether to order the grant of access. This point was raised in the case of *Durant v Financial Services Authority*. At first instance, it was indicated by the judge that, even if he were to accept that the claimant had a right of access to the personal data in question, he would not have made an order to this effect for three reasons:

> First, I cannot see that the information could be of any practical value to the appellant. Secondly, the purpose of the legislation...is to ensure that records of an inaccurate nature are not kept about an individual. A citizen needs to know what the record says in order to have an opportunity of remedying an error or false information. In this case the appellant seeks disclosure not to correct an error but to fuel a separate collateral argument that he has either with Barclays Bank or with the FSA, litigation which is in any event doomed to failure. [Thirdly,] I am entirely satisfied on the facts of the case that the FSA have acted at all times in good faith, and indeed there has been no suggestion to the contrary from the appellant; his argument is with Barclays Bank, not with the FSA.[85]

Assuming that a £10 access fee would cover the costs incurred by most users in satisfying access requests, it may be doubted whether this provision will be utilised to any extent. It has also been suggested, however, that a campaign of mass access requests might be used as a part of an industrial or other campaign directed against a data user. In the field of local government, for example, a spokesman for one authority has suggested that a concerted campaign causing several thousands of applications to arrive simultaneously would create major problems in complying with the legislation's time limits.[86]

On behalf of the claimant, it was argued that the Data Protection Directive requires that Member States 'guarantee' the right of access and that the exercise of any discretion to refuse access would apply only where it was considered that one of the exemptions described above applies. The Court of Appeal disagreed with Lord Justice Auld, holding that the discretion conferred by Section 7(9) was 'general and untrammeled'. It was added, however, that:

> as a corollary to my comment in paragraph 66 on the subject of reasonableness of disclosure of information about a third party under Section 7(4)(b), that it might be difficult for a court to conclude under that provision that it was reasonable to comply with a data subject's request so as to disclose such information, yet exercise its discretion under Section 7(9) against ordering compliance with that aspect of the data subject's request.

Rectification of inaccurate data

Data will be considered inaccurate if they are false or misleading as to any matter of fact. In such an event, the data subject may request the court to order the controller

---

[84] Data Protection Act 1998, s 21(8).
[85] [2003] EWCA Civ 1746 at para. 69.
[86] *Glasgow Herald*, 28 December 1987.

to 'rectify, block, erase or destroy'[87] the data in question.[88] These remedies may also be invoked when the data controller has acted in such a fashion as would give the subject an entitlement to claim compensation under the Data Protection Act 1998. Additionally, the controller may be ordered to amend any statement of opinion which appears to be based on the inaccurate data. Where data constitutes an accurate transcription of information received from a third party, the court may make one of the above orders. Alternatively, it may permit the data to be retained but be supplemented by a further statement of the true facts as determined by the court.[89] Where the court determines that data is inaccurate and requires that it be rectified, blocked, erased, or destroyed, it may, where this is considered reasonably practical, order that the controller notify details of the changes to any third party to whom the data has previously been disclosed.[90] Such a remedy may provide a valuable audit trail, allowing the detrimental consequences of inaccurate data to be minimised.

Compensation

Under the Data Protection Act 1984, data subjects were entitled to claim compensation for damage and distress resulting from inaccuracy in data or from their unauthorised destruction or disclosure. These rights were seldom utilised,[91] the requirement in particular to demonstrate both damage and distress proving a substantial hurdle.

The Data Protection Act 1998 adopts a more extensive approach in terms of the basis for liability. Compensation may be claimed in respect of losses caused through any breach of the legislation. Except, however, in the situation where a claim arises as a result of the processing of data for media purposes (the 'special purposes'), the 1998 Act retains the requirement that damage be demonstrated as a prerequisite to any claim alleging distress. In all cases, the controller will have a defence if it can be shown that reasonable care was taken to avoid the breach.

Although the claim was ultimately rejected, consideration was given by the court of first instance in the case of *Johnson v Medical Defence Union*.[92] The background to the case has been described above. Essentially, the complainant alleged that his personal data had been subject to unfair processing and that this had caused him some pecuniary damage and also distress and damage to his professional reputation.

---

[87] The distinction between erasure and destruction of the data may relate to the nature of the storage medium involved. Manual files may well be destroyed through burning or shredding. With computer records, the concept of erasure is more relevant, given that data may only be completely destroyed following complete reformatting of the storage device.

[88] Section 14(1).

[89] Section 14(2).

[90] Section 14(3).

[91] The *Fourteenth Report of the Data Protection Registrar* (1998) cites one case where a credit reference agency wrongly registered adverse data against the complainant. The mistake continued for some considerable time and the report indicates that, following the Registrar's intervention, 'a substantial ex gratia payment was made' (p. 88).

[92] [2006] EWHC 321 (Ch).

Considerable discussion took place on the issue of whether the Act fully implements the provisions of the Data Protection Directive which requires in Article 23 that:

1. Member States shall provide that any person who has suffered 'damage as a result of an unlawful processing operation or of an act incompatible with the national provisions adopted pursuant to this Directive is entitled to receive compensation from the controller for the damage suffered.

The Directive, it was suggested, used the term 'damage' as encompassing any form of damage, whether pecuniary in nature or not. Evidence was presented to the court indicating that the status of implementation of this provision across the EEA was unclear. Some states provided limited compensation awards to pecuniary damage, whilst others took a more liberal approach. Whilst not commenting on the proper interpretation of the Directive, the conclusion was reached that Section 13(1) provided an entitlement to compensation only for pecuniary damage. This heading excluded any compensation for general damage to reputation. After examining and rejecting a range of headings of expenditure, the only item potentially accepted by the court related to a sum of £10.50 spent paying for breakfast for an MDU officer who the complainant had been asked to meet. This small sum could have served as the trigger to a more substantial claim for distress under the provisions of Section 13(2), although it was noted that:

> I also consider, however, that any compensation under that head must be exclusively in respect of any distress associated with the damage for which recovery is in principle recoverable under Section 13(1). In particular, having concluded that Mr Johnson is not entitled to recover general compensation under Section 13(1) for his claimed loss of professional reputation, I would regard it as inconsistent to permit the recovery under Section 13(2)(a) of compensation in respect of the distress claimed to be suffered by reason of Mr Johnson's perception that the non-renewal of his membership had damaged his reputation.[93]

In respect of other forms of distress, the main claim was to the effect that the complainant had been left without insurance cover for a period of some two months following termination of his MDU membership and that this had caused him anxiety and distress. It was indicated that had the substantive elements of the complainant's case been upheld, compensation of £5,000 might have been awarded. Before the Court of Appeal[94] the size of this figure was criticised, although given that the complainant's case had failed, it 'would be an undue use of judicial time to reason the matter out'.[95]

Other subject rights

Right to request an assessment of processing

Section 42 of the Data Protection Act provides that anyone directly affected by processing—typically the data subject—may request the Information Commissioner

---

[93] Para. 236. [94] [2007] EWCA Civ 262. [95] Para. 77.

to conduct an assessment of the processing in order to determine whether it is being conducted in conformity with the requirements of the legislation. It is the practice of the Information Commissioner to treat any complaint received from a data subject as a request under Section 42. The complainant is to be informed of the result of the assessment and of any action which has been taken.

Right to resist enforced subject access

The situation whereby access rights imprison rather than empower the data subject has long been the subject of criticism, not least by the Data Protection Registrar. Devising an appropriate method of control has proved more difficult. The major difficulty facing any attempt to control the practice is the imbalance of power typically existing in such situations. If the subject is seeking employment, for example, a request that the information be supplied may carry as much weight as a demand. The initial drafts of the Data Protection Directive provided that data subjects should be entitled:

> ...to refuse any demand by a third party that he should exercise his right of access in order to communicate the data in question to that third party.

In the final text, the Directive contained the somewhat enigmatic provision that data subjects should be guaranteed the right to exercise access 'without constraint'.[96] Other language versions of the Directive make it clearer that the provision is intended to apply to enforced access, the German text, for example, requiring that access be provided *frei und ungehindert*.

Although the government indicated the intention to act against enforced subject access from the earliest stages of the Data Protection Act 1998's parliamentary passage, finding an appropriate form of prohibition proved a difficult task. A variety of possibilities were considered. Subject access might, for example, be provided only in person rather than in writing. This would, of course, have made a dramatic change to the whole system of subject access and would have caused great inconvenience in the event, for example, that a data subject was located in Glasgow and the data controller in London. An alternative suggestion canvassed was that all access requests should be filtered through the Commissioner. Again, practical constraints might make this solution unworkable. Ultimately, however, it was determined that the only feasible approach was to make the practice criminal. The prohibitions apply, however, only in respect of certain forms of records—criminal records, prison records and Department of Social Security (DSS) records—and in respect of a limited range of situations. A person must not require the provision of information obtained following a request for access (a relevant record) in connection with the recruitment or continued employment of the data subject or with any contract under which the subject is to provide services. Similarly, when the person is concerned with the provision of goods, facilities, or services to members of the public, it is prohibited to require the production

---

[96] Directive 95/46/EC, Article 11(a).

of any relevant records as a condition for the provision of such goods, facilities, or services.[97] It is further provided that any contractual terms will be void insofar as they purport to require the production of any medical information obtained pursuant to an access request.[98] Although it is provided that these categories may be extended by statutory instrument,[99] it may be queried whether the provisions comply fully with the Data Protection Directive's requirements.[100]

In this, as in other areas, the provisions of the Data Protection Act 1998 will not operate in isolation. Under the provisions of the Police Act 1997, new arrangements have been made for providing access to criminal records. Three categories of access are created. A basic certificate may be sought by any applicant and will reveal details of any convictions which are not spent under the Rehabilitation of Offenders Act 1974. A more extensive 'criminal record certificate', adding details of spent convictions, will be issued upon the joint application of the individual and an organisation which is exempted from the provisions of the 1974 Act. This will include professional organisations, such as the Law Society, in respect of their roles in determining whether individuals might be considered suitable for admission to the profession. The most extensive certificate, the 'enhanced criminal record certificate', will include police intelligence data and details of acquittals, and will be reserved for situations where an individual is seeking to work with children or vulnerable adults (or other sensitive positions, such as those related to gambling or judicial appointments).

Given the large numbers of requests for access relating to criminal records, there will clearly be a close relationship between the access provisions of the Police Act 1997 and those of the Data Protection Act 1998. It was stated in Parliament that the provisions of the Data Protection Act 1998 will not be implemented before those of the Police Act 1997. It is unclear when this may happen. In his Annual Report for 2003, the Information Commissioner noted:

> Whilst we are keen that Section 56 should be brought into effect as soon as possible there appear to be two obstacles. Firstly, there is the question of Northern Ireland. Although the Criminal Records Bureau (CRB) has been established for England and Wales and a similar arrangement is in place in Scotland, as far as we are aware there are no plans to introduce a comparable system in Northern Ireland. Secondly, it appears likely that as a result of an independent review of the Criminal Record Bureau's strategies and operations the launch of basic disclosures in England and Wales is to be postponed indefinitely. It therefore seems that the day on which the relevant sections of the Police Act 1997 are all in force across the whole of the United Kingdom might never arrive.[101]

It was suggested that the government might bring S56 into force, even though the prescribed condition had not been met. It was recognised that this might require primary

---

[97] Section 56.
[98] Section 57.
[99] Section 56(8).
[100] Directive 95/46/EC, Article 11(a).
[101] *Annual Report and Accounts 2003*, at p. 37.

legislation, something which to date has not been forthcoming. It is undoubtedly disappointing that such a significant element of the legislation is still not in force almost a decade after the Act's enactment. As was recognised in the Information Tribunal decision of the Chief Constables of West Yorkshire, South Yorkshire, and North Wales Police, and the Information Commissioner,[102] 'the overwhelming majority of the 200,000 odd police subject access requests per year are currently enforced'.[103] Foreign embassies are major 'beneficiaries' of enforced subject access and it was recognised that even the bringing into force of Section 56 might have little practical effect, as embassies are not subject to national law.

Rights to object to data processing

Direct marketing

It is a little-known fact that those persons who purchase black-ash furniture are twenty times more likely to respond to a fashion promotion than those whose tastes are less exotic. Such nuggets of information may constitute interesting trivia to most people, but to those engaged in the retail industry they can represent the path to fortune. Direct marketing is one of the fastest-growing sectors of the economy. Although it tends to be referred to under the epithet of 'junk mail', each item delivered represents a not inconsiderable investment on the part of the sender. In many instances, retailers will possess information linking an individual to a purchase and may use this in order to attempt to stimulate further sales. The purchaser of a motor vehicle, for example, is likely to receive a communication from the seller around the anniversary of the purchase in the hope that the buyer might be considering buying a new model. The increasing use of store-based credit cards coupled with the utilisation of laser-scanning cash points provides retailers with detailed information about their customers and their purchases. There are few technical barriers in the way of processing data so as to be able to 'talk to every customer in his or her own life style terms'.[104] It has been suggested, for example, that 'intelligent shopping trolleys' might guide customers towards promotions which analysis of their previous purchases suggests might prove alluring.[105] Assuming that the data users involved have registered the fact that they intend to process personal data for sales and marketing purposes, the only legal barrier to such techniques might come from a determination that such processing is unfair.

The use of personal data for purposes of direct marketing has been the cause of some recent controversy. Reference has previously been made to the *Innovations* case[106] and the data protection implications of list broking. Additionally, however, organisations are seeking to exploit their customer databases by entering into agreements to provide

---

[102] <http://www.informationtribunal.gov.uk/Documents/decisions/north_wales_police.pdf>
[103] At para. 82.
[104] Roger Hymas, GE Capital Executive Director, quoted in *Financial Times*, 4 April 1991.
[105] *Financial Times*, 4 April 1991.
[106] *Innovations (Mail Order) Ltd v Data Protection Registrar* Case DA/92 31/49/1 (see Chapter 7).

mailings on behalf of other companies. This may take a variety of forms. Analysis of, for example, purchases made with a credit card may indicate that an individual frequently stays in hotels. The credit card company may then enter into an agreement with a hotel chain to include a promotional leaflet with its statement of account. In this example, no personal data will be transferred between the companies. In a Guidance Note relating to Direct Marketing,[107] the Registrar has indicated that in certain circumstances use of financial data for such purposes might constitute a breach of confidence.[108] More recently, action has been taken against a number of utilities engaging in the practice of cross-selling, with enforcement notices being served against a number of utilities which sent offers of other products and services to their customers. Significantly, the fact that the utilities offered customers the opportunity to opt out of these offers was not considered sufficient, the Registrar arguing that an opt-in system should apply.[109]

Treatment of data obtained and used for the purposes of direct marketing constituted one of the most controversial aspects of the Data Protection Directive.[110] As originally drafted, the legislation would have imposed strict obligations on data controllers to inform subjects whenever data was to be used for such a purpose. The proposals were weakened in subsequent drafts and as enacted, the Directive offers Member States a choice of control regimes. It may be provided that data subjects be given the right to object to a controller's intention to process or to disclose data for the purposes of direct marketing. No fees are to be charged in this event.[111] It is arguable that this reflects current United Kingdom practice, especially after the decisions of the Data Protection Tribunal in the *Innovations* and *Linguaphone* cases.[112] As an alternative, the Directive provides that controllers might be required to give specific notice to data subjects before data is used by or on behalf of third parties for direct marketing purposes.[113] This is coupled with the requirement that steps be taken to inform data subjects of their rights.

The Data Protection Act 1998 adopts the second of these options, providing that:

> An individual is entitled at any time by notice in writing to a data controller to require the data controller at the end of such period as is reasonable in the circumstances to cease, or not to begin, processing for the purposes of direct marketing personal data of which he is the data subject.[114]

Other forms of processing

In the case of direct marketing data, the subject's wishes are absolute. With other forms of processing, the subject may serve notice requiring the cessation of processing

---

[107] October 1995, available from the Registrar's website at <http://www.open.gov.uk/dpr/dprhome.htm>
[108] Paras 81–8.
[109] *Thirteenth Report of the Data Protection Registrar* (1997), pp. 26–7.
[110] Directive 95/46/EC.
[111] Article 14(b).
[112] *Innovations (Mail Order) Ltd v Data Protection Registrar* Case DA/92 31/49/1; *Linguaphone Institute v Data Protection Registrar* Case DA/94 31/49/1.
[113] Article 14(b).
[114] Section 11(1).

on the basis that this is likely to cause substantial and unwarranted damage or distress. This right will not apply:

- where the subject has previously consented to the processing;
- where the processing is necessary to conclude or perform a contract with the data subject;
- where it is necessary to comply with any legal obligation on the data controller; or
- where the processing is necessary to protect the vital interests of the data subject.[115]

The Secretary of State may specify other situations in which the right to object is to be withdrawn.[116] Upon receipt of such a notice, the controller must respond in writing within twenty-one days, either indicating that the subject's request will be granted or giving reasons why or to what extent this should not be the case.[117] A negative response may be appealed to the courts, which may make such order for ensuring compliance as it thinks fit.[118]

Whilst the principle that the data subject should be entitled to exercise control over the situations in which personal data is processed must be welcomed, the requirement that 'substantial and unwarranted damage or distress' be demonstrated, coupled with the exceptions described above, may remove much of the value from the provision. It may be noted that the Data Protection Directive, in providing for the right to object, states that this is to be based on 'compelling legitimate grounds'.[119] Whilst this term is not defined in the legislation, it does seem rather less demanding criteria than those adopted in the Data Protection Act 1998.

Automated decision-making

Increasingly, the results of data processing may trigger further actions affecting the data subject with minimal intervention from any human agency. A trivial example may be taken from the operation of automated cash-dispensing machines. A customer may approach a machine at midnight, insert a bank card, enter a personal identifier number (PIN), and request a sum of money. Details of the customer's account will be checked with the bank's computer system and if the customer is sufficiently in funds, cash will be dispensed. If the customer is not in funds, no money will be issued. There will be no human involvement at any stage of the transaction. In other instances, it is possible that human agents may be reduced to little more than a cipher. An example might be seen in the operation of systems of credit scoring. Here, an applicant for credit is required to fill in a form giving information about matters such as marital

---

[115] Data Protection Act 1998, s 10(1).
[116] Data Protection Act 1998, s 10(2).
[117] Section 10(3).
[118] Section 10(4).
[119] Directive 95/46/EC, Article 14.

status, employment, and housing status, etc. Points are allocated depending on the answers. A married person, for example, may be awarded one point, a single person two, and a divorced person three. The pointage values are based upon an assessment of the risk of default. Each creditor may establish a predetermined acceptance level. If a customer's total falls below this, the application will be rejected.

The operation of credit scoring has been criticised by the Director General of Fair Trading on the basis of perceived unfairness to persons whose profile may not fit the automated model, yet whose credit history may be flawless, and the recommendation has been made that those operating the technique should build in an appeals procedure. A similar approach is adopted in the Data Protection Directive which, drawing on provisions in the French Data Protection Act, provides that individuals must be granted the right:

> ...not to be subject to a decision which produces legal effects concerning him or significantly affects him and which is based solely on automated processing of data intended to evaluate certain personal aspects relating to him, such as his performance at work, creditworthiness, reliability, conduct, etc.[120]

Inevitably, this general statement is subject to exceptions, the Directive continuing to provide that automated decisions are permissible in the course of entering into or performing a contract, so long as the outcome is favourable to the subject or provision is made to safeguard 'legitimate interests'. An appeals procedure such as that referred to above, allowing the subject to present additional information, would appear to meet this requirement. It is further provided that other automated decisions may be sanctioned by law, so long as this also contains safeguards for the subject's legitimate interests.

Although there might be debate about how significant any element of human intervention in a decision-making process is required to be, most applications should pose few intractable problems in that a delay in implementing a decision will not cause significant problems for either data controller or subject. The cash-dispensing example cited above may be a more difficult issue. In the event a customer is denied funds late at night, there seems little doubt that the statutory criteria will be satisfied. It may be doubted whether there is any realistic prospect of providing an immediate right of appeal. In Lord Denning's memorable phrase from *Thornton v Shoe Lane Parking*,[121] the customer 'may protest to the machine, even swear at it; but it will remain unmoved'.

Conclusions

Under the Data Protection Act 1984, the right of access to data, coupled with rights to require the correction of inaccurate data and very restricted rights to compensation, constituted the major innovation from the standpoint of data subjects. By moving to

---

[120] Directive 95/46/EC, Article 15.
[121] [1971] 1 All ER 686.

what are described as 'subject information rights', the Data Protection Act 1998 does confer new entitlements on data subjects. The right to object to data processing and to resist attempts to compel the exercise of access rights also constitute significant advances. That said, what the opening paragraphs of a section confer is often removed by the exceptions and qualifications which tend to litter subsequent paragraphs. It would not be practicable or desirable to permit a data subject an absolute right to require that data not be processed, otherwise an individual with a long history of bad debts could require that a credit reference agency expunge all records from its files. Nevertheless, the statutory provision appears somewhat mean-spirited. Much the same can be said of the provisions relating to enforced subject access. Certainly, it must be admitted that it will be very difficult to stamp out such practices. In many cases, such as the making of an application for employment, the imbalance in power between an employing data controller and applicant data subject will be such that a mere expression of desire might be sufficient to make the subject feel compelled to comply. Undoubtedly, the data subject is in a stronger position under the Data Protection Act 1998 than has hitherto been the case. The criticism may be that the level of improvement has not been more pronounced.

7

Sectoral aspects of data protection

Introduction

The application of data protection principles to particular sectors of activity can be a difficult task. Notions of fairness, for example, are highly context-dependent. This chapter will consider two topics concerned with the application of data protection principles within the media and electronic commmunications sectors. In the case of the media, the issue is principally concerned with the application of what might be regarded as 'traditional' data protection principles in the context of activities where different priorities might legitimately be identified. With the increasing importance of the electronic communications sector—as epitomised by the fact that there are now more mobile phones in use in the United Kingdom than there are people[1]—more and more data processing activities are being conducted over some communications network. Increasingly, as will also be discussed in the following chapter, the need is to ensure that data protection principles are formulated in such a way that they can realistically be enforced within a network environment.

Data protection and the media

The application of data protection provisions in respect of media activities raises a number of complex issues. At the stage of gathering information with a view to publication, investigative journalism in particular may involve the use of tactics and techniques which would normally be stigmatised as unfair (if not unlawful). At almost the other end of the publication spectrum, many newspapers and journals now maintain copies of issues in electronic format. These will certainly come within the scope of the Data Protection Act 1998, under whose general provisions a subject would be entitled to require the rectification of any errors, coupled with a reformulation of any resultant statements of opinion. Whilst generally desirable, the rewriting of documents which claim to represent data as published on a certain date calls to mind the operation of George Orwell's Ministry of Truth.

[1] <http://www.ofcom.org.uk/research/cm/cmr07/telecoms/telecoms.pdf>

The Data Protection Act 1984 made no special provision for the media. In large measure, this approach was justified by the limited use of computer equipment for journalistic purposes, the existence of the text-processing exemption and the limited nature of the definition of processing. Time and technology have moved on. A 1992 study produced for the Council of Europe[2] identified a range of practices within Member States regarding the treatment of media activities within data protection legislation. Some countries, such as the Netherlands and Sweden, provided a total exemption from data protection laws; others provided partial exemption, in the case of Germany, for example, requiring only that media users comply with requirements relating to data security. Other regimes, including that of the United Kingdom, provided no form of special treatment. The study identified a potential conflict between the provisions of the European Convention on Human Rights relating to freedom of expression and the right to seek out and impart information and those concerned with the right to privacy. Identifying problems is normally easy but providing solutions is a more difficult task and the Council of Europe contented itself with a recommendation that the potential conflict should be borne in mind in framing legislation.

The Recitals to the Data Protection Directive,[3] which also recognise the conflicts inherent in the area state that:

> Whereas the processing of personal data for purposes of journalism or for purposes of literary or artistic expression, in particular in the audiovisual field, should qualify for exemption from the requirements of certain provisions of this Directive in so far as this is necessary to reconcile the fundamental rights of individuals with freedom of information and notably the right to receive and impart information, as guaranteed in particular in Article 10 of the European Convention for the Protection of Human Rights and Fundamental Freedoms.[4]

The Recitals continue to suggest that national laws should provide for alternative measures—such as the submission of reports to the supervisory agency—to ensure that data subjects' rights are not abused. In terms of the articles, themselves, the Directive is somewhat imprecise. Article 9 states that:

> Member States shall provide for exemptions or derogations from the provisions of this Chapter, Chapter IV and Chapter VI for the processing of personal data carried out solely for journalistic purposes or the purpose of artistic or literary expression only if they are necessary to reconcile the right to privacy with the rules governing freedom of expression.

It is clear that this formula empowers rather than requires Member States to act, but for the United Kingdom, the decision was taken to include special provisions for these activities, described as the 'special purposes' in the Data Protection Act 1998.

---

[2] 'Data Protection and the Media', a study prepared by the Committee of Experts on Data Protection.
[3] Directive 95/46/EC.
[4] Recital 37.

Scope of the provisions

Section 3 of the Data Protection Act 1998 defines the concept of 'special purposes'. These relate to the processing of personal data:

(a) for the purposes of journalism;

(b) artistic purposes; and

(c) literary purposes.

It was stressed in Parliament that no qualitative criteria would be applied to determine whether a work could be classed as artistic, journalistic, or literary. Although much of the debate in Parliament focused on the activities of the media, this definition recognises that literary and artistic works also raise issues of freedom of expression. The prime purpose of the Act's exceptional provisions is to place limits on the ability of data subjects to invoke statutory rights to impede publication of a work. Similar restrictions are placed upon the powers of the Information Commissioner, with modified provisions for the service of information and enforcement notices. Once the work is in the public domain, the provisions of the general law will apply, including the law of defamation, although, as indicated in Chapter 8, the 1998 Act does provide new rights of compensation for distress caused as a result of processing carried out in connection with one of the special purposes.

Activities covered

The Data Protection Act 1998 applies a three-stage test to determine whether processing for a special purpose should benefit from exemption. Personal data must be subject to processing:

(a) ...with a view to the publication by any person of any journalistic, literary or artistic material;

(b) the data controller reasonably believes that, having regard in particular to the special importance of the public interest in freedom of expression, publication would be in the public interest; and

(c) the data controller reasonably believes that, in all the circumstances, compliance with (statutory provisions) is incompatible with the special purposes.[5]

It was suggested in Parliament that:

We have deliberately placed on the face of the Bill, I believe for the first time in an Act of Parliament in this country, that the public interest is not the narrow question of whether this is a public interest story in itself but that it relates to the wider public interest, which is an infinitely subtle and more complicated concept.[6]

In determining whether belief that publication is in the public interest might be considered reasonable, it is provided that account is to be taken of any relevant code of

[5] Section 32(1).   [6] 585 HL Official Report (5th series), col. 442, 2 February 1998.

practice. Power is conferred on the Secretary of State to designate codes which are to be taken into account in this way. The Data Protection (Designated Codes of Practice) Order 2000[7] lists five codes:

- The Code on Fairness and Privacy issues by the Broadcasting Standards Commission in 1998 under the terms of the Broadcasting Act 1996.
- The ITC Programme Code issued by the Independent Television Commission in 1998 under the terms of the Broadcasting Act 1990.
- The Press Complaints Commission's Code of Practice published in 1997.
- The Producers' Guidelines issued by the British Broadcasting Corporation in 1996.
- The Programme Code issued by the Radio Authority in 1998 under the terms of the Broadcasting Act 1990.

Citation of codes in this manner is a novel feature of the Data Protection Act. It may additionally be noted that whilst three of the codes have some form of statutory basis, the remaining two have no such backing.

Scope of the exemption

Section 31 of the Data Protection Act defines a range of provisions which will not apply where processing is carried out for the special purposes. With the exception of the seventh principle relating to data security, the data protection principles will not operate, neither will the subject access provisions nor those enabling a data subject to object to data being processed. Also excluded are the provisions of s 12, relating to subject rights in respect of automated decision making, and the general provisions of s 14, relating to the subject's rights to compensation. These latter provisions are substituted, however, by special and more extensive rights.

These exceptions are wide-ranging. One consequence will be that even the unlawful obtaining of personal data will not expose the controller to action under the Data Protection Act—although other criminal sanctions, such as a charge of theft, may be imposed in respect of the offending conduct.

Procedural aspects

The question of whether processing is covered by one of the special purpose exemptions is likely to arise in the course of legal proceedings. In this regard, it is provided that proceedings must be stayed when the data controller claims, or it appears to the court, that the data are being processed for a special purpose and:

> With a view to publication by any person of any journalistic, literary or artistic material which, at the time twenty-four hours immediately before the relevant time, had not previously been published by the data controller.[8]

---

[7] SI 2000/418.   [8] Data Protection Act 1998, s 32(4).

The relevant time will be the moment at which the controller makes the claim for protection or the court determines that the processing is for a special purpose.

It will be recognised that there is no requirement that the controller's claim that processing is covered by the special purpose should have any merit. As discussed below, procedures for the lifting of such a stay are complex, and the Commissioner has criticised the situation whereby an unscrupulous party could delay proceedings for a period of months, if not years, with little justification.[9]

Once a court has determined that procedures should be stayed, the focus of attention switches to the Commissioner, who will be required to make a written determination as to whether the processing is being conducted only in connection with one of the special purposes or with a view to the publication of material not previously published by the data controller.[10] In obtaining evidence necessary to reach such a view, the Commissioner may require to exercise powers conferred under the legislation to serve a special information notice. Service of such notice may itself be the subject of an appeal to the Information Tribunal. If the Commissioner determines that the processing is not exempt, this finding may itself be appealed to the Tribunal. It will only be when appeal procedures have been exhausted that the determination will come into effect and the court will be in a position to lift the stay.

The application of the Data Protection Act's provisions relating to media processing was at issue in the case of *Campbell v Mirror Group Newspapers Ltd*. Finding in favour of the claimant in the High Court,[11] Moreland J held that information relating to her drug addiction was sensitive personal data, that the defendant had failed to show that its processing of the data conformed with any of the provisions of Schedule 3 setting out conditions for the lawful processing of personal data or with the Press Complaints Commission code of practice, an instrument which had been designated by the Secretary of State under Section 32. In respect of the defence provided by Section 32 it was held that, whilst this would operate in order to prevent a claimant from stopping publication, its benefit ceased at this point and did not confer any form of immunity in respect of a subsequent action for damages on the basis that the unfair or unlawful processing had caused distress to the data subject. Damages of £3,500 were awarded in respect both of the contravention of the Data Protection Act 1998 and of the claimant's claim that the publication constituted a breach of confidence.

The judge's findings in respect of the Data Protection Act were overturned by the Court of Appeal.[12] Delivering the judgment of the court, Lord Phillips MR was critical of the structure of the Data Protection Act 1998. Echoing the views of Moreland J, who described the interpretative task as akin to 'weaving his way through a thicket', the Act was described as 'a cumbersome and inelegant piece of legislation'.[13]

---

[9] Briefing Note, 'Media Exceptions', 16 February 1998.
[10] Data Protection Act 1998, s 45.
[11] [2002] EWHC 499 (QB), [2002] All ER (D) 448 (Mar).
[12] *Campbell v Mirror Group Newspapers Ltd* [2002] EWCA Civ 1373, [2003] QB 633.
[13] [2002] EWCA Civ 1373, [2003] QB 633 at [72].

Before the Court of Appeal, the appellant did not seek to argue that their processing of Ms Campbell's personal data complied with the requirements of Schedule 3 to the Data Protection Act—as was stated, 'much of their argument was founded on the submission that it was virtually impossible for journalists to comply with the requirements of the Act'[14]—but argued that the effect of the Section 32 defence was to confer immunity in respect of any action for damages made subsequent to publication. It was argued for the appellants that the result of the High Court's ruling would be that:

> Without the consent of the data subject, a newspaper would hardly ever be entitled to publish any of the information categorised as sensitive without running the risk of having to pay compensation. Indeed, it would be difficult to establish that the conditions for processing any personal information were satisfied. If this were correct, it would follow that the Data Protection Act had created a law of privacy and achieved a fundamental enhancement of Article 8 rights, at the expense of Article 10 rights, extending into all areas of media activity, to the extent that the Act was incompatible with the Human Rights Convention.[15]

Analysing the provisions of the Section 32 defence, the Court of Appeal first focused on Subsections (4) and (5). These were described as procedural measures designed to provide for the stay of proceedings brought against a publisher until after publication and there was no dispute that 'the purpose of these provisions is to prevent the restriction of freedom of expression that might otherwise result from gagging injunctions'.[16]

The court continued to examine the provisions of Section 32(1)–(3) which, it was stated:

> ... on their face, provide widespread exemption from the duty to comply with the provisions that impose substantive obligations upon the data controller, subject only to the simple conditions that the data controller reasonably believes (i) that publication would be in the public interest and (ii) that compliance with each of the provisions is incompatible with the special purpose—in this case journalism.[17]

It was concluded that:

> If these provisions apply only up to the moment of publication it is impossible to see what purpose they serve, for the data controller will be able to obtain a stay of any proceedings under the provisions of Subsections (4) and (5) without the need to demonstrate compliance with the conditions to which the exemption in Subsections (1) to (3) is subject.[18]
>
> ...
>
> For these reasons we have reached the conclusion that, giving the... provisions of the Subsections their natural meaning and the only meaning that makes sense of them, they apply both before and after publication.[19]

14 *Campbell v Mirror Group Newspapers Ltd* [2002] EWCA Civ 1373, [2003] QB 633 at [74].
15 [2002] EWCA Civ 1373 at [92].
16 *Campbell v Mirror Group Newspapers Ltd* [2002] EWCA Civ 1373, [2003] QB 633 at [117].
17 *Campbell v Mirror Group Newspapers Ltd* [2002] EWCA Civ 1373, [2003] QB 633 at [118].
18 [2002] EWCA Civ 1373 at [118].
19 [2002] EWCA Civ 1373 at [121].

Support for this approach was taken from the comments of the responsible govern-ment minister as recorded in the *Hansard* report of the debate of the second reading of the Bill. Here it was indicated that:

> Following the meetings to which I referred, we have included in the Bill an exemp-tion which I believe meets the legitimate expectations and requirements of those engaged in journalism, artistic and literacy [*sic*]activity. The key provision is Clause 31. This ensures that provided that certain criteria are met, before publication—I stress 'before'—there can be no challenge on data protection grounds to the processing of personal data for the special purposes. The criteria are broadly that the processing is done solely for the special purposes; and that it is done with a view to the publication of unpublished material. Thereafter, there is provision for exemption from the key provi-sions where the media can show that publication was intended; and that they reason-ably believe both that publication would be in the public interest and that compliance with the bill would have been incompatible with the special purposes.[20]

Although it was indicated that the court, mindful of the dicta of Lord Hoffmann in *Robinson v Secretary of State for Northern Ireland* that reference to *Hansard* should be a matter of 'last resort',[21] did not base its decision on this passage, it may be queried whether the comments do fully support the interpretation that the s 32 defence applies totally, pre- and post-publication. As indicated by the court, the section 32 is indeed a measure in two parts. Subsections (4) and (5) provide a very straightforward method of protection against gagging orders. Subsections (1)–(3), it is submitted, should swing into action only after publication. In conformity with the Data Protection Directive's strictures that:

> Member States shall provide for exemptions or derogations from the provisions of this Chapter, Chapter IV and Chapter VI for the processing of personal data carried out solely for journalistic purposes or the purpose of artistic or literary expression only if they are necessary to reconcile the right to privacy with the rules governing freedom of expression.[22]

The use of the words 'only' and necessary' must indicate both that exemptions may be provided only when and to the extent strictly necessary to reconcile the competing rights. This may involve allowing publication to take place but cannot, it is submitted, justify a removal of rights to compensation (and rectification) after the event. As was stated by the Article 29 Working Party:

> The Directive[23] requires a balance to be struck between two fundamental freedoms. In order to evaluate whether limitations of the rights and obligations flowing from the Directive are proportionate to the aim of protecting freedom of expression particular attention should be paid to the specific guarantees enjoyed by the individuals in rela-tion to the Media. Limits to the right of access and rectification prior to publication

---

[20] 585 HL Official Report (5th series), col. 442, 2 February 1998.
[21] [2002] UKHL 32, [2002] All ER (D) 364 (Jul) at [40].
[22] Directive 95/46/EC, Article 9.
[23] 95/46/EC.

could be proportionate only in so far as individuals enjoy the right to reply or obtain rectification of false information after publication.

Individuals are in any case entitled to adequate forms of redress in case of violation of their rights.[24]

The basis for the individual's claim to compensation is laid down in Section 13 of the Act. This provides that compensation is payable for distress caused as a result of processing for the special purposes which is conducted in breach of any of the Act's provisions. It is further provided that:

In proceedings brought against a person for breach of this Section it is a defence to prove that he had taken such care as in all the circumstances was reasonably required to comply with the requirement concerned.

Perhaps more significantly, the Data Protection (Processing of Sensitive Personal Data) Order 2000,[25] adds to the Schedule 3 list of factors legitimising processing of sensitive personal data in the situation whereby:

(1) The disclosure of personal data—

    (a) is in the substantial public interest;

    (b) is in connection with—

        (i) the commission by any person of any unlawful act (whether alleged or established),

        (ii) dishonesty, malpractice, or other seriously improper conduct by, or the unfitness or incompetence of, any person (whether alleged or established), or

        (iii) mismanagement in the administration of, or failures in services provided by, any body or association (whether alleged or established);

    (c) is for the special purposes as defined in Section 3 of the Act; and

    (d) is made with a view to the publication of those data by any person and the data controller reasonably believes that such publication would be in the public interest.[26]

Whilst not conferring immunity upon data controllers, this provision does provide a defence in situations where disclosure can be justified in the public interest.

Special information notices

A modified form of information notice applies where data is being processed for a special purpose. Acting either in response to a request from a data subject for an assessment of whether data is being processed in accordance with the principles,[27] or where

---

[24] Recommendation 1/97 'Data Protection Law and the Media'.
[25] SI 2000 No. 417.
[26] Schedule, Para. 3.
[27] Section 42.

there are reasonable grounds for suspecting that a data controller has wrongfully claimed the benefit of the special purpose, for example, to refuse a request for access, the Commissioner may serve a 'special information notice'.[28] The notice will require that the controller supply the Commissioner with specified information to enable the Commissioner to determine whether the processing is being conducted for a special purpose or with a view to publication of new information. The notice must indicate the ground upon which the Commissioner is making the request and give notice of the controller's rights of appeal. The notice will not come into effect until the expiry of the period allowed for the lodging of appeals. Under the Data Protection Act 1984, this period is twenty-eight days.[29] The period under the Data Protection Act 1998 will be fixed by Order.[30] In cases of urgency, it is provided that the notice may require that information be supplied within seven days.[31]

Having received the information required, the Commissioner will make the determination referred to above as to whether processing is being conducted only for the special purposes. If the determination is that this is not the case, the Commissioner may serve the normal form of information notice seeking information to be supplied allowing a determination whether processing is lawful.[32]

Enforcement notices

Whether following service of an enforcement notice or otherwise, a determination by the Commissioner that processing is unlawful may be followed by service of an enforcement notice. Once again, different procedures apply in relation to the special purposes. An enforcement notice may only be served with the leave of the court.[33] Leave will only be granted if the court is satisfied that 'the Commissioner has reason to suspect a contravention of the data protection principles which is of substantial public importance', and that 'except where the case is one of urgency', notice has been given to the controller of the Commissioner's intention to apply for leave.[34]

Individual rights and remedies

As discussed above, the Data Protection Act 1998 gives extended rights to data subjects to institute proceedings before the courts seeking compensation for damage and distress resulting from a breach of any of the Act's requirements.[35] In the case of processing for the special purposes, damages may be awarded for distress without the need for any related damage. The data subject may also bring action in the normal manner

---

[28] Section 44.
[29] Data Protection Tribunal Rules 1985, SI 1985/1568, Article 4.
[30] Schedule 6.
[31] Section 44(6).
[32] Data Protection Act 1998, s 46(3).
[33] Ibid., s 46(1).
[34] Section 46(2).
[35] Section 13(1).

seeking rectification, blocking, or erasure of inaccurate data.[36] The question of whether and to what extent such remedies are provided is at the discretion of the court, and it may be assumed that account will be taken of the requirements of the special purposes so that, for example, the court will not order the alteration of the contents of a database containing the contents of stories which have been published in a newspaper. Even where a story contains errors, a notice of correction appended to the file would appear a more appropriate course of action.

Granting of assistance by the Commissioner

Section 53 of the Data Protection Act 1998 confers a new power on the Commissioner to provide assistance following an application from a party to proceedings relating to the special purposes.[37] This will include all the forms of proceeding described above, with the assistance taking the form of a contribution towards the costs of legal advice and representation and with indemnification against any award of costs to the other party.[38] The criterion for the award of such assistance is that the Commissioner is of the opinion that 'the case involves a matter of substantial public importance'.[39] The Commissioner's decision of whether or not to grant support must be transmitted to the applicant as soon as practicable. If the Commissioner decides not to grant assistance, reasoned notification to this effect must be given.[40]

Data protection in the electronic communications sector

In the early days of telecommunications, all calls were required to be connected by human operators. In order to bill customers accurately, the operator would monitor the communication, making a record of when the call was connected, the number to which it was made, and of when it was terminated. It was not unknown for operators to eavesdrop on the conversation itself; indeed, the motivation for Joseph Strowger to invent the world's first automatic telephone exchange is reported to have lain in the discovery that the wife of a competitor who was employed as a telephone operator was intercepting his calls in order to redirect business to her husband.

With the introduction of automated exchanges, first in respect of local, and then from 1979 when the United Kingdom's system of subscriber trunk dialling (STD) was completed for long-distance calls, what might be regarded as a 'golden age' of communications privacy dawned. Calls were connected without human intervention and whilst each telephone line had its own meter located in the telephone exchange, the operation of these was analogous to electricity and gas meters in that they merely recorded the number of units of connection time consumed. If for whatever reason the

---

[36] Section 14.
[37] Section 53(1).
[38] Schedule 10.
[39] Section 53(2).
[40] Section 53(3)–(4).

authorities wished to be able to identify the destination of calls, a special device referred to as a 'call logger' was required to be attached to an individual line.[41] Following the passage of the Interception of Communications Act 1985, a reasonably strict regime was introduced whereby any attempt to monitor telephone conversations required the issuance of a warrant by a High Court judge.[42]

From the 1980s, the telephone network began a changeover to the use of digital technology, with the United Kingdom becoming 'totally digital' with the closure of the last analogue exchanges on 11 March 1998.[43] Whilst the use of digital technology has brought considerable benefits both in terms of reliability and the range of services offered, an inevitable by-product is that increasing amounts of data are collected about customers. Perhaps the best example can be seen with the introduction of itemised billing. Customers now take for granted the fact that they will be presented with a bill describing, at least for long-distance calls, details of time, duration, and the cost of individual calls. Whilst useful for monitoring usage of the telephone, the retention and processing of the data has implications for individual privacy.

With the emergence of mobile networks, even more data concerning user behaviour is generated and retained. When switched on, each mobile phone transmits a signal…every few minutes. All base stations of that network within range respond and the firm allocates the phone to one station. At present, phones can normally be tracked to within several hundred metres—although with the use of appropriate software by the network operator, this might be reduced to perhaps 50 metres. Third generation (3G) mobile phones offer almost automatic location tracking, capable of locating a handset to within a range of 15 metres. This data can be retained almost indefinitely and, as will be discussed below, governments are increasingly taking powers to require that it be retained for periods of years against the eventuality that access may be sought in connection with criminal or national security investigations.

Beyond use for law enforcement purposes, operators are also beginning to develop plans to allow access to location data to commercial parties for use for marketing purposes. Cinemas and restaurants, for example, might want to send text messages promoting their services, perhaps making special offers to persons passing close to their premises. Others, it is reported, have rather more ambitious plans in seeking to combine location data with other forms of personal information to target people with adverts customised to match their preferences.[44]

A further, and perhaps in quantitative and qualitative terms the most extensive source of communications data, is the Internet. As discussed previously, every transmission, whether in the form of sending an email or the accessing and browsing of websites, gives out information about the user. Every web page viewed will be recorded by the site owner. In the context, for example, of an e-commerce site, the data recorded

---

[41] The use of a call logger was central to the prosecution's case in *R v Gold* [1987] 3 WLR 803, one of the first and most high-profile cases brought against alleged computer hackers.

[42] Call logging was not regarded as involving interception and did not require the grant of a warrant.

[43] *United Kingdom Telephone History*, available from <http://web.online.co.uk/freshwater/histuk.htm>

[44] <http://news.bbc.co.uk/1/hi/sci/tech/874419.stm>

is analogous to that which might be obtained by a physical retailer who follows a customer around the store noting not only what goods are purchased but any others that are looked at during the course of the visit. The use of cookies allows this data to be processed by reference to particular individuals and in respect of what may be multiple visits to the site. With regard to email, and perhaps even more to text messaging—although these are often regarded by users as akin to voice communications in terms of speed and informality—unlike telephone communications, electronic communications of this kind do not exist only in real time. Whereas anyone wishing to monitor a telephone conversation must do so whilst the messages are being transmitted, copies of emails will be made at various stages of the transmission process and may be recovered with relative ease days, months, or even years after their transmission.

All of these activities raise data-protection-related issues, whilst other forms of behaviour relating to the use of communication networks fall more naturally into the wider topic of personal privacy. The increasing number of unsolicited calls received by many consumers is frequently seen as an infringement of domestic privacy. Similar considerations apply with faxes and emails and proposals to regulate the use of these have been highly controversial.

Although many aspects of communications networks are regulated under the general provisions of data protection law, at the time that the Data Protection Directive[45] was being formulated, the EU identified a need for a more specialised form of regulation—to 'particularise and complement'[46] the general data protection regime. A major factor is the combination of data processing on the network combined with that by customers who will determine the use to which data is put. Systems such as 'caller id', for example, present users with information regarding the source of an incoming call. This data may be processed and used by an individual to avoid being disturbed by unwanted calls or by a commercial organisation to 'capture' telephone numbers for later use for marketing purposes. The provisions of the general Directive were therefore supplemented by more specific provisions in the form of the Directive of 15 December 1997 'Concerning the Processing of Personal Data and the Protection of Privacy in the Telecommunications Sector'.[47] This Directive was implemented in the United Kingdom by the Telecommunications (Data Protection and Privacy) (Direct Marketing) Regulations 1998[48] and the Telecommunications (Data Protection and Privacy) Regulations 1999.[49]

It is testimony to the pace of developments in the sector (and perhaps also of the slow pace of the legislative process) that less than two years after the adoption of the Telecoms Data Protection Directive,[50] the 1999 Communications Review commented that:

The terminology used in the Telecoms Data Protection Directive, which was proposed in 1990, is appropriate for traditional fixed telephony services but less so for

---

[45] Directive 95/46/EC.
[46] Directive 97/66, Article 1(2).
[47] Directive 97/66/EC, OJ 1998 L 24/01 (the Telecoms Data Protection Directive).
[48] SI 1998/3170.
[49] SI 1999/2093.
[50] Directive 97/66/EC.

new services which have now become available and affordable for a wide public. This creates ambiguities and has led in practice to divergence in national transposition of the Directive. To ensure a consistent application of data protection principles to public telecommunications services and network [*sic*] throughout the EU, the Commission proposes to update and clarify the Directive taking account of technological developments converging markets.

In April 2000, a Working Document was produced describing these issues in greater detail.[51] In some instances, the 1997 Directive[52] was seen as unduly restrictive. It contained, for example, an outright prohibition against the use of traffic data for purposes other than those of the network operator. The Commission now proposed to permit:

> processing of traffic data... for the purpose of value added services with the consent of the subscriber or user. With the extension of the data protection safeguards to traffic data generated by any transmission network for electronic communications, the existing possibility for further processing of traffic data, has become too narrow. Today, value added services have been developed and can be offered based on particular traffic data and there is no reason to prohibit such services in cases where the subscriber has consented with the use of traffic data for the purpose of these services.[53]

In other instances, the nature of communications was seen to be changing user perceptions and wishes. With directory information, for example, the assumption underpinning the Telecoms Data Protection Directive[54] had been that most subscribers would wish details of their fixed telephone number to be included in a directory. The Directive provided that details could be recorded in directories unless the customer chose to opt out. In the age of mobile phones and email addresses, it was suggested a majority of customers might not want these details to appear in a public document and so the system should move to one whereby publication would require the customer's positive assent.

A point which comes out strongly throughout the document is that data relating to communications is becoming both more extensive and more valuable. It is in the interests of the emerging information society that the maximum use should be made of valuable resources. As the volume of data traffic takes up a greater and greater percentage of telecommunications traffic, so there is a clear need to reformulate provisions drawn up even a few years ago when voice telephony was still dominant. It is equally clear, however, that with systems such as the Internet, vast amounts of data may be collected concerning the actions of individuals and processed and used in ways which may not

---

[51] Available from <http://ec.europa.eu/archives/ISPO/infosoc/telecompolicy/review99/review99.htm>

[52] Directive 97/66/EC.

[53] European Commission Working Document on The Processing of Personal Data and the Protection of Privacy in the Electronic Communications Sector at p. 3.

[54] Ibid.

be considered desirable. The establishment of effective legal controls and safeguards is a matter of great importance.

It is indicative of the controversial nature of many of the issues involved that whilst the remainder of the Directives making up the new communications regulatory Framework were adopted in February 2002, agreement could not be reached between the European institutions regarding the proposed data protection measure, and its adoption was delayed until July 2002. Particular points of controversy concerned the nature of the legal response to unsolicited commercial emails (spam) and the imposition of requirements on communications providers to retain traffic and billing data for possible access by law enforcement and national security agencies. One timetabling consequence is that, whilst the bulk of the Directives required to be implemented in the Member States by July 2002, the Directive 'Concerning the Processing of Personal Data and the Protection of Privacy in the Electronic Communications Sector (Directive on Privacy and Electronic Communications)'[55] (hereafter, the Communications Privacy Directive) did not require to be implemented until 31 October of that year. Once again, the United Kingdom was dilatory in acting, with implementation taking the form of the Privacy and Electronic Communications (EC Directive) Regulations 2003,[56] which came into force on 11 December 2003.

Aim and scope of the Privacy and Electronic Communications Directive

The Privacy and Electronic Communications Directive's proclaimed aim is to harmonise:

> the provisions of the Member States required to ensure an equivalent level of protection of fundamental rights and freedoms, and in particular the right to privacy, with respect to the processing of personal data in the electronic communication sector and to ensure the free movement of such data and of electronic communication equipment and services in the Community.[57]

As was also the case in respect of the earlier Telecommunications Data Protection Directive, the 2002 measure's stated aim is to 'particularise and complement' the provisions of the general Data Protection Directive.[58] It also expands the scope of this measure in one important respect by providing at least some rights for legal as well as private persons.[59]

Whilst this chapter will concentrate on the specific elements of the communications sector, it is important to bear in mind throughout that activities will also need to comply with the requirements of the general measure in respect of topics such as fair processing, accuracy of data, and subject access. Also important will be the activities of the supervisory agencies, in the case of the United Kingdom the Information Commissioner.

---

[55] Directive 2002/58.OJ 2002 L201/37.   [56] SI 2003/2426.
[57] Directive 2002/58/EC, Article 1.   [58] Article 1(2).   [59] Ibid.

The scope of the Communications Data Privacy Directive[60] is defined in Article 3 as extending to:

the processing of personal data in connection with the provision of publicly available electronic communications services in public communications networks in the Community.

Personal data is defined in the Data Protection Act 1998[61] and Data Protection Directive[62] as any information which relates to a living identifiable individual. In the context of communications-related activities, it may be assumed that individuals will often by identifiable by reference to telephone numbers or email addresses, matched to lists of subscribers maintained by network providers or ISPs.

The definition of processing is also found in the general data protection law, the Data Protection Act 1998, providing that the concept encompasses the:

obtaining, recording or holding the information or data or carrying out any operation or set of operations on the information or data, including—

(a) organisation, adaptation or alteration of the information or data,

(b) retrieval, consultation or use of the information or data,

(c) disclosure of the information or data by transmission, dissemination or otherwise making available, or

(d) alignment, combination, blocking, erasure or destruction of the information or data.[63]

Given the breadth of this definition, it is difficult to conceive of any communications-related activity which will not involve processing and, save perhaps in the situation where a payphone is used, will be carried out by reference to an identifiable individual.

Security and confidentiality

The first substantive obligation imposed under the Communications Data Privacy Directive,[64] is that the provider of a public communication network or service must 'take appropriate technical and organisational measures' to ensure the security of the network and any messages transmitted over it.

The most obvious security risk undoubtedly will be that of an unauthorised person obtaining access to data being transmitted. Beyond interception of voice traffic, perhaps the most significant and certainly the most high-profile risks associated with modern communications are those associated with the Internet, with concerns frequently being raised about the security of personal and financial data transmitted

---

[60] Directive 2002/58/EC.

[61] Section 1.

[62] Directive 95/46/EC, Article 2.

[63] Section 1.

[64] Directive 2002/58/EC, Article 4.

in the course of an e-commerce transaction. The obligations imposed upon service providers are twofold. First, appropriate security measures must be put in place to protect data and, second, customers must be warned of the risks involved and advised about self-help measures such as encryption which may be used and of the likely costs of such measures.

Whilst the provisions regarding data security are addressed to network and service operators, obligations are imposed upon governments to ensure that legal sanctions may be imposed against those who breach the confidentiality of communications. Legal prohibitions are to be imposed against 'listening, tapping, storage or other kinds of interception or surveillance of communications' other than any measures which are necessary in connection with the transmission of data. Exceptions are sanctioned in cases where interception is necessary in the interests of national security, law enforcement, and 'the unauthorised use of electronic communications systems'.[65] It is also permissible to record commercial communications where this is 'carried out in the course of lawful business practice for the purpose of providing evidence of a commercial transaction'.

For the United Kingdom, the provisions of the Telecommunications (Lawful Business Practice) (Interception of Communications) Regulations[66] will be relevant in this situation. Made under the auspices of the Regulation of Investigatory Powers Act 2000, these provide legal authority for the monitoring or recording of a wide range of electronic and voice communications. Examples would include recording of telephone calls received by businesses and the monitoring of employees' telephone and email communications by employers to determine compliance with policies regarding usage of these facilities.

Although the Regulations[67] and Directive[68] do provide legal authority for substantial forms of monitoring, it should be recalled that the Data Protection Act 1998's requirement is that processing should be both fair and lawful. Whilst employer-directed monitoring of the kind described above may well satisfy the second requirement, the Information Commissioner has suggested that processing carried out without giving proper notice to the individuals affected might well be considered unfair.

A further requirement relating to confidentiality illustrates the breadth of the Communications Data Privacy Directive's[69] provisions but also, perhaps, the problems which may be encountered in attempting to enforce these. Article 5(3) provides that:

> Member States shall ensure that the use of electronic communications networks to store information or to gain access to information stored in the terminal equipment of a subscriber or user is only allowed on condition that the subscriber or user concerned is provided with clear and comprehensive information in accordance with Directive

---

[65] Ibid., Article 15.
[66] SI 2000/2699.
[67] Ibid.
[68] Directive 2002/58/EC.
[69] Ibid.

95/46/EC, *inter alia* about the purposes of the processing, and is offered the right to refuse such processing by the data controller.

The Recitals to the Communications Data Privacy Directive make it clear that this applies to prohibit the use of:

> spyware, web bugs, hidden identifiers and other similar devices [which] can enter the user's terminal without their knowledge in order to gain access to information, to store hidden information or to trace the activities of the user and may seriously intrude upon the privacy of these users.[70]

Beyond the rather sinister sounding technologies specifically identified, it would appear that the placing of cookies may well violate the prohibition. The test will be whether the user is offered the opportunity to object to the placing of such devices. The major difficulty may well be that the default setting of Internet browsers such as Microsoft Explorer is set to accept cookies. In many cases, even if the user changes the setting either to require notice of and approval for the placing of a cookie or to refuse to accept any cookies, the effect will be to render access to many websites difficult or even impossible. For users the choice may be between accepting cookies or doing without access to a site. In such cases, consent might not be considered either informed or freely given.

Beyond issues of consent, a final question concerns the feasibility of enforcing prohibitions. A high percentage of websites are located in the United States or, indeed, in other countries outwith the jurisdiction of the EU. It is difficult to conceive of any feasible manner in which the prohibition may be enforced.

Traffic data

The term 'traffic data' encompasses any data processed in connection with the transmission of signals over a communication network. It will include data relating to the point of origin of a communication, its destination, and the duration of the communication. In the case of a fixed-line telephone, the point of origin will be obvious. With mobile communications, as has been referred to previously, the location of the user may constantly be changing. Data transmitted periodically from the telephone will allow the network to remain aware of the phone's location. This is clearly necessary in order to be able to make and receive calls but the retention and processing of location data raises serious issues for the individual's right to privacy.

Undoubtedly reflecting its origins in the pre-mobile era, the Telecoms Data Protection Directive[71] referred only to traffic data and provided that it might be processed subsequent to a communication only for billing purposes, or—with the consent of the customer—limited items of data might be processed by the telecommunications service provider for marketing purposes.[72]

---

[70] Directive 2002/58/EC, Recital 24.   [71] Directive 97/66/EC.

[72] The Annex to the Directive contained a list of the types of data which might be processed. This included data relating to the volume of calls but not the destination or duration of individual calls.

The term traffic data was not defined in the Telecoms Data Protection Directive.[73] The Communications Data Privacy Directive, however, provides that it is to consist of:

> any data processed for the purpose of the conveyance of a communication on an electronic communications network or for the billing thereof.[74]

This will encompass both data relating to use of a telephone and any data which might be processed by an ISP concerned with Internet usage.

The Directive retains the basic prohibition against processing but extends the range of permissible uses. Article 6 provides that:

> For the purpose of marketing electronic communications services or for the provision of value added services, the provider of a publicly available electronic communications service may process the data referred to in paragraph 1 to the extent and for the duration necessary for such services or marketing, if the subscriber or user to whom the data relate has given his/her consent. Users or subscribers shall be given the possibility to withdraw their consent for the processing of traffic data at any time.

'Value added services' are defined as communication services requiring the processing of data 'beyond what is necessary for the transmission of a communication or the billing thereof'.[75] This would include services such as the downloading of ringtones for mobile phones or the provision of information services. User consent is required and must be given on the same basis as that needed in the Data Protection Directive, which demands a 'freely given, specific and informed indication of his wishes by which the data subject signifies his agreement to personal data relating to him being processed'.[76] The key requirement is that the subject be informed of the uses proposed. In this eventuality, it is acceptable for the processing to take place, unless the subject actively indicates objection (opting out). Consent can be withdrawn at any time.

Additionally, the Communications Data Privacy Directive makes provision for the handling of location data, defined as:

> any data processed in an electronic communications network, indicating the geographic position of the terminal equipment of a user of a publicly available electronic communications service.[77]

Beyond use for the purpose of network operation, location data may be processed only when it is rendered anonymous or, with user consent, for the provision of a value added service. Information must be provided to the user of the type of data which will be processed, the purposes for which it will be used, the duration of any further use and whether this will involve a transfer to third parties.

---

[73] Directive 97/66/EC.
[74] Directive 2002/58/EC, Article 2(b).
[75] Ibid., Article 2.
[76] Ibid.
[77] Ibid.

Although this provision may seem at first glance to provide considerable assistance to users, it is likely that the information may be provided in a relatively lengthy and complex list of standard conditions associated with provision of the overall communications service. Albeit this, prior to the implementation of the Communications Data Privacy Directive, one of the major mobile networks used a clause empowering them to:

> Contact you or allow carefully selected third parties to contact you with information about products and services by post, telephone, mobile text message or email (subject to any preferences expressed by you).

Given that the processing of data will take place in real time and be associated with the movements and location of the user, the processing might be considered rather more sensitive than is the case where traffic data is used for marketing purposes. It is perhaps unfortunate that the requirement is not that the provider seek a positive indication of consent (opt in).

In addition to providing users with the right to opt out of such uses of their data, the Communications Data Privacy Directive requires that users must be given the possibility 'of temporarily refusing the processing of such data for each connection to the network or for each transmission of a communication'.[78] It is likely that this right could be exercised in a manner similar to that currently applying in relation to the use of systems of 'caller id', where prefixing a number with 141 will prevent details of the caller's number being made available to the recipient.

Significant inroads on the level of protection conferred by the Communications Data Privacy Directive came with the inclusion at a late stage in the legislative process of the acceptance by the European Parliament of an amendment permitting Member States to 'adopt legislative measures providing for the retention of data for a limited period justified on the grounds laid down in this paragraph'.[79] The grounds referred to include the safeguarding of 'national security, defence, public security, and the prevention, investigation, detection and prosecution of criminal offences or of unauthorised use of the electronic communication system'.

In the United Kingdom, the provisions of the Regulation of Investigatory Powers Act 2000 empower a senior police officer to require a communications provider to disclose any communications data in its possession where this is considered necessary in the interests of national security, the prevention, or detection of crime or a number of other situations.[80] The term 'communications data' is defined broadly to include traffic and location data, although as was stated by the Home Office:

> It is important to identify what communications data does include but equally important to be clear about what it does *not* include. The term communications data in the Act does not include the content of any communication.[81]

---

[78] Ibid., Article 9(2).
[79] Ibid., Article 15.
[80] Section 22.
[81] Consultation Paper on a Code of Practice for Voluntary Retention of Communications Data, March 2003.

The procedures to be followed in requesting or requiring disclosure are laid down in a Code of Practice on the Acquisition and Disclosure of Communications Data, which was brought into force by the Regulation of Investigatory Powers (Acquisition and Disclosure of Communications Data: Code of Practice) Order 2007.[82]

The Regulation of Investigatory Powers Act 2000 did not require that providers retain data, although concerns had been expressed that mobile phone operators were retaining data for a period of months, and in some cases years. The conformity of this practice with the requirements of the Data Protection Act 1998 that:

> Personal data processed for any purpose or purposes shall not be kept for longer than is necessary for that purpose or those purposes[83]

had been doubted. The passage of the Anti-Terrorism, Crime and Security Act 2001 provided a legal basis for the retention of data. The Act conferred power on the Secretary of State to draw up a code of practice, specifying periods of time during which communications providers would be required to retain communications data.[84] Although the Secretary of State is granted legislative power, it was envisaged that a voluntary code would be agreed between the government and the communications industry.

Initial proposals by the government for the establishment of a code of practice received heavy criticism, both in terms of the period of time within which data might be required to be retained and in terms of the range of government agencies which might be granted access to this data. An initial draft code was withdrawn in July 2002, and a further draft was published in September 2003[85] and entered into force on 5 December 2003, pursuant to the provisions of the Retention of Communications Data (Code of Practice) Order 2003.[86] The code provides authority for the retention of communications data in the interests of national security or the detection or prevention of crime for periods after the business case for retention might have expired up to a maximum period of twelve months.

Compliance with the 2003 code was voluntary. This situation changed upon the implementation of the European Directive 'on the retention of data generated or processed in connection with the provision of publicly available electronic communications services or of public communications networks'[87] (the Data Retention Directive). This Directive, which was introduced in the aftermath of the Madrid and London bombings in 2004 and 2005, respectively, amends the provisions of Directive 2002/58 concerned with privacy in electronic communications networks. Recital 9 to the Directive explains:

> Because retention of data has proved to be such a necessary and effective investigative tool for law enforcement in several Member States, and in particular concerning serious matters such as organised crime and terrorism, it is necessary to ensure that

---

[82] SI 2007 No. 2197.

[83] Schedule 1, fifth data protection principle.

[84] Section 102.

[85] Available from <http://www.opsi.gov.uk/si/si2003/draft/5b.pdf>

[86] SI 2003 No. 3175.

[87] OJ 2006 No. L105/54.

retained data are made available to law enforcement authorities for a certain period, subject to the conditions provided for in this Directive.

Article 5 of the Directive specifies a very wide range of items of communications data relating to the source and destination of telephone calls, emails, and Internet access. The Directive provided that Member States might opt out of applying its provisions to all the forms of communications listed and the United Kingdom, along with a number of other states, issued a declaration to the effect that:

> it will postpone application of that Directive to the retention of communications data relating to Internet access, Internet telephony and Internet e-mail.

The periods for which items of data are to be retained are to be specified by Member States within the range of six months to two years. The Directive was implemented in the United Kingdom by the Data Protection (EC Directive) Regulations 2007,[88] which entered into force on 1 October 2007. Rather than the voluntary retention scheme applying under the Code, Regulation 5 requires that data must be retained relating to:

(a) the telephone number from which the telephone call was made and the name and address of the subscriber and registered user of that telephone;

(b) the telephone number dialled and, in cases involving supplementary services such as call forwarding or call transfer, any telephone number to which the call is forwarded or transferred, and the name and address of the subscriber and registered user of such telephone;

(c) the date and time of the start and end of the call; and

(d) the telephone service used.

Additional information is required to be retained in respect of mobile calls:

(a) the International Mobile Subscriber Identity (IMSI) and the International Mobile Equipment Identity (IMEI) of the telephone from which a telephone call is made;

(b) the IMSI and the IMEI of the telephone dialled;

(c) in the case of pre-paid anonymous services, the date and time of the initial activation of the service and the cell ID from which the service was activated;

(d) the cell ID at the start of the communication; and

(e) data identifying the geographic location of cells by reference to their cell ID.

This data must be retained for a period of twelve months.[89]

Itemised billing

The issue of itemised billing is rather less contentious than that of data retention but does serve to illustrate some of the changes which have occurred in the communications

---

[88] SI 2007 No. 2199.   [89] Ibid. Reg. 5(2).

sector over the past decade and also some potential conflicts between rights to privacy and to information.

The initial provision of the Communications Data Privacy Directive may appear somewhat strange. Subscribers, it is provided, 'will have the right to receive non-itemised bills'.[90] Whilst few people may want to exercise the option, the rationale lies perhaps in the fact that it has become very much the norm for individuals to receive itemised bills. In this situation, given that the Directive is seeking to provide for exceptions, the logical approach is to assume the provision of itemised bills and confer a right to refuse these.

Whilst it is almost inevitably the case that the person responsible for a communications bill would be interested in information regarding the calls made, other persons may have different preferences. The Communications Data Privacy Directive uses two terms—'subscriber' and 'user'. The term 'subscriber' is not defined in the Directive,[91] although it clearly appears that it must refer to the party who has contracted for the provision of services. Perhaps rather inconsistently, the Directive does provide a definition of the term 'user' as 'any natural person using a publicly available electronic communications service, for private or business purposes, without necessarily having subscribed to this service'.[92]

In a household, it will be common for one member to be classed as the subscriber but for other family members to use the equipment. Whilst the former may wish to be able to analyse what calls have been made, the latter may have an interest in maintaining the privacy of their communications. Whilst in many cases it may be accepted that the wishes and interests of the subscriber should prevail, there may be instances, for example where calls have been made to counselling or support agencies, perhaps arising from the behaviour of the subscriber towards the user. The Communications Data Privacy Directive requires that national implementing measures should seek to reconcile the interests of the parties involved 'by ensuring that sufficient alternative privacy enhancing methods of communications or payments are available to such users and subscribers'.[93]

Even by the general standards of EU Directives, this formulation is opaque. In the United Kingdom, there are some 750,000 payphones and it might be argued that this provides sufficient access to telecommunications for users who do not want details of their calls made available to third-party subscribers. The Recitals to the Communications Data Privacy Directive also recommend that Member States:

encourage the development of electronic communication service options such as alternative payment facilities which allow anonymous or strictly private access to publicly

---

[90] Directive 2002/58/EC, Article 7.

[91] The Telecoms Data Protection Directive (Directive 97/66/EC) did define the term as 'any natural or legal person who or which is party to a contract with the provider of publicly available telecommunications services for the supply of such services' (Article 2).

[92] Directive 2002/58/EC, Article 2.

[93] Ibid., Article 7(2).

available electronic communications services, for example calling cards and facilities for payment by credit card.[94]

A further possibility canvassed is that itemised bills may delete 'a certain number of digits' from the lists of called numbers. This might well prove useful in the situation, for example, that calls are made to a medical or emotional support helpline. Again, however, it is difficult to see why such an option would be attractive to subscribers and in the event that only certain numbers were censored, the presence of these might in itself be a cause for suspicion. One reasonable option, however, would appear to be to provide that calls made to freephone numbers (0800) should not appear on bills. These are frequently provided by support agencies. Given that such calls do not involve any cost implications for the subscriber, the balance of interests may be seen as lying with potential users.

Directory information

When the 1997 directory was adopted, virtually the only form of communications directories were telephone directories published by major telecommunications operators. In the past six years, there has been a massive increase in the number of telephones in use due to the continuing growth in the mobile market. Tens of millions of individuals have also acquired email addresses, as this form of electronic communication has expanded to the extent that the volume of email communications dwarfs that carried by the postal networks. Beyond an increase in the range of materials which might be contained in communications directories there has been a similar growth in the level of sophistication of directory services. Increasingly provided in electronic form, directories may include facilities such as reverse searching. Whilst a traditional directory can be searched only in the manner structured by the compiler, typically by alphabetical order, an electronic directory might, for example, allow a user to enter a telephone number and be presented with the name and address of the person to whom it has been allocated.

Traditionally certain individuals—Oftel have estimated the figure to be as high as 37 per cent of residential customers[95]—have sought to keep their contact details out of the public domain. There may be a variety of reasons for this. Members of certain professions, such as law and medicine, may not wish to be contactable at home by their clients. In other instances, individuals may fear being harassed by ex-partners.

The Telecoms Data Protection Directive provided that the information contained in public directories should be limited to that necessary to identify particular customers, that there should be a right to require that details be withheld from the directory, and also that customers should be able to indicate:

> that his or her personal data may not be used for the purpose of direct marketing, to have his or her address omitted in part and not to have a reference revealing his or her sex, where this is applicable linguistically.[96]

---

[94] Ibid., Recital 33.

[95] Directory Information <http://www.oftel.gov.uk/publications/1995_98/consumer/dqchap.htm>

[96] Directive 97/66/EC, Article 11.

The first element of this requirement was met through the establishment of the telephone preference service, which enabled customers to indicate their wish not to receive calls for marketing purposes.[97] Under the Telecommunications (Data Protection and Privacy) Regulations 1999,[98] it is provided that marketing-related communications must not be made to a telephone number which appears on a list maintained by the Director General of Communications of subscribers who have indicated objection to this practice.[99] Breach of this requirement will constitute a contravention of the Data Protection Act 1998 and may entitle the subscriber to compensation for any damage caused. It does not appear that any party has to date obtained compensation for burnt meals caused by unwarranted interruptions by telephone marketers. In 1999, the Director entered into a contract with the Telephone Preference Service for the compilation and maintenance of the list. Effect was given to the remaining requirements of the Directive by the Telecommunications (Data Protection and Privacy) Regulations 1999.[100] Over 1 million subscribers have now registered with the service.

The Communications Data Privacy Directive adopts a somewhat different approach. Subscribers are to be informed of the nature and purposes of the information which will be made available in a public directory or directory information service and 'of any further usage possibilities based on search functions embedded in electronic versions of the directory'. This information must be supplied prior to publication of the directory.[101]

Having been informed of the purposes envisaged, subscribers are to have the right to require that their details be removed in whole or in part. No charge is to be made for this or for compliance with the subscriber's request that errors be corrected.

Especially with electronic directories, it is possible that third parties may seek to copy significant amounts of information and use these for their own purposes. The body of the Communications Data Privacy Directive makes no provision in this respect, although the Recitals indicate that:

> Where the data may be transmitted to one or more third parties, the subscriber should be informed of this possibility and of the recipient or the categories of possible recipients. Any transmission should be subject to the condition that the data may not be used for other purposes than those for which they were collected. If the party collecting the data from the subscriber or any third party to whom the data have been transmitted wishes to use the data for an additional purpose, the renewed consent of the subscriber is to be obtained either by the initial party collecting the data or by the third party to whom the data have been transmitted.[102]

Although not a direct legal requirement, the Telecommunications Directory Information Fair Processing Code, drawn up by the then Data Protection Registrar

---

[97] <http://www.tpsonline.org.uk/tpsr/html/default.asp>
[98] SI 1999/3170.
[99] Regulation 9.
[100] SI 1999/2093.
[101] Directive 2002/58/EC, Article 12.
[102] Ibid., Recital 39.

in 1998, is likely to be very relevant. This provides, inter alia, that controllers should take steps to prevent information being misused. Bulk copying might be inhibited by technical measures designed to limit the number of records which can be accessed and copied by a single search. It is also suggested that encryption techniques might be used and, perhaps now outdated, that there should be no online interface to directories. Encryption of data might also be used to prevent reverse searching.

Although not legally binding, a failure to comply with the Code may be regarded as constituting unfair processing under the Data Protection Act 1998 and result in the service of an enforcement notice by the Information Commissioner. Under the Telecommunications (Open Network Provision) (Voice Telephony) Regulations,[103] an undertaking required (effectively BT) on directory information to a third party was required to obtain an undertaking that the recipient would comply with the Code. Any breach of the undertaking would render the third party's processing unfair. A similar effect is now provided by condition 22 of the General Conditions of Entitlement. This provides that every communications provider is obliged to supply details of its subscribers to any other provider upon reasonable request. This obligation is expressly stated to be 'subject to the requirements of relevant data protection legislation'.

Calling and connected line identification

Systems of calling line identification, often referred to as 'caller id', allow a user to identify the number from which a call originates prior to answering the call. A related system allows a user to discover details of the last call made to the telephone by dialling 1471. As with itemised billing, the systems offer major benefits to individuals, not least as a means of deterring the making of hoax or malicious calls, but there may also be good reason why a party making a call may not wish details to be available to a called party. At a trivial level, a husband may not wish his wife to be aware that rather than a call originating from the office where work demands are requiring a late departure, it is coming from a local pub. Following the break-up of a relationship, one party may wish to contact the other but not to allow the possibility of the call being returned or—especially in an era of reverse searchable directories—to allow their physical location to be discovered. Caller id is also used extensively for commercial purposes. Some companies use systems linked to a database of customers so that the caller's identity is known at the time the call is answered. Many taxi companies use such systems to simplify the task of despatching vehicles and also to provide some check against the making of hoax calls. Less desirable perhaps is the situation where a company 'captures' phone numbers from persons calling to inquire about goods or services and uses these for subsequent marketing activities.[104] The situation may therefore arise where subscribers may wish to know who is calling them but, at least in certain situations, may not want their telephone number to be made available to the party they are calling.

---

[103] SI 1998/1580.

[104] Such processing may, of course, be considered unfair under the provisions of the Data Protection Act 1998.

As well as presenting the called party with information about the origin of a call, the same technology—referred to in this case as connected line information—allows the caller to see the actual number at which the call is answered. Although in the majority of cases this will be the number which was dialled, it may also be the case that calls are forwarded to another number. Whilst in the vast majority of cases the practice will be unobjectionable, there may be situations where the called party is reluctant for this to happen. Out-of-hours calls to a doctor's surgery may be forwarded to the physician's home number, and there may be reluctance to allow patients to know this number.

In respect of caller id, the Communications Data Privacy Directive requires that subscribers and users be presented with a range of options. Users are to be offered the option, free of charge, of blocking the presentation of the number from which they are making a call. In the United Kingdom, this is normally accomplished by prefixing '141' to the telephone number called. Users should also be offered the option of blocking the display of information on a permanent basis, although a charge may be levied for this.[105]

Whilst callers will be entitled to block presentation of their identity, the Communications Data Privacy Directive sets the scene for what might almost be regarded as a battle of the systems by providing that subscribers are to be offered the option to reject incoming calls where the caller has chosen to prevent display of his or her number.[106] One limitation of this approach is that identification details may be withheld either by the deliberate act of the caller or—as typically happens in a work environment—because outgoing calls will be routed through a central switchboard. Even though each instrument may have its own number which can be dialled directly by callers from outside the premises, the identification details will be stripped out in respect of outgoing calls.

In exceptional cases, it may be provided that attempts by callers to conceal details of the number from which a communication originates can be overridden. This may take place on a temporary basis in the event that a subscriber requests the assistance of the service provider in tracing the origin of malicious or nuisance calls and permanently in respect of lines used by the emergency services.[107]

Broadly similar provisions apply in respect of connected line identification. Here, subscribers must be offered the possibility, 'using a simple means and free of charge of preventing the presentation of the connected line information'.[108]

Unsolicited communications

For many persons, receipt of unsolicited commercial communications, whether by post, telephone, fax, or email, is a major cause of aggravation. Oftel research has indicated that up to 20 per cent of customers choosing to remove their details from

---

[105] Directive 2002/58/EC, Article 8(1).
[106] Ibid., Article 8(2). BT currently charges £3.33 per month for use of this facility.
[107] Ibid., Article 10.
[108] Ibid., Article 8(4).

telephone directories do so in order to minimise the numbers of unsolicited marketing calls.[109] As indicated above, very considerable numbers of persons have signed up
to the telephone and fax preference service. Currently, much publicity has attached to
the use of the Internet for unsolicited or junk emails, generally referred to as spam.
The amount of spam was estimated to have increased by 80 per cent in 2002,[110] with
current estimates suggesting that 30 per cent of all Internet-based emails are spam.[111]
Some commentators have predicted that continued growth in the volume of email
would 'render the Internet unusable by 2008'.[112] According to a recent Harris poll, 80
per cent of Internet users claimed to be 'very annoyed' about spam with 74 per cent of
those surveyed favouring a legal ban.[113]

A further tactic, which has not been widely used in the United Kingdom to date,
concerns the use of automated calling systems. With these, numbers are dialled automatically and when the call is answered, a recorded message is played to the recipient.
Beyond any nuisance value, these systems have been implicated in at least one fatality
in Canada, where a fire broke out in a property just at the moment an automated call
was received. Although the householder attempted to terminate the call so that the
emergency services might be summoned, the message continued to be transmitted
with the result that the user was unable to make an outgoing call.

Controls over the use of electronic communications services for marketing purposes
were introduced in the Telecoms Data Protection Directive.[114] As indicated above,
prohibitions were imposed against the use of the telephone to contact individuals who
had expressed a preference not to receive marketing calls. The use of automated calling
machines was also prohibited, except in situations where consumers had specifically
requested such communications.

A similar 'opt in' approach was adopted in respect of the use of fax machines for
the purposes of unsolicited marketing. The rationale for treating fax transmissions
more restrictively than voice communications was an economic one. Whilst receipt
of a telephone call does not have any cost implications for the subscriber, paper and
ink will require to be used to print out the contents of a fax. This was undoubtedly a
more significant consideration in 1990 when the Telecoms Data Protection Directive
was initially drafted, as at that time fax machines required to use special and very
expensive paper.

Perhaps unsurprisingly, the Telecoms Data Protection Directive[115] made no reference to email. Both with the growth in Internet usage and with the expansion in the
scope of the legislation, inclusion of provisions concerning email has been a major
and contentious feature of the new legislation. As originally introduced, the explana-

---

[109] Directory Information <http://www.oftel.gov.uk/publications/1995_98/consumer/dqchap.htm>
[110] <http://news.bbc.co.uk/1/hi/technology/2409855.stm>
[111] <http://news.bbc.co.uk/1/hi/technology/2688619.stm>
[112] <http://www.theregister.co.uk/content/archive/21846.html>
[113] <http://news.zdnet.co.uk/story/0,t269-s2128193,00.html>
[114] Directive 97/66/EC.
[115] Ibid.

tory memorandum accompanying the draft Communications Data Privacy Directive indicated that:

> Four Member States already have bans on unsolicited commercial e-mail and another is about to adopt one. In most of the other Member States opt-out systems exist. From an internal market perspective, this is not satisfactory. Direct marketers in opt-in countries may not target e-mail addresses within their own country but they can still continue to send unsolicited commercial e-mail to countries with an opt-out system. Moreover, since e-mail addresses very often give no indication of the country of residence of the recipients, a system of divergent regimes within the internal market is unworkable in practice. A harmonised opt-in approach solves this problem.

Accordingly, a prohibition was proposed except in respect of individuals who had indicated the wish to receive commercial emails. This approach was highly controversial and in October 2001 the European Parliament voted in favour of an 'opt out system'. In December 2001, however, the Council voted to reinstate the 'opt in' approach and the Communications Data Privacy Directive was finally adopted with this format, the Directive providing that the sending of:

> electronic mail for the purposes of direct marketing may only be allowed in respect of subscribers who have given their prior consent.[116]

Although the term 'prior consent' might appear compatible with the use of an 'opt out' approach where failure on the part of a user to indicate a preference would equate to consent, the Recitals make reference to the need to ensure that the 'prior explicit consent of the recipients is obtained before such communications are addressed to them'.[117] Use of the adjective 'explicit' clearly imposes a heavier burden upon persons wishing to send emails.

The Communications Data Privacy Directive does provide for one situation where commercial emails can be sent without prior consent. This applies where there has been a previous commercial relationship between the parties and:

> a natural or legal person obtains from its customers their electronic contact details for electronic mail, in the context of the sale of a product or a service—the same natural or legal person may use these electronic contact details for direct marketing of its own similar products or services provided that customers clearly and distinctly are given the opportunity to object, free of charge and in an easy manner, to such use of electronic contact details when they are collected and on the occasion of each message in case the customer has not initially refused such use.[118]

Use of a hypertext link in the emails allowing recipients to 'click here to unsubscribe from mailings' would suffice to meet with this requirement.

Even where consent has been given to the transmission of commercial emails or where the email is sent to a previous customer, the Directive imposes a final

---

[116] Directive 2002/58/EC, Article 13(1).
[117] Ibid., Recital 40.
[118] Ibid., Article 13(2).

requirement that commercial emails should be clearly identifiable as such and that they should always use a valid return address.[119] In many cases, it may be obvious from the heading of the email that its subject is commercial. A trawl through the author's mailbox reveals subjects such as:

Need a NEW Computer? No Credit—No Problem

Earn $75/hr with Your Own Home Based Business Processing

sample the weight loss patch—on us!

Nothing more need be done in these situations. Other spammers, perhaps aware that messages with obviously commercial headings may be deleted unread, make use of headings such as:

Please get back to me

re your enquiry

Hello

Headers such as this are now unlawful under the Communications Data Privacy Directive.

Whilst well meaning, it is uncertain how effective the Directive's approach will be. A very considerable percentage of commercial email originates from the United States or from other countries outwith the EU. Unless and until these legal systems adopt a similar approach, there will be little that can practically be done to bring proceedings against spammers. Even within the EU, given the ease with which persons can set up email accounts, the task of tracking down offenders will be a difficult one.

Conclusions

Those using communications services justifiably have an expectancy that the privacy of their communications will be respected. There are, of course, significant issues concerned with the intrinsic security of certain forms of communication. Transmitting an email has been analogised, for example, with using a postcard to send a communication by post. Although the Communications Data Privacy Directive[120] is relevant in respect of these issues, perhaps its most important role relates to the use of traffic data generated as a consequence of the use of networks. Although subject to the inevitable exceptions in the interests of national security and law enforcement, these will provide a reasonable degree of protection.

Undoubtedly, the most publicised provisions in the Communications Data Privacy Directive[121] are those dealing with the processing of junk mail and other forms of

---

[119] Ibid., Article 13(4). Many spammers attempt to conceal the genuine address from which the message is sent to avoid possible action by the ISP involved, which may well have an anti-spam condition in its contract of supply.

[120] Directive 2002/58/EC.

[121] Directive 2002/58/EC.

unsolicited commercial communications. Whilst likely to be welcomed by the majority of users, it may be queried as to how effective the prohibition against unsolicited email communications is likely to be. Although estimates as to the costs incurred by industry in dealing with email spam are legion,[122] it is doubtful whether these stand serious comparison with losses due to improper or wasteful use of other resources, such as telephones, stationery, or even heating and lighting. It is difficult to justify the adoption of an opt-in approach for this specific sector whilst other forms of unsolicited communication using media such as the mail or telephone can continue to operate on an 'opt out' basis.

[122] One estimate puts the global cost at $9 billion per year: see <http://news.bbc.co.uk/1/hi/technology/2983157.stm>

8

Transborder data flows

Introduction

During the nineteenth century, the development of telegraph networks provided a medium for the speedy transfer of data, both nationally and internationally. The possibility that messages might be sent into or out of the jurisdiction without the possibility of control caused concern to many governments. A response was to require a physical break in the telegraph network at the national border and to require that messages be:

> —sent to the terminal at the border, decoded and walked across to the next country where the message was again encoded and sent on to the terminal at the next border and so on.[1]

The International Telegraph Union (ITU) (now the International Telecommunications Union) was established as the world's first international organisation in 1865, in large measure to promote governmental confidence in the integrity of the system and to avoid such artificial barriers to the use of communications technology.

In keeping with history's tendency to repeat itself, concerns at the implications of transborder data flows have evolved, paralleling the development of national data protection statutes. Typically, the fear is expressed that an absence of control may result in the evasion of national controls. As has been stated:

> —protective provisions will be undermined if there are no restrictions on the removal of data to other jurisdictions for processing or storage. Just as money tends to gravitate towards tax havens, so sensitive personal data will be transferred to countries with the most lax, or no data protection standards. There is thus a possibility that some jurisdictions will become 'data havens' or 'data sanctuaries' for the processing or 'data vaults' for the storage of sensitive information.[2]

Controls over transborder data flows have been a feature of almost all national data protection statutes, with restrictions being justified on the basis of safeguarding the position of individuals. In the Swedish Data Act of 1973, it was provided that personal

---

[1] J. N. Pelton, *Global Talk* (Alphen aan den Rijn, 1981), p. 233.
[2] C. Millard, *Legal Protection of Computer Programs and Data* (London, 1985), p. 211.

data might be transferred abroad only with the prior consent of the Swedish Data Inspection Board. Section 11 of the law provided that:

> Personal data in a personal file may not be disclosed if there is reason to assume that the data will be used for automatic data processing contrary to this Act. If there is reason to assume that personal data will be used for automatic data processing abroad, the data may be disclosed only after permission from the Data Inspection Board. Such permission may be given only if it may be assumed that the disclosure of the data will not involve undue encroachment upon personal privacy.

As concern at the impact of national controls over telegraphic and then voice traffic led to the establishment of the ITU, so international initiatives have sought to establish what are effectively free trade zones in respect of personal data. In 1980, the OECD adopted 'Guidelines on the Protection of Privacy and Transborder Flows of Personal Data'. These Guidelines have been supplemented by a Declaration on Transborder Data Flows, adopted in 1995, which declared its signatories' intention to 'avoid the creation of unjustified barriers to the international exchange of data and information'. As discussed above, the Council of Europe Convention on the Automated Processing of Personal Data was the first legally binding international instrument. The Convention states that:

> A Party shall not, for the sole purpose of the protection of privacy, prohibit or subject to special authorisation transborder flows of personal data going to the territory of another Party.[3]

Ratification of the Convention prompted an amendment to the Swedish data protection law, adding a sentence to Section 11 to the effect that:

> Permission is not required, however, if personal data are to be used for automatic data processing solely in a State which has acceded to the Council of Europe's convention for the protection of individuals with regard to automatic processing of personal data.

Regulating transborder data flows

The Council of Europe Convention has been shaped by the experiences and practices of the Western European states which have adopted data protection legislation. Such legislation has three major features: first, it applies to all sectors of automated data processing; second, it contains substantive provisions regulating the forms of processing which can take place and the rights and remedies available to individuals; and, finally, it provides for the establishment of some form of supervisory agency. As indicated above, a different approach has prevailed in other countries, notably the United States.

Initially, the discrepancies in approach between Europe and the rest of the world were of limited practical significance. The Council of Europe makes no explicit reference to the imposition of controls over data to non-signatory states. Although some states such as Sweden required some form of prior approval, others, such as the United

---

[3] Article 12(2).

Kingdom, provided only a power for the supervisory agency to block a transfer if it was satisfied that a proposed transfer was likely to result in a contravention of the data protection principles. In the decade-and-a-half that the legislation was in force, this power was invoked only once.[4] The Data Protection Directive adopts a different and significantly more rigorous approach. Although recognising that:

> ...cross-border flows of personal data are necessary to the expansion of international trade; whereas the protection of individuals guaranteed in the Community by this Directive does not stand in the way of transfers of personal data to third countries which ensure an adequate level of protection; whereas the adequacy of the level of protection afforded by a third country must be assessed in the light of all the circumstances surrounding the transfer operation or set of transfer operations.

Article 25 of the Directive lays down as a basic principle the requirement that:

> The Member States shall provide that the transfer to a third country of personal data which are undergoing processing or are intended for processing after transfer may take place only if, without prejudice to compliance with the national provisions adopted pursuant to the other provisions of this Directive, the third country in question ensures an adequate level of protection.

Effect is given to this provision by the Data Protection Act 1998's eighth data protection principle which provides that:

> Personal data shall not be transferred to a country or territory outside the European Economic Area unless that country or territory ensures an adequate level of protection for the rights and freedoms of data subjects in relation to the processing of personal data.

By including the matter in the principles, it follows that any breach, or anticipated breach, can be answered by service of an enforcement notice. The need, therefore, for an additional transfer prohibition notice disappears. Controllers intending to transfer personal data outside the EEA are required to indicate this fact in their notification. If transfer to ten or fewer countries is envisaged the names of these countries must be notified, where more extensive transfers are planned notification should be given that transfers may take place on a 'worldwide' basis.[5]

Procedures for determining adequacy

The uniform application of the Data Protection Directive would clearly be threatened if the decision on whether third countries offered an adequate level of protection was

---

[4] A transfer prohibition notice was served in 1990, requiring the cessation of the transfer of personal data in the form of names and addresses to a variety of United States organisations bearing such titles as the 'Astrology Society of America', 'Lourdes Water Cross Incorporated', and 'Win With Palmer Incorporated'. These companies, which had been involved in the promotion of horoscopes, religious trinkets, and other products in the United Kingdom, were the subject of investigations by the United States postal authorities, alleging wire fraud and a variety of other unsavoury trading practices.

[5] *Notification Handbook*, available from <http://www.ico.gov.uk/upload/documents/library/data_protection/detailed_specialist_guides/notification_handbook_final.pdf>

to be made by each Member State. It is provided, therefore, that the Member States and the Commission are to inform each other of any cases where they feel that a third country does not provide an adequate level of protection.[6] In practice, general decisions regarding adequacy will be made at a Community level. Article 29 of the Directive establishes a Working Party on the Protection of Individuals with regard to the Processing of Personal Data. This Working Party is to be:

> ...composed of a representative of the supervisory authority or authorities designated by each Member State and of a representative of the authority or authorities established for the Community institutions and bodies, and of a representative of the Commission.

And will, inter alia:

> (a) give the Commission an opinion on the level of protection in the Community and in third countries.

If the Working Party determines that a third country does not provide an adequate level of protection, a report is to be made to a committee established under Article 31 of the Data Protection Directive.[7] Consisting of representatives of the Member States and chaired by the Commission, the Committee will consider a proposal from the Commission for action on the basis of the Working Party's findings and deliver an opinion. The Commission may then adopt legal measures. If these are in accord with the Committee's opinion, the measures will take immediate effect. If there is any variation, application will be deferred for three months, within which time the Council of Ministers may adopt a different decision. Member states are obliged to take any measures necessary to prevent data transfers to the country involved.[8]

To date, no country has been specifically identified as failing to provide an adequate level of protection. Given the reference in the Directive to the role of 'sectoral rules', 'professional rules and security measures', it is perhaps unlikely that there will be many 'black listings' affecting all data processing activities in a particular jurisdiction. More significantly, the Directive also provides for the procedures described above to be used to identify countries which do provide an adequate level of protection[9] and there has been extensive activity in this respect.

Defining adequacy

Although, as will be discussed below, a range of exemptions are provided, determination as to whether a third country provides an adequate level of protection is a key issue and effectively opens the way for data transfers to and from that country. The first attempt to define criteria for determining questions of adequacy was made in the Article 29 Working Party's Working Paper 4, 'First Orientations on Transfers of

---

[6] Article 25(3).
[7] Directive 95/46/EC.
[8] Article 25(4).
[9] Article 25(6).

Personal Data to Third Countries—Possible Ways Forward in Assessing Adequacy', published in 1987.[10] The ideas raised in this document were presented in an expanded form in Working Paper 12, 'Transfers of Personal Data to Third Countries: Applying Articles 25 and 26 of the EU Data Protection Directive', which was published in July 1998,[11] and remains the most significant document in the field. In terms of the general approach, it is suggested that:

> Using directive 95/46/EC as a starting point, and bearing in mind the provisions of other international data protection texts, it should be possible to arrive at a 'core' of data protection 'content' principles and 'procedural/enforcement' requirements, compliance with which could be seen as a minimum requirement for protection to be considered adequate.

In terms of substantive legal requirements, the Working Party identifies five core principles which reflect very closely the provisions of the Data Protection Directive:

1) **the purpose limitation principle**—data should be processed for a specific purpose and subsequently used or further communicated only insofar as this is not incompatible with the purpose of the transfer.

   ...

2) **the data quality and proportionality principle**—data should be accurate and, where necessary, kept up to date. The data should be adequate, relevant and not excessive in relation to the purposes for which they are transferred or further processed.

3) **the transparency principle**—individuals should be provided with information as to the purpose of the processing and the identity of the data controller in the third country, and other information insofar as this is necessary to ensure fairness....

4) **the security principle**—technical and organisational security measures should be taken by the data controller that are appropriate to the risks presented by the processing. Any person acting under the authority of the data controller, including a processor, must not process data except on instructions from the controller.

5) **the rights of access, rectification and opposition**—the data subject should have a right to obtain a copy of all data relating to him/her that are processed, and a right to rectification of those data where they are shown to be inaccurate. In certain situations he/she should also be able to object to the processing of the data relating to him/her....

6) **restrictions on onward transfers**—further transfers of the personal data by the recipient of the original data transfer should be permitted only where the second

---

[10] Available from <http://ec.europa.eu/justice_home/fsj/privacy/docs/wpdocs/1997/wp4_en.pdf>
[11] Available from <http://ec.europa.eu/justice_home/fsj/privacy/docs/wpdocs/1998/wp12_en.pdf>

recipient (i.e. the recipient of the onward transfer) is also subject to rules affording an adequate level of protection.[12]

In terms of procedural requirements, the key requirements are that the agencies established in the third country should be in a position:

1) To deliver a **good level of compliance** with the rules.

2) To provide **support and help to individual data subjects** in the exercise of their rights.

3) To provide **appropriate redress** to the injured party where rules are not complied with.[13]

Activity in determining adequacy

To date, the Article 29 Working Party has published opinions indicating that an adequate level of protection is provided under the regimes operating in Argentina,[14] Canada,[15] Guernsey,[16] the Isle of Man,[17] and Switzerland.[18] The Hungarian regime was also accepted as being adequate,[19] although Hungary's subsequent membership of the European Union has made this finding otiose as the adequacy procedures apply only to transfers to or from non-Member States. A further opinion indicated that the regime in Australia[20] did not provide a sufficient level of protection to justify a finding of adequacy. Commission decisions[21] have subsequently given effect to the Working Party's positive findings but no further action has been taken in respect of Australia.

In addition to its work in assessing national legal provisions, the Article 29 Working Party was also involved in the discussions leading to a Commission declaration that the Safe Harbor principles, developed as a result of negotiations between the Commission and the United States Department of Commerce, provided an adequate level of protection in respect of those organisations which had committed themselves to complying with the principles.

The 'safe harbor' principles

As has been discussed throughout this section, significant differences exist between the United States and European systems of data and privacy protection. Following the adoption of the Data Protection Directive, discussions took place between the Commission

---

[12] At p. 5.
[13] At p. 7.
[14] <http://ec.europa.eu/justice_home/fsj/privacy/docs/wpdocs/2002/wp63_en.pdf>
[15] <http://ec.europa.eu/justice_home/fsj/privacy/docs/wpdocs/2004/wp88_en.pdf>
[16] <http://ec.europa.eu/justice_home/fsj/privacy/docs/wpdocs/2003/wp79_en.pdf>
[17] <http://ec.europa.eu/justice_home/fsj/privacy/docs/wpdocs/2003/wp82_en.pdf>
[18] <http://ec.europa.eu/justice_home/fsj/privacy/docs/wpdocs/1999/wp22en.pdf>
[19] <http://ec.europa.eu/justice_home/fsj/privacy/docs/wpdocs/1999/wp24en.pdf>
[20] <http://ec.europa.eu/justice_home/fsj/privacy/docs/wpdocs/2001/wp40en.pdf>
[21] Available from <http://ec.europa.eu/justice_homefsj/privacy/thirdcountries/index_en.htm>

and the United States Department of Commerce with a view to devising mechanisms to avoid the prospect of a transatlantic data war. The discussions centred on the quest to agree to a set of conditions, generally referred to as the 'safe harbor' principles, observance of which by United States-based companies would be accepted by the Commission as ensuring conformity with European data protection requirements.

Throughout the negotiations between the Commission and the Department of Commerce, the Article 29 Working Party issued a number of documents concerned with the proposed agreement.[22] These demonstrated a significantly greater degree of scepticism concerning the effectiveness of enforcement mechanisms than was exhibited by the Commission. In Opinion 7/99, published in December 1999, the Working Party indicated the view that the then version of the principles did not constitute a satisfactory basis for action. Referring to previous reports, it stated that:

> The Working Party notes that some progress has been made but deplores that most of the comments made in its previous position papers do not seem to be addressed in the latest version of the US documents. The Working Party therefore confirms its general concerns.

The Working Party's major concerns centred on the limitations of a system of self-certification and also concerns that the jurisdiction of the Federal Trade Commission is restricted to activities 'in or affecting commerce', with the consequence that:

> This seems to exclude most of the data processed in connection with an employment relationship (FAQ 9) as well as the data processed without any commercial purpose (e.g.: non-profit, research).

The nebulous nature of the assertion that other Federal and State laws might be applicable in certain situations was also criticised.

In a further Opinion[23] on the topic delivered in May 2000, the Working Party, whilst recognising that the negotiating process had resulted in significant improvements to the documents, expressed reservations about a considerable number of points. The proposals were subsequently approved by the Article 31 Committee consisting of representatives of the Member States, although in July 2000 the European Parliament passed a resolution indicating that it felt that the principles required to be strengthened before they could be considered acceptable. In spite of this view, the Commission issued a Decision on 27 July,[24] stating that:

> 1. For the purposes of Article 25(2) of Directive 95/46/EC, for all the activities falling within the scope of that Directive, the 'Safe Harbor Privacy Principles' (hereinafter 'the Principles'), as set out in Annex I to this Decision, implemented in accordance with the guidance provided by the frequently asked questions (hereinafter 'the FAQs') issued by the United States Department of Commerce on 21 July 2000 as set out in

---

[22] See Documents WP15, WP19, WP21, and WP23.
[23] Opinion 4/2000.
[24] Decision 2000/520/EC OJ 2000 L 215/7.

Annex II to this Decision are considered to ensure an adequate level of protection for personal data transferred from the Community to organisations established in the United States, having regard to the following documents issued by the United States Department of Commerce:

(a) the safe harbour enforcement overview set out in Annex III;

(b) a memorandum on damages for breaches of privacy and explicit authorisations in United States law set out in Annex IV;

(c) a letter from the Federal Trade Commission set out in Annex V;

(d) a letter from the United States Department of Transportation set out in Annex VI.[25]

The safe harbor principles basically encapsulate the contents of the Data Protection Directive's[26] principles relating to data quality. They require that notice must be given of the fact that data is held and the purposes for which it will be processed, and relevant 'opt out' opportunities must be given where it is intended that data will be used or disclosed for purposes other than envisaged or notified at the time of collection. Requirements relating to data security and integrity must also be accepted, as must the principle of subject access.[27] Supplementing the principles are a set of fifteen Frequently Asked Questions (FAQs), which provide detailed guidance on the interpretation of a range of issues, such as the scope of the concept of sensitive data and the manner in which subject access should be provided.

The principles are very much compatible with the contents of the OECD Guidelines. Given the extensive involvement of the United States in the work of this organisation, it is not surprising that discussions with the EU on the principles themselves did not prove particularly contentious. Most of the difficulty centred on the issue of enforcement. As has been discussed, the United States has tended to reject the concept of specialised supervisory agencies, which is integral to the European data protection model. In respect of enforcement, the principles state that:

> Effective privacy protection must include mechanisms for assuring compliance with the principles, recourse for individuals to whom the data relate affected by non-compliance with the principles, and consequences for the organization when the principles are not followed. At a minimum, such mechanisms must include (a) readily available and affordable independent recourse mechanisms by which each individual's complaints and disputes are investigated and resolved by reference to the principles and damages awarded where the applicable law or private sector initiatives so provide; (b) follow up procedures for verifying that the attestations and assertions businesses make about their privacy practices are true and that privacy practices have been implemented as presented; and (c) obligations to remedy problems arising out of

---

25 Article 1.

26 Directive 95/46/EC.

27 Copies of the safe harbor documents, together with much useful background material can be found on the United States Department of Commerce website at <http://www.export.gov/safeharbor/>

failure to comply with the principles by organizations announcing their adherence to them and consequences for such organizations. Sanctions must be sufficiently rigorous to ensure compliance by organizations.

The FAQ indicate that points (a) and (c) in this paragraph may be satisfied by the organisation indicating a willingness to cooperate with European Data Protection Authorities. Under the terms of FAQ 5, a Data Protection Panel has been established as an 'informal grouping' of seven European data protection authorities (including the United Kingdom's Information Commissioner),[28] which will provide advice to United States organisations ('harborites') concerning the operation of the scheme and investigate and seek to resolve disputes between European data subjects and such organisations. In the case where human resource data is transferred, FAQ 9 provides that there should be direct cooperation with the data protection authority from the Member State(s) concerned where these authorities have indicated agreement so to act. Only five supervisory authorities, again including the Information Commissioner, have signed up to this obligation.

In order to participate in safe harbor, United States-based organisations self-certify their intention to observe the safe harbor principles. This is done by means of a letter to the Department of Commerce, indicating as a minimum the:

1. name of organization, mailing address, email address, telephone and fax numbers;
2. description of the activities of the organization with respect to personal information received from the EU;
3. description of the organization's privacy policy for such personal information, including:
   (a) where it is available for viewing by the public,
   (b) its effective date of implementation,
   (c) a contact person for the handling of complaints, access requests, and any other issues arising under the safe harbor,
   (d) the specific statutory body that has jurisdiction to hear any claims against the organization regarding possible unfair or deceptive practices and violations of laws or regulations governing privacy,
   (e) name of any privacy programs in which the organization is a member,
   (f) method of verification (e.g. in-house, third party) [footnote omitted], and
   (g) the independent recourse mechanism that is available to investigate unresolved complaints.[29]

Breach of the terms of such a letter may expose the organisation either to action by the Federal Trade Commission under Section 5 of the Federal Trade Commission Act which under 15 USC Section 45(n) prohibits unfair practices in or affecting commerce,

---

[28] <http://circa.europa.eu/Public/irc/secureida/safeharbor/home>
[29] <http://www.export.gov/safeharbor/SH_FAQ6.asp>

a concept defined in terms of a likelihood to cause 'substantial injury to consumers which is not reasonably avoidable by consumers themselves and not outweighed by countervailing benefits to consumers or to competition'.

In accordance with the establishing Commission Decision,[30] the operation of the safe harbor arrangements were to be closely monitored by the Commission. A first report was published in 2002 and a second in 2004. Both reports identified similar strengths and weaknesses in the functioning of the system. The 2002 report commented that:

> Compared with the situation before it was available, the framework is providing a simplifying effect for those exporting personal data to organisations in the Safe Harbour and reduces uncertainty for US organisations interested in importing data from the EU by identifying a standard that corresponds to the adequate protection required by the [Data Protection] Directive.[31]

Concerns were expressed in both reports, supported by a research report produced under contract to the Commission, that a number of organisations which had signed up to the principles did not have or did not publish privacy policies in conformity with its requirements. Concern was also expressed at the lack of enforcement action by the Federal Trade Commission (FTC) and also at the fact that not a single case had been referred to the European Union's Data Protection Panel. It was also noted that around 30 per cent of harborites were engaging in the transfer of human resource data concerning employees and that this form of processing was outside the remit of the FTC. It was also noted that, although the FTC claimed that the breach of undertakings regarding privacy policies would be actionable, this had not been affirmed by the courts.

Initially, take-up of the safe harbor scheme was limited and at the time of the Commission's 2004 report was published, around 400 organisations had signed up to the principles. At the time of writing, just over 1,300 United States companies had signed up to the safe harbor principles, although not all entries on the safe harbor list are current.[32] Although in comparison with figures of those notifying details of processing in Europe—where the United Kingdom has 275,000 notifications and France 700,000—these figures are tiny, there does seem to be an increased awareness of the concept following the accession to the principles by a number of major companies: Microsoft, Intel, Hewlett-Packard, and Procter & Gamble.

The SWIFT case

The activities of financial services companies are excluded from the remit of the FTC. A very major issue arose between Europe and the United States in the course

---

[30] 520/2000/EC of 26 July 2000.

[31] Directive 95/46/EC.

[32] The list of companies which have signed up to the safe harbor principles can be accessed at <http://web.ita.doc.gov/safeharbor/shlist.nsf/webPages/safe+harbor+list>

of 2006, involving the activity of the Society for Worldwide Interbank Financial Telecommunications (SWIFT). SWIFT is a Belgian-based cooperative which processes financial messages for nearly 8,000 financial institutions around the world. SWIFT processes around 2.5 billion messages every year, some two-thirds of which are related to transactions involving parties located in Europe. It has two operating centres, one in Europe and one in the United States, which act as mirror sites for each other. Copies of all messages are retained for 124 days.

Around June 2006, media reports indicated that SWIFT had been providing substantial amounts of data to United States authorities for terrorism investigation purposes since 2001. This data was supplied under the terms of sixty-four administrative subpoenas served on SWIFT in the intervening years in connection with the Treasury's Terrorist Financing Tracking Program (TFTP). When the fact of the transfers came to light, great concerns were expressed within the EU institutions and the Article 29 Working Party launched an immediate investigation. The Working Party's report was published in November 2006,[33] and concluded that the transfers had placed SWIFT and the financial institutions making up its membership in major and continuing breach of its obligations under the Data Protection Directive and the Belgian data protection law to which its operations were subject. As was stated:

> the hidden, systematic, massive and long-term transfer of personal data by SWIFT to the UST in a confidential, non-transparent and systematic manner for years without effective legal grounds and without the possibility of independent control by public data protection supervisory authorities constitutes a violation of fundamental European principles as regards data protection and is not in accordance with Belgian and European law. An existing international framework is already available with regard to the fight against terrorism. The possibilities already offered there should be exploited while ensuring the required level of protection of fundamental rights.

Following negotiations between the Commission and the United States Department of the Treasury, the United States offered a number of undertakings regarding the controls which would be imposed over the use of any data obtained from SWIFT.[34] These included the statements that:

> The program contains multiple, overlapping layers of governmental and independent controls to ensure that the data, which are limited in nature, are searched only for counterterrorism purposes and that all data are maintained in a secure environment and properly handled.
>
> ...
>
> The SWIFT data are maintained in a secure physical environment, stored separately from any other data, and the computer systems have high-level intrusion controls and other protections to limit access to the data solely as described herein. No copies of

---

[33] Opinion 10/2006 'On the processing of personal data by the Society for Worldwide Interbank Financial Telecommunication (SWIFT)'. Available from <http://ec.europa.eu/justice_home/fsj/privacy/docs/wpdocs/2006/wp128_en.pdf>

[34] OJ 2007 C166/18.

SWIFT data are made, other than for disaster recovery back-up purposes. Access to the data and the computer equipment are limited to persons with appropriate security clearances. Even among such persons, access to the SWIFT data is on a read-only basis and is limited through the TFTP on a strict need-to-know basis to analysts dedicated to the investigation of terrorism and to persons involved in the technical support, management, and oversight of the TFTP.

In order to allay European concerns it was suggested that:

As a sign of our commitment and partnership in combating global terrorism, an eminent European person will be appointed to confirm that the program is implemented consistent with these Representations for the purpose of verifying the protection of EU-originating personal data. In particular, the eminent person will monitor that processes for deletion of non-extracted data have been carried out.

The eminent person will have appropriate experience and security clearances, and will be appointed for a renewable period of two years by the European Commission in consultation with the Treasury Department. The eminent person shall act in complete independence in the performance of his or her duties. The eminent person shall, in the performance of his or her duties, neither seek nor take instructions from anybody. The eminent person shall refrain from any action incompatible with his or her duties under this appointment.

The eminent person will report his or her findings and conclusions annually in writing to the Commission. The Commission in turn will report to the European Parliament and the Council as appropriate.

In response, the Commission agreed that:

Once SWIFT and the financial institutions making use of its services have completed the necessary arrangements to respect EC law, in particular through the provision of information that personal data will be transferred for commercial purposes to the United States and, as regards SWIFT, the respect of the 'Safe Harbour' principles, subject to lawful access by the US Treasury Department, SWIFT and the said financial institutions will be in compliance with their respective legal responsibilities under European data protection law.

Further organsiational changes have also been announced, with a further SWIFT operating centre due to open in Switzerland in 2009 to process inter-Eropean messages, obviating any need for these to be held in the United States.[35]

Air passenger data

The handling of data relating to airline passengers was included in the safe harbor agreement and provides a basis for the transfer of passenger information for the purposes of transportation.[36] It has subsequently been the subject of a further agreement between the EU and the United States in the context of transfers of passenger name record (PNR)

---

[35] <http://ec.europa.eu/justice_home/fsj/privacy/news/docs/pr_11_10_07_en.pdf>
[36] FAQ 13.

data to the United States Department of Homeland Security in connection with its anti-terrorism activities. The basis for the agreement lay in a decision by the United States that it would refuse to allow airplanes to enter its airspace unless information concerning all passengers had previously been made available to its authorities. Such data would invariably class as personal data under the Data Protection Directive and, insofar as it could relate to dietary requirements or the need for medical asssistance, could be classed as sensitive personal data. Such transfers would not be sanctioned under the Directive.

Following extensive political negotiations, two Commission Decisions were published in May 2004: the first declaring that an agreement had been reached on the transfer of PNR data and describing its terms; and the second declaring that in the light of undertakings provided by the Department of Homeland Security:

> For the purposes of Article 25(2) of Directive 95/46/EC, the United States' Bureau of Customs and Border Protection (hereinafter referred to as CBP) is considered to ensure an adequate level of protection for PNR data transferred from the Community concerning flights to or from the United States, in accordance with the Undertakings set out in the Annex.

Promulgation of the decisions was controversial within Europe. The Article 29 Working Party had issued a number of critical opinions, although recognising that 'ultimately political judgements will be needed'.[37] Parliament had also expressed opposition, and upon the Decisions being adopted, raised proceedings before the European Court of Justice, seeking the anulment of both measures. In June 2006, the court handed down its judgment in *Parliament v Council*.[38] This declared the Decision to be invalid on the grounds that it had been adopted under an inappropriate article of the Treaty of Rome. The treaty justification for the measure was stated to lie in Article 95, which refers to the functioning of the internal market, an argument which was accepted by the court. In respect of the decision relating to the finding of adequacy, this was grounded in Article 25(6) of the Data Protection Directive but it was held that the subject-matter of the decision was outtside the Directive's scope, Article 3(2) declaring that the measure did not extend to processing:

> in the course of an activity which falls outside the scope of Community law, such as those provided for by Titles V and VI of the Treaty on European Union and in any case to processing operations concerning public security, defence, State security (including the economic well-being of the State when the processing operation relates to State security matters) and the activities of the State in areas of criminal law.

Again, the finding was that the decision should be annuled on the grounds of a lack of legislative competence.

Although the court found in favour of the Parliament, it ruled that 'it appears justified, for reasons of legal certainty and in order to protect the persons concerned,

---

[37] Opinion 4/2003. 'On the Level of Protection ensured in the United States for the Transfer of Passengers' Data'. <Available from http://ec.europa.eu/justice_home/fsj/privacy/docs/wpdocs/2003/wp78_en.pdf>

[38] Joined Cases C-317/04 and C-318/04.

to preserve the effect of the decision on adequacy' for the period of time that would have been required were the EU to have given notice of termination. This continued the validity of the agreement until the end of September 2006. A further short-term agreement was reached in October 2006 to cover the period up until July 2007. On 23 July 2007, a further agreement 'between the European Union and the United States of America on the processing and transfer of Passenger Name Record (PNR) data by air carriers to the United States Department of Homeland Security (DHS) (2007 PNR Agreement),[39] was signed. This indicated that:

> For the application of this Agreement, DHS is deemed to ensure an adequate level of protection for PNR data transferred from the European Union.

On the same day, Council Decision 2007/551/CFSP/JHA[40] was adopted. Based now on Articles 24 and 38 of the Treaty of Rome, this provided that the terms of the Agreement were to enter into force.

As with previous agreements, priovision is made for the United States authorities to access a range of items of passenger data relating to identity and itinerary, together with information as to frequent flier status and details of the method of payment, including details of any credit cards used. As originally agreed, this data would be collecetd on what is referred to as a 'pull system', whereby the United States authorities are enabled to asccess the airline's computer systems and collect the required information. This approach has been the cause of criticism within Europe and the 2007 agreement provides that the:

> DHS will immediately transition to a push system for the transmission of data by such air carriers no later than 1 January 2008 for all such air carriers that have implemented such a system that complies with DHS's technical requirements. For those air carriers that do not implement such a system, the current systems shall remain in effect until the carriers have implemented a system that complies with DHS's technical requirements. Accordingly, DHS will electronically access the PNR from air carriers' reservation systems located within the territory of the Member States of the European Union until there is a satisfactory system in place allowing for the transmission of such data by the air carriers.

The 2007 agreement seems likely to be no less controversial than its predecessors. It has been subjected to perhaps unprecedented criticism by the Article 29 Working Party. Although the Working Party was not consulted prior to the conclusion of the agreement, in an Opinion published in August 2007,[41] it expressed dissatisfaction:

> that the opportunity to have adopted a more balanced approach based upon real need has been missed. While there has been much comment on the new agreement, the

---

[39] OJ 2007 L204/18.

[40] OJ 2007 L204/16.

[41] Opinion 5/2007 on the follow-up agreement between the European Union and the United States of America on the processing and transfer of passenger name record (PNR) data by air carriers to the United States Department of Homeland Security concluded in July 2007. Available from <http://ec.europa.eu/justice_home/fsj/privacy/docs/wpdocs/2007/wp138_en.pdf>

Working Party would have wished for a different outcome of the EU–US negotiations and feels that the new agreement does not strike the right balance to uphold the fundamental rights of citizens as regards data protection.

It concluded that:

the new PNR agreement contains some minor improvements in comparison with the previous accord but it is clearly disappointed at the inadequate data protection standard of the new PNR agreement. The new agreement does not even preserve the level of privacy protection of the previous agreement which was already considered weak by the Working Party in its previous opinions.

The new PNR agreement as analysed in this opinion does not compare favourably with accepted data protection standards, such as those of Convention 108 and of the Directive. It will cause understandable concern for all transatlantic travellers who are worried about their privacy rights.

It may be noted that a less extensive agreement[42] on the transfer of PNR data to the Canadian Authorities received a positive opinion from the Article 29 Working Party.[43]

Consequences of a finding of adequacy

In the event a finding of adequacy is made, the Member States must allow transfers to the third country.[44] The law of a number of Member States continues to require, however, that prior permission must be sought from the data protection authorities, an approach which has been criticised by the Commission on the grounds of inconsistency:

with Chapter IV of the Directive, which aims at guaranteeing both adequate protection and flows of personal data to third countries without unnecessary burdens. Notifications to national supervisory authorities may be required under Article 19, but notifications cannot be turned into de facto authorisations in those cases where the transfer to a third country is clearly permitted either in all cases or in the situation where the law of recipient country does not guarantee an adequate level of protection.[45]

Of the thirty states which are members of the European Economic Area, fifteen—Austria, Bulgaria, Cyprus, Estonia, France, Greece, Iceland, Latvia, Lichtenstein, Lithuania, Malta, the Netherlands, Romania, Slovenia, and Spain—require some degree of prior notification.[46] The controls vary significantly in extent. In some states such as Austria, it is provided that prior permission must be sought from the data protection authorities for all data flows outwith the EEA.[47] In other countries, there may be a requirement to

---

[42] *Official Journal*, 2006 L91/49.

[43] Opinion 1 of 2005, available from L 82/14.

[44] Article 25(6).

[45] As defined by the Commission of the European Communities and discussed more extensively below.

[46] <http://ec.europa.eu/justice_home/fsj/privacy/docs/modelcontracts/sec_2006_95_en.pdf>

[47] Section 13 of the Federal Act Concerning the Processing of Personal Data.

notify the supervisory authority, whilst in others such as the United Kingdom, there are no procedural requirements to notify the Information Commissioner.

The discrepancy between national approaches has been the cause of criticism of national laws by the European Commission, which has argued that this results in 'an inability to audit compliance with the principles relating to transborder data flows'.[48]

> An overly lax attitude in some Member States—in addition to being in contravention of the Directive—risks weakening protection in the EU as a whole, because with the free movement guaranteed by the Directive, data flows are likely to switch to the 'least burdensome' point of export. An overly strict approach, on the other hand, would fail to respect the legitimate needs of international trade and the reality of global tele-communications networks and risks creating a gap between law and practice which is damaging for the credibility of the Directive and for Community law in general.

It has been commented further that:

> it would appear that pending such a formal determination, individual controllers can make this assessment for themselves, and can therefore decide to transfer data to third countries with regard to which there is no formal domestic or European finding of adequacy, if they have come to the conclusion that the country in question ensures an adequate level of protection.[49]

This certainly appears to be an accurate portrait of the system operating in the United Kingdom.

Transfers when an adequate level of protection is not provided

Even allowing for the inclusion of those organisations from the United States, which are party to 'safe harbor', only a very small number of countries have been determined to provide an adequate level of protection. Alternative mechanisms require to be found therefore to legitimise data transfers with the rest of the world, whilst ensuring that the interests of European data subjects are safeguarded. Having laid down a prohibition against data transfers in Article 25, the Directive's Article 26 is headed 'Derogations' and proceeds to lay down a number of situations in which Member States must permit transfers and a further set of situations in which the Member States may authorise transfers. In respect of the first situation, it is provided that transfers are to be permitted when:

(a) the data subject has given his consent unambiguously to the proposed transfer; or

(b) the transfer is necessary for the performance of a contract between the data subject and the controller or the implementation of pre-contractual measures taken in response to the data subject's request; or

---

[48] <http://ec.europa.eu/justice_home/fsj/privacy/docs/modelcontracts/sec_2006_95_en.pdf>

[49] Analysis and impact study on the implementation of Directive EC 95/46 in Member States. Available from <http://ec.europa.eu/justice_home/fsj/privacy/docs/lawreport/consultation/technical-annex_en.pdf>

(c) the transfer is necessary for the conclusion or performance of a contract concluded in the interest of the data subject between the controller and a third party; or

(d) the transfer is necessary or legally required on important public interest grounds, or for the establishment, exercise or defence of legal claims; or

(e) the transfer is necessary in order to protect the vital interests of the data subject; or

(f) the transfer is made from a register which according to laws or regulations is intended to provide information to the public and which is open to consultation either by the public in general or by any person who can demonstrate legitimate interest to the extent that the conditions laid down in law for consultation are fulfilled in the particular case.[50]

In the main, the Act's wording follows that of the Data Protection Directive, but there is a divergence in respect of the exception relating to subject consent. Whilst the Directive requires unambiguous consent, the Act refers merely to the fact that 'the data subject has given his consent to the transfer'.[51] The Act also confers regulatory power on the Secretary of State to define more closely the circumstances under which transfers may, or may not, take place 'for reasons of substantial public interest'.[52]

Substantial guidance concerning the interpretation of the Article 26(1) exceptions has been provided by the Article 29 Working Party in its 'Working document on a common interpretation of Article 26(1)'.[53] This confirms that the provisions of Article 26(1) constitute exceptions from the general principle that data can be transferred only under conditions that will ensure adequacy. As exceptions, they are to be construed narrowly. Referring to the possibilities for providing adequate protection listed in Article 26(2), the Working Party comments:

> The Working Party would find it regrettable that a multinational company or a public authority would plan to make significant transfers of data to a third country without providing an appropriate framework for the transfer, when it has the practical means of providing such protection.

Particularly relevant in this context are the use of contractual provisions and, a more recent development, the concept of adopting binding corporate rules.

The role of contract

The Data Protection Directive provides that:

> ...a Member State may authorize a transfer or a set of transfers or personal data to a third country which does not ensure an adequate level of protection—where the

---

[50] Article 26(1).

[51] The nature of these provisions is similar to those of the Schedule 2 conditions legitimizing the processing of personal data.

[52] Schedule 4, para. 4(2).

[53] WP114, available from <http://ec.europa.eu/justice_home/fsj/privacy/docs/wpdocs/2005/wp114_en.pdf>

controller adduces adequate safeguards with respect to the protection of the privacy and fundamental rights and freedoms of individuals and as regards the exercise of the corresponding rights; such safeguards may in particular result from appropriate contractual clauses.[54]

Any exercise of this power must be reported to the Commission and the other Member States. If any party so informed objects 'on justified measures involving the protection of the privacy and the fundamental rights and freedoms of individuals', a proposal for action may be tabled before the Committee by the Commission and, if approved, will require the Member State involved to take necessary measures to conform.[55]

In implementing this provision, the Data Protection Act 1998 provides in Schedule 4 that transfers will be acceptable when they are:

- Made on terms which are of a kind approved by the Commissioner as ensuring adequate safeguards for the rights and freedoms of data subjects.[56]

- Authorised by the Commissioner as being made in such a manner as to ensure adequate safeguards for the rights and freedoms of data subjects.[57]

Although the Act provides[58] for notification of approvals to be transmitted to the Commission this has not happened to any extent. In its first report on the implementation of the Data Protection Directive,[59] the Commission comments:

National authorities are supposed to notify the Commission when they authorise transfers under Article 26 (2) of the Directive. Since the Directive came into operation in 1998, the Commission has received only a very limited number of such notifications. Although there are other legal transfer routes apart from Article 26 (2), this number is derisory by comparison with what might reasonably be expected. Combined with other evidence pointing in the same direction, this suggests that many unauthorised and possibly illegal transfers are being made to destinations or recipients not guaranteeing adequate protection. Yet there is little or no sign of enforcement actions by the supervisory authorities.

In spite of a Commission Notice sent to the Member States in 2003 urging more extensive notification, matters do not seem to have changed significantly. In 2006, a Commission Staff Working Document noted that:

...the number of notifications received by the Commission services pursuant to Article 26 (3) of the Directive over the last four years is extremely limited: only 78 notifications from seven Member States (the Netherlands (34), Spain (20), Germany (14), Finland (5), Portugal (2), Austria (2) and Belgium (1). In addition, most of these

---

[54] Directive 95/46/EC, Article 26(2).
[55] Article 26(3).
[56] Schedule 4, para. 8.
[57] Schedule 4, para. 9.
[58] Section 54(7).
[59] COM/2003/0265 final, available from <http://eur-lex.europa.eu/LexUriServ/LexUriServ.do?uri=CELEX:52003DC0265:EN:NOT>

notifications concern the use of standard contractual clauses which, as outlined above, are not covered by the notifying obligation.

Since the Directive entered into force in October 1998, the Commission has not received any notifications from the United Kingdom, France, Italy, Ireland, Greece, Sweden or Luxembourg. None of the new ten Member States has yet notified the use of contractual clauses or other adequate safeguards to the Commission.[60]

Authorisation may be given under the above provisions on an individual basis, but may also make reference to the controller's adherence to model contractual terms and conditions. There appears to be a general acceptance that the volume of transborder data flows is such that it is undersirable for decisions as to acceptability to require to be made in the context of individual transfers, and that more general provisions should be laid down.

The Article 29 Working Party produced a report in April 1998, outlining its 'preliminary views on the use of contractual terms in the context of transfers of personal data to third countries'.[61] This document identified a number of elements that must be found in any relevant contract. The contract must provide for observance of the data protection principles. Whilst it was recognised that no system could provide a total assurance of compliance, it would be required that the provisions should provide a reasonable level of assurance, should provide support and assistance for data subjects, and appropriate forms of redress.

Subsequent to the report of the Working Party, proposals for decisions on two sets of contracts, one for transfers between two data controllers and one for transfers between European data controllers and external data processors, were brought forward by the Commission. These were the subject of further Article 29 Working Party opinions in 2001;[62] two Decisions were adopted by the Commission in 2001 and 2002, and Decision 2001/497/EC on Standard Contractual Clauses for the transfer of personal data to controllers in third countries was adopted in June 2001.[63] This required Member States to accept transfers conducted under its terms (i.e. using the standard form contract within the Decision) as satisfying the requirements of adequacy.[64] Decision 2002/16/EC[65] contained standard contract terms relevant to the situation where an EU-based data controller wishes to transfer data to a processor established in a third country.

The annex to both Decisions lays out a set of standard terms. Beyond customisation with the identifying details of the parties, these may not be changed or amended in any way whatsoever. This has been regarded in some quarters as an overly prescriptive

---

[60] SEC (2006) 95. available from <http://ec.europa.eu/justice_home/fsj/privacy/docs/modelcontracts/sec_2006_95_en.pdf>

[61] WP 9, available from <http://ec.europa.eu/justice_home/fsj/privacy/docs/wpdocs/1998/wp9_en.pdf.>

[62] Opinion 1/2001 and 7/2001, available from <http://ec.europa.eu/justice_home/fsj/privacy/workinggroup/wpdocs/2001_en.htm>

[63] OJ 2001 L 181/19.

[64] Article 1.

[65] OJ 2002 L6/52.

approach but in common with any legal documents, it may be virtually impossible to know whether any change might have major or minor implications.

Clause 2 provides for identification of the parties and the nature of the transfer, and Appendix 1 provides a form in which these details may be provided. Clause 3 provides that third parties are to be able to enforce the contract—possibly assisted by a consumer protection agency. The possibility of third-party enforcement of contractual obligations had long been a stumbling block for the use of such contracts under English law. The Contracts (Rights of Third Parties) Act 1999 now provides a mechanism for such enforcement.

The model contract lays down in some detail the nature and extent of the obligations which are to be accepted by the data exporter and importer. The former is to warrant that the data has been processed in accordance with any relevant European data protection law up until the time the export takes place. If the data constitutes sensitive personal data, the subject is to be informed before the transfer of the fact that the legal system of the importer might not guarantee an adequate level of protection. Copies of the contract clauses are to be made available to data subjects and the exporter is to respond to any reasonable requests from its supervisory agency or from a data subject concerning the processing to be carried out on the data.

For the importing controller, it is required that an undertaking be given that the controller has no knowledge that any provisions of its domestic law will prevent fulfilment of obligations accepted under the contract. The processing is to be carried out in accord with a set of mandatory data protection principles specified in the model contract. These effectively provide for measures equivalent to those found in the Directive (and also the Article 29 Working Party's WP12 on assessing adequacy), regarding matters such as limitations on the purpose of processing, the accuracy, and up-to-date nature of data, the availability of subject access, etc). The importer undertakes to cooperate with requests for information from data subjects and relevant European supervisory agencies and also to submit its facilities for audit by the data exported or a professionally qualified inspection agency selected by the exporter.

One of the most contentious provisions in the model contract is Clause 6, which provides that the parties are to accept joint and several liability for any breaches of the contract. The effect of this is that a data subject could choose to take action, either against the contracting parties jointly or hold either party solely liable. Given the problems of raising legal proceedings in a foreign jurisdiction or against a foreign party, the consequence might be that the data exporter may well be targeted by an aggrieved data subject as the sole object of any claim for compensation, even though any culpability might lie with the data importer.

The initial model contracts were criticized by some business interests as being cumbersome, inflexible, and out of touch with business needs. Recital 10 of the Decisions states that:

> The Commission will also consider in the future whether standard contractual clauses submitted by business organisations or other interested parties offer adequate safeguards in accordance with Directive 95/46/EC.

A new set of standard contractual clauses for data transfers was proposed by seven international business associations: the American Chamber of Commerce to the European Union in Brussels (AmCham EU); the Confederation of British Industry (CBI); the European Information and Communications Technology Association (EICTA); the Federation of European Direct and Interactive Marketing (FEDMA); the International Chamber of Commerce (ICC); the International Communication Round Table (ICRT); and the Japan Business Council in Europe (JBCE).

Following negotiations between these associations and the Commission Working Party, a new set of model contracts was approved by the Commission by Decision 2004/915. These sit alongside the initial contracts, with businesses being offered a choice between the two formulations. Welcoming the new Decision the then Single Market Commissioner, Charlie McCreevy, was quoted as saying:

> This is a good example of regulating in cooperation with business. The business community has shown a serious commitment towards data protection and the Commission has carefully listened to business needs. That is good for EU citizens, whose privacy is better protected, and for our companies, whose competitiveness is reinforced.

Commenting on an earlier draft of the terms,[66] the Article 29 Working Party was perhaps less enthusiastic, although still broadly supportive of the initiative:

> The Working Party has doubts that the current proposals satisfy these conditions fully. It also has doubts that these clauses are easier to use by economic operators. The same business associations that criticised the Commission's standard contractual clauses in 2001 as 'unworkable' do not seem to have found better wording for many clauses and when the proposals deviate from Decision 497/2001/CE, the result is not necessarily clearer but rather more uncertain in legal terms.

In a set of frequently asked questions on the Model Contracts, the Commission suggests that:

> Both sets of clauses provide for a similar level of data protection, in other words, individuals are similarly protected by both sets on the basis of the same (adequate) data protection standards and principles. Differences between both sets are mainly of a technical nature (for example, the conditions under which a data protection authority may carry out an audit in the data importer's premises) or related to the differences in the system of liability already explained above.

Perhaps the major variation between the contracts is in respect of the issue of liability. The 2004 contracts state that:

(a) Each party shall be liable to the other parties for damages it causes by any breach of these clauses... Each party shall be liable to data subjects for damages it causes by any breach of third party rights under these clauses. This does not affect the liability of the data exporter under its data protection law.

---

[66] Opinion 8/2003, available from <http://ec.europa.eu/justice_home/fsj/privacy/docs/wpdocs/2003/wp84_en.pdf>

(b) …In cases involving allegations of breach by the data importer, the data subject must first request the data exporter to take appropriate action to enforce his rights against the data importer; if the data exporter does not take such action within a reasonable period (which under normal circumstances would be one month), the data subject may then enforce his rights against the data importer directly. A data subject is entitled to proceed directly against a data exporter that has failed to use reasonable efforts to determine that the data importer is able to satisfy its legal obligations under these clauses (the data exporter shall have the burden to prove that it took reasonable efforts).

Although certainly more favourable towards the business parties involved, it is difficult to see that the provision affords the same level of protection to data subjects as that provided for under the 2001 contract.

Binding corporate rules

Whilst the conclusion of contracts, whether using the Commission's model contracts or a formulation devised by the parties themselves may provide an appropriate solution to the requirements of many data controllers, difficulties have been identified in the situation where multinational organisations operate in a wide range of countries and require to exchange personal data between the legal entities operating in the different countries. A contractual solution here might create a spaghetti forest of agreements between all possible permutations of national legal entities. Although it is possible under the contractual approach to have a single master agreement which is signed by a range of parties, this approach, with a requirement that details of all transfers be recorded, would be difficult to apply in what may well be an organisation subject to continual change and development.

In response to this situation, the Article 29 Working Party has developed the concept of binding corporate rules as an alternative mechanism for demonstrating that data will receive an adequate level of protection. Working Paper 74, applying Article26 (2) of the EU Data Protection Directive to Binding Corporate Rules for International Data Transfers,[67] was published in 2003 and lays down the basic principles which should be found in such rules.The Working Paper is supplemented by a Checklist published in 2004[68] and Recommendation 1 of 2007 containing a 'Standard Application for Approval of Binding Corporate Rules for the Transfer of Personal Data'.[69] As with all methods for ensuring adequacy, the notion of binding corporate rules seeks to ensure that processing takes place under conditions broadly equivalent to those laid down in the data protection principles. In terms of procedural aspects, the requirement is that one member of the undertaking should be given powers and responsibilities to ensure that the rules are observed throughout the organisation. This member must

---

[67] Available from <http://ec.europa.eu/justice_home/fsj/privacy/docs/wpdocs/2003/wp74_en.pdf>

[68] Available from <http://ec.europa.eu/justice_home/fsj/privacy/docs/wpdocs/2004/wp101_en.pdf>

[69] Available from <http://ec.europa.eu/justice_home/fsj/privacy/workinggroup/wpdocs/2007_en.htm>

be located in the EU and will be responsible for seeking approval of the rules from a relevant supervisory agency. In many cases, multinational corporations will be operating in a wide range of EU states, and the Working Paper suggests that supervisory agencies should make use of the cooperation procedures established under Article 28 of the Data Protection Directive to enable a request for approval to be made to only one supervisory agency and, if granted, to be valid throughout all Member States.

Conclusions

The activities described above indicate perhaps how complex is the task of applying national or regional rules regarding data protection in a situation where processing may take place anywhere on the planet. In February 2007, it was widely reported that Google, the world's most widely used search engine, was calling upon the UN to intervene to help protect the privacy of web users.[70]

Given much recent controversy concerning aspects of Googles' own practices, including its data retention policy and its publication on 'Google Street Views'[71] of images of individuals taken without their knowledge or consent, this may seem a classic instance of a poacher turning gamekeeper. As the discussions concerning the concept of binding corporate rules does indicate, organisations operating on a global basis may find it easier to work on the basis of consistent global standards, even though these may place restrictions on their ability to process data in an unrestricted manner. To date, the UN's involvement in the data/privacy protection field has been somewhat peripheral. The Google plea for activity was also addressed to the OECD and certainly this agency has been much more active in the field. In a Ministerial Declaration on the Protection of Privacy on Global Networks on this, the ministers reaffirmed:

> their commitment to the protection of privacy on global networks in order to ensure the respect of important rights, build confidence in global networks, and to prevent unnecessary restrictions on transborder flows of personal data.
>
> They will work to build bridges between the different approaches adopted by Member countries to ensure privacy protection on global networks based on the OECD Guidelines.

In June 2007, the OECD adopted a Recommendation on Cross-border Co-operation in the Enforcement of Laws Protecting Privacy.[72] In its introductory sections, the Recommendation indicates why action was considered necessary:

> When personal information moves across borders it may put at increased risk the ability of individuals to exercise privacy rights to protect themselves from the unlawful use or disclosure of that information. At the same time, the authorities charged with enforcing privacy laws may find that they are unable to pursue complaints or

---

[70] See, for example, <http://www.guardian.co.uk/technology/2007/sep/14/news.google>

[71] <http://maps.google.com/help/maps/streetview/>

[72] Available from <http://www.oecd.org/dataoecd/43/28/38770483.pdf>

conduct investigations relating to the activities of organisations outside their borders. Their efforts to work together in the cross-border context may also be hampered by insufficient preventative or remedial powers, inconsistent legal regimes, and practical obstacles like resource constraints. In this context, a consensus has emerged on the need to promote closer co-operation among privacy law enforcement authorities to help them exchange information and carry out investigations with their foreign counterparts.

The Recommendation continues to indicate that Member States should act to ensure that 'Privacy Enforcement Authorities' are both empowered and obliged to cooperate with other national authorities. It is suggested that a national point of contact should be established in each Member State to facilitate cross-border requests for assistance.

Initially, international transfers generally took the form of couriering or posting packages containing discs or tapes. In the modern networked world, online transfers are the norm. With modern forms of electronic communications, national or even supra-national boundaries are of limited significance and the European Union's attempt to control the flow of data has drawn comparison with the early English King Canute's attempt to order the incoming tide to retreat. The Canute legend, of course, is susceptible of at least two explanations. One refers to the folly of a monarch who believed that he could control the forces of nature and was surprised when he got his feet wet. A second, and more complex explanation, sees the exercise as a considered attempt to demonstrate to over-deferential subjects the limits of what human authority can and cannot do. In this second case, any folly lies more with those who seek to ascribe human agencies with almighty powers and are disappointed when perfection proves to be an unattainable goal. The fact that data protection legislation cannot prevent all forms of malpractice is no reason for not attempting to prevent some. Fear of the consequences of data havens was a motivating force behind much data protection legislation. Where the European model might perhaps be criticised is in substituting the notion of a European data protection heaven. The tale is sometimes told of a discussion between proponents of Rolls Royce motor cars and those of Ford (or any other mass-produced models). The former can point to the quality of build, the levels of comfort, refinement, and reliability. Whilst conceding these points, the opposing case may be that mass-produced cars offer acceptable levels of comfort, refinement, and reliability, with the additional fact that they can be afforded by most of the population. If some reduction in standards is the price to be paid for global acceptance of the importance of the need for data protection, the price may be one that is well worth paying.

Suggestions for further reading

Article 29 Working Party WP 12 (1998); and WP74 (2003).

Commission Staff Working Document on Transborder Data Flows.

PART II

COMPUTER-RELATED CRIME

9

The phenomenon of computer-related crime

Introduction

It appears an inevitable feature of technological developments that criminal applications follow legitimate uses with only a very short time lag. The computer has proved no exception to the rule. The first instances of computer-related crime date back to the 1960s, with the topic beginning to attract the attention of academic and industrial commentators from the early 1970s. Today, just as legitimate computer-based activities penetrate most aspects of life, at least according to much of the media, the Internet and financial institutions are the constant target of fraudsters, the WWW is a haven for paedophiles and pornographers, computer viruses endlessly threaten the survival of computer networks, whilst the most confidential information held on computer systems is at the mercy of the computer hacker and identity thieves. In some respects, what has happened and is happening is a switch in emphasis from using the computer as a means to commit crime or as the victim of criminal conduct, to using computer networks to constitute the environment within which criminal conduct may flourish.

It is typical to regard computer criminals as sophisticated and expert practitioners. This is not always borne out in reality. Even where crimes appear directly linked to computer technology—as is the case with hacking and the creation and dissemination of computer viruses—the element of skill involved is often limited. One of the first significant United Kingdom cases in the field is that of *R v Gold*.[1] Here, a hacker accessed the contents of an electronic information service after visiting a computer exhibition where the system was being demonstrated by an engineer. A spell of what is referred to as 'shoulder surfing' enabled the password details to be memorised, a task made easier by the fact that it consisted of the letter 'A' repeated several times. With computer viruses, there has been the emergence of websites which:

> contain downloadable prepared viruses, worms and Trojans. These 'point and click' attack tools have removed the need for detailed knowledge of computer code

---

[1] [1988] 1 AC 1063.

programming, and have allowed a new breed of much younger hackers, nicknamed Script Kiddies to develop.[2]

The phenomenon of deskilling is clearly not limited to more legitimate forms of employment!

This chapter will outline the major forms of computer-related crime and give an overview of the most significant national and international legal responses to these. The following chapters will consider the nature and extent of key legal provisions in rather more detail.

The United Kingdom's National Criminal Intelligence Service (NCIS) published a report in 2003 called *United Kingdom Threat Assessment of Serious and Organised Crime*.[3] This set out to identify the environment within which high-technology crime may take place. This was defined as involving 'networked computers and Internet technology'. Tools and techniques, it is suggested, can either be 'misused criminally or used legitimately in support of criminal activity'. The former scenario might see the creation of a computer virus, whilst the use of email as a communication channel to plot the commission of a bank robbery would be an example of the latter. With such a broad-ranging approach it is not surprising that the report suggests that:

> The range of crimes that can be committed, either through or with the support of hi-tech tools and techniques is limited only by the imagination and capability of the criminals.[4]

Insofar as conduct clearly has criminal connotations there are few issues of legal significance. The NCIS report refers to the 'new tools, old crimes' phenomonen. Two propositions may initially be put forward for consideration:

- Where conduct would be regarded as criminal in the absence of a computer, it should be criminal where a computer is involved.

- Where conduct is not criminal in the absence of a computer, the involvement of the computer should not change that result.

In the former situation, what may be required is for any lacunae in the coverage of legislation to be eliminated. An example of this, which will be discussed in more detail below, concerns the question of whether the offence of obtaining services by deception could be committed where the perpetrator's only contact was with a computer. At a perhaps more threoretical level, the increasing popularity of virtual reality environments raises questions of whether an individual's virtual persona can be the victim of assault or whether virtual property garnered in the course of a virtual reality game could form the subject-matter of theft. In the event gaps are identified in the coverage of the criminal law, one further question is whether reform should take the form of adopting computer-specific legislation or whether amendment should be made to general legal principles.

---

[2] United Kingdom Threat Assessment of Serious and Organised Crime. Copies of the report are available from <http://www.ncis.co.uk/ukta/2003/default.asp>

[3] Copies of the report are available from <http://www.ncis.co.uk/ukta/2003/default.asp>

[4] Para. 8.1 at <http://www.ncis.co.uk/ukta/2003/default.asp>

The second situation is more problematic. At first glance, it is difficult to disagree with the proposition, but the issue has arisen in the context of hacking where a decision has to be made whether to criminalise the mere act of obtaining unauthorised access to data or whether some further act is required. The Council of Europe's Convention on Cybercrime, which again will be considered in more detail below, instructs its signatory states to the effect that:

> Each Party shall adopt such legislative and other measures as may be necessary to establish as criminal offences under its domestic law, when committed intentionally, the access to the whole or any part of a computer system without right. A Party may require that the offence be committed by infringing security measures, with the intent of obtaining computer data or other dishonest intent, or in relation to a computer system that is connected to another computer system.

In most cases, obtaining unauthorised access to information will not be a criminal offence unless it is obtained through some form of burglary or involves the taking away of documents. For a variety of reasons, many computer crime laws, including those in the United Kingdom, provide that unauthorised access, per se, will be unlawful in the computer context.

A further issue concerns the nature of the computer environment. With increasing processing power, as any film viewer will be aware, computers are able to generate more and more spectacular and lifelike images. Many modern films, such as the *Lord of the Rings*, rely for a great deal of their visual impact upon computer-generated images. The capacity of the computer to process and manipulate images has raised questions in the context of child pornography. Originally, criminal sanctions were applied to the taking or possession of photographs. Making or possessing a drawing would not generally be unlawful. The concept of 'pseudo photograph' is now used to criminalise computer-generated or processed images.

Prior to considering the legal treatment of computer-related conduct, it might be helpful to provide an account of the major forms of activity involved. Any scheme of categorisation has elements of subjectivity and in many instances, a course of conduct will involve a range of activities. A hacker might, for example, seek to obtain access to credit card details, use these to obtain goods or services and, in the attempt to conceal details of the activity, seek to delete records from the victim computer system. Recognising the limitations of the approach, examination will be made below of the concepts of computer fraud, computer hacking, and damage to data.

Forms of computer-related crime

Computer fraud

As in real life, one of the major categories of computer-related crime involves the attempt to secure some form of unauthorised and unwarranted financial benefit. Given that banks and other financial institutions were amongst the first large-scale computer users in the private sector, it is not surprising that much early attention was paid to this aspect of the topic. One of the first cases cited as an instance of computer fraud involved the Equity Funding Corporation in the United States. In its essentials, the fraud was comparatively simple, with the directors and senior staff of an insurance company engaging in a sustained and substantial scheme of embezzlement. Equity Funding operated in the so-called reinsurance sector, and when it issued new policies, would transfer them to other insurers in return for an upfront payment of part of the premiums which would be received over the life of the policy. Equity Funding would then have to make annual payments to the other insurer. In effect, they would obtain an immediate financial benefit at the expense of incurring ongoing financial commitments. Having stolen money from the company, the fraudsters used the company's computers to generate records of fictitious life insurance policies which were then sold on to other insurance companies. The fraud was assisted by the fact that auditors and regulators accepted computer printouts as definitive evidence of policies and did not ask to see original documentation. As with all schemes of this nature, the fraud ultimately spiralled out of control and by the time the fraud was discovered, some 64,000 out of 97,000 policies allegedly issued by the company were false. Perhaps unrealistically, it was calculated that if the scheme had continued for another five years, fictitious policies would have had to be created for every man, woman, and child living in the United States.[5]

Early computers, such as those used in Equity Funding were massive devices which could only be operated by persons in direct physical proximity to the machine. Beginning in the 1970s, communications capabilities began to be installed, allowing computers to be accessed and operated remotely. With the development of global communications networks, computer fraud—as with other forms of computer-related crime—is increasingly adopting an international dimension. In one case,[6] banking computers located in the United States were penetrated by hackers located in St Petersburg, accounts belonging to a company from Indonesia were fraudulently debited and the proceeds diverted to accounts in Finland, Germany, Israel, the Netherlands, and the United States. One of the individuals suspected of involvement in the scheme was subsequently arrested at Stansted Airport in England and extradition proceedings were initiated by the United States. Not surprisingly, extradition proceedings proved prolonged and protracted, with the key questions being concerned with the issue of when and where offences were committed.

Attempts to target directly financial instutions are relatively rare. With customers increasingly engaging in online banking, these are seen as the weak link and as the bank's own security may increase, customers more and more become the target for attempts at fraud. One of the highest profile forms of conduct is that of identity theft. In November 2007, massive publicity was given to the loss of data concerning some 25 million United Kingdom residents when two CDs were lost in transit between the

---

[5] The case has been widely reported. A useful account is to be found in A. R. D. Norman, *Computer Insecurity* (London, 1983), p. 119.

[6] *Re Levin* [1997] QB 65. The case is discussed in more detail below.

Customs and Revenue Service and the National Audit Office. Other instances may operate on a smaller scale but the intent of would-be identity thieves is to garner sufficient information about individuals to be able to use it to obtain goods or services, such as loans or credit cards, masquerading as another individual. Social networking sites such as Facebook can prove a valuable resource for would-be identity thieves. Generally, it has been suggested, users are blissfully unaware of the sensitivity of the data which they are uploading and its potential utility to those with criminal implications. Items such as an email address, date of birth, marital status, and occupation are frequently supplied, all items that could be invaluable to an identity thief.[7]

Once again, this may represent a case of people taking all too little care to protect themselves. Very frequently, the names of pets or children are used as passwords for even sensitive purposes and a brief perusal of a social networking site may provide a fraudster with much of the material needed to obtain unauthorised access.

As with almost all elements of fraud, it is impossible to assess exactly the scale of the problem. In 2002, a study carried out for the Cabinet Office[8] estimated annual losses of £1.3 billion. A follow-up study published in February 2006 increased this figure to £1.7 billion.[9] Research commissioned by Sainsbury's Bank and published in December 2006 estimated that 4.1 million United Kingdom citizens had been the victim of identity theft. The average loss associated with each theft was put at just over £3,000,[10] although in the majority of cases the loss would have been borne by a financial institution rather than the individuals concerned. A study commissioned for the Association of Chief Police Officers reported in 2007 that:

> Over three-quarters of victims had experienced more than one offence against them (though this may have been why they ended up registered as an identity fraud victim). Over half of the respondents spent less than 24 hours rectifying the situation, significantly less than times given in US-based studies: but 11 per cent took longer than a week and given the small number of respondents, this skewed the average time to 201 hours. About a half of the victims (but fewer victims over 61 and with higher incomes) said that their experience had a big impact on their stress and health levels, and slightly more claimed that it caused them great inconvenience. Levels of inconvenience caused and impact on health or stress levels increased with the time it took to rectify the situation. When asked about personal losses, 17 per cent stated that they had suffered financial repercussions through having to pay postage, make telephone calls, or use printer ink/fuel etcetera in contacting agencies about their case and in replacing documentation.[11]

---

[7] Neil Munroe, External Affairs Director for Equifax, quoted at <http://news.bbc.co.uk/1/hi/uk/6910826.stm>

[8] Identity Fraud.

[9] <http://www.identity-theft.org.uk/ID%20fraud%20table.pdf>

[10] <http://www.vnunet.com/vnunet/news/2170720/million-uk-hit-id-theft>

[11] M. Levi, J. Burrows, M. H. Fleming, and M. Hopkins, *The Nature, Extent and Economic Impact of Fraud in the United Kingdom*, at p. 30. Available from <http://www.acpo.police.uk/asp/policies/Data/Fraud%20in%20the%20UK.pdf>

In many respects, the term 'identity fraud' is used as a generic descriptor for a range of instances of computer-related fraud. Much useful work in assessing the scale and extent of computer fraud has been conducted by the Audit Commission, which has published triennial surveys on the topic since 1981. Adopting a definition of computer fraud as any fraudulent behaviour connected with computerisation by which someone intends to gain financial advantage,[12] the reports are replete with accounts of instances of crimes. One report referred to:

> an incident at a computer centre which was responsible for printing cheques. On a Friday evening prior to a bank holiday weekend, the staff, it was reported, 'left the computer suite without any authority and in breach of regulations to go to the pub'. Whilst they were away, a theft occurred and pre-signed cheques with a value of £931,000 were stolen. The losses resulting were estimated at almost £230,000.[13]

This would be classed as identity theft as thieves would require to pass themselves off as the legitimate recipients of the cheques. It does not, however, represent use of any level of techological expertise.

Slightly more sophisticated forms of conduct involve the use of so-called 'phishing'[14] attacks. This entails sending emails to thousands of addresses at random, purporting to come from a financial institution and asking the recipient to supply personal details. A wide range of examples can be found on the BankSafe Online website.[15] It is reported that there 'were 14,156 phishing incidents targeted against United Kingdom banks and building societies in 2006, up from 1,713 in 2005'.[16]

More sophisticated still are 'Trojan Horse attacks'. These involve the attempt to install software on the victim's computer, frequently by persuading them to link to a website. In much the same manner as websites may download 'cookies' onto a computer, a site associated with a Trojan Horse will transmit a file, perhaps enabling the controller to examine the contents of the victim machine and perhaps record the user's activities in order to discover details of passwords and accounts. In total, it has been estimated that:

> In 2006 total losses for online banking fraud from scams such as phishing and Trojans reached £33.5 million; an increase of 44% from 2005.

Although substantial, these figures have to be taken in the context of an estimated loss through all forms of fraud of more than £12 billion per annum.[17]

---

[12] This definition has been utilised throughout the Audit Commission's surveys. See, for example, the 1987–90 survey, para. 7.

[13] Case 40 cited in the 1981–87 survey.

[14] The term 'phishing' comes from the analogy that the fraudsters are 'fishing' for information in the sea of Internet users and the 'ph' spelling has its origins in the hacking community when phone 'phreakers' used to manipulate telephone exchanges to gain free calls. See <http://www.banksafeonline.org.uk/faqs/faqs_1.html>

[15] <http://www.banksafeonline.org.uk/phishing_examples.html>

[16] <http://www.apacs.org.uk/resources_publications/documents/FraudtheFacts2007.pdf>

[17] *The Nature, Extent and Economic Impact of Fraud in the United Kingdom*, available at <http://www.acpo.police.uk/asp/policies/Data/Fraud%20in%20the%20UK.pdf>

Hacking

Following the financial sector, telephone companies were other early users of computer systems to control the operation of their networks, and the practice referred to as 'phone phreaking' revolved around attempts by users to manipulate telephone networks and their controlling computers in such a way as to obtain free telephone calls. Developing from extremely basic origins, when it was discovered that a toy whistle supplied as a free gift with packets of breakfast cereal mimicked exactly the frequency used by telephone network codes, practitioners developed more elaborate electronic techniques to bypass charging mechanisms.

Once again, the activities involved could be characterised as a species of fraud and a number of individuals were prosecuted and convicted on this basis. As the number of computer systems increased, new forms of conduct became possible. By the early 1980s, communication between geographically separate computer systems was possible, and with it the possibility of external access to computer systems. Although the terms 'hacking' and 'hacker' have a lengthy and, indeed, respectable pedigree in computer technology, they have now become largely synonymous with the act of obtaining unauthorised access to a computer system and, more specifically, obtaining this access by means of a telecommunications connection from another computer.

Viruses (and other nasties)

In some cases, the obtaining of unauthorised access to a computer system is seen as an end in itself, with hacking being considered, at least by its perpetrators, as a form of intellectual pursuit. In other instances, the motives of hackers are considerably less benign. Obtaining access may well be used as the precursor to some fraudulent scheme, or may be followed by conduct intended to corrupt or destroy data held on the computer. This latter effect may not require direct human access to a computer system. Often linked in the public mind with the activity of hacking is the promulgation of computer viruses. The *Concise Oxford Dictionary* defines the word virus as:

> ...the transmitted cause of infection: a pathogenic agent, usually a proteincoated particle of RNA or DNA, capable of increasing rapidly inside a living cell.

For the computer equivalent, a simple definition refers to 'malicious software which replicates itself'. Although some viruses can be relatively harmless (and, indeed, it has been suggested that the programming techniques incorporated in some forms of virus could usefully be used for purposes such as copying documents), there is no doubt that the concept has entered into popular demonology. Like their human equivalent, computer viruses can readily be transmitted from one computer to another. Initially, the act of dissemination would typically occur as the result of the exchange of infected disks, but, increasingly, the Internet has become the chosen method of transmission. A virus may be transmitted when an unsuspecting individual visits a website, but most incidents of viral infections have been spread by means of attachments to email messages. In Spring 2000, for example, the 'Melissa' virus infected around 100,000 computer systems. In common with a number of more recent viruses, it relied for its effect on the integration between various aspects of the Microsoft operating system and applications programs. Once infected with the virus, a computer would automatically send copies of a Word document to the first fifty names in the user's Microsoft Outlook email address book. Once opened by the recipients, the process would be repeated. Although most virus attacks have followed a similar technical pattern, the more recent 'Sasser' virus adopted a new approach. Although, as has been the case with most viruses, it achieved its effects through exploiting a weakness in the Windows operating system, it was capable of infecting any computer which connected to the Internet without the owner needing to take any further action, such as opening an email attachment. The NCIS report estimates that 'the next major virus attack on the United Kingdom will cost business in the region of £2.1 billion and that 2.2 million office days will be lost in downtime'.[18]

Denial of service attacks

In the case of some viruses such as 'Melissa' and the 'I Love You' attachment, the main consequence has been to create such a surge in the volume of email traffic that network performance has been significantly degraded. A closely related form of activity consists of what is generally referred to as a 'denial of service' attack. Often aimed at businesses engaging in e-commerce or at hacker 'bogey figures', such as Microsoft, the aim is to generate such a volume of spurious messages that the victim site becomes clogged up and is unable to accept messages from genuine users wishing to place orders for goods or services. The technique is analogous in many respects to repeatedly dialling someone's telephone number with the intent of occupying the line so that other callers cannot get through. No damage will be caused to data or equipment but in some cases the financial losses caused to system operators can run into many thousands of pounds in terms of lost business and customer goodwill.

Denial of service attacks may sometimes be linked with other elements of criminal conduct. One incident has been reported in which the founder of an online payment system became the target of Russian-based gangsters who threatened to destroy his business unless he made a payment of $10,000. To prove their capabilities, the site was bombarded with around 150 MB of spurious data, which caused its computers to crash. In this particular case, cooperation with the victim's Internet Service Provider managed to block further attacks on the site.[19]

National and international responses to computer-related crime

In considering the application of the criminal law to instances of computer-related conduct, a variety of issues arise. In the early days of computer-related conduct, any

---

[18] Para. 8.10 at <http://www.ncis.co.uk/ukta/2003/default.asp>
[19] <http://management.silicon.com/smedirector/0,39024679,39130810,00.htm>

criminal charge was required to be brought under traditional legal headings. Incidents where damage was caused to the contents of a computer, either directly or by causing it to be infected by a computer virus, were successfully prosecuted as a species of criminal damage under the Criminal Damage Act 1971.[20]

Starting in the 1980s, a trend began for the adoption of computer-specific statute. Perhaps the first was the United States Computer Fraud and Abuse Act, which was enacted in 1984. Within the United Kingdom, the Law Commissions published Consultative Papers and Reports in the 1980s.[21] Although the initial reports identified a case for the introduction of reform, considerable additional impetus came with the failure of the prosecution in the case of R v Gold.[22] The defendant in this case, together with another accused, had obtained password details enabling him to access an online database without paying the charges which would normaly be levied in respect of such usage. The most relevant criminal offence would appear to have been that of obtaining services by deception. As will be discussed in more detail below, there was considerable uncertainty as to whether this offence could be committed when the 'victim' was a machine, and the decision was taken to bring the prosecution under the terms of the Forgery and Counterfeiting Act 1981. The Act provides that:

> A person is guilty of forgery if he makes a false instrument, with the intention that he or another shall use it to induce somebody to accept it as genuine, and by reason of so accepting it to do or not do some act to his own or any other person's prejudice.[23]

The problems identified above relating to the possibility, or impossibility, of deceiving a machine are overcome in this statute, with s 10 providing that attempts to induce a machine to accept the instrument are to be equated with attempts so to induce a person.

The defendants were convicted at trial but their appeals were accepted unanimously, initially by the Court of Appeal and subsequently by the House of Lords. Delivering his judgment in the Court of Appeal, the Lord Chief Justice concluded:

> We have accordingly come to the conclusion that the language of the Act was not intended to apply to the situation which was shown to exist in this case...It is a conclusion which we reach without regret. The Procrustean attempt to force these facts

---

[20] See, for example, R v Whitely ((1991)) Cr App Rep 25). In this case, the appellant had obtained unauthorised access to a number of computer systems and caused significant amounts of data to be deleted. Upholding his conviction on a charge of criminal damage, the Court of Appeal accepted that no physical damage had been caused to any element of the network but held that '[w]hat the Act requires to be proved is that tangible property has been damaged, not necessarily that the damage itself is tangible. There can be no doubt that the magnetic particles upon the metal discs were a part of the discs and if the appellant was proved to have intentionally and without lawful excuse altered the particles in such a way as to cause an impairment of the value or usefulness of the disc to the owner, there would be damage within the meaning of Section 1 [of the Criminal Damage Act 1971]' (at p. 28).

[21] The Law Commission published a Consultation Paper, Computer Misuse in 1988 (No. 110) and a Report of the same title in 1989 (No. 186). Slightly earlier, the Scottish Law Commission had published a Consultative Memorandum, Computer Crime in 1986 (No. 68) and a Report in 1987 (No. 106).

[22] [1988] 1 AC 1063.

[23] Section 1.

into the language of an Act not designed to fit them produced grave difficulties for both judge and jury which we would not wish to see repeated. The appellants' conduct amounted in essence...to dishonestly obtaining access to the relevant Prestel data bank by a trick. That is not a criminal offence. If it is thought desirable to do so that is a matter for the legislature rather than the courts. We express no view on the matter.[24]

Rightly or wrongly, the decision was widely seen as conferring a form of legal immunity on hackers. When the government failed to include proposals for legislation in its legislative programme for the following parliamentary session, a Bill was introduced as a Private Member's measure and, receiving a good measure of governmental support, received the Royal Assent in 1990 as the Computer Misuse Act. This remains the cornerstone of United Kingdom law in the field.

Traditionally, criminal law has been seen as the province of national authorities. As developments in technology gathered pace, it became increasingly apparent that national legislation might be of limited effectiveness. Rather, as was the concern in the field of data protection, the existence of computer crime havens might threaten the effectiveness of national computer crime statutes. A graphic illustration of this fact came in 2000 when the so-called 'I Love You' computer worm affected millions of computers around the world.[25] Although the cost of cleaning up computer systems was estimated to run into billions of dollars, when the alleged creator of the virus was tracked down to the Philippines it proved impossible to bring any criminal charges as at that time, Philippine law did not extend to this form of computer-related conduct.

The Council of Europe Cybercrime Convention

Initial international action was taken by the Council of Europe, whose Convention on Cybercrime was opened for signature on 23 November 2001. The Convention is a substantial document. Its drafting was a lengthy process, occupying some four years and more than fifty meetings of the 'Committee of Experts on Crime in Cyberspace'. The Convention contains a mix of substantive and procedural aspects. In a manner similar to that adopted in the Data Protection Convention, the instrument specifies attributes which must be found in the national laws of its signatory states. It will then be a matter for each state to implement the provisions in domestic law. Although many aspects of the Convention are rather technical and non-contentions, procedural provisions relating to interception and retention of communications data have caused more controversy. The Civil Rights organisation, 'Treatywatch', for example, has commented that:

The Cybercrime Treaty is an international agreement created for the ostensible purpose of helping police cooperate on crimes that take place on the Internet. Unfortunately, the treaty, which was drafted with very little public input, requires signatory nations to cooperate with foreign dictatorships and give invasive new surveillance powers to law

---

[24] [1987] 3 WLR 803 at 809–10.
[25] For a description of the virus see <http://en.wikipedia.org/wiki/ILOVEYOU>

enforcement. It also lacks protections for privacy or other civil liberties, and applies far more broadly than to just the Internet.[26]

Whilst the Convention was opened for signature in November 2001, all substantive work on the Convention was concluded before the attacks of September 11, 2001. In the light of legislative responses to these events, the provisions of the Convention now appear almost mild by comparison.

Although concluded under the auspices of the Council of Europe, the Convention (as is the case with the data protection convention) is open for signature and ratification by non-Member States. To date, 45 countries have signed the Convention, including the non-Member States of Canada, Japan, South Africa, and the United States, and 21 countries (including the United States) have ratified it. The Convention required ratification by 5 states in order to enter into force, a condition which was satisfied when Lithuania gave notice of ratification in July 2004. To date, the United Kingdom has signed but not ratified the Convention, although recent legal changes appear to have put it in a position so to do.

OECD Guidelines for the Security of Information Systems

Also active in the field of computer crime has been the Organisation for Economic Cooperation and Development. As far back as 1986, the organisation published a report on 'Computer-Related Crime: Analysis of Legal Policy'. This identified a range of actions relating to computers which it was suggested should attract criminal sanctions.

In 1992, the Council of the OECD adopted a Recommendation Concerning Guidelines for the Security of Information Systems. These guidelines were replaced by a further set of Guidelines 'For the Security of Information Systems and Networks'.[27] Addressed to all players in the sector, the Guidelines recognise that:

> Participants depend upon interconnected local and global information systems and networks and should understand their responsibility for the security of those information systems and networks. They should be accountable in a manner appropriate to their individual roles. Participants should review their own policies, practices, measures, and procedures regularly and assess whether these are appropriate to their environment.

Recognition that all parties share responsibility for developing and maintaining a culture of security perhaps highlights the close existence which applies between concepts of data protection and computer crime. Many of the Guidelines are aimed primarily at computer users, including advice in matters such as ensuring that virus-checking software is installed and up to date and that any security patches issued by software developers are implemented. Government's involvement is obviously partly at the level of a user, but at the policy level it is suggested that:

> Participants depend upon interconnected local and global information systems and networks and should understand their responsibility for the security of those

---

[26] <http://www.treatywatch.org/>
[27] Available from <http://www.oecd.org/dataoecd/16/22/15582260.pdf>

information systems and networks. They should be accountable in a manner appropriate to their individual roles. Participants should review their own policies, practices, measures, and procedures regularly and assess whether these are appropriate to their environment.

An Implementation Plan for the Guidelines was published in 2003.[28] This recommended that governments should be:

- Enacting a comprehensive set of substantive criminal, procedural and mutual assistance legal measures to combat cybercrime and ensure cross-borders co-operation. These should be at least as comprehensive as, and consistent with, the Council of Europe Convention on Cybercrime.

- Identifying national cybercrime units and international high-technology assistance points of contact and creating such capabilities to the extent they do not already exist; and

- Establishing institutions that exchange threat and vulnerability assessments [such as national CERTs (Computer Emergency Response Teams)].

- Developing closer co-operation between government and business in the fields of information security and fighting cybercrime.

The Guidelines were further supplemented in 2005, with the publication by the Working Party on Information Security and Privacy of a report on *The Promotion of a Culture of Security for Information Systems and Networks in OECD Countries*. This includes a comprehensive account of national measures intended to implement the Guidelines.

EU initiatives

Within Europe, the EU has very limited legislative competence in the criminal field and although, as indicated above, it has been active in respect of Internet content, this has primarily taken the form of encouraging the development of schemes to categorise the contents of websites and of filtering mechanisms which can be used to restrict the range of sites which may be accessed from a particular computer. Typically, parents would be able to restrict their children's access to sites which displayed sexual or violent material.

A more substantive EU development is in the form of a Framework Decision on attacks against information systems.[29] The genesis of this proposal rests in the conclusions of the Lisbon European Council of March 2000, which:

> stressed the importance of the transition to a competitive, dynamic and knowledge-based economy, and invited the Council and the Commission to draw up an eEurope Action plan to make the most of this opportunity This Action Plan, prepared by the

---

[28] Available from <http://www.oecd.org/dataoecd/23/11/31670189.pdf>
[29] COM (2002) 173 final.

Commission and the Council, adopted by the Feira Summit of the European Council in June 2000, includes actions to enhance network security and the establishment of a co-ordinated and coherent approach to cybercrime by the end of 2002.

Acting on this manifesto, the Commission published a Communication entitled 'Creating a Safer Information Society by Improving the Security of Information Infrastructures and Combating Computer-Related Crime'.[30] This proposed a number of legislative and non-legislative measures. In the latter respect, the Commission has published a Communication on 'Network and Information Security: A European Policy Approach'.[31] This analysed the current problems in network security, and provided a strategic outline for action. A Council Resolution of 6 December 2001[32] advocated a common approach to and specific actions in the area of network and information security. More significantly, and perhaps more contentiously in terms of its legislative competence, the Commission also advocated the necessity for the harmonisation of substantive criminal law provisions across the EU. The explanatory memorandum attached to the draft Decision states that it seeks:

> to approximate criminal law in the area of attacks against information systems and to ensure the greatest possible police and judicial co-operation in the area of criminal offences related to attacks against information systems. Moreover, this proposal contributes to the efforts of the European Union in the fight against organised crime and terrorism.[33]

The Framework Decision was adopted in February 2005 and required to be implemented in the Member States by March 2007. In terms of substantive offences, the Decision requires that Member States criminalise the acts of attempting or obtaining illegal access to or perpetrating illegal interference with, information systems, together with acts intended to instigate, aid, or abet the practice.[34] The Decision also contains extensive measures to ensure cooperation between national law enforcement agencies, including the establishment of 24-hour operational points of contact available 24-hours-a-day and seven-days-a-week.[35]

Conclusions

The topic of computer crime has occupied much legislative time around the world. In some respects, the early instances of computer viruses such as the 'I Love You' version cited above, served to provide a wake-up call for many governments, who had to come to terms with the existence of gaps in the coverage of national laws. It did not take

---

[30] COM(2000) 890 final.

[31] Available from <http://europa.eu.int/information_society/eeurope/2002/news_library/new_documents/text_en.htm>

[32] OJ 2002 C 43/02.

[33] COM (2002) 173 final, para. 1.6.

[34] Articles 3–5.

[35] Article 12.

the Philippine authorities long to enact computer misuse legislation. The widespread adoption of the Council of Europe Convention on Cybercrime—certainly compared with the non-existent adoption of its data protection Convention outwith the ranks of the Council's Member States—indicates perhaps that this initiative has struck a chord. The provisions of this Convention, together with the manner in which these are implemented in the United Kingdom, will be considered in more detail in the following chapters.

Suggestions for further reading

Explanatory Memorandum to the Council of Europe Cybercrime Convention.

'Criminalising Computer Misconduct: Some Legal and Philosophical Problems' A.P.L.R. 14(1) (2006), pp. 95–121.

10

Legislating for computer crime

Introduction

As discussed in the previous chapter, the Council of Europe's Convention on Cybercrime has become accepted as the leading international instrument in the field. Its provisions, which are largely replicated in the EU's Framework Decision, will be used in this chapter to indicate the major headings under which computer-related conduct might be prosecuted and to analyse the effectiveness of United Kingdom legislation in the field. In its provisions, the Convention defines four categories of conduct which it requires to be the subject of criminal offences:

- offences against the confidentiality, integrity and availability of computer data and systems;
- computer-related offences;
- content-related offences;
- offences related to infringements of copyright and related rights.

The first three of these will be considered, respectively, in this and the following two chapters, whilst the fourth will be examined later when considering the general operation of intellectual property law. The Convention also contains extensive procedural provisions and these will be described and discussed in Chapter 13.

Offences against the confidentiality, integrity, and availability of computer data and systems

Under this heading, the convention specifies offences relating to illegal access, often involving hacking, illegal interception, and data and system interference, for example as a result of the promulgation of viruses and the misuse of devices. The provisions of Sections 1, 2, and 3 of the Computer Misuse Act, as now amended by the Police and Justice Act of 2006, provide the major United Kingdom activity in this regard.

Illegal access

Article 2 of the Convention requires that:

> Each Party shall adopt such legislative and other measures as may be necessary to establish as criminal offences under its domestic law, when committed intentionally,

the access to the whole or any part of a computer system without right. A Party may require that the offence be committed by infringing security measures, with the intent of obtaining computer data or other dishonest intent, or in relation to a computer system that is connected to another computer system.

This formulation clearly confers considerable discretion upon signatory states. The issue of whether access should require to be attained through overcoming security devices has been extensively debated. Such an approach would be compatible with legal provisions in respect of many other areas of activity. If an unauthorised person walks into an open house, that will not normally render conduct criminal unless and until they engage in further aggravating conduct. Although the Scottish Law Commission in their Report on Computer Crime had proposed that commission of an unauthorised access offence should be contingent upon an intention either to secure a benefit for the perpetrator or to cause loss to the computer owner, the Law Commission argued that the mere fact of obtaining unauthorised access should suffice:

> because of the possibility that any attempted entrant may have had password access to important levels of authority, sometimes to a level which has enabled him to delete records of his activities from the system, any successfiul unauthorised access must be taken very seriously. Suubstantial costs are therefore incurred in (i) taking security steps against unauthorised entry...and (ii) investigating any case, however trivial, where unauthorised activity does in fact occur.

Significantly, however, the Law Commission recommended that the offence should be regarded as a relatively minor one, attracting a maximum penalty of three months' imprisonment. As enacted, the Computer Misuse Act doubled this recommendation and the Police and Justice Act of 2006 increased the maximum penalty to a term of two years' imprisonment.[1]

Although in terms of its penalties, the unauthorised access offence (generally referred to as the 'basic offence') is the least significant of the Computer Misuse Act's provisions, its linkage with other provisions makes it in many ways the most critical element of the legislation. The offence is defined in Section 1 of the Computer Misuse Act 1990, which, as amended by Section 35 of the Police and Justice Act 2006, provides that:

1. A person is guilty of an offence if—

    (a) he causes a computer to perform any function with intent to secure access to any program or data held in any computer or to enable any such access to be secured;

    (b) the access he intends to secure or to enable to be secured, is unauthorised; and

    (c) he knows at the time when he causes the computer to perform the function that that is the case.

---

[1] In cases where the prosecution is on a summary basis, the maximum sentence is 12 months' imprisonment in England and Wales, but only 6 months for Scotland.

In common with other statutory interventions in the computer field, no attempt is made to define the word 'computer'. Many modern appliances make extensive use of microprocessors to control their functioning. A washing machine may, for example, have its operation controlled by such chips, whose circuitry will contain the programs necessary for the performance of their dedicated tasks. In such a situation, it might be argued that an unauthorised person who used the washing machine might be guilty of the unauthorised access offence. Such a prospect was identified in Parliament, where the prospect was welcomed by at least one MP who, in opposing proposals to amend the offence to restrict its scope argued:

> This is a computer misuse Bill. It seeks to tackle unauthorised access to computers which may well include electronic locks...Someone breaking into a car using an electronic key to operate the lock may not be caught under the present legislation if a policeman puts his hand on his shoulder before he gets in and tries to drive away. We are attempting to make it an offence for people to gain unauthorised access to an electronic system. The clause is properly drafted.[2]

It will be seen that in order for the unauthorised access offence to be committed, a variety of conditions have to be satisfied. Three elements call for detailed consideration. The concept of access raises a number of issues and the scope of the definitions are extremely broad. Next, comes the question of whether access is authorised. Finally, it must be established by the prosecution that an accused knew that access was being sought without authority.

Obtaining or enabling access

The first stage in the commission of the offence will consist of causing a computer 'to perform any function with intent to secure access to any program or data held in any computer'. A variety of elements from this definition call for further discussion and comment.

Access will be secured to a program or data when the user, by causing the computer to operate in any manner:

(a) alters or erases the program or data;

(b) copies or moves it to any storage medium other than that in which it is held or to a different location in the storage medium in which it is held;

(c) uses it; or

(d) has it output from the computer in which it is held (whether by having it displayed or in any other manner).[3]

Although the above provisions are somewhat tortuous (and are themselves subject to further definition in the Computer Misuse Act), most actions whereby a user makes

---

[2] HC Official Report, SC C (Computer Misuse Bill), col. 9, 14 March 1990.
[3] Section 17(1).

contact with a computer system will come within its ambit. Thus, the simple act of switching on a computer will cause start-up programs to function and cause various messages to be displayed on the screen.

The popular image of a computer hacker is of someone who accesses computer systems by making a telephone connection from their own computer. This perception caused considerable problems in the first prosecution brought under the Computer Misuse Act 1990. The case resulted in the accused being acquitted of charges under the Act on the direction of the judge. This was based upon an extremely restrictive interpretation of the scope of the unauthorised access offence. The case was referred to the Court of Appeal by the Attorney General, where it is reported as *A-G's Reference (No. 1 of 1991)*.[4] The defendant in this case had been employed as a sales assistant by a wholesale locksmith. He left their employ, but subsequently returned to the premises indicating the intention to purchase an item of equipment. Details of sales transactions were entered into a computer terminal. The defendant was familiar with the use of the system and, taking advantage of a moment when the terminal was left unattended, entered a code into the system. The effect of this was to instruct the computer to give a 70 per cent discount on the sale. The invoice which was subsequently generated charged the sum of £204.76 instead of the normal price of £710.96. Upon these facts coming to light, the defendant was arrested and charged with an offence under the Computer Misuse Act 1990. At trial, the judge dismissed the charge, holding that the phrase in s 1(1)(a) referring to obtaining access to 'any program or data held in any computer' required that one computer should be used to obtain access to a program or data held on another computer.

Given evidence from many computer crime surveys to the effect that most instances of computer misuse are perpetrated by 'insiders', and the fact that most computer systems are not accessible from outside, such a restriction would severely limit the application of the statute. The Attorney General, acting under the authority of the Criminal Justice Act 1972,[5] sought the opinion of the Court of Appeal on the question whether:

> In order for a person to commit an offence under Section 1(1) of the Computer Misuse Act 1990 does the computer which the person causes to perform any function with the required intent have to be a different computer from the one into which he intends to secure unauthorised access to any program or data held therein?

Delivering the judgment of the court, the Lord Chief Justice answered this question in the negative. There were, he ruled:

> ...no grounds whatsoever for implying or importing the word 'other' between 'any' and 'computer', or excepting the computer which is actually used by the offender from the phrase 'any computer'.[6]

---

[4] [1992] 3 WLR 432.
[5] Section 36.
[6] *A-G's Reference (No. 1 of 1991)* [1992] 3 WLR 432 at 437.

Such a view, which is undoubtedly correct but misunderstanding of the scope of the Act's provisions, has been a recurring theme over the years and perhaps indicates a lack of precision in the drafting of the offences.

As originally enacted, the Computer Misuse Act criminalised only the direct attempt to obtain access to a computer. The European Union Framework Decision requires that Member States also criminalise conduct which is intended to aid and abet those commiting offences. Implementing this requirement, the Police and Justice Act introduced the offence of enabling access to be obtained. This was described as applying to the:

> ready criminal market in software tools to gain unauthorised access to others' computers. The intent is therefore to ensure that an offence would be committed where the person's intention is merely to enable someone else to secure unauthorised access—or, for that matter, to enable the person himself to secure unauthorised access at some later time.[7]

Unauthorised access

Access is held to be unauthorised when the user:

(a) is not him or herself entitled to control access of the kind in question to the program or data; and

(b) he or she does not have the consent to access of the kind in question to the program or data from any person who is so entitled.[8]

In many cases, the person entitled to control access will be the owner of the computer system itself. In other cases, a computer system may serve as a 'host', providing storage space and access facilities for programs or data controlled by other parties. In this situation, the question of who has the right to consent to access may be more complex. Most university computer systems provide illustrations of this form of activity. Here, the fact that a student is granted rights of access does not confer any entitlement to transfer these on to a third party.

In many cases, the initial act of making contact with a computer system will not suffice to demonstrate knowledge that access is unauthorised. Even though a hacker contacting computer systems at random (or making use of details supplied by a fellow enthusiast) may well suspect that their attentions may not be welcome; and indeed be reckless whether this would be the case, it may be very difficult to establish that they had actual knowledge that access was unauthorised at the point of initial contact. The dividing line between reckless and intentional conduct may well be crossed once contact is made. A user accessing the main computer system at the author's university is presented with the message 'Unauthorised access to this system is **ILLEGAL**: Computer Misuse Act 1990'. The mere presence of such a notice might be sufficient to

---

[7] HL Official Report, vol. 684, col. 581, 11 July 2006.

[8] Computer Misuse Act 1990, s 17(5).

justify the assumption that any further attempts to operate or access the contents of the system will be conducted in the knowledge that this is unauthorised. The installation of a security system, typically allocating authorised users with passwords and requiring these to be entered at the stage of initial contact, would undoubtedly reinforce this position.

Unauthorised use by authorised users

The Computer Misuse Act prohibits unauthorised access. In the case where an individual has no entitlement to access material, the application of the provision is relatively straightforward. Difficulties have, however, arisen in the situation where an individual is entitled to access information but uses this for an unauthorised purpose. An example might be taken from the case of *R v Thompson* discussed more fully in the following chapter, where a dishonest programmer used his access to his employer's computer to perpetrate a theft. Similar although perhaps less extreme conduct was at issue in the case of *R v Bignell*.[9] Here, two police officers obtained access to data held on the police national computer in order to identify the owner of a number of motor vehicles. The information was sought for the officers' personal interest and was not connected with their duties as police officers. The conduct being discovered, they were charged under Section 1 and convicted at trial. On appeal, although it was not contended that the use to which the data was put was authorised, the Divisional Court accepted submissions to the effect that:

> ...the primary purpose of the Computer Misuse Act was to protect the integrity of computer systems rather that the integrity of information stored on the computers...a person who causes a computer to perform a function to secure access to information held at a level to which the person was entitled to gain access does not commit an offence under S.1 even if he intends to secure access for an unauthorised purpose because it is only where the level of unauthorised access has been knowingly and intentionally exceeded that an offence is committed, provided the person knows of that unauthorised level of access.

The court held that no offence had been committed under the Computer Misuse Act 1990. It was suggested by the court that an offence had been committed under the Data Protection Act 1984. Under the provisions of this Act, any obtaining, holding, disclosure, or international transfer of data by a servant or agent of a data user which contravenes the terms of the latter's entry on the Register will render the individual concerned liable under both criminal and civil law.[10]

The decision in *Bignell*[11] was widely criticised and was reconsidered in the later case of *R v Bow Street Magistrates' Court, ex p Allison*.[12] This case concerned an application

---

[9] *The Times*, 6 June 1997.
[10] Section 5(3).
[11] (1998) 1 Cr App R 1.
[12] [1999] 4 All ER 1. The decision of the Divisional Court is reported at [1999] QB 847.

by the United States authorities for the extradition of the applicant to face charges, inter alia, of securing unauthorised access to the American Express computer system with the intent to commit theft and forgery. The issue before the court was whether the conduct alleged, had it taken place in the United Kingdom, would have constituted a breach of Section 2 of the Computer Misuse Act which established what is referred to as the ulterior intent offence. This provides that:

1. A person is guilty of an offence under this Section if he commits an offence under Section 1 above ('the unauthorised access offence') with intent—

   (a) to commit an offence to which this Section applies; or

   (b) to facilitate the commission of such an offence (whether by himself or by any other person).[13]

The offences referred to in the above passage are defined as being those for which the sentence is prescribed by law[14]—effectively the offence of murder or those for which a person with no previous criminal record might, upon conviction, be sentenced to a term of imprisonment of five years or more.[15] The maximum sentence for commission of the Section 2 offence is itself a term of five years' imprisonment.

The rationale behind the ulterior intent offence is to bring forward in time the moment at which a serious criminal offence is committed. The Law Commission, in their report, identified a number of problems which might arise in the computer field creating circumstances where conduct might not constitute an attempt under the general provisions of criminal law, but which was felt to justify special treatment within the computer context.[16] One example cited concerned a hacker who secured access to a bank's computer system, the system being used for electronic fund transfers. In order to accomplish a transfer, a password would have to be transmitted. The Law Commission hypothesised that the hacker might attempt to transmit a large number of combinations in the hope of finding the correct one. In the event that the password was discovered, used, and a transfer of funds accomplished, the Law Commission were in no doubt that the offence of theft would be committed. The act of transmitting combinations of numbers and letters in the attempt to discover a valid password would not, they considered, be regarded as more than conduct preparatory to the commission of a crime. As such, it would not constitute a criminal attempt, especially in the event that further steps would be required in order to complete the transfer. Reference has previously been made to the speed at which vast sums of money may be transferred using the electronic fund transfer system. In terms of time, it seems clear that the gap between conduct preparatory of a crime and its perpetration may be very short where this form of conduct is at issue.

---

[13] Section 2.
[14] Section 2(2)(a).
[15] Section 2(2)(b).
[16] Law Commission No. 186 (1989) paras 3.52–3.53.

In *Allison*, the defendant had allegedly conspired with another party, Jean Ojomo, who had been employed by American Express. In the course of her work, she was instructed to access specific accounts but once online could access other account information. This was passed on to Allison, who was able to use it to encode credit cards, obtain personal identification numbers, and make withdrawals from automatic teller machines. Allison was arrested in England in possession of forged cards, having been photographed using such a card to make a cash withdrawal. The conduct at issue, it was alleged, would have constituted a breach of ss 1, 2, and 3 of the Computer Misuse Act 1990.[17] Following the decision in *Bignell*,[18] it was held by the Divisional Court that the Section 1 offence had not been committed and therefore there could be no question of a Section 2 offence being committed.

The consequences of the Divisional Court's decisions in *Bignell*[19] and *Allison*[20] for the operation of the Computer Misuse Act 1990 were potentially significant. Most instances of computer fraud (and perhaps fraud in general) are committed by insiders. The decisions, therefore, were seen as conferring a degree of immunity upon such actors. An appeal was made in the case of *Allison* and resulted in a robust rejection by the House of Lords of the notion that the misuse of access rights could not incur criminal sanctions. Delivering the judgment of the House, Lord Hobhouse quoted from the provisions of Section 17, which defines the concept of access and authorisation. This provides that access is unauthorised if a person:

(a) is not himself entitled to control access of the kind in question to the program or data; and

(b) he does not have consent to access by him of the kind in question to the program or data from any person who is so entitled.

In both situations, it was held, account had to be taken of the use to which access was put rather than merely to the data which was accessed. The Section, it was held:

> ...makes clear that the authority must relate not simply to the data or programme but also to the actual kind of access secured. Similarly, it is plain that it is not using the word 'control' in a physical sense of the ability to operate or manipulate the computer and that it is not derogating from the requirement that for access to be authorised it must be authorised to the relevant data or relevant programme or part of a programme. It does not introduce any concept that authority to access one piece of data should be treated as authority to access other pieces of data 'of the same kind'

---

[17] Sections 2 and 3 are considered below. Section 2 creates what is referred to as the 'ulterior intent' offence. This involves securing unauthorised access to programs of data with the intention of using the access to facilitate the commission of a further serious offence. Although extradition could only be authorised for an s 2 offence, the penalties for breach of s 1 being too low to warrant this process, it was necessary for the prosecution to establish commission of the unauthorised access offence as a prerequisite for liability under s 2.

[18] *R v Bignell* [1998] 1 Cr App Rep 1.

[19] *R v Bignell* [1998] 1 Cr App Rep 1.

[20] *R v Bow Street Magistrates' Court, ex p Allison* [1999] 4 All ER 1.

notwithstanding that the relevant person did not in fact have authority to access that piece of data. Section 1 [of the Computer Misuse Act 1990] refers to the intent to secure unauthorised access to any programme or data. These plain words leave no room for any suggestion that the relevant person may say: 'Yes, I know that I was not authorised to access that data but I was authorised to access other data of the same kind.'[21]

In terms which are reflective of the first decision under the Computer Misuse Act 1990, *A-G's Reference (No. 1 of 1991)*,[22] the Divisional Court was criticised for importing words into the statute. The Act, it was held was not concerned with access to 'kinds' of data. It looked rather at the entitlement to access particular programs or items of data. The decision of Kennedy J in the Divisional Court, it was held:

> ...treats the phrase 'entitlement to control' as if it related to the control of the computer as opposed to the entitlement to authorise operators to access to programs and data. He adopts the extraneous idea of an authorised level of access without considering whether, on the facts of the case, it corresponds to the relevant person's authority to access the data in fact accessed. He confines s.1 of the Act to the 'hacking' of computer systems as opposed to the use of a computer to secure unauthorised access to programs or data. Upon a misreading of s.17(5) [of the Computer Misuse Act 1990], he fails to give effect to the plain words of s.1. The meaning of the statute is clear and unambiguous.[23]

The decision in *Allison*[24] undoubtedly closed a significant loophole in the Computer Misuse Act 1990. It is clear that the statute is much more than an 'anti-hacking' measure and that misuse of facilities by authorised users will expose them to the risk of criminal prosecution.

Illegal interception

Article 3 of the Cybercrime Convention provides that:

> Each Party shall adopt such legislative and other measures as may be necessary to establish as criminal offences under its domestic law, when committed intentionally, the interception without right, made by technical means, of non-public transmissions of computer data to, from or within a computer system, including electromagnetic emissions from a computer system carrying such computer data. A Party may require that the offence be committed with dishonest intent, or in relation to a computer system that is connected to another computer system.

The provisions of the Regulation of Investigatory Powers Act 2000, provide in Section 2 for an offence to be committed by a person who, without obtaining a warrant, intercepts any communication transmitted over a public or private communications

---

21 *R v Bow Street Magistrates' Court, ex p Allison* [1999] 4 All ER 1 at 7.
22 [1992] 3 WLR 432.
23 [1999] 4 All ER 1 at 9.
24 *R v Bow Street Magistrates' Court, ex p Allison* [1999] 4 All ER 1.

system. Part 2 of the Act applies to surveillance and by Section 27 provides that intrusive surveillance will be unlawful unless authorised under the legislation. Section 26 provides that:

> surveillance which—
>
> (a) is carried out by means of a surveillance device in relation to anything taking place on any residential premises or in any private vehicle, but
>
> (b) is carried out without that device being present on the premises or in the vehicle, is not intrusive unless the device is such that it consistently provides information of the same quality and detail as might be expected to be obtained from a device actually present on the premises or in the vehicle.

Attempts to determine the data being processed on a computer by detecting electromagnetic emissions could well fall foul of this provision.

In the above situation, it is likely that an offence would be committed under Section 1 of the Computer Misuse Act, as the perpetrator will be causing equipment to perform a function in order to secure access to data on the victim's computer. Although there are no direct precedents, a not dissimilar scenario would see a party attempting to make unauthorised use of a wireless computer network. This appears to be a growing practice, although there appears little doubt that the conduct could constitute an offence under the Computer Misuse Act. In the first case of its kind, a party who accessed a wireless network from his laptop whilst sitting in a car outside the network owner's premises was fined £500.[25]

Damage to data

Anyone possessing a degree of familiarity with computers and their method of operation will be only too well aware of how fragile is the hold on its electronic life of any piece of data. The accidental depression of a key or the placing of a computer disk in undue proximity to a magnetic field as produced by electrical motors, or even telephones, can speedily consign data to electronic oblivion. To the risks of accidental damage must be added those of deliberate sabotage.

The vulnerability of computer users to such events is not questioned. Once again, our concern must be with the legal consequences which may follow such behaviour. The basic scenario involves a party altering or deleting data held on a computer system, such action taking place without the consent of the system owner. Within this, a wide range of activities can be identified. At the most basic level, the perpetrator may use 'delete' or 'reformat' commands or even bring a magnet into close proximity to a computer storage device. Amendment of data may be made for a variety of motives. In some cases, such as that at issue in *R v Thompson*, amendment of data may be a component of a scheme of fraud. Other actions may be driven by the intent to cause disruption to the computer owner's activities. This might involve the manipulation of

---

[25] <http://news.bbc.co.uk/1/hi/technology/4721723.stm>

computer programs through, for example, the insertion of logic bombs, which cause a computer to function in a manner desired by the perpetrator rather than its owner, whilst an ever-expanding range of computer viruses present a continual threat to the wellbeing of computer owners.

During the 1980s, a number of cases involving damage to data had been prosecuted as a form of criminal damage under the Criminal Damage Act 1971. The appropriateness of this approach was confirmed by the Court of Appeal in the case of *R v Whiteley*.[26] Here, a computer hacker had accessed computer networks and, inter alia, deleted a number of files. Upon being detected, he was prosecuted and convicted of the offence of criminal damage. Appealing against conviction, it was argued that his conduct had not caused any tangible form of damage to the victim computers. Rejecting this contention, the Lord Chief Justice ruled that:

> What the Act requires to be proved is that tangible property has been damaged, not necessarily that the damage itself should be tangible. There can be no doubt that the magnetic particles upon the metal discs were a part of the discs and if the appellant was proved to have intentionally and without lawful excuse altered the particles in such a way as to cause an impairment of the value or usefulness of the disc to the owner, there would be damage within the meaning of Section 1. The fact that the alteration could only be perceived by operating the computer did not make the alterations any the less real, or the damage, if the alteration amounted to damage, any the less within the ambit of the Act.[27]

By the time the judgment was handed down, the point was of little practical relevance. In their final report, the Law Commission had indicated that difficulty had been encountered by:

> the police and prosecuting authorities who have informed us that, although convictions have been obtained in serious cases of unauthorised access to data or programs, there is recurrent (and understandable) difficulty in explaining to judges, magistrates and juries how the facts fit in with the present law of criminal damage.[28]

The Law Commission recommended the establishment of an offence of causing an unauthorised modification to programs or data held on a computer and this was implemented in Section 3 of the Computer Misuse Act. The Section was amended by the Police and Justice Act 2006 to take account of the provisions of the Cybercrime Convention and the Framework Decision. Article 4 of the Cybercrime Convention provides that:

1. Each Party shall adopt such legislative and other measures as may be necessary to establish as criminal offences under its domestic law, when committed intentionally, the damaging, deletion, deterioration, alteration or suppression of computer data without right.

[26] (1991) 93 Crim App Rep 25.
[27] Ibid. at p. 28.
[28] Law Commission No. 186 (1989), para. 2.31.

2. A Party may reserve the right to require that the conduct described in paragraph 1 result in serious harm.

Also relevant in this context are the provisions of Article 5, which provides that:

Each Party shall adopt such legislative and other measures as may be necessary to establish as criminal offences under its domestic law, when committed intentionally, the serious hindering without right of the functioning of a computer system by inputting, transmitting, damaging, deleting, deteriorating, altering or suppressing computer data.

There is considerable overlap between the two provisions. In the explanatory report accompanying the Convention, it is indicated that the intention of Article 4 is to 'provide computer data and computer programs with protection similar to that enjoyed by corporeal objects against intentional infliction of damage', and continues: '(t)he input of malicious codes, such as viruses and Trojan horses is, therefore, covered under this paragraph, as is the resulting modification of the data'.[29] Article 5 is also relevant to the situation where viruses impair the operation of computers but it will additionally apply to so-called denial of service attacks.

For the United Kingdom, Section 36 of the Police and Justice Act replaces Section 3 with a new and broader provision headed 'unauthorised acts with intent to impair operation of computer etc.'. This provides that:

1. A person is guilty of an offence if—

   (a) he does any unauthorised act in relation to a computer;

   (b) at the time when he does the act he knows that it is unauthorised; and

a person convicted of the offence may be sentenced to a maximum of 12 months' imprisonment on summary conviction (6 months in Scotland) or ten years on indictment.

The concept of an unauthorised act encompasses both the addition of data or its alteration or erasure. A modification will be regarded as unauthorised if the person causing it is not authorised so to act or does not possess the consent of a person who is so entitled.[30] Again, the possibility of different categories of rights and privileges attaching to different users must be borne in mind. Typically, an employee or a student may be entitled to use the facilities of a computer system but will not be entitled to delete any portions or to add any programs.

The effect of the unauthorised act must be:

   (a) to impair the operation of any computer;

   (b) to prevent or hinder access to any program or data held in any computer;

   (c) to impair the operation of any such program or the reliability of any such data; or

---

[29] At paras 60–1.
[30] Computer Misuse Act 1990, s 17.

(d) to enable any of the things mentioned in paragraphs (a) to (c) above to be done.[31]

The 1990 Act provided that, as with the unauthorised access offence, the prosecution would have to demonstrate that an accused person had acted intentionally. The 2006 modifications reduce the burden somewhat in requiring that conduct may be either intentional or reckless as to whether impairment will be caused.

At the most basic level of activity, this provision would apply in the situation where a user intentionally causes the deletion of programs or data held on a computer. The manner in which this is accomplished will be immaterial. At the simplest level, the user may operate delete functions so as to remove programs or data.[32] In the first prosecution brought under this provision of the Computer Misuse Act 1990, the accused had installed a security package on a computer belonging to a firm which he claimed owed some £2,000 in fees. The effect of the installation was to prevent the computer being used unless a password was entered. As this was not disclosed, the computer was effectively rendered unusable for several days, with resultant losses estimated at some £36,000. The accused was convicted and fined £1,650.[33]

An offence may also be committed when data is added to a computer system. One instance of this, which will be discussed below, occurs when a computer is infected with a virus. The offence will also be committed where logic bombs or other programs are added to the computer system with the intent that these will operate so as to cause inconvenience to the computer user. In one instance, an IT manager added a program to his employer's system which had the effect of encrypting incoming data. The data would automatically be decrypted when it was subsequently accessed. The manager left his employment following a disagreement and some time later the decryption function ceased to operate. Once again, the effect was to render the computer unusable. Despite claims that the encryption function was intended as a security device and that the failure of the decryption facility was an unforeseen error, the manager was convicted of an offence under the Computer Misuse Act 1990.[34]

A further case brought under the legislation concerned a contract for the supply of bespoke software. The customer was late in making payment for the software and shortly afterwards the software stopped working. It transpired that the supplier, anticipating possible problems with payment, had inserted a timelock function. Unless removed by the supplier upon receipt of payment, the software would stop working

---

[31] Section 3(2).

[32] The use of such commands may well remove details of the programs or data from any directories. The program or data will not be removed at that stage, the effect of the command being to render it liable to being overwritten as further programs or data are added to the computer. Such conduct will constitute the unauthorised modification offence, even though the 'damage' may be recoverable.

[33] *R v Whitaker* (1993) Scunthorpe Magistrates' Court. Details of this and a range of other prosecutions under the Computer Misuse Act 1990 are reported in R. Battcock, 'Prosecutions under the Computer Misuse Act', *Computers and Law* 6 (1996), p. 22.

[34] Battcock (1996), p. 22.

from a specified date. This conduct resulted in prosecution and conviction under the unauthorised modification offence.[35]

The issues raised in this case are undoubtedly less clearcut than in a number of the other prosecutions brought under the Computer Misuse Act. It was argued that the use of such timelocks was a legitimate response to the failure of the customer to meet the contractual obligation to pay for the software. A further point which does not appear to have been raised was whether the supplier would retain sufficient intellectual property rights in the software to be entitled to control its continued use. It could also be argued that the action would have been lawful had notice been given to the customer of the fact that the software would stop working if payment was not made timeously.

It may be that the drafting of the offence is sufficiently broad to make the mere act of unauthorised use illegal. An example might concern an employee who types a private letter using their employer's computer. As s 3(5) of the Computer Misuse Act states that the fact whether a modification is permanent or temporary is immaterial, it would not even appear that there is a necessity for the text of the letter to be stored on the computer. In the event that a portion of text is stored on a computer's hard disk, utilising only a minuscule fraction of the disk's storage capacity, any degree of impairment of the computer's capabilities will be similarly minute. The Act, however, does not require that the degree of impairment be substantial or significant. Such conditions would add further levels of complexity and uncertainty to the task of defining the scope of the legislation. It is to be recognised, however, that the act of making an unauthorised act constitutes only one element of the offence and that the prosecution is required, additionally, to establish that the party responsible intended to impair the operation of the computer or was reckless as to whether impairment was caused.[36] In addition to proscribing acts impairing the operation of a computer, the unauthorised act offence may be committed when data held on a computer is modified in a fashion which may affect its reliability. A possible scenario might involve an individual giving false information with a view to causing the modification of an unfavourable entry on a credit reference agency's files. This might render unreliable the data held on the computer and, as such, may constitute an offence under Section 3.

Taking the concept of an unauthorised modification as a whole, it would seem clear that the offence might be committed by a person who creates a computer virus and sends it out into the world with the intention that it will infect other computers. The Computer Misuse Act provides in this respect that:

1. The intent need not be directed at—

    (a) any particular computer;

    (b) any particular program or data or a program or data of any particular kind; or

    (c) any particular modification or a modification of any particular kind.[37]

---

[35] Ibid.   [36] Section 2(2).   [37] Section 3(3).

The virus creator will therefore cause the modification of any computer which is infected, even though they may not be directly responsible for the infection of any particular machine, this being brought about by an unsuspecting (or even reckless) authorised user. To this extent, the phrase 'to cause' must be interpreted in two senses: in respect of the act which causes the effect and also of the act which is proximately responsible for its occurrence.

One of the most publicised cases brought under the Computer Misuse Act involved the prosecution of Christopher Pile. Using the pseudonym 'Black Baron', the accused was reported as having told detectives that 'he had wanted to create a British virus which would match the worst of those from overseas'. A number of viruses were created by Pile and concealed in seemingly innocuous programs which he published on the Internet; from there they would infect any computer onto which they were downloaded. It was estimated that the effects of the virus cost companies in the region of £500,000 and Pile secured the dubious distinction of being the first virus writer convicted under the Act, being sentenced to a term of 18 months' imprisonment.[38]

In addition to being used against those who create a virus, the Computer Misuse Act 1990 could also be used against those who deliberately cause a computer to be infected. Once again, the requirement that the prosecution establish intent may prove difficult to satisfy. In many cases, viruses are spread through users bringing infected disks into offices or educational establishments. Many users now have policies either prohibiting the practice or requiring that disks be checked on a dedicated virus-checking machine prior to being used. If an individual ignores these requirements and causes a viral infestation the conduct might reasonably be characterised as reckless, but this would still fall some way short of the statutory standard.

Whilst there was no doubt that the original Section 3 offence was an effective tool against those disseminating viruses, conduct involving denial of service attacks was widely perceived as more problematic. The All Party Internet Group in their report on the Computer Misuse Act[39] reported that:

> Almost every respondent from industry told us that the CMA is not adequate for dealing with DoS and DDoS attacks, though very few gave any detailed analysis of why they believed this to be so. We understand that this widespread opinion is based on some 2002 advice by the Crown Prosecution Service (CPS) that s3 might not stretch to including all DoS activity.
>
> In contrast the Government, many academic lawyers and also, we understand, the NHTCU (National High Technology Crime Unit), believe that s3 is sufficiently broad to cover DoS attacks. In April 2003 the Internet Crime Forum (ICF) Legal Subgroup pointed out that s3 did not require unauthorised access, merely unauthorised 'modification of the contents of any computer'. They expressed the opinion that the test

[38] M2 Presswire, 24 March 1997.
[39] Available from <http://www.apcomms.org.uk/apig/archive/activities-2004/computer-misuse-inquiry/CMAReportFinalVersion1.pdf>

applied would be whether the attack had rendered unreliable the data stored on a computer or impaired its operation.[40]

The revised wording introduced by the Police and Justice Act by referring to conduct intended to impair or enable the impairment of the operation of any computer is intended to make it clear that denial of service attacks are unlawful. In a manner similar to the applicability of the offence of criminal damage, as the 2006 Act was proceeding through Parliament, the Divisional Court declared unequivocally in the case of *DPP v Lennon*,[41] that denial of service attacks were caught by the original offence. The respondent in the case had admitted downloading a mail-bombing program called Avalanche from the Internet and using this to bombard his former employers with emails. The program has been promoted in the following terms:

> Avalanche is a Windows 3.x and Windows 95/NT based mail-bombing program that was developed by *H-Master*. Unlike the other bombers, Avalanche comes with a number of configuration files that permits the attacker to customize, create, and select random mail headers and messages. Using a sophisticated GUI, the bomber can select the number of mail messages to send or can force the program to send messages continuously until explicitly stopped. For anonymity, Avalanche '*features*' fake mail headers with several built-in anonymous SMTP servers. Avalanche is distributed with over 20 pages of documentation consisting of a detailed user's guide, a *Tips for Bombing* tutorial, and an *Addon Implementation Guide*. The Addon support functionality is a unique feature of Avalanche, which permits the bomber to add new attacks and functionality to the tool without recompiling the source code. Also similar to KaBoom and Up Yours, Avalanche can be used to subscribe Internet citizens to numerous mailing lists without their knowledge.[42]

Over the course of a weekend, around 5 million emails were sent, the majority of which purported to come from the company's human resource manager who had been responsible for dismissing the respondent. Charges were brought under Section 3 of the 1990 Act but the trial judge expressed the view that:

1. Section 3 was intended to deal with the sending of malicious material such as viruses, worms and Trojan horses which corrupt or change data, but not the sending of emails;
2. as D&G's servers were configured to receive emails, each modification occurring on the receipt of an email sent by Mr Lennon was unauthorized.

It appears that the report of the case is in error on this point and that the judge was in fact holding that each modification was authorised. Accordingly, he held that there was no case to answer. The prosecutor appealed against this ruling and the Divisional Court was unequivocally of the view that denial of service attacks were covered by

---

[40] At paras 60–1.
[41] [2006] EWHC 1201 (Admin).
[42] <http://www.silkroad.com/papers/html/bomb/node21.html>

Section 3. Delivering the leading judgment, Mr Justice Jack held that although a party with an email address must give some consent to receipt of emails and for any consequential addition of data to the computer system involved, this:

> plainly does not cover emails which are not sent for the purpose of communication with the owner, but are sent for the purpose of interrupting the proper operation and use of his system. That was the plain intent of Mr Lennon in using the Avalanche program. The difference can be demonstrated in this way. If Mr Lennon had telephoned Ms Rhodes and requested consent to send her an email raising a point about the termination of his employment, she would have been puzzled as to why he bothered to ask and said that of course he might. If he had asked if he might send the half million emails he did send, he would have got a quite different answer. In short the purpose of Mr Lennon in sending the half million emails was an unauthorised purpose and the use made of D&G's email facility was an unauthorised use.

Accordingly, the case was remitted back for trial with the suggestion that:

> One test which the District Judge might consider applying is the answer which Mr Lennon would have expected had he asked D&G whether he might start Avalanche—a point I have referred to in paragraph 9 above. I mention that because it seems to me that it points to the reality of the situation, something which, I consider, has been rather missed in this case thus far.

The respondent was subsequently convicted and sentenced to a two-month period of electronic curfew.

Misuse of devices

As indicated in the *Lennon* case, a wide range of devices may be used in connection with criminal conduct aimed at computers. A market also exists for trading in user names and passwords. The Convention (Article 6) seeks to deter such activities by providing that:

> Each Party shall adopt such legislative and other measures as may be necessary to establish as criminal offences under its domestic law, when committed intentionally and without right:
>
> (a) the production, sale, procurement for use, import, distribution or otherwise making available of:
>
> (i) a device, including a computer program, designed or adapted primarily for the purpose of committing any of the offences established in accordance with the above Articles 2 through 5;
>
> (ii) a computer password, access code, or similar data by which the whole or any part of a computer system is capable of being accessed,
>
> with intent that it be used for the purpose of committing any of the offences established in Articles 2 through 5; and
>
> (b) the possession of an item referred to in paragraphs a.i or ii above, with intent that it be used for the purpose of committing any of the offences established in

> Articles 2 through 5. A Party may require by law that a number of such items be possessed before criminal liability attaches.

The Police and Justice Act 2006 adds a new Section 3(A) to the Computer Misuse Act, providing that:

1. A person is guilty of an offence if he makes, adapts, supplies or offers to supply any article intending it to be used to commit, or to assist in the commission of, an offence under Section 1 or 3.

2. A person is guilty of an offence if he supplies or offers to supply any article believing that it is likely to be used to commit, or to assist in the commission of, an offence under Section 1 or 3.

3. A person is guilty of an offence if he obtains any article with a view to its being supplied for use to commit, or to assist in the commission of, an offence under Section 1 or 3.

4. In this Section 'article' includes any program or data held in electronic form.

In summary proceedings, the offence attracts a maximum penalty of 12 months' imprisonment (6 in Scotland) or two years following conviction on indictment.

Although there has been general support for the principles behind the measure, the manner of its implementation was subjected to extensive criticism in Parliament. The perceived problem lay in the fact that those developing and supplying tools used legitimately for checking computer security know that there is a very strong likelihood that the devices will also prove attractive to those whose intentions are more malign. The United Kingdom approach is perhaps somewhat stricter than that required by the Convention, which refers to articles 'primarily' used for criminal purposes. It is suggested, however, that liability will (or should) arise only in the event that a developer or distributor supplies articles, knowing that it is likely that the particular acquirer will use them for criminal purposes.

Conclusions

Nearly twenty years of computer crime legislation has seen perhaps more than its share of ups and downs. Although a number of judgments limiting the scope of the Computer Misuse Act 1990 have been overturned by the higher courts, it is tempting to recall the words of the Law Commission, arguing that:

> There is recurrent (and understandable) difficulty in explaining to judges, magistrates and juries how the facts fit in with the present law of criminal damage

and reflect that perhaps rather little has changed.

The 2006 changes expand substantially the scope and complexity of the legislation and it may be excessively optimistic to predict an untroubled future.

Suggestions for further reading

'Cyber Crime—A New Breed of Criminal?', *C.L.S.R.* 19(3) (2003), pp. 222–27.

'Cybercrime and the UK', *Companies and Law* 16(2) (2005), 33–6.

'Developing Policies for Cybercrime: Some Empirical Issues', *European Journal Crime Cr. L. Cr. J.* 13(3) (2005), pp. 435–64.

11

Computer forgery and fraud

Introduction

Reference was made in Chapter 9 to the major forms of computer-related fraud and to some of the costs associated with these practices. As with other aspects of the topic, the provisions of the Council of Europe's Cybercrime Convention have significantly influenced United Kingdom law in the field. Title 2 is headed Computer-Related Offences and in Articles 7 and 8 calls for the criminalisation of computer-related forgery and computer-related fraud, providing that:

> Each Party shall adopt such legislative and other measures as may be necessary to establish as criminal offences under its domestic law, when committed intentionally and without right, the input, alteration, deletion, or suppression of computer data, resulting in inauthentic data with the intent that it be considered or acted upon for legal purposes as if it were authentic, regardless whether or not the data is directly readable and intelligible. A Party may require an intent to defraud, or similar dishonest intent, before criminal liability attaches.
>
> Each Party shall adopt such legislative and other measures as may be necessary to establish as criminal offences under its domestic law, when committed intentionally and without right, the causing of a loss of property to another person by:
>
> (a) any input, alteration, deletion or suppression of computer data,
>
> (b) any interference with the functioning of a computer system,
>
> with fraudulent or dishonest intent of procuring, without right, an economic benefit for oneself or for another person.

Computer-related forgery

Although its application proved somewhat disastrous in the case of *R v Gold*,[1] there is no doubt that the provisions of the Forgery and Counterfeiting Act 1981 could successfully be applied to most instances of computer-related forgery. Perhaps the leading authority on the point is the case *of R v Governor of Brixton Prison and Another, ex parte Levin*.[2] This case concerned extradition proceedings, following

---

[1] [1988] 1AC 1063.   [2] [1997] QB 65.

a partially successful attempt by a number of computer hackers based in Russia to access customer account details on computers belonging to Citibank in the United States and to transfer balances to accounts controlled by members of the conspiritors. Although the balances were transferred and some sums of money withdrawn, the conduct was discovered. Some of the conspirators were arrested in the United States and the applicant was arrested by the United Kingdom authorities when he arrived at Stansted Airport, reportedly en route to a computer exhibition in London. The United States sought his extradition and in order for this to be granted, it had to be shown that the conduct alleged would have constituted a criminal offence had it taken place in the United Kingdom. Attention focused on the provisions of the Forgery and Counterfeiting Act 1981. Section 1 of the Act provides that:

> A person is guilty of forgery if he makes a false instrument, with the intention to induce somebody to accept it as genuine to his own or any other person's prejudice.

As in *R v Gold*, the issue before the court concerned the identity of the false instrument. The applicant's conduct had caused modifications to be made to the data held on computer storage devices within Citibank. That constituted an instrument and in response to the issue of whether it should be classed as 'false', the court ruled that:

> We consider the disk embraces the information stored as well as the medium on which it is stored, just as a document consists both of the paper and the printing upon it. Thus by entering false instructions onto the disk it was in our opinion falsified.[3]

Repelling arguments advanced by counsel for the applicant that the House of Lords decision in *R v Gold* indicated that such a disc could not be an instrument, the court referred to Lord Brandon's judgment in the House of Lords and his approval of the comments of the Law Commission, whose report on Forgery and Counterfeit Currency[4] stated that a forged document contained two messages: one as to the nature of the document, and the second relating to the words intended to be acted upon. In the present case it was concluded, unlike the situation in *R v Gold* where data was held in the victim computer only momentarily, the data:

> were inserted onto the disk with the purpose that they should be recorded, stored and acted upon. The instructions purported to be authorised instructions given by Bank Artha Graha to Citibank. They were not authorised and in our view the disk with the instructions recorded and stored on it amounted to a false instrument.[5]

Computer-related fraud

Fraud is a somewhat complex area of the law and is capable of encompassing a wide range of forms of conduct. The simplest, in many respects, is where a perpetrator seeks

---

[3] Ibid. at p. 79.
[4] Law Commission No. 55, 1973.
[5] [1997] QB 65 at p. 80.

to obtain money belonging to someone else by means of some form of trick or unauthorised conduct. In respect of this form of conduct, there will be little doubt concerning its criminality of conduct. Both Law Commissions, for example, expressed the view that 'when a computer is manipulated in order dishonestly to obtain money or other property, a charge of theft or attempted theft will generally lie'.[6] In the event that a cash dispensing card is obtained by means of a trick perpetrated on its owner, the charge of obtaining property by deception has been successfully invoked, although, as will be discussed below, the question of whether a machine, operating without any direct human control, might be deceived has resulted in significant changes in the law of fraud.

If there is little doubt concerning the fact that once another person's property has been obtained, an offence will be committed, one matter which assumes some significance is the question of when the offence is committed. In this respect, the case of *R v Thompson*[7] furnishes a helpful illustration.

Thompson was employed as a computer programmer by a bank in Kuwait. Details of customers' accounts were maintained on the bank's computer system and, in the course of his work, Thompson was able to obtain information about these. Having identified five target accounts, Thompson opened an equal number of accounts in his own name at various branches of the bank. In what might be regarded as a classic form of computer fraud, he compiled a program which instructed the computer to transfer sums from these accounts to accounts which he had opened with the bank. In an effort to reduce further the risks of detection, the program did not come into effect until Thompson had left the bank's employ to return to England. The program was also intended to erase itself and all records of the transactions once this task had been accomplished. Although the law report does not go into detail on this matter, the fact that Thompson stood trial for his actions might indicate that this part of the scheme was not successful.

On his arrival in England, Thompson opened a number of accounts with English banks and wrote to the manager of the Kuwaiti bank, instructing him to arrange for the transfer of the balances from Kuwait to his new English accounts. This was done. Subsequently, his conduct was discovered and charges of obtaining property by deception were brought against him and a conviction secured at trial. An appeal was lodged on the basis that the English courts had no jurisdiction in the matter, as any offence would have been committed in Kuwait.

This plea did not commend itself to the Court of Appeal, which held that the offence was committed at the moment when the Kuwaiti manager read and acted upon Thompson's letter. At this stage, Thompson was subject to the jurisdiction of the English courts. Delivering the judgment of the court, May LJ stated:

> Discard for the moment the modern sophistication of computers and programmes [sic] and consider the old days when bank books were kept in manuscript in large

---

[6] Law Commission Working Paper No. 110 (1988), para. 3.4.
[7] [1984] 3 All ER 565.

ledgers. In effect all that was done by the appellant through the modern computer in the present case was to take a pen and debit each of the five accounts in the ledger with the relevant sums and then credit each of his own five savings accounts in the ledger with corresponding amounts. On the face of it his savings accounts would then have appeared to have in them substantially more than in truth they did have, as the result of his forgeries; but we do not think that by those forgeries any bank clerk in the days before computers would in law have thus brought into being a chose in action capable of being stolen or of being obtained by deception.[8]

The conclusion that no offence involving theft or the fraudulent obtaining of property had been committed at the stage of making the false entry on the computer does not entail that no offence would have been involved. Thompson's conduct, had it taken place in the United Kingdom might have constituted forgery under the terms of the Forgery and Counterfeiting Act. It is also likely that, following the decision in *Allison*, discussed in the previous chapter and in *Levin* discussed above, the appellant would have committed offences under Sections 1, 2, and 3 of the Computer Misuse Act, with the Section 3 offence now attracting a maximum jail term of ten years. More recent reform has come with the enactment of the Fraud Act 2006, following the Law Commission's report on Fraud published in 2002.[9]

Deception of a machine

In part, this issue can be seen as having arisen through a well-meaning, though perhaps short-sighted, incident of law reform. Under the provisions of the Larceny Act 1916,[10] conduct involving a machine might have been prosecuted on the ground of obtaining services by means of a false pretence. This remains the basis of liability in Scots law, and, in its Consultative Memorandum,[11] the Scottish Law Commission expressed the view that in determining whether this offence has been committed, attention should be paid to the conduct of the perpetrator. If the intention is to obtain services dishonestly, the offence will be committed and the fact of whether the conduct operates upon a human or a machine is irrelevant.

In England, the Eighth Report of the Criminal Law Revision Committee recommended a shift from false pretence to deception, on the basis that the word deception:

> ... has the advantage of directing attention to the effect that the offender deliberately produced on the mind of the person deceived, whereas 'false pretence' makes one think of what exactly the offender did in order to deceive.[12]

---

[8] *R v Thompson* [1984] 3 All ER 565 at 569. The decision in *Thompson* has been strongly criticised by T. Smith in *Property Offences* (London, 1994)), paras 325–26, on the basis that if the transaction in Kuwait had been a nullity, its transfer to the United Kingdom could not become the theft of a 'chose in action'.

[9] Law Commission No. 276.

[10] Section 32(1).

[11] Sc Law Commission Consultative Memorandum No. 68 (1986), para. 3.9.

[12] *Theft and Related Offences*, Cmnd 2977 (1966), para. 87.

This report was published in 1966, before the problems of the computer had fully penetrated general legal consciousness. Its recommendations were adopted in the Theft Act 1968, which defines the concept of 'deception' as involving:

> ...any deception (whether deliberate or reckless) by words or conduct as to fact or as to law, including a deception as to the present intentions of the person using the deception or any other person.[13]

Although the point was never definitively settled, it was widely assumed that only a human being could be the victim of deception. In the case of *Davies v Flackett*,[14] a motorist was charged with obtaining car-parking services by deception. The car park in question had an automatic barrier control at its exit. Upon a motorist inserting payment of 5p into a machine, the barrier would be raised, allowing egress. The appellant approached the exit barrier, only to discover passengers from the preceding car forcibly lifting the barrier to allow that car to leave. Considerately, they remained holding the barrier and invited the appellant to follow. This conduct was observed by the police, who proved less charitably disposed, charging the appellant (and presumably the other actors in the drama) with dishonestly obtaining a pecuniary advantage by deception, contrary to s 16 of the Theft Act 1968. The charge against the appellant was dismissed by the justices on the basis that a machine had no mind and therefore could not constitute the victim of a deception. The prosecution appealed, seeking the opinion of the Divisional Court on the question of whether 'an act of deception directed towards a machine in the absence of any human agent is sufficient to support a prima facie case in the preferred information'.[15]

The Divisional Court agreed with the justices that the defendant should be acquitted, but expressed the view that the major flaw in the charge lay in the absence of any evidence that the defendant intended to evade payment. The evidence, it was held, indicated that the defendant had intended to pay when he entered the car park and remained of this intention until the very last moment, when the opportunity to avoid payment was presented to him. The question whether a machine could be deceived was treated very much as a subsidiary question, and differing views were expressed by the judges. Bridge J indicated doubt that this might be the case, commenting 'even if it is possible for a deception to be practised so as to establish that ingredient of the offence under Section 16 [of the Theft Act 1968] without there being a human mind to deceive (though for myself I doubt it)',[16] whilst Acker J, after holding that the case was not properly to be regarded as one involving deception of a machine, stated:

> Nothing which I say expressing my agreement that this appeal should be dismissed in any way suggests that an offence cannot be committed where there is any mishandling of a machine, and thereby an advantage is incurred.[17]

---

[13] Section 15(4).
[14] [1973] RTR 8.
[15] [1973] RTR 8 at 10.
[16] *Davies v Flackett* [1973] RTR 8 at 11.
[17] [1973] RTR 8 at 11.

Rather like a ticking time bomb, the comments in *Davies* were to lie dormant for a period of years but ultimately produce explosive results when, rather than seeking a definitive ruling on the point, the decision was taken to bring the prosecution in the case of *R v Gold*[18] under the terms of the Forgery and Counterfeiting Act 1981. The acquittal of the Prestel hackers gave considerable impetus to the move to introduce computer-specific legislation.

In 2002, the Law Commission published a report on Fraud.[19] This gave extensive attention to the question of whether a machine might constitute the victim in a scheme of deception. Initially, it was commented that:

> A machine has no mind, so it cannot believe a proposition to be true or false, and therefore cannot be deceived. A person who dishonestly obtains a benefit by giving false information to a computer or machine is not guilty of any deception offence. Where the benefit obtained is property, he or she will normally be guilty of theft, but where it is something other than property (such as a service), there may be no offence at all.[20]

Although consideration was given to the possibility that reform should provide that a machine could be deceived, it was concluded that this form of conduct should be criminalised under a new offence of dishonestly obtaining services. This offence will be considered below. In respect of the general law of fraud, it was proposed that there should be a shift from reliance upon the concept of deception to revert to a focus on the behaviour and intentions of the perpetrator. Accepting the Law Commission's recommendations, the Fraud Act was adopted. This provides in Section 2 that:

(1) A person is in breach of this Section if he—

    (a) dishonestly makes a false representation, and

    (b) intends, by making the representation—

        (i) to make a gain for himself or another, or

        (ii) to cause loss to another or to expose another to a risk of loss.

(2) A representation is false if—

    (a) it is untrue or misleading, and

    (b) the person making it knows that it is, or might be, untrue or misleading.

The Law Commission had considered that this provision would have been sufficient to deal with the situation where a person's contact was only (or largely) with a machine. An example might be where a party obtains a credit card and PIN number belonging to someone else and uses this to obtain goods, either over the Internet or by using a chip and PIN machine in a shop. The government argued, however, that:

> We do not want law enforcers to face unreasonably technical choices in making charges and we consider therefore that the Bill should make it clear that a false

---

[18] [1988] 1 AC 1063.
[19] Law Commission No. 276.
[20] Ibid., at para. 3.34.

representation should be an offence whether made to a machine or to a person. This is done by making amendments to provide expressly that representations may be implied and that a representation may be regarded as being made where it or anything implying it is submitted to any system or device, the aim being to clarify, for example, that the entering of a number into a chip-and-pin machine is a representation.[21]

Accordingly, a further Subsection was introduced, providing that:

(5) For the purposes of this Section a representation may be regarded as made if it (or anything implying it) is submitted in any form to any system or device designed to receive, convey or respond to communications (with or without human intervention).

In line with developments in the field of computer crime generally, further provision is made to criminalise various forms of dealings in respect of materials which may be used to facilitate a scheme of fraud. Section 6 of the Act provides that possession of an article for use in the commission of a fraud will itself constitute an offence, whilst Section 7 provides that:

(1) A person is guilty of an offence if he makes, adapts, supplies or offers to supply any article—

(a) knowing that it is designed or adapted for use in the course of or in connection with fraud, or

(b) intending it to be used to commit, or assist in the commission of, fraud.

By Section 8, it is provided that '"article" includes any program or data held in electronic form'. Lists of passwords or PIN numbers would come within the scope of this definition.

The dishonest obtaining of services

Money is not the only thing of value in the world. Increasingly, information may be the most significant asset of many businesses. It has long been the case that where information is linked to some tangible object, the informational content may be taken into account in determining the gravity of any offence. In terms of physical components—paper and ink—there will be virtually no difference between a £5 and a £50 note, but theft of the latter will be a more serious matter than theft of the former. It is well established, however, that information taken in isolation will not constitute property which may serve as the subject-matter for an offence of theft.

A vast market exists for the provision of electronic information services. In the legal field, information services such as 'Lexis' and 'Justis' offer their wares to the legal world—at a price. In a typical scenario, a person wishing to make use of an information service will enter into an agreement with the service provider, and be provided

---

[21] HL Official Report, vol. 679, col. 1106, 14 March 2006.

with a password or other identifier, allowing access to all or part of the contents of the database in return for an agreement to make specified payments.

In the event a party manages to secure unauthorised access to such a database, either by dishonestly obtaining password details or by finding a way to bypass the security system, information will be obtained without proper payment being made. The provisions of Section 2 of the Fraud Act described above will not be applicable to the situation where services are involved as it is provided that the terms 'gain' and 'loss' 'extend only to gain or loss in money or other property'.[22] Services cannot come within the scope of this definition.

Recognising that it is more and more common for services to be supplied in situations where a party's only contact is with a computer or some other form of machine, the Law Commission recommended the establishment of a new offence involving the dishonest obtaining of services. Whilst falling short of providing that information could constitute the subject-matter of theft, the offence is described as being 'theft-like' in nature. It was accordingly recommended that:

> Any person who by any dishonest act obtains services in respect of which payment is required, with intent to avoid payment, should be guilty of an offence of obtaining services dishonestly.[23]

Acting upon this recommendation, the Fraud Act provides in Section 11 that:

(1) A person is guilty of an offence under this Section if he obtains services for himself or another—

  (a) by a dishonest act, and

  (b) in breach of Subsection 2.

(2) A person obtains services in breach of this Subsection if—

  (a) they are made available on the basis that payment has been, is being or will be made for or in respect of them,

  (b) he obtains them without any payment having been made for or in respect of them or without payment having been made in full, and

  (c) when he obtains them, he knows—

    (i) that they are being made available on the basis described in paragraph (a), or

    (ii) that they might be,

  but intends that payment will not be made, or will not be made in full.

In line with general practice, the Act does not provide a definition of the term 'dishonest'. The case of *Ghosh*[24] laid down a two-stage test which is generally accepted

---

[22] Section 5.
[23] Law Commission Report 276 at para. 8.13.
[24] [1982] QB 1053.

as identifying the most appropriate criteria. First, it has to be determined whether conduct would be regarded as dishonest 'according to the ordinary standards of reasonable and honest people'. If that question is answered in the affirmative, it then has to be determined whether the defendant must also have realised that the conduct was dishonest. Although such questions will be a matter for the jury in any particular case, it is difficult to imagine that conduct of the kind at issue in *R v Gold*,[25] involving the surreptitious acquisition and use of a password, would not be classed as dishonest.

Conclusions

In many respects, although of obvious practical importance, issues of computer fraud raise relatively few issues of legal significance. Taking someone else's money without justification will always constitute some form of criminal offence, the exact nature of which will vary dependent upon the nature of the conduct. The situation has been more difficult when the conduct involves evading the charges which would normally be levied in return for the provision of a service. The provisions of the Fraud Act 2006 should serve to close a loophole which had existed in English law since the move in the 1960s to reliance upon the notion of deception as the basis for this form of offence.

Suggestions for further reading

'Criminal Law Tackles Computer Fraud and Misuse', *C.L.S.R.* 23(3) (2007), pp. 276–81.

'The Law and Computer Crime: Reading the Script of Reform', *I.J.L. & I.T.* 13(1) (2005), pp. 98–117.

[25] [1988] 1 AC 1063.

12

The Internet and computer pornography

Introduction

From its earliest days, the Internet has been used for the display and transfer of pornographic and other forms of unsavoury material. Its status as a communication channel largely outside existing schemes of broadcasting and publishing regulation has made it attractive to those whose activities operate on or beyond the edges of legality. In 1995, at the meeting of the British Association for the Advancement of Science, estimates were put forward to the effect that almost half of all searches made using Internet search engines were seeking pornographic material.[1] Although there is no doubt that much material on the Internet is unsavoury in nature, the view that the Internet constitutes no more than a 'heavily used red light district' appears somewhat exaggerated.[2] In most instances, it is questionable whether the involvement of the computer adds a new dimension to the question of whether conduct may be classed as criminal. In early 1995, considerable publicity surrounded the arrest in the United States of a university student who transmitted violent sexual fantasies over the Internet. Charges were brought under a statute prohibiting the transmission of threats across state lines.[3] Less publicity attended the dismissal of these charges in June 1995 by United States District Judge Cohn. Although the messages were 'a rather savage and tasteless piece of fiction', he ruled, they remained protected by the provisions of the First Amendment.[4] The matter, it was suggested, should have been dealt with as a disciplinary matter under the university's computer use policy.

A number of instances of successful prosecutions will be described below. Problems may, however, arise in two areas. First, there is the problem of defining or categorising the Internet. Different forms of regulation have tended to apply to different storage media and means of delivery. In part, this has been dictated by the accessibility of material. A

---

[1] *Independent*, 13 September 1995.

[2] For a comprehensive collection of materials on the topic, see the website at <http://www2000.ogsm. vanderbilt.edu/cyberporn.debate.cgi>

[3] The charges related to the contents of email messages sent by the defendant to another unidentified individual rather than to the Usenet postings.

[4] *National Law Journal*, 3 July 1995.

television broadcast, for example, is more accessible than a film in a cinema and is subject to more stringent regulation. Likewise, a greater degree of tolerance has tended to be given to printed works than to photographic materials. As has and will be discussed, the Internet does not fall easily into existing categories of communications media. A second problem may prove even less soluble. The Internet is a global network. Material may be placed on a server anywhere in the world and accessed anywhere else. In theory, this means that the Internet is perhaps the most heavily regulated sphere of activity in existence, as any country may claim jurisdiction in respect of material accessible from its territory. Claiming jurisdiction is very different from being able to enforce it in any meaningful manner. If material is lawful in the country from which it originates, there may be little that any other jurisdiction can do to regulate it. In a report on the work of the United Kingdom's Internet Watch Foundation, it was suggested that of 453 reports made concerning the presence of pornographic material, in only 67 cases was the material held on a United Kingdom-based server. The bulk of the material was held in the United States with, rather more surprisingly, Japan constituting the second largest host country.[5]

Concern at the possibilities for misuse inherent in the Internet has spawned a number of international, governmental, and industry-based initiatives. In January 1999, the European Commission adopted an 'Action Plan on Promoting Safe Use of the Internet'.[6] This claims as its objective:

> ...promoting safer use of the Internet and of encouraging, at European level, an environment favourable to the development of the Internet industry.[7]

In order to attain this, provision was made for funding to be provided to encourage work to be conducted in the Member States, under the guidance of the Commission, to undertake work in specific fields. Particular reference was made to:

- the promotion of industry self-regulation and content-monitoring schemes (for example, dealing with content such as child pornography or content which incites hatred on grounds of race, sex, religion, nationality or ethnic origin);
- encouraging industry to provide filtering tools and rating systems, which allow parents or teachers to select content appropriate for children in their care while allowing adults to decide what legal content they wish to access, and which take account of linguistic and cultural diversity;
- increasing awareness of services provided by industry among users, in particular parents, teachers and children, so that they can better understand and take advantage of the opportunities of the Internet;
- support actions such as assessment of legal implications; and
- activities fostering international co-operation in the areas enumerated above.[8]

---

[5] Available from <http://www.dti.gov.uk/iwfreview.>
[6] Decision 276/1999, available from <http://158.169.50.95:10080/iap/decision/en.html>
[7] Article 2.
[8] Article 3.

The 'Safer Internet Programme' was originally scheduled to run for a three-year period between 1999 and 2000, with some €38m of funding. This was extended initially for a further two years, and a further four-year extension with a budget of €45 million was established for the period 2005–8 under the title 'Safer Internet *Plus*'.[9]

Much of the EU-funded work has concerned matters such as the development of net filters and the promotion of industry self-regulation. A number of industry initiatives operate in the United Kingdom. UKERNA, which is the agency responsible for the operation of the academic network, JANET, maintains a list of newsgroups which may not be accessed over its facilities.[10] More generally, the Internet Watch Foundation was established by a number of the largest ISPs in 1996.[11] In part, this was a response by the industry to suggestions made by the Metropolitan Police that prosecutions might be brought against ISPs unless the industry took steps to regulate material accessible through its servers. As a number of recent cases have demonstrated, possession of material classed as child pornography is unlawful, whilst ISPs could also be classed as publishers and subject to prosecution under statutes such as the Obscene Publications Act 1964.

The Internet Watch Foundation's activities can be divided into two categories. It seeks to encourage the use of systems of content rating. A number of systems exist, such as PICS (Platform for Internet Content Selection) and RSACi, devised by the Recreational Software Advisory Council.[12] The Foundation also acts to report instances of potentially illegal material to the appropriate ISP and law enforcement agencies. To date, its efforts in seeking to prevent prosecutions being brought against service providers appear to have been successful, although it has been stressed by law enforcement agencies that no guarantee of immunity has been given. Implementation of the EU's Directive on 'Certain Legal Aspects of Information Society Services, in Particular Electronic Commerce, in the Internal Market'[13] might reduce the liabilities of ISPs as a matter of law. Discussed in more detail in Chapter 23, this provides in Article 12 that service providers will not be liable (other than to an injunction regarding future behaviour) where the provider:

(a) does not initiate the transmission;

(b) does not select the receiver of the transmission; and

(c) does not select or modify the information contained in the transmission.

The Internet and child pornography

Whilst initial concern tended to relate to pornography per se, with relatively conservative countries such as the United Kingdom fearing that national controls might be overwhelmed, attention has tended to become more and more focused on the specific

---

9   <http://ec.europa.eu/information_society/activities/sip/programme/index_en.htm>
10 Available from <http://www.ja.net/operational-services/usenet/banlist.html>
11 <http://www.internetwatch.org.uk/>
12 For information on rating schemes and a demonstration of their use, see <http://www.icra.org/>
13 Directive 2000/31/EC (the Electronic Commerce Directive).

topic of the use of the Internet as a vehicle for disseminating paedophilic material. Incidents such as 'Operation Ore', where the United Kingdom police forces are engaged in an ongoing investigation of several thousand United Kingdom citizens whose credit cards were used to pay for access to paedophilic sites based in the United States,[14] mean that the topic is seldom out of the news. It is perhaps testimony to the extent of public concerns that the Council of Europe's Convention on Cybercrime contains only one provision in its Title 3 Section headed 'Content Related Offences'. This provides that:

1. Each Party shall adopt such legislative and other measures as may be necessary to establish as criminal offences under its domestic law, when committed intentionally and without right, the following conduct:

   (a) producing child pornography for the purpose of its distribution through a computer system;

   (b) offering or making available child pornography through a computer system;

   (c) distributing or transmitting child pornography through a computer system;

   (d) procuring child pornography through a computer system for oneself or for another;

   (e) possessing child pornography in a computer system or on a computer-data storage medium.

2. For the purpose of paragraph 1 above 'child pornography' shall include pornographic material that visually depicts:

   (a) a minor engaged in sexually explicit conduct;

   (b) a person appearing to be a minor engaged in sexually explicit conduct;

   (c) realistic images representing a minor engaged in sexually explicit conduct.

3. For the purpose of paragraph 2 above, the term 'minor' shall include all persons under 18 years of age. A Party may, however, require a lower age-limit, which shall be not less than 16 years.

4. Each Party may reserve the right not to apply, in whole or in part, paragraph 1(d) and 1(e), and 2(b) and 2(c).[15]

The inclusion of this provision in what is intended to be a template for computer crime legislation at a global level, highlights the point that there is near-universal legislative condemnation of child pornography. The Convention on Cybercrime provides no definitions of any of the terms used in Article 9. The explanatory memorandum

---

[14] An indication of the global scale of pornographic activity can be taken from the fact that the United States Postal Inspection Service, a federal agency charged with investigating online paedophile activity, seized records of credit card payments by some 250,000 persons, of whom around 7,000 were resident in the United Kingdom. More than two years after the details were passed to the United Kingdom authorities, although 1,230 individuals have been convicted of offences (only one prosecution having been unsuccessful) with the longest sentence being that of 12 years' imprisonment, 1,300 cases are still under investigation: <http://news.bbc.co.uk/1/hi/uk/3625603.stm> The organiser of the original website was sentenced to 1,335 years' imprisonment.

[15] Article 9.

accompanying the Convention is rather more explicit, although even here, elements of uncertainty persist. It is provided, for example, that:

> The term 'pornographic material' in paragraph 2 is governed by national standards pertaining to the classification of materials as obscene, inconsistent with public morals or similarly corrupt. Therefore, material having an artistic, medical, scientific or similar merit may be considered not to be pornographic. The visual depiction includes data stored on computer diskette or on other electronic means of storage, which are capable of conversion into a visual image.

It is noteworthy that although there is absolute condemnation of those involved in the production, sale, or distribution of material, the Convention on Cybercrime leaves it open to signatory states to determine whether and to what extent the acts of obtaining or possessing material should be considered unlawful. Even in this context, international consensus is limited.

For the United Kingdom, the provisions of the Convention on Cybercrime do no more than restate existing legal provisions. Under the Protection of Children Act 1978, it is provided that it will be an offence for a person:

(a) to take, or permit to be taken or to make, any indecent photograph or pseudo-photograph of a child; or

(b) to distribute or show such indecent photographs or pseudo-photographs; or

(c) to have in his possession such indecent photographs or pseudo-photographs, with a view to their being distributed or shown by himself or others; or

(d) to publish or cause to be published any advertisement likely to be understood as conveying that the advertiser distributes or shows such indecent photographs or pseudo-photographs, or intends to do so.[16]

Only limited defences are made available to a person charged with this offence. Effectively, the burden of proof is partly reversed, with the accused being required to show:

(a) that he had a legitimate reason for distributing or showing the photographs or pseudo-photographs or (as the case may be) having them in his possession; or

(b) that he had not himself seen the photographs or pseudo-photographs and did not know, nor had any cause to suspect, them to be indecent.[17]

Given the manner in which the Internet functions with copies of pages being readily recorded in a computer's memory cache, a claim that a party who had stumbled onto a pornographic website was not aware that a copy was held on his computer is not as infeasible as might initially appear and in a number of cases defendants have been acquitted on this basis.

---

[16] Section 1(1).
[17] Protection of Children Act 1978, s 1(4).

Computer pornography before the courts

In the vast majority of cases, the fact that images or text are recorded and transmitted on digital media rather than on paper or video tape will not affect the determination of whether contents are obscene or pornographic. In similar manner to the topic of computer fraud, the use of computers and computer communications networks such as the Internet to disseminate material considered to contravene criminal statutes relating to obscene or pornographic material, raises comparatively few substantive legal issues. If material is considered to be illegal, this conclusion will generally not be affected by the medium in which it is displayed or disseminated. A number of issues have, however, arisen in recent years which provide useful illustrations of the problems encountered in trying to fit forms of computer-related conduct into regulatory schema devised in the light of previous forms of technology.

Pseudo-photographs

In the Criminal Justice and Public Order Act 1994,[18] provisions were included to extend the ambit of the Criminal Justice Act 1988[19] and the Protection of Children Act 1978[20] to prohibit the possession or distribution of what are referred to as 'pseudo-photographs', where what appears to be an indecent image of a child is made up of a collage of images, modified by the use of computer painting packages, none of the elements of which is indecent in itself. It is now provided that an offence will be committed where:

> If the impression created by a pseudo-photograph is that the person shown is a child, the pseudo-photograph shall be treated for all the purposes of this Act as showing a child and so shall a pseudo-photograph where the predominant image conveyed is that the person shown is a child notwithstanding that some of the physical characteristics shown are those of an adult.[21]

The definition of a photograph extends to 'data stored on a computer disc or by other electronic means'.[22] Although this will certainly cover the situation where images are held on a computer disc on a permanent basis, the case of *R v Gold*[23] discussed above may be relevant as suggesting that a more transitory storage will not suffice. Given the development of communications technologies, possession of data or software is becoming of less importance than the knowledge that it can be accessed whenever desired.

Under the terms of the Protection of Children Act 1978, an offence is committed by a person who distributes such a photograph or who has 'in his possession such

---

[18] Section 84.
[19] Section 160.
[20] Section 1.
[21] Protection of Children Act 1978, s 7(7).
[22] Ibid., s 7(4)(b).
[23] [1988] AC 1063.

photographs or pseudo-photographs with a view to their being distributed or shown by others'.[24] The fact that possession may be a basis for conviction should give service providers cause for concern. A defence is provided that an accused 'had not himself seen the photographs or pseudo-photographs and did not know, nor had any cause to suspect, them to be indecent'.[25] In the situation where users of a service are responsible for loading images, the service provider may be able to make use of this defence. As with other areas of potential liability, it is unclear to what extent a service provider may be entitled to turn a blind eye to activities on the system. The phrase 'nor have any cause to suspect' might impose a higher standard in this area than is the case with liability for defamatory statements or conduct constituting a breach of copyright.

An indication of the conduct which would now be prosecuted under the Criminal Justice and Public Order Act 1994 can be seen in the case of *R v Fellows*.[26] The appellant, who was at the time employed by Birmingham University, had, without its knowledge or consent, compiled a large database of pornographic images of children. The database was maintained on an Internet-linked computer belonging to the university. The conduct in question occurred before the entry into force of the provisions of the 1994 Act. Given these changes to the law, it is now significant in only two respects. First, it appears to have been the first case in which the word 'Internet' appears in the judgment of an English court. Second, it provides an indication of judicial response to the situation where new technology enables forms of behaviour which could not have been foreseen when statutory provisions were enacted.

Under the Protection of Children Act 1978, an offence is committed by a person possessing an indecent photograph of a child.[27] It is provided that 'references to a photograph...include the negative as well as the positive'.[28] The question before the Court of Appeal in *R v Fellows*[29] was whether images stored on a computer disk could be classed as photographs.

Answering this question in the affirmative, two issues addressed by the Court of Appeal call for comment. First, whether graphical files held on a computer fell within the statutory definition of a copy of a photograph for the purposes of the Protection of Children Act 1978, and, second, whether a computer hard disk containing these files could be classed as an 'article' for the purposes of the Obscene Publications Act 1959.

Although aspects of the noun 'photograph' are defined in Protection of Children Act 1978, for example, that 'references to a photograph include the positive as well as the negative version', there is no general definition. In the Copyright Act 1956, 'photograph' was defined as 'any product of photography or of any process akin to photography'.[30] The trial judge and Evans LJ both made reference to dictionary

---

[24] Section 1(1).
[25] Section 1(4)(b).
[26] [1997] 2 All ER 548.
[27] Section 1(1)(c).
[28] Section 7(4).
[29] [1997] 2 All ER 548.
[30] Section 48.

definitions of the term as 'a picture or other image obtained by the chemical action of light or other radiation on specially sensitised material such as film or glass'.[31] On this basis, the data stored on the computer's hard disk could not be classed as a photograph. The statutory prohibitions, however, extended to 'a copy of a photograph'. The computerised images had been produced by scanning 'conventional' photographs and it was held that nothing in the 1978 Act required that the copy of a photograph should itself be a photograph.[32] Given the copyright status of a photograph as an artistic work and the broad definitions of copying applying to such works, there can be little ground to challenge such a finding.

Although this approach sufficed in the particular case, many cameras now record images directly onto disk rather than film. The contents of the disk may then be transferred directly to a computer and the image viewed on screen. There need never be any 'traditional' photograph to act as an original. In such a situation, it may be doubted whether even the most purposive interpretation of the Protection of Children Act 1978 could have sustained a conviction.

The Copyright, Designs and Patents Act 1988 adopted a new definition of photograph as 'a recording of light or other radiation on any medium on which an image is produced or from which an image may by any means be produced, and which is not part of a film'.[33] This marks a significant move away from the dictionary definition referred to above. In 1994, the Criminal Justice and Public Order Act 1994 adopted a different approach, providing that references to a photograph should include 'data stored on a computer disc or by other electronic means which is capable of conversion into a photograph'.[34] Juxtaposition of the two definitions can produce a sense of giddiness, but this aspect of changing technology does justify the need for reform of the Protection of Children Act 1978's provisions. Indeed, as is seen by the introduction of the new concept of a 'pseudo-photograph' in the 1994 Act, it may be queried whether the concept of a photograph remains apposite in the digital age. On this point, there is obiter comment by Evans LJ suggesting that the definition 'seems to us to be concerned with images created by computer processes rather than the storage and transmission by computers of images created originally by photography'.[35] Such a view appears unduly restrictive, and leaves open to question whether it would cover the situation where an original photograph was manipulated electronically so as to change the nature of the image.

Both the Obscene Publications Act 1959 and the Protection of Children Act 1978 were enacted before the impact of computers had permeated the legislature's consciousness. The Court of Appeal's judgment indicates that, providing basic concepts are robust, a purposive interpretation can maintain the relevance of statutory formulations so long as electronic activities retain a connection with tangible acts

---

[31] R v Fellows [1997] 2 All ER 548 at 556.
[32] [1997] 2 All ER 548 at 557.
[33] Section 4(2).
[34] Section 84(4).
[35] R v Fellows [1997] 2 All ER 548 at 557–58.

or items.[36] More substantial problems occur when electronic signals constitute the original record rather than a reproduction of a physical object. Here, law reform will often be required. It is somewhat ironic, however, that in a number of cases concerned with computer-oriented statutes, the purposive interpretative techniques adopted in the present case appear to have been replaced by a much more literal and restrictive approach.

Multimedia products

A further case concerned with the application of obscenity law to computer-related material is that of *Meechie v Multi-Media Marketing*.[37] The defendant company established a club, 'The Interactive Girls Club', described as being an 'organisation dedicated to the production of erotic computer entertainment for broad-minded adults'. One product presented users with a short game. Successful completion of this would cause the display of a series of erotic images. A knowledgeable user would have been able to isolate the game element, moving directly to the erotic display.

Under the provisions of the Video Recordings Act 1984, introduced to control the distribution of so-called 'video nasties', it is an offence to supply video recordings which have not been issued with a classification certificate. No certificate had been sought or issued for the particular game and charges were brought under ss 9 and 10 of the Act, alleging, respectively, supply, and possession with a view to the supply of infringing recordings.

These charges were dismissed before the magistrates, who held that the product in question did not come within the scope of the legislation. Section 1 of the Video Recordings Act 1984 defines a 'video work' as:

> ... any series of visual images (with or without sound)—
>
> (a) produced electronically by the use of information contained on any disc or magnetic tape; and
>
> (b) shown as a moving picture.

Although it was accepted that the disc in question satisfied the requirements of s 1 (a) of the Video Recordings Act 1984, it was held that the images did not constitute a 'moving picture' by reason both of their brevity and of the staccato nature of the presentation, which appeared more akin to a series of still images. It was further held by the magistrates that the work in question was excluded from the legislation by the provisions of s 2, which provides that a video game is not to be subject to the classification requirements.

Both of these findings were reversed by the Divisional Court.[38] In a finding which may be contrasted with the dicta of the House of Lords in *R v Gold*[39] to the effect that

---

[36] *R v Fellows* [1997] 2 All ER 548.
[37] (1995) 94 LGR 474.
[38] *Meechie v Multi-Media Marketing* (1995) 94 LGR 474.
[39] [1988] AC 1063.

the term 'recording' required storage for a more than transient period of time, it was held that the short duration of the images in no way prevented their being regarded as a 'moving picture'. A significant development arising from the advent of fast and powerful personal computers has been the linkage between text, sound, and graphics. In the present case, this relates to a computer game and picture sequences, but the same could be said of most multimedia products. It would appear arguable following the decision of the Divisional Court that many multimedia products could also be classed as video recordings, and hence be required to seek classification under the regulatory schema. Although there may be an argument in favour of such an approach, it would be difficult to explain to average computer users that their multimedia encyclopaedias are in reality video recordings.

The exemptions under the legislation apply to computer games and to works 'designed to inform, educate or instruct'. In the present case,[40] the court was able to separate the picture sequences from the game-playing element and so remove the former from the scope of the exemption. It must be likely that in the future there will be instances where video images are integrated more fully with the elements of a game, thereby making the classification more difficult. This will almost inevitably be the case with multimedia products. The court's dicta, which must be seen as affording a very restricted scope to the exemption, may make this of limited significance, and it would be arguable that many examples of multimedia products dealing with medical or artistic topics would be taken outside its scope.

A further point which may be a cause for future difficulty concerns the definition of a moving picture. Although the finding of the court to the effect that the duration of a recording is of minimal significance in determining whether it is to be classed as a 'moving picture', there cannot have been many traditional recordings with a running time of less than 30 seconds. In the present case,[41] the images could be analogised to a more traditional cinematographic recording. In other computer-related products, the duration of individual picture sequences may be very much shorter. Even more problematically, a user may be afforded the opportunity to select particular aspects of an image for expansion or, perhaps, to manipulate the form of the still image. Such activities may present the impression of movement, but it is not clear how they should be regarded for the purpose of the legislation.

Jurisdictional issues

A further, and perhaps more significant, issue concerns the difficulty of applying localised concepts of obscenity, which are dictated by cultural, religious, and societal values in the global environment of the Internet. Attempts by Nottingham County Council to prevent publication on the Internet of a copy of a summary of a report into the handling

---

[40] *Meechie v Multi-Media Marketing* (1995) 94 LGR 474.
[41] Ibid.

by social work officials of a case of alleged Satanic abuse illustrate graphically the near impossibility of such an endeavour.[42] Following publication of a copy of the report on a United Kingdom-based website, the Council obtained a High Court injunction preventing publication of the report on the basis that its reproduction infringed their copyright. It was stated that the order extended to any hypertext links to other sites maintaining copies of the report. Although the order was observed within the United Kingdom, by the time it was issued, copies of the report were also to be found on a number of other websites around the world. A letter from Nottinghamshire's County Solicitor to the operator of a United States website threatening legal proceedings unless its copy was removed drew a somewhat stinging response. Admitting to the presence of a copy of a report, it was pointed out that the Council:

> ...ignore the fact that I and my website are located in Cleveland, Ohio, in the United States of America, a locus where the writs of the courts of the United Kingdom have never run.

Numerous other instances could be cited of the failure of attempts to impose national controls. In the so-called *Homulka* case in Canada, a husband and wife were accused of committing a horrendous double murder and were to be the subject of separate trials—the wife tendering a plea of 'guilty' to the charge of manslaughter. An order was made prohibiting the publication in Canada of any report of the hearings involving the wife until the husband's trial had been concluded. Once again, the ban was of some effect where traditional media were concerned, but served to prompt the establishment of a number of Usenet newsgroups, which carried full details of the case.

Other developments in the United States raise a further issue which is of wider significance. The individual states retain the power to determine what constitutes obscene material. This has raised questions of whether the operators of online services may be subjected to the most restrictive laws of the range of jurisdictions where the service is made available. Whilst this may be the case in the situation where a service provider has a physical point of presence in a particular locality, in other instances, a perceived danger is that there might be a 'race to the bottom' as countries compete to attract online business by offering a minimum set of regulatory requirements.

Against this argument, however, the case of *United States v Thomas*[43] illustrates that parties located within one jurisdiction but offering services or facilities over the Internet may find themselves subject to the most restrictive legal regime reached by their activities. In this case, the defendants operated a computer bulletin board allowing subscribers to download pornographic images (which appear to have been placed on the system in breach of copyright in the original pictures). Subscribers, who were required to submit a written application giving details of name and address, could

---

[42] For a comprehensive collection of material on the case, see <http://samsara.law.cwru.edu/comp_law/#Not>
[43] 1997 United States App LEXIS 12998.

also order videos which would be delivered by post. Under United States law, a federal statute provides that an offence is committed by a person who:

> ...knowingly transports in interstate or foreign commerce for the purpose of sale or distribution, or knowingly travels in interstate commerce, or uses a facility or means of interstate commerce for the purpose of transporting obscene material in interstate or foreign commerce, any obscene, lewd, lascivious, or filthy book, pamphlet, picture, film, paper, letter, writing, print, silhouette, drawing, figure, image, cast, photograph, recording, electrical transcription or other article capable of producing sound or any other matter of indecent or immoral character. (Title 18 USC 1465)

The interpretation of this provision may vary between states, the Supreme Court having accepted that the determination of whether material is obscene is to be made having regard to 'contemporary community standards'. The material in question was considered lawful in California.

Following a number of complaints, a postal inspector in Tennessee subscribed to the bulletin board under an assumed name. In return for a fee of $55, he was able to download a number of images. The defendants were charged and convicted before the Tennessee courts of breach of the federal statute cited above. Appealing against conviction, it was argued that material had not been transported by the defendants. Alternatively, it was contended that the trial court had erred in applying Tennessee standards of morality. Both arguments are clearly significant in the context of WWW activities.

The argument against transportation is essentially a simple one. The material in question remained on the defendants' bulletin board. All that was transmitted was a series of intangible electrical impulses, whilst the terms of the statute related to tangible objects. This argument was rejected by the Court of Appeal:

> Defendants focus on the means by which the GIF files were transferred rather than the fact that the transmissions began with computer-generated images in California and ended with computer-generated images in Tennessee. The manner in which the images moved does not affect their ability to be viewed on a computer screen in Tennessee or their ability to be printed in hard copy in that distant location.[44]

A similar approach would appear to apply in the United Kingdom. In July 1999, an individual pleaded guilty to several specimen charges of publishing obscene materials contrary to the provisions of the Obscene Publications Act 1959.[45] The pornographic materials in question were stored on computers in the United States but could be accessed by customers in the United Kingdom (or anywhere else in the world) upon payment of a fee of around £20 per month.

Two contentions were critical to the defendant's case. First, it was argued that publication of the material took place in the United States. This argument was dismissed, with the judge ruling that publication took place whenever the images were

---

[44] *United States v Thomas* 1997 United States App LEXIS 12998.
[45] *R v Graham Waddon* (1999, Southwark Crown Court, unreported).

downloaded onto a computer in the United Kingdom.[46] A further claim related to evidential requirements. As will be discussed in Chapter 16, the Police and Criminal Evidence Act 1984 requires that evidence be led indicating that a computer whose output is relied upon was operating properly at the relevant time. It was argued that this would have obliged the prosecution to lead information relating to the operation of the servers in the United States. Once again, the judge ruled against the defence, holding that the requirement was limited to demonstrating the reliability of the computer used to access the materials in the United Kingdom.

Although of limited precedential value, the case, coupled with the United States decision in *Thomas*,[47] provides useful evidence that the 'lowest common denominator' standard will not always prevail. The prosecutions, however, could only succeed because the defendants were or could be brought within the court's jurisdiction. Where service provider and user are located in different jurisdictions, enforcement will become much more problematic. Invariably, extradition will only be sanctioned by national authorities where the conduct complained of would constitute an offence if committed on its own territory. If the service providers had been resident in the United States and had not made the mistake of entering the United Kingdom, it is unlikely that any prosecution could have been brought. In the Press Association report of the case, it was noted that:

> Vice Officers are increasingly finding that porn sites siphon subscription money through companies based in countries such as Costa Rica to avoid the attentions of authorities in Britain and the States. And while Internet Service Providers in Britain shut down sites after they are contacted by the police, Scotland Yard's appeals to American companies have fallen on deaf ears in a country where adult porn, however base, remains legal in some states.[48]

With the development of Internet banking, it is a relatively simple matter for accounts to be opened and maintained in offshore locations. Location is becoming an irrelevant consideration for e-commerce and in this, as in many other fields of activity, the prospects for effective national control are limited. As has been seen with Operation Ore, however, where the United States authorities passed on details of credit card payments to their United Kingdom counterparts, there is evidence that international cooperation is increasing in this respect.

Conclusions

From media coverage, it is tempting to believe that Internet pornography poses massive challenges to the law. This is perhaps misleading. What has become clear over the past two decades is that it is difficult for nation states to enforce their own policies regarding what is or is not acceptable. There is no doubt that a computer user in the United Kingdom can readily access material which could not lawfully be purchased

---

[46] See also the ruling in the defamation case of *Godfrey v Demon* [1999] EMLR 542.
[47] *United States v Thomas* 1997 United States App LEXIS 12998.
[48] *Press Association Newsfile*, 30 July 1999.

over (or under) the counter in a shop. There is very little that law enforcement agencies can do in this situation. Matters assume a different perspective when there is a commonality of approach between the jurisdiction where material is hosted and where it is accessed. In this, as in many other respects, the Council of Europe Convention on Cybercrime is a significant, albeit limited, development.

Suggestions for further reading

'The Online Protection of Minors and the Right to Privacy: U.S. and E.U. Perspectives', *W.D.P.R.* 6(2) (2006), pp. 18–22.

'Internet Content Regulation: is a Global Community Standard a Fallacy or the Only Way Out?' *I.R.L.C.T.* 21(1) (2007), pp. 15–25.

'Sentencing Controlling Internet Child Pornography and Protecting the Child', *I. & C.T.L.* 12(1) (2003), pp. 3–24.

13

Detecting and prosecuting computer crime

Introduction

The preceding chapters have considered a variety of forms of conduct which may affect adversely the interests of computer users. A number of computer-specific or general criminal offences have been identified as potentially relevant in such situations. Assuming that the fact of damage may be established, a variety of practical and legal problems may face the task of establishing the identity of the wrongdoer and obtaining sufficient evidence to support a criminal conviction. Issues of jurisdiction will also be of considerable significance in the situation where access is obtained to a computer system by means of some telecommunications link. In this situation, it is very possible that the perpetrator may be located in one jurisdiction and the victim in another. As was stated in the Explanatory Report to the Council of Europe's Convention on Cybercrime:

> One of the major challenges in combating crime in the networked environment is the difficulty in identifying the perpetrator and assessing the extent and impact of the criminal act. A further problem is caused by the volatility of electronic data, which may be altered, moved or deleted in seconds. For example, a user who is in control of the data may use the computer system to erase the data that is the subject of a criminal investigation, thereby destroying the evidence. Speed and, sometimes, secrecy are often vital for the success of an investigation.[1]

The Convention contains extensive provisions relating to procedural matters concerned with the detection of computer-related crime and elements of international cooperation. Also relevant at a more general level is the UN Convention against Transnational Organized Crime and its Protocols,[2] which was opened for signature in 2000 and entered into force in 2003, whilst at the political level extensive work has been carried out under the auspices of the G8, which established the so-called Lyon Group of Senior Experts on Transnational Organized Crime.[3] Within the EU,

---

[1] At para. 133.
[2] Available from <http://www.unodc.org/unodc/en/treaties/CTOC/index.html>
[3] For a useful account of the G8's work, see <http://www.g8.utoronto.ca/adhoc/crime99.htm>

the establishment of Europol[4] provides a basis for cooperation between law enforcement agencies and, at a rather limited level, the Framework decision on information security[5] contains some provisions relating to procedural aspects.

Obtaining evidence of criminality

Interception of communications

In the situation where the conduct occurs entirely on the premises of the victim, as in the case of *A-G's Reference (No 1 of 1991)*,[6] no particular problems may be anticipated in the acquisition of evidence. All matters will be within the control of the computer user and, assuming their willingness to cooperate, there are no legal problems facing the acquisition of evidence.

Greater difficulties arise where access is obtained remotely. The cases of *R v Gold*[7] and *R v Whiteley*[8] might be taken as illustrative of such situations. In both instances, the intruders obtained access to computer systems from their own homes. Certainly, in such a situation, it is open to the victim to make available to the police and prosecution authorities any evidence within their control. This might include details of the time at which access was obtained to the computer system and details of activities undertaken in respect of the system. In such cases, however, it may be considered necessary to monitor and intercept communications. In this respect the Council of Europe Convention provides that:

> Each Party shall adopt such legislative and other measures as may be necessary, in relation to a range of serious offences to be determined by domestic law, to empower its competent authorities to:
>
> (a) collect or record through the application of technical means on the territory of that Party, and
>
> (b) compel a service provider, within its existing technical capability:
>
>   i. to collect or record through the application of technical means on the territory of that Party, or
>
>   ii. to co-operate and assist the competent authorities in the collection or recording of, content data, in real-time, of specified communications in its territory transmitted by means of a computer system.

The Regulation of Investigatory Powers Act 2000 is the major United Kingdom statute setting out the circumstances under which a range of communications data might legitimately be intercepted. This statute replaced the Interception of Communications

---

[4] <http://www.europol.europa.eu/>
[5] Decision 2005/222/HJA. *Official Journal*, 2005 L69/7.
[6] [1992] 3 WLR 432.
[7] [1988] 1 AC 1063.
[8] (1991) 93 Cr App Rep 25.

Act 1985, which itself marked a somewhat belated attempt to bring the United Kingdom's laws into conformity with the requirements of the European Convention on Human Rights. The provisions of the earlier statute had been designed to cover situations where voice telephony messages were intercepted in the course of their transmission over a telecommunications network. In a number of respects, the application of this statute has been overtaken by developments in technology. A particular factor has been the explosion in electronic communications. Unlike voice messages, which are transmitted and require to be intercepted in real time, email communications will be passed from one mail server to another en route to their destination. Copies of the messages will be made at each stage of the journey and may also be held on equipment belonging to an Internet Service Provider, even after they have been read by the designated recipient. Such factors render easier the task of discovering the contents of email messages. Against this, however, the emergence of systems of cryptography as a tool which can be used by the average person means that interception of a message may reveal no useful or usable information.

The Regulation of Investigatory Powers Act 2000 retains the basic structure for the provision of warrants to authorise the interception of communications where this is considered by the Secretary of State to be necessary:

(a) in the interests of national security;

(b) for the purpose of preventing or detecting serious crime;

(c) for the purpose of safeguarding the economic well-being of the United Kingdom; or

(d) for giving effect to international mutual assistance agreements in connection with the prevention or detection of serious crime.[9]

Differences between the nature of voice and data traffic has promoted the decision to adopt a different basis for interceptory techniques in respect of the latter sector. Here, rather than seeking to intercept email and similar messages in the course of transmission, the Regulation of Investigatory Powers Act 2000 provides for this to take place at the premises of, and on the equipment of, ISP (or similar operators). The approach is justified on grounds of cost and efficiency. Individuals, it is suggested, may use a variety of methods to access services such as email. With systems such as 'hotmail', for example, it is a major selling point that users can access their accounts from anywhere in the world. It is argued that:

These developments and others are resulting in a far more diverse range of technologies being used for access to the Internet. It may be expected that this diversity will increase further in the future.

2.4.7. The approach of intercepting Internet services in the telecommunications network, which requires a different interception solution for each service, will become less cost-effective as service diversity increases. It will also be

---

[9] Section 5.

difficult for the interception community to keep up with rapidly developing communication services.

2.4.8. It is also likely that a selected subscriber will utilise Internet services (e.g. a single email account) using multiple access technologies. Invocation of interception will therefore be more straightforward at the Internet Service Provider, rather than in multiple access networks.

...

2.4.11. There are a number of anonymous communication services that selected subscribers may exploit to access Internet services. Examples include pre-pay mobile phones and Internet cafés.

2.4.12. In these cases where a selected subscriber may not be identified through their access telecommunication service, interception of the selected subscriber's traffic may only be effected by intercepting the Internet service directly, e.g. access to a known email account or authentication with an ISP.[10]

It may be argued to what extent these factors differ from those associated with voice traffic. Very many individuals will have land-based and mobile telephones and can also make use of public call boxes. The suspicion may be that the involvement of ISPs creates the potential for more effective and cost-efficient surveillance of electronic communications. In seeking to give effect to this policy, the Regulation of Investigatory Powers Act 2000 provides that:

1. The Secretary of State may by order provide for the imposition by him on persons who—

   (a) are providing public postal services or public telecommunications services; or

   (b) are proposing to do so

of such obligations as it appears to him reasonable to impose for the purpose of securing that it is and remains practicable for requirements to provide assistance in relation to interception warrants to be imposed and complied with.[11]

Such obligations are only to be imposed following a system of statutory consultation[12] and subject to parliamentary approval.[13] It is provided that grants are to be given to ISPs to cover additional costs incurred in providing the interceptory capabilities required under the Act.[14]

These provisions were the subject of extensive parliamentary debate and controversy. Questions were raised concerning the practicality of intercepting messages sent

---

[10] 'Technical and cost issues associated with interception of communications at certain communication service providers', report produced for the Home Office in conjunction with the Regulation of Investigatory Powers Bill, available from <http://www.homeoffice.gov.uk/oicd/techcost.pdf>

[11] Section 12.

[12] Section 12(9).

[13] Section 12(2).

[14] Section 14.

using the packet switching system (PSS), given that these may be split into many different sections and routed in as many different ways. Concerns were also expressed that the requirement to maintain an interceptory capacity in systems would create a ready-made opening for hackers. Additionally, concerns were raised that the cost implications of introducing such facilities would impose a substantial burden upon United Kingdom-based ISPs and would therefore conflict with the government's oft-stated intention of making the country the world's most e-commerce-friendly environment. Against this, the argument was put by the government that obligations to provide for interception of communications have traditionally been imposed upon telecommunications companies and that ISPs are licensed under the same regime. Whilst correct, it may be noted that there are very significantly more small and medium-sized ISPs than there are telecommunications companies. It was suggested in Committee[15] that such providers would be compensated for marginal costs incurred in providing the necessary facilities. Implementing the Regulation of Investigatory Powers Act 2000's provisions, the Regulation of Investigatory Powers (Maintenance of Interception Capability) Order 2002,[16] applies to companies that provide a public telecommunications service to more than 10,000 customers. This will include mobile phone companies and ISPs. Such companies may be required by the Secretary of State to maintain a capability to intercept communications at a level permitting the simultaneous interception and transmission to law enforcement agencies of transmissions in a ratio of one for every 10,000 users. Responses are to be provided within one working day of receipt of a request for interception.

More discussion surrounded the provisions of Chapter 2 of the Regulation of Investigatory Powers Act 2000, which provides for law enforcement agencies to seek access to communications data. Such access may be sought under less restrictive conditions than those required to authorise interception of communications. With modern communications systems, especially mobile networks, data of the kind at issue might be used to track the movements of subscribers, whilst the detailed records of calls made and received could allow a detailed picture to be developed concerning the activities and relationships of individuals. The Regulation of Investigatory Powers (Acquisition and Disclosure of Communications Data: Code of Practice) Order 2007 approves such a code, which specifies the procedures under which a request for access may be made.

Further provisions regarding access to communications data were made in the Anti-terrorism, Crime and Security Act, which was rushed through Parliament in the aftermath of the attacks of September 11, 2001. This provides that a code of practice is to be issued by the Secretary of State regarding the retention of communications data by service providers.

The final provision of the Regulation of Investigatory Powers Act 2000 which should be commented on in the context of information technology law concerns its provisions

---

[15] HC Official Report, SC F (Regulation of Investigatory Powers Bill), 28 March 2000 (morning).
[16] SI 2002/1931.

regarding encryption. The use of encryption is widely seen as providing a weapon to criminals to enable their plans to be communicated with minimal risk that, even if the communication is intercepted, its content could be deciphered. Various suggestions have been made by law enforcement agencies as to how the use of encryption might be regulated. One system which was proposed in the United States would have seen users depositing a copy of their encryption keys with an escrow organisation which could, in response to a warrant issued to a law enforcement agency, transmit the key to that agency. Within the United Kingdom, the development of cryptography support systems (or trusted third parties) would see such details being held by agencies. The Act provides that where encrypted material has been intercepted in accordance with its provisions and there are reasonable grounds to believe:

(a) that a key to the protected information is in the possession of any person;

(b) that the imposition of a disclosure requirement in respect of the protected information is—

i. necessary on grounds falling within Subsection (3); or

ii. necessary for the purpose of securing the effective exercise or proper performance by any public authority of any statutory power or statutory duty;

(c) that the imposition of such a requirement is proportionate to what is sought to be achieved by its imposition; and

(d) that it is not reasonably practicable for the person with the appropriate permission to obtain possession of the protected information in an intelligible form without the giving of a notice under this Section,

the person with that permission may, by notice to the person whom he believes to have possession of the key, require a disclosure requirement in respect of the protected information.[17]

Notices under this heading may be served, either on the owner of the key or on any third party who holds a copy. As an alternative to disclosing the cryptographic key, a copy of the information in decrypted format may be supplied.[18] A deliberate failure to comply with such a notice will constitute an offence.[19] A Code of Practice for the investigation of protected electronic information was approved by Parliament in October 2007,[20] specifying the procedures and circumstances under which these powers might be invoked.

It remains uncertain how effective, or indeed how intrusive, the provisions of the Regulation of Investigatory Powers Act 2000 will be. There is no doubt that there is

---

[17] Section 49.

[18] Section 50(1).

[19] Section 53.

[20] Available from <http://security.homeoffice.gov.uk/ripa/publication-search/ripa-cop/electronic-information?view=Binary>

concern at the extent to which new communications technologies are threatening the effectiveness of traditional forms of law enforcement. As was said by the Minister of State at the Home Office in Committee:

> I should emphasise what the Home Secretary stated on Second Reading: we expect law enforcement to suffer as a result of the development of new technologies. That is a fact of life. That applies not only to encryption, which has been widely discussed, but to more fundamental developments in communications technology. We are trying to preserve as much as we can of valuable intelligence, while always focusing on the key purposes set out in clause 5 and remaining consistent with our e-commerce objectives. We should not adopt—and the Hon. Gentleman is not proposing—a philosophy of despair, of saying that we can do nothing about the matter or make any progress. However, we acknowledge that law enforcement will suffer from the development of new technology. Communications will be missed. We cannot establish a system that is totally rigid.[21]

The challenge for any new legislation in this field is to provide for effective systems of crime prevention and detection without affecting adversely the rights of the vast majority of totally innocent individuals. It does seem clear that as more and more personal information is recorded in electronic format, so the balance will have to be struck between protecting personal privacy and making use of what can be a valuable intelligence resource for law enforcement agencies.

Search warrants

Provisions relating to the grant of search warrants are contained in the Police and Criminal Evidence Act 1984 and, in respect of the basic offence, in the Computer Misuse Act 1990 itself. The provisions of the Copyright, Designs and Patents Act 1988[22] may also be relevant in respect of cases where software piracy is suspected. The offences under ss 2 and 3 of the Computer Misuse Act 1990 may class as serious arrestable offences for the purposes of the 1984 Act.[23] In this event, an application may be made to a justice of the peace for a search warrant, who, if satisfied that a serious arrestable offence has been committed and that evidence relevant to the case is likely to be found on specified premises, may issue a search warrant.[24] Such a warrant will, with the exception of specified material,[25] empower the seizure of any item of property which is reasonably considered to relate to the offence under investigation. In addition, it is provided that where information is contained in a computer, the constable exercising the warrant may require that a printout be taken of that information if it is considered 'necessary to do so in order to prevent it being concealed, lost, tampered with or destroyed'.[26]

---

[21] HC Official Report SC F (Regulation of Investigatory Powers Bill), 28 March 2000 (morning).
[22] Section 9.
[23] Section 116.
[24] Section 8. In certain cases, as prescribed in s 17, a search may take place without a warrant.
[25] Section 14.
[26] Section 19(4).

In the United States, seizure of computers and software was at issue in the celebrated *Steve Jackson* case, where the prolonged detention of the equipment was held by the courts to violate the constitutional guarantees of free speech.[27] Although the submission of the Association of Chief Police Officers suggests that innocent service providers should not be penalised for the actions of their users, there have been suggestions that extensive use has been made of the power of search and seizure. Under the provisions of the Police and Criminal Evidence Act 1984, it is provided that: 'Nothing may be retained...if a photograph or copy would be sufficient for that purpose.'[28] One barrister has been quoted as saying that more extensive and prolonged seizures have been justified on the basis that the equipment itself is needed as evidence at the trial.[29]

In respect of the basic offence, the Law Commission's recommendation was that there should be no provision for the issuing of a search warrant. In parliamentary debate, the case was argued that such a facility would be needed if there were to be any realistic possibility of the Computer Misuse Act 1990, s 1 offence being enforced. Particular reference was made to the situation where premises were subject to multiple entry. Although search warrants are not generally made available in respect of summary offences, the Minister of State accepted that:

> ...the basic hacking offence...is not untypically committed in a private house, remote from public gaze and with no one else present. I am not saying that this is a unique offence, but I cannot immediately think of many others that are committed in private houses to which the police have no access and that do not involve some party other than the offender.[30]

An amendment was accordingly made to the Bill, providing that a search warrant might be issued by a circuit judge where there are 'reasonable grounds for believing' that a Computer Misuse Act 1990, s 1 offence has been or is about to be committed in the premises identified in the application.[31] This provision does not extend to Scotland, it being stated in Parliament that equivalent powers already existed in Scotland, where applications for a warrant would be made to a Sheriff.

Jurisdictional issues

A practical problem relating to the prosecution of computer crime has previously been identified, in as much as the perpetrator of the conduct and the victim computer may be located within different jurisdictions. This is not, of course, an issue which is peculiar to instances of computer crime, but may occur in respect of many instances of fraud. A very simple example might see a person resident in Liverpool ordering goods

---

[27] *Steve Jackson Games Inc v United States Secret Service* 816 F Supp 432 (1993); affirmed 36 F 3d 457 (1994).

[28] Section 22(4).

[29] Alistair Kelman, quoted in 'Privacy: The Strong Arm of the Law', *Guardian*, 22 September 1994.

[30] HC Official Report, SC C (Computer Misuse Bill), col. 65, 28 March 1990.

[31] Section 14.

from a mail order firm based in Edinburgh tendering in payment a cheque which is known to be worthless.

In both England and Scotland, the status of the law relating to jurisdiction is unclear. The Law Commission have called for urgent reform in the area, arguing that:

> International fraud is a serious problem...It is essential that persons who commit frauds related to this country should not be able to avoid the jurisdiction of this country's courts simply on outdated or technical ground, or because of the form in which they cloak the substance of their fraud.[32]

The Scottish Law Commission indicated that the approach of the Scottish courts has been to claim jurisdiction in the event that the 'main act' of the offence occurred within Scotland.[33] Until recently, the view has been taken that the 'main act' occurs when the fraud produces its result. In the example given, this would happen in Edinburgh when the goods were posted to the customer. A somewhat different approach is evident in the recent case of *Laird v HM Advocate*.[34] This concerned a complex case of fraud in which individuals resident in Scotland fraudulently induced other parties to enter into a contract for the sale of a quantity of steel, the steel to be supplied from England. In this situation, the application of the 'main act' test would appear to dictate that the Scottish courts would not be entitled to claim jurisdiction. In the event, criminal proceedings were instituted and convictions secured in Scotland. An appeal against conviction based on the lack of jurisdiction was rejected by the High Court. Two main points can be identified in the decision of the Lord Justice Clerk (Wheatley). First, it was suggested, where a 'continuous crime' is involved there may be dual jurisdiction within both countries concerned. In terms of the circumstances under which the Scottish courts might claim jurisdiction, he commented:

> where a crime is of such a nature that it has to originate with the forming of a fraudulent scheme, and that thereafter various steps have to be taken to bring that fraudulent plan to fruition, if some of these subsequent steps take place in one jurisdiction and some in another, then if the totality of the events in one country plays a material part in the operation and fulfilment of the fraudulent scheme as a whole there should be jurisdiction in that country.[35]

The concept of joint jurisdiction is one which the Scottish Law Commission recommended should be adopted in respect of any new statutory offences which might result from their deliberations. In similar vein, the Law Commission recommended that the English courts should enjoy jurisdiction when either the perpetrator or the victim computer was located within England.[36] This approach has been adopted in the Computer Misuse Act 1990, although the enabling provisions are somewhat

---

[32] Jurisdiction over Fraud Offences with a Foreign Element (1989), Law Commission No. 180, para. 2.7.
[33] Sc Law Consultative Memorandum No. 68 (1986), para. 7.1.e.
[34] 1984 SCCR 469.
[35] 1984 SCCR 469 at 472.
[36] Law Commission Report No. 186 (1989), para. 4.2.

tortuous. Separate provision is made for Scotland, England and Wales, and Northern Ireland.

The basis for any court to claim jurisdiction will be the existence of a 'significant link' with the country in question.[37] In this respect, the provisions relating to jurisdiction can be divided into two categories with the Computer Misuse Act 1990, s 1 and s 3 offences being considered together. In respect of these, a domestic court will have jurisdiction if either the accused person was located in the territory at the time the conduct complained of occurred or the computer to which access was obtained or whose data or programs were modified was so located.

The provisions relating to Computer Misuse Act 1990, s 2 offences are considerably more complicated. Under these, a domestic court may claim jurisdiction in three circumstances:[38]

1. All aspects of the conduct take place in that country.

2. The further offence referred to in s 2 is intended to take place in that country, regardless of whether the 'significant link' required for the establishment of the unauthorised access component of the offence can be established. Effectively, this means that the victim computer will be located in the territory.

3. The 'significant link' requirement can be satisfied in respect of the domestic country and the further offence will be committed (either wholly or in part) in a country (or countries) which recognise such conduct as constituting an offence. In this event, it will also be necessary for the further conduct to satisfy the s 2 requirements of seriousness.

Extradition

The basis for the United Kingdom's laws relating to extradition is found in the Extradition Act of 2003, which replaced a series of statutes dating back to the Extradition Act of 1870. The Act repeals the provisions of Section 15 of the Computer Misuse Act 1990, which had previously provided that extradition would be permissible in cases where conduct alleged to have occurred in a foreign country would have constituted an offence under either Sections 2 or 3 of the Computer Misuse Act. The Explanatory Notes to the 2003 Act[39] state that:

> Crime, particularly serious crime, is becoming increasingly international in nature and criminals can flee justice by crossing borders with increasing ease. Improved judicial co-operation between nations is needed to tackle this development. The reform of the United Kingdom's extradition law is designed to contribute to that process.[40]

---

[37] Section 5.

[38] See s 7 (adding a new s 1(1A) to the Criminal Law Act 1977 for England and Wales, s 13 for Scotland and s 16 for Northern Ireland).

[39] Available from <http://www.uk-legislation.hmso.gov.uk/acts/en2003/2003en41.htm>

[40] Para. 6.

As was commented by the Home Secretary, in a Foreword to the Home Office document presenting the Extradition Bill, the existing extradition laws:

date from an age when suspicion and distrust characterised relationships between European nations and the courts saw their role as to protect those fleeing from despotic regimes.

The result is that nowadays the overlapping avenues of appeal mean it can take years to extradite someone who is suspected of a serious crime. It recently took nearly six years to send someone back to France to face charges of drugs trafficking.

This hampers the fight against crime and goes against the interests of justice and the victims of crime. It also reflects badly on the United Kingdom.[41]

For the purposes of the Act, the world is effectively divided into two categories. Within the EU, the Act gives effect to the Framework Decision on the European Arrest Warrant,[42] creating a fast-track extradition arrangement with Member States of the EU and Gibraltar (Category 1). The Decision includes in Article 3 a list of offences which will be covered. This includes 'computer related crime', albeit subject to a requirement that the offence should carry a penalty of 12 months' imprisonment. For the remainder of the world, power is conferred upon the Secretary of State to place countries in a Category 2 list; the Extradition Act 2003 (Designation of Part 2 Territories) Order 2003[43] gives initial effect to this power. The basic criteria for extradition is that the accused is charged with commission of an 'extradition offence'. This occurs when, inter alia:

the conduct would constitute an offence under the law of the relevant part of the United Kingdom punishable with imprisonment or another form of detention for a term of 12 months or a greater punishment if it occurred in that part of the United Kingdom.[44]

With the extension of the Acts penalties in the Police and Justice Act 2006, this will now encompass conduct which could be prosecuted under Sections 1, 2, or 3 of the Computer Misuse Act were it to have occurred in the United Kingdom.

The computer in court

In many cases, the major evidence indicating that a crime has been committed will be generated by a computer. In cases where a computer fraud has been perpetrated, the evidence may be found in the computer records themselves. In such instances, it will be vital for the prosecution's case that they should be permitted to produce such evidence in court. Two situations will be considered in which difficulties may arise. The first concerns the situation when the computer serves to record information supplied

[41] <http://www.homeoffice.gov.uk/crimpol/oic/extradition/bill/>
[42] OJ 2002 L 190/1.
[43] S.I. 2003 No. 3334.
[44] S 137.

by some person. Here, any records which may subsequently be obtained from the computer might be regarded as falling under the prohibition against hearsay evidence. The second situation concerns the situation where the evidence is effectively generated by the computer itself. Many breath-analysing devices used to detect instances of drink-driving use microprocessors to process a sample of breath, providing a printout of the resultant analysis. Here, the challenge to the evidence may be based more on considerations of reliability.

Hearsay evidence

One of the landmark cases in the law of evidence is that of *Myers v DPP*.[45] The case concerned an alleged conspiracy to deal in stolen motor vehicles. Evidence produced by the vehicle manufacturers at the time of the production of the vehicles was critical to the prosecution's case. As the vehicles moved along the production line, workers recorded details of the serial numbers of the various components fitted to a particular vehicle. These details were recorded on a card by the worker responsible. Eventually, the completed card was photographed and recorded on microfilm. By a 3–2 majority, the House of Lords held that this evidence would be inadmissible as hearsay. As the prosecution had failed to produce evidence demonstrating reason why the workers responsible for making the original records could not give evidence, there was no justification for admitting the microfilm.

The Criminal Evidence Act 1965

The decision in *Myers*[46] was effectively and speedily reversed by the enactment of the Criminal Evidence Act 1965. This short measure provided that documentary hearsay evidence could be admitted where the document was:

1. created in the course of a trade or business;
2. from information supplied by a person who might reasonably be supposed to have personal knowledge of the information contained therein; and
3. where the person in question is dead, beyond the seas or could not reasonably be expected to have any recollection of the matters contained in the record.[47]

This would be the case in a situation such as *Myers*, where it would be unreasonable to expect a factory worker to have any direct recollection of the numbers entered on to one card when they may well have entered hundreds of such numbers every working day.

The provisions of the Criminal Evidence Act 1965 were first tested in a computer context in the case of *R v Pettigrew*.[48] Pettigrew was convicted of theft of a quantity

---

[45] [1965] AC 1001.
[46] *Myers v DPP* [1965] AC 1001.
[47] Section 1.
[48] (1980) 71 Cr App Rep 120.

of money. Critical evidence was contained in a computer printout from the Bank of England, which indicated that the banknotes found in Pettigrew's possession had been sent to a bank in Newcastle. The records had been generated by a machine in the bank which fulfilled two functions. A quantity of banknotes would be inserted by a bank employee. The machine would check the notes for validity, rejecting any defective specimens. It would then divide the notes into bundles of 100 and produce a printout showing the serial number of the first and the last note in each bundle, together with a note of the numbers of any rejected notes. It was accepted that the notes would be numbered sequentially. Pettigrew having been convicted, an appeal was made on the issue of the admissibility of the computer evidence. This appeal succeeded, the Court of Appeal holding that the requirements of s 1 were not satisfied, as the bank employee responsible for operating the machine had no personal knowledge of the information produced.

The decision in Pettigrew[49] was subjected to extensive criticism. In particular, it was argued that the evidence in question should not have been classed as hearsay evidence, but rather as evidence generated directly by the machine. This view was supported by a subsequent decision of the Court of Appeal in the case of R v Wood.[50] This case concerned the admissibility of computer-processed evidence concerning the composition of a quantity of metals which were alleged to have been stolen by the appellant. It was held by the Court of Appeal that the provisions of the Criminal Evidence Act 1965 were not applicable. The analysis in question had been carried out by scientists acting on behalf of the prosecution authorities. As such, they were not acting in the course of a trade or business. The evidence should rather, it was held, be considered as direct evidence. The computer was being used as a calculator and the question for the court was whether sufficient evidence had been submitted indicating that its output could be relied upon. This was held to be the case.

In Wood, the case of Pettigrew[51] was distinguished almost out of existence, the Lord Chief Justice indicating that it was to be considered authority only for the proposition that:

> ...where it is sought to make a document admissible under the Act, the requirements of the Act have to be satisfied and one of those requirements is a personal knowledge of the person or persons who supplied the information to the record keeper.[52]

The application of the Criminal Evidence Act 1965 was undoubtedly critical in the case of R v Ewing.[53] In this case, the appellant had been convicted of theft on the basis, inter alia, of computer printouts generated by a bank's computer detailing transactions in respect of particular accounts. Before the Court of Appeal, counsel for the appellant contended on the authority of Pettigrew that this evidence should not have

[49] R v Pettigrew (1980) 71 Cr App Rep 120.
[50] (1983) 76 Cr App Rep 23.
[51] R v Pettigrew (1980) 71 Cr App Rep 120.
[52] R v Wood (1983) 76 Cr App Rep 23 at 29.
[53] [1983] 2 All ER 645.

been admitted. This contention was rejected, the court holding that all the statutory conditions required for the admissibility of the evidence had been satisfied. *Pettigrew* was once again distinguished as a case decided on the basis of a particular factual situation.

The provisions of the Criminal Evidence Act 1965 remain in force for Scotland. This was the cause of some judicial criticism in the case of the *Lord Advocate's Reference (No 1 of 1992)*,[54] although the case also demonstrates a more robust attitude towards the admissibility of computer-generated evidence. Two persons had been accused and acquitted of charges of fraud against a building society. In the course of the trial, computer-generated evidence had been held inadmissible as hearsay by the Sheriff. The Lord Advocate sought the opinion of the High Court on the question as to whether evidence of the kind at issue should be admissible.

The computer evidence in question had been generated by computers operated by a health authority. In line with the finding in *Wood*,[55] it was held that this took it outside the scope of the Criminal Evidence Act 1965, as the records were not made in the course of a trade or business. The High Court considered the judgment of the House of Lords in *Myers*[56] and concluded that the judgments of the dissenting minority more accurately reflected Scots law on this point. The High Court, it was stated by the Lord Justice General:

> ...has shown itself willing to adapt the criminal law of this country in order to meet changes in social conditions and attitudes...In my opinion that is a proper exercise of the judicial function and it is within the inherent power of this court.[57]

The information in question had been generated through the activities of a number of employees. It was impossible to state which employee had been responsible for entering a particular piece of information. The procurator had sought to present the evidence of the health authority's computer operations controller regarding the contents of the information. This evidence was rejected as hearsay by the Sheriff. The High Court disagreed, with the Lord Justice General, holding that the computer evidence would be admitted as the best available evidence, subject to it being established that it would be impossible to produce any other witnesses. It was not considered appropriate for the court to try to define the circumstances under which this might be the case, but the suggestion was made that:

> ...the reliability and sophistication of modern systems for the storage and retrieval of information electronically may well result in impossibility. Hard copy may be destroyed because it can be assumed that there is no need to refer to it, and checks carried out at the time of entry may make the keeping of references to its authorship unnecessary.[58]

---

[54] 1992 SLT 1010.
[55] *R v Wood* (1983) 76 Cr App Rep 23 at 29.
[56] *Myers v DPP* [1965] AC 1001.
[57] *Lord Advocate's Reference (No. 1 of 1992)* 1992 SLT 1010 at 1017.
[58] *Lord Advocate's Reference (No. 1 of 1992)* 1992 SLT 1010 at 1018.

The Police and Criminal Evidence Act 1984

If judicial activism has provided a Scottish response to the perceived limitations of the Criminal Evidence Act 1965, the English approach to reform was contained in the Police and Criminal Evidence Act 1984. Following the recommendations of the Roskill Committee on Fraud Trials,[59] the provisions of the Criminal Justice Act 1988[60] introduced more liberal rules for the admissibility of documentary evidence. Initially, the Police and Criminal Evidence Act 1984 contained provisions relating to documentary evidence in general. These provisions, as now contained in the 1988 Act, provide for its admissibility in circumstances broadly similar to those envisaged under the Criminal Evidence Act 1965, but applying in situations where the document is produced other than in the course of a trade or business. Additionally, the Police and Criminal Evidence Act 1984 provides in s 69 that:

> In any proceedings, a statement in a document produced by a computer shall not be admissible as evidence of any fact stated therein unless it is shown—(a) that there are no reasonable grounds for believing that the statement is inaccurate because of improper use of the computer; (b) that at all material times the computer was operating properly, or if not, that any respect in which it was not operating properly or was out of operation was not such as to affect the production of the document or the accuracy of its content.

It is further provided that rules of court may be made to require that a statement to this effect be given in a prescribed form. Schedule 3 to the 1984 Act provides that where a certificate is tendered as evidence of any of the matters referred to above:

> ...a certificate (a) identifying the document containing the statement and describing the manner in which it was produced; (b) giving such particulars of any device employed in the production of that document as may be appropriate for the purpose of showing that the document was produced by a computer; (c) dealing with any of the matters mentioned in Section 69(1) above; and (d) purporting to be signed by a person occupying a responsible position in relation to the operation of the computer, shall be evidence of anything stated in it.[61]

The provisions of the Police and Criminal Evidence Act 1984 were at issue before the Court of Appeal in the case of *R v Minors, R v Harper.*[62] The court considered the status of ss 68 and 69 of the Act, commenting that:

> In the courts below, it was assumed by all that Section 69 constitutes a self-contained code governing the admissibility of computer records in criminal proceedings.[63]

This, it was held, was not the case, the statutory requirements being cumulative rather than alternative. In the first appeal, the appellant had been convicted of offences

---

[59] HMSO, 1986.
[60] Section 24.
[61] Part III, para. 8.
[62] [1989] 2 All ER 208.
[63] [1989] 2 All ER 208 at 212.

of attempted deception and the use of a false instrument. These offences involved the use of a passbook. The conduct had related to a building society. A computer print-out produced by the building society indicated that the last four entries in the pass-book were false. Although evidence was led concerning the reliability of the computer equipment used to produce the printout, no attempt was made to establish the requirements of s 68 of the Police and Criminal Evidence Act 1984. This, it was held by the Court of Appeal, rendered the evidence inadmissible, although the conviction was sustained on the basis of other evidence.

In the second appeal, the appellant had been convicted of handling stolen goods in the form of a London Transport travel pass. Details of the pass were recorded on a computer operated by London Transport and a printout was supplied to the court. The printout was produced by a revenue protection official who had no knowledge of the manner in which the computer functioned and could not testify as to its reliability. The judge ruled that this evidence satisfied the requirements of s 69 of the Police and Criminal Evidence Act 1984. The Court of Appeal disagreed, holding that the witness was not suitably qualified to testify to matters coming within the ambit of s 69. Additionally, it was held that the evidence should have been declared inadmissible as no attempt had been made to satisfy the requirements of s 68.

The linkage identified by the Court of Appeal[64] between the requirements of the Police and Criminal Evidence Act 1984, ss 68 and 69, was further at issue in the case of *R v Spiby*.[65] Once again, the Court of Appeal was faced with a question of the admissibility of computer-generated evidence. In this case, the evidence took the form of an automatically produced printout of details of telephone calls made from a hotel room. The equipment was used by the hotel to bill its customers for any telephone calls made. Upholding the findings of the Recorder in the Crown Court, it was held that given the automated nature of the equipment in question, the evidence had to be regarded as real, as opposed to hearsay evidence. In this case, it was held, the provisions of s 69 of the 1984 Act were not applicable.

More recently, the application of the Police and Criminal Evidence Act 1984 has been discussed by the House of Lords in the case of *R v Shepherd*.[66] The appellant had been convicted of theft by shoplifting. Significant evidence in the case against her had been constituted by the printouts from computer-controlled tills. These purported to show that no goods of the kind alleged to have been stolen by the appellant had been sold on the day in question. Evidence as to the till receipts and their reliability was led by a store detective. This witness explained the manner in which the tills operated and the procedures which had been conducted in order to examine the till receipts. It was also stated that no problems had been identified with the operation of the equipment.

The evidence of the store detective being held admissible, the appellant was convicted. An appeal against conviction being dismissed by the Court of Appeal, a final

---

[64] *R v Minors, R v Harper* [1989] 2 All ER 208.
[65] (1990) 91 Cr App Rep 186.
[66] [1993] 1 All ER 225.

appeal was made to the House of Lords.[67] This proved no more successful, although their Lordships expressed a measure of disagreement with the earlier decisions of the Court of Appeal in this area.

The point of divergence centred upon the relationship between ss 68 and 69 of the Police and Criminal Evidence Act 1984. In *R v Minors*, the attempt to link the requirements of ss 68 and 69 led to the statement that:

> to the extent to which a computer is merely used to perform functions of calculation, no question of hearsay is involved and the requirements of ss 68 and 69 do not apply.[68]

Delivering the leading judgment in the House of Lords, Lord Griffith stated that no authority existed to support this proposition.[69] In so far as this dictum had been followed by the Court of Appeal in *Spiby*,[70] that decision was overruled. The application of s 69 of the Police and Criminal Evidence Act 1984, it was held, extended to all cases where the admissibility of computer-generated evidence was at issue, not merely to cases when the evidence was hearsay in nature.

The next issue to be determined was whether the evidence submitted in the present case satisfied the requirements of the Section. Although the evidence of a revenue protection official had been declared inadmissible in the case of *R v Harper*, that of the store detective was held admissible. Making reference to the provisions of Schedule 3 to the Police and Criminal Evidence Act 1984 regarding the issuance of a certificate relating to the operation of a computer, it was held that a person giving oral evidence need not possess the qualifications which would be required of such a signatory. Particular stress was laid upon the point that the evidence of such a witness might be challenged in the course of cross-examination. Lord Griffiths commented that:

> Documents produced by computers are an increasingly common feature of all business and more and more people are becoming familiar with their uses and operation. Computers vary immensely in their complexity and in the operations they perform. The nature of the evidence to discharge the burden of showing that there has been no improper use of the computer and that it was operating properly will inevitably vary from case to case. The evidence must be suited to meet the needs of the case.[71]

The decision of the House of Lords in *R v Shephard*[72] has been criticised as rendering too easy the task of tendering computer-generated evidence in criminal cases. Such criticism may be unfair. Almost since the enactment of the Police and Criminal Evidence Act 1984, calls have been made for the replacement of formal rules of admissibility by more general codes of practice relating to the weight properly to be attached

---

[67] *R v Shepherd* [1993] 1 All ER 225.
[68] [1989] 2 All ER 208 at 212.
[69] *R v Minors* [1989] 2 All ER 208 at 212.
[70] *R v Spiby* (1990) 91 Cr App Rep 186.
[71] [1993] 1 All ER 225 at 231.
[72] [1993] 1 All ER 225.

to items of computer evidence.[73] Mechanistic formulations as to the forms of evidence deemed acceptable are always likely to run the risk of being rendered obsolete by developments in technology. Recent judicial tendencies in both Scotland and England might, at least on one analysis, demonstrate a welcome degree of flexibility in allowing the admission of evidence to the judicial forum wherein its weight might legitimately be challenged.

Conclusions

New tools create new opportunities for criminals and require the application of new techniques by those who seek to apprehend them. There is no doubt that the widespread availability of systems of strong encryption allow criminals or terrorists to conceal evidence of their intentions or actions in a highly effective manner. With global communications networks there is clear need and justification for extensive international cooperation amongst law enforcement agencies. The difficulty, as has been a recurring theme throughout this book, is how best to safeguard the rights of the average person to respect for private life and correspondence with the aspirations of law enforcement agancies. As with most aspects of the topic, time has certainly not stood still, and it is perhaps a sad reflection upon the times we live in that the procedural provisions of the Council of Europe Convention on Cybercrime, which were criticised at the time of their drafting as being too draconian, now seem a beacon of liberality in the context of post-2001 developments.

Suggestions for further reading

'Computer Evidence: Admissibility of Evidence and Jurisdiction Relating to Online Fraud' *C.L.S.R.* 14(1) (1998), pp. 29–33.

'Legal Policies and Pitfalls in the Use of Electronic Information', *Corp. Brief,* 12(5) (1998), pp. 9–11.

'Evidence—Documentary Evidence Held on Computer', *Crim. L.R.* Oct. (1998), pp. 750–51.

Admissibility of computer evidence in criminal proceedings: I.P. & I.T. Law 1998, 3.

---

[73] See the VERDICT and APPEAL studies carried out by the Central Computer and Telecommunications Agency and summarised in S. Castell, 'The Legal Admissibility of Computer Generated Evidence', *Computer Law and Security Report* 2 (1984), pp. 2–6.

PART III

INTELLECTUAL PROPERTY ISSUES

14

Intellectual property law

Introduction

The subject of intellectual property has had a long and varied history. Developed during the Middle Ages, it initially aroused considerable controversy, largely because it was seen as a device for promoting the interests of those in authority. From the eighteenth century onwards, however, it almost faded from the popular consciousness. Even for lawyers it was often seen as a somewhat esoteric subject. Until recently, few law degrees exposed students to more than the most cursory examination of its scope and role, and fewer legal practitioners would have any dealings with the topic.

As this book has sought to describe, times are changing and the needs of the information society differ from those of its industrial predecessor. Information has become a commodity as valuable as coal or steel in previous eras. It was during the late 1980s, that the proportion of the gross domestic product (GDP) of countries such as the United States and the United Kingdom relating to the manufacturing sector dropped below 50 per cent for the first time since the early stages of the Industrial Revolution. This trend continues and the services sector is now responsible for most of the national income. Software (and electronic information services) makes up a significant and growing element of the sector. In its Green Paper, *Copyright and Related Rights in the Information Society*,[1] the EC indicates that 'activities covered by copyright and related rights account for an estimated 3–5% of Community gross domestic product'. The European information services market itself has been valued at almost €2.2 billion (approximately £1.5 billion) per annum. Intellectual property has become an important element in international trade, to the extent that it is the subject of a protocol to the GATT (General Agreement on Tariffs and Trade) agreement.[2] As will be discussed, the GATT and the World Trade Organization, which was established under its auspices, are playing significant roles in the development of intellectual property law.

The nature and purposes of intellectual property rights have evolved over centuries. Copyright in particular has proved to be a very flexible concept, being extended over

---

[1] <http://www.ispo.cec.be/infosoc/legreg/com95382.doc>

[2] *Agreement on Trade Related Aspects of Intellectual Property Rights, Including Trade in Counterfeit Goods.* This agreement obliges signatories to recognise the main forms of intellectual property rights in their domestic laws and to 'accord to the nationals of other Members treatment no less favourable than that it accords to its own nationals' (Article 3).

time to forms of recording technologies which could scarcely have been envisaged when the system originated. Even the most pliable objects, however, have a breaking point, and in respect of copyright some commentators would suggest that notions which were appropriate in an analogue age when the information industry was a relatively minor player on the national and global stage, may not be appropriate for the information society. Although there is no doubt that intellectual property is currently of greater importance than ever before, a system which is based on the notion of exclusive rights sits uneasily with the distributive nature of increasingly networked societies.

Forms of intellectual property rights

In general terms, the phrase 'intellectual property' can be regarded as encompassing anything emanating from the working of the human brain: ideas, concepts inventions, stories, songs—the list is almost unending. A basic distinction has to be drawn between intellectual property—which, as indicated above, covers a vast range of material—and intellectual property rights, which delimits the subject to encompass those aspects of the topic which receive a measure of legal protection.

Three main forms of right have traditionally been identified as operating in this area of the law:

- Patents
- Copyright
- Trade marks.

In terms of terminology, a distinction is sometimes drawn between industrial and intellectual property rights. The former term refers to topics which are of practical application and importance. One of the key criteria for the award of a patent, for example, is that the subject-matter should be capable of 'industrial application'. Trade marks, which seek to protect a holder's economic interests in some form of trading name or sign, can also be classed under this heading, as can the law of designs which protects aspects of the design of products, such as a motor car or a table. Although beauty is always in the eye of the beholder, the essential feature of these systems is that they protect items which serve some functional purpose. Intellectual property rights, principally the copyright system, are concerned with the protection of rights in some aesthetic or artistic work. Protection of literary, artistic, musical, and dramatic works is at the core of the copyright regime. If consideration is given to the nature of computer software, it will be apparent that it exists at the interstices of the industrial and intellectual property systems. Software, especially at the level of operating systems, is concerned with function, yet concepts such as 'ease of use' are also of great importance. Recognising this situation, the term 'intellectual property law' will be used throughout this book as denoting all forms of intellectual and industrial property rights.

Development of intellectual property law

At the outset, it may be stated that the role of intellectual property rights is to confer rights on the person responsible for conceiving ideas and reducing these to some usable format. In some situations, most notably concerned with the patent system, the right is close to the monopoly entitlement associated with the ownership of items of real property. In the case of copyright, however, the right is much more limited. The difference between the two regimes might be illustrated by reference to the story of Alexander Graham Bell and Elisha Grey. Both men invented the telephone. Alexander Graham Bell[3] allegedly reached the United States Patent Office slightly ahead of Grey. The patent system works in large measure on the principle 'first come, first served'. Bell was awarded a patent and the exclusive right to exploit the technology described therein. Even though Grey had worked totally independently, he was unable to exploit his own work as this would have conflicted with Bell's patent. In the event that the case should have centred on a copyright claim, Bell's protection would have been limited to preventing the copying of his work. Grey would not have infringed Bell's copyright and would, indeed, have obtained his own copyright for his own work. Patents, it might be concluded, confer a monopoly, whereas copyright can only be invoked to prevent copying or certain other forms of unfair exploitation of the work.

Until recently, the law of copyright was seen as having the most relevance to information-related products and activities. At a time when software development was widely seen as an art or craft rather than an industrial process, it was a relatively simple step to class computer programs as a form of literary work—an approach which features in many national and international copyright instruments. The patent system has always been seen as applying to the industrial sector and, initially, was regarded as having little application in the computer field. This approach was relatively easy to support and apply in the days when computers were large, stand-alone machines used mainly for the making of mathematical calculations. With the spread of computers and the introduction of microprocessors, it is a rare industrial process which is not influenced by some form of computer program. We invariably talk in terms of 'the software industry' and the software company, Microsoft, is now the world's most valuable company. The exclusion of software from the patent system has become increasingly difficult to defend.

The question of whether and to what extent software should be considered patentable has been the subject of considerable debate over the past two decades. During the 1970s and 1980s, when the judicial tendency appeared to favour the liberal application of provisions of copyright law, the role of the patent system seemed to have been marginalised. More recent decisions in both the United States and Europe have marked a retrenchment in this line of judicial thinking. In the leading United States authority of *Computer Associates v Altai*,[4] the Court of Appeals opined that:

> Generally we think that copyright registration, with its indiscriminating availability—
> is not ideally suited to deal with the highly dynamic technology of computer science

---

[3] See *The Telephone Gambit*, by Seth Sullivan (Norton, 2008), which argues strongly that Grey was the real inventor of the telephone.
[4] 982 F 2d 694 (1992).

...patent registration, with its exacting up-front novelty and non-obviousness requirements, might be the more appropriate rubric of protection for intellectual property of
this kind.[5]

Decisions by the patent authorities and courts in a range of countries have indicated increasing willingness to allow patents to be granted for what are frequently
referred to as 'software-related inventions'. Whilst the criteria for the grant of a patent
are considerably more demanding than those relating to the acquisition of copyright,
the greater legal strength of this form of protection is making the patent route increasingly the preferred option for software developers.

If copyright and patents can be seen as overlapping to some extent, the role of trade
mark law is significantly different. In the first edition of this book, written no more than
seven years ago, the topic received only the most passing mention.[6] The role of a trademark is to serve to distinguish the goods or services offered by one party from those of
anyone else. The current United Kingdom law concerning trade marks is to be found
in the Trade Marks Act 1994, which itself seeks to implement the EU Directive to approximate the laws of the Member States relating to trade marks.[7] Also relevant is the
common law doctrine of 'passing off'. As the name suggests, this operates to prevent a
party using names or other indicators which are likely to mislead third parties as to the
true identity of the person with whom they are dealing. Typically, the impression will
be given that a person is connected with some well-known and regarded organisation.

A trade mark may consist of anything which may be recorded in graphical format.
Traditionally, marks have tended to take the forms of names or logos, but the scope
is increasing, with sounds and even smells forming the subject-matter of trade mark
applications. For the present purpose, attention can be restricted to the use of names.
Given the increasing commercialisation of the Internet, organisations frequently
seek the registration of a domain name which creates an obvious link with their real-
life activities. The software company Microsoft, for example, can be found at http://
microsoft.com. In many cases indeed, firms have obtained trade mark registration for
their domain name as such. Amazon.com, for example, is a registered trade mark in
the United States.

As will be discussed in the following chapters, the task of fitting software and software-related applications into traditional forms of intellectual property law has not
been a simple one. In some areas, the attempt has been made to develop new, specialised forms of protection. The two main areas in which this has been attempted have
been in the fields of database and semiconductor chip design protection. In both areas,
the impetus for reform in the United Kingdom has lain in EU Directives. Whilst providing specialised or *sui generis* forms of protection, both regimes draw heavily on the
principles and policies of copyright law.

---

[5] 982 F 2d 694 (1992) at 712.

[6] To note that the names of IT companies such as Apple and Microsoft were protected by trade marks,
along with devices such as logos.

[7] Directive 89/104/EEC (the Trade Mark Directive), OJ 1998 L 40/1.

Conclusions

In our fast-changing societies, it is tempting to conclude that history has few lessons to teach us. Much depends, perhaps, on whether we see change as evolutionary or revolutionary. Prior to considering where and how intellectual property should develop, it is perhaps useful to look back to consider how and why the systems developed. The first intellectual property statutes were motivated very much by economic and trade considerations. In the English patent system, for example, invention took second place to the need to overcome by force of law the obstacles placed by local tradesmen against those seeking to apply techniques and technologies, established in other countries but novel in England.

A similar trend can be mapped in respect of the copyright system. Essentially a product of the invention of the printing press, this seeks to protect a range of interests. The world's first copyright statute was the United Kingdom's Statute of Anne, enacted in 1709. The date of the Act's passage is significant. Although the notion of copyright had been developed under the English common law, it had not featured significantly in Scots law. Under the Act of Union between Scotland and England in 1707, an eighteenth-century equivalent of the European Single Market was established, with Scottish producers enjoying access to the economically stronger English market. Scots law was retained under the Act of Union and Scottish publishers discovered a useful source of income by producing what today would be regarded as 'pirate' copies of leading English literary works. One of the motives of the Statute of Anne was to introduce copyright notions into Scots law and prevent what was seen as a form of unfair competition.

Matters have not, perhaps, changed greatly over the past three centuries. In 1707, a relatively poor country saw little benefit in systems of intellectual property law and some advantage in their absence. Its richer, more powerful neighbour used economic and political muscle to cause the introduction of intellectual property laws. Today, it is not self-evidently to the benefit of the developing world to enforce intellectual property rights, which primarily benefit first world owners. The price of entry to the World Trade Organization and access to first world market under the GATT and GATS (General Agreement on Trade and Services) treaties is, however, that they accept the World Trade Organization Protocol on Trade Related Aspects of Intellectual Property Rights (TRIPS). This obliges signatories to recognise intellectual property rights and to provide enforcement mechanisms in the event rights are nor observed. This obligation has been the cause of considerable controversy, most notably perhaps in relation to the production and distribution of anti-AIDS drugs, which are invariably protected by patent rights.

Perhaps surprisingly, almost no empirical evidence exists whether the patent system is effective in either economic terms or in ensuring that information regarding technical innovations enters into the public domain. Some studies have suggested that small and medium-sized enterprises make little or no use of patent specifications as a source of information regarding developments in their field of activity. In cases such as DNA research, it may be argued whether the publication of details of an end product adds anything to the sum of human knowledge and, as such, whether the award of a patent adequately advances the aims of the patent system. A recent study conducted for the Commission on 'The Economic Impact of Patentability of Computer Programs'[8] considered the literature on the economics of the patent system before concluding:

> The economics literature does not show that the balance of positive and negative effects lies with the negative. All it says is that there are grounds for supposing that the negative forces are stronger relative to the positive forces in this area than in some others and that any move to strengthen IP protection in the software industry cannot claim to rest on solid economic evidence.

In fields such as software and with projects such as the mapping of the human genome it may be questioned how far the award of patents serves the end of encouraging further innovation. As in the example cited above involving Elisha Grey and Alexander Graham Bell, different people may be working independently on the same idea simultaneously. It may be a matter of chance who stumbles on a practical method of implementation first. It may be questioned whether the interests of society in the development of technology are likely to be best served by the grant of a monopoly to one person or whether the existence of at least one competitor might have served as a spur to more rapid developments.

Suggestions for further reading

The Gowers Report on Intellectual Property.

The Economic Impact of Patentability of Computer Programs' EC Commission Study.

---

[8] Study Contract ETD/99/B5-3000/E/106, available from <http://www.europa.eu.int/comm/internal_market/en/intprop/indprop/study.pdf>

15

Key elements of the patent system

Introduction

The patent system is the oldest form of intellectual property right. Its development has been at times a convoluted and complex one and the concept featured in some of the major political upheavals in the late Middle Ages, testimony to the fact that the element of monopoly conferred upon the holder of a patent has at least the potential to provide very significant economic benefits. This chapter will consider in general terms the nature and manner of operation of the patent system, whilst the following chapter will focus upon the somewhat complex manner in which the system has operated in respect of so-called software-related inventions.

The first recorded patent was issued in Florence in the fifteenth century. We are told that:

> Filippo Brunelleschi, the architect of Florence's remarkable cathedral, won the world's first patent for a technical invention in 1421. Brunelleschi was a classic man of the Renaissance: tough-minded, multi-talented and thoroughly self-confident. He claimed he had invented a new means of conveying goods up the Arno River (he was intentionally vague on details), which he refused to develop unless the state kept others from copying his design. Florence complied, and Brunelleschi walked away with the right to exclude all new means of transport on the Arno for three years.[1]

As adopted in England, the purpose of the patent system was somewhat different. In the early Middle Ages, each town would have its guilds of craftsmen, who would guard access to the various trades jealously. Only a member of the appropriate guild could, for example, act as a butcher or carpenter. One of the major weaknesses of such an approach was that the guilds stifled innovation. Recognising that the country was lagging behind its continental rivals in terms of technology, the practice began whereby the Sovereign would encourage foreigners to come to England, bringing with them their advanced technical skills. To overcome the objections of the craft guilds, letters patent would be issued. Signed with the Royal seal, these would command any

---

[1] R. King, *Brunelleschi's Dome: The Story of the Great Cathedral of Florence* (London, 2001), p. 3.

citizen to refrain from interfering with the bearer in the exercise of the technical skills referred to in the letter. The first recorded English patent of this kind was issued to a Flemish glazier who came to the country to install stained glass windows in Eton College. Unlike Brunelleschi's patent, the technology covered by the patent was new to the country rather than new in itself.

In the sixteenth and seventeenth centuries the system fell increasingly into disrepute. Although some patents were granted in respect of what might be regarded as inventions (the first recorded patent of this kind being awarded to an Italian émigré, Annoni, who developed a novel system of fortification, used to safeguard the town of Berwick against the Scots invaders), the system was all too often used to boost the Royal revenues by conferring a monopoly in respect of basic commodities for a fee. A prime example was the grant of a patent in respect of playing cards. In 1602, the courts declared unlawful a Royal monopoly relating to the manufacture of playing cards and in 1623 the Statute of Monopolies rendered illegal all monopolies except those:

> ...for the term of 14 years or under hereafter to be made of the sole working or making of any manner of new manufactures within this Realm to the true and first inventor; monopolies should not be 'contrary to the law nor mischievous to the State by raising prices of commodities at home or hurt of trade'.[2]

It was almost another hundred years, however, before it was settled that in return for the award of a patent, the inventor was required to specify details of the manner in which the invention functioned, and not until the enactment of the Patent Act 1902 that even a rudimentary form of examination of patent applications was made with a view to establishing novelty.

In recent United Kingdom statutes, it has been made absolutely clear that the element of invention is critical for any award and that a balance is to be struck whereby in return for putting details of the manner in which the invention functions into the public arena, the inventor is to receive a temporary monopoly in respect of its exploitation. An oft-quoted description of the modern system explains that:

> The basic theory of the patent system is simple and reasonable. It is desirable in the public interest that industrial techniques should be improved. In order to encourage improvement, and to encourage the disclosure of improvements in preference to their use in secret, any person devising an improvement in a manufactured article, or in machinery or methods for making it, may upon disclosure of the improvement at the Patent Office demand to be given a monopoly in the use for a period of years. After that period it passes into the public domain; and the temporary monopoly is not objectionable, for if it had not been for the inventor who devised and disclosed the improvement nobody would have been able to use it at that or any other time, since nobody would have known about it. Furthermore, the giving of the monopoly encourages the putting into practice of the invention, for the only way the inventor can make a profit from it (or even recover the fees for his patent) is by putting it into practice; either by using it

---

[2] Section 6.

himself, and deriving an advantage over his competitors from its use, or by allowing others to use it in return for royalties.[3]

Today, the United Kingdom's patent system is based primarily on the Patents Act 1977. This statute was enacted in part to reform and update the United Kingdom law relating to patents but also in order to bring domestic law into conformity with the provisions of the European Patent Convention, opened for signature in 1973, which, as will be discussed below, provides for a measure of harmonisation in matters of substance and procedure amongst signatory states.

Whilst there is no doubt that inventiveness is a key requirement of the patent system, what has been more debatable has been the application of the system to software-related inventions—innovations where novelty resides primarily or exclusively in software components. Concern has tended to focus on two elements: first, whether software developments fit conceptually into the industrial nature of the system, and, second, whether the library and related resources exist to allow claim to novelty to be adequately assessed. This remains the most problematic aspect of the subject and will be discussed in more detail below.

Patents in the international arena

Until recent times, patent systems tended to be found only in the developed world. The advent of the World Trade Organization has resulted in many more countries introducing systems of patent protection. Although there is some element of harmonisation, this is at a lower level than provided for under the Berne Copyright Convention, first adopted in that city in 1886 and subject thereafter to periodic revisions, which provides for almost worldwide protection to be conferred automatically on literary, dramatic, and musical works. A United Kingdom patent will be valid within the United Kingdom but of no effect in Japan or the United States, and vice versa. A person wishing to secure widespread patent protection for an invention will have to undergo the time-consuming and expensive process of seeking to obtain a patent from each country where protection is desired.

The oldest international instrument is the Paris Convention (an instrument signed by ninety-six states, including all of the major industrial states).[4] This provides that the submission of an application for patent protection in one signatory state will serve to establish priority for the applicant in the event that equivalent applications are submitted in other signatory states within twelve months.[5] Although such a facility is of considerable value for inventors, the practical problems involved in obtaining patent

---

[3] T. A. Blanco White, *Patents for Inventions* (London, 1983), p. 1. For a good description of the history of the United Kingdom patent system, see the Patent Office website at <http://www.patent.gov.uk/dpatents/fivehund.html>

[4] The Convention was first opened for signature on 20 March 1883, with the most recent revision occurring in Stockholm in 1968.

[5] Article 4.

protection on anything like a worldwide basis are immense, and a number of subsequent agreements have sought to ease the task facing applicants.

The Patent Co-operation Treaty

The Patent Co-operation Treaty, which was opened for signature in 1970, prescribes basic features which are to be found in the national laws of signatory states. Under the provisions of the Patent Co-operation Treaty, an application may be directed to the patent authorities in any state and will indicate the countries within which patent protection is sought.[6] The national authority will then transmit the application to an International Searching Authority (the national patent offices of Austria, Australia, Japan, Russia, Sweden, and the United States, together with the European Patent Office).[7] The procedure to be adopted subsequently will depend upon the extent to which the state in question adheres to the Treaty. At the most basic level, the International Searching Authority will carry out a prior art search and submit reports to the designated national authorities.[8] Signatory states are given the option to adhere to a more significant regime which will permit the searching authority to conduct a preliminary examination.[9] Once again, reports will be sent to the designated national authorities. The Patent Co-operation Treaty does not contain any specific prohibition against the award of patents for computer programs,[10] but does state that an International Searching Authority is not to be obliged to conduct a search of the prior art in respect of a computer program 'to the extent that the International Searching Authority is not equipped to search prior art concerning such programs'.

The operation of the Patent Co-operation Treaty serves to eliminate a measure of the duplication of searches and examinations which would otherwise face an international applicant. Ultimately, however, the decision as to whether to grant or refuse a particular application is one for the national authorities.

The European Patent Convention

More extensive rationalisation of the patent system has been carried out within Europe with the adoption of the European Patent Convention. This Convention was opened for signature in 1973, and has been ratified by Belgium, France, Germany, Luxembourg, the Netherlands, Switzerland, and the United Kingdom. The Convention establishes the European Patent Office (located in Munich) and the concept of a European Patent. The title, however, is something of a misnomer. An applicant is required to specify those countries in which it is intended that the patent will apply and, assuming the application is successful, the end product will be the award of a basket of national patents. Effectively, the role of the Convention and the European Patent Office is to centralise the process for the award of national patents, with the costs to applicants rising in line with the number of countries in which protection is sought. As the European Commission

---

[6] Article 3.   [7] Article 12.   [8] Article 15.   [9] Article 31.
[10] Article 33 provides that the subject-matter of a patent may be anything that can be made or used.

has commented, one consequence of this process has been that 'the additional costs of protection for each designated country are prompting businesses to be selective in their choice of countries, with effects that run counter to the aims of the single market'.[11]

Applications for patent protection may be addressed to the European Patent Office. Once again, the applicant must indicate those countries to which they wish the patent to extend.[12] Subsequently, all the examining procedures will be conducted by the European Patent Office, which will then also proceed to make the decision on whether to grant the patent. Although some differences of procedure and style can be identified between the practice of the United Kingdom Patent Office and its European counterparts, the principles which will be applied are virtually identical. The British law relating to patents is to be found today in the Patents Act 1977. This statute was introduced in part to update domestic law, but principally to enable the United Kingdom to ratify the European Patent Convention. The Act provides that judicial notice is to be taken of decisions of the European Patent Office authorities and, as will be discussed below, decisions made within the European Patent Office have proved extremely influential in the domestic system. In one of the leading United Kingdom cases, the view was strongly expressed that:

> It would be absurd if, on the issue of patentability, a patent application should suffer a different fate according to whether it was made in the United Kingdom under the Act or was made in Munich for a European Parliament (United Kingdom) under the Convention.[13]

As will be discussed below, the absurd has become very close to becoming the rule.

The proposed Community Patent

Although the European Patent Convention (the Munich Convention) is sometimes linked with the EU, the two organisations are quite distinct. In the 1970s, it was the intention of the then EU Member States that the Munich Convention should be followed shortly by the establishment of a Community Patent and the Community Patent Convention (the Luxembourg Convention) was signed in 1975. This sought to establish a unitary patent system operating throughout the EU. The system would, however, be administered through the European Patent Office. In spite of the conclusion in 1989 of a further Agreement (the Luxembourg Agreement), the Convention has never entered into force, having been ratified by only seven of the current Member States (Denmark, France, Germany, Greece, Luxembourg, the Netherlands, and the United Kingdom). Over the past decade, however, the European Commission has sought to become more involved in the field. During 1997, the Commission published a Green Paper, *Community Patent and the Patent System in Europe*.[14] This document sought views on future EU action in the field of intellectual property law, exploring the possibility that a new EU patent regime might be established by Regulation. In

---

[11] Green Paper, *Community Patent and the Patent System in Europe* (1997), available from <http://europa.eu/documents/comm/green_papers/pdf/com97_314_en.pdf>

[12] Article 79.

[13] Per Nicholls J in *Gale's Application* [1991] RPC 305.   [14] COM (97) 314 final.

spite of regular appearances on the agenda of meetings of the Council of Ministers, the Regulation has not been adopted,[15] with the Council meeting of 25 and 26 March 2004 concluding that:

> agreement on the Community Patent is now long overdue and the European Council calls for further efforts to complete work on this proposal.

The Community patent continues to be bogged down in the European legislative process. In a Commission Communication published in April 2007, it was recognised that the costs involved, principally in providing for translations of an application into other Community languages, continued to constitute a significant barrier, although it was again indicated that further measures would be introduced during 2008.

Although the Community Patent Convention is not in force, the provisions of EU law are of considerable significance in the field of intellectual property rights. In particular, the EU's competition policy will prevent the owner of a patent from using the rights conferred thereby to impede the flow of goods between Member States. Effectively, if a product has been lawfully marketed in one Member State, it may be bought and sold in other states, irrespective of any patent rights which might otherwise apply in those territories.[16]

Intellectual property in the GATS and WTO

Since shortly after the end of the Second World War, the General Agreement on Tariffs and Trade has provided a legal mechanism for international trade. Reform to the system in the 1990s brought services into the international agreement for the first time and also introduced provisions relating to intellectual property rights. The Trade Related Aspects of Intellectual Property Rights (TRIPS) Protocol[17] to the General Agreement on Tariffs and Trade (GATT) requires signatories to make patents:

> ...available for any inventions, whether products or processes, in all fields of technology, provided that they are new, involve an inventive step and are capable of industrial application...patents shall be available and patent rights enjoyable without discrimination as to the place of invention, the field of technology and whether products are imported or locally produced.[18]

This provision was included at the behest of the developed world, and was prompted by concern that companies were suffering losses through audio, software, and video piracy in developing countries, with little legal recourse because concepts of intellectual property law were not recognised by national laws. Effectively, TRIPS requires these states to introduce intellectual property statutes as the price for benefiting from

---

[15] The draft regulation is available from <http://europa.eu.int/comm/internal_market/en/indprop/patent/index.htm>

[16] See Chapter 25.

[17] Adopted in 1994, entering into force on 1 January 1995. The text of TRIPS is available from <http://www.wto.org/wto/intellec/1-ipcon.htm>

[18] Article 27.

the free trade provisions of the GATT. Although not technically binding on either the EU or the European Patent Office, there is no doubt that its provisions requiring that patents be made available 'for any inventions' have proved highly influential in an on-going debate concerning the patentabilty of software-related inventions.

Requirements for patentability

A patent may be awarded in respect of an invention. The invention may relate either to a new product or to a novel process. The Patents Act 1977 does not define the word 'invention', but it does specify attributes that any invention must possess. These require that:

(a) the invention is new;

(b) it involves an inventive step;

(c) it is capable of industrial exploitation; and

(d) the grant of a patent for it is not excluded.[19]

As will be discussed extensively below, the categories of excluded subject-matter are of great significance in the case of software-related inventions. Initially, however, attention will be paid to the positive attributes which must be possessed in order for a product or a process to be considered patentable.

Novelty

The question of novelty is assessed against the existing state of human knowledge. Account will be taken of any material within the public domain which might indicate that the concept of the claimed invention did not originate with the particular applicant. It is not necessary that all the details of the alleged invention should have previously appeared in a single document. The test which will be applied is sometimes referred to as the 'mosaic' test. The analogy might also be drawn with a jigsaw puzzle. This consists of a number of pieces. Once completed, the subject-matter will be readily identifiable, as will the manner in which the constituent pieces fit together. Such a result might not have been apparent to someone who merely saw a pile of unassembled pieces.

An indication of the complexity of the task of determining whether a claimed invention is novel or whether key elements have been anticipated in earlier products or publications can be taken from the case of *Quantel Ltd v Spaceward Microsystems Ltd*.[20] This concerned a challenge to the validity of a patent awarded in respect of a computer-based device permitting the production of graphical images for display on television screens. The end products of the system can be viewed every day in the captions and graphical montages which appear on almost all television programmes.

A competing product having been placed on the market, proceedings were instituted alleging breach of patent. In defending this action, the defenders alleged, inter

---

[19] Section 1(1).   [20] [1990] RPC 83.

alia, that the patent had been incorrectly awarded to a development that was not novel. A variety of material was presented in support of this contention, including a thesis submitted by an American student and deposited in the library of Cornell University. Although the validity of the patent was ultimately upheld by the court, when account is taken of the number of such works produced each year and the very limited publicity afforded to them, the incident demonstrates the magnitude of the task of determining whether an alleged invention is truly novel. The case also provides an excellent illustration of the fact that the grant of a patent may be only the first step for the inventor, who may be faced with a challenge to its validity in the course of any subsequent legal proceedings.

A further aspect of novelty concerns the question of whether details of the alleged invention might previously have been brought into the public domain by the applicant. Any significant disclosure of the features of an invention prior to the submission of an application for a patent will lead to its rejection. The Patent Office advise inventors:

> If you are thinking of applying for a patent you should not publicly disclose the invention before you file an application because this could be counted as prior publication of your invention. Any type of disclosure (whether by word of mouth, demonstration, advertisement or article in a journal), by the applicant or anyone acting for them, could prevent the applicant from getting a patent. It could also be a reason for having the patent revoked if one was obtained. It is essential that the applicant only makes any disclosure under conditions of strict confidence.[21]

Inventive step

The application of this test is as much a matter of art as of science and is linked to a considerable extent with the criteria of novelty. The Patents Act 1977 states that an invention:

> ...shall be taken to involve an inventive step if it is not obvious to a person skilled in the art, having regard to any matter which forms part of the state of the art.[22]

It is very much a question of fact whether the advance involved in a particular invention would have been 'obvious'. Again, the attempt has to be made to apply the test without engaging in the use of hindsight, but by reference to the state of the art at the time the invention was made.

An excellent example of a situation where the requirement of an inventive step was not satisfied can be seen in the case of *Genentech Inc's Patent*.[23] A research programme conducted by Genentech resulted in the identification and mapping of elements of DNA (one of the basic building blocks of life). The research furthered the knowledge of this basic structure and could be used as the basis for the production of anti-coagulant drugs. Genentech sought to patent the results of its efforts, the application ultimately

---

[21] <http://www.patent.gov.uk/dpatents/canipub.html>
[22] Section 3.
[23] [1989] RPC 147.

failing when the Court of Appeal held that the work did not involve an inventive step. Mustill LJ referred to Genentech's activities in the following way:

> ...they won the race. The goal was known and others were trying to reach it. Genentech got there first.[24]

Whilst the achievement of a goal (equivalent, perhaps, to setting a new world record in a sporting event) would constitute evidence of novelty, if the target was widely known, winning the race might tell no more than that the winner was richer or more determined or luckier than others working in the same area. To this extent, therefore, the expenditure of time and effort in making a breakthrough will not, of itself, be conclusive evidence of the existence of an inventive step.[25]

Such arguments are of considerable relevance in the information technology field, where vast sums of money are being expended by large research units throughout the world, all pursuing the goal of faster, more powerful computing devices. A distinction can be drawn between this situation, where the goal can be expressed only in abstract terms, and that applying in *Genentech*,[26] where the target of the research was much more precisely defined. Even on this restricted analysis, the situation appears a little inequitable. The achievement of the goal of running a mile in less than three minutes might not be inventive, but would certainly be meritorious and deserving of recognition. The problem will be encountered in a number of areas and the traditional precepts of intellectual property may not fit well with developments in information technology, yet the effect of denying access to intellectual property rights is to deny any form of legal recognition and protection for the work in question.

Also at issue in the *Genentech*[27] litigation was the identification of the notional persons 'skilled in the art'—those persons to whom the making of the steps leading to the claimed invention would have been 'obvious'. It was recognised that, in respect of advanced areas of technology, the collected knowledge of a team of researchers might be the relevant factor rather than the knowledge possessed by any particular individual. The question also arises of whether the person or persons 'skilled in the art' should themselves be credited with possessing any inventive qualities. In the case of *Valensi v British Radio Corpn Ltd*,[28] it was stated that:

> ...the hypothetical addressee is not a person of exceptional skill and knowledge, that he is not to be expected to exercise any invention nor any prolonged research, inquiry or experiment. He must, however, be prepared to display a reasonable degree of skill and common knowledge of the art in making trials and to correct obvious errors in the specification if a means of correcting them can readily be found.[29]

---

[24] [1989] RPC 147 at 251.
[25] [1989] RPC 147 at 278.
[26] *Genentech Inc's Patent* [1989] RPC 147.
[27] *Genentech Inc's Patent* [1989] RPC 147.
[28] [1973] RPC 337.
[29] [1973] RPC 337 at 377.

A more expansive view of the abilities of the skilled person was adopted by Mustill LJ in *Genentech*. In a comment which is especially relevant in relation to developments in information technology, he held that:

> Where the art by its nature involves intellectual gifts and ingenuity of approach, it would, I believe, be wrong to assume that the hypothetical person is devoid of those gifts.[30]

Capacity for industrial application

The final requirement which must be satisfied in order for a patent application to proceed is that the invention involved should be capable of industrial application. This requirement is, in many respects, at the heart of the patent system. However novel an idea might be, it will be of little practical benefit if it cannot usefully be applied. Application may take two forms, with the subject-matter of the patent application referring to a product or a process (sometimes referred to as apparatus and means). In many instances, applications will combine the two elements. A helpful illustration is provided in Laddie J's judgment in the case of *Fujitsu Ltd's Application:*[31]

> ...it may be useful to consider what the position would be in a case where someone had invented a new way of mowing grass which involved designing a new type of motor with micro sensors and blade adjustment motors on it, the sensors being used to determine both the softness of the grass to be cut and the height of it above the ground and then produced an output which operated the motors so as to adjust the height of the cut, the angle of the blades and the speed at which they rotated...considerations of novelty aside, such a device would be patentable and, so it seems to me, would be the mowing method itself.

In a software context, the claim may often be that the equipment operating in accordance with the program's instructions constitutes a novel product, whilst the algorithmic steps prescribed by the implementing programs represent a novel process. Virtually any product will be capable of being sold or otherwise disposed of and, in this respect, will satisfy the applicability test. With a process, slightly different considerations will apply. If the end result of the application of the process will be a product, it is likely that the process will be considered capable of industrial application. An illustration of the kind of development which will be excluded from patent protection can be found in the provisions of the Patents Act 1977, which states that:

> ...an invention of a method of treatment of the human or animal body by surgery or therapy or of diagnosis practised on the human or animal body shall not be taken to be capable of industrial application.[32]

Thus, the intangible concept is not patentable. In the event, however, that new surgical tools or equipment are invented to facilitate the application of the new

---

[30] *Genentech Inc's Patent* [1989] RPC 147 at 280.
[31] [1996] RPC 511.
[32] Section 4(2).

techniques, these will, assuming the other statutory criteria are complied with, be regarded as patentable.

Matters excluded from patent protection

In addition to defining the elements that must be found in an invention, the Patents Act 1977 lists a number of features which will not qualify for the grant of a patent. Section 1(2) (which mirrors Article 52 of the European Patent Convention) provides that patents are not to be awarded for:

(a) a discovery, scientific theory or mathematical method;

(b) a literary, dramatic, musical or artistic work or any other aesthetic creation whatsoever;

(c) a scheme, rule or method for performing a mental act, playing a game or doing business, or a program for a computer; or

(d) the presentation of information.

Given the appearance of the phrase 'a program for a computer' in this listing, it may appear surprising that the topic should be of any significance in a text on information technology law. Matters, however, are not so straightforward. After reciting the list of prohibited subject-matter, both the Patents Act 1977 and the European Patent Convention continue:

>...but the foregoing provision shall prevent anything from being treated as an invention for the purposes of this Act only to the extent that a patent or an application for a patent relates to that thing *as such* [emphasis added].

In his judgment in *Fujitsu Ltd's Application*,[33] which was subsequently affirmed by the Court of Appeal,[34] Mr Justice Laddie analysed the rationale behind a number of the statutory exceptions. The prohibition against the grant of a patent to a discovery illustrates perfectly the problems inherent in this area. The obvious objection to awarding a patent for a discovery, for example, of a new mineral, is that there is no discernible inventive step. However, as was pointed out in the judgment:

>...most inventions are based on what would be regarded by many people as discoveries. Large numbers of highly successful and important patents in the pharmaceutical field have been and continue to be based upon the discovery of new strains of micro-organisms which exist naturally in the wild.[35]

Recognising this fact, the statutory prohibition against the grant of a patent is restricted to the case where the application relates to the discovery 'as such'.[36]

---

[33] 1996 RPC 511.
[34] *The Times*, 14 March 1997.
[35] [1996] RPC 511 at 523.
[36] Patents Act 1977, s 1(2).

In principle, such an approach must be correct. Its practical application has proved more difficult, with particular problems surrounding the treatment of what are frequently referred to as 'software-related inventions'. In part, the problem may lie with the fact that both the Patents Act 1977 and the European Patent Convention were enacted in the 1970s. At that time, it was considered that computer programs could be separated from the hardware components and should be excluded from the patent system. Both the report of the Banks Committee in the United Kingdom and the initial Guidelines for Examiners produced by the European Patent Office make this point clearly. Over the last twenty-odd years, the nature of computer programs has changed and expanded, and the division between software and hardware has become a matter of choice as much as one of technology.

To complicate matters further, as the relevance of the obvious prohibition has declined, so it has also become apparent that software-related inventions are vulnerable to challenge under a range of the statutory exceptions. Applications have been rejected on the basis that they relate to a mathematical method, a method of doing business, the presentation of information and a method for performing a mental act, all of which are excluded from the award of a patent. It is difficult to think of any other form of technology whose nature and range of application is sufficiently chameleon as to bring it within so many of the statutory prohibitions. Not unnaturally, those seeking patent protection for software-related inventions have sought to lay as much emphasis as possible on the task performed by the invention, and as little as possible on the contribution made by computer programs. The criterion applied by both the European Patent Office and the United Kingdom authorities is to require that the claimed invention produced a 'technical contribution' to the state of the art (also referred to as a 'technical effect' or 'technical application'). The next question, of course, is whether the mere presence of a technical contribution can outweigh the explicit prohibition against patentability.

Patenting software

Notwithstanding the present prohibitions, there is no doubt that software-related inventions can be patented. In the United Kingdom, approximately 100 patent applications in their name are published each year. In proceedings before the European Patent Office, this figure rises to 100 per month.[37] The report of the Parliamentary Office of Science and Technology on 'Patents, Research and Technology'[38] indicates that 'in the last 10 years the EPO has granted around 10,000 patents for software-related inventions, and has refused only 100 applications'.[39] In 2003, it was estimated

---

[37] I am grateful to Mr J. Houston, Intellectual Property Rights Officer of the University of Strathclyde, for the provision of these statistics.

[38] March 1996.

[39] P. 31. The Follow-up to the Green Paper on the Community Patent refers to the existence of 13,000 patents in Europe.

that up to 30,000 software patents had been issued by the European Patent Office;[40] although, in part because the existence of the statutory prohibitions requires that software-related inventions be catalogued by reference to their field of application rather than the software component, any calculation is a somewhat subjective assessment. Even more substantial figures are quoted for the number of patents awarded in the United States, and there is no doubt that patents have a significant role to play in the field of information technology.

The process of obtaining and enforcing a patent

The application

The act of making an invention will confer no rights upon an inventor. A person wishing to secure protection is required to make application for a patent and to pursue this through all the stages of the patent procedure.[41] The key components of the process are described in the following paragraphs.

Specification and statement of claim

The key elements of any patent application are the provision of a specification and a statement of claim(s).[42] The specification consists, essentially, of a description of the invention. It will describe the state of the technical art in the field and indicate the improvements which the invention makes and the manner in which this is accomplished. The specification should be formulated in such a manner as to permit the product to be made or the process operated by 'a person skilled in the art'.

The specification serves to indicate what may be regarded as the inventor's opinion regarding the optimum embodiment of its principles. Beyond this, claims for protection may be made regarding the functioning of the product or process—effectively, what the invention does. The drafting of these claims is critical to the success of a patent. Any claim alleging infringement of a patent will relate to the claims rather than to the specification. If the claims are drawn too broadly, the patent application may be rejected on the grounds that the applicant is seeking protection, either for matters which have not been disclosed in the specification or for matters which are not novel or inventive. If the claims are drawn more narrowly, the patent may well be awarded, but prove worthless, as competitors evade its scope by making minor changes to the design of the invention. In many cases, an applicant will submit a considerable number of claims, commencing with extremely broad references to the technology at issue, with subsequent claims narrowing down the level of protection, ending with a claim to protection for the invention 'substantially as described'.

---

[40] <http://eupat.ffii.org/>

[41] Where an invention is made in the course of employment, the employer will be regarded as the inventor for the purpose of making a patent application.

[42] Section 14(2).

An example of a failure in this regard has been reported concerning the patents granted to what has become the market-leading telephone modem. Modems play a vital role in the transfer of data between computers.[43] Just as with human telephone conversations, a basic requirement of data transmissions is the ability to identify when a communication has been completed and thereupon terminate the connection. This is referred to as the escape sequence. A particular sequence had been developed in which the initiating modem would transmit three + signs. Such a transmission would be most unlikely to occur in the course of a message and would signal to a compatible receiving modem that the communication had concluded. In this, as in many other areas of the intellectual property field, the question of compatibility is critical. Although it was not selected at random, the 3+s message possessed no unique qualities. The commercial success of the modem produced consumer demand for modems which transmitted and recognised this sequence. In laying claim to a patent for the modem design, the developers failed to claim in respect of the specific escape sequence. This proved a costly error. The resulting patent protection certainly prevented competitors from copying the specific design features of the modem, but the same effect, that of transmitting and receiving data communications, could readily be achieved using alternative and non-infringing means. Having done this, the absence of a claim in respect of the escape sequence left competitors free to utilise this, thereby acquiring compatibility with the market-leading product to their own commercial advantage.

The lodging of an application with the Patent Office serves to initiate the procedures leading to the grant of a patent. Until the Patent Act 1902, although substantial procedural requirements had to be observed, a patent would be awarded without the invention being subjected to any form of scrutiny. From 1902, increasingly stringent procedures have been introduced, whereby an application will be examined with a view to making a determination on whether it complies with the statutory criteria. Under the Patents Act 1977, a two-stage process operates, with applications being subjected to preliminary and substantive examinations.

Preliminary examination

The first purpose of the preliminary examination is to ensure that the application complies with all the formal requirements of the legislation.[44] If this is the case, the examiner will turn to consider the merits of the application. At the stage of the preliminary examination, the examiner's main task is to identify those documents and information sources which it is considered are likely to prove of assistance in applying the criteria of novelty and inventiveness. Having identified relevant documents, the examiner is to scrutinise the documents to such extent as is considered will serve a purpose in determining the application.[45] The results of the preliminary investigation are to be reported to the Comptroller of Patents and to the applicant.[46]

---

[43] *Guardian*, 9 February 1989.
[44] Patents Act 1977, s 17(2).
[45] Section 17(4)–(5).
[46] Section 17(2).

This initial report will be non-judgemental. It may indicate grounds for objecting to or refusing the grant of a patent. In such circumstances, it might become apparent to an applicant that the chances of the application being granted are minimal and the decision taken to withdraw the application.

Publication of the application

Unless notice of withdrawal is given, details of the specification and claims will be published 'as soon as possible' after the expiry of eighteen months from the date of application.[47] In most cases, an applicant will receive the report of the preliminary examination before the application is due to be published. Whilst publication will have no detrimental effect in the event that the patent is ultimately granted, if the application is unsuccessful, the consequence will be that the inventor will have disclosed information to the public without securing any benefit in return. Equally seriously, publication may adversely affect the prospects of any modified application which the inventor might wish to make. Under the present United States system, no details of an application are published until the patent is ultimately awarded. Although this may seem fairer to the applicant, problems have been encountered with what are referred to as 'submarine patents'. Even assuming a relatively straightforward application, it will be quite normal for the process to take two to three years. With more complex cases, perhaps including modification of the original application, this period may increase to ten years, or even longer. The essence of a submarine patent is that, originally describing what has been described as 'science fiction technology', it lurks unseen in the patent office awaiting the widespread application of the technology by third parties (perhaps being modified better to describe their applications). At this time, the patent surfaces with claims of patent infringement being fired at any users.

Substantive examination

In the event that the applicant wishes the process to continue, a request must be made for a substantive examination.[48] It is at this stage that the examiner will make a full study of whether the claimed invention is novel, involves an inventive step, is capable of industrial application, and does not fall within one of the prohibited categories. The request for a substantive examination must be made within six months of the date of publication.[49]

Although, as has been said, the determination of whether an invention is novel has to be made by reference to any material in the public domain, it would be unreasonable to expect patent examiners to be aware of every book or article deposited in any library anywhere in the world. The basic tool for examiners will be collections of patents previously awarded in the world's major patent offices.

---

[47] Patents Act 1977, s 16.
[48] Patents Act 1977, s 18(1).
[49] Patents Rules 1995, SI 1995/2093, r 33.

It is at the stage of the substantive examination that a decision will be made regarding the patentability or otherwise of the invention. The examiner will make a report to the Comptroller of Patents. In the event that this report makes objection to aspects of the application, the applicant must be afforded the opportunity to make observations or to amend the application so as to take account of the examiner's objections. In the event that the applicant fails adequately so to do, the Comptroller may refuse the application.[50]

Third-party involvement

The Patents Act 1977 contains no provisions for the formal involvement of third parties in the processes leading to the grant or refusal of a patent. It is provided, however, that in any interval between publication of the application and the decision on grant, a third party may submit written observations to the Comptroller, who must take these into account in reaching a decision.[51]

Award of a patent

In the event that a patent is awarded, the Comptroller is required to cause a notice to this effect to be published in the *Official Journal (Patents)*. The maximum term of validity of a patent is twenty years, commencing from the date when the application is first submitted.[52] It should be noted, however, that a patent is not awarded for such a period. Protection will be awarded for an initial period of four years; thereafter annual applications will require to be made (accompanied by a fee) to retain the patent's validity. Only a small percentage of patents remain in force for the full twenty-year period, the average lifespan of a patent being in the region of eight years.[53] By this time, it will have become apparent either that the patent has been overtaken by newer technologies or that the invention is of limited practical utility.

Infringement of patents

The definition of infringement is of critical importance. Under the terms of the Patents Act 1977, infringement may be either direct or indirect. Direct infringement occurs when a party, without the consent, express or implied, of the proprietor of the patent 'makes, disposes or offers to dispose of, uses, keeps, or imports' a product constituting the subject-matter of the patent. Similar prohibitions apply in the event that the patent covers a process.[54]

---

[50] Patents Act 1977, s 18(3).

[51] Section 21.

[52] Patents Act 1977, s 20.

[53] For an excellent analysis of the lifespan of patents, see J. Phillips and A. Firth, *An Introduction to Intellectual Property Law*, 3rd edn (London, 2001).

[54] Section 60(1).

Indirect infringement occurs where a party supplies or offers to supply any equipment which constitutes an essential part of the invention in the knowledge (or having reasonable grounds to believe) that infringement will result.[55]

The question of whether a subsequent product infringes the provisions of a patent is essentially one of fact. It will seldom be the case that the subsequent product is an exact copy of a patented object. In the event that any infringement is innocent, with the product being the result of the competitor's own researches, it is unlikely that every detail of the original will be replicated. Should the subsequent producer have been aware of and seek to evade the provisions of the patent, it is again likely that differences of detail will be introduced in an effort to conceal the fact of infringement.

In the event that products are not identical, the task for the court is to examine the patent specification and statement of claim in order to identify the essential features or integers possessed by the patented product. These are then compared with those of the competing product. If the latter replicates the essential elements, infringement may be established even though the product may differ in other respects. An example of the operation of this principle can be seen in the case of *Beecham Group Ltd v Bristol Laboratories Ltd*.[56] Here, the plaintiffs held a patent for a pharmaceutical product possessing a particular chemical structure. The defendant company produced a product possessing a slightly different structure, but the evidence established that the latter product became converted to the patented product upon being absorbed into the bloodstream. In these circumstances, it was held that there was a patent infringement.

In the case of *Catnic Components Ltd v Hill and Smith Ltd*,[57] the plaintiffs had been granted a patent in respect of a design of lintel. The patent made specific reference to the fact that the support member was to be vertical. The defendants subsequently produced a lintel possessing most of the features of the original design, but with the change that the support was angled slightly from the vertical. The alteration made the design slightly less effective, although the difference was of no practical significance. It was held that the similarity between the two designs was sufficient for infringement to be established.

The fact that the addition of further integers increases the efficiency of the product will not necessarily defeat a claim of infringement. As was stated by Bower LJ in the case of *Wenham Gas Co Ltd v Champion Gas Lamp Co Ltd*,[58] 'the superadding of ingenuity to a robbery does not make the operation justifiable'. More difficult issues may arise in the event that the subsequent product substitutes or modifies some of the essential integers of the patented product. Here, the determination of whether there is any infringement will be strongly influenced by any expert evidence presented by the parties. If it can be established that it would have been obvious to the mythical 'workman, skilled in the art', presented with details of the modification at the date of

55 Patents Act 1977, s 60(2).
56 [1978] RPC 153.
57 [1982] RPC 183.
58 [1891] 9 RPC 49.

publication of the patent, that the substitution of one feature for another would not have had a significant effect on the operation of the patented invention, infringement may be established.

Remedies for infringement of a patent

Four basic forms of remedy may be available to the holder of a patent. At the initial stage of legal proceedings, an interdict may be sought to prevent the defender continuing with the alleged infringement. When the dispute comes to trial, three further remedies may be applicable. An order may be sought requiring the delivery up to the patentee of any infringing copies. In terms of financial compensation, the patentee may seek either an accounting of profits from the infringer or an award of damages.

Revocation of a patent

A patent may be revoked by the court or the Comptroller on the application of any person if it is established:

1. that the invention is not a patentable invention;
2. that the patent was granted to a person or persons who were not the only persons qualified to obtain such a grant. Such an action may only be brought by a person or persons who would have been entitled to be granted the patent or to have shared in such a grant. The action must be brought within two years from the date of the patent grant unless it is established that the patent holder was aware that he or she was not entitled to the proprietorship of the patent;
3. the specification does not disclose the invention sufficiently clearly and completely for it to be performed by a person reasonably skilled in the art;
4. the matter disclosed in the patent specification is more extensive than that disclosed in the patent application; or
5. the protection conferred under the patent has been extended by an amendment which should not have been allowed.[59]

Although it is possible that a challenge to the validity of a patent may be brought in isolation, it will more commonly be raised as an issue in the course of proceedings by the patent holder alleging infringement. Effectively, therefore, the trial may provide the forum for reconsideration of the question of whether the application for patent protection should be granted.

This possibility is particularly relevant in the information technology sector, where substantial criticism has been made of the abilities of patent offices to identify all materials relevant to determinations of novelty and inventiveness. To this extent,

---

[59] Patents Act 1977, s 72.

acquisition of a patent may mark only the first stage in a continuing battle to establish its validity and enforce its terms.

Conclusions

The processes for obtaining a patent are frequently lengthy and expensive. Although the United Kingdom Patent Office introduced a 'fast track' process in 1995, which aimed to make a decision on the patentability of an application within twelve months,[60] the patent process will normally occupy a period in excess of two years. Fees must be paid at all stages of the patent process.[61] In addition, the complexity of the processes may compel applications to make use of the services of patent agents—something which is recommended by the Patent Office.

Faced with these factors, coupled with the requirement in the European and United Kingdom systems that details of an invention be published prior to the decision being taken on whether to award a patent, it might be queried where the value of the patent system lies for those working in the software field. Given the pace of technical development, it will certainly be the case that, for many applications, the technology will be rendered obsolete before the patent is awarded. The United States case of *Microsoft v Stac* provides perhaps the best example of the value of the patent system.[62]

At issue in the case was a patent describing novel techniques for the practice of data compression. As the name suggests, this technique is used to reduce the amount of storage space necessary to hold data. A recent application of compression technology can be seen with the MP3 system. MP3 is an audio compression format that enables audio files to be stored and transferred on a computer with a relatively small file size. Typically, three minutes of music recorded in digital format would require some 30MB of storage space. Use of the MP3 mathematical techniques, which are themselves patented in the United States[63] and the source of potential litigation, reduces the space required to about 3MB. Such a reduction makes it feasible to place musical tracks on, and download from, the Internet.

In the particular case, Stac held two United States patents for a compression system which was sold under the name 'Stacker'. Interestingly, especially given the controversy which has existed concerning the eligibility of software-related inventions for patentability within the United Kingdom, one of the patents was originally issued in the United Kingdom to a British company, Ferranti, and was subsequently assigned to Stac. Microsoft wished to incorporate a compression system in a new version of their operating system. Negotiations followed with Stac but these proved unsuccessful, largely because Microsoft was unwilling to offer any payment for the use of the Stac system.[64] When the new version of the operating system appeared on the market, it

---

[60] <http://www.patent.gov.uk/dpatents/pataccel.html>

[61] For current details, see <http://www.patent.gov.uk/sservice/ukpatnt.html>

[62] For details of the case, see <http://www.vaxxine.com/lawyers/articles/stac.html>

[63] See <http://www.mp3.com/news/095.html>

[64] For details of Stac's claim, see <http://www.vaxxine.com/lawyers/articles/stac.html>

did contain a compression system. It transpired that it was based on the Stac system. Microsoft's claim was that this had been used initially, but they had subsequently devised their own code. In copyright law, as will be discussed below,[65] this claim may well have succeeded and might at least have resulted in extensive litigation. As the techniques were protected by patents, all that Stac had to establish was that Microsoft had used these. In a jury trial, Stac was awarded $120 million in compensation.[66]

The litigation brought by Stac marked—at least until the antitrust litigation brought by the United States authorities—the most significant legal finding against Microsoft. As such, it is eloquent testimony to the strength of a patent. Software patents have been, and remain, an extremely controversial subject, especially in the United States. Objections appear to be based on a number of grounds. The system, it is argued, is inequitable in the situation where different people are working independently in the same field. The first one to obtain a patent is then in a position to stop others exploiting their own work. As can be seen from the example of Alexander Graham Bell and Elisha Grey cited above, this is not a new phenomenon. A further ground of objection is founded in the perception that the inability of the Patent Offices to make comprehensive searches in the field has resulted in the award of patents in respect of technology which is not truly novel or inventive. This is a more difficult ground to assess. It may be noted that examination is a relatively novel feature of the patent system. Until the twentieth century, the system was effectively one of registration. The fact that a patent is granted is not conclusive evidence of its validity. It may be challenged at any time. Against this, it should be stated that the onus of proving a patent to be invalid lies with the challenger, and patent litigation can be prolonged and expensive. These issues will be considered in more detail in the following chapter, which will consider the manner in which patent law has evolved in relation to patents for software-related inventions.

Suggestions for further reading

Colston and Middleton (2005), *Modern Intellectual Property Law* (London).

---

[65] See discussion of *Computer Associates v Altai* 982 F 2d 693 (1992).

[66] Ultimately, the two companies signed a cross-licensing agreement. Stac received $43 million in cash from Microsoft and Microsoft invested $39.9 million in non-voting Stac stock (about 15 per cent of the company's shares)—a total payout of $83 million.

16

Patents and software

Introduction

Given the apparently clear prohibition against the grant of patents for computer programs in both the Patents Act and the European Patent Convention, it might appear that the topic should be of little significance. This is far from the case—and rather as was said by Humpty Dumpty in the well-known legal authority, *Alice in Wonderland*, 'when I use a word it means exactly what I want it to mean'—judges in both the United Kingdom and the European Patent Office have been forced to engage in word gymnastics when attempting to reconcile the words of the Act and Convention with the realities of a world in which software patents have become a reality. The global picture was well described by Lord Justice Jacob in the case of *Aerotel v Telco*[1] when he suggested that, in large part because of the willingness of the United States authorities to grant patents for software-related inventions, '[a]n arms race in which the weapons are patents has set in'.[2]

The first United Kingdom cases involving the eligibility of software-related inventions for patent protection arose under the Patents Act 1949. Not surprisingly given the time the Act was enacted, there is no mention of the words computer, programs, or software. The Act provided rather more simply that patents might be awarded for 'any manner of new manufacture'[3] without seeking to define the concept further. Although some commentators have expressed the view that the categories of qualifying and prohibited subject-matter introduced in the 1977 Act represented a codification of existing precedent, it was stated by Purchas LJ in *Genentech Inc's Patent*[4] that the 1977 Act must be 'viewed in the context of a departure from much of the authority and usage of previous patent law'. What is perhaps clear and worthy of note is that cases brought under the 1949 Act appear to demonstrate a move from initial judicial hostility, to acceptance of the need for and desirability of bringing the embryonic software industry within the scope of the patent system. It is again perhaps noteworthy that in the United States—which continues to be the jurisdiction most friendly towards issuing patents

---

[1] [2006] EWCA Civ 1371.
[2] At para. 18.
[3] Section 101.
[4] [1989] RPC 147 at 197.

for software-related inventions—the patent law in force dates back to 1952 and is based upon principles very similar to those found in the United Kingdom's Act of 1949.

In the final case decided under the Patents Act 1949, that of *International Business Machines Corpn's Application,* a patent had been awarded and the proceedings related to a challenge by the applicants to its validity. After surveying all of the previous United Kingdom authorities and considering the first United States cases concerned with software-related inventions to reach the level of the Supreme Court, the Patent Appeals Tribunal concluded that:

> We proceed upon the basis that the only thing that was novel in connection with the present application was (the) concept of the way in which a price could be fixed, but what he seeks to claim as a manner of new manufacture is a method involving operating or controlling a computer in which, so far as the contested claims are concerned, the computer is programmed in a particular way or programmes in physical form to control a computer so that it will operate in accordance with his method. The method is embodied in the programme and in the apparatus in physical form and in our view the superintending examiner was right in concluding that the claims should be allowed to proceed...an inventive concept, if novel, can be patented to the extent that claims can be framed directed to an embodiment of the concept in some apparatus or process of manufacture.[5]

The essential distinction drawn is one which continues to be at issue today—between a program for a computer and a computer programmed to operate in a particular maner.

Towards the end of the 1960s, it became clear that reform would be needed to the United Kingdom's patent system, both for internal purposes and, perhaps more significantly, to ensure that the country was in a position to participate in the approaching European Patent Convention. In typical manner, a committee, the Banks Committee, was established with the remit to consider the patent system, and make recommendations for reform. The Committee's report was published in 1970, with a chapter being devoted to an examination of the position of computer programs.[6] This concluded that the situation was characterised by considerable uncertainty, but indicated that the majority of the evidence submitted to the Committee was hostile to the notion that programs should qualify for patent protection.[7] This view was endorsed by the Committee, which put forward reasons of both principle and utility for denying protection. In terms of principle, it was argued that no significant distinction existed between programs and methods of mathematical calculation, which had always been excluded from protection. Practical problems were also identified, the Committee commenting:

> ...were programs to be patentable, very real and substantial difficulties would be experienced by the Patent Office in searching applications for program patents even were the search material available in suitably classified form. The issues of novelty and

---

[5] *International Business Machines Corpn's Application* [1980] FSR 564 at 573.
[6] Cmnd 4407 (1970), ch. 17.
[7] Ch. 17, para. 479.

obviousness would be so difficult of determination that patents of doubtful validity would be likely to issue.[8]

Although it appears that this comment is at odds with much of the case law under the 1949 Act, in almost all of the cases, the legal argument was restricted to the question of whether an application was entitled to be considered for the award of a patent. The cases, typically, were not concerned with the question of whether the software developments were truly novel. As will be discussed, one of the major arguments advanced against the application of the patent system to software-related inventions has concerned the difficulty in establishing the true state of the technical art. Especially in the United States, a number of fairly high-profile patent awards have been subject to heavy criticism—in at least one case resulting in the revocation of the patent—on the ground that the technology described was well known to those working in the field. Thirty years of advances in database technology do not appear to have done much to resolve the concerns voiced by the Banks Committee.

In the event, the Banks Committee recommended that:

> A computer program, that is: a set of instructions for controlling the sequence of operations of a data processing system, in whatever form the invention is presented e.g. a method of programming computers, a computer when programmed in a certain way and where the novelty or alleged novelty lies only in the program, should not be patentable.[9]

Such a view clearly conflicts with the judgment of the Patent Appeals Tribunal in the *International Business Machines Corpn's Application* decision,[10] and represents a hardening of attitudes towards the award of patents for software-related inventions. It was not considered, however, that the presence of software components in an otherwise qualifying invention should exclude the latter from patent protection. The report drew a distinction between:

> ...applications for programs *per se* and for inventions of the kind claimed as a computer controlled steelworks...which involve the use of a program. The invention should then be patentable if it does not reside merely in the details of the program.[11]

Although such a distinction may be totally supported, it will be seen that once again the seeds of doubt as to the application of patent protection have been planted. Two propositions can be culled from the report of the Banks Committee. A program per se should never, at least under the United Kingdom and European regimes, be accepted as the basis for a patent. Equally, an invention that would otherwise be considered patentable is not to be barred from protection merely because a program is utilised somewhere in its operations. Inevitably, problems arise at the margins, and especially in the

---

[8] Ch. 17, para. 483.
[9] Cmnd 4407 (1970), ch. 17, para. 487.
[10] [1980] FSR 564 at 573.
[11] Cmnd 4407 (1970), ch. 17, para. 486.

situation where the product functions in a novel and inventive manner, but where this is due in large measure to the operation of the programs contained therein.

The Patents Act 1977 and the European Patent Convention

As indicated in Chapter 18, after specifying the positive attributes which must be evidenced in a patent application, the Patents Act 1977 provides that:

> ...the following (among other things) are not inventions for the purposes of this Act, that is to say anything which consists of—
>
> (a) a discovery, scientific theory or mathematical method;
>
> (b) a literary, dramatic, musical or artistic work or any other aesthetic creation whatsoever;
>
> (c) a scheme, rule or method for performing a mental act, playing a game or doing business, or a program for a computer; or
>
> (d) the presentation of information.[12]

Although the first draft of the European Patent Convention was silent on the point, as the result of representations made by the United Kingdom delegation, the final text contains a very similar list of prohibited subject-matter, providing that:

1. European patents shall be granted for any inventions which are susceptible of industrial application, which are new and which involve an inventive step.

2. The following in particular shall not be regarded as inventions within the meaning of paragraph 1:

   (a) discoveries, scientific theories and mathematical methods;

   (b) aesthetic creations;

   (c) schemes, rules and methods for performing mental acts, playing games or doing business, and programs for computers;

   (d) presentations of information.

3. The provisions of paragraph 2 shall exclude patentability of the subject-matter or activities referred to in that provision only to the extent to which a European patent application or European patent relates to such subject-matter or activities as such.[13]

The minor discrepancy in terminology between the Convention and Act has drawn some judicial criticism, Lord Justice Jacob commenting that:

> Although s.1(2) pointlessly uses somewhat different wording from the EPC no-one suggests that it has any different meaning. So we, like the parties before us, work directly from the source.[14]

---

[12] Section 1(2).

[13] Article 52.

[14] *Aerotel v Telco* [2006] EWCA Civ 1371 at para. 6.

In both the Act and the Convention, however, the list of non-qualifying subject-matter is followed by the proviso that the prohibition applies only to the extent that the application relates to that item 'as such'. It is the interpretation of this latter provision that has been at the heart of the litigation in this area. Typically, as in the cases brought under the Patents Act 1949, the claim has been made that what should be protected is the end product of the program's operation, i.e. what the software plus hardware components accomplish, rather than the manner in which this is done.

To complicate matters further, it has become apparent that software-related inventions are vulnerable to challenge under a range of the statutory exceptions. Applications have been rejected on the basis that they relate to a mathematical method, a method of doing business, the presentation of information and a method for performing a mental act, all of which are excluded from the award of a patent. It is difficult to think of any other form of technology whose nature and range of application is so chameleon-like as to bring it within so many of the statutory prohibitions.

The Patents Act 1977 was enacted in order to enable the United Kingdom to ratify the European Patent Convention and provides, most unusually, that judicial notice is to be taken of decisions of the European authorities.[15] It is further provided that:

> ... the following provisions of this Act ... are so framed as to have, as nearly as practicable, the same effects in the United Kingdom as the corresponding provisions of the European Patent Convention ...[16]

Given this, it is not surprising that it should be stated by Nicholls LJ in *Gale's Application*:[17]

> It would be absurd if, on the issue of patentability, a patent application should suffer a different fate according to whether it was made in the United Kingdom under the Act or was made in Munich for a European Parliament (United Kingdom) under the Convention.[18]

In spite of this recognition, concerns have been raised that software-related applications have been treated more harshly before the United Kingdom patent authorities and courts. Such a matter is difficult to determine with any degree of certainty. In recent years matters have become ever more complex. Whilst in the 1990s, the question was whether the United Kingdom authorities were applying the same criteria as the European Patent Office Boards of Appeal, differently composed Boards of Appeal have adopted significantly different criteria in determining applications before them to the extent that it has proved impossible for national courts to determine a single line of authority to follow.

The quest for a technical contribution

Although the term 'technical contribution' does not appear in either the Patents Act 1977 or the European Patent Convention, it achieved pivotal significance since being

---

[15] Section 91.   [16] Section 130(7).
[17] [1991] RPC 305.   [18] [1991] RPC 305 at 323.

introduced in the Guidelines for Examiners drawn up by the European Patent Office. In the original Guidelines prepared for the assistance of examiners in the European Patent Office, it was stated:

> If the contribution to the known art resides solely in a computer program then the subject matter is not patentable in whatever form it might be presented in those claims. For example, a claim to a computer characterised by having the particular program stored in its memory or to a process for operating a computer under control of the program would be as objectionable as a claim to the program *per se* or the program when recorded on magnetic tape.[19]

By 1985, it was recognised that a fuller exposition was required concerning the European Patent Convention's application to inventions which made use of computer programs. As is the case under the United Kingdom legislation, there is no doubt that a computer program per se is not patentable. The prevailing opinion would suggest that this would be the case, regardless of the specific prohibition contained in Article 52, this being of a declaratory nature. In view of the increasing importance of computer programs, it was considered desirable to offer more precise guidance, both to inventors and to the examiners in the European Patent Office. To this extent, new Guidelines[20] were promulgated which seek to make it clear that the essential prerequisite for the grant of a patent is the making of a 'technical' invention, i.e. a requirement that there be some tangible end product. Thus, although the revised Guidelines provide that:

> A computer program claimed by itself or as a record on a carrier is unpatentable irrespective of its content. The situation is not normally changed when the computer program is loaded into a known computer[.][21]

it is recognised also that inventions in which a computer program constitutes an essential element may qualify for patent protection, subject to the application of the Convention's general rules. The Guidelines continue:

> If, however, the subject matter as claimed makes a technical contribution to the known art, patentability should not be denied merely on the ground that a computer program is involved in its implementation. This means, for example, that program controlled machines and program controlled manufacturing and control processes should normally be regarded as a patentable subject matter. It follows also that, where the claimed subject matter is concerned only with the program controlled internal working of a known computer, the subject matter could be patentable if it produced a technical effect.

The aim of the new approach, it is stated, is to produce a workable system from the standpoint of the European Patent Office (particularly in relation to the search and examination requirements) whilst 'responding to the reasonable desires of industry for a somewhat more liberal line than that adopted in the past'.

---

[19] OJ 1/1978.

[20] The current guidelines were published in 2003 and are available from <http://www.european-patent-office.org/legal/gui_lines/index.htm>

[21] Para. 22.

The first significant case following from the adoption of the new European Patent Office Guidelines was the decision of the European Patent Office Technical Board of Appeal in the case of *Vicom/Computer-Related Inventions* in July 1986.[22] This ruling has been of pivotal importance, being cited in virtually every subsequent European Patent Office and United Kingdom decision. Discussion of the question on how far software-related inventions might be patentable under the Patents Act 1977 must therefore commence with discussion of this case.

The *Vicom* application[23] related to the use of a computer for image-processing purposes. Data representing the image, in the form of electrical signals, would be processed by the computer so as to enhance the quality of the image as displayed on the computer monitor. It was accepted by the applicant that the process could be operated using a standard computer. This application was rejected by the examiner on the grounds, both that it sought protection for a computer program and that it related to a mathematical method. The electrical signal, it was argued, could be represented in mathematical terms, likewise the processed signal.

Appealing against this refusal, the applicants claimed that:

A novel technical feature clearly exists in not only the hardware, but also in the method recited in the claims presented by this appeal. The invention, furthermore, confers a technical benefit namely a substantial increase in processing speed compared with the prior art.

Digital filtering in general and digital image processing in particular are 'real world' activities that start in the real world (with a picture) and end in the real world (with a picture). What goes on in between is not an abstract process, but the physical manipulation of electrical signals representing the picture in accordance with the procedures defined in the claims. There is no basis in the EPC [European Patent Convention] for treating digital filters differently from analogue filters.

The appellants have thus made a new and valuable contribution to the stock of human knowledge and patent protection for this contribution cannot be denied merely on the basis that the manner in which the invention is defined would appear to bring it within the exclusions of Article 52(3) EPC.[24]

Acting on a suggestion from the examiner, amended claims relating both the apparatus and means were submitted for consideration by the Board of Appeal. This held that the claims referred to patentable subject-matter. In respect of the program objection it was held that:

Generally, claims which can be considered as being directed to a computer set up to operate in accordance with a specified program (whether by means of hardware or software) for controlling or carrying out a technical process cannot be regarded as relating to a computer program...

Generally speaking, an invention which would be patentable in accordance with conventional patentability criteria should not be excluded from protection by the mere

---

22 *Vicom Systems Inc's Application* [1987] 2 EPOR 74.
23 *Vicom Systems Inc's Application* [1987] 2 EPOR 74.
24 *Vicom Systems Inc's Application* [1987] 2 EPOR 74 at 77–8.

fact that for its implementation modern technical means in the form of a computer program are used. Decisive is what technical contribution the invention as defined in the claim when considered as a whole makes to the known art.[25]

It was further recognised that a mathematical method could not be protected directly. When the formula existed in isolation, there could be no question of it being granted a patent. Where the formula was applied, however, different considerations arose. It was stated that:

> ...if a mathematical method is used in a technical process, that process is carried out on a physical entity (which may be a material object but equally an image stored as an electronic signal) by some technical means implementing the method and provides as its end result a certain change in that entity. The technical means might include a computer comprising suitable hardware or an appropriately programmed general purpose computer.[26]

What was required was that the mathematical method should be applied within a specific technical context which, being capable of industrial application, would qualify for patent protection. In this event, the mathematical methods could freely be used by third parties for any purpose other than the specified form of image processing. Such an approach overcomes one of the major concerns which has been expressed by opponents of software patents—especially in the United States—that a patent could be infringed by a party working out calculations with pen and paper.

The Board, therefore, was of the opinion that even if the idea underlying an invention may be considered to lie in a mathematical method, a claim directed to a technical process in which the method is used does not seek protection for the mathematical method as such.[27]

In respect of the claims relating to the apparatus, it was conceded that the process could be conducted using conventional computing equipment. The Board of Appeal held, however, that:

> ...a claim directed to a technical process which process is carried out under the control of a program (be this implemented in hardware or in software), cannot be regarded as relating to a computer program as such within the meaning of Article 52(3) EPC [European Patent Convention], as it is the application of the program for determining the sequence of steps in the process for which in effect protection is sought. Consequently, such a claim is allowable under Article 52(2)(c) and (3) EPC.
>
> In arriving at this conclusion, the Board has additionally considered that making a distinction between embodiments of the same invention carried out in hardware or in software is inappropriate as it can fairly be said that the choice between these two possibilities is not of an essential nature but is based on technical and economical considerations which bear no relationship to the inventive concept as such.

---

[25] Ibid., at 80–1.
[26] Ibid., at 79.
[27] Ibid.

Generally speaking, an invention which would be patentable in accordance with conventional patentability criteria should not be excluded from protection by the mere fact that for its implementation modern technical means in the form of a computer program are used. Decisive is what technical contribution the invention as defined in the claim when considered as a whole makes to the known art.[28]

A number of significant features can be identified from the decision in *Vicom*.[29] The applicants' argument might well be noted that they had made 'a new and valuable contribution to the stock of human knowledge'. Protecting such work is at the core of the patent system. In terms of the decision of the Board of Appeal, there is recognition that what an invention does is more important than the manner in which it is achieved. As was stated in the decision, and as is increasingly the case, the distinction between hardware and software implementation of a concept is a matter of choice.

Software-related inventions returned to the European Patent Office Board of Appeal in 1987 in the case of *Koch and Sterzel*.[30] Here, a patent had been awarded in respect of a 'diagnostic X-ray system operative in response to control signals from a stored program digital computer to generate an X-ray beam and to produce an image of the object through which the X-ray beam passes'.[31] The validity of the patent was challenged by two competitor companies, which argued that its subject-matter differed from the state of the art only through the involvement of a novel computer program. The decision in *Vicom*,[32] it was suggested, was erroneous in that an application should not be accepted where the elements of novelty and inventiveness lay only in prohibited subject-matter—in this case a computer program. Support for this contention was found in a decision of the German courts, to the effect that:

> ...a teaching is not technical if in its essence it states a rule that can be carried out without employing controllable natural forces other than human brainpower, even if the use of technical means appears expedient or indeed the only sensible and hence the necessary procedure, and even if reference is made to these technical means in the claims or description.[33]

We will return to this concept in discussing the impact of the prohibition against patenting schemes or rules for performing a mental act. In *Koch and Sterzel*, the Board of Appeal rejected the German approach, holding that:

> ...an invention must be assessed as a whole. If it makes use of both technical and non-technical means, the use of non-technical means does not detract from the technical character of the overall teaching. The European Patent Convention does not ask that a patentable invention be exclusively or largely of a technical nature; in other words,

---

[28] Ibid.
[29] *Vicom Systems Inc's Application* [1987] 2 EPOR 74.
[30] [1988] EPOR 72.
[31] EP0001640.
[32] *Vicom Systems Inc's Application* [1987] 2 EPOR 74.
[33] [1988] EPOR 72 at 74.

it does not prohibit the patenting of inventions consisting of a mix of technical and non-technical elements.[34]

The alternative approach, it was suggested, could result in a situation where technical aspects of an invention, which were themselves novel and inventive, would be denied patent protection because they were connected with non-technical aspects such as computer programs.

The question of where novelty is required to reside was a key issue in the next authority to be considered, the United Kingdom case of *Merrill Lynch's Application*.[35] The case was first considered in the Patents Court prior to publication of the European Patent Office's decision in *Vicom*,[36] with the decision of the Appeal Court following after this landmark opinion.

If *Vicom*[37] constitutes a landmark decision under the European Patent Convention, the decision in *Merrill Lynch's Application*[38] plays a similar role in United Kingdom patent law. The factual content of this case was very similar to that at issue in *International Business Machines Corpn's Application*.[39] Merrill Lynch had developed what was referred to as 'a data processing system for making a trading market in securities and for executing orders for securities transactions'. The application of computerised trading systems in stocks and shares has proved controversial in a number of areas. Some of the blame for the 'crash' of stock exchanges on 'Black Monday' in October 1987 has been apportioned to the operation of systems whereby a fall in share prices automatically triggers the sale of shares which produces a further drop in prices, more selling and a continuation of a downward spiral. Such considerations were not at issue in the present case, which was concerned solely with the question of whether a patent might be awarded in respect of one such system.

The system devised by Merrill Lynch related to:

> ...business systems and, more specifically, to an improved data processing based system for implementing an automated trading market for one or more securities. The system retrieves and stores the best current bid and asked prices; qualifies customers' buy/sell orders for execution; executes the orders; and reports the trade particulars to customers and to national stock price reporting systems. The system apparatus also determines and monitors stock inventory and profit for the market maker.[40]

The specification went on to state that the programs involved could be implemented on a wide range of data-processing equipment. Effectively, what the application was claiming was that a general-purpose computer could operate the computer programs to produce novel effects.

---

[34] Ibid.
[35] [1989] RPC 561, reported at first instance at [1988] RPC 1.
[36] *Vicom Systems Inc's Application* [1987] 2 EPOR 74.
[37] Ibid.
[38] [1989] RPC 561, reported at first instance at [1988] RPC 1.
[39] [1980] FSR 564.
[40] *Merrill Lynch's Application* [1989] RPC 561 at 569.

The application was rejected within the Patent Office on the basis that the subject-matter of the alleged invention fell within the prohibition of s 1(2) of the Patents Act 1977. The principal patent examiner held that the effect of this section was such that it would prevent the award of a patent in the situation where the program was incorporated in some other object (the computer) but where the novelty and inventive step resided in the elements of the program rather than in any of the other attributes of the subject-matter.

This reasoning, which was upheld by Falconer J in the Patents Court, was challenged before the Court of Appeal. The critical issue concerned the interpretation of the concluding passage of s 1(2) of the Patents Act 1977, stating that the prohibitions against patentability extended only 'to the extent that a patent or application for a patent relates to that thing as such'. It was the applicant's contention that the claim related to apparatus operating in accordance with the requirements of the program and, therefore, was for more than the program as such.

Subsequent to the decision of Falconer J at first instance,[41] the Court of Appeal delivered its judgment in the case of *Genentech Inc's Patent*,[42] which also took account of the decision of the European Patent Office Board of Appeal in the case of *Vicom's Application*.[43] Although the subject-matter of this case concerned developments in genetic engineering, the issue of the extent of the prohibition against patentability was also discussed, in this case in the context of a discovery.

As described previously, Genentech had identified elements of DNA and obtained patents for applications based upon this research. These patents were revoked by order of Whitford J sitting in the Patents Court on the ground that, inter alia, the identification of the make-up of the DNA was in the nature of a discovery. Having made the discovery, its application was obvious. The only novelty, therefore, lay in the act of discovery. As discoveries cannot be patented, the patent was invalid.

This interpretation of the legislation was rejected by the Court of Appeal. Although the decision to revoke the patent was upheld on other grounds, it was acknowledged that many developments in the pharmaceutical field could be regarded in the same light. Once it is discovered, for example, that a particular drug has a beneficial effect on stomach ulcers, its application is very obvious. Dillon LJ commented:

> Such a conclusion, when applied to a discovery, would seem to mean that the application of the discovery is only patentable if the application is itself novel and not obvious, altogether apart from the novelty of the discovery. That would have a very drastic effect on the patenting of new drugs and medicinal or microbiological processes.[44]

The Court of Appeal in *Genentech*[45] was referred to the decision of Falconer J in *Merrill Lynch*.[46] Indicating their disagreement with the reasoning applied (although

---

41 *Merrill Lynch's Application* [1988] RPC 1.
42 [1989] RPC 147.
43 *Vicom Systems Inc's Application* [1987] 2 EPOR 74.
44 *Genentech Inc's Patent* [1989] RPC 147 at 239–240.
45 Ibid.
46 *Merrill Lynch's Application* [1988] RPC 1.

concurring with the ultimate result of the case), the court held that so long as the subject-matter of the application as a whole satisfied the requirements for patent-ability, it would not matter that the requisite novelty and inventiveness resided in non-qualifying elements. Effectively, the test concerns what the invention does, as opposed to the manner in which this is accomplished.

Applying the reasoning of the *Genentech* decision[47] and that of the European Patent Offices Technical Board of Appeal in *Vicom*,[48] the Court of Appeal affirmed that an invention could be patentable where the novel or inventive elements lay entirely in a computer program. However, the decision of the Patent Office to refuse Merrill Lynch's application was upheld on another ground. Even though the incorporation of the program in the computer equipment might serve to take it outwith the prohibition against the grant of patents for computer programs, attention had to be paid to the nature of the resulting application. In the present case, the result:

> ...whatever the technical advance may be, is simply the production of a trading system. It is a data processing system for doing a specific business, that is to say mak-ing a trading market in securities. The end result, therefore, is simply 'a method...of doing business', and is excluded by section 1(2)(c) [of the Patents Act 1977]...A data processing system operating to produce a novel technical result would normally be patentable. But it cannot, it seems to me, be patentable if the result itself is a prohibited item under section 1(2). In the present case it is such a prohibited item.[49]

It may be noted that Merrill Lynch subsequently obtained a patent for broadly the same application from the United States Patent Office.[50] The case demonstrates that, not only must the invention produce some technical contribution—in itself no easy thing to define—but the end product must not constitute prohibited subject-matter. In cases such as *Koch and Stertzel*,[51] where the programs control the operation of some product, this test is fairly easily established. In the situation where the effects are either internal or affect information—echoing back to the debate in *Slee and Harris*[52] on whether information can constitute a product—the prognosis for the grant of a patent is much less favourable.

The following sections will consider the recent development of case law in the United Kingdom and before the European Patent Office. In spite of repeated com-ments to the desirability of securing uniformity of treatment of applications between the United Kingdom and European patent authorities, it does appear that signifi-cant divisions have emerged both between the United Kingdom and Europe and also internally within the European Patent Office, with differently composed Boards of Appeal producing incompatible decisions. In the case of *Aerotel v Telco Holdings*[53] which came before the Court of Appeal in 2006 and is discussed extensively below,

[47] *Genentech Inc's Patent* [1989] RPC 147.
[48] *Vicom Systems Inc's Application* [1987] 2 EPOR 74.
[49] *Merrill Lynch's Application* [1989] RPC 561 at 569.
[50] This patent survived a challenge in the United States courts.
[51] [1988] EPOR 72.
[52] *Slee and Harris's Application* [1966] RPC 194.
[53] [2006] EWCA 1371.

the court declared that in the face of conflicting European authorities, the United Kingdom would follow its own precedents.

The development of software patent jurisprudence

Gale's Application

In the case of *Gale's Application*,[54] Mr Gale had developed a new algorithm and sought a patent in respect of an invention entitled 'Improvements and means whereby a binary manipulative system may derive a square root'. Effectively, Gale had devised a simplified process for the calculation of square roots. This process could be implemented in a number of ways. Certainly, where it was intended that the calculations be made by a computer, it would have been possible to store them on a computer disk or tape. As such, the provisions of s 1(2) of the Patents Act 1977 would undoubtedly come into play. In his patent application, Gale sought to overcome this obstacle by describing the operation of the mathematical process as implemented on a ROM (read-only memory) chip. Such a device, he argued, could be distinguished from a computer program in that its physical form was dictated by the specific function that it was designed to perform. Although the difference might be apparent only upon the most minute inspection, a chip produced to Mr Gale's specifications would have an appearance distinct from any other piece of circuitry.

This argument did not commend itself to the Principal Examiner in the Patent Office, who rejected the application on basis that it related to a program for a computer. There was, he ruled, no distinction between a segment of ROM with a program held on it and a disk holding the same data. The latter would not be patentable and neither, in his opinion, should the former. Such a scenario had also been posited by Dillon LJ in *Genentech*, and the view expressed that:

> It would be nonsense for the Act [Patents Act 1977] to forbid the patenting of a computer program, and yet permit the patenting of a floppy disc containing a computer program, or an ordinary computer when programmed with the program; it can well be said, as it seems to me, that a patent for a computer when programmed or for the disc containing the program is no more than a patent for the program as such.[55]

In the Patents Court, Aldous J surveyed the case law under Patents Act 1977 referring to the *Merrill Lynch*[56] and *Genentech*[57] decisions. From this, he concluded that the relevant criterion was whether there was more to the claimed invention than unpatentable subject-matter, in the present case whether *Gale's Application* concerned more than a program for a computer:

> ...the first task of the court is to construe the claim as that is where the invention is defined. If the claim properly construed is drafted so as to relate to any of the matters

54 [1991] RPC 305.
55 [1989] RPC 147 at 240.
56 *Merrill Lynch's Application* [1989] RPC 561 at 569.
57 *Genentech Inc's Patent* [1989] RPC 147.

disqualified by section 1(2) then the invention is not patentable. If, however, the claim is drafted to a process or technique or product and the basis of such process technique or product is a disqualified matter, the court should go on to consider whether the claimed invention is in fact no more than a claim to an invention for a disqualified matter. It is a question of fact to be decided in each case, but if the claimed invention is more than a claim to an invention for a disqualified matter then it qualifies as a patentable invention.

In deciding that question of fact it is always important to consider whether the claimed invention is part of a process which is to be used in providing a technical result. If it is, then the claim cannot be said to be an invention relating to no more than one of the disqualified matters. Similarly, where a claim is directed to a product, it is important to consider whether the product claimed is a new technical product or merely an ordinary product programmed in a different way as in the latter case the claim is in reality to the programme and therefore could not relate to a patentable invention.[58]

Applying this test, it was held that a distinction could be drawn between a computer program and the electronic circuitry specified in the patent application. The circuitry involved was a manufactured item which was dedicated to one function. In the situation where a program was held on a computer disk, the disk served merely as a storage device. In the present case, the program was used as the basis for altering the physical structure of the circuitry, which could then be used to implement the program. Accordingly, the decision of the Principal Examiner that the application fell into one of the prohibited categories under the Act was reversed, and the case was returned to the Patent Office in order for a substantive examination to be made concerning the issues of novelty and inventiveness.

The decision in *Gale* was criticised by a number of commentators, principally on the basis that no significant distinction exists between a disk as a storage device for a program and a segment of ROM. The decision was subsequently appealed successfully by the Comptroller of Patents.[59] Delivering the leading judgment in the Court of Appeal, Nicholls LJ, whilst accepting that an invention would not necessarily be debarred from the grant of a patent where the novelty lay in a computer program (or a discovery or any other prohibited subject-matter), disagreed that the form in which the series of instructions making up the program were stored was of any significance for patent purposes:

To be used in a computer, a series of instructions has to be recorded in a physical form which a computer can understand. Typically, but by no means always, the instructions will be recorded either on a disc inserted in the computer when required or, in the case of sequences of instructions routinely or frequently required, in a ROM which normally is inserted in a computer and not removed. Plainly, however, if the instructions qua instructions are not patentable, a claimant's position is not improved by claiming a disc on which those instructions have been recorded or a ROM in which they have been embodied. The disc or ROM is no more than an established type of artefact

---

[58] *Gale's Application* [1991] RPC 305.
[59] Ibid.

in which the instructions are physically embedded. It is merely the vehicle used for carrying them.[60]

The analogy was drawn with compact discs used for the storage of pieces of music. Each disc will differ physically from other discs holding a different musical composition. These physical differences, however, related only to the use of the disc for its normal purpose, the differences being created through the use of conventional production techniques. Attempts to create distinctions on this basis would, it was held, 'exalt form over substance'.

Although the Court of Appeal was unanimous in the view that the prohibition against the patentability of a computer program could not be circumvented by implementing it in hardware, Parker LJ indicated that he had found the issue to be 'of considerable difficulty'[61] and that '[i]n the course of arguments it appeared to me from time to time that the contentions in favour of patentability should be accepted in preference to those against'.[62] The effect of Mr Gale's chip was, he stated, to allow computers to calculate square roots both faster and to a greater degree of accuracy than had hitherto been possible. Ultimately, however, the fact that the same effect might equally well have been achieved using software and would certainly have been unpatentable in this form proved fatal to the application.

In some respects, the refusal of a patent might appear somewhat inequitable. As a result of Mr Gale's activities, the prospect of a better form of calculator existed. Nicholls LJ noted that:

> Although a computer program as such is not patentable, this is not to say that the instructions comprised in such a program, when recorded in a suitable medium, attract no protection. In this country the writer of the instructions, considered simply as a sequence of instructions, has a measure of protection for the product of his skill and effort, but it lies elsewhere, namely, in the law of copyright.[63]

The copyright system will be considered in more detail in subsequent chapters. Although at the time the decision was delivered in *Gale* the received wisdom was that this branch of intellectual property law provided extensive protection (extending to what was often referred to as the 'look and feel' of software), subsequent decisions have raised the question of whether copyright does provide adequate protection for the skill and effort of the developer.

Hitachi's Application

Hitachi's Application[64] concerned a development in the area of compiler programs. Today, most computer programs are initially written in source code. Depending upon

---

60 [1991] RPC 305 at 325.
61 *Gale's Application* [1991] RPC 305 at 328.
62 [1991] RPC 305 at 330.
63 *Gale's Application* [1991] RPC 305 at 326.
64 [1991] RPC 415.

the computer language used, this may bear close similarities to the normal use of English. In order to be understood by a computer, the source code has to be converted into machine or object code. Special programs known as compilers are available to perform this task.

Computers can operate on the basis of two forms of instructions, known as scalar and vector. The latter was, at least in the late 1980s, a relatively new development, which enabled processing to be conducted at much higher speeds than were possible with their scalar equivalent. The source code of most programs was written in the scalar format. Hitachi's development was a form of compiler that would, in addition to converting source to object code, convert scalar instructions into their vector equivalent. This would obviate the need for the programmer to return to the source code and make the necessary changes by hand. Hitachi sought patents for this development, relating both to a computer programmed with the compiler and to the method of operation employed. It was argued that the claims related to a technical process in that the computer as programmed was operating on a physical entity in the form of the source code program. Such a view, it was argued, was supported by the European Patent Office's decision in *Vicom*.[65] This view was rejected by the Principal Examiner in the Patents Office, who held that although the *Vicom* case had indeed involved the mathematical processing of electronic signals, this had involved three elements:

> ...firstly a mathematical method, secondly numbers—these being the things upon which the mathematical method operates, and thirdly the representation of images by the numbers, the third element being the element that converted the first two into a patentable invention. In the present application, in my view, the compiler program takes the place of the mathematical method, and the thing that the compiler operates upon, i.e. the thing that corresponds to the numbers of Vicom, is the source program. Thus, if the analogy between the present application and Vicom is set up in the way I have just indicated, there is no element in the present application that is analogous to the third element in Vicom, because the present application does not state what the source program represents, and indeed I think it stands alone and cannot properly be said to represent anything other than itself.[66]

Additionally, it was held, the processing involved in *Vicom*[67] could be used for a variety of further purposes, some of which, as in the case of the image processing, could be put to industrial application, whilst others, such as the use of the mathematical techniques for the purpose of making economic forecasts, would not. In the present case, the compiler, which was at the heart of the application, could only realistically work upon computer source code. As was concluded, 'this renders specious any separation of the data that the compiler operates upon and the source program, since they

65 *Vicom Systems Inc's Application* [1987] 2 EPOR 74.
66 *Hitachi's Application* [1991] RPC 415 at 417.
67 *Vicom Systems Inc's Application* [1987] 2 EPOR 74.

are one and the same'. Hitachi's claims, accordingly, were rejected as referring only to unpatentable subject-matter.[68]

When is a program more than a program?

The clear message from cases such as *Vicom*[69] is that in determining whether a software-related invention is patentable, a critical determinant will be what the application achieves. In a case such as *Koch and Sterzel*,[70] this may be relatively easy to identify. The end product in this case could be classed as a better X-ray machine. It is often suggested that the person who invents a better mousetrap will find the world waiting to pay a fortune for the device. It must surely be of little significance if the improved mousetrap relies on a computer program rather than a piece of cheese. More difficult cases arise when, as in *Hitachi*,[71] it is difficult to identify tangible elements as resulting from the operation of the program. A number of cases decided before the European Patent Office involving the computer company IBM illustrate the problem. In *IBM/Homphone Checker*,[72] the application referred to a novel method for correcting homophone errors in a document, for example, the use of the word 'where' when the context of the document required 'wear'. Such a facility is an important feature of speech recognition systems, but is also a process which is carried out (often imperfectly) within the brain of an author. The application, it was held, related only to known and standard apparatus, and was described in functional terms corresponding to the mental steps which would be carried out by a human performing the same text processing operations. Holding it unpatentable, the Board of Appeal ruled that:

> Since the only conceivable use for a computer program is the running of it on a computer, the exclusion from patentability of programs for computers would be effectively undermined if it could be circumvented by including in the claim a reference to conventional hardware features, such as processor, memory, keyboard and display, which in practice are indispensable if the program is to be used at all. In the opinion of the Board, in such cases, patentability must depend on whether the operations performed involve an inventive step in a field not excluded from patentability.[73]

A further decision relating to an application from IBM, *IBM Corpn/Reading Age*,[74] is more explicit. This application concerned a system for checking automatically the text of a document in order to highlight words having a reading age higher than that specified for its readers. The system would go on to present a list of alternative formulations which would meet the appropriate age requirements. Again, the equipment could be seen as replicating functions traditionally carried out by human editors.

---

68 *Hitachi's Application* [1991] RPC 415 at 417.
69 *Vicom Systems Inc's Application* [1987] 2 EPOR 74.
70 [1988] EPOR 72.
71 *Hitachi's Application* [1991] RPC 415 at 417.
72 [1990] EPOR 181.
73 [1990] EPOR 181 at 183.
74 [1990] OJEPO 384.

Although the particular application was rejected, the Board of Appeal held that such a development might be patentable if the technical manner in which the process was conducted involved an advance on the state of the art *even though* (emphasis added) the steps taken might correspond to those performed in the mind of a human.

IBM/Semantically Related Expressions[75] involved an application by IBM, who sought to patent a system for automatically generating a list of expressions semantically related to an input linguistic expression, together with a method for displaying such a list, i.e. a form of thesaurus. The actions of the computer in this case were considered to operate in the field of linguistics rather than to produce a technical contribution to the known art.

The computer's functions were all conventional, described as consisting of:

> ...storing data; comparing input data with an index for finding an address location; storing the address; accessing it with a memory; decoding the addressed data; utilising the decoded data as an address for accessing another memory; displaying the addressed data.[76]

Beyond the technicalities of its performance, all that the computer did was to compare data, in the form of a word, with other data already programmed into a segment of its memory and display the results of any matches. To this extent, its operations were comparable with a person 'searching' his or her memory for an alternative form of expression. The Board of Appeal concluded:

> It remains, of course, true that internally a computer functions technically and this applies also to its display device. However, the effect of this function, namely the resulting information about the existence of semantically related expressions, is a purely linguistic, that is, non-technical result. The appellant agrees that the claimed system can be implemented by pure software and this implementation is the only one described and preferred. No new reconfigured hardware has been shown to be used in this case. As said before, the two memories can be different sections of a single (conventional) memory. In the opinion of the Board, this new reconfiguration by software is not a technical contribution here.[77]

In a further case, *IBM/Data Processor Network*,[78] the application involved the interconnection of a series of computers in such a manner as to facilitate communications between programs and data held in the various computers. Obviously, the basis for the claimed invention lay in the computer programs which controlled these operations. It was accepted that:

> The proposed improved communication facilities between programs and files held at different processors within the known network do not involve any changes in the physical structure of the processors or the transmission network. The necessary control

---

[75] [1989] EPOR 454.
[76] *IBM/Semantically Related Expressions* [1989] EPOR 454 at 458.
[77] *IBM/Semantically Related Expressions* [1989] EPOR 454 at 460.
[78] [1990] EPOR 91.

functions for this purpose, referred to as 'mirror transaction' in the description of the present application, are effected by appropriate software.[79]

In spite of this, it was the opinion of the Board of Appeal that:

> ...an invention relating to the coordination and control of the internal communication between programs and data files held at different processors in a data processing system...and the features of which are not concerned with the nature of the data and the way in which a particular application program operates on them, is to be regarded as solving a problem which is essentially technical. Such an invention therefore is to be regarded as an invention within the meaning of Article 52(1) EPC [European Patent Convention].[80]

In yet another application involving IBM, *IBM/Computer Related Invention*,[81] an application was accepted which referred to a method for causing a computer to display automatically one of a number of predetermined messages relating to the machine's status. The view was taken that:

> ...giving visual indications automatically about conditions prevailing in the apparatus or system is basically a technical problem.

The application proposed a solution to a specific problem of this kind, namely providing a visual indication about events occurring in the input/output device of a text processor. The solution included the use of a computer program and certain tables stored in a memory to build up the phrases to be displayed.[82]

The distinction between this successful application and the unsuccessful claim in *IBM/Semantically-Related Expressions*[83] appears slight. The Board of Appeal was of the view that the present application was more than a computer program, but it is not clear why a development which automatically displays information regarding a computer system's state of health should be so regarded whilst a development which automatically displays the synonyms of a word inputted by a user should be rejected.

Final reference will be made to another IBM application, this time involving a development in what is referred to as text clarity.[84] This consisted of a method by which a computer program would scan text in order to identify incomprehensible or obscure linguistic expressions and suggest alternative formulations. Many authors could benefit greatly from such a facility.

Once again, the Board of Examiners sought to identify whether the claimed invention produced any technical effect. It used, it was held, technical means to substitute for human intellectual acts, but once the steps required to perform the act have been identified, their implementation involved 'no more than the straightforward application of

---

[79] [1990] EPOR 91 at 94.
[80] [1990] EPOR 91 at 95.
[81] [1990] EPOR 107.
[82] [1990] EPOR 107 at 110.
[83] *IBM/Semantically Related Expressions* [1989] EPOR 454.
[84] *IBM/Text Clarity Processing (T38/86)* [1990] EPOR 606.

standard techniques'[85] which would be obvious to a person skilled in the technical art. On this basis, there was no inventive step. The Board of Examiners concluded:

> Since the only conceivable use for a computer program is the running of it on a computer, the exclusion from patentability of computer programs would be effectively undermined if it could be circumvented by including in the claim a reference to conventional hardware features...which in practice are indispensable if the program is to be used at all.[86]

Although the case law of the European Patent Office as discussed above does not appear totally consistent, the number of successful applications, coupled with some of the dicta of the Board of Examiners, created a sense that the criteria were being applied more flexibly. This was the case, not just in respect of the prohibition against the award of patents for computer programs, but also in respect of the prohibition against the award of a patent in respect of a scheme or method for performing a mental act. Given that the effect of many computer programs is to automate processes which would previously have required human intervention, this can be a substantial obstacle to the award of a patent.

Schemes or methods for performing a mental act

Two relevant United Kingdom cases on this point concern applications by Wang and Raytheon. In *Wang*,[87] the claimed invention related to a novel form of expert system. This was held to be unpatentable on the ground that it related to nothing more than a computer program. Reference was also made in the case to the statutory prohibition against the grant of a patent in respect of a scheme or method for performing a mental act. Counsel for Wang argued that the phrase 'scheme, rule or method for performing a mental act' only applied to methods which were capable of being performed in the human mind. The operation of the expert system, although seeking to produce results similar to those arrived at by a human expert, utilised steps and procedures which would not be replicated by such a person. This interpretation was rejected by Aldous J (as he then was), who held that:

> Just as a claim to a disk containing a program can be in fact a claim to an invention for a computer program, so can a claim to steps leading to an answer be a claim to an invention for a method for performing a mental act. The method remains a method for performing a mental act, whether a computer is used or not. Thus a method of solving a problem, such as advising a person whether he has acted tortuously, can be set out on paper, or incorporated into a computer program. The purpose is the same, to enable advice to be given, which appears to me to be a mental act. Further, the result will be the advice which comes from performance of a mental act. The method may well be different when a computer is used, but to my mind it still remains a method

---

[85] *IBM/Text Clarity Processing (T38/86)* [1990] EPOR 606 at 611.
[86] [1990] EPOR 606 at 613.
[87] [1991] RPC 463.

for performing a mental act, whether or not the computer program adopts steps that would not ordinarily be used by the human mind.[88]

Image identifying

The decision in *Wang*[89] was approved in the subsequent case of *Raytheon's Application*.[90] At issue in this case was a method of automatically identifying objects such as ships. The image of the object's silhouette would be captured by some form of imaging device, such as a camera, and be transformed into digital format. The digitised image would then be processed by a standard computer. This process involved making a comparison with a library of images stored on the computer in order to select the most appropriate match. A patent was sought for the process, but was rejected within the Patent Office on the grounds that the application related to no more than a method for performing a mental act using a computer. This interpretation was upheld in the Patents Court, where Mr Julian Jeffs QC (sitting as a deputy judge) held that the phrase 'a mental act' had to be construed in its normal sense. This was equated with the possibility of explaining in words how a mental act had been performed. In some cases, it is a simple task, for example to explain that two times two equals four. Obviously, in a case such as this, much would depend upon the level of complexity required to accompany the answer. In other cases, for example, explaining how we might recognise a friend passing by on the other side of the street, explanation becomes a more convoluted matter. Rather like the definition of the elephant, we might know a friend when we see her but find it hard to explain all the cognitive processes involved. Somewhere in between comes a category, exemplified in the court in terms of defining the smell of an orange. Here, chemical analysis could explain most of the elements but such a process could not be equated with the human method.

The approach developed in *Wang*[91] and *Raytheon*[92] would deny protection to any software-related innovation performing a function which, *in principle*, could be carried out within the human brain even though this would not reflect the normal process of human reasoning. This approach sits uneasily with at least some of the jurisprudence of the European Patent Office and, during the 1990s, concerns were raised in a number of forums concerning the state of United Kingdom law and whether the stated objective to ensure compatibility with the case law of the European Patent Office was being met. The most recent United Kingdom decision is that of *Fujitsu's Application*. The scrutiny of the High Court[93] and Court of Appeal[94] was welcomed, not least by the patent authorities, it being commented before the High Court that the Patent Office had encountered

---

[88] [1991] RPC 463 at 473.
[89] [1991] RPC 463.
[90] [1993] RPC 427.
[91] [1991] RPC 463.
[92] [1993] RPC 427.
[93] [1996] RPC 511.
[94] [1997] RPC 608.

difficulties in applying the concepts of technical advance and contribution. These difficulties had been compounded by the fact, to which we will return later, that decisions of the European patent authorities had applied a more liberal interpretation of the
concepts than had previously been considered the case. Additionally, it was suggested,
strict interpretation of the statutory guidelines would deny patentability to many applications which did appear to provide 'substantial contribution to the sum of human
knowledge'.[95] The present case was seen as a good example of this phenomenon.

It is very debatable whether these hopes have been realised, although the decision in
Fujitsu remains the most important predent in the United Kingdom's patent law.

Fujitsu's Application

The technology at issue in *Fujitsu*[96] will be familiar to anyone with a recollection of
chemistry lessons at school and the use of three-dimensional lattices to depict molecular structures. Fujitsu's invention sought to bring this concept into the age of virtual
reality, allowing chemists to depict and manipulate crystal structures on a computer
screen. The effect would be to allow the analysis of the properties of new compounds
without the need to create these in the real world. The novelty in the claimed invention
lay only in the relevant computer programs.

The patent application was rejected in the Patent Office on two grounds: first, that
the application related to a program for a computer; and second, that it constituted a
method for performing a mental act—that of visualising molecular structure.

The computer program exception

Relying on the *Vicom* decision,[97] Counsel for Fujitsu suggested that what was required
to bring prohibited subject-matter, such as computer programs or schemes for performing mental acts, within the patent system was that these should be tied to some
technical application. In the present case,[98] as in *Vicom*, the technical component was
that the application resulted in the manipulation of images. In *Vicom*, images of physical objects were processed; in the present case, images of molecular structure.

After surveying relevant United Kingdom and European Patent Office authority,
Laddie J concluded that four propositions could be drawn relating to the patentability
of software-related inventions:

1. Any claimed invention which relied upon excluded subject-matter for its functioning would be excluded from patentability, regardless of whether the end product
was something which performed a technical act.

2. The exclusion from patentability is concerned with substance rather than form.
The fact that a computer program might be recorded on some physical (or technical)

95 [1996] RPC 511 at 521–2.
96 *Fujitsu Ltd's Application* [1996] RPC 511.
97 *Vicom Systems Inc's Application* [1987] 2 EPOR 74.
98 *Fujitsu Ltd's Application* [1996] RPC 511.

device would not render it patentable when the program, *per se*, would have been excluded.

3. At one level of analysis it could well be argued that a computer running one program was a different machine from a computer running another. At a very simple level, a computer running a word processing program was effectively a word processor, whilst the same machine running a spreadsheet program was morphed into a calculating machine. Even accepting that argument, it was held, there remained a requirement that the computer, as programmed, should produce a novel technical contribution.

4. Following from the above, where a computer was programmed to perform a novel function in the field of data processing, it should not be excluded from patentability on the ground that it related to nothing more than a computer program, but might well be challenged on the basis that what the computer, as programmed, was accomplishing was not more than something which was excluded from patentability under Section 1(2).

Applying these factors to the present case it was held that:

> The real issues it seems to me is whether the application also avoids the other exclusions...If it does not, the application will fail. Whether in those circumstances, the grounds of failure are stated to be that the invention is only for a program or that it is, for example, a method for performing a mental act is a matter of semantics.[99]

The *Fujitsu Application*, it was held, was excluded from patentability, although it is not clear from the judgment whether this conclusion was based upon a finding that it related to a computer program or to a scheme or method for performing a mental act. An appeal was lodged against this finding and the issue was considered rather more directly in the Court of Appeal, where Aldous LJ held that the application should be rejected on both. Comparing the claimed invention with that at issue in *Vicom*,[100] he concluded that:

> In Vicom, the technical contribution was provided by the generation of the enhanced display. In the present case, the combined structure is the result of the directions given by the operator and use of the program. The computer is conventional as is the display unit. The displays of crystal structures are provided by the operator. The operator then provides the appropriate way of superposition and the program does the rest. The resulting display is the combined structure shown pictorially in a form that would in the past have been produced as a model. The only advance is the computer program which enables the combined structure to be portrayed quicker.[101]

It might be suggested that a quicker method of producing a display of molecular structure should be regarded as patentable in the same way as would a better mousetrap or a method for producing better quality images. Certainly, the comments made

---

[99] Ibid., at 532.
[100] *Vicom Systems Inc's Application* [1987] 2 EPOR 74.
[101] *Fujitsu Ltd's Application* [1997] RPC 608 at 618–19.

regarding the conventional nature of the computer and the fact that 'virtual reality' displays are substituting for traditional three-dimensional models might be ground for challenge on the issues of novelty and inventiveness, but the distinction drawn with the situation in *Vicom*[102] exacerbates rather than clarifies the issue of what is required to produce a technical effect.

Schemes or methods for performing a mental act

Holding also that the *Fujitsu Application* related to no more than a scheme or method for performing a mental act, Laddie J stated that:

> In Vicom,[103] the Board explained that a mathematical method could be distinguished from a patentable process based on it in that the former involved an abstract concept in which numbers were worked on to produce new numbers whereas in a patentable process a physical entity was worked on and a new physical entity was produced. Very similar concepts apply to the distinction between methods for performing mental acts and processes methods or apparatus based upon such acts. Excluded mental acts must include those mental activities which involve a significant level of abstraction and intellectual generality. Rules as to the planting of potatoes in which the operator is instructed to measure and evaluate matters such as the type of soil, location, weather and availability of irrigation is a method for performing a mental act. Directions to plant one seed potato every metre is not. It is a precise process.
>
> In this case, Fujitsu's application leaves it to the operator to select what data to work on, how to work on it, how to assess the results and which, if any, results to use. The process is abstract and the result of use of it is undefined. What is produced is not an inevitable result of taking a number of defined steps but is determined by the personal skill and assessment of the operator. As such it consists in substance of a scheme or method for performing a mental act and is unpatentable.[104]

The decision in *Fujitsu*[105] provides no specific answer to the definitional questions raised above. It does appear to support a restrictive view of the scope of patentability. In some respects, the result seems somewhat paradoxical. A computer-controlled potato-planting machine which plants a potato every metre might be patentable. Were the identical machine to have more sophisticated software allowing account to be taken of factors such as soil conditions, weather, and the presence of other crops, no patent could be awarded, even though this second machine might appear more technologically advanced and deserving of protection. Again, reference to the role of the Fujitsu system in presenting information for the operator to act upon might be compared with many other pieces of machinery. The example might be presented of a novel form of navigational aid incorporated on an aircraft flight deck. This might present the pilots with information as to height, speed, and direction of flight. Assuming

---

102 *Vicom Systems Inc's Application* [1987] 2 EPOR 74.
103 Ibid.
104 *Fujitsu Ltd's Application* [1996] RPC 511 at 532.
105 Ibid.

that the device made use of mechanical components, there would be no bar to its patentability.

New millenium, new patent law?

Although it is always possible to identify points of difference between judgments, until the end of the twentieth century there was very considerable similarity in terminological approach both between the United Kingdom and the European authorities and also internally between differently composed Boards of Appeal within the European Patent Office. All authorities shared the view that any patent application required to demonstrate some technical contribution—although what constitutes a technical contribution is sometimes far from clear. Starting with the decision in *IBM's Application*, matters have become more confusing within the European Patent Office, although for the United Kingdom, the decision of the Court of Appeal in *Aerotel v Telco*[106] brings at least a measure of clarity to the situation.

IBM's Application

At issue in this case was an application for a patent for developments in relation to the use of 'windows' as a means for presenting information on a computer monitor. The advantage of IBM's programs, it was claimed, was that it rearranged the information held in one window so that it remained visible even when another window was opened on top of it. The application was rejected by the examiner on the ground that it related to a program per se and an appeal made to the Board of Appeal.

IBM's appeal was based on a number of grounds. It was argued that:

> ...the reason for the exclusion of computer programs as such from patent protection under the European Patent Convention was because there was already adequate and clear protection in the form of copyright, but that if the claims sought to protect something which would not attract copyright protection then the objection to patentability must fall. It was also argued that this approach was consistent with TRIPS. The appellants further argued that since the European Patent Office allowed a claim defining an invention by way of a technical feature, even if that feature was embodied in a computer program, once such an intellectual construction had been accepted as an invention, the provisions of Article 52 of the EPC were satisfied and would no longer justify constraining the applicant as to how to claim the invention.[107]

The issue concerning the availability of copyright for developments such as the IBM software was not pursued by the Board of Appeal. Whilst there is no doubt that computer programs are protected by copyright, this does not extend to the underlying concepts.

The TRIPS agreement provides that computer programs are to be protected by copyright. However, it requires also that 'patents shall be available for any inventions,

---

[106] [2006] EWCA Civ 1371.
[107] Case T0935/97 [1999] RPC 861 at 862.

whether products or processes, in all fields of technology, provided they are new, involve an inventive step and are capable of industrial application'.[108] There is no equivalent to the European Patent Convention's list of prohibited subject-matter.

It is national states (and the EU) who are signatories to TRIPS. The Agreement, therefore, is not binding upon international organisations such as the European Patent Office. The Board of Appeal held, however, that its provisions should be taken into account:

> ...since it is aimed at setting common standards and principles concerning the availability, scope and use of trade-related intellectual property rights, and therefore of patent rights. Thus TRIPS gives a clear indication of current trends.[109]

Reference was made also to developments in the United States and Japanese Patent Offices, which had adopted a more liberal approach towards the granting of patents for software-related inventions. Whilst recognising that these offices worked under legal provisions different from those applying in Europe, the developments, it was considered, 'represent a useful indication of modern trends' which 'may contribute to the further highly desirable (worldwide) harmonisation of patent law'. The clear implication would appear to be that the European Patent Office was out of step with other major offices in its treatment of software-related inventions.

Turning to the substance of the particular application, reference was made to the fact that computer programs were excluded only to the extent that the invention related to the program 'as such'. This formulation, it was held, indicated that the 'legislators did not want to exclude from patentability all programs for computers'. In previous decisions, the European Patent Office had laid stress on the requirement for a technical contribution. In the present case, attention focused on the interpretation of the phrase 'as such'. This phrase, it was held had to be construed as meaning that excluded programs were merely abstract creations which did not possess any technical character. 'As such' they could not be considered an invention as this term necessarily implied some technical character. It was held, however, that where programs demonstrated a technical character, they had to be considered eligible for protection.[110]

The question, therefore, was to determine when a computer program constituted more than an abstract creation and exhibited a technical character in its own right, independent of linkage with tangible objects. What was required was that the program should have the potential to cause the occurrence of a technical effect. A patent might be granted where a computer program operates to cause a computer to control some industrial process or the operation of a piece of machinery. Additionally, it was held, a patent may be granted when the computer program constituted a necessary part of the device for which protection was sought, even though the technical effect was

---

[108] Article 5.
[109] Case T0935/97 [1999] RPC 861 at 868.
[110] Ibid., at 870.

achieved purely by means of the internal functioning of the computer. Consequently, it was held that:

> ...on condition that they are able to produce a technical effect in the above sense, all computer programs must be considered as inventions within the meaning of Article 52(1) of the EPC [European Patent Convention], and may be the subject-matter of a patent if the other requirements provided for by the EPC are satisfied.[111]

It was recognised that the Guidelines for Examiners stated that a 'computer program claimed by itself or as a record on a carrier is not patentable'. For the future, however, the Board's decision was that:

> ...a computer program claimed by itself is not excluded from patentability if the program, when running on a computer or loaded into a computer, brings about, or is capable of bringing about, a technical effect which goes beyond the 'normal' physical interactions between the program (software) and the computer (hardware) on which it is run.[112]

The decision in *IBM's Application* might be seen as marking the culmination of a line of authority stretching back directly to *Vicom*. In very large measure, it might be seen as restating the law as laid down by the United Kingdom authorities in the final years of the 1949 Patents Act. Subsequently, three further decisions have been issued by the European Patent Office, which mark divergences in the approach which should be adopted in determining issues of technical contribution.

Pensions benefits[113]

In a decision handed down in September 2000, the Board of Examiners considered an appeal against the rejection of a patent application for a system designed to manage pension benefit programmes. It was claimed that the combination of hardware and software specified in the application was 'radically different' from existing pension management programmes:

> reducing the financial and administrative burdens for both sides, the employers and the employees, and achieving significant advantages over the former pension systems.

Criticising the decision of the patent examiner that the application fell to be classed as a method of doing business and demonstrated insufficient technical character it was argued that:

> relying on the 'technical character' of inventions was not justified, since such a criterion was not set up by the European Patent Convention as a requirement for patentability.

Reference was also made to the fact that the exclusion of business methods from patentability had been abandoned in many non-European jurisdictions, with specific reference made to the United States.

---

[111] Ibid., at 871.
[112] Ibid., at 877.
[113] Case T0931/95.

In its decision, the Board of Appeal accepted that the application was, prima facie, eligible for protection.

> In the Board's view a computer system suitably programmed for use in a particular field, even if that is the field of business and economy, has the character of a concrete apparatus in the sense of a physical entity, man-made for a utilitarian purpose and is thus an invention within the meaning of Article 52(1) EPC.
>
> This distinction with regard to patentability to between a method for doing business and an apparatus suited to perform such a method is justified in the light of the wording of Article 52(2)(c) EPC, according to which 'schemes, rules and methods' are non-patentable categories in the field of economy and business, but the category of 'apparatus' in the sense of 'physical entity' or 'product' is not mentioned in Article 52(2) EPC.
>
> This means that, if a claim is directed to such an entity, the formal category of such a claim does in fact imply physical features of the claimed subject-matter which may qualify as technical features of the invention concerned and thus be relevant for its patentability.
>
> Therefore the Board concludes that:
>
> > An apparatus constituting a physical entity or concrete product suitable for performing or supporting an economic activity, is an invention within the meaning of Article 52(1) EPC.

Although the Board held that a computer programmed to operate in a particular was not barred from patentability per se, the application was ultimately rejected on the basis that the programs used to bring about the desired effects were themselves not inventive.

Hitachi[114]

The decision in Hitachi concerned an application for a patent in respect of a method for conducting electronic auctions requiring minimal intervention on the part of bidders. As is described in the report:

> The auction starts with preliminary steps of data exchange between the client computers and the server computer in order to collect bids from the participants. Each bid comprises two prices, a 'desired price' and a 'maximum price in competitive state'. After this initial phase the auction is automatic and does not require that the bidders follow the auction on-line. An auction price is set and successively lowered (which is typical for so-called Dutch auctions) until it reaches the level of the highest bid or bids as determined by the 'desired price'. In case of several identical bids the price is increased until only the bidder having offered the highest 'maximum price' is left. He is declared successful.
>
> Therefore, taking into account both that a mix of technical and non-technical features may be regarded as an invention within the meaning of Article 52(1) EPC and that prior art should not be considered when deciding whether claimed subject-matter is such an invention, a compelling reason for not refusing under Article 52(2) EPC subject-matter

---

[114] Case T0258/03.

consisting of technical and non-technical features is simply that the technical features may in themselves turn out to fulfil all requirements of Article 52(1) EPC.

[3.7] For these reasons the Board holds that, contrary to the examining division's assessment, the apparatus of claim 3 is an invention within the meaning of Article 52(1) EPC since it comprises clearly technical features such as a 'server computer', 'client computers' and a 'network'.

[4.6] The Board is aware that its comparatively broad interpretation of the term 'invention' in Article 52(1) EPC will include activities which are so familiar that their technical character tends to be overlooked, such as the act of writing using pen and paper. Needless to say, however, this does not imply that all methods involving the use of technical means are patentable. They still have to be new, represent a non-obvious technical solution to a technical problem, and be susceptible of industrial application.

Determining the technical contribution an invention achieves with respect to the prior art is therefore more appropriate for the purpose of examining novelty and inventive step than for deciding on possible exclusion under Article 52(2) and (3).

Microsoft[115]

The most radical decision of the European Patent Office came with the decision in respect of an application for Microsoft for a new form of clipboard operation which, used in its Windows operating system, would enable data held in one format (for example, a graphic) to be copied into another application which is using a different format (for example, text). An application for the grant of a patent was rejected by the examiner on the grounds of lack of novelty and inventiveness. The Board of Examiners disagreed. Initially it was confirmed that:

> Claim 1 relates to a method implemented in a computer system. T 258/03—*Auction method/Hitachi* (OJ EPO 2004, 575) states that a method using technical means is an invention within the meaning of Article 52(1) EPC. A computer system including a memory (clipboard) is a technical means, and consequently the claimed method has technical character in accordance with established case law.
>
> Moreover, the Board would like to emphasise that a method implemented in a computer system represents a sequence of steps actually performed and achieving an effect, and not a sequence of computer-executable instructions (i.e. a computer program) which just have the potential of achieving such an effect when loaded into, and run on, a computer. Thus, the Board holds that the claim category of a computer-implemented method is distinguished from that of a computer program. Even though a method, in particular a method of operating a computer, may be put into practice with the help of a computer program, a claim relating to such a method does not claim a computer program in the category of a computer program.

The Board next considered the issues of novelty and inventiveness. In *Pensions Benefits* and *Hitachi*, these requirements had proved an insurmountable obstacle, with

---

[115] Case T0424/03.

the Board holding that the novel computer program should be regarded as if it constituted part of the prior art. No trace of this holding is to be found in *Microsoft*, with
the Board accepting that the previous version of Windows (Windows 3.1) constituted
the most relevant prior art. Compared to the features found in this, the new clipboard
was considered novel and inventive and the case was remitted to the examiner with the
instruction that a patent should be awarded.

Let a thousand flowers bloom?

The phrase, 'let a thousand [or in some sources, a hundred] flowers bloom, let a hundred ideas compete', is attributed to the legendary Chinese leader Chairman Mao. In
his case, the application of the principle proved problematic and when individuals took
him at his word and put forward ideas critical of current policy the response took the
form of the so-called Cultural Revolution, which sought to clamp down ruthlessly on
any blossoms other than those expressly approved by authority. Whilst not predicting
similar consequences, the varying approaches of the European Patent Office Boards of
Appeal may bring confusion rather than enlightenment. The situation has caused difficulties and perhaps a measure of irritation amongst national courts. This was clearly
expressed in the United Kingdom in the case of *Aerotel v Telco*, the outcome of which
might perhaps be seen as declaring a measure of conditional independence from the
internal disagreements within the European Patent Office.

   The facts in *Aerotel* can be relatively briefly stated. Aerotel had developed and sought
a patent for a method for making telephone calls from phones without using cash. A
user would deposit funds with the provider in advance and establish a credit balance.
Upon dialing a particular code, the call would be routed to a special exchange. Upon
entering a PIN number, the user would have calls connected up to the level of his
credit. Although it is not specified in the report, the system could be used by indirect
telephone service providers who might, especially for international calls, purchase
capacity from BT and sell this on to customers. As with mobile phones, the pay as you
go approach would obviate the need for complex contractual and billing procedures.

   Aerotel were awarded a patent for the system and subsequently sued a competitor for
infringement. The other party counter-claimed, alleging that the patent was invalid as
relating to nothing more than a program for a computer. Although the case was settled,
Aerotel appealed to the Court of Appeal, seeking reinstatement of the patent.

   Delivering the judgment of the court, Lord Justice Jacob provided an extensive survey of the development of the law relating to software-related patents. The
approaches adopted within the United Kingdom and before the European Patent
Office were summarised succinctly:

(1) The contribution approach
Ask whether the inventive step resides only in the contribution of excluded matter—if
yes, Article 52(2) applies.

   This approach was supported by Falconer J in *Merrill Lynch* but expressly rejected
by this Court.

(2) The technical effect approach

Ask whether the invention as defined in the claim makes a technical contribution to the known art—if no, Article 52(2) applies. A possible clarification (at least by way of exclusion) of this approach is to add the rider that novel or inventive purely excluded matter does not count as a 'technical contribution'.

This is the approach (with the rider) adopted by this Court in *Merrill Lynch*. It has been followed in the subsequent decisions of this Court, *Gale* and *Fujitsu*. The approach (without the rider as an express caution) was that first adopted by the EPO Boards of Appeal, see *Vicom, IBM/Text processing* and *IBM/Data processor network*.

(3) The 'any hardware' approach

Ask whether the claim involves the use of or is to a piece of physical hardware, however mundane (whether a computer or a pencil and paper). If yes, Article 52(2) does not apply. This approach was adopted in three cases, *Pensions Benefits, Hitachi*, and *Microsoft/Data transfer* (the 'trio'). It was specifically rejected by this Court in *Gale*.

However, there are variants of the 'any hardware' approach:

(3)(i) Where a claim is to a method which consists of an excluded category, it is excluded by Article 52(2) even if hardware is used to carry out the method. But a claim to the apparatus itself, being 'concrete' is not so excluded. The apparatus claim is nonetheless bad for obviousness because the notional skilled man must be taken to know about the improved, excluded, method.

This is the *Pensions Benefits* approach.

(3)(ii) A claim to hardware necessarily is not caught by Article 52(2). A claim to a method of using that hardware is likewise not excluded even if that method as such is excluded matter. Either type of claim is nonetheless bad for obviousness for the same reason as above.

This is *Hitachi*, expressly disagreeing with *Pensions Benefits* about method claims.

(3)(iii) Simply ask whether there is a claim to something 'concrete' e.g. an apparatus. If yes, Article 52(2) does not apply. Then examine for patentability on conventional grounds—do not treat the notional skilled man as knowing about any improved excluded method.

This is *Microsoft/Data Transfer*.[116]

Faced with such a baffling range of authorities, it was considered that, although it was a requirement to place great weight on decisions of the European Patent Office Board of Appeal, the contradictory nature of the jurisprudence made it impossible to do so. Rather than relying on European Patent Office authority, reference was made to the decisions of the Court of Appeal in *Gale, Merril Lynch*, and *Fujitsu's Applications*.[117] These, it was held, adopted the technical effect approach, with

---

[116] [2006] EWCA Civ 1371 at para. 26.
[117] [2006] EWCA Civ 1371.

the additional qualification or rider that novelty could not lie only in the otherwise excluded subject-matter.

Turning to the manner in which this principle should be applied, Lord Justice Jacob accepted a submission by counsel for the Commissioner of Patents which required the decision maker to:

1. *Properly construe the claim.*

This is a basic step for any patent application and requires identification of the nature and scope of the subject-matter of the patent and the extent of the monopoly which is sought.

2. *Identify the actual contribution.*

This involves an assessment of the problem which the applicant claims to have solved, the manner in which the invention works and the advantages which it claims to offer over existing technologies. Lord Justice Jacob summarised the requirement in the following terms '[w]hat has the inventor really added to human knowledge?'

3. *Ask whether it falls solely within the excluded subject-matter.*

This relates to the provision in the Act and Convention that inventions containing excluded subject-matter are ineligible for patent protection only to the extent that they contain nothing more than excluded subject-matter.

4. *Check whether the actual or alleged contribution is actually technical in nature.*

In many cases, it was suggested, the answer to this question would be obvious from that of the previous one.[118]

The four-stage test, it was stated, was a reformulation of the approach followed by the Court of Appeal in *Fujitsu*.

Applying these tests, the *Aerotel Application*, it was held, was patentable. The system specified was novel in itself and not merely because of its application to the handling of telephone calls. This meant that it satisfied the second and third criteria. The system required the use of hardware components and so was technical in nature.

Following the decision in *Aerotel*, the Patent Office stated that the case:

> must be treated as a definitive statement of how the law on patentable subject matter is now to be applied in the United Kingdom (United Kingdom). It should therefore rarely be necessary to refer back to previous United Kingdom or EPO case law.

In the subsequent case of *IGT v Commisioner of Patents*,[119] the *Aerotel* approach was adopted, albeit with comment to the effect that:

> The Court of Appeal has recently developed the approach which the courts should adopt to the correct interpretation of Article 52(2) and (3). Whether or not the application of the Article is now more or less straightforward, or clear, than it was before is perhaps a matter on which minds may differ.

---

[118] [2006] EWCA Civ 1371 at para. 40.
[119] [2007] EWHC 1341 Pat.

Following his concerns at the range of approaches adopted by the European Patent Office, Lord Justice Jacobs, with the support of the United Kingdom Patent Office, made a request to the President of the European Patent Office that an extended Board of Appeal be convened and asked to determine:

1. What is the correct approach to adopt in determining whether an invention relates to subject-matter that is excluded under Article 52?

2. How should those elements of a claim that relate to excluded subject-matter be treated when assessing whether an invention is novel and inventive under Articles 54 and 56?

3. And specifically:

   (a) Is an operative computer program loaded onto a medium such as a chip or hard drive of a computer excluded by Article 52(2) unless it produces a technical effect, if so what is meant by 'technical effect'?

   (b) What are the key characteristics of the method of doing business exclusion?

The request, however, was declined. Subsequently, disagreements between the European Patent Office and the Court of Appeal appear to have become even more pronounced. In the case of *Duns Licensing Associates' Application*,[120] the Board of Appeal—whilst rejecting an application for a patent in respect of method for estimating sales activities at outlets in the absence of actual returns (effectively by compiling a database allowing comparison to be made with other sales outlets of similar size and in similar locations) on the basis that it related only to a method for doing business—was highly critical of the decisions in *Aerotel v Telco*. The Court of Appeal's adoption of the 'technical effect approach (with rider)' criterion, it was claimed, was 'irreconcilable with the European Patent Convention'[121] and 'inconsistent with a good-faith interpretation of the European Patent Convention in accordance with Article 31 of the Vienna Convention on the Law of Treaties'.[122]

A request by the applicant in *Duns Licensing Associates* for a referral to an Enlarged Board of Appeal was rejected. Referral, it was held, could be justified only in order to ensure uniform application of the law or if an important point of law could be identified. The Rules of Procedure established under the European Patent Convention provided for a referral if a Board of Appeal proposed to deviate from a previous decision of an enlarged board. Disagreements between differently composed Boards of Appeal or with national authorities was not of itself a reason for making a referral. Hence, it was held:

> the legal system of the European Patent Convention gives room for evolution of the jurisprudence (which is thus not 'case law' in the strict Anglo-Saxon meaning of the

---

[120] Case T 0154/04.

[121] At para. 13.

[122] At para. 12. Article 31 of the Vienna Convention lays down principles to be used in interpreting treaties providing, inter alia, that: 'A treaty shall be interpreted in good faith in accordance with the ordinary meaning to be given to the terms of the treaty in their context and in the light of its object and purpose.'

term) and leaves it to the discretion of the boards whether to give reasons in any decision deviating from other decisions or to refer a point of law to the Enlarged Board.[123]

This perhaps is the crux of the issue and the disagreements. The European Patent
Office, in common with the approach in civil law jurisdictions, has less respect for precedent than the United Kingdom courts, and has tended to modify its interpretation
of the Convention in the light of developments in technologies and circumstances.
As was said by Lord Justice Jacobs in *Aerotel*, 'An arms race in which the weapons
are patents has set in.'[124] As will be discussed below, given a considerable willingness on the part of the United States authorities to grant patents for software-related
inventions, and given the importance of that country within the world's software industry, it is perhaps not surprising that the European Patent Office should modify its
approach. It is not surprising either that—given the strength of the doctrine of precedent and an approach to statutory interpretation which pays respect to the words used
in a legal instrument rather than seeking to determine what its framers would have
intended had the measure been redrafted in the light of changing circumstances—the
United Kingdom courts should adopt a more conservative approach. Differences may
exist only at the margins and it is noteworthy that the appellant in *Duns Licensing
Associates*, cited the decision in *Aerotel* in support of his application, in apparent
contradiction of the received wisdom that the European Patent Office is more recep-
tive to software patents.

Conclusions

It was suggested at the beginning of this chapter that the patent system was based
largely on the notion of national patents. This is likely to remain the case, and even
the proposed Community patent would exist alongside, rather than replace, national
patents. The increasingly global nature of commerce and industry is serving to bring
about an increasing degree of harmonisation and, as shown in the discussion above of
the most recent European Patent Office case law, the TRIPS Agreement is providing
a legal basis for harmonising initiatives. The trend throughout the world is clearly to
accept that software should be brought within the ambit of the patent system. In some
senses, there is almost an element of competition between states as to who can provide
the strongest protection. As was said in the United States case of *Lotus v Paperback*:

> It is no accident that the world's strongest software industry is found in the United
> States, rather than in some other jurisdiction which provides weaker protection for
> computer programs.[125]

It is now thirty years since patent law was reformed by the Patents Act 1977. At
that time, although the status of computer programs was certainly discussed in the

---

[123] At para. 2.
[124] [2006] EWVA Civ 1371 at para. 18.
[125] 740 F Supp 37 (1990).

preceding report of the Banks Committee,[126] it was not a matter of massive importance. In the intervening years, not only has the technology permeated into every
aspect of life, the development of microprocessors has rendered almost redundant
distinctions between hardware and software—to the extent that the term 'computer
program' is seldom used today. From a situation of existing as a rather small adjunct to
the industrial society, information technology has become pivotal to the information
society. Software development has changed from a craft to an industry. The turnover
and profits of software companies such as Microsoft dwarf those of the vast majority of
industrial enterprises. The development of satisfactory forms of protection is a matter
of great importance.

As will be discussed in the following chapters, one of the legislative trends of the
1980s was to provide that computer programs are protected under the law of copyright. Certainly copyright provides an acceptable and appropriate form of protection
for most computer programs which do not possess significant elements of novelty or
originality. Copyright, however, particularly given precedents in the United States
and the United Kingdom placing limits on the scope of protection against non-literal
copying, is less suitable as a vehicle for protecting innovative works. Competitors can
readily discern the underlying—and unprotected—ideas and replicate these without
the necessity to engage in literal copying of any of the code used in the original. In such
situations, the attractions of the patent system are apparent. In return for disclosing
details of the techniques employed, the patent holder secures monopoly protection
against reproduction of the novel ideas.

When the topic of the patentability of computer programs was discussed by the
Banks Committee in the 1970s, the issue was agreed to be finely balanced. Ultimately,
the Committee recommended against eligibility on grounds both of principle and
practice. In terms of principle, it was argued that no significant distinction existed
between programs and methods of mathematical calculation, which had always been
excluded from protection.

These arguments cannot be discounted. It may have been preferable had the relatively hard line against patentability advocated by Banks been enforced by the courts.
Once the dam had been broken by the EPC decisions in *Vicom*[127] and *Genentech*,[128] the
line has proved impossible to hold. In *Fujitsu*,[129] Mr Justice Laddie commented that the
distinction between the prohibition against programs and that relating to methods for
performing a mental act was 'a matter of semantics'. In respect of many of the decisions
and distinctions drawn, it may be suggested that the issue of patentability has been sub-
merged in a semantic sea. Whilst accepting that there may be reasons of principle why
no software patents should be issued, it is more difficult to accept at this level that an
image-processing system should qualify whilst a virtual reality system would not.

---

[126] Cmnd 4407 (1970).
[127] *Vicom Systems Inc's Application* [1987] 2 EPOR 74.
[128] *Genentech Inc's Patent* [1989] RPC 147.
[129] *Fujitsu Ltd's Application* [1996] RPC 511.

The Schleswig-Holstein Question refers to a series of disputes which arose in the nineteenth century concerning the relationship of the Duchies of Schleswig and Holstein and Denmark and the Confederation of German States.[130] The origins of the dispute dated back to the twelfth century and, as with many such disputes, matters became ever more complex as time passed. The Schleswig-Holstein Question has become a byword for insoluble problems and the then British Foreign Secretary famously commented that the question was of such a level of complexity that only three people had ever understood it:

> The first was Albert, the Prince Consort and he is dead; the second is a German professor, and he is in an asylum: and the third was myself—and I have forgotten it.

In many respects, the issue of software patents, at least in Europe, is fast approaching the dimensions of the Schleswig-Holstein Question. As attitudes harden on both sides of the divide, so the attempt to rationalise the treatment of applications becomes more and more complex. When leading and eminent judges can accuse each other of a failure to understand basic concepts, there is little hope for the rest of us to make sense of the situation. In many respects, the European situation contrasts unfavourably with that applying in the United States where, although the topic is certainly not without its controversies, the basics are relatively clear.

One of the issues that has been raised periodically throughout this book has been whether computer-related matters should be regulated by the general law or whether the need could be identified for the enactment of technology-specific measures. The European Patent Convention, and statutes such as the United Kingdom's Patents Act which are based on its provisions, have perhaps attained the worst of all possible worlds. Like the Schleswig-Holstein Question, the origins of the decision to include a prohibition against the grant of patents to computer programs is lost in history, although, as indicated above, the finger of suspicion may point at the United Kingdom.

The point has also been made throughout this book that computer technology has advanced with incredible speed. Computers and computer programs in the late 1960s and early 1970s bore no resemblance to the modern industries. Indeed, the fact that it is universal practice to talk about the 'software industry' indicates how far events have moved on. It is perhaps unlikely that had the drafters of the European Patent Convention been gifted with the power of prophecy the same approach would have been adopted, but such a guess does not provide any form of resolution to the present problems. Attempts have been made. In 2000, a diplomatic conference considered a proposal to remove the exclusion of computer programs from the European Patent Convention. The attempt failed, principally for the valid reason that it would be wrong to treat the computer program exclusion in isolation from the other grounds, such as schemes or methods for performing a mental act laid down as bars to patentability. A further attempt was made by the European Commission to introduce a Directive on Software Patents which would have required the Member States to adopt

---

[130] Cited in <http://thinkexist.com>

a liberal approach towards the award of patents for software-related inventions. This was rejected by the European Parliament in 2005 and no moves have been brought to bring forward new proposals. By way of contrast, United States patent law remains based on a 1952 statute which, as was the case with the previous United Kingdom legislation, restricts itself to providing that:

> Whoever invents or discovers any new and useful process, machine, manufacture, or composition of matter, or any new and useful improvement thereof, may obtain a patent therefor, subject to the conditions and requirements of this title.[131]

Although the statute lays down requirements of novelty[132] and non-obviousness,[133] there is no list of prohibited subject-matter.

There is no doubt that the United States Patent and Trademark Office, largely driven by case law from the Court of Appeals for the Federal Circuit, has the highest United States judicial authority other than the Supreme Court, and has been a leading proponent of the application of patents for software-related inventions. The value of the solution remains largely unproven. In *Aerotel v Telco*, it was commented:

> despite the fact that such patents have been granted for some time in the United States, it is far from certain that they have been what Sellars and Yeatman would have called a 'Good Thing'. The patent system is there to provide a research and investment incentive but it has a price. That price (what economists call 'transaction costs') is paid in a host of ways: the costs of patenting, the impediment to competition, the compliance cost of ensuring non-infringement, the cost of uncertainty, litigation costs and so on. There is, so far as we know, no really hard empirical data showing that the liberalisation of what is patentable in the USA has resulted in a greater [*sic*] rate of innovation or investment in the excluded categories. Innovation in computer programs, for instance, proceeded at an immense speed for years before anyone thought of granting patents for them as such.[134]

Statistics produced by the United States Patent and Trademark Office indicate a steady increase in the number of challenges made to patents in the form of a request that the office re-examines their validity. Such an approach, it is suggested, is quicker and cheaper than instituting legal proceedings seeking the same effect. Although the percentage of patents that are challenged represents a small proportion of the numbers awarded each year, the statistics indicate that in a large majority of cases, the result of the re-examination is either the removal or at least the weakening of the patent. The key problem remains, as was identified in the Report of the Committee on Patents as far back as 1970, for patent examiners to be able adequately to identify and assess the state of the art in order to determine whether an application is truly novel and sufficiently inventive to qualify for the award of a patent.

---

[131] Title 35 United States Code Section 101.
[132] Section 102.
[133] Section 103.
[134] [2006] EWCXA Civ 1371 at para. 20.

It would be facile to suggest that patent law—which involves an amalgam of legal and technical requirements—can ever be simple. Its application to software arouses strong passions on both sides of the argument. There is a well-known tale of a motorist stopping to ask a passer-by directions to a particular location, only to be told after many attempts to describe a route, 'If I were you I wouldn't have started from here in the first place.' In many respects, this perhaps sums up where software patents are now. Radical reform of the patent system could be a massive undertaking and securing the necessary international consensus would be a Herculean task. Providing to some extent a mirror image of developments in patent law, significant changes have taken place in the law of copyright, which has been seen as the most appropriate form of protection for the majority of computer programs.

Suggestions for further reading

'Court of Appeal Parts Company with the EPO on Software Patents' *C.L.S.R.* 23(2) (2007), pp. 199–204.

'The Patentability of Computer Implemented Inventions in Europe', *I.P.Q.* (2007), pp. 92–116.

17

Copyright protection

Introduction

Although there appears globally to be an increasing willingness to bring software-related inventions within the ambit of the patent system, discounting all other issues and problems, only a small proportion of computer programs will display the necessary degree of novelty and inventiveness to qualify for that form of protection. Virtually every program, however, will qualify for the award of copyright as well as every email, message or web page. In addition to software being protected by copyright, information recorded in electronic format such as email messages, multimedia packages, and web pages will also be protected by copyright.

The essence of copyright can be deduced from the name itself. The owner of copyright in a work possesses the right to copy and, by inference, the right to prevent others from copying. Until the invention of moveable-type printing by Gutenberg in 1450, the issue of copying was of little legal importance. The beginning of mass publishing of literary works brought with it new forms of regulation and control. Initially in the United Kingdom, use of the new technology was controlled by a requirement that printing be restricted to authorised printers and that the publication of individual books be licensed by the Crown. This scheme continued until 1695. With its abolition, petitions were presented to Parliament at the behest of the Stationers' Company, which had enjoyed an effective monopoly of publishing but which would now be subjected to competition. Responding to these representations, the first copyright Act, the Statute of Anne, was enacted in 1709. This Act granted the author (or assignee) the exclusive right to reproduce the work. In respect of existing works, this right would subsist for 21 years, with new works being protected for up to 28 years, subject to these being registered with the Stationers' Company. The registration scheme was a comparatively shortlived component of the United Kingdom copyright regime, although it continues to be a feature of the United States system.

The copyright system has developed over the centuries, largely following changes in recording technology. As it became possible to record different forms of work in permanent form, so copyright law has tended to be extended to regulate the sector. In 1734, engravings became the first form of artistic work to be protected under the terms of the Engraving Copyright Act. In 1814, sculptures were brought within the copyright system by the Sculpture Copyright Act, and the Dramatic Copyright Act 1833 extended protection still further to encompass the public performance of musical and dramatical compositions. The Fine Art Copyright Act 1862 marked a significant recognition of the intervention of technology, with protection being extended to photographs. Study of the various copyright statutes enacted in the twentieth century indicates a steady expansion in the range of subject-matter covered, normally following close on the heels of technological developments. In the Copyright Act 1911, reference is made to:

> ...any record, perforated roll, cinematography film or other contrivance by which the work may be mechanically performed or delivered.[1]

The Copyright Act 1956 extended protection to television and radio broadcasts made by the BBC or the Independent Television Authority.[2] During the 1980s, albeit motivated as much by the desire to introduce significant criminal sanctions as by uncertainty on whether the subject-matter was protected under existing provisions of copyright law, the Copyright (Computer Software) (Amendment) Act 1985 brought this subject-matter unequivocally within the ambit of copyright law.[3] The current United Kingdom copyright law is to be found principally in the Copyright, Designs and Patents Act 1988. As was the case with the Patents Act 1977, a variety of motives prompted the introduction of the new legislation. The previous statute, the Copyright Act 1956, had been subjected to piecemeal amendment and a need could be identified for a consolidating piece of legislation, coupled with a measure of reform to take account of specific problems which had been encountered concerning the extent to which protection might be extended towards functional works such as the design of product components. These problems were manifested in the decision of the House of Lords in the case of *British Leyland Motor Corpn Ltd v Armstrong Patents Co Ltd*.[4] Finally, reform of the United Kingdom's copyright system, in the shape of the introduction of a system of 'moral rights', was required to permit ratification of the 1971 and 1979 revisions to the Berne Convention. In contrast, the situation with patent law where protection is offered on a national basis, the Berne Convention, which has been signed by all the world's major countries, provides for the recognition of copyright in all signatory states.

Although the Copyright, Designs and Patents Act 1988 remains the major statute in the copyright field, further reform has been introduced pursuant to the requirements of the European Directive 'On the Legal Protection of Computer Programs'.[5] Effect has been given to the Directive's requirements by the Copyright (Computer Programs) Regulations 1992,[6] which make a number of amendments to the text of the 1988 Act. A further European Directive, 'On the Legal Protection of Databases', introducing a *sui generis* form of protection for the contents of electronic databases was adopted in

---

[1] Section 1(2)(d).

[2] Section 14.

[3] Section 1.

[4] [1986] AC 577.

[5] Directive 91/250/EC, OJ 1991 L 122, p. 42.

[6] SI 1992/3233. Despite their title, these regulations were introduced under the authority of the European Communities Act 1972, as opposed to the Copyright, Designs and Patents Act 1998.

1996 and required to be adopted within the Member States by 1 January 1998.[7] The Copyright and Rights in Databases Regulations implemented the Directive within the United Kingdom.[8] Further changes to domestic law have also been made by the Copyright and Related Rights Regulations 2003,[9] in order to satisfy the requirements of the Directive 'On the Harmonisation of Certain Aspects of Copyright and Related Rights in the Information Society'.[10] The provisions of these Directives and their implementation within the United Kingdom are discussed in the following two chapters.

This chapter will initially outline the key features of the copyright system and will then continue to analyse the manner in which these have been applied within a software context. In many respects, the development of copyright protection for software displays almost a mirror image of the situation described in the previous chapter in respect of patents. Starting with a denial of patentability, the application of the patent system has grown over time. With copyright, early cases accepted a very high level of protection but with the passage of time this has been steadily weakened.

Copyright basics

In contrast to the patent system, the copyright regime is noteworthy for a near complete lack of procedural formalities. The substantive requirements will be considered in more detail below, but at the outset it may be stated that protection begins at the moment that a work is recorded in some material form. Copyright lasts during the lifetime of the author and continues for a period of up to 70 years after the author's death. During this time, civil and criminal penalties may be imposed upon a party who, without the consent of the copyright owner, reproduces all or a substantial part of the work or engages in one or more of a list of other prohibited acts.

Forms of protected work

The Copyright, Designs and Patents Act provides that:

1. Copyright is a property right which subsists in accordance with this Part in the following descriptions of work—

   (a) original literary, dramatic, musical or artistic works,

   (b) sound recordings, films, broadcasts or cable programmes, and

   (c) the typographical arrangement of published editions.[11]

Although the Act refers to copyright constituting a 'property right', it is accepted that it is a specialised and limited right, the scope of which is to be found exclusively in the

---

[7] Directive 96/9/EC, OJ 1996 L 77/20.
[8] SI 1997 No 3032.
[9] SI 2003 No. 2498.
[10] Directive 2001/29/EC, OJ 2001 L 167/10.
[11] Section 1.

copyright legislation.[12] Although it is commonplace to talk about software theft and, indeed, the leading organisation set up to protect the interests of copyright owners is the Federation Against Software Theft (FAST),[13] dealings in copyright material cannot be the subject of a charge of theft—although the legislation does provide significant criminal penalties for incidents of breach of copyright.

The provisions relating to copyright in typographical arrangements does not require further consideration in this book. All of the other headings can impact upon software, however, although, as will be discussed below, the most significant category has been that of a literary work.

The requirement of originality

The Act provides that only 'original' works are to be protected. Semantically, the word might be equated with the requirement of novelty applying under the patents regime. In reality, the requirement of originality has been construed as requiring only that the work is that of the author, i.e. has not been copied from any other source. In *University of London Press Ltd v University Tutorial Press Ltd*,[14] Petersen J held that:

> The word 'original' does not mean that the work must be an expression of original or inventive thought. Copyright Acts are not concerned with the originality of ideas, but with the expression of thought, and, in the case of 'literary work', with the expression of thought in print or writing. The originality which is required relates to the expression of the thought. But the Act does not require that the expression must be in an original or novel form but that the work must not be copied from another work—that it should originate from the author.[15]

Under the United Kingdom's copyright system, the most crass and unedifying piece of prose (or the most error-ridden computer program) is as entitled to the benefit of copyright protection as the most illustrious example of the species (although it may fare less well in the marketplace). In the case of *Shetland Times v Willis*,[16] it was accepted without debate that the headlines of newspaper reports could qualify for protection, and the case of *Exxon Corp v Exxon Insurance Consultants International Ltd*[17] provides a very rare illustration of a situation in which the requirement of originality was not met. Here, it was held that copyright could not subsist in the single word, Exxon, albeit that it had been selected after lengthy and expensive public research to find a name to replace the well-known brand Esso. This was a requirement of United States antitrust litigation, although the name Esso continues to be used in the United Kingdom.

---

[12] See *C.B.S. Songs Ltd and Others v Amstrad Consumer Electronics Plc. and Another* [1988] A.C. 1013 [1988].

[13] <http://www.fast.org.uk/>

[14] [1916] 2 Ch. 601.

[15] [1916] 2 Ch. 601 at 608–9.

[16] 1997 SC 316.

[17] [1982] Ch. 119.

This approach is to be contrasted with that applying in Germany, where the application of strict qualitative criteria resulted, prior to the EC Directive on the Legal Protection of Computer Programs,[18] in an estimated 95 per cent of computer programs being denied protection on the ground that they were not original. The Directive would appear to endorse the United Kingdom position on the legal protection of computer programs, stating in its Preamble that 'no tests as to the qualitative or aesthetic merits of the program should be applied' and providing subsequently that:

A computer program shall be protected if it is the author's own intellectual creation. No other criteria shall be applied to determine its eligibility for protection.[19]

The phrase 'intellectual creation' is more reflective of the civil law's system of authors' rights than the common law notions of copyright, and it might prove sufficiently vague to allow a measure of discretion in this area. It remains uncertain, therefore, whether the Directive on the Legal Protection of Computer Programs will secure its objective of eliminating 'differences in the legal protection of computer programs offered by the laws of the Member States (which) have direct and negative effects on the functioning of the common market as regards computer programs'.[20]

Ownership of copyright

The author of a work will, subject to one exception, be the first owner of any copyright which may subsist in it.[21] Where a work is the product of two or more authors, any copyright arising will be the joint property of the authors.[22] The criterion for determining the existence of joint authorship is whether the individual contributions of the authors can be distinguished.[23] In this case, each author will possess individual copyright in his or her portion of the work. This may be a matter of some significance in the software field, where in the case of a program intended for use in a specific area of business, production may require both programming skills and knowledge of the subject area. Unless suitable contractual arrangements are negotiated, the result could be the existence of two separate copyrights, each useless without the other.

Employee-created works

An exception to the principle that the author is the first owner of copyright in a work applies where the work is created in the course of the author's employment. In this event, copyright will, subject to any contractual provision to the contrary, vest in the

---

[18] Directive 91/250/EC.
[19] Article 1(3).
[20] Directive 91/250/EC, Preamble.
[21] Copyright, Designs and Patents Act 1988, s 11(1).
[22] Section 10(3).
[23] Section 10(1).

employer.[24] This approach marks a change from the position under previous copyright statutes, where the employer's rights in respect of employee-created works were limited in the situation where the work was created for publication in a newspaper, magazine, or other periodical.[25] Although the employer would possess copyright in the publication containing the work, all other rights in respect of it would remain with the author. Thus, the inclusion of the work in a database would require the author's permission. Today, many newspapers make copies of previous issues available in the form of an electronic database. Under the provision described above, the consent of the author of every piece of information appearing in the database would have been required. Responding to lobbying on the part of media interests, the Copyright, Designs and Patents Act 1988 eschews any exceptions to the general rule conferring unrestricted copyright on the employer.

Computer-generated works

Computers are frequently used to assist in the production of a work. In many instances, this will not affect copyright in the work at all. This book, for example, was typed on an Apple Macintosh™ computer, using Microsoft Word™ software. In this, and in many other situations, the computer is merely a tool and the author of the text acquires full copyright in the completed work. In *Express Newspapers plc v Liverpool Daily Post and Echo plc*,[26] another case determined at interlocutory level, the plaintiff ran a competition 'Millionaire of the Month' in its newspaper. A number of other national newspapers operated similar competitions. In each case, the key feature was that competitors would have to check the newspaper each day to see whether numbers allocated to them matched winning numbers. The defendant republished all the winning numbers with the obvious intention that readers could participate in the competitions run by other publishers without having to purchase copies of the newspaper. In defence to an action alleging copyright infringement, the defendant claimed that as the numbers were selected by a computer program, they were not entitled to protection. Dismissing this defence, Whitford J (as he then was) held that a great deal of skill and labour had been required to develop the computer program (not least to ensure that too many winning numbers were not selected). As with the word processing example cited above, the computer was no more than a tool giving effect to the intentions of its human controller.

In other instances, the role of the computer may move beyond that of recording a user's work and may serve to embellish the creation. An example concerns the practice of digital sampling. Other applications in the musical field might concern the use of electronic synthesisers. Without delving into the technical details concerning the manner in which these products function, it is sufficient to note that the involvement of the computer is at a qualitatively greater level than that occurring in word processing applications.

[24] Copyright, Designs and Patents Act 1988, s 11(2).
[25] Copyright Act 1956, s 4(2).
[26] [1985] 1 WLR 1089.

A further situation which may raise questions of the ownership of copyright might apply where a database or expert system program is acquired. The program will require the addition of data by the user and the combination of the program and the user-supplied data will produce a new product in the form of the processed output. Again, this finished product will owe a considerable amount to the underlying program.

The Copyright, Designs and Patents Act 1988 contains a provision which appears to be unique in copyright statutes. It introduces a specific category of computer-generated work and provides:

> In the case of a literary, dramatic, musical or artistic work which is computer-generated, the author shall be taken to be the person by whom the arrangements necessary for the creation of the work are undertaken.[27]

The concept of a computer-generated work is defined as one where 'the work is generated by computer in circumstances such that there is no human author of the work'.[28]

It is unclear when this provision might be applicable. Few, if any, works will be created by a computer in the absence of any human involvement. In circumstances such as those identified above, human involvement will be required. The question which may have to be determined by a court in the event of any dispute is whether the input of any of the parties is sufficiently substantial to qualify them for sole ownership of copyright (as will almost certainly be the case with a piece of text produced on a word processor) or whether there might be joint ownership of copyright. In many instances, the enabling computer programs may be sold under the terms of a contract which prescribes the use to which a completed work may be put. Typically, the purchaser of the program will be entitled to use it for his or her own purposes but prohibited from selling or disposing of any work thereby created without the further agreement of the supplier.

In determining whether there is no human author of a work, two issues may be relevant. The first would be whether there is no human involvement of any kind in the production of the work. It is difficult to conceive of situations where the computer will act entirely on its own initiative. Once the possibility of some human intervention is accepted, the statutory provision might appear otiose. The general criterion for a literary or other work to be protected requires that it be the author's 'original' work. Although the requirement of originality has little application in the general field, the concept of computer-generated works can have meaning only if this is interpreted so as to exclude a human computer operator from qualifying for authorship where they make no intellectual contribution to the work. An example of such a situation might be where a computer program operates to produce a drawing on a completely random basis, with the operator's only contribution being to initiate its operation. In this case, the operator, or a person who instructed that person to carry out the task, will become owner of the computer-generated work.

---

[27] Section 9(3).
[28] Section 178.

The duration of copyright will depend upon the particular form of the work. In the case of a literary, dramatic, or musical work, copyright will subsist during the lifetime of the author and for a period of 70 years after the author's death.[29] In the event that the work is computer-generated, copyright will last for 50 years from the end of the calendar year in which the work is produced.[30] The same period of protection extends to films, sound recordings, and broadcasts,[31] whilst a shorter period of 25 years is applicable to the typographical arrangements of a published work.[32]

The lifespan of copyright is clearly much greater than that of a patent, although it must be doubted whether a period of protection which, depending upon the age and longevity of the author, may subsist for a century or longer is of any practical significance in the information technology field. Given the pace of technological development, it is unlikely that any piece of software will retain commercial value for more than a few years, although, as the publicity surrounding the Millennium Bug evidenced, many programs have enjoyed a longer lifespan than originally expected. Even in the case of the author's own word processing package, Microsoft Word, the copyright notice refers to versions of the program dating back to 1983.

Infringement of copyright

As discussed in the preceding chapters, the award of a patent serves to confer upon the successful applicant a monopoly in respect of the exploitation of its subject-matter. Although judicial references have been made to copyright conferring a monopoly—in the case of *Green v Broadcasting Council of New Zealand*,[33] Lord Bridge, delivering the judgment of the Privy Council, stated that '[t]he protection which copyright gives creates a monopoly'—it is generally accepted that the copyright owner possesses only the exclusive right to perform certain acts in respect of the work. These comprise the rights:

- to copy the work or any substantial part of it;[34]
- to issue copies of the work to the public;[35]
- to perform, show, or play the work in public;[36]

---

[29] Copyright, Designs and Patents Act 1988, s 12(1). The only exception to this rule applies in favour of the work, *Peter Pan*. Copyright in this work was bequeathed upon the author's death to the Great Ormond Street Children's Hospital, with the revenue accruing from royalty payments, etc. constituting a significant portion of the hospital's income. The author, J. M. Barrie having died in 1937, copyright would normally have expired at the end of 1987. In what may be a unique provision, s 301 and Sch 6 of the Act provide, not inappropriately given the nature of the work's main character, that elements of the copyright in Peter Pan will never die.

[30] Section 12(3).
[31] Section 13.
[32] Section 15.
[33] [1989] 2 All ER 1056.
[34] Copyright, Designs and Patents Act 1988, s 16(1)(a).
[35] Section 16(1)(b).
[36] Section 16(1)(c).

- to broadcast the work or include it in a cable programme service;[37] and

- to make an adaptation of the work or do any of the above in relation to an adaptation.[38]

The nature of copying

The act of copying is defined as involving the reproduction of the work, or a substantial part of the work in any material form.[39] This is to include 'storing the work in any medium by electronic means'.[40] Thus, for example, the use of some form of scanning device to transform text into electronic format will constitute an infringement of copyright in the original text.

A popular saying is to the effect that if enough monkeys are given enough typewriters, eventually one monkey will hit the keys in such an order as to reproduce the works of Shakespeare. Discounting the inconvenient fact that the works of Shakespeare are out of copyright, and the considerable uncertainty as to whether a monkey could own copyright, the end product would not infringe copyright for the reason that it represents an independent composition.

The question of whether one work infringes copyright in an earlier work is determined on the basis of objective criteria. It is not necessary that the act should have been deliberate. A number of cases have been brought in which the allegation has been made (and sometimes established) that a musical work was derived from an earlier composition which might well have been heard by the second composer, who retained a subconscious memory of the melody. The fact that the copying or plagiarism was unintentional will not serve as a defence. The key factors which will have to be established by a party alleging copyright infringement are that the alleged copyist would have had access to the work and that there are substantial similarities between the works which are not explicable by factors other than copying.

In situations where two or more people are working on the same topic, for example, a history of the Second World War, it is likely that similarities will exist between the finished works. In a non-fictional work, the ending must be the same and there is likely to be consensus regarding the key events of the conflict. Greater levels of similarity may raise suspicions that one author has relied too heavily on the work of the other.

In the United States copyright system, a distinction is drawn between ideas—which are not protected by copyright—and particular forms of expression. In similar manner, the European Directive on the Legal Protection of Software provides that:

> Protection in accordance with this Directive shall apply to the expression in any form of a computer program. Ideas and principles which underlie any element of a computer

---

[37] Section 16(1)(d).
[38] Section 16(1)(e).
[39] Section 17(2).
[40] Section 17(3).

program, including those which underlie its interfaces, are not protected by copyright under this Directive.[41]

Often referred to as the 'idea/expression dichotomy' this element has featured in many cases concerned with copyright infringement in software. Generally, however, although providing a useful sound bite, the idea/expression dichotomy can offer only limited assistance in determining whether copyright infringement has occurred.

Fair and unfair use of an earlier work

Beyond those situations in which it may be apparent that a protected work has been copied, translated or adapted, situations may arise in which it is clear that the work has been used in the course of producing another work, but where the conduct cannot equivocally be regarded as involving any of the acts prohibited in the legislation. In a variety of cases concerned with literary works, the courts have adopted a broad view as to the scope of copyright protection, extending it to conduct which is regarded as involving the inequitable exploitation of the work of another—what might in everyday language be referred to as 'plagiarism'.

In the case of *Harman Pictures NV v Osborne*,[42] the plaintiff owned the screen rights in respect of a book dealing with the Charge of the Light Brigade. Negotiations had taken place with a view to the defendants acquiring the rights. The negotiations came to nothing, but some time later, the defendants indicated their intention to produce a film on the same theme. The screenplay for the film was written by the first defendant. The plaintiff sought an injunction to prevent the film's distribution, alleging that the screenplay infringed their copyright.

Comparison of the screenplay with the book revealed points both of similarity and dissimilarity. The defendant did not deny having knowledge of the plaintiff's work, but argued that their screenplay had been based upon a much wider variety of sources.

Whilst accepting that it was permissible for a later author to make use of an existing work, it was held that this could not be utilised as a substitute for the expenditure of independent effort. As was stated by Sir William Page Wood V-C in the case of *Jarrold v Houlston*:[43]

> I take the illegitimate use, as opposed to the legitimate use, of another person's work on subject matters of this description to be this: If, knowing that a person whose work is protected by copyright has, with considerable labour, compiled from various sources a work in itself not original, but which he has digested and arranged, instead of taking the pains of searching into all the common sources and obtaining your subject matter from them, you avail yourself of the labour of your predecessor, adopt his arrangements, adopt moreover the very questions he has asked or adopt them with but a slight degree of colourable variation, and thus save yourself pains and labour by

---

[41] Article 1(2).
[42] [1967] 2 All ER 324.
[43] (1857) 3 K&J 708 at 716–17.

availing yourself of the pains and labour which he has employed, that I take to be an illegitimate use.

In the present case, the issue was whether the defendant had worked independently to:

> ...produce a script which from the nature of things has much in common with the book, or did he proceed the other way round and use the book as a basis, taking his selection of incidents and quotations therefrom, albeit omitting a number and making some alterations and additions by reference to the common sources and by some reference to other sources? [44]

Considering these matters, Goff J determined that the similarities between the two works were sufficient to justify the grant of an interlocutory injunction, with terms preventing the defendants from 'exhibiting, releasing or distributing any film of or based on [the screenplay]'.[45]

The question of the use which can be made of an earlier work was again at issue in the case of *Elanco Products Ltd v Mandops Agricultural Specialists Ltd*.[46] Elanco had invented and secured patent protection for a herbicidal product. During the currency of the patent's validity, both the plaintiff and independent research institutions had made extensive studies of the herbicide's application. Some of the information derived from these studies was incorporated in the form of instructions which were supplied with the product.

Upon the expiry of the patent, the defendant commenced production and marketing of the herbicide. Initially, they produced an accompanying instructional leaflet that was a virtual copy of the plaintiff's. The plaintiff objected to this action, alleging that it infringed copyright in their compilation of instructions, and the leaflet was withdrawn. A revised version was produced which also brought objections. When a third version was still considered objectionable, the plaintiff sought an injunction. Although the final version of the defendant's leaflet used terminology different from that of the plaintiff's, it was alleged that it remained based upon their material, thereby constituting an infringement of their copyright.

Holding in favour of the plaintiff, Goff LJ agreed that there was an arguable case of copyright infringement:

> It may well be that if the respondents had in fact at the start simply looked at the available information...and from that decided what they would put in their literature and how they would express it, the appellants would at least have had considerable difficulty in bringing home any charge of infringement, even, having regard to the evidence, if the results had been extremely similar and the selection of items had been the same. But they chose, on the evidence as it stands at the moment, to proceed by making a simple...copy, and then they proceeded to revise it. It may well be that the result produced that way is an infringement.[47]

[44] *Harman Pictures NV v Osborne* [1967] 2 All ER 324 at 334.
[45] [1967] 2 All ER 324 at 337.
[46] [1980] RPC 213.
[47] *Elanco Products Ltd v Mandops Agricultural Specialists Ltd* [1980] RPC 213 at 228.

Concurring, Buckley LJ ruled:

> As I understand the law in this case, the defendants were fully entitled to make use of
> any information, of a technical or any other kind which was in the public domain, for
> the purpose of compiling their label and their trade literature, but they were not enti-
> tled to copy the plaintiffs' label or trade literature thereby making use of the plaintiffs'
> skill and judgement and saving themselves the trouble, and very possibly the cost, of
> assembling their own information, either from their own researches or from sources
> available in documents in the public domain, and thereby making their own selection
> of information to put into that literature and producing their own label and trade
> literature.[48]

In one significant respect, the decision in *Elanco*[49] must be approached with a
measure of caution. The fact that the defendant had originally produced a near total
copy of the plaintiff's work must have cast a shadow over their subsequent conduct.
One aspect of the case would, however, appear apposite in a software context. As is the
case with much software, the literary works were functional in nature. Unlike the situation where works are created with a view to the reader's entertainment, their purpose
was to provide instruction. In the situation where a user has become familiar with the
instructions issued by one producer, the use of semantic variations may result in unnecessary confusion. Whereas diversity of expression may be a valuable attribute in
literature, its virtues are less obvious in a more technical arena.[50]

To issue copies of the work to the public

The owner of copyright in a work has the right to determine whether copies of that
work might be made available to the public. This right extends only to the first occasion upon which the work is made available and not to any subsequent dealings in the
work by way of importation, distribution, sale, hire, or loan.

In most cases, a person who has lawfully come into possession of a copy of a protected work will have the right, either to resell the copy or to make it available to
members of the public on a rental basis. The Copyright, Designs and Patents Act 1988
provides an exception to this rule in the case of the rental of computer programs,
sound recordings, and films.[51] Essentially, such works may be hired only under the
terms, either of an order made by the Secretary of State or according to the provisions
of a licensing scheme devised by the copyright owners and approved by the Copyright

---

[48] [1980] RPC 213 at 231.

[49] *Elanco Products Ltd v Mandops Agricultural Specialists Ltd* [1980] RPC 213.

[50] Some recognition of the different status of product instructions can be seen in the case of *Wormell
v RHM Agriculture (East) Ltd* [1987] 3 All ER 75. Once again, a pesticide product was at issue, with the
purchaser alleging that its failure to eradicate weeds rendered it unmerchantable in terms of s 14 of the
Sale of Goods Act 1979. Although this action failed, the court accepted that the adequacy or otherwise of
instructions constituted a relevant factor in determining questions of merchantability. This approach may
be contrasted with the general refusal of the courts to consider claims that the quality of a written work is
unacceptably low quality.

[51] Section 66.

Tribunal. Either procedure will prescribe terms upon which the rental may occur and the royalty that will be payable to the copyright owner. The justification for this provision lies with the ease with which copies of software may be made. To this extent, the provisions for royalty payments can be seen as offering some compensation for losses which may result from such activities.

To perform, show, or play the work in public

The acts of performing or showing the protected work in public are reserved to the copyright owner. The issue of what is a public performance is not defined in the legislation. It would seem clear, however, that the operation of a computer game program within, for example, a public house or an amusement arcade would constitute an infringing act if committed without the consent of the copyright owner.

To broadcast the work or include it in a cable programme service

Although this may appear unlikely to be of great application in a software context, the case of *Shetland Times v Willis*[52] provides some authority for the proposition that a website is to be classed as a cable programme service, with individual pages being classed as cable programmes. The Act defines a cable programme service as:

> a service which consists wholly or mainly in sending visual images, sounds or other information by means of a telecommunications system, otherwise than by wireless telegraphy, for reception—
>
> (a) at two or more places (whether for simultaneous reception or at different times in response to requests by different users), or
>
> (b) for presentation to members of the public[53]

with any item included in such a service being classed as a cable programme. The case concerned two websites, the *Shetland Times*, which was the electronic form of an established newspaper, and the *Shetland News*, which existed only in electronic form. The *Shetland News* website copied headlines from the *Shetland Times* site (something which in itself was held to be a breach of copyright) and placed hypertext links allowing users to go to the appropriate section of the *Shetland Times* website. The case did not proceed to the stage of a full hearing, the judge accepting that there was a prima facie case that the *Shetland News* was in breach of the *Shetland Times*' rights in this regard.

To make an adaptation of the work

In respect of computer programs, it is provided that adaptation 'means an arrangement or altered version of the program or a translation of it'.[54] Producing, for example, a version of a program originally designed to run under Microsoft Windows to operate

[52] 1997 SC 316.
[53] Section 7.
[54] Copyright, Designs and Patents Act 1988, s 21(4).

on Apple computers will, in the absence of authorisation from the copyright owner, constitute unlawful adaptation.

The development of software copyright

Questions about the eligibility of computer programs for copyright protection began to emerge in the 1960s. Prior to this time, hardware and software tended to be supplied by the same party and generally equipment was rented by the customer (often with the manufacturer supplying staff to maintain the machine), rather than bought. In such an environment, there was little interest in issues of ownership of intellectual property rights. In 1969, prompted by antitrust investigations by the United States competition authorities, IBM, the dominant player in the computer market, announced that it was to separate its hardware and software operations. This has been seen as a pivotal move in the development of a distinct software industry and today there is little doubt that companies such as Microsoft and Google are more significant players than hardware producers. Indeed, IBM itself has sold off most of its hardware production businesses and is focusing on consulting and re-engineering services.

Once a distinct market began to develop in software, issues of legal protection were not far behind. One of the striking features of software is that it can be massively expensive to develop but can be reproduced quickly and at very low cost. Although there were debates in the 1970s and 1980s as to whether computer programs were a proper subject for protection under the copyright system, the fact that the underlying source code was written in a form of English meant that there was—at least from the perspective of the United Kingdom system, which imposes almost no qualitative requirements for the grant of copyright—little dispute that software should be protected as a form of literary work. The Copyright, Designs and Patents Act 1988, the EC Directive on the Legal Protection of Computer Programs,[55] the Berne and World Intellectual Property Organisation (WIPO) Copyright Conventions, and the World Trade Organizations Agreement on Trade Related Aspects of Intellectual Property Rights (TRIPS) now all provide that computer programs are to be protected on this basis.

As enacted, the Copyright, Designs and Patents Act 1988 provided simply that the term 'literary work':

> ...means any work, other than a dramatic or musical work, which is written, spoken or sung, and accordingly includes—
>
> (a) a table or compilation; and
>
> (b) a computer program.[56]

In common with many other aspects of the subject, the term 'computer program' is not defined in the legislation. This may have been a matter of limited importance in 1988, but is becoming more significant in our digital age. A computer program may

---

[55] Directive 91/250/EC.
[56] Section 3(1).

be developed which will itself cause images to be displayed on screen. Many computer games will fall into this category and the technique is increasingly used to create or enhance images in feature films. Recent examples include the films *Titanic* and *Gladiator*, whilst the film *Toy Story 2* is reported to be the first production which exists entirely in digital format. No actors were involved, with all the images being produced within a computer environment. Copies of the film are recorded on computer storage media and projected directly from this. As will be discussed in more detail below, in such instances, it is difficult to tell where the computer program ends and the film begins.

In the course of producing a computer program, a good deal of other material may be developed. The process may begin with a general formulation of the intended purpose of the program. Subsequently, a detailed specification may be written down, describing all the functions and manner of operation to be provided in the completed work. This may take the form of a flow chart depicting the structure and sequence of the operations to be carried out. Drawings may also be made depicting various aspects of the screen displays to be produced.

It is almost certain that such preparatory works would have been protected under the original formulation of the Copyright, Designs and Patents Act 1988. As will be discussed at various stages below, the United Kingdom requires a very low degree of originality or literary merit in order to award copyright protection, and there is little doubt that even a few scribbles on a piece of paper would be protected. The situation was less clear in other EU Member States, and the Directive on the Legal Protection of Computer Programs made special provision for the protection of such materials.[57] In implementing the measure, the Copyright (Computer Programs) Regulations 1992[58] added a new section 3(1)(c) to the 1988 Act, referring to:

(c) preparatory design material for a computer program.

In some respects, the amendment may create more problems than it solves. Where the preparatory work is in the form of lines of code and written descriptions of the intended functions, there will be no problem in offering protection on this basis. The preparatory material may also take the form of flow charts or drawings of possible screen displays. In the Copyright, Designs and Patents Act 1988, the term 'artistic work' is defined as including 'any painting, drawing, map, chart or plan'.[59] Whilst it may be that artistic copyright will continue to exist in these elements, the rationale for protecting plans and drawings as something which they clearly are not appears somewhat obscure.

Applying copyright principles to software

In discussing the extent to which activities relating to software might contravene copyright law, three categories of potential infringement can be considered. The first

---

[57] Directive 91/250/EC, Article 1(1).
[58] SI 1992/3233.
[59] Section 4(2).

two relate to what is called literal copying of software. In the first instance, this involves the making of a direct copy of software. This may be done for commercial gain, and will be discussed under the heading of software piracy. Also involving direct reproduction is the act of using software. Every time a program is used, a copy of its contents is required to be taken from its storage location on the computer to the machine's active processing memory. This creates problems for the relationship between copyright owner and user, and has led in part to the emergence of software licences. These documents, which are an almost inevitable companion to mass-produced software packages, typically confer use rights, but at the expense of seeking to oblige the user to accept other provisions limiting or excluding liabilities in the event that the software fails to operate in a satisfactory manner and thereby causes some form of injury or damage to the user. Although the Copyright, Designs and Patents Act 1988 as enacted was silent on all questions concerned with users' rights other than the somewhat nebulous concept of fair dealing, implementation of the EC Directive on the Legal Protection of Computer Programs[60] has brought about significant changes. Although the extent of some of the rights remains unclear, lawful users of software acquire a number of entitlements, ranging from a right to use software to the ability to reverse engineer and decompile, albeit in limited circumstances.

The third category of infringement raises the most interesting legal issues. It concerns the situation whereby two programs exhibit similarities at the level of screen displays but not at the level of code. Although the phrase has rather fallen out of legal favour, the argument might be put in terms that one program has copied the 'look and feel' of another. This topic might also be considered at two levels. In the first—and more common—case, the alleged infringer will have had some access to the original program's code. Typically, a programmer will have worked on the development of one package, moved to another employer and been involved with the development of a competing program. In the second category, the parties will act much more at arm's length, with the only access obtained by the alleged infringer being to the working copy of the program.

Software piracy

The term 'software piracy' encompasses a range of forms of conduct. The Business Software Alliance (BSA), an organisation which includes most of the major Western software producers amongst its membership, has identified a range of forms of conduct:

- *Multiple Installation*
  This is where you install more copies of a software program than you have licences. For example, if you buy 10 single-user licences for a product yet install it onto 20 machines, you are using 10 illegal copies.

---

[60] Directive 91/250/EC.

- *End-User Piracy*
  Similar to multiple installation, this involves an end-user (or company employee) copying programs illegally or using unlicensed software in the workplace.

- *Client/Server Piracy*
  Occurs when a program is run off a server (rather than from individual PCs) and is accessed by more end-users than the company has bought licenses for.

- *On-line Piracy*
  This happens when software is downloaded from the web and installed but not paid for. There are other types of software piracy (grey software, counterfeit software, etc.).[61]

Essentially, any conduct which can be considered an infringement of copyright will come within these definitions. As the term 'piracy' would suggest, there is little doubt that the conduct at issue is unlawful. A considerable number of studies have sought to assess the scale of the problem. Most have been conducted by or on behalf of organisations such as the BSA. The fourteenth piracy study conducted by the Business Software Alliance and IDA was published in May 2007[62] and gives statistics up to 2006.

The study indicated that the global piracy rate in 2006 was 35 per cent. Although indicating that one-third of all software packages in use were unauthorised copies, the figures for piracy have declined markedly over recent years, the comparable figure for 2002 being 39 per cent, and 49 per cent in 1994. Wide variations exist between countries and regions in respect of the level of piracy. The 'distinction' of topping the piracy charts falls to Armenia, with a 95 per cent rate. Other significant offenders are China and Nigeria, with an 82 per cent rate, and Russia at 80 per cent. In general, Central Eastern Europe is the region with the highest rate of pirate software at 68 per cent. At the other end of the spectrum, the United States posts a rate of 21 per cent, the United Kingdom stands only slightly higher at 27 per cent, with Western Europe generally averaging at 34 per cent.

In economic terms, the total loss is estimated at $39.5 billion. Given the scale of software use within North America and Europe, it is not surprising that the regions with the highest financial losses were North America and Western Europe, although a worrying trend identified is that the biggest increases in software use is now coming from areas which have much higher piracy. A further estimate of the impact of piracy can be taken from a further study produced for the BSA by Price Waterhouse in 1998.[63] This calculated that:

> Reducing software piracy rates by realistic levels from the 1996 Western European average of 43 per cent for PC business software to the corresponding U.S. average of 27 per cent, and equivalent reductions in other software categories would generate as many as 258,651 more job and $13.9bn additional tax revenues by the year 2001, in addition to forecast market growth.

---

[61] <http://www.bsa.org/uk/types>
[62] Available from <http://w3.bsa.org/globalstudy//upload/2007-Global-Piracy-Study-EN.pdf>
[63] Available from <http://www.bsa.org/uk/studies/europe_study98.pdf>

User rights in respect of software

Whilst the application of provisions of copyright law to software-based products is less contentious than is the case with the application of the patent system, the principles of the copyright system were designed for application in the literary and artistic fields. Information technology products operate in the practical arena, and it may be argued that fundamental concepts such as reproduction or adaptation require to be applied in a modified form in such circumstances. Two particular difficulties can be identified.

The essence of copyright is that it prohibits the copying of a work without the consent of the copyright owner. In the case of most works, this does not impinge upon a third party's normal use of the work. The purchaser of a book can read it without requiring to make any form of copy. Likewise, a television broadcast can be watched and an audio cassette listened to without the need for any form of copying. Software (and indeed other digital products, such as CDs) operates in a different manner. Any form of use requires that the contents of the work be copied from a storage location to be processed within the equipment. Normal use requires copying, a fact which creates complications, not just in the field of copyright but also—through the widespread use of software licences—in the area of liability.

Fair dealing

Much is written and spoken of concerning the right of a user to copy a work to such an extent as is justified under the heading of 'fair dealing' for the purposes of research or private study.[64] Few of these expressions receive any form of definition in the legislation. The concept of fair dealing will undoubtedly permit a degree of copying of a protected work, but the supplementary question 'how much?' cannot definitively be answered. At one time, the United Kingdom publishing industry suggested that the copying of up to 10 per cent of a book might be regarded as fair dealing. This was, however, an informal indication which was subsequently withdrawn. It would not appear that the extent of copying permitted under this heading has been at issue in any case.

Whilst the concept of private study is not one which will be of great practical significance in the software field, that of research is potentially much more so. It is to be noted that the word 'research' precedes the phrase 'private study' in the Copyright, Designs and Patents Act 1988. It would appear to follow, therefore, that its application is not restricted to the area of individual research, but will extend into the commercial sphere.

In the case of a traditional literary work, such as a book or article, the acts which encompass fair dealing can readily be identified. Clearly, researchers must be able to read the work and to quote small portions of it in any work which they themselves might compile. In the course of this task, they may copy portions of the work, perhaps by means of a photocopier, although infringement may occur equally well if the work

---

[64] Copyright, Designs and Patents Act 1988, s 29.

is copied by hand. It must be accepted that the concept of fair dealing in a literary work cannot extend to the making of a copy of the complete work. Different considerations may apply in respect of software.

Two arguments can be put forward in support of such a proposition. First, whilst it is a very simple task to copy portions of a book—indeed it is much easier to copy a part than the whole—the reverse is the case with respect to a computer program. A second argument operates at a utilitarian level. The user of a book would generally be considered as having no legitimate need to take a second copy of the work in case the original suffers damage. This view would be justified on the basis that although the cosmetic appearance of a book may easily be harmed, for example, through the spillage of a cup of coffee, the damage will seldom be such as to prevent its continued use. Software is a much more fragile creature and, especially if research is being conducted as to its make-up, terminal damage may easily result. In such an event, the making of a back-up copy might appear a reasonable precaution.

In concluding the examination of the fair dealing exception, the point must be stressed that any of the actions referred to above will be sanctioned only to the extent that they are carried out in connection with research. It is specifically provided that decompilation of a program will not be permitted under the fair use provisions.[65] Assuming that a copy of software may legitimately be made for research purposes, its status will change in the event that the research ends and the copy is put to operational use.

A use right for software?

Reference has previously been made to the fact that copying or adapting a protected work constitutes an infringement of copyright. This raises one significant issue in relation to software. Whenever a computer program is operated, the process requires that its contents be copied from the storage disk upon which it normally resides into the hardware's memory. The act of using software in its normal manner is capable, therefore, of constituting a breach of copyright.

Prior to 1992, this was arguably the case, although it is submitted that a persuasive case could have been made out for implying at least a basic use right. Substantial precedent exists for such judicial creativity under patent law, where it has been held that the purchaser of a patented product may exercise all the normal rights of an owner, including the right to resell, unless specific notice has been given of restrictions.[66] With most software products, the response of producers to the uncertain state of the law was to seek to incorporate the terms of a licence into the contract with the end user. The status of software licences will be considered in more detail in the context of liability issues. Essentially, the licence would grant permission for the use of software in specified circumstances, but would frequently couple this with clauses limiting or excluding liability in the event the performance of the software was defective. In 1992,

---

[65] Copyright, Designs and Patents Act 1988, s 29(4).

[66] See, for example, *National Phonograph Co of Australia v Menck* (1911) 28 RPC 229.

the provisions of the Copyright Designs and Patents Act 1988 were amended in order
to implement the provisions of the EC Directive on the Legal Protection of Computer
Programs.[67] The Copyright (Computer Programs) Regulations 1992[68] add a new s 50C
to the 1988 Act, providing that:

> It is not an infringement of copyright for a lawful user of a copy of a computer program
> to copy or adapt it, providing that the copying or adapting—
>
> (a) is necessary for his lawful use; and
>
> (b) is not prohibited under any term or condition of an agreement regarding the
> circumstances under which his use is lawful.

In the European Commission's explanatory memorandum to the 1989 proposal for
the Directive, it was argued that it was not clear:

> ...whether the practice of so-called, 'shrink wrap licensing' where use conditions are
> attached to a product which is, to all intents and purposes 'sold' to the user, constitutes
> a valid licence in all circumstances and in all jurisdictions.
>
> It is therefore proposed that... [w]here 'sale', in the normal sense of the word occurs,
> certain rights to use the program must be taken to pass to the purchaser along with the
> physical copy of the program.[69]

whilst the Preamble to the Directive on the Legal Protection of Computer Programs[70]
states that:

> Whereas the exclusive rights of the author to prevent the unauthorized reproduction
> of the work have to be subject to a limited exception in the case of a computer program
> to allow the reproduction technically necessary for the use of the program by the law-
> ful acquirer.
>
> Whereas this means that the acts of loading and running necessary for the use of
> a copy of a program which has been lawfully acquired...may not be prohibited by
> contract.

It may be queried how far the text of the Directive implements this. Article 4 makes
it clear that the copyright owner retains the right to authorise the:

> ...permanent or temporary reproduction of a computer program by any means and
> in any form, in part or in whole. Insofar as loading, displaying, running, transmission
> or storage of the computer program necessitates such reproduction, such acts shall be
> subject to authorization by the rightholder.

Whilst Article 5 provides for an exception to this provision, stating that:

> In the absence of specific contractual provisions, the acts referred to in Article 4... shall
> not require authorization by the rightholder where they are necessary for the use of the
> computer program by the lawful acquirer in accordance with its intended purpose.

---

[67] Directive 91/250/EC.
[68] SI 1992/3233.
[69] COM (88) 816 final—SYN 183, paras 3.4–3.5.
[70] Directive 91/250/EC.

In implementing the Directive on the Legal Protection of Computer Programs,[71] the United Kingdom government substituted the term 'lawful user'[72] for the original 'lawful acquirer'. Another change was to substitute reference to 'lawful use'[73] for the Directive's 'intended use'. These changes undoubtedly complicate matters. The concept of 'lawful use', in particular, is defined as applying where a person has '(whether under a licence to do any act restricted by the copyright in the program or otherwise)...a right to use the program'.[74] This formulation relates to the status of the user as much as to the nature of the application, thereby producing a somewhat circular effect. Although there seems no doubt that the Directive sought to confer a use right, it is less clear whether the United Kingdom implementing legislation secures this and it is possible that the issue may some day have to be resolved before the courts.

Although a basic use right will now be implied, difficulties may arise in a number of areas. Increasingly, computers are being networked. The communications facilities provided by such a development means that one copy of a program may be used by a considerable number of different people. Depending upon the nature of the program and the network, use may be either simultaneous or successive. A further difficulty may arise in the situation where a user has two computers, typically, one at home and one at work. In this case, the user may well wish to use the same software (perhaps a word processing program) on both computers. In these situations, the need and justification for licences will continue.

Error correction

It is received wisdom that every computer program contains errors or 'bugs'. In accordance with the requirements of the EC Directive on the Legal Protection of Computer Programs,[75] it is provided that an authorised user may copy or adapt a program 'for the purpose of correcting errors in it'.[76] This provision might appear to give a user a carte blanche to copy a program in the quest to discover errors. An alternative, and perhaps preferable, view is that the right will extend only in respect of particular errors which have been discovered by the user in the course of running the program in a normal manner.

Even on this basis, uncertainties remain as to the extent of the user's rights. Computer programs are not like other literary works. A typing or grammatical error occurring in a book may be corrected without the act having any impact upon the remainder of the work. The relationship between the various elements of a computer program is much more complex. If an error is discovered in the course of running a program, its cause may lie almost anywhere in the program. If the source of a particular error is detected

[71] Ibid.
[72] Copyright, Designs and Patents Act 1988, s 50A.
[73] Section 50A.
[74] Section 50A(2).
[75] Directive 91/250/EC.
[76] Copyright, Designs and Patents Act 1988, s 50C(2).

and a correction made, it cannot be certain that the effects of the change will not manifest themselves in an unexpected and undesirable fashion elsewhere in the program. There is, indeed, a school of thought in software engineering that suggests that when errors are detected, rather than amending the program, operating procedures should be changed to avoid the conditions which it is known cause the specific error to occur.

Back-up copies

Computer programs are frequently supplied, and invariably held, on some storage device, such as a disk or tape. Such storage media are notoriously fragile and it is all too possible that their contents might be accidentally corrupted or erased. In such circumstances, it might not appear unreasonable for a user to seek to take a second, or back-up, copy of the work, with the intention that this will be stored in a safe location and brought into use in the event that the original copy of the software be destroyed.

As enacted, the United Kingdom Copyright, Designs and Patents Act 1988 (in contrast to several other copyright statutes) made no mention of the possibility that a user might make a back-up copy of a program which had been lawfully acquired. Although, once again, it is possible to argue that such a term must be implied into any relevant contract, the argument is more tenuous than that relating to the implication of a basic use right.

Implementation of the provisions of the Directive on the Legal Protection of Computer Programs[77] has brought about a measure of reform, the Copyright, Designs and Patents Act 1988 now providing that a back-up copy may be made by a user where this is 'necessary...for the purposes of his lawful use'.[78] It is unclear how useful this provision might be. The making of a back-up copy will invariably be a wise precaution, but it is difficult to envisage any situation where the presence of a second copy is 'necessary' for the functioning of the original.

Some small measure of consolation may be offered to a user by the fact that the copyright owner may not validly restrict or exclude the operation of the provisions regarding the making of back-up copies.[79] It is doubted, however, whether the new provisions will alter significantly either the law or the practice in this area.

Reverse engineering and decompilation

When software is supplied to a customer, it will be in a form known as object or machine-readable code. If this were to be viewed by a user, it would appear as a series (a very long series) of zeros and ones. Obtaining sight of these digits will give little indication as to the manner in which the program is structured. Although it is possible for a program to be written in object code, much more programmer-friendly techniques are available and almost universally utilised. A number of what are referred to as 'high level' languages exist—examples are BASIC and FORTRAN. These allow

---

[77] Directive 91/250/EC.
[78] Copyright, Designs and Patents Act 1988, s 50A(1).
[79] Ibid., s 296A(1)(b).

programmers to write their instructions in a language which more closely resembles English, although the functional nature of computer programs limits the variations in expression which are a hallmark of more traditional literary works.

Most users, of course, will be concerned only with what a program does rather than the manner in which this is accomplished. Some, however, may have different motives. The practice of reverse engineering has a lengthy history in more traditional industries and, typically, involves the purchase and dismantling of the products of a competitor. In the computer context, reverse engineering may involve the study of the operation of a computer program in order to discover its specifications. This is essentially a process of testing and observation and might involve pressing various keys or combinations of keys in order to discover their effects. The technique known as decompilation may be used as part of this process. Normally involving the use of other computer programs to analyse the object code, the technique seeks to reproduce the original source code.

The two leading English authorities on the topic of reverse engineering point are *LB (Plastics) Ltd v Swish Products Ltd*[80] and *British Leyland Motor Corpn v Armstrong Patents Co Ltd*.[81] Although in the *LB Plastics* case, the alleged infringers had obtained a degree of access to the product drawings, in neither case was it argued that these had been reproduced directly. Instead, the case was based on the contention that by reproducing the finished object, respectively furniture drawers and a vehicle exhaust system, the provisions of s 48(1) of the Copyright Act 1956 had been breached. This provided inter alia: 'that copyright in a two-dimensional work, the product drawings, will be infringed by converting these into a three-dimensional form'.[82]

In *LB (Plastics)*,[83] the plaintiff designed and produced a drawer system. The key feature was that the drawers could be supplied to customers (generally, furniture manufacturers) in what was referred to as 'knock-down' form. This offered considerable benefits at the transportation and storage stages, whilst the design facilitated swift and easy assembly of the drawers by the final producer. The concept proved commercially successful and some time later, the defendant introduced a similar range of products. It was alleged that this was achieved by copying one of the plaintiff's drawers.

In the High Court, Whitford J accepted that the resulting product infringed the plaintiff's copyright in two of the original product drawings. Although this ruling was reversed by the Court of Appeal, which held that an insufficient causal link existed between the drawings in question and the defendant's product, it was reinstated by the House of Lords.[84] A significant factor underpinning the judgment would appear to have been the recognition that although the defendant was required by commercial dictates to ensure that their drawers were functionally compatible with those produced by the plaintiff, this could have been attained in ways which required less in the way of replication of the original design.

---

[80] [1979] RPC 551.

[81] [1986] RPC 279.

[82] Section 48 (1) Copyright Act 1956.

[83] *LB (Plastics) Ltd v Swish Products Ltd* [1979] RPC 551.

[84] Ibid.

The decision in *LB Plastics*[85] was approved in the subsequent case of *British Leyland Motor Corpn v Armstrong Patents*.[86] Here, the plaintiff manufactured motor vehicles. The multitude of parts which make up each vehicle were produced in accordance with detailed designs drawn up by the plaintiffs. The defendant specialised in the manufacture of spare parts, in the particular case an exhaust system, which would be offered for sale to motor-vehicle owners. In order to allow the replacement systems to be fitted to the plaintiff's vehicles, their design required to be virtually identical to that of the original component. This was achieved by taking an example of the plaintiff's exhaust system and examining its shape and dimensions.

The plaintiff's exhaust system was not itself eligible for copyright protection; neither was protection available under the law of patents or of registered designs.[87] The court's attention was directed, therefore, to the question of whether copyright subsisted in the original engineering designs and, if so, whether the defendant's conduct constituted an infringement.[88] Holding in favour of the plaintiff on the issue of copyright infringement, the court (Lord Griffiths dissenting on the basis that, although the majority's opinion was in line with precedent, the case was one which justified the application of the 1966 Practice Direction) held that the defendant's conduct amounted to indirect copying of the designs, constituting a breach of s 48(1) of the Copyright Act 1956. This provides that the conversion of a two-dimensional work into one of three dimensions will constitute reproduction.

A further relevant case on this point is that of *Plix Products Ltd v Frank M Winstone*,[89] a case heard before the High Court of New Zealand, whose decision was upheld on appeal to the Privy Council. This case concerned the design of containers for the transport of kiwi fruits. During the 1960s and 1970s, the plaintiff designed and produced a number of containers which offered significant advantages in respect of the safe storage and transportation of the fruit. The New Zealand kiwi fruit industry is subject to tight regulation, with the New Zealand Kiwi Fruit Authority having power to prescribe, inter alia, standards of packing. This power was exercised, with the standards being based on the plaintiff's designs. The defendants wished to penetrate this potentially lucrative market. Being aware of the potential intellectual property

---

[85] Ibid.

[86] [1986] RPC 279.

[87] The Copyright, Designs and Patents Act 1988 introduced the concept of a design right which will apply to drawings such as those at issue in *British Leyland Motor Corpn v Armstrong Patents* [1986] RPC 279. This right will substitute for copyright but, significantly, does not extend to any aspects of the design which enable the finished article to be 'connected to, or placed in or around or against, another article so that either article may perform its function' (s 213(3)).

[88] The plaintiff's action ultimately failed on a second ground, the House of Lords holding that their claim to copyright was defeated by the right of a purchaser of their vehicle to obtain spare parts as economically as possible. The relationship between the provisions of intellectual property and competition law is assuming some significance in EC law. Recent dicta would suggest that, whilst a refusal to grant competitors licences in respect of the use of intellectual property rights will not constitute an abuse of Article 82 of the Treaty of Rome, any element of discrimination may render the conduct an abuse of a dominant position.

[89] [1986] FSR 63.

pitfalls, they sought to avoid infringement by engaging a designer who had no knowledge of the plaintiff's product. The designer was given the Fruit Authority's standards, together with samples of kiwi fruit and instructed to produce an appropriate design. Strict instructions were given that the project was not to be discussed with any other party and that no examination should be made of any existing product. Effectively, therefore, the designer was given a set of written specifications and instructed to begin work on a clean sheet of paper. Perhaps not surprisingly, the end result was a series of designs which, when put into production, resulted in a container extremely similar in appearance to the plaintiff's.

Holding that the plaintiff's copyright had been infringed, the High Court of New Zealand ruled that copyright in an artistic design could be infringed by a party who had been provided with a written or verbal description of the work in the event that the description provided was sufficiently detailed to convey the form (expression) of the work, as opposed to outlining the concept.[90] An illustration of the latter situation can be taken from the case of *Gleeson and Gleeson Shirt Co Ltd v H R Denne Ltd.*[91] Here, the plaintiff had designed a novel form of clerical shirt. The design proved commercially successful. A competing firm was asked by one of its clients whether it could produce a similar product. To this end, a general description of the shirt was given to one of its employees who had previously produced shirts containing similar features (although not in a single specimen). The resulting product was alleged to infringe the plaintiff's copyright in the artistic designs relating to its shirt. Dismissing this claim, it was held that the instructions given related only to the underlying ideas and that the application of the employee's own skill and knowledge had resulted in the creation of an independent piece of work. A second factor which appeared to influence the Court of Appeal in reaching this conclusion was the fact that the drawings upon which the plaintiff's copyright was founded were more in the nature of sketches than designs intended to serve as the blueprint for production. To this extent, the notion of an 'idea' and its distinction from 'expression' becomes blurred. As was stated in *Plix Products*:

> There are in fact two kinds of 'ideas' involved in the making of any work which is susceptible of being the subject of copyright. In the first place there is the general idea or basic concept of the work. This idea is formed (or implanted) in the mind of the author. He sets out to write a poem or a novel about unrequited love or to draw a dog listening to a gramophone... Then there is a second phase—a second kind of 'idea'. The author of the work will scarcely be able to transform the basic concept into a concrete form—i.e. 'express' the idea—without furnishing it with details of form and shape. The novelist will think of characters, dialogue, details of plot and so forth. All these modes of expression have their genesis in the author's mind—these too are 'ideas'. When these ideas... are reduced to concrete form, the forms they take are where the copyright resides.[92]

90 *Plix Products Ltd v Frank M Winstone* [1986] FSR 63.
91 [1975] RPC 471.
92 [1986] FSR 63 at 93.

Even so, the distinction between protected and unprotected aspects of a work remains obscure. A significant factor relates to what might be termed the 'added value' element introduced by the author. Where the idea is expressed in simplistic or general terms (as with the sketches in *Gleeson*), a considerable degree of reproduction may be considered legitimate. In the event, however, that the expression is 'ornate, complex or detailed', the would-be plagiariser must beware, as 'the only product he can then make without infringing may bear little resemblance to the copyright work'.[93]

Although the cases of reverse engineering are of considerable relevance to the present topic, one major point of distinction may be identified. It will be recalled that the legislation specifically provides that computer programs are to be protected as a species of literary work. Although no criterion of literary merit is applied, the protection must extend to a particular combination of letters and numbers. As stated above, in the situation where access is obtained to these, it is arguable that a claim for breach of copyright will succeed, even though the literary aspects of the second work bear little resemblance to the original. Where there is no question of access, merely the assertion that the operation of the second program replicates the 'look and feel' of the original, and where there is little evidence of literal similarity, it is difficult to argue that the traditional reverse engineering cases referred to above have any applicability. In each case, the cornerstone of the copyright owner's claim has been that, albeit indirectly, protected drawings have been reproduced. In the event that the operation of a computer program is studied and the attempt made to replicate its functions, there may be no substantial similarity between the two sets of code which make up the programs.

A closer analogy with computer software may be found with the case of *Green v Broadcasting Corpn of New Zealand*.[94] The plaintiff, Green, had been author, producer, and presenter of a popular British television show, *Opportunity Knocks*. The show operated according to a specific format and considerable use was made of catchphrases. Some years later, a programme with the same title was produced in New Zealand, making use of the same formats and catchphrases. With the interpolation of a new presenter, the programme, it might be stated, mimicked the 'look and feel' of the original. Upon discovering this, Mr Green instituted proceedings alleging, inter alia, that the later programme infringed his copyright in the original production. This action was rejected in the High Court of New Zealand, which held that, in the absence of evidence that scripts for the programmes had been reduced to writing, details of the dialogue could not be regarded as protected. An alternative head of claim concerned the dramatic format of the original programme, the various items which were included, and the order in which they appeared. This claim was also rejected, the court referring to the views of a United States commentator to the effect that:

> Formats are thus an unusual sort of literary creation. Unlike books, they are not meant for reading. Unlike plays, they are not capable of being performed. Unlike synopses, their use entails more than the expansion of a story outline into a script. Their unique

---

[93] [1986] FSR 63 at 94.
[94] [1989] RPC 469.

function is to provide the unifying element which makes a series attractive—if not addictive—to its viewer.[95]

With minimal substitution of terminology, these sentences would seem to describe exactly the nature and role of many items of computer software. Whilst the case would not provide authority for the proposition that the reproduction of every aspect of a user interface will be sanctioned, it does suggest that a considerable degree of commonality may be permitted.

Reverse engineering and computer programs

Computer programs can be divided into two broad categories—operating systems and application programs. An operating system—the best known examples are perhaps MSDOS or Microsoft Windows—contains the basic instructions necessary for a computer to operate. A very simple analogy might be made with a railway system. The gauge of the track and the height and width of tunnels and bridges might be regarded as equivalent to an operating system. They set down basic parameters which must be respected by anyone wishing to build a train to operate on the system. If the track gauge is 4ft 8ins, no matter how technologically advanced an engine might be, it will be quite useless if its wheels are set seven feet apart. In the computer field, programs such as word processing and spreadsheet packages constitute the equivalents of railway engines. They work with the operating system to perform specific applications and must respect its particular requirements.

A producer intending to develop an applications package for use on a particular operating system must be aware of its functional requirements. In most instances, the information necessary will be made available by the producer of the operating system, whose own commercial interests will be best served by the widest possible availability of applications to run on the system. In the event that the information is not readily available—or that it is suspected that only partial information has been made available—the attempt may be made to reverse engineer the operating system.

A second occasion for the use of reverse engineering occurs at the level of applications packages. Programs such as word processors and spreadsheets store data in a particular format. In the case of basic text, a widely used standard exists—ASCII (American Standard Code for Information Interchange). The text of most word processed documents is a much more complex creature. Particular fonts, type size, and line spacing will be used. Portions of the text may be printed in italics or may be emboldened or underlined. These matters are not standardised. A producer intent on developing a new word processing program may wish to discover the codes used by rival producers so that conversion facilities may be built into the new product. From a commercial perspective, existing users are more likely to change to a new program if they can still use documents created using their existing program.

---

[95] R. Meadow, 'Television Formats—The Search for Protection', *Californian Law Review* 58 (1970), 1169 at 1170.

The final form of reverse engineering is the most controversial. Here, the object of the reverse engineering is to discover information about the user interface of an applications package, which may then be used as the basis for the attempt to produce a substantially similar package. In early court cases on the point in the United States, it was often asserted that the intent was to reproduce the 'look and feel' of the original package.

Given that a lawful user cannot be prevented from using a program for its normal purpose, some aspects of reverse engineering must be considered legitimate. A user who operates the program in a normal fashion in order to study its various aspects will not infringe copyright. Subject to strict conditions, a user will also be given the right to attempt to decompile a program's object code when this is done in order to produce a further program which will be interoperable with the copyright owner's. This would apply with respect to the first and second forms of reverse engineering discussed above. The right cannot be excluded by contract, but will apply only where the information required has not been made 'readily available' by the copyright owner. The term 'readily available' appears imprecise, and indeed was a key issue in the anti-trust action brought by the European Commission against Microsoft, discussed in Chapter 21 below. It would not seem to require that the information be supplied free of charge. The levying of excessive charges would obviously be incompatible with the provision, but the question will arise of what level is to be so considered. In most cases where interchange information is used in, for example in the word processing programs referred to above, it would appear that this is done under the terms of cross-licensing agreements between the parties involved.

A second issue raises more technical questions. Producers of operating systems will normally find it in their own commercial interest to make the information available to those who wish to produce applications to run on the system. In some cases, the producer of an operating system will also produce applications packages. The best known example is Microsoft. Although sufficient information concerning its operating system is made available to other producers, the systems have a number of what are referred to as 'undocumented calls' and it is frequently asserted that these are used by Microsoft's own applications packages. The situation might be compared with producing a road map of the British Isles which omitted all reference to motorways. A motorist who relied totally on the map would certainly be able find a route between Glasgow and London, although the journey might take considerably longer than one making use of the motorway network. Returning to the computer context, it may be queried whether the provision of incomplete information will resurrect the decompilation right. Against this, it may be noted that the legislation makes no mention of the quality of the interconnection which is to be enabled. If comparison is made with the patent system, which requires that an inventor disclose details of the manner in which the invention functions, the duty here is to disclose an effective manner of performing the invention, and not necessarily the optimum method. Any claim relating to the sufficiency of disclosure above and beyond that necessary to achieve interoperability might more reasonably lie under the heading of competition law.

The activities carried out in reliance on the decompilation right are to be restricted to the minimum necessary to obtain the information.[96] Again, this may be a difficult matter to determine. It might be that the user can determine which elements are essential to their legitimate goals only after the entire program has been decompiled. A further restriction imposed upon the user provides that information derived from the decompilation may not be passed on to any third party, except where this is done in order to produce the new interoperable program.[97]

The final restriction concerns the format of the finished program. This, it is provided, is not to be substantially similar in its expression to the original.[98] This is not to be implied as meaning that the program may not compete with the original. The producer of a word processing program may decompile existing programs to discover details of their format so as to permit the new program to accept text files produced using the earlier program. What is not permitted is the production of a program which infringes copyright in the original. The question of how far copyright extends to the appearance and manner of functioning of computer programs is discussed below.

Literal and non-literal copying

The question of when a basic idea is refined sufficiently to become a protected work is one of the most difficult issues in the field of copyright law. In the United States, what is invariably referred to as the 'idea/expression dichotomy' has assumed statutory form, with the United States Code providing that:

> In no case does copyright protection for an original work of authorship extend to any idea, procedure, process, system, method of operation, concept, principle or discovery, regardless of the form in which it is described, explained, illustrated or embodied in such work.[99]

The EC Directive on the Legal Protection of Computer Programs[100] applies this principle in the specific context of computer programs, providing that:

> ...protection...shall apply to the expression in any form of a computer program. Ideas and principles which underlie any element of a computer program...are not protected by copyright.[101]

For the United Kingdom, although Lord Hailsham indicated in *LB (Plastics) Ltd v Swish Products Ltd* that 'it is trite law that there is no copyright in ideas', he continued, 'But, of course, as the late Professor Joad used to observe, it all depends on what you mean by "ideas"'.[102] The notion of a formal separation between ideas and expressions is found nowhere in United Kingdom copyright law. Indeed, although the United Kingdom has incorporated most aspects of the Directive into national law—even where, as in the case of the application of protection to preparatory material, it is arguable that no specific provisions were required, no attempt was made to include this formulation in the implementing regulations.

---

[96] Copyright, Designs and Patents Act 1998, s 50B(3)(b). [97] Section 50B(3)(c).
[98] Copyright, Designs and Patents Act 1998, s 50B(4). [99] Title 17 USC at 102(b) (1982).
[100] Directive 91/250/EC. [101] Article 1(2). [102] [1979] RPC 551 at 629.

The main justification for refusing protection to an idea lies in the belief that ideas as such are too intangible, too ethereal, to be protected. It is only when a thought or an idea is committed to paper or some other form of recording device, or even spoken in a public forum, that any evidence becomes available of the existence of what might be a protected interest. Even where this occurs, policy considerations operate to limit the scope of protection. Many legal journals (and academic CVs) would be much thinner if the first person to conceive of the notion of writing a learned article on the idea/expression dichotomy in copyright law had been granted a monopoly concerning the subject. The approach adopted under the law, both of patent and of copyright, has been to regard ideas as an unprotected step along the road to the protection of some concrete or practical manifestation of the concept. The grant of a patent requires a description of a practical application of the idea, whilst copyright law serves to protect a particular sequence of letters, words, figures, or symbols which constitute the application or expression of the underlying idea.

A second area of difficulty concerns the extent of the protection offered under copyright. There is no doubt that direct or literal copying of the work will constitute infringement. A less certain matter concerns the extent of the protection in respect of what is sometimes referred to as 'non-literal copying'. During the 1980s and early 1990s, this was regarded as the most critical issue in intellectual property law. From a high-water point of perceived protection in 1990, the effect of subsequent decisions in the United Kingdom and the United States has been to reduce the scope of protection. The increasing use of graphical interfaces and the application of text and graphic-rich applications such as multimedia products and, indeed, the WWW has brought with it a switch in emphasis from indirect protection of the underlying code to direct protection of the end product. Given the ease with which material held in electronic format may be copied, attention has also tended to switch from the exercise of the exclusive rights which are pivotal to the copyright regime, to the issue of how copyright may be managed in the interests of both owners and users. An indication of the scale of the issue and the problems can be taken from a WIPO estimate presented to the European Commission's Legal Advisory Board that some 90 per cent of the costs incurred in producing a multimedia product made up of existing materials were related to the management of the intellectual property interests involved.

From a legal perspective, there is no doubt that the complete reproduction of software packages will constitute infringement of copyright. In other cases, elements of an earlier work may be reproduced. A typical scenario will see an employee changing jobs and subsequently producing software which incorporates routines from earlier works, the copyright in which will, of course, vest in the original employer. The issues involved here essentially concern the questions of whether a substantial amount of the previous work has been reproduced and whether any similarities can be explained by reasons other than that of deliberate copying. Particularly in the case of computer programs, a variety of producers may be operating in the same field. In such a situation, and especially given the technical constraints which may operate, close similarities between two works may occur in the absence of deliberate copying or plagiarism.

Similarities in the educational background of different programmers might also result in the production of substantially similar portions of program.

The rise and fall of look and feel protection

With the emergence of the PC, the possibilities for copyright infringement increased dramatically. As has been discussed above, in the situation where one party makes a complete or literal copy of a program, there is no doubt that infringement has occurred. A more difficult issue arises where there is an element of independent creative activity on the part of the second producer.

Starting in the late 1970s, a number of cases of this nature were raised in courts in the United Kingdom and the United States. The disputes can reasonably be placed into two categories. In the first, a person or persons would have been employed to work on the development of a particular computer program. The employment would come to an end and the individual, either in his or her own right or as an employee of another company, would be involved in the development of a similar program. The program might well be written in a different computer language, providing limited evidence of literal similarities, and would often incorporate additional features or refinements not found in the original. The contention on the part of the original copyright owner would be that a substantial part of the original program had been copied into the new version.

A second category of case, which to date has arisen only in the United States, would see parties acting very much at arm's length. The alleged infringer will have had the opportunity to see a copy of the original program in operation and will have set out to create from scratch a competing product which will replicate all or parts of the on-screen appearance of the original.

The computerised pharmacist

In the first category of disputes, there is no doubt that the individual responsible for the development of the allegedly infringing product will have had access to all significant elements of the original program. The English case of *Richardson v Flanders*,[103] which was the first case concerned with software copyright to reach the stage of trial in the High Court, might be considered as a typical example of the species.

At issue in this case was a computer program designed for use by pharmacists. The program, which was developed to run on the then popular BBC microcomputers, performed a number of tasks. Principally, when the computer was attached to a printer it would automate and simplify the task of preparing dosage instructions to be supplied with medicines. The program's other major function was to assist in stock-keeping by keeping a record of the drugs dispensed. The program was marketed by the plaintiff, who had also performed a significant amount of work on the original program. Subsequently, the first defendant was employed to work on the project. It was accepted that all relevant copyrights in the work belonged to the plaintiff.

[103] [1993] FSR 497.

The program achieved considerable commercial success. Relationships between the plaintiff and the defendant were not so happy. The defendant resigned from his position, although he continued to perform some work for the plaintiff as an independent contractor for a further period of time. With the advent of the IBM PC, one of the plaintiff's major customers expressed interest in a version of the program capable of running on this machine and which could be sold on the Irish market. Following discussions, the plaintiff decided not to proceed with the project but suggested that the defendant might be willing to perform the work. The program was completed and was sold in Ireland. The defendant subsequently contacted the plaintiff offering him the rights to market the product in the United Kingdom. These discussions proved fruitless and the defendant proceeded to market a modified version of the program in the United Kingdom. At that stage, the plaintiff initiated proceedings alleging that the new product infringed copyright in his original program.

Because of the fact that the programs had been developed to run on different computers, examination of the code used would have revealed few evidences of similarities. The programs did perform the same functions and had very similar appearances when operating on their respective hardware.

In the absence of any relevant United Kingdom precedent, the judge placed considerable reliance on United States authority, notably the case of *Computer Associates v Altai*.[104] The court, it was held, should conduct a four-stage test designed to answer the questions.[105] This would seek to answer the following questions:

1. Whether the plaintiff's work was protected by copyright.

2. Whether similarities existed between the plaintiff's and the defendant's programs.

3. Whether these were caused by copying or whether other explanations were possible.

4. In the event that copying was established, whether the elements copied constituted a significant part of the original work.

Given what has been said above regarding the willingness of United Kingdom courts to confer copyright protection on a work, it is not at all surprising that the first question could be answered quickly and definitively in the affirmative. Consideration of the other issues was a more difficult task.

Examining the operation of the original program, the judge identified thirteen aspects of the functioning of the original program leading to the printing of the label for a drug container. This program also offered a stock control function and some seventeen other features allowing a pharmacist to customise the program in accordance with any particular requirements. When the same analysis was applied to the revised program, seventeen points of similarity were identified between the two

---

[104] 982 F 2d 693 (1992).
[105] *Richardson v Flanders* [1993] FSR 497.

programs which would require further investigation to determine whether they were the product of copying.

These similarities were identified from an examination of the screen displays and key sequences. The judge did not attempt to compare the underlying codes. Although an expert witness for the plaintiff had presented an analysis of alleged similarities between the source codes of the two programs, the judge indicated that he found this 'extremely difficult to understand'. Counsel for the plaintiff failed to pursue an invitation to attempt further explanation, and the analysis formed no part of the final decision.

One obvious cause of similarities, that of deliberate copying, was rejected by the judge. It was accepted, however, that the defendant must have retained considerable knowledge of the plaintiff's program and that if similarities resulted from the unconscious use of this material, infringement might be established.

Examining the similarities between the two programs, most were considered explicable by reasons other than copying. The two programs, for example, presented dates in a similar format. Conventions for the presentations of dates are well established and the fact that two works utilise a similar format is more likely to be caused through adherence to such conventions rather than by copying.

In a second aspect, the original program had presented the pharmacist with the option of placing a date other than the current date on a label. This feature was reproduced in the revised program. Although the judge held that it was likely that this had been copied from the original, he held that, given there were a very limited number of ways in which the idea could be expressed, the fact that the two programs utilised very similar approaches did not establish infringement.

In total, six of the seventeen similarities identified by the judge were considered explicable by reasons other than copying. The remaining eleven items it was considered, with varying degrees of conviction, might have been copied from the original program. Eight of these, however, referred to matters which in the opinion of the judge did not amount to a substantial part of the program. One element found in both programs gave users an indication that their instructions have been accepted. In both programs, the message 'operation successful' would appear on the screen and the computer would emanate a double-beep sound. This aspect of the original program, it was held, 'lacks originality and cannot have required any significant skill or effort to devise it'.

Ultimately, infringement was established in respect of only three of the points of similarity, comprising editing and amendment functions and the use of dose codes. The similarities in respect of the editing function were perhaps especially noticeable as it operated in the same idiosyncratic (and probably erroneous) manner in both programs. The dose code facility allowed the user to abbreviate certain instructions regarding the dosage and the manner in which the medication was to be taken. Thus, in both programs, use of the abbreviation AC (*ante cibum*) would cause the instruction 'before food' to be printed on the label. Although a number of the abbreviations were held to be obvious, the fact that 84 out of 91 codes found in the original program were reproduced in an identical format in the later version, with only minor changes in another 5, was held to raise an inference of copying.

Although copyright infringement was ultimately established, the plaintiff's victory was heavily qualified.[106] The copying was described as constituting 'a fairly minor infringement in a few limited respects and certainly not...slavish copying'. Although some of the processes adopted clearly differ from those in *Computer Associates*,[107] the effect of the judgment is similar in recognising that for functional works, external forces may well be the cause of similarities, thereby excusing conduct that might otherwise appear to constitute a breach of copyright.

Agricultural software

Allegations of copyright were again before the High Court in the case of *Ibcos Computers v Barclays Mercantile Highland Finance*.[108] Again, there was a background of the major defendant having worked for the plaintiff on the development of a software product intended for use by agricultural dealers, which was marketed under the name ADS. On leaving its employment, he developed a further and competing product which was marketed under the name of Unicorn. The plaintiff alleged that sufficient features of this were copied from the original to constitute an infringement of copyright.

In determining the criteria which would be applied in determining the question of whether infringement had occured,[109] Jacobs J was somewhat critical of the extensive references to the United States decision in *Computer Associates*,[110] and warned against 'overcitation of United States authority based on a statute different from ours'. The approach to be adopted was for the court to determine whether there was a sufficient degree of similarity between the two works which, coupled with evidence of access to the original work, would establish an inference of copying. The onus would then switch to the defendant to establish that the similarities were explicable by causes other than copying. Evidence that 'functional necessity' served to narrow the range of options open to the defendant would be relevant. Trivial items may well provide the most eloquent testimony. As was said in *Bilhofer v Dixon*:

> It is the resemblances in inessentials, the small, redundant, even mistaken elements of the copyright work which carry the greatest weight. This is because they are the least likely to have been the result of independent design.[111]

In the present case, evidence was presented that the same words were misspelled in the same manner, the same headings were used in the two programs, and both shared the same bit of code which served no useful purpose for the functioning of the

---

[106] Ibid.

[107] *Computer Associates v Altai* 982 F 2d 693 (1992).

[108] [1994] FSR 275.

[109] *Ibcos Computers v Barclays Mercantile Highland Finance* [1994] FSR 275.

[110] *Computer Associates v Altai* 982 F 2d 693 (1992).

[111] [1990] FSR 105 at 123.

program. Beyond this, there were considerable similarities at the level of the code it-self. In respect of one element of the programs, it was held that:

> ...there are 22 identical variables, 8 identical labels, 1 identical remark, 31 identical code lines and one identical redundant variable. This to my mind plainly indicates copying and enough in itself to constitute a significant part.[112]

The court recognised in *Ibcos*[113] that copyright protection must extend beyond the literal aspects of the program code to aspects of 'program structure' and 'design fea-tures'. In the case of the former element, it was held that copyright subsisted in the compilation of individual programs which made up the ADS system. Although some differences existed between ADS and Unicorn, it was held that the defendant had taken 'as his starting point the ADS set and that set remains substantially in Unicorn'. Although the two programs had a different visual appearance and it was recognised that 'Unicorn is undoubtedly to the user a much friendlier program than ADS was at the time', the defendant, it was held, had taken 'shortcuts by starting with ADS and making considerable additions and modifications'.

Financial markets

A further significant decision was delivered by the High Court in April 1999, in the case of *Cantor Fitzgerald International v Tradition United Kingdom Ltd.*[114] Both com-panies involved in the case operated in the financial services market. The plaintiff had developed a computer package which was used in the course of its bond-broking activ-ities. Much of the work in respect of this had been carried out by its Managing Director, a Mr Howard, and a team of programmers appointed by him. The Managing Director was dismissed in 1991. He subsequently secured employment with the defendants, in large part because of his suggestion that he could develop a similar system for them. On taking up employment, he secured the recruitment of three other members of the plaintiff's programming team.

The defendant obtained computers of the same type as those used by the plaintiff, and the employees (who were also defendants in the litigation) began work. In a period of less than three months, a working system was produced. Action alleging copyright infringement and breach of confidence was initiated by the plaintiffs, who argued that it would have been impossible for the programs involved to have been written from scratch in the time available.

Initially, the programmers denied that they had had access to any of the plaintiff's other source code. When the process of discovery highlighted evidence suggesting copying of certain modules, the truth emerged that the programmers had taken a copy of the plaintiff's source code with them. The defendant dropped its initial denial

---

[112] *Ibcos Computers v Barclays Mercantile Highland Finance* [1994] FSR 275 at 308.
[113] *Ibcos Computers v Barclays Mercantile Highland Finance* [1994] FSR 275.
[114] [2000] RPC 95.

of any copyright infringement and the case proceeded on the basis of how extensive the copying had been.

Expert witnesses were appointed by both parties. The witness for the plaintiff was subjected to severe criticism by the trial judge, Pumphrey J, who opined that the witness had held back relevant information and had acted as an advocate for the plaintiff rather than as an objective and impartial expert. The defendant's witness, on the other hand, was regarded as 'an admirable expert'. His conclusions were perhaps surprising, and were summarised by the judge:

> The Tradition system comprises some 77,000 lines of source code divided into some 363 'modules'. A total of 2,952 lines of code are admitted to have been copied, of which some are repeated copies of a single block of code. In addition Dr McKenzie has identified some 1,964 lines of code which he says are questionable, although he says that the majority of the questionable code was probably not copied. This means that if the admissions are exhaustive, the copied code represents 2 per cent of the system by number of lines. If all the questionable code is included as well, the figure is about 3.3 per cent.[115]

Faced with this report, the plaintiff restricted its claim of copying to 35 of the systems modules. The question, therefore, was whether what was copied constituted a substantial part of the original program. It also made two claims alleging breach of confidence in respect of the techniques used for developing programs of the kind at issue and also in respect of the code itself, arguing that if the programmers had used their access to the plaintiff's code to 'increase their confidence' in the accuracy of their new work, that would of itself constitute misuse of confidential information, regardless of whether the code was subsequently copied.

Initial reference was made to the decision of Jacobs J in *Ibcos Computers v Barclays Mercantile Highland Finance*,[116] laying down the steps to be followed in deciding an action for infringement of copyright:

(1) What are the work or works in which the plaintiff claims copyright?

(2) Is each such work 'original'?

(3) Was there copying from that work?

(4) If there was copying has a substantial portion of that work been reproduced?

The situation in *Cantor*[117] was in many respects more complex than in *Ibcos*.[118] Although the start point may have been the same, it was more questionable both of whether the end product could be regarded as the product of copying of a substantial part of the original programs and, indeed, of whether what had been copied satisfied the criterion of originality required for copyright to come into existence. Pumphrey

---

[115] *Cantor Fitzgerald International v Tradition United Kingdom Ltd* [2000] RPC 95 at 102.
[116] [1994] FSR 275.
[117] *Cantor Fitzgerald International v Tradition United Kingdom Ltd* [2000] RPC 95 at 102.
[118] *Ibcos Computers v Barclays Mercantile Highland Finance* [1994] FSR 275.

J expressed some doubt as to whether the application of criteria developed in a literary context was a proper approach when dealing with a functional product such as software:

> A program expressed in a computer language must not contain errors of syntax (or it will not compile) and it must contain no semantic errors. Computers do not have the capacity to deduce what the author meant when they encounter errors in the kind of software with which this action is concerned. If the software contains semantic errors it will produce the wrong answer or no answer at all: it may merely fail to run. The only opportunity that the programmer gets to express himself in a more relaxed way is provided by the comments in the code, which are for the benefit of the human reader and are ignored when the code comes to be compiled.[119]

It might be suggested from this that every line of code in a program should be considered essential for its operation and, therefore, that any copying would involve reproduction of a substantial part of the original. The Australian case of *Autodesk v Dyson*[120] was cited as authority for this proposition. For the United Kingdom, however, the court was not willing to follow such a line of argument. Whilst it was accepted that every line of a program was essential in order for it to function, the view of the court was that the determination of whether a substantial part of the work had been copied required to be made by reference to qualitative rather than to quantitative criteria:

> In the general case it is well established that a substantial part of the author's skill and labour may reside in the plot of a novel or play; and to take that plot without taking any particular part of the particular manner of its expression may be sufficient to amount to copyright infringement.[121]

For software, it was suggested:

> It seems to be generally accepted that the 'architecture' of a computer program is capable of protection if a substantial part of the programmer's skill, labour and judgment went into it. In this context, 'architecture' is a vague and ambiguous term.[122]

Two possible meanings were identified for the term, the first relating to the overall description of the system at a high level of abstraction. It could also mean, as was at issue, the overall program structure. Here, functions which it was agreed between the parties were essential elements of the particular software package were grouped into programs, with copyright being recognised in the 'compilation of the programs'.

In spite of the somewhat reprehensible nature of the programmer's work in *Cantor*[123] (which included documenting plans to alter code so as to disguise the fact that it had originated in the plaintiff's program), only a very limited degree of copyright infringement was established. The defendant had accepted liability for the

---

[119] [2000] RPC 95 at 130.
[120] [1992] RPC 575.
[121] *Cantor Fitzgerald International v Tradition United Kingdom Ltd* [2000] RPC 95 at 134.
[122] [2000] RPC 95 at 134.
[123] *Cantor Fitzgerald International v Tradition United Kingdom Ltd* [2000] RPC 95.

points of similarity identified by its expert witness and in all other respects the finding of the court was that there was no infringement. Similarities were considered either to relate to insubstantial pieces of work or to be explicable by reasons other than copying.

The judgment in respect of the claims of breach of copyright follows what appears to be a general trend to limit the scope of copyright protection to little more than direct or literal copying. As such, it might appear to leave a copyright owner with limited protection. The alternative claim relating to breach of confidence fared better. Although it was held that the techniques used in the development of the original programs were not sufficiently novel or unusual to be regarded as trade secrets and entitled to protection on this basis, it was found, albeit without any detailed explanation, that the use of the original code as an aide-memoire constituted breach of confidence.

Arm's length reproduction

In all of the cases cited above, there had been some prior relationship between the parties which had given the alleged copyist access to the underlying source code of the original software packages. This eliminates any issue of whether the alleged copyist had had access to the protected work. Although there was a history of dealings between the parties, the High Court decision in *Navitaire Inc v easyJet Airline Company and Bulletproof Technologies Inc.*[124] provided the first occasion where a copyright infringement case arose from a situation where the alleged infringers had enjoyed no significant access to the source code of the original program, but had based their work upon analysis of the operation of the program. The claimant, Navitaire had developed a computerised reservation system, 'OpenRes', designed for use in the airline environment. The defendant, easyJet, one of the United Kingdom's biggest airlines, had licensed this program for use in the course of its operations. After a period of time, it decided to develop its own system and employed the second defendants, a Californian-based software development company to develop the programs which were completed and put into use under the name of 'eRes'. It was common ground between the parties that 'easyJet wanted a new system that was substantially indistinguishable from the OpenRes system, as easyJet used it, in respect of its "user interface"'. The claimant alleged that 'eRes' infringed its copyright in 'OpenRes'.

The infringement proceedings were prolonged and complex. In the final analysis, although some small elements of infringement were established, the great preponderance of the judgment was in favour of easyJet. The judge, Mr Justice Punphrey commented:

> I consider that the better approach is to take the view that it is not possible to infringe the copyright that subsists either in the source code for a parser or in the source code for a parser generator by observing the behaviour of the final program and constructing

[124] [2004] EWHC 1725 (Ch.).

another program to do the same thing. In expressing this view, I am verging on drawing a distinction between the 'idea' of the program and its 'expression'.

Such an approach had not previously been a feature of United Kingdom copyright
law but support was taken from the provisions of Article 1(2) of the European Software
Protection Directive stating that:

> Protection in accordance with this Directive shall apply to the expression in any form
> of a computer program. Ideas and principles which underlie any element of a computer
> program, including those which underlie its interfaces, are not protected by copyright
> under this Directive.

Much legal ink and judicial time has been spent on discussion of the question of
when an unprotected idea becomes sufficiently detailed and specific to be classed
as a protected form of expression. Counsel for the claimants placed reliance upon a
number of authorities concerned with the topic of non-literal copying. In the case of
Harman Pictures v Osborne,[125] for example, the owner of copyright in a book about
the Crimean War was successful in a claim of copyright infringement against the producers of a film which depicted the same incidents as those described in the book. In
all the cases cited, the critical difference from the present case was that the alleged
infringer had enjoyed access to the copyright work.

Computer programs, it was suggested by the judge, could not easily be analogised
with other forms of work. The difficulty, it was stated, was that, unlike any other form
of literary work, there was limited linkage between the letters and words used in the
original code and the end product as displayed and operating on a computer screen.
Two completely different sets of code could produce virtually identically functioning
computer programs, even though the creator of the second had not had any form of
access to the code of the first program.[126]

In the final analysis, the decision was reached that:

> Navitaire's computer program invites input in a manner excluded from copyright
> protection, outputs its results in a form excluded from copyright protection and
> creates a record of a reservation in the name of a particular passenger on a par-
> ticular flight. What is left when the interface aspects of the case are disregarded is
> the business function of carrying out the transaction and creating the record, be-
> cause none of the code was read or copied by the defendants. It is right that those
> responsible for devising OpenRes envisaged this as the end result for their program:
> but that is not relevant skill and labour. In my judgment, this claim for non-textual
> copying should fail.

Such a conclusion, it was stated, was not reached with any form of regret. It was
the stated policy of the European Software Directive that computer languages and
the ideas underlying computer programs should not qualify for copyright protection.
It would be wrong for these exclusions to be circumvented by seeking to identify some

---

[125] [1967] 1WLR 723.
[126] At para. 125.

overall function behind the program when this was a direct consequence of the operation of the unprotected elements. Additionally, it was held:

> As a matter of policy also, it seems to me that to permit the 'business logic' of a program to attract protection through the literary copyright afforded to the program itself is an unjustifiable extension of copyright protection into a field where I am far from satisfied that it is appropriate.[127]

Initially, it was indicated that an appeal would be lodged against this decision. The parties, however, reached an out-of-court settlement. Similar issues did reach the Court of Appeal in the subsequent case of *Nova Productions Ltd v Mazoooma Games Ltd and Others*.[128] The appellant in this case was a software game developer who had produced a computer game, based upon the game of pool, for use in arcade machines. A player would be presented with the image of balls on a pool table and using an electronic cue would attempt to strike the cue ball in such a manner as to cause it to knock one of the object balls into a pocket. Cash prizes would be paid depending upon the player's degree of success. The various defendants were responsible for the development of another game of pool and its use in arcade gaming machines. Although it was not alleged that the defendants had had any form of access to the original code, it was argued that they had seen the original and appropriated elements of its manner of operation sufficient to constitute infringement of copyright. These claims were rejected in the High Court, where the judge held that no features had been copied from the original game. Although a number had been 'inspired' or 'affected' by the study of the original this was not sufficient to establish breach of copyright. An appeal was lodged with the Court of Appeal with an initial request, which was rejected, that a number of questions be referred to the European Court of Justice for a preliminary ruling.[129]

Delivering the judgment of the court, Lord Justice Jacob reviewed the law relating to the protection of computer programs. In similar manner to his comments on the Patents Act and the European Patent Convention cited above, he lamented the fact that the drafts of the statutory instrument which implemented the software Directive into the United Kingdom had strayed from its exact wording thereby adding additional levels of complexity to the task of interpreting its meaning. In particular, although not of major importance to the case, the United Kingdom Regulations appeared to treat computer programs and their preparatory materials as the objects of two different forms of copyright, whereas the Directive envisaged only a single copyright in the program, including any preparatory materials.[130]

The key question related to whether what had been taken (if anything) was restricted to unprotected ideas or whether it formed elements of the expression of the software. For the appellant, it was suggested that elements of their game, such as the feature where the appearance of the cue 'pulsed' in proportion to the level of force which the player intended to put into a shot, was sufficiently detailed to merit protection. This

---

[127] At paras 129–30.
[128] [2007] EWCA Civ 219.
[129] [2006] EWCA Civ 1044.
[130] At para. 28.

claim was rejected. Although the original program may have been inventive, this was a criterion which was applicable in patent law rather than copyright. The claim for infringement of the program as a literary work failed on the ground that what was found to have inspired some aspects of the defendants' game is just too general to amount to a substantial part of the claimants' game.[131]

Although the issue was not analysed in great detail, it was also stated that the appeal would fail through the application of the principles laid down in *Navitaire v easyJet*. This, it was stated, was a stronger case 'yet the claimants lost'.[132] The judge in *Navitaire*, it was held, 'was quite right to say that merely making a program which will emulate another but which in no way involves copying the program code or any of the program's graphics is legitimate'.[133]

Lord Justice Jacob's concluding remarks perhaps mark the final nail in the coffin of look and feel protection for software. Noting that it was agreed by all parties that the case had significance for the whole computer games industry, he acknowledged that counsel for the cliamant had suggested that if the trial judge's decision was upheld, the consequence would be that computer games would be denied any effective form of protection in respect of conduct involving anything other than literal reproduction of the program code. Whilst this might be the case, consideration had to be given to the original nature and purpose of copyright and the concept of a balance being struck between protecting the work of an author and encouraging the creative works of others. The famous scientist, Sir Isaac Newton, once wrote, 'If I have seen further, it is because I stood on the shoulders of giants.'[134] In like manner, Lord Justice Jacobs recognised that almost all literary work was derivative to some extent and acknowledged the importance of the fact that copyright law should not stifle the creation of new works, concluding:

> If protection for such general ideas as are relied on here were conferred by the law, copyright would become an instrument of oppression rather than the incentive for creation which it is intended to be. Protection would have moved to cover works merely inspired by others, to ideas themselves.[135]

Computer programs as visual works

In addition to protecting literary works, as indicated above, copyright has steadily been extended to cover other forms of recorded work, closely following developments in technology. The 1988 Act ptovides that:

> Copyright is a property right which subsists in accordance with this Part in the following descriptions of work—
>
> (a) original literary, dramatic, musical or artistic works,
>
> (b) sound recordings, films, broadcasts or cable programmes.

---

[131] At para. 44.   [132] At para. 46.   [133] At para. 52.

[134] Letter to Robert Hooke (a rival scientist), 15 February 1676, cited in the *Concise Oxford Dictionary of Quotations*.

[135] At para. 55.

In the early days of computers, very little was provided in the way of visual content. The first computers were effectively calculating machines with no form of visual display unit. Even when these became commonplace, and even with the move to applications such as word processing, the small amounts of memory and limited processing capacity of computers meant that there was little interest in the aesthetic appearance of a computer program. The world today, of course is very different with many computer games utilising sophisticated graphics.

Two issues are of relevance in this context: first, the question of whether an image generated through the operation of a computer program might be classed as an artistic work, and, second, whether moving images might be classed as films.

The issue of artistic copyright in software was discussed by the Court of Appeal in the case of *Nova Productions Ltd v Mazooma Games Ltd and Others*.[136] The facts of the case have been described above. The games, although not identical, shared a number of elements and it was the claimant's contention, inter alia, that the defendants' games infringed its artistic copyright in 'Pocket Money'. The case hinged upon the subset of artistic work referred to as 'graphic works',[137] and centred upon the individual screen frames. It was accepted that comparison of individual frames did not demonstrate any substantial degree of similarity but it was argued that 'there was in effect a further kind of artistic work, something beyond individual freeze-frame graphics'.[138] What the defendants had done, it was argued, was to 'create a 'dynamic reposing' of the original game, changing some of the level of details but retaining 'an essential artistic element of the original'.[139] At trial, the judge was prepared to accept that this was an arguable point, although he went on to hold that there had been no infringement in the particular case. Delivering the judgment of the Court of Appeal, Lord Justice Jacobs disagreed:

> 'Graphic work' is defined as including all the types of thing specified in s.4(2) which all have this in common, namely that they are static, non-moving. A series of drawings is a series of graphic works, not a single graphic work in itself. No-one would say that the copyright in a single drawing of Felix the Cat is infringed by a drawing of Donald Duck. A series of cartoon frames showing Felix running over a cliff edge into space, looking down and only then falling would not be infringed by a similar set of frames depicting Donald doing the same thing. That is in effect what is alleged here.
>
> This reasoning is supported by the fact that Parliament has specifically created copyright in moving images by way of copyright in films. If (the claimant's argument was accepted), the series of still images which provides the illusion of movement would itself create a further kind of copyright work protecting moving images. It is unlikely that Parliament intended this.[140]

There would be no doubt that reproduction of the individual frames would have constituted infringement.

[136] [2007] EWCA Civ 219.
[137] Section 4(1).
[138] At para. 13.
[139] Ibid.
[140] At paras 16–17.

To date, there have not been any cases involving the claim that a computer program classes as a film. Many modern films make very extensive use of computer-generated images, to the extent that some characters, such as Gollum in the *Lord of the Rings*, are entirely computer-generated.[141] There appears to be little doubt that the programs responsible would qualify for protection as a film. Films, of course, enjoy copyright protection in their own right and there might be little benefit in bringing a claim for infringement on the basis of the software rather than the end product. There is a further factor to be taken into consideration which perhaps influences much of what will be discussed in the remainder of the chapter concerning protection of software as a literary work. Discounting the concept of piracy, whereby all of a work is copied and passed off as an original, there is limited value for a later party to slavishly copy elements of an earlier work of entertainment. Copying the appearance and actions of the character of Gollum from the *Lord of the Rings* and inserting this in a film on a different topic would not be likely to increase the appeal of the later film; rather the reverse as audiences who had seen Gollum would prefer to view a novel character. Different considerations apply with software products which are functional in nature and a user who has acquired familiarity with one form of interface will not unnaturally want to be able easily to transfer skills to another package produced by a different developer.

Conclusions

In many resects, developments in the field of software copyright provide a mirror image to the situation with software patents. In the latter case, at least at the level of decisions in the European Patent Office and even more so in the United States, there has been a move from an initial denial of patentability to a much more liberal approach. With copyright, whilst there has never been any significant doubt that software is eligible for protection, recent judicial decisions have significantly limited the scope of protection so that it will extend to little more than direct copying. As cases such as *Navitaire v easyJet* illustrate, a complex balancing act often requires to be performed, considering the interests of software developers, users, and in many instances, end consumers.

Whilst copyright may no longer extend to cover the 'look and feel' of a program, there is no doubt that it does prohibit direct copying of the underlying code. Although at first sight unobjectionable, this does create problems for users. Unlike any other form of literary work, use of software requires copying. In this respect, software, which in the case of application packages such as word processing or spreadsheet programs, is effectively a tool sits rather uneasily in the context of a form of protection designed for literary or artistic works. As the *Gowers Report* on the future of Intellectual Property Law points out, for a user to burn the contents of a CD which he or she has bought onto an MP3 player, constitutes a breach of copyright. Few users, it may be assumed, are aware of this and it may be doubted whether (m)any of those who do, care. A situation

---

[141] For an account of developments in the field see <http://en.wikipedia.org/wiki/Computer-generated_imagery>

where conduct which almost everyone would regard as acceptable is in breach of the law can serve only to bring the law into discredit. Conversely, of course, software, given its digital format, is massively vulnerable to large-scale copying at little or no cost to the copyist. There is a need to rethink some of the basic tenets of copyright law and the following chapter will consider the provisions of the rather grandly named 'Copyright in the Information Society' Directive.

Suggestions for further reading

Software Copyright—A Comprehensive Current Analysis of Software 'Look and Feel' Protection.

LAI, S. (2000), *The Copyright Protection of Computer Software in the United Kingdom* (Oxford).

18

Copyright in the information society

Introduction

Issues of intellectual property have been at the forefront of much of the debate concerning legal aspects of the 'information society'. An indication of the relative importance and complexity of the issues involved can be taken from a WIPO estimate that no less 90 per cent of the total investment in a multimedia product was expended in dealing with intellectual property issues.[1] In its *Follow-Up to the Green Paper on Copyright and Related Rights in the Information Society*, the Commission has estimated that:

> The market for copyright goods and services ranges Community-wide from between 5 and 7% of the GNP. This market is comprised of a large variety of products and services, containing protected subject matter, ranging from traditional products, such as print products, films, phonograms, graphic or plastic works of art, electronic products (notably computer programs) to satellite and cable broadcasts, CD and video rental, theatres and concert performances, literature and music, art exhibitions and auctions.[2]

For the United Kingdom, the then Prime Minister indicated in 1999 that the country's cultural sector is a greater source of revenue than the steel industry.[3] In its review of the operation of the Database Directive published in December 2005, the Commission reported estimates of the value of copyright products, as indicated in Figure 18.1.

The total turnover of the database and directory publishing industries in 2000 amounted to €8.2 billion; the software and databases industries (including electronic publishing based upon those databases) and print media industries contributed in excess of 1 per cent to the EU GDP.[4] Further statistical information comes in the form of the *Gowers Report* on Intellectual Property, which was commissioned by the

[1] 'The Information Society: Copyright and Multimedia', Proceedings of a meeting held under the auspices of the Legal Advisory Board, Luxembourg, 16 April 1995.

[2] COM (96) 568 final, p. 6.

[3] <http://www3.europeparl.eu.int/omk> Debates of Tuesday, 9 February 1999.

[4] Section 4.2.1.

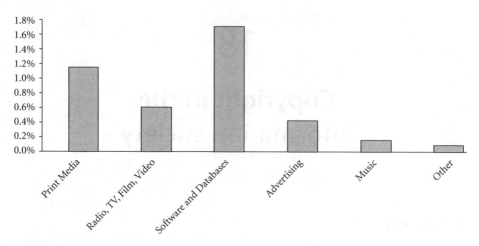

Fig. 18.1 Gross value added by EU copyright industry sectors as per cent of total GDP, 2000

Source: 'The contribution of copyright and related rights to the European Economy' (2003)
<http://ec.europa.eu/internal_market/copyright/docs/studies/etd2002b53001e34_en.pdf>

Treasury[5] to make recommendations on possible reforms to the United Kingdom's system of Intellectual property rights. This reported that:

> Knowledge based industries have become central to the UK economy—in 2004 the Creative Industries contributed 7.3 per cent of UK Gross Value Added, and from 1997 to 2004 they grew significantly quicker than the average rate across the whole economy.[6]

Whilst managing intellectual property rights is complex and time-consuming for those who wish to remain within the law, the ease with which digital information may be copied renders the owners of copyright in literary, artistic, and musical works vulnerable to the making and dissemination of unauthorised copies of a work in electronic format. If the invention of the printing press resulted in a move from an oral to a written tradition at the price of chaining information to the pages of a book, the information revolution frees information in the sense that it may be readily transferred with minimal need for linkage to paper or any other form of storage device.

To date, the attempt has generally been made to bring technological applications within the scope of the intellectual property system, most notably in the field of copyright. As has been discussed, copyright has proved an extremely flexible instrument, having been extended from literary works through to sound recordings, films, terrestrial broadcasts, satellite and cable broadcasts, and onto computer programs. Even the most flexible tool, however, has limits to its elasticity, and as the information society becomes more and more entrenched, so the relevance of the system, especially with its

---

[5] Text available from <http://www.hm-treasury.gov.uk/media/6/E/pbr06_gowers_report_755.pdf>

[6] *Gowers Report*, para. E2.

notion of exclusive rights, becomes open to challenge. This chapter will look at some of the emerging issues in the attempt to consider whether, and to what extent, copyright principles have a future in this information society.

The Directive on Copyright in the Information Society

A Green Paper entitled *Copyright and Related Rights in the Information Society* was published by the Commission in July 1995.[7] This was followed by a proposal for a Directive 'On the Harmonisation of Certain Aspects of Copyright and Related Rights in the Information Society', which was submitted by the Commission to the European Parliament in January 1997.[8] A number of aspects of the proposal were criticised in the Parliament, and an amended proposal was tabled in May 1999.[9] The Directive was finally adopted in May 2001,[10] with Member States being obliged to implement its provisions by 22 December 2002. In common with a number of other Member States, the United Kingdom failed to meet this deadline, with implementation occurring through the medium of the Copyright and Related Rights Regulations 2003,[11] which entered into force on 31 October 2003. The Regulations make a number of changes to the provisions of the Copyright, Designs and Patents Act 1988.

The Explanatory Memorandum to the original proposal for a Directive[12] identified discrepancies in the level of protection offered within the Member States, not so much at the level of fundamental principles, but in respect of detailed implementation and the provision of exceptions. Thus, all Member States accept that a right holder possesses the exclusive right to reproduce material, but differ in respect of issues such as whether a temporary reproduction will constitute infringement. Variations occur also in respect of concepts such as fair dealing and the provision of special regimes for the educational sector.

Beyond the issue of reproduction, significant issues concern the extent of rights to distribute a work or to communicate its contents to the public. With the development of 'on demand' services for the delivery of digital information in the form of audio or video material, lacunae exist between provisions relating to private communications and broadcasting. The Directive on Copyright in the Information Society[13] sets out to make provision for these matters and to harmonise existing national provisions, keeping always in line with the provisions of the Berne Convention and the 1996 WIPO Treaty on Copyright and Performances and Phonograms. In essence, the Directive is evolutionary rather than revolutionary in its contents. As Recital 5 indicates:

> Technological development has multiplied and diversified the vectors for creation, production and exploitation. While no new concepts for the protection of intellectual

---

[7] COM (95) 382 final.

[8] OJ 1998 C 108, p. 6.

[9] COM (1999) 250 final.

[10] Directive 2001/29/EC, OJ 2001 L 167/10 (the Directive on Copyright in the Information Society).

[11] SI 2003/2498.

[12] Available from <http://europa.eu.int/comm/internal_market/en/intprop/intprop/1100.htm>

[13] Directive 2001/29/EC.

394 | INTELLECTUAL PROPERTY ISSUES

property are needed, the current law on copyright and related rights should be adapted and supplemented to respond adequately to economic realities such as new forms of exploitation.

Reflecting this approach, the initial articles of the Directive do little more than confirm existing copyright realities, especially as they have developed in the United Kingdom. Article 2 provides authors, performers, producers, and broadcasters with the exclusive right to prohibit direct or indirect, temporary or permanent reproduction of the protected work by any means or in any form. Article 3 provides for similar exclusive rights in respect of the communication of all or part of a work to the public by wire or wireless means. It is specifically provided that the provision is to extend to the situation where the works are communicated in such a way that 'members of the public may access them from a place and at a time individually chosen by them', for example, over the Internet. Article 4 provides for authors to enjoy the exclusive right to control the distribution of works to the public by sale or otherwise.

Caching

The most controversial section of the Directive is contained in Article 5, which provides an exception from the prohibitions against reproduction in respect of:

1. Temporary acts of reproduction referred to in Article 2, which are transient or incidental [and] an integral and essential part of a technological process and whose sole purpose is to enable:

    (a) a transmission in a network between third parties by an intermediary, or

    (b) a lawful use of a work or other subject-matter to be made, and which have no independent economic significance, shall be exempted from the reproduction right provided for in Article 2.

Recital 33 indicates the intent behind this provision:

The exclusive right of reproduction should be subject to an exception to allow certain acts of temporary reproduction, which are transient or incidental reproductions, forming an integral and essential part of a technological process and carried out for the sole purpose of enabling either efficient transmission in a network between third parties by an intermediary, or a lawful use of a work or other subject-matter to be made. The acts of reproduction concerned should have no separate economic value on their own. To the extent that they meet these conditions, this exception should include acts which enable browsing as well as acts of caching to take place, including those which enable transmission systems to function efficiently, provided that the intermediary does not modify the information and does not interfere with the lawful use of technology, widely recognised and used by industry, to obtain data on the use of the information. A use should be considered lawful where it is authorised by the rightholder or not restricted by law.

A range of situations might be envisaged in which this provision will be applicable. The act of viewing information on a web page will involve the making of a temporary copy of that data on the user's own equipment. The nature of the Internet, again, will mean that transient copies of email messages will be made at various stages of the message's journey from sender to recipient. Such copying clearly falls within the criteria of 'integral' and 'essential' used in Article 5 and poses no legal difficulty. The practice of caching, which is specifically referred to in the Recital,[14] raises more difficult issues, and the inclusion of the phrase 'an integral and essential part' might be seen as robbing the provision of much of its meaning.

Caching involves the making of copies of materials originating on another site on a local machine. A user seeking access to the materials will be presented with a local copy, rather than having the request transmitted over the Internet to the original host site. Typically, the materials copied will be those for which there is the greatest demand, and the practice serves both to speed access for the user and reduce traffic over what is often a congested Internet. The problem that may be faced under the Directive's provisions is that although the use of caching may be advantageous, it cannot be considered essential.

The legality of caching is also provided for in the EU's Electronic Commerce Directive.[15] This introduces the concept of an 'information society service'. This is defined as 'any service normally provided for remuneration, at a distance, by electronic means and at the individual request of a recipient of services'.[16] In respect of the practice of caching, however, it provides that:

> Where an Information Society service is provided that consists in the transmission in a communication network of information provided by a recipient of the service, Member States shall provide in their legislation that the provider shall not be liable, otherwise than under a prohibitory injunction, for the automatic, intermediate and temporary storage of that information, performed for the sole purpose of making more efficient the information's onward transmission to other recipients of the service upon their request, on condition that:
>
> (a) the provider does not modify the information;
>
> (b) the provider complies with conditions on access to the information;
>
> (c) the provider complies with rules regarding the updating of the information, specified in a manner consistent with industrial standards;
>
> (d) the provider does not interfere with the technology, consistent with industrial standards, used to obtain data on the use of the information; and
>
> (e) the provider acts expeditiously to remove or to bar access to the information upon obtaining actual knowledge of one of the following:
>
> - the information at the initial source of the transmission has been removed from the network;
>
> - access to it has been barred; or
>
> - a competent authority has ordered such removal or barring.[17]

---

[14] Directive 2001/29/EC, Recital 33.
[15] Directive 2000/31/EC, OJ 2000 L 178/1.
[16] Directive 98/48/EC, OJ 1998 L 217/218.
[17] Article 13.

In most cases, it may be assumed that the creator of a material on the WWW will seek its wide distribution, and the practice generally raises few objections. The Electronic Commerce Directive goes on to make further provisions relating to the need to ensure that cached copies are kept up to date and that access to these does not impinge on the original user's ability to monitor access to the material. This last point will be of particular importance where a website is commercial in nature. Increasingly, such sites carry advertising material and the advertising income may be dependent upon evidence being supplied of the number of persons accessing and using the site.

Copy protection and Digital Rights Management (DRM)

The use of copy protection devices was a feature of many early software products. A wide range of techniques was utilised in the attempt to ensure that only an authorised user could make use of software. In some cases, anti-copying techniques would have been embedded in the software itself, in other cases physical devices were used. The absence of a uniform approach between producers meant that there was almost invariably a non-protected version of software available on the market and, given that the use of such devices normally made software more difficult to use, market forces compelled most producers to abandon such tactics. With devices such as Digital Video Discs (DVDs) there are signs that the technique is returning to favour. Here, manufacturers of discs embed a code corresponding to the region of the world in which the disc is marketed. DVD players are also coded in a similar manner, so the effect is intended to be that only discs marketed in one region can be played on equipment marketed in that area. A variety of techniques can be used to overcome this form of protection and the Directive sets out to provide legal sanctions against such acts. Article 6 provides that:

1. Member States shall provide adequate legal protection against the circumvention of any effective technological measures, which the person concerned carries out in the knowledge, or with reasonable grounds to know, that he or she is pursuing that objective.

2. Member States shall provide adequate legal protection against the manufacture, import, distribution, sale, rental, advertisement for sale or rental, or possession for commercial purposes of devices, products or components or the provision of services which:

   (a) are promoted, advertised or marketed for the purpose of circumvention of, or

   (b) have only a limited commercially significant purpose or use other than to circumvent, or

   (c) are primarily designed, produced, adapted or performed for the purpose of enabling or facilitating the circumvention of, any effective technological measures.

Measures will be considered effective when:

the use of a protected work or other subject-matter is controlled by the rightholders through application of an access control or protection process, such as encryption, scrambling or other transformation of the work or other subject-matter or a copy control mechanism, which achieves the protection objective.

Section 296 of the Copyright Designs and Patents Act 1988 already provided a copyright holder who publishes work in an electronic form which is copy-protected with a right of action against a person who:

(a) makes, imports, sells or lets for hire, offers or exposes for sale or hire, or advertises for sale or hire, any device or means specifically designed or adapted to circumvent the form of copy-protection employed, or

(b) publishes information intended to enable or assist persons to circumvent that form of copy-protection,...

This provision with its limitation to devices 'specifically designed or adapted' is rather more restrictive than the Directive's provisions, which refer to an article's primary purpose.[18] Accordingly, whilst retaining the original formula in respect of computer programs (which are outside the scope of the Directive) the regulations introduce a number of somewhat complex provisions—new Sections 296ZA (circumvention of technological measures), 296ZD (rights and remedies in respect of devices and services designed to circumvent technological measures), and 296ZE (remedy where effective technological measures prevent permitted acts).[19]

With traditional forms of literary work, it is customary to incorporate copyright details into the printed text. Where work is distributed in electronic format, the use of rights management information would see details identifying copyright owners being embedded in the work, and a facility included to record the use made of the work. This would facilitate the tasks of establishing copyright and the extent of any infringing use of the work. As the Directive's Recitals indicate:

(55) Technological development will facilitate the distribution of works, notably on networks, and this will entail the need for rightholders to identify better the work or other subject-matter, the author or any other rightholder, and to provide information about the terms and conditions of use of the work or other subject-matter in order to render easier the management of rights attached to them. Rightholders should be encouraged to use markings indicating, in addition to the information referred to above, inter alia their authorisation when putting works or other subject-matter on networks.

---

[18] Albeit, in a slightly different context, see the discussion of *CBS Songs Ltd v Amstrad Consumer Electronics plc* below, where the fact that a twin cassette deck had some legitimate uses provided a defence to a claim of copyright infringement, even though it might be argued that most purchasers would use the equipment for unlawful purposes.

[19] SI 2003/2498, Reg. 24.

(56) There is, however, the danger that illegal activities might be carried out in order to remove or alter the electronic copyright-management information attached to it, or otherwise to distribute, import for distribution, broadcast, communicate to the public or make available to the public works or other protected subject-matter from which such information has been removed without authority. In order to avoid fragmented legal approaches that could potentially hinder the functioning of the internal market, there is a need to provide for harmonised legal protection against any of these activities.

To guard against this, Article 7 requires that:

Member States shall provide for adequate legal protection against any person performing without authority any of the following acts:

(a) the removal or alteration of any electronic rights-management information; or

(b) the distribution, importation for distribution, broadcasting, communication or making available to the public, of copies of works or other subject matter protected under this Directive[20] or under [the Database Directive[21]] from which electronic rights-management information has been removed or altered without authority, if such person knows, or has reasonable grounds to know, that by so doing he is inducing, enabling or facilitating an infringement of any copyright or any rights related to copyright as provided by law, or of the *sui generis* right provided for in [the Database Directive].

In order to implement this provision, the regulations add a further new Section (296ZG) to the Copyright, Designs and Patents Act 1988. This provides that an offence will be committed by:

a person (D) who knowingly and without authority, removes or alters electronic rights management information which—

(a) is associated with a copy of a copyright work, or

(b) appears in connection with the communication to the public of a copyright work, and

(c) where D knows, or has reason to believe, that by so doing he is inducing, enabling, facilitating or concealing an infringement of copyright.[22]

Offences will also be committed by parties concerned with the importation, distribution, or communication to the public of copies from which electronic rights information has been removed.

Private copying in the digital age

In many jurisdictions, a measure of tolerance has traditionally been extended in respect of copying activities carried out by private individuals. In some European

---

[20] Directive on Copyright in the Information Society, Directive 2001/29/EC.

[21] Directive on 'The Legal Protection of Databases', Directive 96/9/EC, OJ 1996 L 77/20 (the Databases Directive).

[22] SI 2003/2498, Reg. 25.

jurisdictions, such conduct is specifically authorised, often in parallel with the imposition of some form of levy on the costs of recording devices such as cassette tapes, the proceeds of which will go to authors' rights organisations to be distributed or used for the benefit of copyright owners, thereby providing at least some compensation for losses caused by copying.

Although at one stage it was proposed to introduce a similar scheme in the United Kingdom, the objection has always been that the devices can be used for lawful as well as for infringing purposes. An individual might, for example, use a cassette recorder and tape to record his or her own compositions, rather than to make a copy of a third party's work. In such a situation, it is difficult to identify equitable grounds for requiring payment to be made to copyright owners. The *Gowers Report* comments:

> Downloading music and films from the Internet is now the most common legal offence committed by young people aged between 10 and 25 in the United Kingdom. Up to 80 per cent of music downloads are not paid for, even though most consumers recognise it to be illegal. According to a report commissioned by the British Phonographic Industry (BPI), file-sharing cost the music industry £414 million in lost sales in 2005, on total retail sales of £1.87 billion. These losses have risen steeply from £278 million in 2003.[23]

Even though the United Kingdom does not legitimise domestic copying,[24] a measure of tolerance is shown by the fact that the criminal penalties applicable in the event of copying for commercial purposes do not extend to private persons. Such an approach can be justified in the context of analogue copying. It would be a rare person who has not infringed copyright at some stage through over-zealous use of a photocopier. Most readers will be familiar with the limitations of the copying technology. A photocopy of an article in a journal or a chapter of a book will invariably be of lower quality than the original. Slight movement of the page as the copy is being made will cause blurring of lines, the size of the book being copied and the paper being used in the photocopier may differ, again with adverse consequences for the appearance of the copy. Problems will be exacerbated if a photocopy is itself copied and by the time the process is repeated over a few generations of copies, the final version will be virtually indecipherable. Similar factors will apply when a cassette copy is made of a musical recording or television or film production. In general, with equipment normally available to the domestic copyist, the copying process is a laborious one and the results inferior in quality to the original work.

Where information is recorded in digital format, the task of the copier is very much easier. A copy of a digital work will be identical in terms of quality to the original, and the same result will apply no matter how many generations of copies are produced. The speed with which copies may be made is also generally increased, whilst the emergence of the Internet makes it possible for a program to be placed on a website and copied by tens or even hundreds of thousands of users around the world. The popular encryption

---

[23] At para. 217.
[24] Save in the case of use of a video recorder to record a television broadcast 'solely' in order to allow it to be viewed at a more convenient time (Copyright, Designs and Patents Act 1988, s 70).

program PGP was released to the world in this manner in order to pre-empt attempts by the United States authorities to prevent its distribution. Not even the might of the United States could put the technological genie back in that particular bottle. Today, much debate focuses on the presence on the Internet of copies of audio recordings in MP3 format. As will be discussed below, one legal response to the problem has been to seek to impose liability on commercial third parties whose equipment or facilities are regarded as facilitating the infringing acts of private individuals. The question arises also, as to what should be the level of liability imposed on the individual's concerned.

The Directive on Copyright in the Information Society[25] contains provisions which, if adopted, may require significant changes to present United Kingdom law and practice, Recital 38 stating that:

> Member States should be allowed to provide for an exception or limitation to the reproduction right for certain types of reproduction of audio, visual and audio-visual material for private use, accompanied by fair compensation. This may include the introduction or continuation of remuneration schemes to compensate for the prejudice to rightholders. Although differences between those remuneration schemes affect the functioning of the internal market, those differences, with respect to analogue private reproduction, should not have a significant impact on the development of the information society. Digital private copying is likely to be more widespread and have a greater economic impact. Due account should therefore be taken of the differences between digital and analogue private copying and a distinction should be made in certain respects between them.

It would seem that this provision empowers rather than requires Member States to introduce licensing or similar schemes. Regulation 26 of the Copyright and Related Rights Regulations 2003[26] provides for an extension of the scope of criminal offences. Previously, an offence was committed only when a copyright infringer acted in the course of a business. The Copyright, Designs and Patents Act 1988 is now amended to provide that:

> (2A) A person who infringes copyright in a work by communicating the work to the public—
>
>   (a) in the course of a business, or
>
>   (b) otherwise than in the course of a business to such an extent as to affect prejudicially the owner of the copyright, commits an offence if he knows or has reason to believe that, by doing so, he is infringing copyright in that work.[27]

As the Gowers Report comments, however:

> The fact that the letter of the law is rarely enforced only adds to the public sense of illegitimacy surrounding copyright law. Yet copyright is essential for protecting the

---

[25] Directive 2001/29/EC.
[26] SI 2003/2498.
[27] Section 107.

investment that UK creative industries make in artists, performers and designers. If uses such as transferring music from CDs to an MP3 player for personal use are seen to be illegal, it becomes more difficult to justify sanctions against copyright infringement that genuinely cost industry sales, such as from freely downloading music and films using the Internet.[28]

Third-party liability for copyright infringement

In terms of the question of whether infringement of copyright has occurred, there is little doubt that the individual responsible for copying a work in electronic format will incur liability where this act is done without the authority of the copyright owner. An individual who downloads a copy of a software program or the text of an article from a bulletin board or other form of online service will infringe copyright. A constant thread in discussions of audio, video, or software piracy has concerned the impossibility, and, indeed, the desirability, of bringing proceedings against thousands if not millions of individual infringers. Much attention has been paid to the possibility of holding liable those parties who provide the equipment or facilities used for infringing acts.

The question of how far an ISP may be held responsible for the activities of its users is of considerable significance for the industry. In the United Kingdom, the decision of the House of Lords in the case of *CBS Songs Ltd v Amstrad Consumer Electronics plc*[29] is a relevant precedent. The respondents in this case produced audio equipment. Included in their range was a hi-fi unit containing two cassette decks. This feature allowed a user to copy the contents of one cassette tape onto another, a prospect which caused considerable concern to the owners of copyright in works recorded on cassette, a sector of the audio market which had hitherto enjoyed a considerable degree of immunity from the ravages of home copying. The concern was exacerbated by a further feature which allowed the contents of a tape to be copied in half the normal playing time. Action was brought alleging that Amstrad had, by their production of the equipment and the use of marketing strategies[30] described by Lord Templeman as being 'deplorable', 'cynical' and 'open to severe criticism',[31] purported to authorise users to make copies of protected works in disregard of the rights of the copyright owners and in breach of the provisions of the Copyright Act 1956.

This contention was rejected by the House of Lords. The critical issue, it was held, was whether equipment could be put to legitimate as well as to illegitimate purposes. Where this was the case, even the most ambiguous marketing strategy could not be regarded as purporting to authorise its use for illegal purposes. 'By selling the recorder', it was held, 'Amstrad may facilitate copying in breach of copyright but do not

---

[28] At para. 327.

[29] [1988] AC 1013.

[30] One advert claimed that the system 'features "hi-speed dubbing" enabling you to make recordings from one cassette to another, record direct from any source and then make a copy and you can even make a copy of your favourite cassette'.

[31] [1988] AC 1013 at 1053.

authorise it.'[32] A similar approach can be seen in the earlier case of *CBS Records v Ames Records and Tapes*,[33] where a record library which lent out records and simultaneously offered blank cassette tapes for sale at a reduced price was held not to have purported to authorise customers to make infringing copies. Applying these principles in the context of Internet-based activities, it would seem that an ISP whose facilities were used by customers for purposes which would constitute infringement of copyright—for example, through the posting of MP3 audio files—will not be liable. This conclusion is strengthened by the provisions of the Electronic Commerce Directive,[34] which states that:

> Where an Information Society service is provided that consists in the storage of information provided by a recipient of the service, Member States shall provide in their legislation that the provider shall not be liable, otherwise than under a prohibitory injunction, for the information stored at the request of a recipient of the service, on condition that:
>
> (a) the provider does not have actual knowledge that the activity is illegal and, as regards claims for damages, is not aware of facts or circumstances from which illegal activity is apparent; or
>
> (b) the provider, upon obtaining such knowledge or awareness, acts expeditiously to remove or to disable access to the information.[35]

Even more helpfully for ISPs, the Electronic Commerce Directive goes on to provide that no obligation is to be imposed on ISPs requiring that they monitor the contents of their site with a view to determining whether material might be considered unlawful.[36] The line between unknowingly facilitating copyright infringement and assisting it in a more concrete manner may be difficult to define. In 2003, an internet café, Easy Internet Café, was held liable in damages to the British Phonographic Industry—representing a large number of copyright owners, in respect of its practice whereby it would charge customers £5 to allow then to download a CD of music from the Internet. Damages of £80,000 (and £130,000 in legal costs) were awarded to the Claimant.[37]

Although it does not raise any issues of legal precedent, it may be noted that copyright owners have recently begun taking action directly against individuals who engage in copyright infringement, typically by making materials available for downloading using peer to peer (P2P) web services. One case was reported in 2006 in which a defendant was ordered to pay damages of £5,000 and legal costs of £13,500 following detection of his file-sharing activities.[38]

---

[32] [1988] AC 1013 at 1053.

[33] [1982] Ch. 91.

[34] Directive 2000/31/EC.

[35] Article 14. The implications of the requirement in para. (b) are discussed in more detail in the context of defamatory material in Chapter 31.

[36] Directive 2000/31/EC, Article 15.

[37] <http://www.theregister.co.uk/2003/01/28/easyinternetcafe_loses_cd_burning_court/>

[38] <http://www.pcpro.co.uk/news/83041>

Conclusions

In our fast-changing societies, it is tempting to conclude that history has few lessons to teach us. Much depends, perhaps, on whether we see change as evolutionary or revolutionary. Prior to considering where and how intellectual property should develop, it is perhaps useful to look back to consider how and why the systems developed. The first intellectual property statutes were motivated very much by economic and trade considerations. In the English patent system, for example, invention took second place to the need to overcome by force of law the obstacles placed by local tradesmen against those seeking to apply techniques and technologies, established in other countries but novel in England. In order to encourage foreigners to ply their trade in the country, a monopoly in respect of the particular technology would be conferred. As the system developed, the monopoly element became increasingly abused. Exclusive rights were conferred in respect of the manufacture and sale of well-established goods. A particularly unpopular patent related to the manufacture of playing cards. The abuses of the patent system played a part in the enactment of the Statute of Monopolies in 1623, which limited the grant of patents to the situation where a new product or process was invented. From there the patent system developed along well-known lines, with the national dimension of the system remaining very much applicable today.

A similar trend can be mapped in respect of the copyright system. Essentially a product of the invention of the printing press, this seeks to protect a range of interests associated with the creation and publication of literary, musical, and dramatic works. If we look back to the world's first copyright statute, the Statute of Anne of 1709, we see that its scope is limited to the direct and complete reproduction of books. The statute is a very short instrument but one which repays examination. Its Preamble recites the reasons behind the statute's introduction:

> Whereas Printers Booksellers and other Persons have of late frequently taken the Liberty of printing reprinting and publishing or causing to be printed, reprinted or published Books and other Writings without the consent of authors or proprietors of such Books and Writings to their very great Detriment and too often to the ruin of them and their Families. For preventing therefore such Practices for the future and for the Encouragement of learned Men to compose and write useful Books ... [Capitalisation and [lack of] punctuation as in original.]

A number of other features of the legislation deserve brief comment. In the event of infringement, although any infringing copies were to be handed over to the copyright owner for destruction, the financial penalties imposed on the infringer took the form of a penalty payable to the Crown. The copyright owner, also, was not free to demand such price as was thought fit for the book. The Statute of Anne 1709 allowed any person to make complaint to one or more high officials (including the Archbishop of Canterbury and the Lord Chief Justice) that the price demanded by a bookseller or printer was 'too high and unreasonable'. In the event that the complaint was upheld, the price would be reduced to a specified amount. Any subsequent attempt to charge a higher price would be punishable by fine. It is interesting to speculate how such a provision might be applied in the context of today's software and information products.

In general, it may be stated that the approach in the Statute of Anne 1709 is more consistent with the attempt to balance competing interests rather than to confer exclusive rights. It seeks specifically to promote learning. Over the centuries, the range of works protected by copyright has expanded steadily, as has the protection afforded to copyright owners and the extent of their remedies. Less and less emphasis is placed on the educative goals of the system or on the rights of those who seek to use the protected works.

Whilst the basic notion that a work should not be copied for commercial gain remains valid, the application of copyright law is hindered by the fact that digital technology operates in a different manner than its analogue equivalent. Although one motive behind statutes such as the United States Digital Millennium Copyright Act and the Directive on Copyright in the Information Society[39] is to confer a measure of legal immunity on users and service providers, it is difficult to see why a user's freedom to act in a reasonable manner should depend upon exceptional provisions.

The problem may not be one only for users. Another aspect of digital technology is that it puts extensive copying facilities in the hands of private individuals. The existence of systems such as Napster and MP3 provides eloquent testimony to this. In the Council of Europe's Cybercrime Convention, when providing for the imposition of criminal sanctions for various forms of copyright infringement, the instrument eschews the traditional formula that copying take place for commercial purposes with the requirement that copying take place on a commercial scale. This undoubtedly reflects the fact that a single individual with an Internet connection can, without seeking to secure any direct financial gain, cause significant loss to copyright owners.

Whilst there will always be those users who wish to obtain something for nothing, a perception of imbalance between the rights afforded to producers and users can only encourage disregard of the law. It may be that just as software companies have reduced levels of piracy in part through offering added value in the form of upgrades and customer support services to legitimate users of software packages, so the wider information industries might require to make use of similar techniques. The purchaser of a music CD might, for example, qualify for reduced price admission or preferential access to concerts performed by the artist(s) involved.

At a more legalistic level, in the English case of *R v Gold*,[40] the House of Lords had to consider the question of whether the transitory holding of data in part of the memory of a computer system satisfied a requirement that data be 'recorded or stored'. Holding that this was not the case, the court ruled that the process required 'a degree of continuance'. It may be that the implementation of a similar approach could resolve at least some of the issues arising in respect of digital information. In general terms, there

---

[39] Directive 2001/29/EC.
[40] [1988] 1 AC 1063.

requires to be recognition that whilst an author or other inventor may choose to keep a work out of the public domain, once the decision has been taken to make it available, rights have to be balanced against those of other parties, especially those who invest time or money in order to use the work. As is often noted in the context of human rights law, rights are accompanied by responsibilities. It is difficult either in law or in practice to see that these are currently in balance in the intellectual property field.

19

Protection of databases

Introduction

Since 1 January 1998, a new form of intellectual property right has been established in United Kingdom law. Implementing the provisions of the EC Directive of 11 March 1996 on 'The Legal Protection of Databases',[1] the Copyright and Rights in Databases Regulations 1997[2] may reduce the level of copyright protection available to database owners, substituting this with a new *sui generis* right effective against the extraction and/or reutilisation of a substantial part of the database contents.

What is a database?

The concept of a database is one which does not receive specific mention in the United Kingdom's copyright legislation. The term tends to be used with specific reference to computers, the *Concise Oxford Dictionary* definition it as a '[l]arge body of information stored in a computer which can process it and from which particular bits of information can be retrieved as required'. The initial draft of the EC's Database Directive adopted a similar approach, limiting its application to:

> ...a collection of work or materials arranged, stored and accessed by electronic means, and the electronic materials necessary for the operation of the data base such as its thesaurus, index or system for obtaining and presenting information.[3]

Although there might be pragmatic reasons for limiting the scope of legislation, there is no reason in principle why more traditional forms of data storage, such as a card index file, should not also be classed as a database. In the final version of the Database Directive,[4] and in the Copyright and Rights in Databases Regulations 1997, which implement the provisions of the Directive for the United Kingdom, a broader definition applies, referring to:

> ...a collection of independent works, data or other materials which:
>
> (a) are arranged in a systematic or methodical way; and

---

[1] Directive 96/9/EC, OJ 1996 L 77/20 (the Database Directive).
[2] SI 1997/3032.
[3] COM (92) 393 final, Article 1.
[4] Directive 96/9/EC.

(b) are individually accessible by electronic or other means.[5]

The Preamble to the Database Directive expands on this definition somewhat, stating that:

> Whereas the term 'database' should be understood to include literary, artistic, musical or other collections of works or collections of other material such as texts, sound, images, numbers, facts, and data; whereas it should cover collections of independent works, data or other materials which are systematically or methodically arranged and can be individually accessed; whereas this means that a recording or an audio-visual, cinematographic, literary or musical work as such does not fall within the scope of this Directive.[6]

Examples of databases

Starting with non-automated systems, a paper telephone directory can be classed as a database. Here, data in the form of names, addresses, and telephone numbers are arranged in alphabetical order, and may be retrieved by users through opening the directory at the appropriate page. Card index systems, such as those catalogue systems which used to occupy significant areas of floor space within libraries, also function in a similar manner. On the basis of the definition cited above, one might even class the contents of the library itself as a database.

With the dawning of the digital revolution and the ability to record and store any form of information in electronic format, the range and commercial value of databases has increased dramatically. Introducing the proposed regulations in Parliament, the Minister of State stated that:

> The database sector is a major United Kingdom industry. Estimates of the size of the UK database market range up to £10 billion but even that may be an underestimate. It is growing at more than 11% a year. About 350 firms are believed to be active in the sector, 30 of which are large suppliers and the rest small and medium-sized enterprises. UK suppliers have a share of the wider European Union market which has been put at more than 50%.[7]

Many electronic databases are accessible on an online basis. Most lawyers will, for example, be familiar with the 'Lexis' database. Located in Dayton, Ohio, this represents the world's largest collection of case law and statutory material. The parallel 'Nexis' service provides access to electronic copies of the contents of a vast range of newspapers and journals. Also on the market is a wide range of CDs. Such capacity devices typically have a storage capacity of around 650MB of data. A 500-page book would occupy somewhere in the region of 2.5MB. A single CD could, therefore, contain the text of some 300 volumes, although this figure would drop if pictures and illustrations were to be embedded in the text.

---

[5] SI 1997/3032, Reg. 3.

[6] Directive 96/9/EC, Recital 17.

[7] Fourth Standing Committee on Delegated Legislation, 3 December 1997.

Databases and new technology

Traditionally, one of the basic requirements for a functional database has been that its contents are stored in accordance with a predetermined structure. A similar requirement applies to many automated databases, where data is stored in predetermined fields. With developments in retrieval software and what are referred to as relational databases, it is less and less necessary for information to be stored in accordance with a predetermined structure. In general, the tendency is to allow users maximum flexibility in using a database rather than requiring searches to be formulated in accordance with predetermined structures. Once again, the telephone directory may provide an apposite example. With a paper directory, a user can search effectively only by means of the structure devised by the publisher—effectively in alphabetical order by reference to subscribers' surnames. CD directories typically allow searches by reference to any item of data—or to a combination of items. Reverse searching is a popular feature which allows names to be identified from telephone numbers or a listing produced of all subscribers resident in a particular street.[8]

Where a database comprises an amalgam of data and retrieval software, it will be necessary for the software to compile indexes of words used in the data, such indexes being used in subsequent acts of retrieval. Such a system is likely to come within the definition. More problematic issues will arise where the retrieval software is separate from the data being searched. The WWW, for example, consists of tens of millions of individual items of data controlled by millions of users. It is difficult to think of a less structured network than the WWW, yet search engines such as Alta Vista provide increasingly sophisticated searching facilities. Whilst it must be likely that many items on the WWW will qualify for copyright protection in their own right, others may not, for example law reports or copies of statutes from countries which regard such materials as being in the public domain. It may be that the list of materials identified by a search engine as meeting the user's request will itself constitute a database. In this instance, there might be a further issue, discussed below—who is to be considered owner of any resulting database right?

Traditional forms of protection for databases

The rationale behind the Database Directive lies in the belief that 'databases are at present not sufficiently protected in all Member States by existing legislation'.[9] This may certainly have been the case in some other Member States, notably Germany, which have required strict qualitative criteria for the award of copyright, but it is less applicable in a United Kingdom context. The basis for the legal protection of databases lies in the copyright system. As we have seen, Section 3 of the Copyright, Designs and Patents Act 1988 defines a literary work so as to include 'a table or compilation'.

---

[8] See, for example, British Telecom's (BT) online directory at <http://www.bt.com/phonenetuk/> and the more extensive service at <http://www.192.com/>

[9] Recital 1.

Although there is little precedent on the point, there seems little doubt that a database would fall within the latter category.

Copyright in respect of the contents of a database may arise in two ways. First of all, the individual pieces of work located therein may qualify for copyright protection in their own right. An example might be of a database consisting of a collection of poems. Each poem, it may be assumed, will be protected by copyright. Additionally, the database may qualify for protection in its own right, a matter which may acquire particular importance if portions of the subject material are not so protected, for example, because the author has been dead for more than seventy years or, in the case of collections of factual material, because the nature of the data excludes copyright protection. The names of individual companies, for example, will be unlikely to be protected by copyright, but a compilation such as the FTSE 100 will enjoy protection as a compilation. Again, as was at issue in the case of *Ladbroke (Football) Ltd v William Hill (Football) Ltd*,[10] although the names of individual football teams will not be protected by copyright, a compiled fixture list will be eligible for protection.

Discounting the issue of whether the contents of a database might qualify for protection in their own right, the issue arises of whether the degree of effort which accompanies the compilation of a database is sufficient to qualify for such a grant. Traditionally, a major element of the task facing the compiler of a database has been to determine the order in which the material is to appear and subsequently give effect to this concept. Using modern technology, text can be scanned and converted into digital format. Whereas traditional compilations such as directories will require to be carefully structured to make it easy for users to find particular items of information, the utilisation of appropriate software will mean that the entire contents of a database may be scanned with reference to a particular word or phrase. In such a case, there is less need for the database compiler to expend effort in arranging the layout of the database.

It is also one of the features of many computerised services that they seek to take advantage of the processing and storage capabilities of computers in order to present a comprehensive collection of materials. The goal of a legal database such as Lexis is to provide a transcript of every High Court decision delivered in the English courts. Similarly, the website of the Scottish Courts Administration[11] provides the text of every High Court and Court of Session judgment. This is to be contrasted with the more traditional law reports, which contain only a comparatively small number of decisions, and where some skill and labour will be expended by the publishers to determine which cases are of sufficient importance to warrant a place in a particular volume.

The 'sweat of the brow' doctrine

In the event that a database seeks to provide a comprehensive coverage of its chosen subject area, it may be difficult to evidence any originality in the selection process. It

---

[10] [1964] 1 WLR 273.
[11] <http://www.scotcourts.gov.uk/pages/opinions_intro.htm>

is here that a significant divergence exists between the United Kingdom approach and that adopted in almost every other copyright system. As has been stated, the United Kingdom system imposes minimal qualitative requirements relating to originality. In the case of a compilation, the traditional justification for extending protection has been the effort that has gone into selecting the works to be incorporated therein; what has been referred to in the United States as the 'sweat of the brow' doctrine. This approach is well illustrated in the case of *Waterlow Publishers v Rose*.[12] The plaintiff, under contract to the Law Society, had published listings, arranged geographically, of English solicitors and barristers in a publication, the *Solicitors' Diary and Directory*. A listing of all solicitors was supplied to the plaintiff by the Law Society, and this was used to send out forms seeking further information about areas of specific expertise.

Prior to 1984, a company owned by the defendant had been contracted to print copies of the directory. Following a takeover of the plaintiff, this work was transferred to another firm. The defendant thereupon determined to publish a similar work, the *Lawyers' Diary*, which would compete with the plaintiff's publication. The defendant's manner of work was to commence with the *Solicitors' Diary*, which constituted the only comprehensive public listing of the names and addresses of solicitors. A copy of the entry in the *Solicitors' Diary* would be sent out to the individuals concerned and they would be asked to reply, either confirming the accuracy of the information or making any changes that were felt desirable. The plaintiff alleged that this method of work meant that the resultant publication infringed their copyright.

In deciding the case, the court had to consider, first, the question of whether copyright subsisted in the compilation of names, addresses, and other information published in the *Solicitors' Diary*, and, second, whether the defendant's conduct constituted infringement. Although it was recognised that the nature of compilations was such that it might be difficult to identify a single person as author, the fact that the plaintiff was identified as publisher established a presumption that copyright was owned by it. Regarding the issue of infringement, the Court of Appeal held that:

> Mr Rose argued that he only used the existing directory to get in touch with the solicitors and that his work was then based upon the forms returned to him...There were something like 50,000 forms and the names and addresses to which they were sent were all obtained from the Solicitors' Diary 1984...In my judgement that goes beyond lawful use of an existing publication and amounted to an infringement of the plaintiff's copyright.[13]

The effect of this and of similar decisions is that extensive copyright protection is afforded to databases compiled in the United Kingdom. A similar approach had been followed in the United States, until the landmark Supreme Court case of *Feist Publications Inc v Rural Telephone Service Co Inc*[14] signalled a significant change of direction.

---

[12] [1995] FSR 207.
[13] *Waterlow Publishers v Rose* [1995] FSR 207 at 221.
[14] 111 S Ct 1282 (1991).

The case concerned the extent of copyright protection in a telephone directory. The respondent, Rural, was a telephone service provider which was required under the terms of its operating licence to publish a directory of its subscribers. A substantial number of service providers operate in the United States, each publishing directories covering a small geographical area. The appellant, Feist, was a publishing company which specialised in publishing directories which covered a wider geographical area than that of a typical small-scale provider such as Rural. It entered into negotiations seeking licences to publish from eleven different telephone utilities. Only Rural refused permission.

Despite Rural's refusal, Feist went ahead with the publication, extracting the necessary information from Rural's directory. Although it added some items of information and attempted to verify other items independently, 1,309 entries in the Feist directory were identical to their Rural counterparts. More damningly, four of these were fictitious entries inserted by Rural in order to provide a means of detecting unauthorised copying.

Rural's action alleging copyright infringement succeeded before the lower courts. The Supreme Court took a different view.[15] Infringement, it was held, could occur only when what was copied was protected under the copyright regime. Although the level of originality required as the basis for protection was low, there was 'a narrow category of works in which the creative spark is utterly lacking or so trivial as to be virtually non-existent'. Rural's telephone directory, it was held, fell into this category. Its selection of listing 'could not be more obvious'. Rural, it was held, 'expended sufficient effort to make the...directory useful, but insufficient creativity to make it original'.

The decision in *Feist*[16] produced considerable comment and controversy within the United States and prompted a significant tightening up of the criteria for the award of copyright generally. Certain aspects of the court's reasoning are potentially significant for the United Kingdom system. In particular, the court explicitly rejected the notion that the expenditure of effort, the 'sweat of the brow', could suffice for the grant of copyright. Even so, the court makes it clear that only a modicum of creativity is required. Although copyright does not subsist in an alphabetical listing of subscribers, subsequent cases have held that 'yellow pages'-type listings, where subscribers are grouped according to the nature of their business or profession, will attract protection.

A further illustration of the new United States approach can be found in the case of *ProCD v Zeidenberg*.[17] As was stated in the case report:

> Plaintiff spent millions of dollars creating a comprehensive, national directory of residential and business listings. Plaintiff compiled over 95,000,000 residential and commercial listings from approximately 3,000 publicly available telephone books. The listings include full names, street addresses, telephone numbers, zip codes and

[15] *Feist Publications Inc v Rural Telephone Service Co Inc* 111 S Ct 1282 (1991).
[16] Ibid.
[17] 86 F 3d 1447 (1996).

industry or 'SIC' codes where appropriate. Plaintiff sells these listings on CD-ROM discs under the trademark 'Select Phone TM', as well as under other trade names and trademarks.[18]

The plaintiff's pricing strategy was to sell copies of the CD at a low price for consumer use, but levy higher rates for those seeking to make commercial use of the product. The defendant purchased a copy of the consumer CD, which retailed for less than $100. Using its own retrieval software, it placed a copy of the plaintiff's listings on an Internet site, from where it allowed users to extract up to 1,000 listings free of charge. More extensive access, typically for commercial purposes, could be obtained at a cost less than that charged by the plaintiff. The site was soon attracting up to 20,000 visitors a day and, fearing significant adverse effects on sales of its CD, the plaintiff sought an injunction preventing its continued operation. Although at first instance the injunction was refused, the Court of Appeals eventually found in favour of the plaintiff on the ground that the defendant was bound by the terms of a licence accompanying the CD which prohibited its use for commercial purposes; it was common ground that no copyright subsisted in the data itself.

More recently, litigation has been initiated by the legal database supplier, Lexis, against an Internet-based company, Jurisline.[19] In the United States, Lexis markets compilations of law reports in CD format. Jurisline admittedly copied the contents of these CDs and placed the material on a website. Access to the site is free of charge, with the intention being that the site's costs will be met by advertising. As in the *ProCD* case,[20] the CDs in question are supplied subject to the terms of a licence which restricts the use to which the materials may be put. It appears, however, that the terms of the licence are not made accessible to the user until after the CD is purchased. An additional argument advanced on behalf of Jurisline is to the effect that Law Reports in the United States are regarded as being in the public domain so that:

> ...the limitations built into Lexis' licensing agreement attempt to control an 'essential facility' in violation of federal antitrust law.
>
> Lexis may not use a contract to take public domain material such as court opinions—which are explicitly not covered by the federal copyright law—and create a level of protection that is tantamount to a federal copyright.[21]

At the time of writing, the case appears to be in its early stages, but already it indicates the complexity of some of the issues involved. Whilst there is little scope for originality in the production of a comprehensive collection of law reports, denial of protection for the efforts and investment required to gather the material together might dissuade commercial publishers from making the initial effort. Such a decision would deny copyists their raw material, but would also produce the same effect for the public.

---

[18] 86 F 3d 1447 at 1447 (1996).
[19] The Jurisline site is at <http://www.jurisline.com>
[20] *ProCD v Zeidenberg* 86 F 3d 1447 (1996).
[21] Cited in D. Wise, 'Lexis Battles Web Upstart', *New York Law Journal*, 8 February 2000.

As indicated in *ProCD*,[22] one of the consequences of the *Feist*[23] decision has been the emergence of a new market in the United States for CD and Internet-based compilations of telephone directories. Selling for a few dollars, these will contain hundreds of millions of names and numbers, often providing additional facilities such as a reverse search option allowing a person's address to be identified from a telephone number. In the United Kingdom, BT has continued to assert copyright in telephone directories and has threatened copyright actions against parties planning to introduce competing products. This situation has now changed, not through the operation of copyright law but as a result of the actions of the Director General of Telecommunications, who inserted a clause in BT's licence requiring them to make directory information available to third parties.[24]

A major goal of the Database Directive[25] is to eliminate obstacles to the creation of a single market by harmonising the level of protection afforded to databases. Although not explicitly stated in the Preamble, there was undoubtedly the feeling that the United Kingdom's 50 per cent share of the EU database market was due in part to the fact that strong legal protection provided an incentive for database producers to locate their businesses in the United Kingdom. An alternative explanation might refer to the advantages of working in the English language and the larger market available to such databases.

The new database regime

The provisions of the Database Directive can be grouped into three categories. First, it makes provision regarding the application of copyright to the contents of databases; second, it provides for the extent of and exceptions to such copyrights. Finally, a new *sui generis* right is established to benefit some databases that are excluded from the copyright regime.

Copyright and databases

Article 1 of the Database Directive[26] provides that:

> ...databases which, by reason of the selection or arrangement of their contents, constitute the author's own intellectual creation shall be protected as such by copyright.

The key phrase in this provision refers to work being 'the author's own intellectual creation'. This term is not defined further. In the implementing United Kingdom regulations, it is provided that:

> For the purposes of this Part, a literary work consisting of a database is original if, and only if, by reason of the selection or arrangements of the contents of the database the database constitutes the author's own intellectual creation.[27]

---

[22] *ProCD v Zeidenberg* 86 F 3d 1447 (1996).
[23] *Feist Publications Inc v Rural Telephone Service Co Inc* 111 S Ct 1282 (1991).
[24] See <http://www.oftel.co.uk/dq998.htm>
[25] Directive 96/9/EC.
[26] Ibid.
[27] SI 1997/3032, Reg. 6 introducing a new s 3A(2) into the Copyright, Designs and Patents Act 1988.

The formula that work will be protected when it is the author's 'own intellectual crea-tion' is also used in the EC Directive on 'The Legal Protection of Computer Programs',[28] which provides that these are to be protected as literary works. When the Directive was implemented into United Kingdom law, this phrase was not included. Introducing the regulations in Parliament, however, the Minister of State commented that:

> Some people felt that no amendment of the [Copyright, Designs and Patents Act 1988] was needed to introduce the test and that the current test for the originality of literary works was enough.
>
> The Government do not share that view. The Directive is clear. It requires copyright protection for databases 'which by reason of selection or arrangement of their con-tents, constitute the author's own intellectual creations'.
>
> This is intended to exclude so-called sweat of the brow databases—that is, ones that involve time, money or effort but no intellectual creation, such as the white pages tele-phone directory.[29]

Assuming this view is correct, it gives rise to the suggestion that the United Kingdom has failed to implement the Database Directive[30] adequately. If the view is incorrect, the effect of the regulations has been to introduce unnecessary complexity into copy-right law. Prior to implementation of the Directive, s 3(1) of the Copyright, Designs and Patents Act 1988 provided that the term 'literary work' was to encompass:

> ...any work, other than a dramatic or musical work, which is written, spoken or sung, and accordingly includes:
>
> (a) a table or compilation;
>
> (b) a computer program; and
>
> (c) preparatory design material for a computer program.[31]

This is now amended to read:

> ...any work, other than a dramatic or musical work, which is written, spoken or sung, and accordingly includes:
>
> (a) a table or compilation other than a database;
>
> (b) a computer program;
>
> (c) preparatory design material for a computer program; and
>
> (d) a database.[32]

For the purposes of this Part, a literary work consisting of a database is original if, and only if, by reason of the selection or arrangements of the contents of the database the database constitutes the author's own intellectual creation.[33]

---

[28] Directive 91/250/EC, OJ 1991 L122/42 (the Software Protection Directive).

[29] Fourth Standing Committee on Delegated Legislation, 3 December 1997.

[30] Directive 96/9/EC.

[31] Section 3, as amended by the Copyright (Computer Programs) Regulations 1992, SI 1992/3233.

[32] Copyright, Designs and Patents Act 1988, s 3(1).

[33] SI 1997/3032, Reg. 6, introducing a new s 3A into the Copyright, Designs and Patents Act 1988.

Given that databases were hitherto regarded as a form of compilation, this approach might not be considered entirely satisfactory, and it is unclear where the division between the two categories lies. The Preamble to the Database Directive recites that:

> ...as a rule, the compilation of several recordings of musical performances on a CD does not come within the scope of this Directive, both because as a compilation, it does not meet the requirements for copyright protection and because it does not represent a substantial enough investment to be eligible under the *sui generis* right.[34]

Under previous United Kingdom law, there is little doubt that such a work would benefit from protection as a compilation. The question discussed below is whether implementation of the Directive will alter this situation.

Licensing and databases

In the first draft of the Database Directive,[35] provision was made for database owners to be required to grant licences to users in certain circumstances:

> If the works or materials contained in a database which is made publicly available cannot be independently created, collected or obtained from any other source, the right to extract and re-utilize, in whole or substantial part, works or materials from that database for commercial purposes shall be licensed on fair and non-discriminatory terms.[36]

It was also provided that licenses should require to be issued:

> ...if the database is made publicly available by a public body which is either established to assemble or disclose information pursuant to legislation or is under a general duty to do so.[37]

At least in respect of the first category, compulsory licences would only be available in very limited circumstances. It might be commented, in particular, that in most cases where only one party could obtain data, this might fall into the category of confidential information or be regarded as a trade secret, and would certainly not be made available to the public. In the event, the proposal was dropped following objections from Parliament, although it is provided that the issue is to be kept under review by the Commission, which had to report to the Council and Parliament within the first three years of the Database Directive's[38] operation, indicating whether the operation of the new regime:

> ...has led to abuse of a dominant position or other interference with free competition which would justify appropriate measures being taken including the establishment of non-voluntary licensing arrangements.[39]

---

[34] Directive 96/9/EC, Recital 19.
[35] Directive 96/9/EC.
[36] COM (92) 393 final, Article 8(1).
[37] Article 8(2).
[38] Directive 96/9/EC.
[39] COM (92) 393 final, Article 16(3).

Extensive provisions are made in the Copyright, Designs and Patents Act 1988[40] for the handling of licensing agreements between copyright owners and those wishing to make use of their materials. The Copyright Tribunal is established to determine disputes as to the nature and extent of such schemes. The regulations extend the scope of the statutory provisions and of the Tribunal's jurisdiction to matters relating to database licences.[41]

Other copyright changes

A number of other changes are made to the provisions of the Copyright, Designs and Patents Act 1988. In order to implement the provisions of the Software Protection Directive,[42] amendments were made by the Copyright (Computer Programs) Regulations 1992,[43] which had the effect of allowing the lawful user of a program to perform acts which might otherwise be restricted by copyright. In particular, this would sanction such copying of the program as was necessary for its use. Similar considerations will apply with electronic databases (whether online or held on disc) and the regulations add equivalent authorising provisions to the 1988 Act. Any attempt contractually to restrict or exclude the operation of these rights is now declared void.[44]

The database right

Implementation of the Database Directive[45] will have the effect of removing the protection of copyright from certain databases. Balancing this, a new database right is created which will arise when:

> ...there has been a substantial investment in obtaining, verifying or presenting the contents of the database.[46]

The maker of the database will be the first owner of the database right except in the case where the work is created by an employee, in which event the employer will own the right.[47]

It is not clear how much investment will be required to justify application of the adjective 'substantial'. The Database Directive's[48] assertion that a musical compilation will not require substantial investment has been cited above. Dependent upon the popularity of the music involved, it may be, however, that a high price will need to be paid to obtain the necessary copyright licences.

[40] See Chs VII and VIII.
[41] SI 1997/3032, Reg. 25.
[42] Directive 91/250/EC.
[43] SI 1992/3233.
[44] Regulation 9, inserting a new s 50D into the Copyright, Designs and Patents Act 1988.
[45] Directive 96/9/EC.
[46] SI 1997/3032, Reg. 13.
[47] Regulation 14.
[48] Directive 91/250/EC.

The database right is not presently found in any international agreements, although WIPO have proposed a draft treaty which would establish such a right. Pending the adoption of this instrument (which has been the subject of considerable hostility from certain quarters in the United States, where it is seen as marking a retreat from the principles of free access to data enshrined in the *Feist*[49] decision), protection is limited to individuals or undertakings who are nationals of, or incorporated in a state within, the European Economic Area (EEA).[50] Assuming that the effect of the changes to the Copyright, Designs and Patents Act 1988 discussed above do have the effect of taking databases outwith the scope of copyright protection, the effect will be to reduce the level of protection afforded to databases owned by non-EEA nationals or undertakings, without conferring the compensatory benefit of the new database right. To this extent, non-EEA database owners may be significant losers under the new regime. This may cause difficulties where databases are maintained on the WWW. Implementation of the Database Directive[51] in the United Kingdom might have the effect of removing some such databases from the copyright regime, but where the database is controlled by a non-EEA national, the compensatory database right will not be available. The effect of the new regime will be, therefore, to reduce the level of protection afforded within the United Kingdom to, for example, United States-based database providers.

It is immaterial for the existence of this right, which is stated to be a 'property right' whether the database or its contents are protected by the law of copyright. The right will be infringed by a person who:

> ...without the consent of the owner...extracts or reutilises all or a substantial part of the contents of the database.[52]

This may take the form either of a single act or of a succession of smaller extractions. Where conduct by a lawful user would not infringe the database right, it is provided that any term or condition which seeks to restrict this will be null and void. The traditional copyright exemption permitting such use as comes under the heading of fair dealing is restated in modified form for the new right. This provides that:

> Database right in a database which has been made available to the public in any manner is not infringed by fair dealing with a substantial part of the database for the purposes of illustration for teaching or research, other than teaching or research for a commercial purpose, provided that the source is indicated.[53]

Infringement of the database right will expose the perpetrator to actions for damages, injunctions, or accounting of profits as specified in s 96 of the Copyright, Designs and Patents Act 1988.[54] Significantly, however, although the Database

---

[49] *Feist Publications Inc v Rural Telephone Service Co Inc* 111 S Ct 1282 (1991).
[50] SI 1997/3032, Reg. 18.
[51] Directive 96/9/EC.
[52] SI 1997/3032, Reg. 16.
[53] Directive 96/9/EC, Article 9, as implemented by SI 1997/3032, Reg. 20.
[54] SI 1997/3032, Reg. 23.

Directive[55] confers considerable discretion on Member States as to the nature of the rights and remedies adopted in respect of the new right, the 1988 Act's provisions relating to criminal penalties do not extend to infringements of the database. Also unavailable are the rights of seizure of infringing copies and the right to demand delivery up. It may be that such rights are of limited relevance to online databases but, as has been discussed, the right extends to a wide range of electronic and manual products.

Duration of the right

The right will come into existence when a database is made available to the public and will subsist for a period of 15 years. It is provided, however, that:

> Any substantial change to the contents of a database, including a substantial change resulting from the accumulation of successive additions, deletions or alterations, which would result in the database being considered to be a substantial new investment shall qualify the database resulting from that investment for its own term of protection.[56]

The application of this provision should be non-problematic where databases (perhaps a telephone directory) are issued on an annual basis. Its application to online databases may be more contentious, and the provision cited above was amended from earlier proposals to try to cover the situation where a database was subject to continual minor amendment. The example might be taken of an online database of law reports such as Lexis. In most areas, cases are stored for a period of 50 years. If reports are added on a daily basis, each day will see a database which is very slightly different from the earlier one. On a rough and ready calculation, the change from one day to another will be in the region of 0.0001 per cent of the total database. This can surely not be considered substantial. As additions accumulate and are accompanied, perhaps, by changes to the structure of the database itself, it must be likely that the criteria will be satisfied before the expiry of the 15-year period. Assuming continuing development of the database, it will obtain perpetual protection.

In practice, it must be likely that the issue of whether the contents of a database remain protected by the database right will be significant only when legal proceedings are brought alleging infringement. A database might, for example, be made available to the public in the year 2000 and subjected to continual minor amendments. In 2020, the database owner might institute proceedings against a third party, alleging breach of the database right. In this event, evidence could be submitted to the court of the state of the database in 2000 compared with its 2015 incarnation. In the event this indicated substantial additional investment, the court would have to conclude that a new period of protection began in 2015 and that infringement had occurred.

---

[55] Directive 96/9/EC.
[56] Ibid., Article 10(3), as implemented by SI 1997/3032, Reg. 17.

The database right in the courts

The extent of the database right was at issue before the English Courts in the case of *British Horseracing Board Ltd, the Jockey Club and Weatherbys Group Ltd v William Hill Organization Ltd.*[57] The claimant in this case is the body responsible for the operation of the horse-racing industry in the United Kingdom. The defendants are a major firm of bookmakers. As part of its activities, the claimants compiled and maintained databases of horses and jockeys scheduled to participate in horse races. The databases were extremely large and subject to a process of continual updating. It was estimated that some 800,000 entries were added or revised each year. The cost of the work was put at some £4 million annually.

The database had been used by the defendant and other betting operators for a number of years. No complaint had been made regarding this. As with so many other aspects of life, the emergence of the Internet—in the particular case as a medium for betting—changed circumstances. William Hill published information concerning horses and riders competing in particular races taken from the database on its website, only for the claimants to allege that this constituted unauthorised extraction and reutilisation of a substantial part of the database. Each day's use of the data, it was argued constituted extraction and reutilisation of a substantial part of the database. Alternatively, it was argued that even if the individual extracts were not to be considered substantial, the totality of the defendant's practices amounted to repeated and systematic extraction or reutilisation of insubstantial elements of the database, a practice which was prohibited by Article 7(5) of the Database Directive.

For the defendant, it was argued that a distinction had to be drawn between the protected elements of the database, a concept which was described as its 'database-ness', and the underlying information which was not protected. Factual information such as the names of horses and riders and the races in which they were registered to compete could not be the subject of protection under the Directive.

Expanding upon the definition of the concept, it was suggested that:

> Since no right is created in the works, data or other materials, the 'database-ness' of a database must lie in the fact that the independent materials are arranged in a systematic or methodical way, and are individually accessible...the acts amounting to infringement of a database must in some way take unfair advantage of this 'database-ness'. Any acts which do not make any use of the arrangement of the contents of the database, nor take advantage of the way in which the maker has rendered the contents individually accessible, cannot infringe the database right.[58]

This is perhaps the crux of the debate. Whilst early database software packages required that great attention be paid to the structure and layout of the database, modern techniques permit searching to be carried out independently of structure. The idea that a predetermined structure was necessary for the establishment of protection was rejected by Mr Justice Laddie, who ruled that there was nothing in the Directive to

---

[57] [2001] 2 CMLR 12.   [58] Ibid.

support the existence of a concept of 'databases-ness' which, he held, converged two distinct concepts:

> the feature of form which have to exist before a database will be recognised as existing and the features of content or investment which are protected once a database is held to exist. Thus a database consists of a collection of data brought together in a systematic or methodical way so as to be individually accessible by electronic or other means.

The form of the database, might be protected by copyright rather than the database right. As regards the contents of the database, he stated, it was made clear in the Recitals to the Directive that a user was not entitled to take the contents and rearrange them. As was provided in Recital 40:

> the object of this *sui generis* right is to ensure protection of any investment in obtaining, verifying or presenting the contents of a database for the limited duration of the right; whereas such investment may consist in the deployment of financial resources and/or the expending of time, effort and energy.

In the particular case, the claimant had expended considerable effort in taking details of horses and riders from its existing database, placing them in the context of a specific race and verifying the accuracy of the resulting lists of horses and riders. The essential reason why the defendant's conduct infringed the database right was not that they had copied details of horses and riders but that they had relied upon the investment made by the claimant to ensure that the data was accurate.

The claimants also succeeded in their second contention that the defendant's conduct amounted to repeated and systematic extraction and/or reutilisation of insubstantial parts of the database. For the defendants, it was argued that there was not one single database but that as it was continually updated, there was in effect a whole series of works. Each act of extraction and reutilisation had to be considered as occurring in respect of a novel database. The judge was not convinced. The Directive, it was held:

> has to be construed to make sense... There is nothing in the Directive which suggests that it was not to apply to dynamic databases in just the same way as it applies to ones which are built and modified in discrete, well defined steps. Many of the most valuable databases are those which are under constant revision...

The claimant's database, it was ruled, was a single database which was constantly being refined. This, of course, raises the spectra of continuous protection for databases. If protection were to begin anew each time new items of data were included, the consequence would be that for at least some forms of database—and the one at issue in the present case would furnish a prime example—protection might be eternal, at least for so long as the database was maintained:

> In my view the BHB Database is a single database which is in a constant state of refinement. It seems to have been so regarded by all the witnesses. An attempt to split it into a series of discrete databases, besides being impossible to do, would not reflect reality. Its contents change with time and without any obvious break. So too, the term

of protection changes. As new data are added, so the database's term of protection is constantly being renewed. However, an unlicensed third party who takes only older data from it only faces a database right which runs from the date when all of that older data was present in the database at the same time. This does not render Article 10(3) meaningless. First, it emphasises that the term keeps being renewed as the database is renewed. Secondly, it makes clear that if someone takes an existing database and adds significantly to it, he obtains protection for the database incorporating his additions. This would be so even if the new author is not the same as the author of the original database...[59]

Repeated references in the judgment make it clear that the purpose of the new right is to protect investment rather than creativity. In determining whether a substantial part of the database had been extracted, account was to be taken of qualitative and quantitative aspects. No hard and fast rule could or should be laid down for the task of balancing quantitative and qualitative aspects. As was stated:

No useful purpose would be served by trying to assess this issue first on a quantitative basis and then, separately, on a qualitative basis. They should be looked at together.

The importance of the information to the alleged infringer is not irrelevant. In some cases, of which this is an example, 'the significance of the information to the alleged infringer may throw light on whether it is an important or significant part of the database'.[60]

Following the decision in the High Court, the defendants appealed to the Court of Appeal which stayed proceedings[61] to request the European Court of Justice to issue a preliminary ruling on a set of eleven questions relating to the scope of the Database Directive. The court delivered its opinion in November 2004.[62] Largely disregarding the opinion of the Advocate General, the court adopted a very restrictive view as to the scope of the database right.

Initial consideration was given to the second and third questions posed by the Court of Appeal. These asked:

(2) What is meant by 'obtaining' in Article 7(1) of the Directive? In particular, are the facts and matters (at issue in the case) capable of amounting to such obtaining?(3) Is 'verification' in Article 7(1) of the Directive limited to ensuring from time to time that information contained in a database is or remains correct?

The court referred to the Recitals to the Directive which referred to the intention to promote investment in systems which contribute to the development of the information market. A distinction was drawn between the expenditure of resources to compile and verify existing material which it compiled into a new database, and the use of

---

[59] Ibid. at 244.
[60] Ibid. at 235.
[61] [2001] EWCA Civ 1268.
[62] [2004] EUECJ C–203/02.

resources for the creation and verification of new materials. In the present case, the activity fell into the latter category.

The court was also asked to consider where the distinction should lie between substantial and insubstantial acts of reproduction and when repeated acts of extraction could be taken to unreasonably prejudice the rights of the database owner as laid down in Article 7(5) of the Directive. Again, the court's interpretation was restrictive. The prohibition against repeated acts of extraction, it was held, applied only where the end result would be the recreation of the whole or a substantial part of the database. Although William Hill's acts were systematic and repeated, there was not, it was held, any:

> possibility that, through the cumulative effects of its acts, William Hill might reconstitute and make available to the public the whole or a substantial part of the contents of the BHB database.

Following the decision of the European Court of Justice, the Court of Appeal overturned the ruling of the High Court,[63] albeit with a measure of reluctance, Lord Justice Clarke commenting:

> I am conscious that in doing so I have agreed to allow an appeal against a decision which I was inclined to think was correct when the case was last before the Court of Appeal in July 2001.[64]

The claimant's case, it was stated, rested on the approach that the Directive covered all aspects of the process of compiling the databases. The European Court ruling, however, in the words of Lord Justice Jacobs:

> implicitly rejected that approach. It focussed on the final database—that which is eventually published. What marks that out from anything that has gone before is the BHB's stamp of authority on it. Only the BHB can provide such an official list. Only from that list can you know the accepted declared entries. Only the BHB can provide such a list. No one else could go through a similar process to produce the official list.
>
> ...So if one asks whether the BHB published database is one consisting of 'existing independent materials' the answer is no. The database contains unique information— the official list of riders and runners. The nature of the information changes with the stamp of official approval. It becomes something different from a mere database of existing material.[65]

The Directive, it was held, did not protect the claimant's database.

Conclusions

Since the United States Supreme Court moved away from the 'sweat of the brow' doctrine in its decision in *Feist*,[66] the United Kingdom (and to an extent, Commonwealth

---

[63] [2005] EWCA Civ 863.
[64] At para. 37.
[65] At paras 129–30.
[66] *Feist Publications Inc v Rural Telephone Service Co Inc* 111 S Ct 1282 (1991).

jurisdictions) have been isolated in terms of the extent of copyright protection. Copyright has been held to extend to subjects such as a football fixture list, whilst the threat of copyright litigation was used by BT during the latter years of the twentieth century to deter parties who were planning to publish competing telephone directories in CD format. There is perhaps little doubt that the British Horse Racing Board could have succeeded in an action for copyright infringement under the old United Kingdom regime. The fact that the case was litigated to the extent that it has may be indicative that, as was stated by Mr Justice Laddie:

> These propositions dovetail with a more general point, namely that database right is to be construed so as to be narrower than the protection which used to be afforded to compilations under English copyright law.[67]

Given the increasing economic importance of the informational content of databases, this is a rather paradoxical conclusion. As has been the case in other areas, there is a degree of tension between the common and civil law legal traditions. It is arguable that if the United Kingdom afforded too much protection to works possessing little or no literary worth, other Member States afforded too little protection. The result, in the form of the Database Directive, has been a compromise. Only time will tell whether the compromise will be a successful one. In 2005, the Commission published a review of the working of the Database Directive.[68] This accepted that the scope of the *sui generis* right had been 'severely curtailed' by the decision of the Court of Justice in the *William Hill* and similar cases. The basic purpose of the Directive was to promote the development of the European database market and the evaluation aimed to determine:

> whether the European database industry's rate of growth increased after the introduction of the new right; whether the beneficiaries of the new right produced more databases than they would have produced in the absence of this right; and whether the scope of the right was drafted in a way that targets those areas where Europe needs to encourage innovation.[69]

The evidence for the success of the Directive was limited. Although a majority of those expressing views felt that databases were more strongly protected under the Directive than previously (presumably excluding the United Kingdom), the report stated:

> The economic impact of the '*sui generis*' right on database production is unproven. Introduced to stimulate the production of databases in Europe, the new instrument has had no proven impact on the production of databases. Data taken from the GDD (Gale Directory of Databases)... show that the EU database production in 2004 has fallen back to pre-Directive levels: the number of EU-based database 'entries' into

---

[67] *British Horseracing Board Ltd, the Jockey Club and Weatherbys Group Ltd v William Hill Organization Ltd* [2001] 2 CMLR 12 at 232.

[68] Available from <http://ec.europa.eu/internal_market/copyright/docs/databases/evaluation_report_en.pdf>

[69] At Section 1.2.

the GDD6 was 3095 in 2004 as compared to 3092 in 1998. In 2001, there were 4085 EU-based 'entries' while in 2004 there were only 3095.[70]

Views were sought on four options for change. These involved: the repeal of the Directive, the repeal of the *sui generis* right, the modification of the *sui generis* right, or the maintenance of the status quo. Fifty-five comments were received, with the Commission reporting in 2006 that:

> 8 contributions support Option 1, 3 contributions support Option 2, 26 support Option 3 and 26 support Option 4.[71]

To date, there has been no indication from the Commission that anything other than maintenance of the status quo is under active consideration.

Suggestions for further reading

'Databases *sui generis* Right: Should We Adopt the Spin-off Theory?', *E.I.P.R.* 26(9) (2004), pp. 402–13.

'The *sui generis* Database Right Clarified at Last?', *I.P. & I.T. Law* 9(4) (2004), pp. 3–14.

'Information technology; Intellectual property Databases: Is *sui generis* a Stronger Bet than Copy Right?', *I.J.L. & I.T.* 12(2) (2004), pp. 178–208.

---

[70] At Section 1.4.
[71] <http://ec.europa.eu/internal_market/copyright/prot-databases/prot-databases_en.htm>

20

Trade mark and domain name issues

Introduction

Along with patents and copyright, trade marks constitute a key component of the system of intellectual property rights. In the United Kingdom, the system originated in the Trade Marks Registration Act 1875. The present law is to be found in the Trade Marks Act 1994, which was introduced in order to enable the United Kingdom to comply with its obligations under the 1988 EC Directive 'To Approximate the Laws of the Member States Relating to Trade Marks'.[1] The 1993 Council Regulation 'On the Community Trade Mark'[2] established a Community Trade Mark to operate in parallel with national systems. At the international level, the Madrid Agreement Concerning the International Registration of Marks provides for a system of international registration of trade marks.[3]

As defined in the Trade Marks Act 1994, a trade mark is:

> ...any sign capable of being represented graphically which is capable of distinguishing goods or services of one undertaking from those of other undertakings.
>
> A trade mark may in particular, consist of words (including personal names), designs, letters, numerals or the sale of goods or their packaging.[4]

Details of trade marks are recorded in the Register of Trade Marks, a document which is open to public inspection.

The scope of this definition is broader than might initially appear to be the case. In our digital age, virtually everything is capable of being represented in graphical form. The process of 'sampling', for example, would allow any sound to be depicted in graphical format. A trade mark has been awarded for the distinctive sound of the telephone which features in advertising for the Direct Line Insurance company. In similar vein, the Chanel No 5 perfume smell has been trade marked under the description:

> The scent of aldehydic-floral fragrance product, with an aldehydic top note from aldehydes, bergamot, lemon and neroli; an elegant floral middle note, from jasmine, rose,

---

[1] Directive 89/104/EC, OJ 1989 L 40/1 (the European Trade Mark Directive).

[2] Regulation 40/94/EC, OJ 1994 L 11/1. Although dated '94' the Regulation was adopted on 20 December 1993.

[3] The text of the Agreement is available from <http://www.wipo.org/eng/madrid/texts.htm>

[4] Section 1(1).

lily of the valley, orris and ylang-ylang; and a sensual feminine base note from sandal, cedar, vanilla, amber, civet and musk. The scent also being known by the written brand name No 5.

This latter description illustrates a difficulty with the system. Although the description may identify the ingredients used, it makes no reference to the relative proportions of the ingredients or to the manner of manufacture. It would be possible to perform a chromatographic analysis and provide a much more detailed and specific description of the product. This might also prove useful to would-be counterfeiters. In the particular instance cited, inspection of the Register of Trade Marks would be of little assistance to anyone wishing to determine whether a product infringed the Chanel trade mark. This could only be determined by an inspection of samples of the perfumes involved. What is protected may not be apparent from scrutiny of the register.

In terms of their manner of issuance, trade marks fall somewhere between patents and copyright. Registration of the trade mark (in the United Kingdom, responsibility for the system vests in the Patent Office) is an essential requirement. This distinguishes the system from the copyright regime, where the right arises as soon as work is recorded in some manner. Although there are provisions relating to what form of marks may or may not be used, these requirements fall short of the exacting requirements of novelty and inventiveness applied under the patent system. The Register of Trade Marks is divided into forty-two categories and an applicant will be required to specify those in respect of which he or she would wish the trade mark to apply. A sliding scale of fees will apply, depending on the number of categories applied for.

Once accepted for registration, a trade mark will be valid indefinitely. The first trade mark was issued in 1876 in respect of the red triangle symbol found on containers of Bass beer and remains valid to this day. The two main threats to trade mark owners are that the mark will fall into disuse or, at the other end of the spectrum, will become so widely used on account of the proprietor's failure or inability to take action against infringers, that it takes on a generic meaning rather than 'distinguishing goods or services of one undertaking from those of other undertakings'. The word 'aspirin', for example, was once a registered trade mark (and remains so in France) owned by the German Bayer company. The trade mark rights in the United Kingdom were lost in the First World War, and the term may now be used to describe any painkiller containing the drug aspirin.

At the international level, the Madrid Agreement Concerning the International Registration of Marks provides for a system of international registration of trade marks. The Agreement provides that the owner of a trade mark in one signatory state may request the national authority to present an application for international registration to the International Bureau of WIPO, indicating those countries in which recognition of the mark is sought. In turn, the International Bureau notifies each state referred to which must give notice of a refusal to accept the trade mark, generally within a period of twelve months. The effectiveness of the international system is limited by the fact that many significant countries, including the United States, are not signatory to its various constituent agreements and protocols.[5]

Effect of trade marks

As with other forms of intellectual property, trade marks constitute 'property rights', conferring upon the proprietor the exclusive right to certain forms of use of the mark.[6] A trade mark will be infringed in two main situations:

> Where an identical or similar mark is used in respect of goods or services which are identical or similar to those forming the subject of the trade mark and where there is a consequential likelihood of confusion on the part of the public.
>
> Where the identical or similar mark is used; where the goods or services are not identical or similar to those forming the subject of the trade mark but where the trade mark has a reputation in the United Kingdom and where its reproduction 'takes unfair advantage of, or is detrimental to the distinctive character or repute of the trade mark.'[7]

In the first situation, dispute is likely to centre upon the issue of whether an allegedly infringing mark is sufficiently similar to confuse members of the public. Thus the name 'OXOT' has been held to infringe the trade mark 'OXO'. In most cases, the fact that the mark is used in respect of different categories of goods or services will defeat a claim of infringement. Where the trade mark has widespread recognition, infringement may occur when the use of the name (or a similar name) is regarded as seeking to benefit unfairly from association with the brand name or is likely to reduce its standing. In one United States case, use of the name 'Dogiva' for dog biscuits was held actionable on the first of these grounds by the proprietors of the trade mark 'Godiva', representing the well-known Belgian chocolates.

Passing off

By no means every name or indication of origin can be protected under the law of trade marks. Although United States practice appears to be somewhat more liberal, in the United Kingdom, popular names and geographic indicators cannot be protected as trade marks, as these are considered insufficiently descriptive of the origin of goods or services. Thus, a name such as McDonald cannot be protected by trade mark, although, as is the case with regard to the well-known fast food supplier of that name, trade marks encompass almost every other aspect of the business, from the 'Golden Arches' symbol through styles of writing and design to the names of individual dishes, for example 'BigMac'. On occasion, in deciding on the eligibility of a name submitted for trade mark registration, the Patent Office has had recourse to documents such as telephone directories in order to determine whether a name is in common usage.

---

[5] The text of the Agreement (as amended on a number of occasions, is available from: <http://www.wipo.int/clea/docs_new/en/wo/wo015en.html>

[6] Trade Marks Act 1994, s 2.

[7] Section 10.

A trader finding that it is unable to register its name as a trade mark will not be deprived of legal protection. The doctrine of 'passing off' is a common law creation located in the law of tort and is based on the premise that 'nobody has any right to represent his goods as the goods of somebody else'. The action is effectively one of unfair competition and will lie where a competitor markets goods or services in such a manner that the public are likely to be confused as to their origins. In the case of *Erven Warnink v Townend*,[8] Lord Diplock identified five requirements for a successful action:

(1) a misrepresentation

(2) made by a trader in the course of trade,

(3) to prospective customers of his or ultimate consumers of goods or services supplied by him,

(4) which is calculated to injure the business or goodwill of another trader (in the sense that this is a reasonably foreseeable consequence) and

(5) which causes actual damage to a business or goodwill of the trader by whom the action is brought or . . . will probably do so.

Although the doctrine of passing off is limited to use of a name in a manner which will harm commercial interests, recent decisions under the Internet domain name dispute resolution procedures indicate that protection may extend to private interests in respect of the practice sometimes described as 'cybersquatting'.

Trade marks and information technology

As with many other forms of products and services, information technology products are likely to seek the protection of trade mark law. Many product names are trade marked—Apple and Microsoft, for example, are both registered trade marks, together with symbols such as the famous Apple logo. In these situations, the application of trade mark law raises no novel issues.

With the emergence and increasing commercialisation of the Internet, many businesses have sought to establish a presence in cyberspace. Typically, they will seek to register a domain name which incorporates their real-life identity. British Airways, for example, can be found at http://www.britishairways.com. In some cases, businesses which exist wholly or primarily on the Internet have sought to register aspects of the domain name structure as a trade mark, an example being Amazon.com, where the .com element is part of the registered mark. The United Kingdom Patent Office has published notices on 'Practice on Trade Marks Incorporating the Word Net'[9] and on 'Registration of Internet Domain Names as Trade Marks'.[10] The notices indicate that

---

[8] [1979] FSR 39.

[9] Available from <http://www.patent.gov.uk/snews/notices/tmnet.html>

[10] Available from <http://www.patent.gov.uk/snews/notices/tmnames.html>

in deciding whether a mark should be registered, elements such as http, www, .com, .co.uk are to be discounted in determining the eligibility of the mark. The term will then fall to be judged on normal criteria. Initially, applicants should show that the mark is distinctive of their business or that goods or services have been supplied under the name in such a manner as to show factual distinctiveness.

Where novel issues have arisen is in the relationship between trade mark rights and the allocation of Internet domain names.[11] As the systems of allocating domain names developed, the responsible agencies adopted a first come, first served policy. As the commercial attractiveness of the WWW has increased, so more and more commercial organisations have sought to develop a presence. The impact of a web presence will obviously be enhanced by use of the organisation's trading name, something which may well be protected by trade marks. What many have discovered is that, whether by accident or design, the name is already in use. In such instances, consideration may well be given to the possibility of raising an action alleging infringement of the trade mark. Unfortunately, the application of trade mark law to the operation of the Internet is not without its difficulties.

Problems are exacerbated by a number of features of the system of Internet domain names. In many instances, the names of undertakings may be shared by many individuals. There are in excess of 2,000 Macdonalds listed in the Glasgow telephone directory alone. Although the existence of sub-domains such as .co and .ltd means that the same name might be used in these various sectors, there may not be enough sub-domains to go around. Even where domain names identical to a trade mark have been obtained by another commercial undertaking, there may be no question of infringement when this undertaking's activities are conducted in different sectors. Again, domain names cannot incorporate a distinctive type font or style of presentation of a name or identifying badges or signs.

Additional problems exist in respect of the generic top level domain names such as .com. These may be obtained by anyone from anywhere in the world. This global system sits uneasily with the trade mark system which, albeit with mechanisms for international co-operation, is still based on the notion of national rights. It may well be the case that the same trade mark is owned by different persons or undertakings in different states. An example is Budweiser beer. Although this is currently the subject of a dispute between United States and Czech-based brewers, for historical reasons, the name has been used by two distinct parties.

In considering the relationship between trade marks (and other legal rights such as passing off) and domain names, consideration will first be given to a number of cases which have been brought before the courts in the United Kingdom. Following this, reference will be made to the dispute resolution procedure adopted by Internet regulatory agencies.

---

[11] See Chapter 2 for a description of the function of Internet domain names and the manner in which these are allocated.

Internet-related trade mark disputes

Most of the disputes which have reached the courts have concerned the question whether use or possession of a domain name including a trade mark constitutes infringement. Two situations might arise, the first concerned with cases of domain-name hijacking as discussed above, and the second with the more problematic case of honest concurrent usage.

Domain-name hijacking

As indicated above, domain registries have operated (and to a considerable extent, continue to do so) on the basis of accepting the first application for registration of a particular domain name. This has been open to exploitation by street- (or Internet-) wise users, who have sought to register large numbers of popular names. Names such as Macdonalds, Hertz, and Rolex were issued to applicants with no connection with the well-known firms. The practice of seeking a domain name corresponding with a well-known organisation is generally referred to as 'domain-name hijacking'. As the commercial usage of the Internet has increased, so the benefits of obtaining a domain name which is readily identifiable with the owner's business has become recognised. It is reported that one domain name (pizza.com) has been sold for no less than £1.3 million,[12] with a number of firms conducting online auctions for the sale of attractive domain names.[13]

In the case of a number of the names mentioned above, the return of these to their 'rightful' owners has been accompanied by the making of payments to charity. Other 'hijackers' have acted from less altruistic motives. The first Internet-related dispute to come before an English court provides an illustration. In *Harrods v Lawrie*,[14] the plaintiff successfully asked the High Court to order the defendant to give up all claim to the domain names Harrods.com and Harrods.co.uk. It was noted that the defendant had also registered the names ladbrokes.com and cadburys.com. A spokesman for Harrods suggested:

> There can be only two purposes in him registering the name. One is to demand money from us to relinquish it, and the other to stop us using it. Either purpose is, we think, illegal and we believe that the existing laws of this country should be sufficient to establish that a company may protect its name and reputation on the Internet.

The decision in this case was handed down in the absence of the defendant and is of very limited precedential value. A non-Internet-related case which may be of relevance in illustrating the issues involved is that of *Glaxo plc v Glaxowellcome Ltd*.[15] Here, a merger had been proposed between two pharmaceutical companies, Glaxo and Wellcome. The news was announced in a press release on 23 January 1995, which

---

[12] <http://www.news.bbc.co.uk/1/world/americas/7331042.stm>
[13] See, for example, <http://www.part.to/index.html>
[14] *Daily Telegraph*, 14 January 1997.
[15] [1996] FSR 388.

stated that the new company would trade under the name Glaxo-Wellcome plc. The following day, one of the defendants, who acted as a company registration agent registered a company under the name Glaxowellcome Ltd. The defendant's normal business was to create 'shell' companies which would be sold for a fee of £1,000. The plaintiffs discovered the details of the registration which would have prevented their own use of the name. The defendants refused to sell the rights in the name for their standard fee, but indicated 'without prejudice' that this might be arranged for a fee of £100,000. The plaintiffs alleged that the defendants were guilty of the tort of 'passing off' and sought an order requiring the defendants to change the name of their company to something 'which did not contain the names "Glaxo" or "Wellcome" or any other confusingly similar words'.

This order was granted in the High Court, Lightman J holding that the plaintiffs were not obliged to follow the statutory procedures for challenging the registration of a company name with the Registrar of Companies, proceedings which could well be lengthy. The court, he stated:

> . . . will not countenance any such pre-emptive strike of registering companies with names where others have the goodwill in those names, and the registering party then demanding a price for changing the names. It is an abuse of the system of registration of companies' names[16]

and granted an injunction 'specifically requiring the company and subscribers to take all such steps as lie within their power to change or facilitate the change of name'.

A more significant and directly relevant decision is that of the Court of Appeal in *British Telecommunications plc, Virgin Enterprises Ltd, J Sainsbury plc, Marks & Spencer plc and Ladbroke Group plc v One in a Million*.[17] The defendant, One in a Million, together with four other companies, acted as dealers in Internet domain names. Included in the names registered by them were:

ladbrokes.com	bt.org
sainsbury.com	virgin.org
sainsburys.com	marksandspencer.co.uk
j-sainsbury.com	britishtelecom.co.uk
marksandspencer.com	britishtelecom.net
cellnet.net	britishtelecom.com

The plaintiff companies alleged that the defendants' conduct constituted both threats to engage in and completed acts of passing off and trade mark infringement. Judgment was granted in their favour in the High Court, with the judge accepting that the defendants' conduct demonstrated a consistent and deliberate pattern of registering domain names which were either identical or confusingly similar to names and

---

[16] *Glaxo plc v Glaxowellcome Ltd* [1996] FSR 388 at 391.
[17] [1999] FSR 1. The decision at first instance is reported at [1998] FSR 265.

marks owned and used by other persons. In the absence of any evidence justifying acquisition of the names, the plaintiffs were awarded a permanent injunction.[18]

The defendants lodged an appeal but the Court of Appeal upheld the initial judgment in all respects. In respect of the allegation that the defendant had engaged in passing off, it was argued that the mere act of registering names was not sufficient. Although the defendants had in the past registered and sold domain names, there had been no attempt to offer the present names for sale—perhaps because the plaintiffs were so quick to seek an injunction. For the defence, it was argued that until some attempt was made to use or sell the names, there could be no element of threatened trade mark infringement or risk of deception to the public. This contention was rejected. Delivering the judgment of the court, Lord Justice Walker identified the criteria that should be applied by a court in deciding whether to grant relief:

> The court should consider the similarity of the names, the intention of the defendant, the type of trade and all the surrounding circumstances....If, taking all the circumstances into account the court should conclude that the name was produced to enable passing-off, is adapted to be used for passing-off and, if used, is likely to be fraudulently used, an injunction will be appropriate.[19]

The judge proceeded to examine the activities of the defendant in some detail. As indicated above, a considerable number of instances were identified when names of well-known companies had been registered and subsequently offered for sale. British Telecommunications had been offered the domain bt.org for about £5,000. This had itself resulted in threats of legal action by British Telecommunications, which culminated in the defendants agreeing to the transfer of the domain name. Burger King was also reported to have been offered the domain burgerking.org for a 'mere' £25,000. After considering a number of similar cases where he considered there was an express or implicit threat to sell the domain names to a third party, Walker LJ described the defendants' conduct as evidencing 'systematic registration' of well-known brands names with the intention of 'extracting money from the owners of the brands'.

In respect of a number of the domain names, the defendant argued that there could be other legitimate holders of the name:

> there are people called Sainsbury and Ladbroke and companies, other than Virgin Enterprises Ltd, who have as part of their name the word Virgin and also people or firms whose initials would be BT.[20]

Even the defendant had to concede that this argument could not apply in respect of the name marksandspencer.co.uk. The court was also unimpressed with the arguments relating to the other companies. Once again, the pattern of the defendants' behaviour was damning.

---

[18] [1998] FSR 265 at 273.

[19] *British Telecommunications plc, Virgin Enterprises Ltd, J Sainsbury plc, Marks & Spencer plc and Ladbroke Group plc v One in a Million* [1999] FSR 1 at 8.

[20] Ibid. at 23.

A number of the plaintiffs also brought action alleging trade mark infringement. Section 10(4) of the Trade Marks Act 1994 defines what constitutes use of a trade mark:

For the purposes of this section, a person uses a sign if, in particular, he—

(a) affixes it to goods or the packaging thereof;

(b) offers or exposes goods for sale, puts them on the market or stocks them for those purposes under the sign, or offers or supplies them under the sign, or offers or supplies services under the sign;

(c) imports or exports goods under the sign; or

(d) uses the sign on business papers or in advertising.

In *One in a Million*,[21] Walker LJ took the view that the use was in connection with the defendant's business of supplying services. Counsel for the defendant argued that in order to constitute infringement there had to:

...be a trade mark use in relation to goods or services, in the sense that it had to denote origin. He also submitted that the use had to be confusing use.[22]

These issues are potentially significant in the Internet context. In the present case, the defendant's conduct again told against them, it being held that:

I am not satisfied that Section 10(3) [of the Trade Marks Act 1994] does require the use to be trade mark use nor that it must be confusing use, but I am prepared to assume that it does. Upon that basis I am of the view that threats to infringe have been established....

The domain names were registered to take advantage of the distinctive character and reputation of the marks. That is unfair and detrimental.[23]

The issue of 'trade mark use' and the possibility of confusion were discussed in more detail in the Scottish case *of Bravado Merchandising Services Ltd v Mainstream Publishing (Edinburgh) Ltd.*[24] An author had written a book about the pop group, 'Wet Wet Wet'. The group had trade marked its name in categories relating to printed matter. The book's title was *A Sweet Little Mystery—Wet Wet Wet—The Inside Story*. It was alleged that this constituted trade mark infringement.

Delivering judgment, Lord McCluskey made frequent reference to the criterion of whether the name was used 'in a trade mark sense'. He pointed out that:

...a travel writer who wrote an article about a fortnight's hill walking in the Lake District might well, if he had been unlucky enough, give it the title 'Wet Wet Wet'.

---

[21] *British Telecommunications plc, Virgin Enterprises Ltd, J Sainsbury plc, Marks & Spencer plc and Ladbroke Group plc v One in a Million* [1999] FSR 1.

[22] [1999] FSR 1 at 25.

[23] [1999] FSR 1 at 25.

[24] [1996] FSR 205.

Such usage would be descriptive of the topic and would not constitute use in a trade mark sense. In the present case, however:

> The repeated reference to 'Wet' has nothing to do with moisture or political timidity. On the contrary, the use of 'Wet Wet Wet' is avowedly and obviously a use of the name which the group has registered. Accordingly, even if the use is appropriate to indicate the subject matter of the book on whose cover it appears that use does not thereby cease to be used in a trade mark sense.[25]

If use of a trade mark as the title of a book constitutes trade mark use, there can be little doubt that use as a domain name would be similarly regarded. Lord McCluskey went on, however, to consider the defence provided by s 11(2) of the Trade Marks Act 1994. This sanctions:

> ...the use of indications concerning the...intended purpose of goods or services...provided the use is in accordance with honest practice in industrial or commercial matters.

In the present case, the use of the trade mark was to indicate the subject-matter of the book. The judge commented that:

> In the course of the discussion, as I noted earlier, such names as Ford, Disney and Guinness were discussed. It would be a bizarre result of trade marks legislation, the primary purpose of which is to 'guarantee the trade mark as an indication of origin', if it could be used to prevent publishers from using the protected name in the title of a book about the company or product. If that had been the intention of Parliament, I would have expected it to be made plain.[26]

Accordingly, the claim of trade mark infringement was dismissed. It is perhaps unlikely that a defendant such as One in a Million could satisfy the Trade Marks Act 1994, s 11(2) defence, but the issue may be more open in the case where a site contains material about a trade mark owner. If the author's book could legitimately use the group's name as its title, the same might be said of a website containing information or comment about the group. On the same basis, someone establishing a website to discuss the current United States antitrust litigation involving Microsoft might well wish to include reference to the company in the domain name.

Honest concurrent use

In the cases discussed above, there appears little doubt that the parties seeking to register the domain names were acting, at the least, in bad faith and without possessing any colourable title to use of the name. Other circumstances may be less clear-cut, with two or more parties possessing rights in respect of a name. The problem may arise in a number of ways. With forty-two categories of goods and services in the Trade Mark Register, the same name may have been allocated to a number of persons. The

---

25 *Bravado Merchandising Services Ltd v Mainstream Publishing (Edinburgh) Ltd* [1996] FSR 205 at 213.
26 Ibid. at 216.

existence of many national trade mark regimes is likely to result in further duplication, whilst in the case of trade marks which can be used as human surnames, tens of
thousands of persons may have an entitlement to the name.

A number of actions have reached the courts involving disputes between parties
as to the right to a particular Internet domain name. Many of the disputes have also
involved the organisations responsible for the administration of the system of domain
names and, as will be discussed in the telecommunications module, these have devised
a bewildering range of policies in the attempt to limit their exposure in trade mark disputes. If a name is retained following a challenge from a trade mark owner, there is the
possibility that the registered owner may regard them as jointly liable with the name
holder. If the name is withdrawn following a complaint, an action may be brought by
the registered owner alleging breach of contract. The case of *Pitman Training Ltd v
Nominet United Kingdom*[27] is illustrative of the situations that are likely to arise.

The Pitman publishing company was established in 1849 and expanded to cover a
range of publishing and training activities. In 1985, the various divisions of the business
were sold, the publishing business being acquired by Pearsons, the second defendant in
the present case, and the training business by the plaintiff. An agreement was reached at
that time providing for the continued use of the Pitman name by the new owners.

In February 1996, a request was submitted to Nominet United Kingdom, the organisation which administers much of the .uk domain name system, by an ISP, Netnames,
acting on behalf of the publishing company and seeking registration of the names 'pit-
man.co.uk' and 'pitman.com'. The application was accepted. Although the publishers
had plans to establish a website and reference to its new domain names was used in
some of their advertising, it does not appear that any significant use was made of the
Internet.

In March 1996, another ISP acting on behalf of the plaintiff, Pitman Training, made
a totally independent request for the allocation of the domain name 'pitman.co.uk'.
Under the allocation rules operated by Nominet, a system of 'first come, first served'
applied. Under this provision, the plaintiff's request should have been rejected. Owing
to some administrative mishap, however, the request was accepted and the original
registration was removed and reallocated to the plaintiff, who promptly made extensive
use of the name, sending out significant mailings and publishing adverts inviting email
responses to the 'pitman.co.uk' address. From a commercial perspective, the exercise
was not successful. Only two replies had been received by the date of the trial.

It was not until December 1996 that the second defendant discovered that its domain
name had been withdrawn. It made a complaint to its ISP, requiring reinstatement
of its name. Prolonged negotiations followed, involving all of the parties to the case
but without an acceptable solution being reached. Finally, on 4 April 1997, Nominet,
applying their 'first come, first served' rule, indicated that the domain name would be
removed from the plaintiff and reallocated it to the second defendant. Matters then
switched to the High Court.

[27] [1997] FSR 797.

On 11 April, a consent order was made restraining Nominet from transferring the domain name pending a full hearing or further order. In May 1997, the matter returned to the High Court, where the Vice-Chancellor held that the injunction should be withdrawn on the basis that the plaintiff had not demonstrated a reasonable prospect of succeeding in its action. As was stated:

> It is trite law and, of course, common ground that interlocutory relief in an action can only be granted in support of some viable cause of action. If a plaintiff cannot show a reasonably arguable cause of action against a defendant the plaintiff cannot obtain any interlocutory relief against that defendant however convenient the grant of that relief might appear to be.[28]

In terms of intellectual property, the plaintiff's main ground of action was that the defendant had committed the tort of passing off. This contention was not accepted by the judge. The name Pitman had been used for publishing for almost 150 years. The agreement at the time of the break-up of the original company provided for its continued use in this context. Indeed, it was suggested, given the terms of the agreement, if any party was guilty of passing off it was more likely to be the plaintiff. He concluded:

> That there may be some confusion experienced by some members of the public is undoubtedly so. But that confusion results from the use by both companies, PTC and Pitman Publishing, of the style Pitman for their respective trading purposes. No viable passing off claim against Pitman Publishing arising out of the future or past use by Pitman Publishing of the 'pitman.co.uk' domain name has, in my judgment, been shown.[29]

In many respects, it may be considered that the problems of trying to apply national trade mark law in the context of the Internet are intractable. Final reference may be made to the case of *Prince PLC v Prince Sports Group*.[30] The plaintiff was a United Kingdom company providing a range of computer consultancy and training services. The defendant was a major United States-based sports goods manufacturer which possessed United States and United Kingdom trade marks in respect of the use of the name Prince for sports goods.

In 1995, the plaintiff applied for and was awarded an Internet domain name as Prince. com. In 1997, the defendant became aware of this fact and its attorneys wrote a letter to the plaintiff, indicating that a failure on its part to relinquish rights in the name would constitute trade mark infringement and impliedly threatening legal proceedings:

> Dear Sirs:
>
> We represent Prince Sports Group, Inc, with respect to trademark and other intellectual property matters. Prince is the owner of the famous PRINCE trademark, which has been used in connection with tennis rackets, squash rackets, other sporting items and clothing for at least the past 20 years in the United States. Prince is the owner

---

[28] *Pitman Training Ltd v Nominet United Kingdom* [1997] FSR 797 at 806.
[29] Ibid. at 807.
[30] [1998] FSR 22.

of several US registrations for the PRINCE mark, many of which are incontestable, e.g., Registration Nos 1,049,720; 1,074,654; 1,111,008; 1,103,956; 1,233,680; 1,284,452; 1,290,202; and 1,290,217. Our client has also registered the PRINCE mark in many other countries throughout the world, including the United Kingdom.

Through extensive sales and advertising under the PRINCE mark and the excellent quality of our client's products, the PRINCE mark has become an asset of immeasurable goodwill and value to our client.

It has come to our client's attention that you have registered 'PRINCE.COM' as a domain name with Network Solutions Inc, (NSI) thereby preventing our client from registering its house mark and trade name as a domain name. We are writing to advise you that your company's use and registration of PRINCE as a domain name constitutes infringement and dilution of our client's trademark rights in PRINCE, as well as unfair competition, under the Lanham Act, 15 USC 1051 *et seq*.

This matter can be amicably resolved by an assignment of the PRINCE.COM domain name to Prince Sports Group, Inc, in accordance with the procedures of NSI and an agreement not to use PRINCE as part of any new domain name you may select. While we are willing to wait for your orderly transition to a new domain name, we must have your immediate written agreement to assign the PRINCE.COM domain name to Prince Sports to avoid litigation.

We look forward to hearing from you or your attorneys in the very near future.[31]

The plaintiff considered that the letter related to proceedings in the United Kingdom. Under United Kingdom trade mark law, an unjustified threat to institute infringement proceedings is actionable, s 21 of the Trade Marks Act 1994 providing that:

1. Where a person threatens another with proceedings for infringement of a registered trade mark other than—

   (a) the application of the mark to goods or their packaging;

   (b) the importation of goods to which, or to the packaging of which, the mark has been applied; or

   (c) the supply of services under the mark any person aggrieved may bring proceedings for relief under this section.

2. The relief which may be applied for is any of the following—

   (a) a declaration that the threats are unjustifiable;

   (b) an injunction against the continuance of the threats; or

   (c) damages in respect of any loss he has sustained by the threats.

The plaintiff sought all three remedies plus a further declaration that its conduct did not constitute trade mark infringement. It achieved significant but not total success. Although the plaintiff's letter made extensive reference to United States trade marks and to provisions of United States law, it was considered that it could also reasonably be understood as relating to proceedings in the United Kingdom. The threat of action

---

[31] *Prince PLC v Prince Sports Group* [1998] FSR 21 at 24.5.

did not come under the headings in s 24(1) of the Trade Marks Act 1994. Although the plaintiff's business involved the supply of services, the threat of action was general in its terms. The court therefore awarded the remedies under s 24(2)(a) and (b). It rejected the request for a more extensive declaration of non-infringement, holding that such a determination was not appropriate for interim proceedings. As regards damages, the court was of the view that the plaintiff had not suffered any financial loss sufficient to sustain a claim for damages.[32]

Reverse domain-name hijacking

Whilst there is little doubt that the attempt wrongfully to utilise a trade mark or similar identifier as a domain name will be struck down, the practice referred to as reverse domain-name hijacking has acquired some publicity, albeit without any significant legal authority. The practice has been defined by Internet Corporation for Assigned Names and Numbers (ICANN) as the attempt to use procedures 'in bad faith to attempt to deprive a registered domain-name holder of a domain name'.[33] An example of the application of this doctrine can be seen in a dispute between the Driver and Vehicle Licensing Agency (DVLA) in the United Kingdom and a United States based company, DVL Automation. Although it owned the domain name DVLA.gov.uk, the DVLA objected to the registration of the domain DVLA.com by the United States company and instituted arbitration procedures before WIPO under the Uniform Dispute Resolution Rules (discussed in more detail below). It was argued that:

> Ignoring the '.com' domain name extension, <dvla.com> is identical to the Complainant's famous DVLA name and trademarks. There is no difference between the Respondent's chosen domain name and the Complainant's trade name and trademarks. The impression given to web users is that the Respondent's domain name and the Complainant's marks are one and the same, that is, that any associated goods or services are sponsored by, endorsed by, or affiliated with the Complainant.

It was further argued that as the respondent traded under the name DVL Automation it would have a legitimate interest in the name DVL.com but not DVLA.com. It was also asserted that the respondent had no trade make registered in the name DVLA and no legitimate interest in its use. These arguments were unequivocaly rejected by the arbiter:

> The Complainant claims that the Respondent cannot have a legitimate interest in the domain name since it does not have a trademark in 'DVLA'. However, the Policy does not require, and has never required, that the Respondent have a registered mark for it to have a legitimate interest in a domain name. Alternatively the Complainant argues that the Respondent's trading name is 'DVL Automation' rather than 'DVLA', and therefore there is 'no reason why the Respondent should have any interest in a domain name incorporating "DVLA".' It is hard to know how to respond to this

---

[32] *Prince PLC v Prince Sports Group* [1998] FSR 21.
[33] <http://www.icann.org/dndr/udrp/uniform-rules.htm>

sort of assertion, except to say that if this were the standard by which a Respondent's legitimate interest was assessed then almost no Respondent could ever hope to retain its domain name. It is an unsupportable statement, on a par with the Complainant's assertion that the Respondent has no legitimate interest in the domain name 'since the Respondent trades as DVL Automation and not as DVLA.'

The Complainant's final assertion, that there 'is no evidence that the Respondent is making a legitimate non-commercial or fair use of the Domain Name' is dangerously close to an outright lie. The Complaint specifically discloses that the Complainant has seen the website at 'dvla.com', which the Respondent is using for its clearly bona fide business purposes, and which is utterly removed from vehicle licensing or any other usage which might be characterized as illegitimate. The Respondent is a registered company, doing business at a domain name which has an obvious connection with its company name. The Complainant notes as much in its Complaint, and yet it maintains this position. It cannot do so in good faith.

The conclusion was damning:

I consider that the Complainant has brought this action in bad faith. . . . the Complaint discloses that the Complainant is aware of the business and corporate status of the Respondent, and has examined the website available at the domain name. The domain name was registered over 6 years ago, and is being used for a legitimate business.

The DVLA case is in some respects a typical example of the issues which have arisen when a party seeks to stretch the level of protection conferred by trade marks. An alternative form of the practice as occurred in several cases is where the target of the complaint is what is generally referred to as a .sucks website. These are typically established by dissatisfied customers of an organisation and, prefixed with the name of a company, provide a forum for the ventilation of complaints against the company. The basic purpose of trade mark law is to prevent confusion in the minds of the public about the origin of goods or services and increasingly of a website. Perhaps reflecting the early and evolving nature of the cases, decisions have been contradictory and, as with the DVLA case, have been brought in the course of dispute resolution procedures established by ICANN or by national domain name registries. Consideration will next be given to the manner in which these procedures have been operated.

The Uniform Dispute Resolution Rules

A feature of early disputes concerned with rights relating to domain names was the attempt by domain name registries such as Network Solutions and Nominet to devise policies designed to render them immune from legal action. In many respects, the agencies were put in difficult legal positions. In the *Pitman* case[34] discussed above, for example, the domain name registry, Nominet, was threatened with legal action by one party unless the name was reassigned and with action by the other in the event that it was reassigned. A classic example of a 'no win' situation.

---

[34] *Pitman Training Ltd v Nominet United Kingdom* [1997] FSR 797.

With the emergence of ICANN as the co-ordinating body for the system of domain names, a new approach has been adopted to the problem of trying to resolve domain name disputes without invoking national courts. Any organisation wishing to act as a registry in respect of the generic domain names is obliged to conduct business according to the 'Uniform Domain Name Dispute Resolution Policy'.[35] This requires applicants for domain names to submit to mandatory dispute resolution procedures before approved dispute resolution service providers in the event of any claim that:

(i)   your domain name is identical or confusingly similar to a trademark or service mark in which the complainant has rights;

(ii) you have no rights or legitimate interests in respect of the domain name; and

(iii) your domain name has been registered and is being used in bad faith.

The onus is on a complainant to establish all of these heads of claim.[36]

Originally, four organisations were recognised as offering dispute resolution services under the ICANN rules:

The Asian Domain Name Dispute Resolution Centre[37]

CPR Institute for Dispute Resolution[38]

The National Arbitration Forum[39]

The World Intellectual Property Organisation.[40]

The CPR Institute and the National Arbitration Forum—which described itself as the 'largest provider of domain name dispute resolution in North America'—are no longer active in the field. Throughout, the major player has been the World Intellectual Property Organization, which as of 2007 had received almost 12,000 complaints concerning the use of domain names.

An early decision of the WIPO dispute resolution panel in the case of *Jeanette Winterson v Mark Hogarth* illustrates how these requirements might be applied. In this case, the complainant, a well-known author, objected to the registration of the domain names:

jeanettewinterson.com

jeanettewinterson.net

jeanettewinterson.org

by the respondent, a Cambridge University academic.[41]

---

[35] Available from <http://www.icann.org/udrp/udrp.htm>
[36] Uniform Dispute Resolution Rules, r 4a.
[37] <http://www.adndrc.org/adndrc/index.html>
[38] <http://www.cpradr.org/ICANN_Menu.htm>
[39] <http://www.arbforum.com/domains/>
[40] <http://arbiter.wipo.int/domains/>
[41] A copy of the decision can be obtained from <http://arbiter.wipo.int/domains/decisions/index.html>

In circumstances similar to those at issue in the *One in a Million* case,[42] the registrant had registered a range of domains, making use of the names of well-known authors. Contact had been made with a number of these; in the case of one, Joanna Trollope, a letter was sent to her literary agent indicating the intent to auction the names to third parties, but giving the author a right of 'first refusal' to acquire the names for a fee of 3 per cent of her 1999 gross book sales. Similar communications were made to the complainant.

In answering to complaints, the respondent wrote to the effect that:

> The Complainant also contends that the Respondent has no rights to or legitimate interests in respect of the domain names in issue, that the Complainant has not consented to use of the Mark by the Respondent and that the Respondent has registered and is using the domain names in bad faith.

The respondent stated that:

> ...he registered the domain names in issue in the belief that JEANETTE WINTERSON was not a trade mark or a service mark and that the domain names in issue were registered with a view to developing a website devoted to the work of the Complainant.

It was held by the panel that the Uniform Domain Name Dispute Resolution Policy required that a complainant establish all three grounds specified, namely, use of an identical or confusingly similar mark, in breach of a trade or service mark in which the respondent has no rights, and in circumstances evidencing bad faith.

It is clear that the name used is effectively identical to the complainant's name. More significant was the finding of the panel in respect of the next ground. Here, it was ruled that:

> The Rules do *not* require that the Complainant's trademark be registered by a government authority or agency for such a right to exist.

The complainant being resident in England, it was ruled, English law had to be applied to determine the extent of rights. The doctrine of passing off, it was held could also be invoked:

> 6.11 There are a number of English cases dealing with passing-off the names of well-known individuals and personalities, which all—as may be expected—turn on the facts. These include, the Uncle MAC case [*Mcculloch v Lewis A May (Produce Distributors) Ltd* [1947] 2 All ER 845]; the KOJAK case [*Taverner Rutledge v Trexpalm* (1975) FSR 479]; the WOMBLES case [*Wombles Ltd v Wombles Skips Ltd* [1977] RPC 99]; the ABBA case [*Lyngstad v Anabas Products* [1977] FSR 62]; and the Teenage Mutant Ninja Turtles case [*Mirage Studios v Counter Feat Clothing Co Ltd* [1991] FSR 145]. The case for decision here does not concern whether or not passing-off has occurred *but*

---

[42] *British Telecommunications plc, Virgin Enterprises Ltd, J Sainsbury plc, Marks & Spencer plc and Ladbroke Group plc v One in a Million* [1999] FSR 1.

whether the Complainant (Jeanette Winterson) has rights in her name sufficient to constitute a trade mark for the purposes of para. 4a of the Policy.

6.12 In the Panel's view, *trademarks* where used in para. 4a of the Policy is not to be construed by reference to the criteria of registrability under English law [the ELVIS PRESLEY case] but more broadly in terms of the distinctive features of a person's activities, in other words, akin to the common law right to prevent unauthorised use of a name. Thus, applying English law the Complainant clearly would have a cause of action to prevent unauthorized use of the Mark JEANETTE WINTERSON in passing-off.

The other tests being satisfied, the panel ordered that the registrations should be transferred to the complainant.

The decision in this case appears in line with the authorities cited. The complainant was a well-known and successful author and the effect of the registrations complained of would satisfy the criteria for the award of a remedy by the English courts. The English courts have never, however, accepted that any general right to personality exists which can be infringed by use of a name or other indications of identity.[43] It must remain an open question whether any action would lie against registrations such as those reported to have been made in the name of the recent Prime Minister Tony Blair's youngest son ('leoblair.com' and 'leoblair.co.uk').

Some time after the development of dispute resolution schemes for WWW sites within the generic top-level domains, a similar scheme was adopted to deal with disputes within the .uk top-level domain. Operated by the domain name registry, Nominet, a panel of around thirty experts act as adjudicators, with individual cases being heard by a single person.[44] The basis for any complaint is that there was 'abusive registration of a domain name'. This encompasses a domain name which either:

i. was registered or otherwise acquired in a manner which, at the time when the registration or acquisition took place, took unfair advantage of or was unfairly detrimental to the Complainant's Rights; OR

ii. has been used in a manner which took unfair advantage of or was unfairly detrimental to the Complainant's Rights.

Beyond substituting the perhaps more pejorative term 'abusive registration' for the ICANN criterion of 'bad faith', the substance of the policy is broadly similar.

The first decision under the new procedure was delivered in 2001. The pharmaceutical company, Eli Lilly, was successful in its application to have rights in the domain xigris.ci.uk transferred to it. Eli Lilly had obtained a European Community Trade Mark in the name Xigris in 1999. The domain name had been registered by an ex-employee in June 2001. No representations were made by the employee in response to Eli Lilley's complaint and although there was no evidence available as to the purpose for which the registration might have been made, the expert held that the

---

[43] See discussion in W. Cornish and D. Llewelyn, *Intellectual Property: Patents, Copyrights, Trademarks and Allied Rights* (London, 2007), paras 16.33–16.34.

[44] <http://www.nominet.org.uk/disputes/drs/>

circumstances surrounding the case were such that a prima facie case of abuse had been made out and that in the absence of any attempt at explanation, the request for transfer should be granted.[45]

In total, more than 6,000 disputes have been referred to the United Kingdom dispute resolution service, although around 25 per cent of these have been declared invalid on procedural grounds and did not therefore proceed to any form of dispute resolution. Following receipt of a valid complaint, the first step in the process is to attempt mediation and more than half of the cases are resolved at this stage. As of September 2007, 728 cases had proceeded to the stage of a hearing before an expert. In almost 80 per cent of cases the decision was in favour of the complainant but in three cases, as well as finding for the respondent, the expert made the determination that reverse domain-name hijacking had taken place. Appeals may be made against the decision of an individual expert. These will be heard before a panel of three experts. To date, twenty appeals have been made, half being determined in favour of the appellant and half sustaining the original decision. The roll-call of complainants includes some of the best-known names in the United Kingdom's commercial and public life, featuring organisations such as Harrods, Vodaphone, Barclays Bank, Nokia, the Royal Marines, and Interflora. It appears almost to be the case that an incident of cybersquatting is an integral consequence of commercial success.

Conclusions

With the emergence of global and national dispute resolution procedures, trade mark disputes involving the use of domain names appear to have largely vanished from the legal system. Although most disputes are settled, statistics from the dispute resolution organisations do show that the majority of decisions reached are in favour of the complainant. Given the nature of many of the incidents referred which involve blatant hijacking of the name of a business, this rate is not in itself a source of surprise. What may be a greater cause for concern is the fact that the law applied in a number of instances appears to be almost, but not quite, trade mark law. In one sense, disputes are being hijacked from the courts to tribunals which are strongly supported by commercial pressures. The approach, especially concerning the allocation of generic domain names, may represent a way forward for dispute resolution in what is an increasingly globalised society, but great care needs to be taken to ensure that it acquires a considerable measure of legitimacy and is not seen as the captive of particular interest groups.

Suggestions for further reading

'International Domain Name Disputes: Rules and Practice of the UDRP', *E.I.P.R.* 25(8) (2003), pp. 351–65.

'Domain Name Disputes: A Review of the Case Law', *Bar Review* 6(9) (2001), pp. 502–8.

[45] The full text of the decision can be obtained from <http://www.nic.uk/DisputeResolution/Decisions/EliLillyAndCompany-v-DavidClayton.html>

21

Competition and intellectual property issues

Introduction

It is an essential ingredient of intellectual property law that a right holder receives some form of exclusive right in respect of the subject-matter. In the case of patents, it is fair to say that the protection is monopolistic in nature, whilst even though the protection afforded under copyright law is restricted to the copying (or translation or adaptation) of a work, in practice the protection is again strong and there is no doubt that a copyright owner is in a position of dominance concerning the manner in which a work may be exploited.

The promotion of free and fair competition is a key objective of the EU and indeed of most national governments, certainly including the United Kingdom. There is a considerable degree of tension between the provisions of intellectual property law, which, it must be recalled, do constitute property rights and as such are not to be restricted without good cause and the provisions of competition law. From a relatively slow and tentative start, the relationship between the two concepts has recently assumed considerable importance and a good measure of controversy in the context of proceedings instituted by the European Commission against the United States-based software giant, Microsoft. This chapter will consider the development of case law in the sector and conclude with an assessment on whether the application of competition law principles might overcome some of the problems and difficulties identified with the operation of the copyright system in the context of software.

Initial developments

Whilst the provisions of the Treaty of Rome which established the EU do not impact upon the existence of intellectual property rights, the European Court has held that the provisions of Articles 81 and 82 (formerly Articles 85 and 86), dealing, respectively, with anti-competitive agreements between undertakings and conduct which is abusive of a dominant position, may restrict the extent to which they can be exercised. An illustration of the relationship between the concepts of competition and intellectual property law can be seen in the case of *Volvo v Veng*[1] involving a dispute between the well-known motor car manufacturer and Veng, who specialised in the supply of replacement body panels for use in the repair of damaged vehicles. As part of this business, Veng imported into the United Kingdom panels for Volvo cars, only for Volvo then to institute proceedings before the Patents Court, alleging breach of its registered design right in the panels in question. In their defence, Veng argued, inter alia, that Volvo's refusal to grant them a licence to manufacture the components in question on reasonable terms constituted an abuse of a dominant position.

The question of the compatibility of Volvo's conduct with the requirements of Article 86 of the EC Treaty was referred to the Court of Justice for a preliminary ruling. Holding that there was no infringement of Article 86, the court held that:

> the right of the proprietor of a protected design to prevent third parties from manufacturing and selling or importing, without its consent, products incorporating the design constitutes the very subject matter of his exclusive right. It follows that an obligation imposed upon the proprietor of a protected design to grant to third parties, even in return for a reasonable royalty, a licence for the supply of products incorporating the design would lead to the proprietor thereof being deprived of the substance of his exclusive right, and that a refusal to grant such a licence cannot in itself constitute an abuse of a dominant position.[2]

The court went on to suggest, however, that Article 86 of the EC Treaty might be invoked in response to:

> ...certain abusive conduct such as the arbitrary refusal to supply spare parts to independent repairers, the fixing of prices for spare parts at an unfair level or a decision no longer to produce spare parts for a particular model even though many cars of that model are still in circulation, provided that such conduct is liable to affect trade between Member States.[3]

The issue has subsequently returned to the European Court, most recently in the context of proceedings brought by the European Commission against Microsoft. Initial consideration will be given, however, to the case of *Radio Telefis Eireann (RTE) v European Commission*,[4] which established for the first time situations in which the use of intellectual property rights could amount to a contravention of Article 82.

Television listings

In the time before satellite television, viewers in the Republic of Ireland and some parts of Northern Ireland were able to choose from six television channels: the then four available on the British mainland broadcast by the British Broadcasting Corporation (BBC) and by Independent Television (ITP) and, in addition, RTE and RTE2, which

---

[1] [1988] ECR 6211.
[2] *Volvo v Veng* [1988] ECR 6211 at 6235.
[3] *Volvo v Veng* [1988] ECR 6211.
[4] [1995] All ER (EC) 416.

are broadcast by Radio Telefis Eireann (RTE) within the Irish Republic. At the time of the case, in neither part of Ireland was there available any comprehensive guide to all programmes scheduled to be broadcast. Each company distributed its own separate guide in which copyright was claimed under the respective United Kingdom and Irish Copyright Acts. Although newspapers were provided with programme details to allow them to print daily schedules, the broadcasters retained exclusive rights to publish and distribute weekly programme schedules.

In May 1986, a company called Magill Publications produced a magazine containing weekly programme schedules for all the television channels available in Ireland. The ITP, BBC, and RTE unsuccessfully applied to an Irish court for an injunction to prevent continued publication of this guide on the ground that it infringed the copyright in the companies' programme schedules. These were held to be the result of a process of planning, preparation, and the use of expert appraisal of content and layout and, as such, entitled to protection as compilations.

Prior to this decision, Magill had registered a complaint with the European Commission under Articles 85 and 86 of the EC Treaty, arguing that the ITP, BBC, and RTE were abusing a dominant position by refusing to allow third parties to publish their television listings. This complaint was investigated by the Commission, which issued a Decision on 21 December 1988.[5] This upheld Magill's complaints, finding that the ITP, BBC, and RTE did hold a dominant position within Article 86, that third parties were being prevented from competing by the existence of the monopoly enjoyed by the broadcasting companies, and, further, that by claiming copyright, an economic monopoly had been reinforced by a legal monopoly. The Commission rejected the argument that copyright was justified and stated its view that copyright was being used to prevent free competition. The broadcasting companies were ordered to permit reproduction of their programme schedules by granting licences to third parties. The three organisations involved brought an appeal against this decision before the European Court.

A number of the arguments concerned the definition of the relevant market. In respect of the claim that the invocation of the appellants' intellectual property rights constituted an abuse under Article 86 of the EC Treaty, it was argued that action taken to protect the subject of their intellectual property right could not constitute an abuse, and claimed that the Treaty did not affect such rights as were given in the Member States. The existence of copyright allowed them to retain an exclusive right to reproduce the subject of the copyright protection.

The Commission rejected this view of the scope of copyright. The national rules granting copyright to television schedules, it was argued, allowed broadcasting companies to gain an unlawful monopoly on the production of weekly guides and prevented the publication of any competing guide. To this extent, the existence of copyright would obstruct the achievement of a single market in broadcasting services. To resolve the conflict between copyright and competition, the Commission indicated that the correct approach was to identify the 'specific subject matter' of the intellectual

---

[5] Decision 89/205/EEC, OJ 1989 L 78, p. 43.

property right, which might qualify for special protection and which might justify an exception to the Community rules on competition.

The Commission first asserted that the television guides were not 'secret, innovative or related to research' and stated that the only reason for retaining copyright was to 'reserve a monopoly'. The sole reason for refusing to authorise the Magill guide was to prevent the publication of a competing product. The fact that programme information was distributed by the broadcasting companies to daily newspapers which do not compete with weekly guides was held to be arbitrary and discriminatory. A copyright holder could not choose to allow reproduction of its daily information and yet seek to prevent publication of a competing weekly guide. Enforcement of copyright was being used to restrict competition.

A distinction was drawn between the *Volvo* case[6] discussed above and the situation presently at issue. In the former case, the manufacturer reserved to itself the exclusive right to manufacture spare parts, i.e. no third parties were authorised to utilise the designs. By way of contrast, the television companies involved had authorised newspapers and other periodicals to publish their listings on a daily basis. This rendered their refusal to offer licences to Magill arbitrary. It was further pointed out that whilst the market for spare parts fell within the main part of a motor manufacturer's activities, the publishing of details of television broadcasts was an activity separate and downstream from that of broadcasting, which constituted the *raison d'être* of the appellants. Finally, the Commission pointed out that the effect of the appellants' conduct was to prevent the appearance of a new product (a general listings magazine) for which there was public demand. In the *Volvo* case, the products were available to the public whilst considerable competition remained both between independent repairers and from other manufacturers.

After presenting this analysis, the Commission commented significantly, if ambiguously, to the effect that:

> ...its analysis of the abuse of copyright applies also to situations different from that at issue in this case, in the area of computer software for example.[7]

The Court of First Instance upheld the Commission's Decision in all respects. Referring to previous decisions, it held that the reconciliation between the provisions of intellectual property law, which remained a matter for national authorities,[8] and the Treaty provisions relating to the free movement of goods and the maintenance of competition, required that a distinction be drawn between legitimate and illegitimate aspects of the exercise of the rights. In principle, it was accepted that:

> ...the two essential rights of the author, namely the exclusive right of performance and the exclusive right of reproduction are not called in question by the rules of the [EC] Treaty.[9]

---

[6] *Volvo v Veng* [1988] ECR 6211.

[7] *Independent Television Publications v EC Commission* Case T–76/89 [1991] 4 CMLR 745 at 761.

[8] Subject now to a partial exception in the case of the Commission Directive on the Legal Protection of Computer Programs and Data, 91/250/EC, OJ 1991 L 122, p. 42.

[9] *Warner Bros Inc v Christiansen* [1988] ECR 2605 at 2629.

However, the court went on to state that:

> ...while it is plain that the exercise of the exclusive right to reproduce a protected work is not in itself an abuse, that does not apply when, in the light of the details of each individual case, it is apparent that the right is exercised in such ways and circumstances as in fact to pursue an aim manifestly contrary to the objectives of Article 86. In that event, the copyright is no longer exercised in a manner which corresponds to its essential function...which is to protect the moral rights in the work and to ensure a reward for the creative effort, while respecting the aims of, in particular, Article 86 [of the EC Treaty].[10]

The concept of a distinction between the essential functions of intellectual property rights and any remaining attributes is one which may prove easier to define in principle than in practice. In terms of its application to software, whilst there is no doubt that a copyright owner may take action to prevent the direct copying of their work, it might be that attempts to prevent non-literal reproduction might infringe Article 86 of the EC Treaty. Again, and always assuming that the copyright owner is accepted as occupying a dominant position, a refusal to issue licences to third parties to produce programs that were functionally compatible with the original might be considered unlawful.

An appeal was lodged by the television companies against the Court of First Instance's ruling. In 1994, the Advocate General (Gulmann) delivered an opinion supporting the appeal. After analysing relevant case law concerning the relationship between the Community's competition policy and the system of intellectual property rights, he concluded that:

> The specific subject matter of copyright does unreservedly include a right to refuse to grant licences and the imposition of a compulsory licence pursuant to Article 86 constitutes interference with the specific subject matter.[11]

It was only in the situation where an intellectual property right holder sought to exercise rights to prevent the development of a work which did not compete with the subject-matter of the right that there would be any prospect that the provisions of Article 86 of the EC Treaty could overrule this basic aspect of the copyright system. Continuing, the Advocate General addressed an argument advanced by the Commission that a distinction should be drawn between literary and artistic works and functional products such as computer programs. Concern was expressed by the Commission that a failure to grant licences in the software field could prevent effective competition and argued that the solution to such a problem should lie with legislation rather than a strained interpretation of the Treaty. Accordingly, he recommended that the decision of the Court of First Instance should be reversed.

---

[10] *Independent Television Publications v Commission of the European Communities* [1991] CMLR 745 at 767.

[11] [1991] 4 CMLR 745 at para. 53.

Notwithstanding the strong recommendations of the Advocate General, the Court of Justice affirmed the judgment of the Court of First Instance. Whilst:

> ...in the absence of Community standardisation or harmonisation of laws, determination of the conditions and procedures for granting protection of an intellectual property right is a matter for national rules. Further, the exclusive right of reproduction forms part of the author's rights, so that refusal to grant a licence, even if it is the act of an undertaking holding a dominant position, cannot in itself constitute abuse of a dominant position.[12]

In 'exceptional circumstances', however, it was held that the exercise of an exclusive right might constitute abusive conduct. This was the case in the present action, with the court determining that the appellant's conduct was such as to prevent a new form of product from appearing on the market. Stress was also laid on the fact that the market for TV guides constituted a secondary market to the appellant's broadcasting operations. Under these situations, a breach of Article 82 of the Treaty had occurred.

The Microsoft litigation

The decision in *Radio Telefis Eireann (RTE) v European Commission* established the principle that limits could be applied concerning the extent to which intellectual property rights could be invoked. Because the activity of publishing was somewhat peripheral to the broadcasting functions of the appellants, uncertainty remained as to the extent to which competition law might limit the extent to which the owner of intellectual property rights could utilise these to prevent competition in its core markets. The long-running dispute between the European Commission and Microsoft reached its conclusion with the decision of the European Court of Justice in September 2007, a decision which may have significant consequences for the information technology industry.

The origins of the case date back to 1998, when Sun Microsystems, themselves a major player in the IT sector filed a complaint with the Commission regarding Microsoft's alleged refusal to supply it with information necessary to allow it to ensure that its products would operate properly with Micosoft's Windows operating system. The Sun products at issue were classed as work group servers. These devices effectively network a number of personal computers to provide a potentially wide range of services, including printing, Intranet and Internet content, email, databases, and shared access to software products such as word processing packages. Microsoft itself produces work group servers and the gist of Sun's complaint was that by failing to make available to competitors all the information required for effective interoperability, it was attempting to lever its dominant position in the market for PC operating system software into the more competitive market for work group software by virtue of the fact that its server software was better integrated with Windows. An indication of the

---

[12] Ibid. at para. 49.

effectiveness of the strategy might be taken from the fact that between 1999 and 2007, the Microsoft share of the server market rose from 35 to 75 per cent.[13]

The Commission commenced an investigation which expanded to encompass other aspects of Microsoft's behaviour and a further complaint was lodged concerning Microsoft's practice of including Windows Media Player in its operating system. Such an approach, it was argued, made it difficult for the producers of competing products, such as Real Player, to develop market share.

Following prolonged investigations and negotiations, the Commission adopted a decision in March 2004.[14] This found Microsoft to be in breach of Article 82 in respect of both the grounds of complaint and imposed a fine of nearly €500 million (about £370 million). Microsoft was ordered to make interoperability information available to its competitors in respect of the work group software and also to make available a version of its Windows operating system without its media player. Microsoft lodged an appeal against the decision and sought suspension of the application of the decision, pending conclusion of the appeal proceedings. An initial stay was adopted but following an interim decision from the Court of First Instance[15] in March 2005, it was held that the Decision should be enforced. In a further Decision of November 2005, the Commission gave Microsoft a period of 35 days to comply with the further sanction of additional fines of €2 million for each day of continuing non-compliance. In the Commission's view, Microsoft continued to fail to comply and in July 2006, it was announced that a penalty payment of €238 million would be invoked in respect of the time which had elapsed since the entry into force of the November 2005 decision and that the level of fines was to be increased to €3 million a day.[16] The penalties continued until 22 October 2007, when the Commission announced that it considered Microsoft to be in compliance with the original decision.

The final decision of the Court of First Instance confirmed the Commission decision in all substantive respects. In respect of the exceptional situations in which the requirements of competition law might prevail over the exercise of intellectual property rights, it was held that three factors had to be present:

- in the first place, the refusal relates to a product or service indispensable to the exercise of a particular activity on a neighbouring market;

- in the second place, the refusal is of such a kind as to exclude any effective competition on that neighbouring market;

- in the third place, the refusal prevents the appearance of a new product for which there is potential consumer demand.[17]

---

[13] <http://www.betanews.com/article/EU_Microsoft_Exhibiting_Abusive_Behavior/1174580417>

[14] Decision 2007/53/EC OJ 2007 L32/23. The text of the decision, which runs to 302 pages, is available from <http://ec.europa.eu/comm/competition/antitrust/cases/decisions/37792/en.pdf>

[15] Case T–201/04. Judgment available from <http://curia.europa.eu>

[16] <http://ec.europa.eu/comm/competition/antitrust/cases/decisions/37792/art24_2_decision.pdf>

[17] At para. 332.

The first task facing the court in any competition case is to define what constitutes the relevant market. This can be a complex task, with questions on whether one product might be seen by users as a substitute for another. In one leading case, for example, the European Court of Justice held that consumers might accept a glass of wine as an alternative to a glass of beer. In the present case, the matter was less complicated. Three markets were identified. First, that for PC operating systems. Here, it was found that Microsoft had in the region of a 90 per cent market share, something which clearly equated to a position of dominance. Second, was the market for work-group server software designed to provide 'basic infrastructure services' to computers on small- to medium-sized networks. There was some debate as to what features were to be found in such software but the issue was not critical to the judgment. Again, the Commission had concluded that Microsoft had a dominant position in this market, with a share of around 60 per cent. The third market was that for streaming media services. The first argument was that Microsoft had a dominant position in the PC software market and that it had abused this position of dominance by refusing to provide competitors with sufficient information to allow their work-group server software to achieve sufficient interoperability with computers running Microsoft Windows. The second argument was broadly similar, claiming that Microsoft had abused its dominant position in the PC operating system market by including an application package in the form of Media Player, thereby making it difficult for third-party producers of this form of product to compete with Microsoft.

In respect of the work-group server market, Microsoft contended that it had made sufficient information available to competitors to allow them to achieve interoperability with Windows-based PCs and that to require the provision of more information would mean:

> that its competitors' operating systems must function in every respect as a Windows server operating system. That situation could be achieved only if those competitors were allowed to 'clone' its products, or some of their features, and if information on the internal mechanisms of its products were communicated to those competitors.

Such a requirement, it was asserted, would render Microsoft's intellectual property rights of little value.

Much of the discussion before the court focused on the extent of the concept of interoperability at the qualitative level. Reference was made to market research surveys which suggested that users believed that the Microsoft server software integrated better with Windows than did its competitors, although in terms of the quality of the work-group servers, per se, the Microsoft products were less highly regarded than most of their competitors. This suggested that the level of information made available to competitors was not sufficient and the court upheld the Commission's decision, requiring that Microsoft make available:

> The complete and accurate specifications for all the *Protocols* implemented in *Windows Work Group Server Operating Systems* and that are used by *Windows Group Servers* to deliver file and print services and group and administration services, Active Directory services and Group Policy Services to *Windows Group Networks*.

The term 'protocol' is defined to encompass:

> A set of rules of interconnection and interaction between various instances *of Windows Work Group Operating Systems* and *Windows Client PC Operating Systems* running on different computers in a *Windows Work Group Network*.[18]

Such a requirement, it was emphasised, would not allow the competitors to copy any element of Microsoft's software. In many respects, the decision, or at least the form of conduct envisaged might be seen as akin to that at issue in *Navitaire v easyJet* in Chapter 17 discussed above.[19]

The second element of the case concerned the bundling of Windows Media sofware in copies of Windows. One of the practices prohibited under competition law is that of tying unrelated obligations into a contract for the supply of one item. A simple example might see a drinks manufacturer refusing to supply these goods unless the customer also agrees to buy crisps and peanuts from them. Microsoft argued that the concept and nature of computer operating systems had expanded over the years and that a product such as a media player which would previously have been regarded as an applications program should now be regarded as an integral part of the operating system. It was pointed out that other major operating systems such as that developed by Apple included media players as an integral element. This contention was rejected by the Commission and the court. What other system suppliers did was of limited relevance as they did not enjoy Microsoft's position of dominance in the market. The fact that other suppliers, notably Real Player, offered media players as a stand-alone product indicated, it was held, that the markets were separate and it was held that Microsoft's intention in bundling the products was to secure a competitive advantage. The court concluded that:

> The Commission is correct to make the following findings:
>
> – Microsoft uses Windows as a distribution channel to ensure for itself a significant competitive advantage on the media players market...;
>
> – because of the bundling, Microsoft's competitors are a priori at a disadvantage even if their products are inherently better than Windows Media Player (ibid.);
>
> – Microsoft interferes with the normal competitive process which would benefit users by ensuring quicker cycles of innovation as a consequence of unfettered competition on the merits.[20]

Having found that Microsoft's conduct constituted a breach of Article 82, the court upheld the Commission's ruling to the effect that Microsoft should make available to its customers a version of Windows which did not incorporate Media Player.

It is unclear how effective the ruling will prove in practice. Microsoft are expressly permitted to continue supplying Windows with Media Player included, and given that

---

[18] Decision 2007/53/EC Article 1. OJ 2007 L32/23.

[19] easyJet 2004 EWHC 1725 (Ch).

[20] At para. 1088.

it has been indicated that the price for the inclusive version of Windows will be exactly the same as that for the version with Media Player removed, it is difficult to see why any customer would choose the latter option.

Conclusions

The Microsoft litigation demonstrates clearly the tensions which can exist between intellectual property rights and competition policy. It should be stressed that it is only in exceptional cases that the provisions of the latter branch of the law will prevail. Few companies enjoy the position of dominance that Microsoft possesses in the market for PC software. It appears that the dispute between Microsoft and the Commission may still have some distance to run. In January 2008, it was announced that a further investigation was being instituted concerning Microsoft's bundling of its web browser, Internet Explorer, with the Windows operating system. The investigation follows complaints received from the developer of an independent web browser, 'Opera'.

PART IV

LEGAL ISSUES OF THE INTERNET

22

Internet regulation and the rise, fall, and rise of .com

Introduction

This chapter will attempt to address some of the legal implications arising both from the emergence of the Internet and the uses to which it may be put. As stated, the communications sector has always been regulated and the Internet is no exception. In some respects, it may be argued that the Internet is the most heavily regulated electronic communications network in that activities carried out over it are subject, in theory if not always in practice, to a mass of legal regulation. When it comes to the issue of regulation of the overall network, reference to specific legal provisions is limited. Reference to the Internet is entirely lacking in the Communications Act 2003, which provides the basis for the regulation of electronic communications networks and services and, indeed, government ministers were at pains on numerous occasions to point out that the measure was not intended to regulate the Internet. Communications regulation has tended to operate at a national level, with international agencies such as the International Telecommunications Union operating at a functional rather than a policy level in respect of international communications. Almost from its outset, the Internet has functioned on an international basis and the question of who controls it assumes considerable political and legal importance. Depending on the perspective of the commentator, for most of its existence, the Internet could be described either as being governed on the basis of consensus amongst Internet users or directed by an unelected, self-perpetuating clique. Regulatory structures have tended to evolve rather than develop in any structured manner, and a baffling range of organisations and acronyms need to be confronted in any attempt to understand the manner in which the Internet operates and is controlled. This chapter will initially describe the nature of the organisations which have been involved in Internet regulation and seek to analyse the legal basis for their activities.

In its early days, Internet-based operations made little impact upon the average person. Whilst its initial status as almost a form of private members' club continues to influence debate as to the future shape and form of regulation, with some users calling for the law to provide the same freedom for internal self-regulation as is afforded to voluntary organisations, the prevailing view is that the Internet's effect on the wider world is such as to call for a greater degree of legal involvement. One of the major forces for change has undoubtedly been the increasing use of the Internet for commercial purposes. At the beginning of the twenty-first century there seemed to be no limits to the potential growth of commercial activities on the Internet. Investors rushed to take a stake in any and every form of business and share values soared to dizzying levels. In November 1999, *Fortune* magazine reported that the Internet bookseller Amazon's share capital was seventeen times greater than that of the world's largest 'bricks and mortar' book chain-store, Barnes and Noble, and that it had a market value five times greater than Barnes and Noble. The so-called dot com phenomenon was widely seen as an unstoppable force, which would revolutionise the world of commerce. Contemporaneously with a more general fall in worldwide share values, what has come to be referred to as e-commerce saw its progress come to a halt, with many of the pioneering ventures finding their future in the bankruptcy courts rather than in the company of established retail giants.

More recently, there has been something of a renaissance in the scale and perceived utility of e-commerce as organisations have come to realise where the strengths and weaknesses of this form of activity lie. It has been suggested that ecommunications involve a switch from 'bricks and mortar' to 'clicks and mortar' and the true value of e-commerce lies in the facility to provide information-based products and services. This definition encompasses subjects such as airline tickets, where leading budget airlines provide figures showing that more than 90 per cent of flights are purchased over the Internet. Even more traditional airlines are moving to systems of electronic ticketing, although the increased security requirements being imposed on airlines in the aftermath of September 11 are making paperless travel a largely unattainable goal. Whilst some product retailers continue—such as Amazon, which has recently announced its first trading profits—these do tend to operate either in niche markets or in fields where the value of goods is primarily determined by content rather than by weight. The second section of the chapter will consider the nature and legal implications of applications of e-commerce.

The emergence of Internet regulation

It is often stated that the person who controls access to files and records is the most powerful individual in any organisation or, indeed, state. In large part, Internet traffic is carried over communications networks owned and controlled by a range of public and private sector communications providers. The decision of the European Commission prohibiting a proposed merger between the United States-based telecommunications companies, MCI/Sprint and Worldcom, provides much useful information about the nature of the technology underpinning the Internet. Although frequently viewed as a network in which all users are equal, the Commission decision shows that this is far from the case at the level where individuals and Internet Service Providers (ISPs) are connected to the global network. As the decision states:

> The Internet is an interconnected 'networks of networks' that carries bits of data between two or more computers through thousands of interconnected networks. Approximately 300 networks providing Internet connectivity operate long distance

transmission networks that, together, form the global Internet's international 'back-bone'. A handful of these operate networks that connect to multiple countries in more than one region. It is estimated that the ten largest Internet connectivity providers control 70 percent of international Internet bandwidth. Below the top tier providers are a number of Internet connectivity providers that operate at regional level (Europe, USA and Asia).[1]

Whilst communications companies may carry traffic, for any form of two-way communication it is a basic necessity that the parties should be able to identify each other. Once there is a movement from direct contact to the involvement of some form of intermediary to act as a conduit for the transmission of a message there is need for some unique and individual form of identification. This may take the form of indica-tors, both of individual identity and of geographical location. An obvious example is that of a postal address. As time has moved on, so there has been a move from an emphasis on names to one where numbers become the prime identifier. From house names, the vast majority of addresses are now identified by some form of number, whether identifying the location of a flat within a larger building or a particular house in a street. Above all, perhaps, the ubiquitous postcode serves as one of the closest equivalents to an identity card in current British society.

From a human perspective, names offer many benefits, especially in the form of ease of recognition and recollection. Perhaps indicative of human limitations, the average person has a greater facility for remembering words than numbers. From an efficiency standpoint, however, numbers possess overwhelming advantages. Names may often be duplicated so that there are, for example, towns called Glasgow in Jamaica, South Africa, and Zimbabwe. In the United States, there are Glasgows in Alabama, Minnesota, Delaware, Iowa, California, Georgia, Illinois, Missouri, Ohio, Oregon, West Virginia, Kentucky, Missouri, Montana, North Carolina, Virginia, and Pennsylvania.[2] There is, however, only one city of Glasgow with the telephone dialling code of 0141.

Until the 1960s, most telephone exchanges were referred to using an abbreviated form of the area covered. Telephone numbers for the town of Kirkintilloch, for exam-ple, would use the code KIR.[3] In reality, of course, as those familiar with sending text messages on mobile phones will be aware, the letters matched to numbers on the telephone dial or keypad.[4] Given that each number typically occupies the space

---

[1] Case No. COMP/M. 1741-MCI at para. 16.

[2] <http://bmcphee.com/glasgow_places.htm>

[3] For more information on old dialling codes, see <http://www.telephonesuk.co.uk/old_dialing_codes. htm#ODC>

[4] Recently, a number of companies have sought to obtain telephone numbers which relate to letters in such a way as to promote their business. In evidence before the Select Committee on Trade and Industry in 1999, the Director General of Telecommunication cited the case of a travel agency called Boomerang Travel, whose telephone number translated to '4 Australia'. Two practical problems were identified with this tech-nique. First, many fixed-line phones are marked solely with numbers. Second, even when letters are used, the Director reported that there are four different variations in the manner in which the letters ABCDEF are presented. Depending on the pattern used, the consequence might be a wrong number.

associated with three or four letters, the number of memorable combinations was severely limited, even at the national level. The *Oxford English Dictionary*, for example, references some 290,000 words and 615,000 word forms. As the telephone network expanded and as it became possible for users to dial directly on an international basis, so the complexity of numbers increased. Clearly, there cannot be enough memorable words to go around as telephone identifiers and for the past thirty years, the United Kingdom telephone system has worked solely on the basis of numbers.

In some ways, the emergence of the Internet has seen a reversion towards names as a means of identifier. Although at the technical level the Internet functions exclusively through the processing of IP numbers, the system of domain names has been adopted as a more 'user friendly' form of identifier. In similar manner to the system of telephone names, letters are effectively translated into numbers, although unlike telephone dials, there is no direct correlation between letter and number.

The TCP/IP protocols enable any user to connect to the Internet. There are no social or political controls over the making of a connection and cost implications are minimal. All computers linked to the Internet are allocated a unique identifier known as an IP number. At present, these are 32 binary digits in length (normally in the region of eight or nine decimal numbers). Just as Oftel required to insert an extra '1' into all United Kingdom telephone numbers in 1994 in order to secure what appears to be temporary relief from a shortage of available numbers, so has the exponential rate of growth in Internet usage, compounded by the increasing availability of Internet access via mobile phones, led to the introduction of a new numbering system known as IP V6. An increase in number length to 128-bit numbers is calculated to provide capacity for some 340 billion, billion, billion, billion computers. Even at the Internet's (and mobile phone networks') current rates of expansion, this should be sufficient for the foreseeable future, although take-up of the new system remains slow.

The issuance of IP numbers is a relatively non-problematic task. As with phone numbers, although some combinations might be more memorable than others, this is a matter of limited importance. Initially, all Internet connections were referred to solely by IP number. As the number of users increased, so pressure grew for a more memorable means of identification. In 1987, the system of domain names came into effect. Typically, users will seek to use some form of name which has a connection with their real-life existence. In the educational sector, for example, most institutions will make use of some form of abbreviation of their name. Strathclyde University, for example, uses the designator 'strath', whilst Southampton can be found at 'soton'. With the increasing commercialisation of the Internet, firms will also wish to have their real-life identity mirrored in their Internet address.

At the outset, it should be stressed that for the working of the Internet, it is a user's IP number which is critical. Typing an address such as http://itlaw.law.strath.ac.uk in a web browser initiates a process of trying to match the name with the appropriate IP number. Initially, the attempt will be made by the ISP's own equipment. If it fails to make a match, the query will be passed on to more comprehensive name servers, a process known as domain name resolution. The definitive tables of names and numbers are maintained on what are referred to as root servers. There are thirteen of these machines. Ten are located in the United States, with the remaining three being in England, Japan, and Sweden. The key root server is maintained by Network Solutions, with the other servers downloading information about new domains from this server on a daily basis. Although many ISPs will maintain their own Domain Name Server, the information on this will invariably have been copied, perhaps with a delay of a few days, from the root servers. In order to be accessible to the Internet world, therefore, it is imperative that a user be issued with an IP number and that the registered name and domain be accepted by the Network Solutions root server.

Whilst, as discussed above, the supply of IP numbers is virtually inexhaustible, words are in rather shorter supply. A typical directory might contain in the region of 200,000 words. At the level of personal names, large numbers of individuals coexist happily under the same identifiers. The Glasgow telephone directory, for example, lists some twenty pages of McDonalds. Because each domain name has to be mapped with a specific IP number, the Internet is not nearly as flexible. Although, as will be discussed below, the domain name structure offers a range of categories based both on national origin and nature of activity, the issue of allocation of and rights to particular domain names remains one of the most problematic aspects of the Internet and its regulation.

The domain name structure

Two initial categories of domain name can be identified—generic and country code. There are currently ten generic domain names, some widely available but others limited to fairly narrow categories of users. Technical support for each domain name is provided by an organisation known as a registry. Effectively, each registry will maintain the definitive database of all names allocated and their associated IP numbers:

- .aero—(restricted to certain members of the glob\l aviation community) sponsored by Société Internationale de Télécommunications Aéronautiques SC (SITA);
- .biz—(restricted to businesses) operated by NeuLevel;
- .com—operated by Verisign Global Registry Services;
- .coop—(restricted to cooperatives) sponsored by Dot Cooperation LLC;
- .info—operated by Afilias Limited;
- .museum—(restricted to museums and related persons) sponsored by the Museum Domain Management Association (MuseDoma);
- .name—(restricted to individuals) operated by Global Name Registry;
- .net—operated by Verisign Global Registry Services;
- .org—operated by Public Interest Registry; and
- .pro—(restricted to licensed professionals) operated by Registry Pro.

Additionally, the domains .edu, .gov, and .mil are reserved for United States users, and the domain .int for recognised international agencies.

These names carry no indication of country of origin. Although it is sometimes assumed that the names 'belong' to the United States,[5] this is not the case and many companies operating on an international basis see value in possessing a non-country-specific identifier. British Airways, for example, has a website at http://www.britishairways.com.

There also exists what are referred to as country code domain names. Based on ISO standard 3166, these consist of a two-letter denominator for every country in the world. The United Kingdom, for example, is referred to as .uk, France as .fr, and Germany as .de. It should be noted that there is no requirement that a company be established or operate in a particular country in order to register a domain name in that location. One country domain name with an interesting tale is that of Tuvalu. Tuvalu is a collection of nine, small coral atolls in the Pacific Ocean close to Fiji. It is classed as a 'Least Developed Country', with a population of about 10,000 and a GDP of $11 million. Its only export is copra. It has one computer connected to the Internet. It also 'possesses' the ISO code of TV and, in 1998, entered into a deal worth $50 million with a Canadian company to licensing rights to the domain .tv. The company planned to sell domain names to television companies wishing to establish a web presence. Sadly for the Tuvaluans, the deal fell through when the company failed to make payments, although it has recently been announced that a similar, albeit less valuable, agreement has been concluded. Other locations which have proved popular 'homes' for websites are Tonga, whose ISO code is .to, and Italy, with the designator .it.

In most countries, there is a further indicator of the nature of the business. In the United Kingdom, domain names may be registered in the following categories:

Name	Intended usage
ac.uk	Academic
co.uk	Commercial
gov.uk	Governmental
ltd.uk	Limited liability companies
mod.uk	Ministry of Defence
net.uk	Internet networks
nhs.uk	National Health Service
plc.uk	Public limited companies
police.uk	Police
sch.uk	Schools

Administration of domain names

The allocation of IP numbers was initially administered by an organisation, the Internet Assigned Numbers Authority (IANA), which is part of the Information

---

[5] Two other generic codes, .gov and .mil, are restricted to United States governmental and military organisations. A further code, .edu, is primarily, although not exclusively, used by United States educational establishments.

Science Institute within the University of Southern California. Its web page[6] proclaims that it is: 'Dedicated to preserving the central co-ordinating functions of the global Internet for the public good.'

Initially, IANA also allocated domain names but from 1993, although it continued to play what has been described as a coordinating role, the task has been conducted by a range of domain name registries. Whilst some of these are based in the public sector, the majority are private sector companies. In respect of most of the generic domain names, the United States National Science Foundation, which sponsored much of the pioneering development work on the Internet, entered into a five-year contract with a commercial organisation, Network Solutions Inc,[7] for the management of most of the generic domains.

The operation of the system of domain names has been the source of much controversy and some litigation in recent years. As indicated above, although we are all used to domain names such as strath.ac.uk, there is no technical reason why this is required, the name being merely an alias for the critical IP number. Some organisations have sought to set up alternative domain structures. One such company is Name.Space which offers no fewer than 517 top-level domains, including such delights as .beer and .president.[8] The main problem that the company has faced has been the refusal of the keepers of the Internet root servers to include details of its users on their machines. Effectively, this significantly limits the range of persons with whom their users can communicate.

Faced with this refusal to include its details, a lawsuit was raised, *PGMedia, Inc D/B/A Name.Space v Network Solutions Inc and the National Science Foundation*.[9] The basis for the complaint was that the defendants were in breach of United States antitrust law and, by preventing the claimant and its customers using such names as they wished, were in violation of the United States Constitution's guarantee of free speech. The claims were dismissed by the United States District Court in March 1999 and a subsequent appeal was also rejected.

Although the District Court upheld the role of Network Solutions and the National Science Foundation, changes have been occurring from other directions. Concern at the working of the system of Internet domain names had been rising, not least prompted by the limited number of domains creating scarcity of what were perceived as suitable domain names. To give an example, the domain name aba.com is registered to the American Bankers Association, aba.org to the America Birding Association, and aba.net to a company, Ansaback, which provides email auto-respond services. All appear bona fide organisations, but there is no room left for the perhaps better-known (at least to lawyers) American Bar Association, whose WWW site has to use the less intuitive domain name abanet.net.

---

[6] <http://www.iana.org/>
[7] <http://www.networksolutions.com/>
[8] See <http://namespace.autono.net/>
[9] 202 F 3d 573 (2000).

National domain names

The situation with regard to the national domains is rather more complex, with a mix of public and private sector organisations playing the role of domain name registry. In the United Kingdom, this role is played by a non-profit-making company Nominet.[10] As with much of the Internet, the legal basis for its actions is unclear, it being stated that:

> Nominet UK derives its authority from the Internet industry in the UK and is recognised as the UK registry by the Internet Assigned Numbers Authority (IANA) in the USA.

Reform of Internet regulation

Given the increasing economic importance of the Internet, concern grew from the mid-1990s over the somewhat nebulous legal status under which it operated. Concerns were also expressed at the extent of United States dominance over the working of what was becoming a vital global communications network. This was especially noticeable in the field of domain names dispute resolution policies. Network Solutions, which possessed a monopoly concerning the registration of names in the .com domain, adopted a range of procedures which afforded greater weight to United States trademark rights than to those emanating from other jurisdictions.

The Internet International Ad Hoc Committee (IAHC) was established in 1996 'at the initiative of the Internet Society, and at the request of the Internet Assigned Numbers Authority', with the remit to:

> resolve a difficult and long-standing set of challenges in the Domain Name System, namely enhancing its use while attempting to juggle such concerns as administrative fairness, operational robustness and protection of intellectual property.

The IAHC recommended that administration of the .com domain should be removed from the sole control of Network Solutions and made available to a number of competing registries. It also recommended an expansion in the number of generic domains. At the conclusion of its work, the IAHC put forward for signature by the various interest groups a Generic Top Level Domain Memorandum of Understanding. The work of the IAHC culminated in the conclusion of a Generic Top Level Domain Memorandum of Understanding (gTLD-MoU). The Memorandum, which is published in the name of the 'Internet Community' endorsed the final report of the IAHC, which recommended expansion of the number of generic top-level domains and adopted a set of six principles:

- the Internet Top Level Domain (TLD) name space is a public resource and is subject to the public trust;
- any administration, use and/or evolution of the Internet TLD space is a public policy issue and should be carried out in the interests and service of the public;

---

[10] <http://www.nic.uk/>

- related public policy needs to balance and represent the interests of the current and future stakeholders in the Internet name space;
- the current and future Internet name space stakeholders can benefit most from a self-regulatory and market-oriented approach to Internet domain name registration services;
- registration services for the gTLD name space should provide for global distribution of registrars;
- a policy shall be implemented that a second-level domain name in any of the CORE-gTLDs which is identical or closely similar to an alphanumeric string that, for the purposes of this policy, is deemed to be internationally known, and for which demonstrable property rights exist, may be held or used only by, or with the authorization of, the owner of such demonstrable intellectual property rights. Appropriate consideration shall be given to possible use of such a second-level domain name by a third party that, for the purposes of this policy, is deemed to have sufficient rights.[11]

In January 1998, the United States Department of Commerce published a Green Paper, *A Proposal to Improve Technical Management of Internet Names and Addresses*.[12] This proposal studiously avoided making any reference to the work of the IAHC and the Global Memorandum of Association. It received a lukewarm response from the EU, which commented that the Paper appeared to be seeking to retain United States dominance over the Internet. A further United States White Paper, *Management of Internet Names and Addresses*,[13] published in June 1998, moved much closer to the proposals of the IAHC and the terms of the Global Memorandum and drew the speedy response from the Commission that it:

can now confirm that the EU should act to participate fully in the process of organization and management of the Internet that has been launched by the US White Paper.[14]

Ultimately, agreement was reached that yet another new body be set up, the Internet Corporation for Assigned Names and Numbers (ICANN), which was established in October 1998. It is described as:

a non-profit, private sector corporation formed by a broad coalition of the Internet's business, technical, and academic communities. ICANN has been designated by the U.S. government to serve as the global consensus entity to which the U.S. government is transferring the responsibility for coordinating four key functions for the Internet: the management of the domain name system, the allocation of IP address space, the assignment of protocol parameters, and the management of the root server system.[15]

---

[11] Section 2, available from <http://www.gtld-mou.org/gTLD-MoU.html>

[12] Available from <http://www.ntia.doc.gov/ntiahome/domainname/dnsdrft.htm>

[13] Available from <http://www.ntia.doc.gov/ntiahome/domainname/6_5_98dns.htm>

[14] <http://www.ispo.cec.be/eif/dns/com98476.html>

[15] <http://www.icann.org/general/fact-sheet.htm>

Following this quite precise job description, there is a reversion to platitude with the comment that:

> ICANN is dedicated to preserve the operational stability of the Internet; to promote competition; to achieve broad representation of the global Internet community; and to coordinate policy through private-sector, bottom-up, consensus-based means.

In terms of legal status, ICANN is a company registered under the law of California.

Effectively, ICANN has taken over the role of IANA by means of a Memorandum of Understanding[16] and subsequently a contract was entered into with the United States government.[17] The agreement removed the monopoly of Network Solutions in respect of the .com domain. Whilst the first part of the process was carried out smoothly, negotiations with Network Solutions were more difficult, with legal action being threatened by Network Solutions on more than one occasion. Agreement was eventually reached in November 1999 and at the time of writing, thirty-two organisations were accredited to act as registries for the .com domain.[18] In order to qualify to act as a registrar,[19] an organisation must provide evidence of financial and technical stability.

Given an increasing number of registries located throughout the world, the possibility for domain name disputes is exacerbated. In an effort to control the problem, all registrars are obliged to operate the ICANN Uniform Domain Name Dispute Resolution Policy.[20] This obliges applicants to agree that any disputes will be adjudicated by an approved dispute resolution service. At present, three organisations operate such services:

- the World Intellectual Property Organization;[21]
- E-Resolution;[22] and
- the National Arbitration Forum.[23]

A considerable number of cases have already been referred to these agencies.[24] In addition to providing for a degree of priority to be given to trade mark owners, provision is also made for names to be withdrawn when a party registers the name in bad faith. Bad faith will be evidenced by:

(i) circumstances indicating that you have registered or you have acquired the domain name primarily for the purpose of selling, renting, or otherwise transferring the domain name registration to the complainant who is the owner of the trademark or service mark or to a competitor of that complainant, for

---

[16] Available from <http://www.icann.org/general/icann-mou-25nov98.htm>
[17] See <http://www.icann.org/general/iana-contract-09feb00.htm>
[18] For an up-to-date list see <http://www.icann.org/registrars/accredited-list.html>
[19] For full details of the accreditation process, see <http://www.icann.org/registrars/accreditation.htm>
[20] Available from <http://www.icann.org/udrp/udrp.htm>
[21] <http://arbiter.wipo/int/domains/>
[22] <http://www.eresolution.ca/>
[23] <http://www.arbforum.com/domains/>
[24] For a complete list see <http://www.icann.org/udrp/proceedings-list-name.htm>

valuable consideration in excess of your documented out-of-pocket costs directly related to the domain name; or

(ii) you have registered the domain name in order to prevent the owner of the trade-mark or service mark from reflecting the mark in a corresponding domain name, provided that you have engaged in a pattern of such conduct; or

(iii) you have registered the domain name primarily for the purpose of disrupting the business of a competitor; or

(iv) by using the domain name, you have intentionally attempted to attract, for commercial gain, Internet users to your web site or other on-line location, by creating a likelihood of confusion with the complainant's mark as to the source, sponsorship, affiliation, or endorsement of your web site or location or of a product or service on your web site or location.[25]

These provisions will allow action to be taken against the activity generally described as 'cybersquatting' and against other improper uses of the domain name system. An example of an action brought under these proceedings is a dispute heard before the WIPO panel involving the mark ABTA.[26] Generally associated with the Association of British Travel Agents who own trade marks in the acronym, the domain name ABTA.net was registered by a hotelier. In the event, the WIPO panel found for ABTA on a range of grounds, including use of a mark 'identical or confusingly similar' to a trade mark. The Panel also found in favour of ABTA on the bad faith issue. Key elements here were that the name was not being used and that the holder had not evidenced any plans to make use of the name. 'The concept of a domain name being used in bath faith', it was held, 'is not limited to positive action: inaction is within the concept'.'

The future of ICANN and Internet regulation

At the time of its establishment, ICANN was seen in some quarters as providing a blueprint for a more democratic form of Internet regulation. Provision was made for a number of its directors to be elected by those Internet users. In the hard light of experience, these hopes were unrealistic and the work of ICANN has been subject to considerable criticism.

At a basic level, ICANN was established by unilateral action on the part of the United States government, albeit with the tacit support of the European Commission. As Internet penetration has increased in other areas of the world, this narrow focus has been a cause for complaint. ICANN's role is in respect of the generic domain name codes but in more recent times country-level codes have begun to assume greater importance and the relationship between ICANN and the agencies responsible for the administration of country codes has at times been difficult.

---

[25] ICANN Uniform Domain Name Dispute Resolution Policy, para. 4b.
[26] <http://arbiter.wipo.int/domains/decisions/html/d2000–0086.html>

In autumn 2002, the initial contract between the United States Department of Commerce expired. It was extended for a further year[27] but on condition that ICANN introduced substantial reforms to its procedures and on the understanding that its progress would be closely monitored. In an accompanying statement,[28] the Department expressed concern that:

> ICANN has been troubled by internal and external difficulties that have slowed its completion of the transition tasks and hampered its ability to garner the full support and confidence of the global Internet community.

It continued:

> ICANN's reputation in the Internet community has suffered. In particular, ICANN has been criticized for over-reaching, arbitrariness, and lack of transparency in its decision making. Concerns have been raised about ICANN's lack of accountability and that it is inserting itself too much into the pricing and nature of services offered by, and business practices of, domain name companies. Some consider ICANN too slow to act on various issues, especially the roll-out of new gTLDs. There has also been growing concern that ICANN's structure, processes, and inability to make progress on other key DNS issues have undermined its effectiveness and legitimacy. Not surprisingly, many in the Internet community have called for ICANN to review its mission, structure, and processes for efficacy and appropriateness in light of the needs of today's Internet.

Extensive reforms have been put in place by ICANN but the future of the organisation remains uncertain. Given the importance of the Internet for all aspects of modern life, it cannot be considered satisfactory that a central coordinating body should continue in existence on a year-by-year basis and longer-term resolution is required. It may be that for the longer term, an agency similar to the International Telecommunications Union should assume responsibility for the technical aspects of the work. Although the Union's structures might themselves be criticised as providing excessive weight to governmental interests in an era of increasing private sector involvement in the communications sector, its deliberations do bring together public and private sector interests.

From Armageddon to cyberspace—the growing commercialisation of the Internet

Until 1991, the Internet remained the exclusive province of the academic/military/governmental sectors. The prime justification for this approach was that the infrastructure used for data transmission was funded by the public sector. Aspects of the technology have been used in the private sector for a number of years. The computerised legal information retrieval service 'Lexis', for example, began operations in

---

[27] <http://www.ntia.doc.gov/ntiahome/domainname/agreements/Amend5_09192002.htm>
[28] <http://www.ntia.doc.gov/ntiahome/domainname/agreements/docstatement_09192002>

1973. Services such as 'CompuServe' and 'America Online' also began operations in the 1980s, using proprietary communications software and operating over the normal telephone network. Effectively, this would mean that a CompuServe member could send emails to another member, but not to a subscriber to another service.

In 1991, the decision was taken in the United States to allow commercial users to access the Internet. Almost without exception, organisations such as CompuServe and America Online have migrated to the Internet through the adoption of the TCP/IP standards, and have been joined by many thousands of other organisations offering individual subscribers the possibility of Internet access. At the time of writing, there are around 150 ISPs operating in the United Kingdom. The range of services provided by these organisations varies significantly. Some provide significant value-added services. These might include technical help desks and access to proprietary information services, as well as access to the Internet. Users pay fees, generally based upon the level of usage. More recently, a large number of operators have come into the market offering free Internet access (except for the telephone charges incurred by the user whilst online). A number of ISPs are now offering free connections (by means of an 0800 number) to the Internet during the evenings and at weekends. At present, it is estimated that around 18 per cent of local telephone calls are made for the purpose of establishing connection with the Internet, a figure which is likely to rise significantly. It is perhaps not surprising that domestic Internet usage is considerably higher in the United States, where local telephone calls are generally free of charge.

Why is the Internet valuable for commercial users?

Today, the .com domain, which hosts websites of commercial relevance, is the largest single Internet domain, with some 12 million hosts. In 1998, of those sites registered, 84 per cent were in the .com domain.[29] In the United Kingdom domain, however, the academic domain .ac.uk remains the largest sector, with slightly over 700,000 hosts, as opposed to 585,000 in .co.uk.

A number of elements can be identified which make the Internet valuable for the commercial sector. As many users of email will be aware, the Internet provides marketers with a cheap promotional device, albeit referred to under the derogatory epithet of 'spamming'. Also, from the marketing perspective, the owner of a website can, through the judicious use of 'cookies', obtain a considerable amount of information about those visiting the site. More directly, of course, the Internet can be used for the conclusion of contracts for the sale and supply of goods and services.

One of the most notable aspects of e-commerce has been the facility it offers for relatively small and newly established companies to establish what is effectively a global presence. An excellent example is the electronic bookshop, Amazon.com. Located in Seattle (chosen because this city is home to some of the biggest book wholesalers in the United States), Amazon originally consisted of little more than a computer and

---

[29] <http://www.domainstats.com/>

small warehouse. It can compete, however, with more traditional booksellers around the globe and, in November 1999, towards the height of the 'dot com' boom, *Fortune* magazine reported that Amazon's share capital was seventeen times greater than that of the world's largest bricks-and-mortar book chain, Barnes and Noble, and that it had a market value five times greater than Barnes and Noble. At a more basic level, many small businesses which would never previously have contemplated international trade are now in a position to do so. An example, close to the heart of the author, is the company miracleblanket.com which from its base in Oregon supplied a wonderfully successful baby swaddling blanket to very appreciative parents in Glasgow.

In discussing this aspect of the Internet's role, a distinction can be drawn between three forms of transaction. In the first category, as epitomised by the online sale of books, Internet businesses allow contracts of sale to be entered into electronically, with the goods involved being delivered using traditional mechanisms. Such transactions can be equated with existing forms of catalogue system and, save for the introduction of an international dimension, raise few novel legal issues.

A second category relates to the provision of services. As with the previous situation, the contract will be concluded electronically but there will remain some element of physical performance of the contract. Perhaps the best example, and one of the major sectors of e-commerce, concerns the sale of aeroplane tickets. Most airlines now operate a system of online booking of aeroplane tickets. Such a facility can provide considerable cost benefits to the airline, which will require to employ and support fewer reservations staff and, in a number of cases, passengers are offered a discount for ordering online. In many cases, the next step is for the airline to post tickets to the customer, who then completes the journey in the normal manner. There is increased reliance, however, on what are referred to as electronic tickets. On receiving electronic confirmation of a successful booking, the customer will receive a booking number. No ticket will be issued and, on arrival at the airport, the customer need only quote the booking number in order to receive a boarding pass for the flight. Many 'low cost' airlines such as Ryanair and Easyjet actively promote themselves as ticketless carriers, although increased security demands in the aftermath of September 11 have brought with them requirements that passengers carry some official form of photographic identification such as a passport or driving licence. Similar cost benefits to the service provider can be identified in many sectors. A recent survey by Salomon, Smith Barclay has suggested that the costs to a bank of an average transaction carried out within a branch is 67.5p; with telephone banking the cost is reduced to 37p; and with Internet banking there is a further reduction to 2p. It is scarcely surprising that many banks are promoting the merits of this form of service.

The trend towards increasing dematerialisation of the contract performance phase reaches its ultimate in the third category of contracts. The phenomenon of digitisation is concerned with the practice whereby information is recorded in digital format. Any form of information, images, sound, or text may be recorded in this way. In addition to software itself, we are all familiar with musical CDs and electronic encyclopaedias such as *Microsoft Encarta* or *Britannica Online*.

The scale of Internet commerce

Increasingly, e-commerce is being conducted over the Internet, with websites offering a range of products and services. As the range of services expands, so it appears does the number of estimates as to its scale. It has been estimated that 75 per cent of United Kingdom consumers engage in some form of Internet-based shopping. The value of these transactions is estimated to amount to £40 billion, a figure which it is predicted will rise to £80 billion.[30]

Whilst impressive in terms of raw numbers, these figures represent a relatively small portion of total retail transactions, currently amounting to perhaps £300 for every person in the country. In further figures published in 2002 by the Office of National Statistics, it was suggested that:

> [b]usinesses are continuing to experience difficulties in providing estimates of online sales. The value of orders received over the Internet by United Kingdom non-financial sector businesses increased by 39 per cent between 2001 and 2002, from £16.8bn to £23.3bn (1.2% of total economic activity in the sectors).[31]

Some 27 per cent of this figure represented transactions between business and consumers, generally referred to as B–C transactions. This sector, then, is a small, albeit increasing sector of the e-commerce economy, with the bulk of transactions relating to contracts between businesses, referred to as B–B. The largest sector of this (66 per cent) relates to the supply of physical goods, with the electronic component effectively operating as a contracting and ordering mechanism. The supply of services made up 29 per cent of transactions, with 5 per cent relating to 'digitised products'. Although small, this represented a fivefold increase on figures for the previous year, and, given the growth in sectors such as online audio supply sites, is likely to have increased further in subsequent years.

Conclusions

The Internet has developed to an extent which could never have been foreseen in the pioneering days of the 1970s. In little more than a quarter of a century, it has become an essential component of the global economy. However, even so, it continues to defy definition. We can identify individual attributes, but the overall picture remains elusive.

Any predictions are dangerous, but the notion of convergence discussed in this chapter and in Chapter 1 perhaps offers a hint of where the future lies. The Internet is about communications and, from a stage where differing forms of communication were transmitted over different media and regulated in different ways, we can predict a single, all-purpose network, to the extent that it will be impossible to tell when a

---

[30] Internet Statistics Compendium, 2008.
[31] Value of e-trading by non-financial sector businesses.

database ends and a newspaper begins or when a video film transforms into a television broadcast.

Regulation will increasingly be the critical issue. With the emergence of organisations such as ICANN, the regulation of the network has been put on a rather more solid legal foundation. The problem, however, is not so much the technology. The TCP/IP protocols are essentially neutral. As will be discussed in the remaining chapters of this book, the key issue for the law is to regulate activities carried out in the context of networked technologies.

Suggestions for further reading

Three Degrees of Internet Regulation (Legal Issues). Information Today.

SMITH, G. J., *Internet Law and Regulation*, 3rd edn (London, 2002).

23

International and European initiatives in e-commerce

Introduction

Although in the e-commerce sector it is frequently difficult to distinguish hype from reality, there is no doubt that an increasing range of contracts will be concluded using some form of electronic communication. In many cases concerned with services, delivery, and perhaps performance, will also take place within an electronic environment.

In the context of traditional business activities, it is often stated that the three attributes most critical to commercial success are 'location, location, and location'. It is regarded as one of the hallmarks of e-commerce that issues of location, at least at the physical level, are of no significance. Paradoxically, however, when consideration is given to legal issues, location returns very much to the forefront. The most important questions concern the determination when and where a contract is made and which laws and tax regimes will govern the transaction.

International initiatives

Given the international nature of the topic, it is not surprising that many of the activities in the field of e-commerce have been initiated by international organisations. The UN Commission on International Trade Law (UNCITRAL) adopted a model law on e-commerce in 1996, whilst in December 1999, the OECD agreed Guidelines on Electronic Commerce.[1] The goal of the guidelines, it is stated:

> ...is that consumers shopping on-line should enjoy transparent and effective protection that is not less than the level of protection that they have in other areas of commerce. Among other things, they stress the importance of transparency and information disclosure.

The model law and the guidelines have no binding force. In focusing on regulatory activity, attention must concentrate on the activities of the EU and of national

---

[1] Available from <http://www.oecd.org/news_and_events/release/guidelinesconsumer.pdf>

legislatures. EU involvement in the field of e-commerce can be traced primarily to a Commission Communication, 'A European Initiative in Electronic Commerce', published in April 1997.[2] Itself building on earlier information society initiatives, this outlined a programme for regulatory action across a range of topics. In what might be considered chronological order, action was required in order to ensure that organisations were enabled to establish electronic businesses in any of the Member States, that legal barriers to electronic trade should be removed, that provision should be made for the manner in which contracts should be negotiated and concluded. Finally, legislation might be required in the field of electronic payments.

The mechanics of e-commerce constitute one aspect of the regulatory task. It was also recognised that other more general principles would require to be applied in the context of commercial applications. Issues such as data protection arise whenever personal data is transmitted and received. Again, as will be discussed in Chapter 24, the use of cryptographic techniques as a means for enhancing security, both to preserve privacy and to enhance consumer and business confidence in the integrity of electronic communications, raises significant and controversial regulatory questions.

Although it is tempting to regard e-commerce as a new phenomenon, this is to neglect a significant existing market sector—that dealing with mail order or catalogue selling. Especially in the United States, there is a substantial tradition of sales being conducted on this basis—dating back to the Wild West days beloved of cyberspace analogists. Given the federal nature of the United States Constitution, such sales also occurred across state boundaries. The oft-cited Uniform Commercial Code was first promulgated in 1940 to provide means to overcome jurisdictional and substantive problems arising when a supplier located in one jurisdiction contracted with a customer in another. Subject to some variations, it provides a common body of rules applicable throughout the fifty states. Recent (and highly controversial) developments in the United States have resulted in proposals to amend the venerable provisions of the Uniform Commercial Code to take account of the special nature of software sales.[3] Most initiatives seeking to amend the Code are the joint product of two bodies, the American Law Institute (ALI) and the National Conference of Commissioners on Uniform State Laws (NCCUSL). Originally, it was proposed to table an amendment to Article 2 of the Code. This provision deals with the law relating to the sale of goods. During 1999, a division occurred between the two drafting bodies, with the ALI taking the view that the proposal as drafted was too heavily weighted in favour of the interests of software developers and suppliers. The NCCUSL proceeded with the proposal, which was changed into a stand-alone statute, the Uniform Computer Information Transactions Act.[4] The measure has been passed to the fifty states, although it has been enacted in only two (Maryland and Virginia).

---

[2] Available from <http://www.cordis.lu/esprit/src/ecomcom.htm>

[3] For a vast range of materials and comments on the proposed new law, see <http://www.2bguide.com/legart.html>

[4] Text available from <http://www.law.upenn.edu/bll/ulc/ucita/cita10st.htm>

European initiatives

A number of measures adopted or proposed by the EU are relevant to any discussion of e-commerce. Three are of particular relevance. The Distance Selling Directive[5] and substantive law elements of the Electronic Commerce Directive[6] will be discussed in the present chapter. The Electronic Commerce Directive also contains provisions relating to the legal recognition of electronic contracts in cases where national laws require that contracts be concluded in a particular form. These matters, which are also covered in the Directive on 'A Community Framework for Electronic Signatures',[7] will be discussed in Chapter 24.

The Distance Selling Directive

The market for distance selling through catalogues is a well-established one, especially in remote areas where retail outlets are few and far between. The sector is particularly well established in the United States, and it is anticipated that businesses with experience of these forms of transactions will be well placed to benefit from the move to e-commerce. Over the past decade, the telephone, fax machine, and, most recently, email and the WWW have been used to solicit consumer contracts. One of the most important European legal instruments is the Directive on 'The Protection of Consumers in Respect of Distance Contracts'.[8] The Directive applies to all forms of distance selling, but contains some provisions relating specifically to the use of electronic communications. A number of these have been supplemented by the terms of the draft Electronic Commerce Directive.[9] The Distance Selling Directive were required to be implemented within the Member States by June 2000.[10] The Preamble makes its rationale clear:

> Whereas the introduction of new technologies is increasing the number of ways for consumers to obtain information about offers anywhere in the Community and to place orders; whereas some Member States have already taken different or diverging measures to protect consumers in respect of distance selling, which has had a detrimental effect on competition between businesses in the internal market; whereas it is therefore necessary to introduce at Community level a minimum set of common rules in this area.[11]

---

[5] Directive 97/7/EC.

[6] Directive 2000/31/EC.

[7] Directive 99/93/EC, OJ 2000 L 13/12.

[8] Directive 97/7/EC, OJ 1997 L 144 (the Distance Selling Directive). A further proposal for a Directive concerns the distance selling of financial services, COM (98) 468 final of 14.10.98.

[9] Directive 2000/31/EC.

[10] Two consultation papers have been published by the Department of Trade and Industry seeking views on the United Kingdom's implementation policy. The first, published in June 1998, is available from <http://www.dti.gov.uk/CACP/ca/distcon.htm>, and the second, published in November 1999, from <http://www.dti.gov.uk/cacp/ca/distance/index.htm>

[11] Recital 4.

The Distance Selling Directive defines the term 'distance contract' as:

Any contract concerning goods or services concluded between a supplier and a consumer under an organized distance sales or service-provision scheme run by the supplier, who, for the purpose of the contract, makes exclusive use of one or more means of distance communication up to and including the moment at which the contract is concluded.[12]

Annex 1 contains an illustrative list of communication technologies. In addition to traditional categories, such as letters and press advertisements, reference is made to the use of systems of videotext, email, and facsimile transmission.

The Distance Selling Directive's provisions commence at the stage where the consumer's entry into a contract is solicited, the principal requirement here being that promotional techniques must pay due regard to the consumer's privacy, conform to the 'principles of good faith' and provide 'clear and unambiguous information' regarding the nature of any product or service, its price, and the identity of its supplier.[13] In the case of telephone communication, the supplier is obliged to make its identity, and the fact that the call is commercial in nature, clear at the commencement of a call.[14]

The Distance Selling Directive also provides that two forms of technology, automated calling systems and fax machines, may be used only with the prior consent of the consumer—what might be referred to as an 'opt-in' system.[15] Automated calling systems involve the use of a computer system to call numbers and on answer, play a pre-recorded message to the recipient. Such technologies are effectively prohibited in the United Kingdom as their use would require a licence from OFTEL, which has indicated objections to the practice. In the case of other forms of communication, it is provided that these are to be made only when the consumer has not indicated a clear objection to receipt of solicitations.[16] The operation of an 'opt-out' system would be compatible with this requirement.

The rationale behind the selection of specific prohibited technologies is not clear. Recital 17 of the Distance Selling Directive[17] asserts that the consumer's right to privacy should extend to 'freedom from certain particularly intrusive means of communication'. It is difficult to argue, however, that a pre-recorded telephone message is intrinsically more intrusive than other forms of telephone canvassing. Unsolicited faxes also are unlikely to be seen as invasive of privacy, and perhaps a more persuasive basis for restricting these lies in the fact that the recipient of a fax incurs cost in terms of the paper and ink used for its reproduction. This was, perhaps, more of a factor with previous generations of fax machines, which required the use of special (and expensive) paper.

---

[12] Directive 97/7/EC, Article 2(1).
[13] Ibid., Article 4(2).
[14] Article 4(3).
[15] Directive 97/7/EC, Article 10(1).
[16] Article 10(2).
[17] Directive 97/7/EC.

Assuming that discussions between supplier and consumer extend beyond the initial contact, there is clear need to ensure that the latter is made aware of the terms and conditions associated with a particular contract. The Distance Selling Directive[18] provides for two approaches, the first of which is outwith the scope of the present study, requiring the grant of a 'cooling off' period following the conclusion of the contract.[19] More relevant are provisions requiring that the consumer be given information as to terms. Article 4 specifies the items of information which must be given. These relate primarily to the identity of the supplier, the nature and cost of the goods or services, and any arrangements for delivery. These are relatively easily satisfied in traditional mail order or catalogue sales, but in respect of electronic communications, Recital 13 states that:

> Whereas information disseminated by certain electronic technologies is often ephemeral in nature insofar as it is not received on a permanent medium; whereas the consumer must therefore receive written notice in good time of the information necessary for proper performance of the contract.

Whilst the comment regarding the transient nature of information displayed on a website, for example, is basically true, the text of an email message can be as locatable as any written message. It would seem somewhat Luddite were a party engaging in e-commerce to be required to supply confirmation details on paper. The Distance Selling Directive requires that confirmation be supplied in writing or:

> ...in another durable medium available and accessible to him.[20]

It may be that the transmission of an email which may be stored on the consumer's computer would satisfy this requirement. This is the view which has been adopted by the Department of Trade and Industry, which commented in its second consultation paper:

> We consider that confirmation by electronic mail would meet the definition of confirmation in 'another durable medium available and accessible to [the consumer]', where the order has been made by means of e-mail. We have not however specified this in the Draft Regulations since the Directive is not specific on the point, and only a court can determine the meaning of the wording.[21]

The Electronic Commerce Directive

The proposal for a Directive on 'Legal Aspects of Electronic Commerce' was introduced in November 1998.[22] The proposal was debated in the European

---

[18] Ibid.
[19] Article 6.
[20] Directive 97/7/EC, Article 5.
[21] Para. 3.9.
[22] OJ 1999 C 30.

Parliament[23] and following its comments, an amended proposal was introduced in September 1999,[24] becoming law on its adoption by the Council of Ministers in May 2000.[25] It is implemented in the United Kingdom by the Electronic Commerce (EC Directive) Regulations 2002.[26] The regulations follow very closely the wording and format of the Directive.

The scope of the measure is broad ranging. It applies to what are referred to as 'Information Society Services'. These are defined in Directive 98/34/EC, laying down a procedure for the provision of information in the field of technical standards,[27] which refers to:

> . . . any service normally provided for remuneration, at a distance, by electronic means and at the individual request of a recipient of services.

For the purposes of this definition three fundamental requirements apply:

> 'at a distance' means that the service is provided without the parties being simultaneously present;
>
> 'by electronic means' means that the service is sent initially and received at its destination by means of electronic equipment for the processing (including digital compression) and storage of data, and entirely transmitted, conveyed and received by wire, by radio, by optical means or by other electromagnetic means; and
>
> 'at the individual request of a recipient of services' means that the service is provided through the transmission of data on individual request.

It is specifically provided that the definition is not to apply to radio or television broadcasting services. A television 'shopping channel' will, therefore, not be governed by the Directive. Beyond this, however, the Commission have commented that:

> The Directive covers all Information Society services, both business to business and business to consumer, and services provided free of charge to the recipient e.g. funded by advertising or sponsorship revenue and services allowing for on-line electronic transactions such as interactive tele-shopping of goods and services and on-line shopping malls.
>
> Examples of sectors and activities covered include on-line newspapers, on-line databases, on-line financial services, on-line professional services (such as lawyers, doctors, accountants, estate agents), on-line entertainment services such as video on demand, on-line direct marketing and advertising and services providing access to the World Wide Web.[28]

---

[23] A copy of the report and proceedings is available from <http://www.ispo.cec.be/e-commerce/legal/legal.html>

[24] COM (99) 427 final.

[25] Directive 2000/31/EC, OJ 2000 L 178/1 (the Electronic Commerce Directive). The text of the measure can be obtained from <http://europa.eu.int/comm/internal_market/en/media/eleccomm/index.htm>

[26] SI 2002/2013.

[27] OJ 1998 L 204/37, as amended by Directive 98/48/EC, OJ 1998 L 217/18.

[28] 'Commission welcomes final adoptions of legal framework Directive': <http://europa.eu.int/comm/internal_market/en/media/eleccomm/2k-442.htm>

No authorisation is generally required in connection with the establishment of an information society service. Article 5 of the Electronic Commerce Directive[29] provides that:

1. Member States shall lay down in their legislation that access to the activity of Information Society service provider may not be made subject to prior authorisation or any other requirement the effect of which is to make such access dependent on a decision, measure or particular act by an authority.

This provision is subject to an exception where authorisation will be required in connection with the establishment of any business in a sector, i.e. a legal or financial services firm.

When and where is a contract made?

In order for a contract to be concluded, it is required that there should be an unconditional offer and acceptance. In many instances, of course, there may be several iterations of offer and counter-offer before the parties reach agreement on all important matters concerned with the contract.

In the situation where a customer purchases goods in a shop, there is little problem in determining the question where a contract is made. The question when the contract is concluded is a little more problematic. In the situation where goods are displayed in retail premises, it is normally the case that the display constitutes an invitation to treat. An offer to purchase will be made by the customer, which may be accepted (or rejected) by the seller. There are sound reasons for such an approach, not least due to the possibility that goods might be out of stock or that the wrong price tag may have been placed on an item by mistake (or through the action of some third party). In practical terms, it can be said that a contract will typically be concluded when the customer's offer of payment is accepted by the seller.

Subject to any other mechanism agreed between the parties, it is generally the case that acceptance becomes effective when it is communicated to the offeror. Clearly, in the case of a face-to-face transaction, this occurs at the point where the acceptor indicates—whether by words or actions—that the offer is acceptable. Matters become rather more complex when the parties to the transaction are at a distance. Here, two sets of rules have been developed, depending on the nature of the communications technology employed. The rule relating to postal contracts form a well-established feature of the legal system. Here, it is provided that the contract is deemed to have been concluded at the moment the acceptance is placed into the postal system. The main rationale for such an approach is that once the message has been posted, it moves out of the control of the sender. The effect of this is, of course, that a contract will be concluded before the offeror is aware of the fact of acceptance. It is also the case that having been posted, an acceptance cannot be withdrawn, even

---

[29] Directive 2000/31/EC.

though this may have been brought to the attention of the offeror prior to delivery of the acceptance.

The postal rule is to be contrasted with another rule relating to the use of forms of technology which might be classed as involving 'instantaneous communication'. In *Entores Ltd v Miles Far East Corpn*,[30] the question at issue was where a contract made following communications by telex should be regarded as having been concluded. The plaintiffs, who were located in London, had made an offer which had been accepted by the defendants in Amsterdam. Holding that the contract was made when the acceptance was received by the plaintiffs in London, Parker LJ held that where:

> ...parties are in each other's presence or, though separated in space, communication between them is in effect instantaneous, there is no need for any such rule of convenience. To hold otherwise would leave no room for the operation of the general rule that notification of the acceptance must be received. An acceptor could say: 'I spoke the words of acceptance in your presence, albeit softly, and you did not hear me'; or 'I telephoned to you and accepted, and it matters not that the telephone went dead and you did not get my message'...So far as Telex messages are concerned, though the despatch and receipt of a message is not completely instantaneous, the parties are to all intents and purposes in each other's presence just as if they were in telephonic communication, and I can see no reason for departing from the general rule that there is no binding contract until notice of the acceptance was received by the offeror.[31]

This view was endorsed by the House of Lords in the case of *Brinkibon Ltd v Stahag Stahl und Stahlwarenhandel GMBH*,[32] although it was recognised by Lord Wilberforce that the result might have to be reviewed in the event that it could be established that there was:

> ...some error or default at the recipient's end which prevents receipt at the time contemplated and believed in by the sender...No universal rule can cover all such cases; they must be resolved by reference to the intentions of the parties, by sound business practice and in some cases a judgement where the risks should lie.[33]

In the context of the present work, the key question will be whether emails and other forms of message transmitted over the Internet will be classed as coming under the postal rule, or whether the provisions relating to instantaneous communications will apply. Although the issue of determining when an email contract is concluded might appear to be of the 'number of angels on a pinhead' category, this is not always the case, especially when—as in the *Entores*[34] and *Brinkibon*[35] cases—transactions possess an international dimension. In such cases, the questions will arise of which law will govern the transaction and which courts will have jurisdiction in the event

---

[30] [1955] 2 All ER 493.
[31] [1955] 2 All ER 493 at 498.
[32] [1982] 1 All ER 293.
[33] [1982] 1 All ER 293 at 296.
[34] *Entores Ltd v Miles Far East Corpn* [1955] 2 All ER 493.
[35] *Brinkibon Ltd v Stahag Stahl and Stahlwarenhandel GMBH* [1982] 1 All ER 293.

of a dispute. In the event that a contract is silent on the point, the location where a contract is concluded will be a major factor in determining the choice of law question. This issue will be considered in more detail below.

In terms of speed of transmission, email might generally be equated with fax or telex transmission. In the event of problems or congestion on the networks, messages may be delayed by hours or even days and, in terms of the nature of transmission, the more accurate parallel may be with the postal system. An email message will be passed on from point to point across the network, with its contents being copied and forwarded a number of times before being delivered to the ultimate recipient. There is no single direct link or connection between sender and receiver.

The Electronic Commerce Directive provides what appears to be a somewhat complex mechanism for determining the moment at which a contract is concluded. It is stated that:

> Member States shall lay down in their legislation that, save where otherwise agreed by professional persons, in cases where a recipient, in accepting a service provider's offer, is required to give his consent through technological means, such as clicking on an icon, the contract is concluded when the recipient of the service has received from the service provider, electronically, an acknowledgment of receipt of the recipient's acceptance.[36]

Such an approach would pose problems for the United Kingdom system which, as stated above, sees offers emanating from the customer rather than the supplier. There appears also to be an element of unnecessary complication by adding the requirement of acknowledgement of receipt of acceptance as a condition for the conclusion of a contract. The original proposal was even more prolonged, stating that the contract would not be concluded until acknowledgement was made of receipt of the acknowledgement! Receipt of acceptance would seem quite sufficient for this legal purpose. An alternative, and perhaps preferable, approach is advocated by the International Chamber of Commerce, whose draft Uniform Rules for Electronic Trade and Settlement propose that:

> An electronic offer and/or acceptance becomes effective when it enters the information system of the recipient in a form capable of being processed by that system.[37]

Albeit intended primarily for business to business contracts rather than the EU's consumer contract focus, this approach seems to achieve the legal requirements in a rather simpler fashion. Simplest of all, however, would be the United Kingdom approach, which would allow the seller to combine acceptance of the customer's offer with acknowledgement of the terms of the transaction.

A further obligation is proposed in the EC Electronic Commerce Directive. Member States are required to ensure that national laws require that:

> ...the service provider shall make available to the recipient of the service appropriate means that are effective and accessible allowing him to identify and correct handling

---

[36] Directive 2000/31/EC, Article 11.
[37] Article 2.1.1.

errors and accidental transactions before the conclusion of the contract. Contract terms and general conditions provided to the consumer must be made available in a way that allows him to store and reproduce them.[38]

Whilst the provision is well meaning, it is difficult to identify how the result might be achieved. The provisions relating to the moment of formation of contract discussed above require that 'the service provider is obliged to immediately send the acknowledgment of receipt'. We can assume that in most cases this will be transmitted automatically. This affords very little time for the customer to identify and seek to correct any mistakes which have been made.

An alternative approach would be to provide consumers with a 'cooling off' period within which a contract might be terminated. The Distance Selling Directive provides for a seven-day period, beginning with the date upon which goods supplied under the contract were received by the consumer.[39] The provision does not, however, apply to contracts for the provision of services where 'performance has begun with the consumer's agreement, before the end of the seven-day working period'. This will exclude contracts for the electronic delivery of software. Exemption is also provided in respect of contracts 'for the supply of audio or video recordings or computer software which were unsealed by the consumer'. The legitimate concern in all these cases is that the consumer would have the ability to copy the material before returning the originals to the supplier and seeking a refund of the purchase price.

Choice of law issues

As has been stated frequently, location is irrelevant in e-commerce. It is also the case that the largest body of sites offering to supply goods or services is in the United States. A consumer located in the United Kingdom and wishing to engage in e-commerce is almost inevitably going to require to deal with United States-based companies. International trade, which hitherto has been almost exclusively the preserve of large commercial operators, is assuming a significant consumer dimension.

In any situation where buyer and seller are located in different jurisdictions, two key legal issues will arise. The first is to determine which legal system will govern the transaction and the second to determine which courts will be competent to hear disputes arising from the transaction. In many cases, it will be the case that the parties make explicit contractual provision for both matters. In a contract between parties in Scotland and France, for example, it might be provided that French law will govern the transaction but that disputes may be raised in the French or the Scottish courts, the latter being required to decide the case according to the relevant principles of French law.

In general, parties have (subject to the legal systems chosen having some connection with the subject-matter of the contract) complete freedom to determine choice of law issues. Different rules apply where consumers are involved. Problems also arise where

---

[38] Directive 2000/31/EC, Article 11(2).
[39] Directive 97/7/EC, Article 6.

the parties fail to make explicit provision for issues of jurisdiction. In this case, the matter may fall to be decided by the courts.

As discussed above in the context of contract formation, the question when and where a contract is concluded is a major factor in determining which legal system is to govern the transaction. Where transactions are conducted over the Internet, the question is not always easy to answer. The Global Top Level Domain name .com gives no indication where a business is located. Even where the name uses a country code such as .de or .uk there is no guarantee that the undertaking is established in that country. It is relatively common practice, based in part upon security concerns, to keep web servers geographically separate from the physical undertaking. A website might, for example, have an address in the German (.de) domain. Its owner, however, might be a United Kingdom-registered company.

The question whether an Internet-based business can be regarded as having a 'branch, agency or establishment' in all the countries from which its facilities may be accessed is uncertain. The OECD has pointed out in the context of tax harmonisation that the notion of permanent establishment, which is of major importance in determining whether an undertaking is liable to national taxes, may not be appropriate for e-commerce.

Within Europe, the Brussels[40] and Rome[41] Conventions make special provision for consumer contracts. The latter provides that a supplier with a 'branch, agency or establishment' in the consumer's country of residence is to be considered as domiciled there. Further, consumers may choose to bring actions in either their country of domicile or that of the supplier, whilst actions against the consumer may be brought only in the consumer's country of domicile.

The Brussels Convention builds on the Rome Convention's provisions and provides that an international contract may not deprive the consumer of 'mandatory rights' operating in the consumer's country of domicile. The scope of mandatory rights is not clear-cut but, given the emphasis placed on the human rights dimension in many international instruments dealing with data protection, it is argued that any attempt contractually to deprive consumers of rights conferred under the Council of Europe Convention and the EC Electronic Commerce Directive[42] would be declared ineffective on this basis.

More recent developments may complicate matters. The Electronic Commerce Directive[43] provides that transactions entered into by electronic means should be regulated by the law of the state in which the supplier is established. This approach is justified on the basis of supporting the development of the new industries, Recital 22 stating that:

> ...in order to effectively guarantee freedom to provide services and legal certainty for suppliers and recipients of services, such Information Society services should only be subject to the law of the Member State in which the service provider is established.

[40] C 189 of 28 July 1990.
[41] OJ 1980 L 266/1.
[42] Directive 2000/31/EC.
[43] Ibid.

At the same time, however, the Commission have adopted, in the form of a Regulation 'On jurisdiction and the recognition and enforcement of judgments in civil and commercial matters',[44] amendments to the Brussels and Rome Conventions which would have the effect of subjecting all consumer contracts to the law of the consumer's domicile.[45] This approach is justified on the basis that the consumer is regarded as the weaker party in any contract with a business organisation.

There appears to be an inescapable conflict between choice of law provisions designed to favour the development of e-commerce by making more predictable the nature of the liabilities incurred by service providers, and giving priority to the interests of consumers by maximising their access to local courts and tribunals. The Explanatory Memorandum to the draft Regulation stated that:

> The Commission has noted that the wording of Article 15 has given rise to certain anxieties among part of the industry looking to develop electronic commerce. These concerns relate primarily to the fact that companies engaging in electronic commerce will have to contend with potential litigation in every Member State, or will have to specify that their products or services are not intended for consumers domiciled in certain Member States.

The intention was announced to review the operation of Article 15 two years after the Regulation's entry into force. In the shorter term, public hearings on the subject were announced and were held in Brussels in November 1999. The hearings attracted an audience of several hundred persons[46] and produced several hundred pages of comments and suggestions.[47] No consensus was—or perhaps could be—reached and the position remains one where different Commission Directorates appear to be promoting different policies.

Alternative dispute resolution

One possible palliative for jurisdictional problems is to try to obviate the need for formal legal proceedings. Two provisions in the Electronic Commerce Directive[48] seek to facilitate this. Article 16 requires Member States and the Commission to encourage the drawing up at Community level of codes of conduct designed to contribute to the implementation of the substantive provisions of the Directive. Such codes, which will be examined by the Commission to ensure their compatibility with Community law, might provide a valuable unifying force throughout the EU. Article 17 obliges Member States to:

> …ensure that, in the event of disagreement between an Information Society service provider and its recipient, their legislation allows the effective use of out of court schemes for dispute settlement, including appropriate electronic means.

---

[44] Regulation 44/2001/EC, OJ 2001 L 12/1.
[45] Article 15.
[46] Available from <http://europa.eu.int/comm/scic/conferences/991104/participants.pdf>
[47] Available from <http://europa.eu.int/comm/scic/conferences/991104/contributions.doc>
[48] Directive 2000/31/EC.

Although a number of online dispute resolution services have been established, these have mainly been in the United States and do not appear to have attracted significant custom. In the United Kingdom, the 'Which Web Trader' scheme operated by the Consumers Association,[49] requires participating traders to observe a code of practice but, in the event of a dispute with a consumer, makes it clear that recourse will have to be sought through the courts.

In 1998, the Commission adopted a 'Communication on the out-of-court settlement of consumer disputes'.[50] A Commission Working Document on the creation of a European Extra-Judicial Network (EEJ-NET)[51] was published in March 2000. This notes that:

> The continuing expansion of economic activity within of the internal market inevitably means that consumers' activities are not only confined to their own country. Greater cross border consumption has arisen due to an increase in consumer travel and the emergence of new distance selling technologies like the Internet. This increase in cross border consumption, especially with the ever-increasing expansion of electronic commerce and the introduction of the Euro, is invariably likely to lead to an increase in cross border disputes. It is, therefore, necessary and desirable to create a network of general application which will cover any kind of dispute over goods and services.

The Commission is now proposing the establishment of a network of National 'Clearing Houses'. These organisations will give consumers wishing to pursue complaints against suppliers located in their jurisdiction information about available facilities for dispute resolution. The Clearing Houses will also assist their own national consumers who are in dispute with a supplier in another Member State by liaising with the relevant Clearing House to provide information about dispute resolution procedures. A further Green Paper on alternative dispute resolution in civil and criminal law was published by the Commission in 2002.[52]

Conclusions

The scope of the Electronic Commerce Directive[53] is broad-ranging and is generally non-controversial. Even matters such as the procedure for concluding a contract may cause theoretical rather than practical problems. The major criticism that might be made of the EU's activity in the field of e-commerce is that initiatives are dispersed across a range of measures. As well as complicating the task of determining what the law is in a particular respect, there is the potential for internal conflict, as has been discussed in relation to the issue of choice of law.

---

[49] Available from <http://www.which.com/webtrader/consumer_guide.html>
[50] COM (98) 198 final.
[51] Available from <http://europa.eu.int/comm/dg24/policy/developments/acce_just acce_just06_en.pdf>
[52] COM (2002) 196 final.
[53] Directive 2000/31/EC.

Perhaps the key message which can be taken from the initiatives discussed in this chapter is that in most cases, the application of traditional legal provisions will be quite adequate in order to regulate e-commerce. The key issue is perhaps the negative one that legal requirements should not impede the operation of e-commerce. This issue primarily arises in the context of formal or procedural requirements that a contract be concluded or evidenced in writing. The issue as to what extent such requirements might be satisfied in an electronic environment has become entangled with the topic of encryption. Both topics will be considered in the following chapter.

Suggestions for further reading

'Article 5 of the Rome Convention on the Law Applicable to Contractual Obligations of 19 June 1980 and Consumer E-Contracts: The Need for Reform', *I. & C.T.L.* 13(1) (2004), pp. 59–73.

24

Cryptography, electronic signatures, and the Electronic Communications Act 2000

Introduction

An issue which is often identified as a factor deterring consumers from participating in e-commerce is the fear that information transmitted over the Internet might be intercepted by computer hackers. Where the data takes the form of, for example, credit and information, the potential for loss is obvious. Reality does not necessarily accord with perception. To date, no instances have been recorded of data being intercepted in transmission, although there are numerous instances of fraud conducted by parties involved in e-commerce. Rather than seeking to intercept messages, for anyone wishing to engage in criminal conduct, it is a much simpler matter to set up a website offering to supply goods or services at attractive prices, solicit orders with payment by credit card, and make off with a rich harvest of numbers.

In addition to concerns relating to the security of payment systems, the ease with which electronic data might be modified without leaving any discernible trace raises concerns regarding the legal status of contracts evidenced only in such format. The situation is not, of course, unique to electronic data. Forgery is a well-established, if disreputable, profession. Whilst most contracts can be constituted in such manner as the parties think fit, there are obvious problems in permitting large contracts with obligations continuing over many years to be concluded in a relatively informal manner. Two parties might well enter into a verbal agreement for the sale and purchase of property. With the passage of time, memory of what was agreed may fade and both parties will at some stage die. The land, of course, goes on forever and either the parties or their successors may at some time have to determine just what was agreed. Taking account of such problems, there have long been requirements in the law that some agreements be reduced to written form and authenticated by the signature of the party or parties responsible for the creation of documents.

Along with the proposals for a Directive on 'Legal Aspects of Electronic Commerce',[1] a draft Electronic Signatures Directive was published by the Commission.[2] This was

---

[1] OJ 1999 C 30.   [2] OJ 1998 C 325.

adopted slightly before the Electronic Commerce Directive,[3] final approval being given in December 1999 to a Directive 'On a Community Framework for Electronic Signatures'.[4] Although Member States were given until 19 July 2001 to implement the measure,[5] with the enactment of the Electronic Communications Act 2000 in May 2000, the United Kingdom would appear to have met all its obligations under the Directive.

The main purpose of the Electronic Signatures[6] and Electronic Commerce[7] Directives and the Electronic Communications Act 2000 is to encourage the development of electronic equivalents to written documents and manual signatures. In considering the impact of the Directives and the Act, consideration might usefully be divided into three sections. First, a brief account will be given of the background to the Electronic Communications Act 2000, a measure which will be pivotal to many of the developments described in this chapter. Next, an examination will be made of provisions relating to requirements for writing. This may relate both to the contractual situation and to other cases, such as the submission of tax returns. Finally, consideration will be given to requirements for signature. The notion of electronic or digital signatures has become inextricably linked with the use of cryptographic techniques and this section will commence with a brief description of this somewhat complex topic.

Background to the Electronic Communications Act 2000

After a number of false dawns and extensive consultation exercises, an Electronic Communications Bill was introduced in the House of Commons in November 1999. The Bill, it was stated in the Second Reading debate:

> will be Britain's first 21st century law. It was the first Bill referred to in the Queen's Speech, it was the first to be introduced; and, tonight, it will become the first to receive Second Reading. It will bring our statute book into the 21st century, provide a sound legal basis for electronic commerce and electronic government, and help to build consumer and business confidence in trading on the Internet.[8]

In the event, the need to introduce emergency legislation to suspend the operation of Northern Ireland's power-sharing Executive meant that the measure was not to be the first statute of the twenty-first century. Once this honour had been removed, some of the sense of urgency which had accompanied the early stages of the Bill seemed to be dissipated and it was not until 25 May 2000 that the measure received the Royal Assent.

The genesis of the measure can be traced to a Consultation Paper published by the previous administration, in March 1997, on the 'Licensing of Trusted Third Parties for the Provision of Encryption Services'. In April 1998, the Department of Trade and

---

[3] Directive 2000/31/EC.

[4] Directive 99/93/EC, OJ 2000 L 13/12 (the Electronic Signatures Directive).

[5] Article 13.

[6] Directive 99/93/EC.

[7] Directive 2000/31/EC.

[8] Patricia Hewitt, Minister for Small Business and E-Commerce, 340 HC Official Report (6th series), col. 4, 29 November 1999.

Industry published a statement on 'Secure Electronic Commerce'. This marked the first occasion when the term Electronic Commerce was used in an official statement. It was indicated that:

2. The Government places considerable importance on the successful development of electronic commerce. It will, if successfully promoted, allow us to exploit fully the advantages of the information age for the benefit of the whole community.

3. The Government is committed to the successful development and promotion of a framework within which electronic commerce can thrive. Electronic commerce, as indicated below, is crucial to the future growth and prosperity of both the national economy and our businesses. Although the prime economic driver for electronic commerce may currently lie with business-to-business transactions, it is clear that consumers (whether ordering books or arranging pensions) will also directly benefit.

Although the statement used the term electronic commerce, its contents were almost exclusively concerned with security issues:

To achieve our goals, however, electronic commerce, and the electronic networks on which it relies, have to be secure and trusted. Whether it be the entrepreneur E-mailing his sales information to a potential supplier or the citizen receiving private advice from their doctor; the communications need to be secure. In a recent DTI survey 69% of UK companies cited security as a major inhibitor to purchasing across Internet.[9]

Security can have a number of components and the statement referred approvingly to BS7799, which was referred to as the 'national standard on information security'. As well as organisational and technical measures, however, the statement focused on encryption policy. As discussed above, this has been, and remains, a contentious political issue and the paper was criticised widely as appearing to promote a scheme of mandatory key escrow.

The next significant event occurred in March 1999, when a Consultation Paper, *Building Confidence in Electronic Commerce*, was published.[10] This indicated that 'The Government is committed to introducing legislation in the current Parliamentary session.' Comments were sought within a three-week period. Although cryptography policy again featured prominently in the document, significant provisions were also introduced concerning procedural issues of e-commerce, specifically relating to the removal of requirements that contracts be concluded in writing or be accompanied by a signature.

The Paper was the subject of critical comment by the House of Commons Select Committee on Trade and Industry.[11] Other organisations made 252 comments.[12] In July 1999, a further consultation document, *Promoting Electronic Commerce*, was

[9] Available from <http://www.fipr.org/polarch/secst.html>
[10] Available from <http://www.dti.gov.uk/cii/ana27p.html>
[11] Tenth Report of the Select Committee on Trade and Industry (1998–99), available from <http://www.parliament.the-stationery-office.co.uk/pa/cm199899/cmselect/cmtrdind/648/64802.htm>
[12] A summary of responses is available from <http://www.dti.gov.uk/cii/elec/conrep.htm>

published. Although a draft Bill (now referred to as the Electronic Communications Bill) was appended to this Paper, the commitment to introduce legislation in the 1998–99 parliamentary session was abandoned, apparently because of the refusal by the opposition to allow it to be certified as non-controversial and thereby permitted to continue its progress over two sessions. Comments this time were requested to be submitted by October 1999. A further report was tabled by the Select Committee in November 1999,[13] and the Electronic Communications Bill was introduced in the House of Commons on 18 November, receiving its Second Reading on 29 November.

As the legislative proposals have developed, the main changes have been in respect of the controls imposed over those operating cryptographic services. Concerns were expressed in many quarters that those using encryption would be required to lodge copies of their keys with agencies, from where they might be passed on to the law enforcement or national security agencies. It would appear that this is now off the legislative agenda. In a speech delivered in September 1999, Patricia Hewitt, the newly appointed Minister for Small Firms and E-Commerce, proclaimed that:

> Let me confirm that mandatory key escrow is NOT part of the bill. Many of you will have taken part in the campaign against mandatory key escrow—the previous cross-party policy to coerce people to give copies of the keys to their encrypted mail to a third party. This issue assumed such importance that the PIU [Performance and Innovation Unit] set up a special taskforce to look at it. Back in May the PIU concluded that these plans were not going to work.
>
> Let me repeat what the Prime Minister said last week:
>
> 'No company or individual will be forced, directly or indirectly, to escrow keys.'
>
> The Electronic Communications Bill is not about key escrow. Mandatory key escrow is off the agenda.

In the event, the provisions relating to the interception of encrypted messages were removed from the Electronic Communications Bill and transferred to the Regulation of Investigative Powers Bill. To emphasise the rejection of mandatory key escrow, the Electronic Communications Act 2000 provides that there shall be no power 'to impose a requirement on any person to deposit a key for electronic data with another person'.[14]

The removal of the provisions relating to interception seems to have drawn the teeth from most of the opposition to the Bill. The remaining provisions have been generally welcomed, with Bill Gates, the President of Microsoft, referring to it as a 'model for Europe'.[15] This may be somewhat exaggerated as, in many respects, the legislation provides only a framework which will require to be filled in by secondary legislation.

The Electronic Communications Act 2000 contains three parts. Part I contains provisions relating to the use of encryption, Part II is designed to facilitate e-commerce,

---

[13] Fourteenth Report of the Select Committee on Trade and Industry (1999–2000), available from <http://www.parliament.the-stationery-office.co.uk/pa/cm199899/cmselect/cmtrdind/862/86202.htm>

[14] Section 14(1).

[15] Cited in 340 HC Official Report (6th series), col. 41, 29 November 1999.

whilst Part III contains miscellaneous provisions, mainly concerned with a change to the telecommunications licensing regime.

Requirements for writing

In a 1990 report, *Preliminary study of legal issues related to the formation of contracts by electronic means*, UNCITRAL identified four reasons which had historically prompted a requirement that contracts be concluded in writing. These were the desire to reduce disputes; to make the parties aware of the consequences of their dealings; to provide evidence upon which third parties might rely upon the agreement; and to facilitate tax, accounting, and regulatory purposes.

A wide range of statutory provisions make provision for information to be supplied 'in writing', for example, company accounts. In a number of instances, specific statutory provision has been made for the acceptance of computer-generated information. In the taxation field, for example, electronic copies of invoices will be accepted for purposes connected with Value Added Tax. As will be discussed, the Electronic Communications Bill seeks to pave the way for greater acceptance of electronic information as satisfying requirements for writing. At present, however, statutory requirements will be subject to the terms of the Interpretation Act 1978, which defines writing as including:

> ...typing, printing, lithography, photography and other modes of representing or reproducing words in a visible form, and expressions referring to writing are construed accordingly.[16]

A document which exists solely in digital form, for example, an email message stored on the hard disk of the recipient's computer, will not be capable of coming within this definition, as the electronic impulses representing its contents are not visible.

It seems clear that the 1978 definition was introduced at a time when communication between computers was limited and, as with other statutory definitions of that era relating to concepts of recording and storage, is ill suited to the modern age. The UN Model Law on Electronic Commerce introduces the concept of 'a data message', which is defined as:

> ...information generated, sent, received or stored by electronic, optical or similar means including, but not limited to, electronic document interchange (EDI), electronic mail, telegram, telex or telecopy.[17]

The UN Model Law goes on to provide that:

> Where the law requires information to be in writing, that requirement is met by a data message if the information contained therein is accessible so as to be usable for subsequent reference.[18]

---

[16] Schedule 1.
[17] Article 2.
[18] Article 6.

The desire to reduce requirements for paper-based documents is a feature of the Electronic Commerce Directive.[19] This provides that:

1. Member States shall ensure that their legislation allows contracts to be concluded electronically. Member States shall in particular ensure that the legal requirements applicable to the contractual process neither prevent the effective use of electronic contracts nor result in such contracts being deprived of legal effect and validity on account of their having been made electronically.

2. Member States may lay down that paragraph 1 shall not apply to the following contracts:

   (a) contracts requiring the involvement of a notary;

   (b) contracts which, in order to be valid, are required to be registered with a public authority;

   (c) contracts governed by family law; and

   (d) contracts governed by the law of succession.[20]

The effect of this provision would be to ensure that most forms of e-commerce can be conducted without requiring to comply with any additional requirements relating to form. This general rule may, at the option of a Member State, be subject to exceptions. The situations specified in the proposed Directive relate to contracts which are regarded as being of special importance. In respect of these, national laws typically require that the terms of the contract be recorded in writing and signed by the contracting parties.

The Electronic Commerce Directive's provisions[21] are implemented in the Electronic Communications Act 2000. This provides ministers (including Scottish ministers) with a general power to modify any statute or statutory instrument:

...in such manner as he may think fit for the purpose of authorising or facilitating the use of electronic communications or electronic storage (instead of other forms of communication or storage) for any purpose mentioned in subsection (2).

   (2) Those purposes are—

   (a) the doing of anything which under any such provisions is required to be or may be done or evidenced in writing or otherwise using a document, notice or instrument;

   (b) the doing of anything which under any such provisions is required to be or may be done by post or other specified means of delivery;

   (c) the doing of anything which under any such provisions is required to be or may be authorised by a person's signature or seal, or is required to be delivered as a deed or witnessed;

---

[19] Directive 2000/31/EC.
[20] Article 9.
[21] Directive 2000/31/EC.

(d) the making of any statement or declaration which under any such provisions is required to be made under oath or to be contained in a statutory declaration;

(e) the keeping, maintenance or preservation, for the purposes or in pursuance of any such provisions, of any account, record, notice, instrument or other document;

(f) the provision, production or publication under any such provisions of any information or other matter; and

(g) the making of any payment that is required to be or may be made under any such provisions.[22]

The power is not to be invoked unless the minister is satisfied that the use of electronic communications provides at least an equal measure of certainty and security as can be garnered through the use of more traditional requirements.[23]

A vast range of transactions might be affected by this power. It was indicated in Parliament that for England and Wales:

The Lord Chancellor is exploring, with the assistance of the Law Commission and the Land Registry, what is necessary to allow conveyancing in particular to be done electronically.[24]

Much publicity has been given to the recognition of electronic signatures, but the power will also extend to permitting firms to supply accounts in electronic form and to give shareholders notice of meetings by email. It may well be that government will be major users of the provision in connection with oft-quoted targets that 25 per cent of government services should be available electronically by 2002, 50 per cent by 2005 and 100 per cent by 2008. It is also indicated that 90 per cent of routine government procurement should be conducted electronically by 2001.[25]

The task of updating the statute book will be a massive one. It has been estimated that there are in the region of 40,000 references to paper signatures, documents, and records.[26] The range of topics covered and the variety of expressions used in these statutes was considered to be such that it would be impracticable for a straightforward abolition of requirements for writing to be considered. What remains uncertain is the timetable for action. It was stated in Committee by the Minister for Small Businesses and E-Commerce that:

I am keen for the powers provided under clause 8 to be used extensively to modernise the statute book as quickly as possible. As I said on Second Reading, my right hon. Friend the Minister for the Cabinet Office, who is responsible for e-government, is already working with other Government departments to ensure that each Department

---

[22] Section 8.
[23] Section 8(3).
[24] HC Official Report, SC B (Electronic Communications Bill), col. 73, 14 December 1999.
[25] Explanatory Notes to the Electronic Communications Bill.
[26] 340 HC Official Report (6th series), col. 41, 29 November 1999.

examines the statutes for which it is responsible in order to ascertain in which cases it can move rapidly to introduce electronic equivalents. A timetable for completing that has not yet been specified, but I am drawing to the attention of my colleagues in different Departments the need to move with considerable urgency. We are leading by example in my own Department, which is already preparing under clause 8 a draft order that relates to company law, to enable us to consult on it early in the new year and have it ready for introduction as soon as the Bill becomes law and clause 8 comes into effect.[27]

Concerns were expressed in Parliament that the provisions of s 8 of the Electronic Communications Act 2000 might be used to compel persons doing business with the government to engage in electronic communications. Section 8(6) provides, however, that any order made 'may not require the use of electronic communications or electronic storage for any purpose'. What may serve as a greater incentive for the use of electronic communications is the provision of some form of discount. Here, it is provided that regulations may make:

> Provision, in relation to cases in which fees or charges are or may be imposed in connection with anything for the purposes of which the use of electronic communications or electronic storage is so authorised for different fees or charges to apply where use is made of such communications or storage.[28]

It has recently been announced in the budget, for example, that taxpayers submitting income tax returns electronically will qualify for a (small) discount of £10.[29] Such reductions seem modest compared with the savings which can be accomplished through the use of electronic communications. It has been estimated that paper documentation and associated handling procedures can represent up to 10 per cent of the total costs of goods. Costs savings on this element of up to 50 per cent can be attained through a switch to electronic communications. Another producer has estimated that it costs $70 to process a paper purchase order, as opposed to 93 cents when the order is submitted electronically. In other cases, the figures might be even higher. In June 1997, the National Audit Office criticised procurement practices within the Ministry of Defence, citing a case where £73.50 was spent processing an order for a padlock worth just 98p.[30]

Implementation of the above statutory provisions will open the way for businesses, individuals, and government agencies to make use of electronic communications for most aspects of their life and work. Whether they utilise this freedom will, of course, depend upon whether there is sufficient confidence in the integrity and reliability of systems of communication. As indicated at the beginning of this chapter, the use of systems of encryption is seen as playing an important role in this respect. The following

---

[27] HC Official Report, SC B (Electronic Communications Bill), col. 75, 14 December 1999.
[28] Section 6(4)(h).
[29] Details can be found at <http://www.inlandrevenue.gov.uk/ebu/info.htm>
[30] Report on 'Improving the Procurement of Routine Items' (June 1997).

sections will describe the nature of the technology and some of the practical and legal problems involved.

The nature of encryption

Techniques of encryption date back many centuries. An early user was Julius Caesar, who wrote his despatches from Gaul in what is now referred to as the Caesar code. This involves shifting letters an agreed number of spaces along the alphabet. For example, placing the two alphabets above each other with a shift of three would give:

ABCDEFGHIJKLMNOPQRSTUVWXYZ
DEFGHIJKLMNOPQRSTUVWXYZABC

The letter C would become F; A become D; and T would become W: so CAT would read FDW.

The Caesar code is an example of what is referred to as a substitution cipher. The other main form of encryption has involved a process of transposition. Effectively, this involves taking a phrase, such as:

WET DAY IN GLASGOW

omitting spaces, and placing the letters into blocks of five letters each, producing:

WETDA YINLA ASGOW

The letters in each block are then shuffled in a predetermined manner. If the first letter is moved to the fourth space, second to fifth, third to first, fourth to second, and fifth to third we arrive at:

TDAWE NLAYI GOWAS

Obviously, a real-life example would require to add far more in the way of complexity but, until recent times, all codes were based on substitution or transposition techniques. Throughout history, there has been a constant battle between those seeking to use encryption to preserve secrecy and those wishing to break the codes. Simon Singh recounts how a critical factor in the decision to try to execute Mary, Queen of Scots was the successful attempt by Hugh Walshingham, Queen Elizabeth's chief secretary, in deciphering coded messages exchanged between Mary and others conspiring to overthrow the English monarch.[31]

In the pre-computer age, the battle between code makers and breakers could well have been regarded as an intellectual pursuit akin to solving a crossword puzzle.[32] The advent of the computer served to change the situation. Much has been written concerning the British and United States cryptographic operations during the Second

---

[31] S. Singh, *The Code Book* (London, 1999). This book provides an excellent account of the history and nature of cryptography and has been drawn on heavily in the preparation of this chapter.

[32] A contest to solve *The Times* crossword puzzle in less than 12 minutes was used by the security service as a front for the quest to find suitable people to work on its attempt to break the German Enigma code.

World War. These led to the development of the world's first practical computing machines. Although limited by today's standards, the processing power of these computers transformed code breaking from what had been an intellectual pursuit into an exercise in number crunching. The analogy might be made with a combination lock on a safe and the contrast between the stereotypical image of a skilled safe breaker using a stethoscope to detect the correct combination and the random selection of numbers continued until the correct combination is achieved. Whilst the effort of trying several million possible combinations would be too great for humans, the task is comparatively simple for a computer.

In response to the vulnerability of traditional forms of encryption, modern systems place reliance upon mathematical techniques. One of the first of a new generation of cryptographic techniques was implemented in the United States Data Encryption Standard, or DES. DES has been a source of some controversy since its inception in 1977, with allegations that its effectiveness was deliberately reduced at the behest of the United States National Security Agency. The level of security is basically as great as the complexity of the encryption software. The analogy might be made with a combination lock. A lock with three dials provides some security, but one with five considerably more so. The original version of DES used what is described as a 56-bit key. This has some 70 quadrillion combinations. A massive figure for human calculators, but one which provides a more manageable challenge to modern computers. The selection of a 56-bit key is rumoured to have been influenced by the United States National Security Agency. The Agency is reported to possess the world's most powerful computers, machines capable of decoding messages encoded using a 56-bit key within a matter of hours. As computer technology develops, it has become possible for other organisations to acquire the processing power required. In 1998, the Electronic Frontier Foundation, a civil liberties pressure group, claimed to have built a 'DES cracker' for $250,000 whilst, in yet another significant demonstration of the power of the Internet, it has been reported that messages have been successfully decoded using several thousand computers linked together over the Internet and operating throughout the night whilst their normal users slept.[33]

DES—and other forms of substitution and transposition codes—are examples of single key or symmetric encryption systems. In the same way that the same key is used to open and lock a door, a message is encoded and decoded using the same key. So long as only the sender and recipient know the key, the system is reasonably secure. Apart from the vulnerability of codes to attack by code breakers, another significant point of weakness has concerned the fact that a single key is used to encode and to decode the message. If a sender wishes the recipient to be able to decipher his or her messages, it is necessary to deliver a copy of the key. The possibility that the key might be intercepted or misused creates another major point of vulnerability. Whilst systems such as DES might be used within closed networks of trusted parties—Electronic Data Interchange (EDI)

---

[33] There were 3,500 computers linked over the Internet, searching possible key combinations at a rate of 1.5 trillion keys per hour. In total, 312 hours of processing were required to find the correct key.

agreements would be an obvious example—it can be of limited value in the wider world of e-commerce. Here, just as is the case in the High Street, the intention is that customers and suppliers who have no prior knowledge of each other can conduct business. Clearly, no sensible users of encryption would send a key to a party they had not met previously.

A solution to this problem emerged with the development of public key or asymmetric cryptography. The concept was initially devised in 1976 by two mathematicians, Whitfield Diffie and Martin Hellman, and was brought to practical fruition by three further mathematicians, Ron Rivest, Adi Shamir, and Leonard Adleman, after whom the RSA system is named. It has recently been reported that similar work had been conducted in the United Kingdom at the GCHQ, although details were withheld on grounds of national security.

The RSA system has proved controversial in a number of respects. Although the system was developed using public funds, the algorithms were patented (the patents expired in the year 2000) by a private company, which marketed the software on a commercial basis. The system was first marketed in 1977, and required levels of processing power which effectively limited its use to large organisations and government departments. A modified form of public key encryption, still based on the RSA algorithms but suitable for use on personal computers, was developed by Phil Zimmerman and is generally referred to by the acronym PGP (Pretty Good Privacy). Zimmerman's original intention was reportedly to offer the system on a commercial basis. In 1991, however, he became concerned at legislative proposals being discussed in the United States Congress which, if enacted, would have restricted the availability of encryption software. Zimmerman's response was to persuade a friend to place a copy of PGP on the Internet. From that date, the cryptographic genie has been well and truly out of the bottle and copies of PGP can be downloaded free of charge from a wide range of Internet sites.

For a number of years, Zimmerman faced threats of patent infringement action by RSA, but eventually the parties concluded a licence allowing the use of the RSA algorithms in non-commercial copies of PGP. This has been dropped. The United States government also places restrictions on the strength of RSA software which may lawfully be exported from the United States and threatened action against Zimmerman. Doubts were raised, however, as to whether causing a copy of PGP to be placed on the Internet constituted an act of exporting as defined in the relevant legislation and, given that the system could not be uninvented, the decision was taken to drop proceedings.

A user of either PGP or RSA software will generate two keys, a public and a private key. The act of generating the keys typically requires nothing more than random movements of the computer mouse. Messages can be encrypted using either key, but possession of the other key will be required in order to decrypt them. Although the mathematics are beyond the comprehension of mere lawyers, the system is claimed to be significantly more secure than single-key systems, although it also operates considerably more slowly.

If consideration is given to the nature of the public key system, strengths and weaknesses can be identified. The scenario might be postulated whereby A receives a message which purports to have been sent by B and encrypted using the latter's private key. Assuming A had details of the public key, the message can be decrypted and A can be certain that the message has not been tampered with following its encryption. A cannot, however, be certain that B has not let the private key fall into a third party's hands. Again, given the ease with which PGP software and email accounts can be acquired or forged, if A and B have not dealt previously, A cannot be confident that B is who he or she claims to be. A final weakness may be most relevant in the commercial context. B may be a company and the key used to encrypt a message ordering 100,000 widgets from A. A will have no means of knowing that the person sending the message on A's behalf is authorised to engage in such transactions.

The same issues will apply in the event that A replies to B, encrypting the message with A's public key. Again, there can be confidence that the message has not been intercepted and amended in transit but less reliance upon the identity of the claimed sender. Indeed, given that the essence of the public key is that it is public, it might be a foolhardy person who would place too much credence on the origin of a message. From the point of view of the sender, he or she may be given details of a public key and told that it belongs to Ian Lloyd, a well-known supplier of memorabilia of Glasgow Celtic Football Club. Encouraged by the prospect of secure communications, credit card details may be transmitted with a view to acquiring a selection of materials. Unfortunately, the key may have been generated by a criminal seeking to acquire valid credit card numbers.

Enter trusted third parties

If the aim of encryption is to authenticate the accuracy of a transmission and to identify its sender, systems of public key cryptography score one out of two. To provide mechanisms for promoting trust in the identity and status of the parties involved, the involvement of trusted third parties (TTPs), also referred to as certification agencies, has emerged. The TTP will seek evidence that the party sending a message is who he or she claims to be and will cause a certificate to that effect to be attached to a message. For the United Kingdom, banks, some solicitors and accountancy firms, and even the Post Office have expressed interest in acting as TTPs.

The basic operation of TTPs is non-controversial and can be equated with traditional professions such as that of notary, or even with the role of a witness to a document. TTPs will almost inevitably obtain information about their customers' keys and some offer of what is referred to as a key recovery service. This effectively involves them keeping secure a copy of a private key. In the event that the user forgets the key or—perhaps more likely—details are destroyed by a disaffected or departing employee, the loss can be made good.

As with many issues concerned with the Internet, initial moves in the field came from the United States. Here, enormous controversy followed proposals to introduce a new system of encryption, the Escrowed Encryption Standard, more commonly referred to as the 'Clipper Chip'. The attraction of this system, which would be based on public key cryptography, would be that any form of digitised data would be encrypted in such a way as to ensure a high level of security. The less welcome aspect of the system was that its structure would enable 'keys' to be made available to government agencies, enabling messages to be readily deciphered. Concerns were expressed as to whether the legal controls envisaged concerning release of the keys would provide adequate safeguards. Although legislation implementing the Clipper proposals did not pass through Congress, it was announced in Autumn 1996 that export controls on encryption software would be reduced in return for an industry commitment to the introduction of a 'key recovery' system requiring that copies of all keys be held by a 'Trusted Third Party'. It would appear in this case that the prime motive was that the third party should be trusted by the government rather than by the contracting parties.

Much of the legislative debate in the late 1990s has concerned the role of TTPs and systems of key recovery and escrow. In March 1997, the Council of the OECD adopted 'Guidelines for Cryptography Policy'.[34] In a manner similar to that adopted in the field of data protection, the guidelines identify eight principles which should inform national legislation in this field:

1. Cryptographic methods should be trustworthy in order to generate confidence in the use of information and communications systems.

2. Users should have a right to choose any cryptographic method, subject to applicable law.

3. Cryptographic methods should be developed in response to the needs, demands and responsibilities of individuals, businesses and governments.

4. Technical standards, criteria and protocols for cryptographic methods should be developed and promulgated at the national and international level.

5. The fundamental rights of individuals to privacy, including secrecy of communications and protection of personal data, should be respected in national cryptographic policies and in the implementation and use of cryptographic methods.

6. National cryptographic policies may allow lawful access to plain text, or cryptographic keys, of encrypted data. These policies must respect the other principles contained in the guidelines to the greatest extent possible.

7. Whether established by contract or legislation, the liability of individuals and entities that offer cryptographic services or hold or access cryptographic keys should be clearly stated.

8. Governments should co-operate to co-ordinate cryptographic policies. As part of this effort, governments should remove, or avoid creating in the name of cryptography policy, unjustified obstacles to trade.

[34] Available from <http://www.oecd.org/dsti/sti/it/secur/prod/crypto1.htm>

A strong relationship can be identified between these principles and a number of those applying in the data protection field. Although the guidelines recognise the need for some legal controls over the use of cryptography, it is stressed throughout that these must 'respect user choice to the greatest extent'. To this extent, the guidelines are seen as moving away from the United States-sponsored notion of mandatory key escrow, a move which is also followed in recent EU and United Kingdom legislation and proposals.

It is not the purpose of this chapter to discuss in detail the political aspects of encryption policy. It is suggested, however, that both sides are failing to come to terms with the reality of modern life. Those advocating extensive powers for law enforcement agencies are, in many respects, looking back to a form of golden age when governments could exercise genuine control over communications. Terrestrial broadcasting was largely a state-controlled monopoly, and the limits of transmitter power meant that foreign broadcasts could be received only in regions close to national borders. Postal and telecommunication services were also state-controlled, and international communications were conducted only on a small scale. The world has moved on and attempts to exert control again are likely to be doomed to failure.

Those opposed to the interception of encrypted messages may suffer from a similarly dated view of the world, harking back to a golden era of individual anonymity. In many Western countries, this can be considered to have reached its apogee in the 1960s. The past thirty years have seen a massive increase in the amount of personal data recorded and processed. Privacy in the traditional sense has largely vanished. In part, this is as a result of public sector activity, but a large and growing threat comes from the private sector. There has never been a situation in which all communications receive immunity from interception. Whilst there is certainly need for controls to be introduced concerning interception and decryption of encoded messages, the notion that individuals should be assured of absolute privacy for their communications has never been a feature of societal life.

The Electronic Signatures Directive

Although its provisions generally conjure up images of systems of public key encryption, the Electronic Signatures Directive[35] seeks to be technologically neutral. Its implementation would have the effect of providing for electronic equivalents to writing and signature to be accepted within the Member States. The Directive is expressly stated to be unconcerned with contractual and other procedural requirements.[36] Its purpose is stated to be:

> ...to facilitate the use of electronic signatures and to contribute to their legal recognition. It establishes a legal framework for electronic signatures and certain

---

[35] Directive 99/93/EC.
[36] See also the provisions of the Electronic Commerce Directive, Directive 2000/31/EC.

certification-services in order to ensure the proper functioning of the internal market.[37]

The Electronic Signatures Directive identifies two forms of signature: electronic and advanced electronic signatures. These are defined as:

1. 'electronic signature' means data in electronic form which are attached to or logically associated with other electronic data and which serve as a method of authentication; and

2. 'advanced electronic signature' means an electronic signature which meets the following requirements:

   (a) it is uniquely linked to the signatory;

   (b) it is capable of identifying the signatory;

   (c) it is created using means that the signatory can maintain under his sole control; and

   (d) it is linked to the data to which it relates in such a manner that any subsequent change of the data is detectable.[38]

The term 'electronic signature' is very broad. It would encompass, for example, the use of scanning equipment to create a digital image of a person's signature, with this image being reproduced at the end of a word-processed letter. Advanced forms of signature will require the use of some form of encryption. The Electronic Signatures Directive refers to this under the heading of 'Secure-Signature-Creation Device'. The technical attributes to be possessed by such devices are specified in Annex 3, whilst the Directive provides that Member States may, acting in accordance with criteria to be specified by the Commission, establish mechanisms to verify the conformity of particular systems of encryption.[39]

In terms of the legal status to be afforded to electronic signatures, the Electronic Signatures Directive provides that:

1. Member States shall ensure that advanced electronic signatures which are based on a qualified certificate and which are created by a secure-signature-creation device:

   (a) satisfy the legal requirements of a signature in relation to data in electronic form in the same manner as a hand-written signature satisfies those requirements in relation to paper-based data; and

   (b) are admissible as evidence in legal proceedings.

---

[37] Article 1.
[38] Directive 99/93/EC, Article 2(1).
[39] Ibid., Article 3(4).

2. Member States shall ensure that an electronic signature is not denied legal effectiveness and admissibility as evidence in legal proceedings solely on the grounds that it is:

– in electronic form; or

– not based upon a qualified certificate; or

– not based upon a qualified certificate issued by an accredited certification-service-provider; or

– not created by a secure signature-creation device.[40]

An advanced electronic signature will give a considerable degree of assurance that the signature is that of a particular person. There cannot be assurance that its use has been authorised by the owner, either generally or in the context of a particular transaction. It might be, for example, that an unauthorised third party has obtained a copy of a private key. Alternatively, a company may have a private key which is used by an employee to place an order for goods but where the employee is acting in excess of his or her authority. To overcome these difficulties, the notion has been advanced that the use of a signature should be certified by an independent agency. The Electronic Signatures Directive identifies criteria which must be met in what is called a 'qualified certificate':

(a) an indication that the certificate is issued as a qualified certificate;

(b) the identification of the certification-service-provider and the State in which it is established;

(c) the name of the signatory or a pseudonym, which shall be identified as such;

(d) provision for a specific attribute of the signatory to be included if relevant, depending on the purpose for which the certificate is intended;

(e) signature-verification data which correspond to signature-creation data under the control of the signatory;

(f) an indication of the beginning and end of the period of validity of the certificate;

(g) the identity code of the certificate;

(h) the advanced electronic signature of the certification-service-provider issuing it;

(i) limitations on the scope of use of the certificate, if applicable; and

(j) limits on the value of transactions for which the certificate can be used, if applicable.[41]

This is in effect creating a role for the TTPs, now known as certification-service-providers, discussed above. Annex 2 of the Directive specifies a wide range of technical

---

[40] Ibid., Article 5.
[41] Directive 99/93/EC, Annex 1.

and organisational attributes which must be demonstrated in order for a certificate issued by a service provider to be recognised as a qualified certificate.

The Electronic Signatures Directive makes it clear that no limitations are to be imposed upon the freedom of anyone to engage in the activity of a certification-service-provider. It is provided, however, that:

> Member States may introduce or maintain voluntary accreditation schemes aiming at enhanced levels of certification-service provision. All conditions related to such schemes must be objective, transparent, proportionate and non-discriminatory. Member States may not limit the number of accredited certification-service-providers for reasons which fall within the scope of this Directive.[42]

It may well prove, of course, that a person wishing to engage in the business of certification-service-provider may find that commercial pressure may dictate that accreditation is sought.

Electronic signatures and the Electronic Communications Act 2000

The Electronic Signatures Directive[43] requires to be implemented in the Member States by July 2001. The United Kingdom met this timetable with the enactment of the Electronic Communications Act, which received the Royal Assent on 25 May 2000. Reference has previously been made to the role of this statute in providing for electronic communications to be taken as satisfying requirements for writing. The Act also provides for recognition of electronic signatures and for the activities of what are referred to as cryptography service providers.

Electronic signatures

The Electronic Communications Act 2000's provisions relating to the recognition of electronic signatures are rather more simple than those found in the Electronic Signatures Directive.[44] The Act eschews the distinction between 'electronic' and 'advanced electronic signatures', instead providing that:

> In any legal proceeding–
>
> (a) an electronic signature incorporated or logically associated with a particular electronic communication or with particular electronic data, and
>
> (b) the certification by any person of such a signature,
>
> shall each be admissible in evidence in relation to any question as to the authenticity of the communication or data or as to the integrity of the communication or data.[45]

---

[42] Ibid., Article 3(2).
[43] Directive 99/93/EC.
[44] Ibid.
[45] Section 7(1).

The term 'electronic signature' is defined in terms similar to those found in the Directive:

> For the purposes of this section an electronic signature is so much of anything in electronic form as—
>
> (a) is incorporated into or otherwise logically associated with any electronic communication or electronic data; and
>
> (b) purports to be so incorporated or associated for the purpose of being used in establishing the authenticity of the communication or data, the integrity of the communication or data, or both.[46]

Effectively, the decision will be left to a court what weight to attach to any particular signature.

In the situation where a signature is required to validate a contract, the provisions of s 8 of the Electronic Communications Act 2000 will again be relevant. As is the case with requirements for writing generally, rather than providing for blanket recognition of electronic signatures, the Act provides that secondary legislation may be made in order to provide for:

> (c) the doing of anything which under any such provisions is required to be or may be authorised by a person's signature or seal, or is required to be delivered as a deed or witnessed by electronic means.[47]

Cryptography service providers

The final, and most controversial, element of the Electronic Communications Act 2000 concerns the provisions made for cryptographic service providers. This term is defined as encompassing:

> ...any service which is provided to the senders or recipients of electronic communications, or to those storing electronic data, and is designed to facilitate the use of cryptographic techniques for the purpose of—
>
> (a) securing that such communications or data can be accessed, or can be put into an intelligible form, only by certain persons; or
>
> (b) securing that the authenticity or integrity of such communications or data is capable of being ascertained.[48]

The service must either be provided from premises within the United Kingdom or be provided to persons carrying on a business in the United Kingdom. A German service provider marketing services to United Kingdom-based companies would come within the second element of this definition.

Anyone is entitled to establish a cryptography support service. Equally, there is no obligation imposed on users of encryption to involve such a service in their

---

[46] Section 7(2).
[47] Section 8(2).
[48] Section 6.

transactions. Especially in cases where parties have a background of previous dealings or operate as part of an EDI network, such third-party involvement may well be rendered otiose.

At present, no restrictions—and virtually no legislation—apply to the use of encryption or cryptography services. Maintenance of the status quo would not justify such flagship legislation. What is envisaged in Part I of the Electronic Communications Act 2000 is the establishment of a voluntary register of accredited cryptography service providers along the lines provided for in the Electronic Signatures Directive.[49] Whilst the decision to seek registration will be a voluntary one, the intention is that the existence of such a scheme will promote public confidence in what must be regarded as an embryonic profession.

The Electronic Communications Act 2000 provides in ss 2 and 3 that responsibility for the establishment of such a register is to vest in the Secretary of State (or such other body to whom performance of the task may be delegated). It has been indicated, however, that the intention is that the register should be operated on a voluntary basis. Section 16 provides that the provisions will come into force on such day as may be fixed by order, but that if no order is made within five years from the date of Royal Assent, the order-making power will lapse.

Government speakers in the Commons indicated a strong desire that a voluntary scheme should be introduced as soon as possible. Discussions with the Alliance for Electronic Business resulted in the establishment of a 'non-statutory self-regulating scheme (tScheme) for Trust services'.[50] The scope of the proposal is described as being 'to operate and enforce a voluntary approval scheme for trust services'. The overall objective is stated to be to provide a mechanism that will:

- set minimum criteria for trust and confidence;
- be responsible for:
  - the approval of electronic trust services against those criteria;
  - the monitoring of approved services;
  - provide a means of redress where services fall below those criteria;
- and thereby promote the benefits of using an approved electronic trust service.

Five organisations are currently approved for the provision of services. An indication of the nature of the likely requirements can be found in Annex 2 of the Electronic Signatures Directive[51] (with which the Electronic Communications Act 2000 is designed to be compatible). This refers to the need for demonstrable reliability of the systems, technologies, and personnel involved in the provision of the service; the acceptance of liability for losses caused through errors in the service provision; and the observance of a proper degree of confidentiality regarding details

---

[49] Directive 99/93/EC.
[50] Available from <http://www.tscheme.org/>
[51] Directive 99/93/EC.

of the customer's business. Further indication regarding the criteria which might be applied can again be taken from the Alliance for Electronic Business Scheme, which states that:

> It is anticipated that the criteria will address business, management, operational and technical issues necessary for approval. Criteria will relate to both the services offered and the organisations offering them and will be based as far as possible on existing criteria in the marketplace.
>
> The actual criteria used for assessment will be a selection of elements from publicly available, and wherever possible international, technical or management standards (e.g. ISO 9000, BS 7799, X.509, FIPS 140; and from other appropriate criteria published by bodies such as FSA and OFTEL).
>
> In addition to adopting previously defined standards the organisation will, when necessary, create criteria not already existing in the marketplace. It is vital to the success of [the] scheme, and its take up by providers, that it does not duplicate existing approval and regulatory structures, but builds on their foundations.
>
> The selection of criteria, termed an Approval Profile, will be unique for each different type of service. Criteria will be selected by reference to specific versions of standards, and reviewed periodically to ensure that the most relevant and appropriate criteria are applied, as the standardisation process and services develop. A list of the criteria selected, including any necessary identifying publication information (e.g. dates, versions, etc.) will be maintained and publicly available.

It is clear from the above that there can be no single scheme of certification. Given the vast range of transactions that may be carried out electronically, such an approach is necessary and desirable. It is to be expected and hoped that standards will emerge over time to give appropriate guidance to the courts and other agencies on what reliance might reasonably be placed upon a particular form of certificate. One thing does seem certain: accreditation will not be a cheap process for service providers. The Minister for Small Business and E-Commerce stated in Committee that:

> An estimate of the possible costs involved for a medium-sized company that is seeking approval for the issue of certificates would be between £10,000 and £30,000.[52]

Conclusions

There seems little doubt that e-commerce will expand significantly in the coming years. It is the author's view that this will take place in spite of concerns regarding lack of security. Consumers run the risk of falling victim to fraud in every aspect of life. The Internet is no better and no worse in this respect. Encryption is frequently used by service providers to enhance security. This is typically done in a manner which makes no demands on the consumer. The complexities of public key cryptography are such that its use is likely to remain restricted to the commercial sector and to techno-freaks.

---

[52] HC Official Report, SC B (Electronic Communications Bill), col. 37, 9 December 1999.

A further development which may enhance consumer confidence in e-commerce relates to the acceptance by credit card providers of the risk of loss due to fraud on the Internet. Under s 75 of the Consumer Credit Act 1974, credit card providers incur joint and several liability with merchants in respect of any claim which a consumer may have in respect of misrepresentation or breach of contract relating to a transaction valued at between £100 and £30,000. This provision will apply to Internet transactions, although there is doubt as to whether it applies in a situation where a consumer resident in the United Kingdom contracts with a merchant located in some other country. In the event that the consumer's details are intercepted by a third party and subsequently misused, s 83 of the Act may be of assistance. This provides that the card holder is not liable for loss arising from third-party use of the credit facility by 'another person not acting as the debtor's agent'. Section 84 does provide that the consumer may be liable (up to a maximum of £50) for misuse of a 'credit token' during the period when it leaves the consumer's control until its loss is reported to the creditor. The term 'credit token' is defined as a 'card, check voucher, coupon, stamp, form, booklet or other document or thing'. This can clearly relate to the physical card rather than the numbers contained thereon.

If the Internet creates the problem, it may also provide the solution. A growing number of credit card suppliers conduct business over the Internet. As described previously, this can result in very considerable cost savings. One card provider, Egg. com,[53] offers its customers a guarantee against the risk of loss through fraud in respect of activities carried out within the card company's own network of approved dealers. Again, the impression is given that the credit card company will be liable only after redress has been sought and refused by the supplier. Section 75 of the Consumer Credit Act 1974 gives the consumer the option of which party to proceed against in the first instance and the case of *Office of Fair Trading v Lloyds TSB Bank Plc and Others*,[54] confirmed that this right applies in respect of all transactions, regardless of where the supplier might be located. In the event that loss follows from a transaction concluded over the Internet with a supplier based in China and using a credit card supplied by a United Kingdom-based financier, the credit card company will incur joint and several liability.

The Commission and United Kingdom proposals regarding electronic signatures may be of greater relevance in the commercial sector, where many requirements of form currently restrict the extent to which companies can maximise the use of electronic communications. However, this may relate more to undertakings' relations with the state than to between themselves. The unanswered question in this—as in many other areas of IT law—is whether legal provisions will be relevant in the face of seemingly remorseless advances in technology.

---

[53] <http://www.egg.com>
[54] [2007] UKHL 48.

25

Contractual liability for defective software

Introduction

Software is undoubtedly the driving force of the information society. By any standards, the sector is a major contributor to national economies and employment and it should be borne in mind that these figures relate to only one part of the information technology industry. The traditional notion of a computer is that it consists of a monitor, processing unit, keyboard, and sundry peripherals such as the ubiquitous mouse. Most people will recognise such a device when they see one. It is less easy to recognise a motor car or video recorder as a computer, yet a modern motor car is in many respects a sophisticated computer system, to the extent it has been calculated that the 'chip cost of a new car is now greater than the metal cost'.[1] A vast range of objects, from domestic appliances to nuclear power stations, is dependent on microprocessors. In many cases, these are, quite literally, built into a structure. Worldwide, it is estimated that there are some 20 billion embedded chips in use, a fact which caused great concern in the context of the Millennium Bug. It has been reported that:

> All buildings built between 1984 (the year when building services started to computerise) and 1996/7 (the period when most new buildings were fitted with systems that were millennium compliant) are likely to be affected by the millennium bug. Bovis Construction Group, one of the biggest building contractors has written to the owners of 870 buildings it has built since 1984 warning them integral systems ranging from ventilation and heating to intruder alarms and connections to the electricity supply network may fail. This is because many building systems use microchips to identify dates for switching machinery on and off and to alert maintenance staff of the need for servicing.[2]

As the importance of software increases, so does the level of societal vulnerability in the event of any failure. In purely economic terms, losses are potentially massive. Although it is tempting to take the example of the Millennium Bug as a case where the degree of risk was exaggerated, even what might be regarded as a false alarm proved

---

[1] <http://www.scl.org/members/emagazine/vol9/iss3/vol9-iss3-peter-cochrane-art.htm>
[2] Cited in evidence to the House of Commons Select Committee on Science and Technology.

an extremely costly exercise. The British Bankers Association estimated that United Kingdom banks spent £1 billion checking and repairing systems. British Telecom budgeted for expenditure of £300 million. Worldwide, costs were estimated at some £400 billion. To put these figures into perspective, these figures exceed the total financial cost of the Vietnam War.[3]

Matters could, of course, have been significantly worse in the event of extensive problems materialising. One estimate suggested that the effect of the bug would cause 8 per cent of Western European companies to fail. The prospect of global recession was frequently raised in reports. Additionally, as indicated above, the application of information technology in a vast range of applications conjured up the spectre of hospital patients dying because of failures of medical devices; trains, planes, and automobiles crashing; massive power cuts; and shortage of food and drink due to failures in retailers' distribution systems. Fortunately, the predictions of computer doom proved unfounded, but the incident may have served a useful, albeit expensive, purpose in bringing home the extent of our society's dependence on information technology. What the incident also achieved was to highlight the fact that where losses arise through the improper operation of systems and equipment, considerations of legal liability will not be far behind.

To date, comparatively few cases concerned specifically with issues of software quality have reached the stage of court proceedings. A variety of explanations may be proposed for this state of affairs. Although parties may not wish to litigate when the answer is certain, excessive uncertainty as to the very basis upon which a court may decide will itself inhibit litigation. Some of the most basic questions concerning the application of provisions of contractual and non-contractual liability in the information technology field admit of no easy or certain solution. With one exception, all of the cases which have reached the stage of High Court proceedings have concerned relatively high-value contracts for software which has, either been developed under the terms of a specific contract (bespoke software) for one or a small number of clients, or has been modified extensively to suit the needs of a particular customer (customised software). To date, there have been no cases concerned with the extent of the liabilities which will apply to mass-produced or standard software packages such as word processing or spreadsheet programs. A further factor complicating such cases is the invariable presence of a software licence. The role of these documents in respect of intellectual property issues has been discussed previously. In respect of liability considerations, the terms of the licence inevitably seek to limit or exclude the producer's liabilities in the event that the performance of the software does not match the user's expectations.

Forms of liability

Two main strands of liability run through the field of private law. The law of contract confers rights and imposes duties upon contracting parties. Whilst the nature and

---

[3] *Sunday Times*, 10 August 1997. The cost of the Vietnam War has been estimated at some £370 billion.

extent of these may be determined in large part by the expressed wishes of the parties, these may be constrained by the provisions of statutes such as the Sale of Goods Act 1979 and the Unfair Contract Terms Act 1977. It is, of course, a basic tenet of the common law that contractual rights can be enforced only by those who are a party to the contract. In the situation where no contract exists, attention must turn to non-contractual remedies. Until recently, the basis of these has rested in the law of tort/delict. The prerequisite for a successful action in tort is evidence of negligence on the part of the defender (absent exceptional circumstances where strict liability has attached to this party's actions). The passage of the Consumer Protection Act 1987 has radically transformed the non-contractual position. Based on the provisions of an EC Directive on 'The Approximation of the Laws, Regulations and Administrative Provisions of the Member States Concerning Liability for Defective Products',[4] this serves to impose a strict liability regime, whereby the producer of a product is held liable for personal injury or damage to non-commercial property resulting from the presence of a defect within the product, irrespective of any fault on their part.

The nature of software defects

Prior to considering issues of legal liability, it might be helpful to attempt a brief analysis of the nature of the differences which exist between software and the tangible products with which society and the law are more familiar. Defects in a traditional product such as a motor car may originate in one of two ways. Design defects relate to some failure at the design stage, with the consequence that the failure node will be exhibited in every species of the product. A more commonplace form of defect is introduced during the production stage. It might be, for example, as happened in the case of *Smedleys v Breed*,[5] discussed below, that a caterpillar found its way into a can of peas somewhere within the canning process. Such defects will be restricted to one or to a limited number of examples of the product. In the *Smedleys* case, for example, only four caterpillars or other foreign bodies had been reported from an annual production of 3.5 million cans.

If a party is trying to establish that a product fails to comply with relevant quality requirements, the task is almost invariably simpler where defects arise in production. In most cases, what a claimant will seek to establish is that compared with other examples of a product, the one at issue is of inferior quality. The case might be put, for example, that 3,499,996 cans of peas did not contain foreign bodies. The four that did should, therefore, be considered exceptional (or exceptionally bad). Evidential burdens are more extensive when all examples of the product exhibit the same properties. A prime example is in the pharmaceutical field, where adverse reactions to a product

---

[4] Council Directive 85/374/EEC, OJ 1985 L 210, p. 29.
[5] [1974] AC 839.

are generally caused because of the properties of the drug, rather than through con-tamination of a particular tablet or bottle of medicine.

Where software is concerned, the nature of the digital copying process is such that there can be a high degree of confidence that every copy of software will be identical. If particular copies are corrupted, the likelihood is that they will not work at all, so that any defect becomes apparent before any damage is caused. If a customer should wish to establish that a copy of a word processing program which has been purchased is not of satisfactory quality, argument will have to proceed by reference to word processing programs produced by other producers and to general standards. Although the task can be accomplished, it is a significantly more onerous burden than that faced by a person claiming the existence of a production defect.

A more general difference may be identified at the level of the testing which may be carried out in respect of a product. With a product such as a motor car, it is possible to test every component so as to provide definitive information about its properties. Often, however, testing entails destruction of the item involved and, even where this is not the case, it will seldom be commercially feasible to test every specimen of the product. In production, it is possible that some components will be of inferior quality to those tested. Only a portion of products will possess any particular defect and these may not be the ones which are selected for inspection. The conclusion from this analy-sis is that it is possible to test one item exhaustively, but that the results have limited applicability regarding other items of the same type.

The situation is radically different where software is concerned. It is impossible to test even the simplest program in an exhaustive fashion. This is because of the myriad possibilities for interaction (whether desired or not) between the various elements of the program. In the world of popular science, much publicity has been given in recent years to what is known as the chaos theory. This suggests that every event influences every other event; that the beating of a butterfly's wings has an impact upon the devel-opment of a hurricane. On such an analysis, totally accurate weather forecasting will never be practicable because of the impossibility of taking account of all the variables affecting the climate. The theory's hypothesis is reality in a software context. Although software can and should be tested, it has to be accepted that every piece of software will contain errors which may not materialise until a particular and perhaps unrepeatable set of circumstances occurs. It is commonplace for software to be placed on the market in the knowledge that it contains errors. Early users, in effect, act as unpaid testers. As faults are reported to the producer, fixes will be developed and incorporated into new versions of the software.[6]

Especially where software is used in safety-critical functions, it is sometimes advocated that where an error is discovered, it is preferable to devise procedures to prevent the circumstances recurring than to attempt to modify the software. The argument is that any change to the software may have unanticipated consequences, resulting in another error manifesting itself at some time in the future. The cause

---

[6] See the discussion of the case of *Saphena v Allied Collection Agencies* [1995] FSR 616.

of a massive failure which paralysed sections of the United States telecommunications system in 1991, was ultimately traced to changes which had been made in the call-routing software.[7] The software contained several million lines of code. Three apparently insignificant lines were changed and chaos ensued. By way of contrast, the operators of London's Docklands Light Railway, whose trains are driven under computer control, took the decision that they would not make any changes to the software after it had passed its acceptance tests. The result was that for several years, trains stopped on an open stretch of line, paused for a few seconds and then continued with their journey. It had been intended to build a station at the site. After the software was accepted, the plans were abandoned, but the trains remained ignorant of this fact.

Forms of software

As indicated above, software is supplied in a variety of situations and under a range of conditions. Viewed across the spectrum, at one end we can identify bespoke or made-to-measure software products. The cost of these may run into many millions of pounds, with the essential feature being that the supplier agrees to design and develop software to suit the needs of a particular customer, or a comparatively small number of identified customers. The software will be supplied under the terms of a written agreement negotiated between the parties. Perhaps not surprisingly, given the costs involved, almost all of the software-related disputes which have reached the courts have been concerned with such forms of contract.

At the far end of the software spectrum are standard software packages. In this category, identical copies will be supplied to users—perhaps tens or even hundreds of thousands in number—often via a substantial distribution chain and at a cost ranging from tens to thousands of pounds. There will seldom be any written agreement negotiated in advance between the parties, with the producer attempting to introduce a set of terms and conditions through the device of a licence. As will be discussed below, the validity of software licences is open to challenge on a number of grounds.

A final and more nebulous category of software is referred to as having been 'customised'. This involves the supplier modifying existing software, developed either by themselves or by a third party, better to suit the requirements of a particular customer. The degree of customisation may vary from making very minor adjustments to a single package, to developing a unique system based on a combination of a number of existing packages. With developments in 'object oriented engineering' it may be expected that the range of customised products will increase substantially as developers base their operations on a 'pick-and-mix' philosophy.

---

[7] Most of the examples of software failure cited in this chapter have been culled from the columns of comp.risks, an Internet-based newsgroup which chronicles the failures of safety-critical systems and the risks they pose to the public.

The legal status of software and software contracts

Throughout this book, use has been made of terms such as 'software industry' and of software being 'produced'. Such terms are in common use. The pages on the Microsoft website describing its software packages are titled 'products',[8] whilst the Price Waterhouse study discussed in the context of copyright law is titled 'The Contribution of the Packaged Software Industry to the European Economies'. The fact that terms are in popular usage does not, of course, mean that their legal interpretation will be the same, and over the years, much legal ink has been spilled in discussion of the question of whether contracts for the supply of software should be regarded as a species of goods or as a form of services.

Much of the discussion regarding status has focused on two decisions of the Court of Appeal. In *Lee v Griffin*,[9] the Court of Appeal was faced with a contract under which a dentist undertook to make a set of dentures for a patient. A dispute subsequently arising, the court was faced with the question of the contract's proper categorisation. Holding the contract to be one of sale, the court held that the essential test was whether anything that could be the subject-matter of a sale had come into existence. In the event, for example, that an attorney was engaged to draw up a deed for a client, it was held that the contract would be one for services. In other situations, however:

> I do not think that the test to apply to these cases is whether the value of the work exceeds that of the materials used in its execution; for, if a sculptor were employed to execute a work of art, greatly as his skill and labour, assuming it to be of the highest description, might exceed the value of the marble on which he worked, the contract would in my opinion, nevertheless be a contract for the sale of a chattel.[10]

On this basis, it would appear that the supply of software on some storage device such as a disk or CD would be classed as involving goods. The increasingly common situation where software is supplied electronically, typically being downloaded from a website, could not, of course, come within the definition.

The distinction between goods and services was again at issue before the Court of Appeal in the case of *Robinson v Graves*.[11] The contract here was one whereby an artist agreed to paint a portrait of his client's wife. On the basis of the situation hypothesised in *Lee v Griffin*,[12] it would appear that such a transaction should be regarded as one of sale. In the event, however, it was held that it should be regarded as one for services. In reaching this conclusion, the court sought to identify the prime purpose of the contract. In the oft-quoted words of Greer LJ:

> If the substance of the contract . . . is that skill and labour have to be exercised for the production of the article and . . . it is only ancillary to that that there will pass from the

[8] <http://www.microsoft.com/office/products.htm>
[9] (1861) 1 B&S 272.
[10] (1861) 1 B&S 272 at 278.
[11] [1935] 1 KB 579.
[12] (1861) 1 B&S 272.

artist to his client or customer some materials in addition to the skill involved in the production of the portrait, that does not make any difference to the result, because the substance of the contract is the skill and experience of the artist in producing the picture.[13]

Although the court in *Robinson*[14] did not overrule, or even distinguish, the earlier authority, it must be doubted how far the two approaches can truly be considered compatible. It would appear that the decision in *Robinson* has been the more influential in recent years but, even so, its application in a software context has not been without its difficulties. Whilst it would seem to suggest that contracts for the development of bespoke software should be regarded as services, standard software exhibits many of the attributes associated with goods.

In the final analysis, the precise categorisation of software contracts may be a matter of limited practical significance. In most of the cases which have come before the courts, the dispute has centred on the interpretation of a specific contract between the parties. The court's task is to determine what the contract said, rather than concern itself unduly with categorisations. Even where no detailed contract exists, there is little difference between the relevant statutory provisions. The Sale of Goods Act 1979 implies terms relating to title description and quality. The Supply of Goods and Services Act 1982 implies requirements that the supplier should exercise reasonable skill and care and that any goods ultimately supplied will comply with identical requirements relating to title, description, and quality as those required under the Sale of Goods Act 1979. Faced with this convergence between the statutory provisions, it is not surprising that Staughton LJ, delivering judgment in the case of *Saphena Computing Ltd v Allied Collection Agencies Ltd*, was able to state:

> It was, we are told, common ground that the law governing these contracts was precisely the same whether they were contracts for the sale of goods or for the supply of services. It is therefore unnecessary to consider into which category they might come.[15]

In the case of *St Albans District Council v ICL*,[16] the Court of Appeal was braver—or more foolhardy. Here, Sir Iain Glidewell posed the question, 'Is software goods?' He continued:

> If a disc carrying the program is transferred, by way of sale or hire, and the program is in some way defective, so that it will not instruct or enable the computer to achieve the intended purpose, is this a defect in the disc? Put more precisely, would the seller or hirer of the disc be in breach of the terms of quality or fitness implied by s. 14 of the Sale of Goods Act [1979].[17]

---

[13] [1935] 1 KB 579 at 587.
[14] *Robinson v Graves* [1935] 1 KB 579.
[15] [1995] FSR 616 at 652.
[16] [1996] 4 All ER 481. Reported at first instance at [1995] FSR 686.
[17] [1996] 4 All ER 481 at 492.

There was, he recognised, no English or indeed any common law precedent on this point. An analogy was drawn, however, with another form of informational product:

> Suppose I buy an instruction manual on the maintenance and repair of a particular make of car. The instructions are wrong in an important respect. Anybody who follows them is likely to cause serious damage to the engine of his car. In my view the instructions are an integral part of the manual. The manual including the instructions, whether in a book or a video cassette, would in my opinion be 'goods' within the meaning of the Sale of Goods Act and the defective instructions would result in breach of the implied terms.
>
>   If this is correct, I can see no logical reason why it should not also be correct in relation to a computer disc onto which a program designed and intended to instruct or enable a computer to achieve particular functions has been encoded. If the disc is sold or hired by the computer manufacturer, but the program is defective, in my opinion there would prima facie be a breach of the terms as to quality and fitness for purpose implied by the Sale of Goods Act.[18]

As will be discussed, this statement will have implications for all of those involved in the information market. In the case of *Wormell v RHM Agriculture Ltd*,[19] the Court of Appeal recognised that where instructions for use were supplied along with a product, the sufficiency and adequacy of these should be taken into account in considering questions of the product's merchantability. *St Albans District Council v ICL*[20] appears, however, to be the first occasion in which instructions per se were subjected to the qualitative requirements of the Sale of Goods Act 1979. It remains uncertain, however, how extensive liability will be. The analogy drawn with a motor instruction book may be appropriate. In the circumstances described, where following the instructions will result in serious damage, there could be little argument that the book is not fit for its purpose. The decision becomes much closer if the complaint is that the book describes an inefficient method for performing work. Another problematic case might be where an instruction is so obviously wrong that no reasonable person would follow it. Equivalents in a software context might be inefficient methods of saving word processed documents or defects which require a user to 'work around' them. Further cases will be required before we can attempt a plausible answer to the question of what these qualitative requirements mean in a software context.

There is, of course, the increasing possibility that software might be downloaded over the Internet so that no tangible objects change hands. Indeed, in the present case, the practice for installing software was that an ICL engineer would visit, load the software from disk, and retain the disk. In such cases, there could be no transfer of goods. In such situations, it was indicated, in determining the extent of the parties' obligations:

> The answer must be sought in the Common Law. The terms implied by the Sale of Goods Act...were originally evolved by the Courts of Common Law and have since by analogy been implied by the courts into other types of contract.
>
>   ...

---

[18] [1996] 4 All ER 481 at 493.   [19] [1987] 3 All ER 75.   [20] [1996] 4 All ER 481.

In the absence of any express term as to quality or fitness for purpose, or of any term to the contrary, such a contract is subject to an implied term that the program will be reasonably fit for, i.e. reasonably capable of achieving the intended purpose.[21]

Given the existence of a specific contract between the parties, these comments must be regarded as *obiter dicta* rather than as binding precedent. They do appear, however, to be in line with a judicial trend to imply requirements that software be fit for its purpose into contracts unless the terms make clear provision to the contrary. Any ambiguities will be interpreted *contra proferentem*, with the case of *Salvage Association v CAP Financial Services*[22] providing a good illustration of how restrictive this doctrine may be. The key issue, therefore, must be to determine what concepts, such as fitness and the newly introduced requirement that goods be of 'satisfactory quality', might mean in an informational context.

Implied terms in software contracts

The Sale of Goods Act 1979 provides for three conditions to be implied into a contract of sale. Although there is room for argument whether software is generally sold by virtue of the fact that intellectual property rights will remain with the original owner, the Supply of Goods and Services Act 1982 provides that the implied terms will extend to any other contract for the supply of goods. Although interpretative problems may remain in the situation discussed above, where software is supplied over the Internet, for example, the categorisation of contracts as forms of sale or rental or loan is of no significance. Reference throughout this section will be to the provisions of the Sale of Goods Act 1979, as amended by the Sale and Supply of Goods Act 1994.

One of the cornerstones of English commercial law has been the doctrine of *caveat emptor* ('let the buyer beware'). Traditionally, no provisions relating to the quality of goods has been implied into contracts of sale. In previous eras, this approach was not as inequitable as it might appear in the twenty-first century. Goods were simple in nature and composition, and it was a feasible task for a buyer to make an assessment of their condition and suitability. As goods became more sophisticated, it became increasingly difficult for an inexpert customer to examine them. Even if a potential buyer were to wish to do this, the reaction of the seller of a computer could well be predicted in the event that a customer was to produce a screwdriver and seek to disassemble the equipment. The notion of the implied term has been developed, first by the courts and now enshrined in statute, as a means for protecting the interests of the consumer. In general law, of course, an implied term is overridden by any contrary express agreement made between the parties. Often such an express term will seek to reduce or exclude the liability of the seller in the event that the performance of the goods is inadequate. Again, the first attempts to control these contractual tactics were made by the courts, with Parliament intervening in 1977 with the passage of the Unfair Contract Terms

---

[21] *St Albans District Council v ICL* [1996] 4 All ER 481 at 494.
[22] (9 July 1993, unreported), CA. The case is reported at first instance at [1995] FSR 654.

Act 1977. The following sections will consider the extent of the obligations implied by law into contracts for the supply of software. Attention will then be paid to the extent to which these might validly or lawfully be reduced by the application of devices such as licences or contractual terms.

Title in software

By virtue of s 12 of the Sale of Goods Act 1979, a seller must guarantee that he or she possesses the right to sell the goods and that full title to the goods will be transferred to the buyer, except for such limitations as are brought to the buyer's attention prior to the contract of sale. In terms of the usage of the goods, it is provided that the buyer is to enjoy 'quiet possession'. This entails that the buyer's freedom to deal with the goods in such manner as might be desired is not to be restricted by virtue of any rights retained by the seller or by some third party. In many cases concerned with software, the sale will be made by a retailer, with the producer retaining ownership of copyright in the work and remaining an interested third party.

The major limitations imposed upon the buyer's freedom to deal with software are found in the copyright legislation. As has been seen, the mere use of software might constitute a breach of copyright. The buyer's right under s 12 of the Sale of Goods Act 1979 is always subject to the caveat that the use proposed is lawful. The terms of the European Directive on the Legal Protection of Computer Programs[23] might have implications for the operation of s 12. Under the Directive, a number of forms of behaviour concerned with software, for example, modification for the purpose of error correction, will be permitted unless the terms of a contract or licence provide otherwise. Where the copyright owner intends to exercise this option and seeks to do so by means of a licence document whose contents are not disclosed to the buyer until after the contract of sale is concluded, the failure to give prior notice might place the seller in breach of s 12.

Description

Section 13 of the Sale of Goods Act 1979 provides that where a sale is by description, there is to be an implied condition that the goods will correspond with this description. In the course of many contracts of sale, a variety of claims may be made concerning the attributes of the product involved. Not all such elements will be incorporated into the final contract. Many laudatory phrases, typically used in promotional materials, will be regarded as too general. A claim that a product is 'user-friendly' might, for example, be regarded as insufficiently precise to be considered as a description, although in such cases it may be that an action will lie on the ground of misrepresentation.

Claims of compatibility with other products, typically that a piece of software will operate on a specified piece of hardware, might be regarded as descriptive. Equally, lists of the features possessed by a product will be considered as part of its description,

---

[23] Directive 91/250/EC, OJ 1991 L 122/42.

although even here the matter may not be beyond doubt. In the case of a popular laser printer, for example, the product specification made reference to a printing speed of four pages per minute. The statement appears true, but what is not made clear is that the printer can only print four copies of the same page in any given minute. The printing process requires that data regarding the contents of any page be transmitted from the computer to the printer. This process takes some time, with the result that the speed for printing a multi-page document slows to little more than a single page per minute. One factor which is relevant throughout all the discussion of liability is the absence of clearly defined industry standards and conventions. In the absence of these in respect of speed of printing or many other attributes concerned with the functioning of information technology systems, it may be difficult to establish liability in respect of claims that are accurate but potentially misleading.

Quality

The Sale of Goods Act 1979 requirements relating to product quality are so well known that little exposition is required. Two partially overlapping conditions will be implied into a contract of sale. Goods must be of satisfactory quality and reasonably fit for any particular purpose for which they are supplied.[24] The requirement that goods supplied be of satisfactory quality was introduced in 1995 in substitution for the concept of merchantable quality. The notion of merchantable quality can be traced back to the Middle Ages. It assumed statutory form for the first time in the Sale of Goods Act 1893 and was retained in the Sale of Goods Act 1979. The latter statute also introduced a new definition, providing that goods would be of merchantable quality if they are:

> ...as fit for the purpose or purposes for which goods of that kind are commonly bought as it was reasonable to expect having regard to any description applied to them, the price (if relevant) and all the other relevant circumstances.[25]

The law relating to sale of goods was the subject of a report by the Law Commissions in 1987.[26] This expressed concerns at the suitability of the venerable concept of merchantability to deal with the complexities inherent in many modern products. Beyond the issue of whether the terminology itself was not unduly archaic, the notion of a general requirement of fitness for purpose (as opposed to the more specific instantiation in the second implied term) was developed in an era of comparatively simple products, which would either work or fail to work. With a modern product, such as a motor car or a software product, the manner or quality of performance is of at least as much importance.

Acting on the Law Commissions' recommendations, the requirement that goods be of satisfactory quality was substituted in the Sale and Supply of Goods Act 1994. The

---

[24] Section 14.
[25] Section 14(6).
[26] A Joint Report was published: Law Commission No. 160, Scots Law Commission No. 104, Cm. 137.

definition of the new requirement retains echoes of its predecessor. It is now provided that:

> ...goods are of satisfactory quality if they meet the standard that a reasonable person would regard as satisfactory, taking account of any description of the goods, the price (if relevant) and all the other relevant circumstances.[27]

The statute goes on, however, to list a number of specific factors which are to be taken into account in determining whether goods are of satisfactory quality:

> ...the following (among others) are in appropriate cases aspects of the quality of goods:
>
> (a) fitness for all the purposes for which goods of the kind in question are commonly supplied;
>
> (b) appearance and finish;
>
> (c) freedom from minor defects;
>
> (d) safety; and
>
> (e) durability.

A number of points from this new definition may be of considerable significance in a software context. Problems have arisen in the past where an object is fit for only some of its normal purposes.[28] An integrated spreadsheet/word processing/database package, for example, might perform satisfactorily in two modes but be unworkable in the third. A design package may be satisfactory for external designs but unsuited for internal design. It is now clearly stated that products must be fit for all the purposes for which they are commonly supplied. Products of the kind mentioned above will fail to meet the statutory requirement. Producers will be well advised to give greater care to the descriptions of their products and, at the risk of blunting their marketing strategy, make clear any design limitations applying to the product.

A number of the other features of the definition of satisfactory quality will also be relevant in a computer context. The criteria relating to appearance and finish might be invoked in respect of the user interface and screen displays of a software product. Perhaps the biggest source of problems may arise with the specific mention of 'freedom from minor defects'. Given that all software products contain defects, this may be of considerable significance. It must be stressed, however, that the Sale of Goods Act 1979 does not require that goods be perfect. The standard relates to the expectations of a 'reasonable person'. The major impact may lie in the fact that the specific mention of minor defects may be expected to draw a court's attention to this aspect of an allegedly defective product. Assessment of software product causes particular difficulties. With most products, defects are likely to be introduced at the production stage. If a complaint relates to the allegedly defective performance of a television set, the item at issue can normally be compared with other examples of the same model produced by

---

[27] Sale of Goods Act 1979, s 14.
[28] *Aswan Engineering v Lupdine* [1987] 1 WLR 1.

the same manufacturer. Given the fact that all copies of a software product are likely to be identical, the only basis for comparison will be with the products of competitors. This creates problems in comparing like with like.

The decision as to whether a product is satisfactory is a factual one. A variety of factors may be taken into account. The question of price is one which is of considerable weight in many cases. In *Rogers v Parish*, Mustill LJ stated that '[t]he buyer was entitled to value for his money'.[29] In the vast majority of cases, one might reasonably expect that a more expensive product will be of better quality than a lower-priced alternative. This approach may break down to some extent in the context of software. The physical components make up such a small part of the value of a package that it is unlikely that any significant variation might be expected here. The point can also be made that it is easier and cheaper to emulate than to innovate. On this basis, and ignoring possible intellectual property complications, it might not be unreasonable to expect a lower-priced derivative package to attain a similar level of quality to that of the original. The speed of development in the entire information technology field also makes difficult the task of determining issues of quality and value for money. A product which might have been regarded as of acceptable quality if sold for £500 on 1 January might be regarded much less favourably if sold for the same amount (or even at a lower price) on the following 31 December.

Further problems may arise in determining the proper purpose of an item of software. Difficulties may be exacerbated by a lack of customer knowledge, as epitomised in the first software disputes to reach the courts, *MacKenzie Patten v British Olivetti*.[30] In this case, the plaintiff, a small firm of solicitors, entered into an agreement for the supply of a computer in the apparent belief that this would be able to access court schedules held on a computer at the Old Bailey. This was notwithstanding the fact that neither computer possessed any form of communications capability. It is also the case, of course, that design limitations are not as apparent in software products as may normally be the case. Under the provisions of the Sale of Goods Act 1979, a customer wishing to receive the benefit of the fitness for purpose condition is obliged to inform the seller if it is intended to put the product to some unusual purpose. No specific mention need be made if the product is intended to be put to its normal use. 'Normal' in this sense may be interpreted in two ways. First, consideration must be given to the normal uses of a product of the type in question. Thus, a screwdriver is to be used to insert and remove screws. Use as a crowbar would not be classed as normal. A second element might relate to the scale of the intended use. Most products might be intended for a specific sector of a market. A low-cost and low-powered electric drill might be suitable for occasional use in domestic circumstances, but would not be fit for intensive use by a professional builder or joiner. With most products of this kind, design limitations will be apparent. A customer putting a product to excessive use might not receive the court's sympathy in the event of a claim that the product was not

---

[29] [1987] 2 All ER 232 at 237.
[30] (1985) 48 MLR 344.

fit for its purpose. With software products, design limitations will be much less transparent. A disc retailing at £10,000 will look no different from a blank disc worth a few pence. The development of cheap personal computers has led to the marketing of 'cut-down' versions of computer programs originally designed for the commercial market. Intended for domestic use, these may be marketed on the back of the original but may lack some of its features and capabilities. This may render the program unfit for use at a commercial level of activity. The limitations will not be as apparent as with the electric drill, and sellers may be faced with a dilemma. If they do not make them clear to potential buyers, they may run the risk that a naïve and inexperienced business user may purchase the product and find it unsuitable, whilst drawing excessive attention to the limitations of the product might not be advisable in marketing terms.

Remedies for breach of the implied terms

In the event of a breach of any of the implied terms, the buyer's claim may be to reject the goods supplied as failing to conform with the contractual requirements. It follows that if the goods are validly rejected, the buyer will be released from any obligation to pay for them. If the seller's breach of contract has resulted in the buyer suffering any further loss, the rejection of the goods may be accompanied by a claim for damages.

The right to reject will be lost where the buyer's conduct indicates acceptance of the goods. The Sale of Goods Act 1979 provides that the buyer is to be given a reasonable opportunity of examining them. This may occur before or after the sale.[31] One factor which may arise in software contracts, given the near certainty that every copy of a particular package will be identical, concerns the problem whether the opportunity to examine a copy in the seller's premises will debar the right of rejection, even though a different copy is supplied to the customer.

The Sale of Goods Act 1979 provides further that the right to reject will cease when the buyer does any act which is inconsistent with the seller's continuing ownership or by the lapse of a 'reasonable time'.[32] In respect of the first of these elements, it might be queried whether the act of completing and returning a licence agreement accompanying the software might be regarded as an act inconsistent with the seller's ownership. In the case of many popular software programs, the disks are contained in an envelope inside the packaging. The envelope bears a legend to the effect that opening it signifies acceptance of a licence agreement. The validity of such techniques will be explored in more detail in the next chapter, but the buyer may be put in the position whereby taking the steps that are physically necessary to use the software might involve an act which is inconsistent with the seller's title. Given that the buyer's right to use the software will otherwise be severely restricted, such a view would appear harsh but by no means illogical.

More difficult still is the question of what will be considered a reasonable time to examine the goods. In the case of *Bernstein v Pamsons Motors (Golders Green) Ltd*,[33]

---

[31] Section 34(1).
[32] Section 35(1).
[33] [1987] 2 All ER 220.

a new motor car was sold to the plaintiff. Some three weeks after delivery, the car suffered a major and potentially dangerous breakdown on a motorway. Examination revealed that a blob of sealing compound had somehow found its way into the vehicle's lubrication system during the course of manufacture. During the course of the engine's short life, the object floated around the system until the occasion when it caused an obstruction, blocking the flow of oil, to the severe detriment of the engine.

Under the terms of the Sale of Goods Act 1979, goods are accepted when the buyer retains them beyond a reasonable length of time without intimating any complaint to the seller. In this case, it was held that the passage of three weeks sufficed to prevent the buyer from rejecting the vehicle. A purchaser, it was held, was entitled to such time as was required to make a general examination of the goods. Although this time would vary depending upon the complexity of the goods, no account would be taken of the nature of the particular defect in question.

The implications of this case for software purchasers are not hopeful. Although particular defects may not manifest themselves for a considerable period of time, it seems unlikely that a general examination of software, of the kind sanctioned in *Bernstein*[34] would occupy a substantial period of time. It must be stressed, however, that the fact that the right to reject is lost does not imply that the buyer possesses no remedies. In the event that goods are unmerchantable or are not fit for their purpose, a remedy will remain in damages. The situation at issue in *Bernstein* is again relevant in a software context. The engine of the motor car suffered significant damage in the incident. The seller was willing to repair those components which had identifiably been affected. The customer, however, expressed the fear that the stresses incurred during the incident might have affected other components, rendering them more likely to fail in the future. This fear served to reduce significantly the customer's confidence in the vehicle. Although the judge accepted that the vehicle was not of merchantable quality and an award of damages was made, it is arguable that this provided an inadequate remedy. In the software context, it might be argued that a customer who discovered significant defects in a software product might justifiably fear that efforts on the supplier's part to correct these might create further problems, alternatively, that other defects might be lying in wait. The fact that software is not susceptible of exhaustive testing, coupled with its intangible nature, makes the issue of customer confidence a significant one.

The fact that a buyer no longer possesses the right to reject goods for non-conformity with contractual obligations does not mean that no remedies are available. An action for damages will always be competent. In respect of the product itself, the measure of damages will reflect the difference between the value of the goods as supplied and the cost of acquiring goods which will conform with the contractual obligations. The implications of this may be significant. An example might be taken of a seller who, having been informed of the buyer's requirements, supplies a system for £4,000. In the event that the system proved not to be fit for that purpose and evidence indicated that a sum of £10,000 might be required in order to meet the requirements, the measure

---

[34] *Bernstein v Pamsons Motors (Golders Green) Ltd* [1987] 2 All ER 220.

of damages would reflect this difference. This may not be an unlikely scenario in the information technology field. One of the criticisms made in the inquiry into the failures of the London Ambulance Service's computer system was that the cost of the system was approximately half of that which might have been expected for such a significant project.

Software quality and the courts

Having outlined the general principles applicable in any contractual action relating to the quality of goods supplied, attention will be paid in the remainder of this chapter to the approach adopted by the courts in the limited number of cases which have reached the High Court or Court of Appeal. Initially, examination will be made of the application of the quality requirements. It is a feature of software contracts that the attempt is normally made to limit or even to exclude liabilities which would normally arise under the application of the law of contract. Such provisions are subject to judicial scrutiny under the provisions of the Unfair Contract Terms Act 1977. In respect both of quality requirements and of the validity of exclusion clauses, a variety of judicial approaches can be identified and even nearly twenty years after the first case reached the Court of Appeal, it remains difficult to lay down precise guidelines concerning the nature and extent of liability. In some respects, the situation may be characterised as similar to that applying in respect of the categorisation of contracts as involving goods and services where two precedents exist rather uneasily in the cases of *Lee v Griffin* [35] and *Robinson v Graves*. [36]

Questions of time

The inclusion of the word 'reasonable' or 'reasonably' in the statutory requirement indicates that a customer may not be entitled to expect perfection. This may be relevant in two respects. The first concerns the condition in which the goods are delivered, and the second, the broader question of the level of quality ultimately attained by the product. In the case of *Eurodynamic Systems v General Automation Ltd*, [37] the High Court was faced with a dispute concerning, inter alia, the quality of an operating system for a computer. Steyn J stated that:

> The expert evidence convincingly showed that it is regarded as acceptable practice to supply computer programmes [sic] (including system software) that contain errors and bugs. The basis of the practice is that, pursuant to his support obligation (free or chargeable as the case may be), the supplier will correct errors and bugs that prevent the product from being properly used. Not every bug or error in a computer programme can therefore be categorised as a breach of contract.

---

[35] *Lee v Griffin* (1861) 1 B&S 272.
[36] *Robinson v Graves* [1935] 1 KB 579.
[37] (6 September 1988, unreported), QBD.

It is not, of course, only with software that a product may originally be supplied suffering from minor defects. Although the continued presence of these after the supplier has been offered the opportunity of repair will eventually lead to a finding that the product is not of satisfactory quality, the courts have tended to require that this opportunity be given. In the Scottish case of *Millars of Falkirk Ltd v Turpie*,[38] a new car was sold to the defendant. Immediately upon taking delivery, he discovered an oil leak emanating from the power-assisted steering unit. Upon being notified, the sellers attempted to repair the defect. This attempt proving unsuccessful, the defendant refused to pay for the vehicle and purported to reject it. Holding that he was not entitled so to do, the Court of Session ruled that although the car as supplied was not of merchantable quality, the seller must be granted a reasonable opportunity to repair the defect. 'Many new cars', it was stated, 'have on delivery to a purchaser, some defects, and it was not exceptional that a car should come from the manufacturer in the condition of the defender's new car on delivery.'[39] As the buyer had failed to allow this, the breach of contract was on his part.

Given the received wisdom that all software contains defects, it would appear that a customer will have to extend reasonable tolerance towards their supplier if or when minor defects manifest themselves. This is well illustrated by the case of *Saphena Computing v Allied Collection Agencies Ltd*,[40] the first software dispute to reach the Court of Appeal. The appellant, Saphena Computing, was a small firm specialising in the supply of third-party hardware and software, either produced or customised by themselves. The respondent was engaged in the business of debt collection. Under an initial contract between the parties, it was agreed that Saphena would supply a quantity of software. The software was ordered in January 1985 and installed between February and April. Despite initial teething problems, it was functioning satisfactorily by May 1985. In August 1985, a second contract was made for the supply of further software. It was intended that this would upgrade the defendant's system. Upon installation of the system, a degree of modification was required as a result of difficulties in attaining compatibility with the existing system and through changes in the defendant's requirements.

Although attempts were made to remedy the problems, it was common ground between the parties that the system was not operating in a satisfactory manner by February 1986. On 11 February, a telephone conversation took place between representatives of the parties. In the course of this, it was agreed that the relationship should be terminated. Unfortunately, untangling the legal consequences was to prove no simple matter, and when the dispute went to trial, proceedings before the High Court lasted for seventeen days.

Subsequent to the termination of the contract, another programmer was contracted to work on the system. In the course of this work, the source code of the programs

---

[38] 1976 SLT (Notes) 66.
[39] 1976 SLT (Notes) 66 at 67.
[40] [1995] FSR 616.

produced by the plaintiff was copied. Responding to this action, the plaintiff instituted proceedings alleging breach of copyright in its programs. It was further claimed that the defendant had acted wrongfully in terminating the contract and that the plaintiff was entitled to the price of the goods or services supplied under the contract. This latter contention was challenged by the defendant, who counterclaimed for damages, alleging that the software supplied was not to be considered fit for its purpose. The plaintiff succeeding in all significant aspects of its claim, the defendant appealed to the Court of Appeal, which unanimously affirmed the findings of the lower court. In particular, it was held, there was an implied term as to the fitness for the purpose for which the software was required. It had to be reasonably fit for such purposes as had been notified to the suppliers before the orders were placed or were notified subsequently and accepted by the supplier. These obligations had not been fulfilled by the supplier at 11 February when the relationship was terminated. Although the software was usable at this stage, it was not entirely fit for the defendant's purposes. There remained faults which required correction. However, the defendant was not entitled, at that stage, to terminate the agreement on this basis. Software, it was held by Staughton LJ:

> ...is not a commodity which is delivered once, only once, and once and for all, but one which will necessarily be accompanied by a degree of testing and modification.[41]

Thus, it would not be a breach of contract to deliver software in the first instance with a defect in it. In this respect, software must be distinguished from other products, in that the concept of delivery is a much more fluid one. In part, this is due to the necessary interaction between supplier and customer:

> Just as no software developer can reasonably expect a buyer to tell him what is required without a process of feedback and reassessment, so no buyer should expect a supplier to get his programs right first time.[42]

The eradication of defects may be a lengthy and laborious process. In the absence of specific provisions relating to acceptance tests and procedures, it is debatable as to how long the buyer must allow this process to continue. Certainly, the message from *Saphena* would indicate that the buyer must exercise caution and restraint before seeking to terminate a contractual relationship. In this instance, the effect of termination was that:

> ...the defendant thereby agreed to accept the software in the condition in which it then was and, by agreement, put it out of the plaintiff's power to render the software fit for its purpose. The original agreements were thereby varied by deleting the fitness term.[43]

In the event, the plaintiff was held entitled to payment of a reasonable sum in respect of their work on the software and were freed from the requirement to conduct any

---

[41] *Saphena Computing v Allied Collection Agencies Ltd* [1995] FSR 616 at 652.
[42] Ibid.
[43] [1995] FSR 616 at 618.

further work on the system. The defendant's counterclaim for damages in respect of losses caused by the alleged unfitness of the software was dismissed.

The final question before the court concerned the extent of the defendant's right to seek themselves to rectify the defects. To effect this process, they would require access to the programs' source code. Although the plaintiff's contractual conditions made it clear that the source code remained their property, in view of the circumstances under which the agreement had been cancelled, the court held that the defendants must be allowed such access to this as would enable them to cure the defects in the software. In so far as the defendant had gone beyond this by copying portions of the code, they were acting in breach of copyright.

The principle lesson which might be taken from the *Saphena* case[44] is that there is need for precision in the drafting of contractual provisions. In this case, the court had to find its way through a number of written agreements, coupled with evidence of verbal negotiations and promises which were considered to have also constituted part of the agreement. In spite of these factors, the parties do not appear to have addressed the basic question of what level of quality was to be expected, how conformity with this was to be established, and what periods of time would be appropriate for testing and the rectification of errors.

Problems with the Community Charge

Although it was held in *Saphena*[45] that the customer could not expect software to work perfectly from the moment it was supplied, the next case to be considered, *St Albans District Council v ICL*,[46] illustrates that this cannot provide a defence in a situation where software proves incapable of meeting its basic purposes.

The background to the case began with the introduction of a new form of local taxation, the Community Charge. This tax, more commonly known as the poll tax, proved one of the less popular forms of taxation in recent British history. In fiscal terms, the tax is no longer operative, but thanks to the litigation in *St Albans*[47] it has made a significant contribution to information technology law. The case was concerned with the acceptability of hardware and software supplied to the plaintiff for the purpose of administering the operation of the tax. The case is undoubtedly the most significant precedent in the field of information technology law and deserves detailed consideration.

The key element of the poll tax was that, subject to a very limited number of exceptions, all those aged 18 or above living in a local government district were required to pay an identical sum. No account was taken of a taxpayer's income, so that a person earning £100,000 would pay the same as a person earning £10,000. In administrative terms, this approach simplified the task of the local authorities. Effectively, all that was

---

44 *Saphena Computing v Allied Collection Agencies Ltd* [1995] FSR 616 at 652.
45 Ibid.
46 [1996] 4 All ER 481. Reported at first instance at [1995] FSR 686.
47 *St Albans District Council v ICL* [1996] 4 All ER 481.

required was to calculate the income required, the number of persons liable to pay the tax, and divide the one by the other.

If ever a task could be seen as made for the computer, this was surely it, and apparently without exception, local authorities invested heavily in IT systems to administer the tax. Many of the authorities, St Albans included, entered into contracts with the computer supplier ICL, who promoted an IT system referred to as 'The ICL Solution'. At the time the contract was signed, the elements of the system required to cope with the specific demands of the Community Charge had not been completed or tested. This fact was promoted as a positive benefit to the authority. The developers would use a seventy-strong development team to produce the necessary software and by entering into the contract, the Council would be able 'to input into the development process in order to be sure that this product meets your specific requirements'.[48]

The contract, valued at some £1.3 million, was concluded subject to ICL's standard terms and conditions, which excluded all liability for consequential loss and limited liability for other losses to a maximum of £100,000. The system was delivered to the council timeously but, as envisaged in the contract, the software required was to be delivered and installed in stages as various elements were completed and in line with legislative requirements relating to the introduction of the new tax. Initial elements were to be completed in Autumn 1988, with the full system being operable by February 1990.

One of the first tasks which needed to be conducted by local authorities was to calculate the number of persons in their area liable to pay the tax. Many local authorities were politically opposed to the new system, and in order to prevent them delaying its introduction, the legislation provided a rigid timetable for the various actions required, with penalties being imposed upon recalcitrant authorities. St Albans Council was, therefore, faced with the requirement to complete its count by a certain date. Once the figure had been calculated, the legislation provided that it could not be altered.

The calculation was carried out using the ICL system in early December 1989 and a figure of 97,384.7 was produced. Unfortunately, the version of the software used had a bug and, for some unknown reason, a new release which would have cured the problem was not installed on the Council's computers prior to the calculation. The correct figure, it was subsequently discovered, was almost 3,000 lower at 94,418.7. The financial effects were significant. The council was effectively caught in a double-edged trap. Their income was reduced because the 3,000 phantom taxpayers would clearly not produce any income. To compound matters, part of the Community Charge income was destined to be transferred to the larger Hertfordshire County Council and this figure was also calculated on the basis that St Albans' taxpaying population was greater than it actually was. When the accounts were finally completed, it was calculated that the loss to St Albans was over £1.3 million.[49]

---

[48] Ibid., at 483.

[49] In the event, ICL were held liable for only some two-thirds of the amount, it being held that the remainder could be recouped from taxpayers by increasing the rate of tax in the next financial year.

Although the defendants did not dispute the fact that the software involved in the calculation had been defective, they argued that their obligation was merely to supply a system which would be fully operative at the end of February 1990. Until then, as was recognised in the contract, the system would be in the course of development. Save where it could be shown that the supplier had acted negligently, it was argued, the case of *Saphena v Allied Collection Agencies*[50] provided authority for the proposition that 'the plaintiffs had impliedly agreed to accept the software supplied, bugs and all'. This contention was rejected, with Nourse LJ stating in the Court of Appeal that:

> Parties who respectively agree to supply and acquire a system recognising that it is still in the course of development cannot be taken, merely by virtue of that recognition, to intend that the supplier shall be at liberty to supply software which cannot perform the function expected of it at the stage of development at which it is supplied.[51]

In the particular case, it was of critical importance that the system should have been able to provide an accurate population count in December 1989.

The defendant's arguments relating to the protection conferred by its exclusion clause will be considered in more detail below. Although it might be argued that the defect in *St Albans*[52] was considerably more serious than the failures in *Saphena*,[53] the tenor of the judgment does seem to be much more 'user friendly' than was the case in the earlier judgment.

Water privatisation

ICL was also the defendant in the most recent case concerned with software quality, *South West Water Services Ltd v International Computers Ltd.*[54] Once again, the origins of the case lay in politics, on this occasion the privatisation of the English water companies. Following the establishment of the Office of the Water Regulator, a formula was devised which would limit the ability of the companies to increase charges to customers. The intention was that the companies would only be able to maintain their profits through efficiency gains. The plaintiff identified its billing system as a candidate for such savings. The introduction of a new IT system, it was considered, would allow forty-six employees to be made redundant.

A prolonged contractual process then followed, although, as was the case in *St Albans*,[55] external factors, in the form of scheduled reviews to be conducted by the Regulator, imposed immutable deadlines for the accomplishment of a working system and its associated cost savings. One false start ensued, with a contract being entered into with a major supplier who quickly discovered that the project could not be completed on time. The contract was cancelled by South West Water (SWW).

[50] [1995] FSR 616.
[51] *St Albans District Council v ICL* [1996] 4 All ER 481.
[52] Ibid.
[53] *Saphena Computing v Allied Collection Agencies Ltd* [1995] FSR 616.
[54] [1999] Masons CLR 400.
[55] *St Albans District Council v ICL* [1996] 4 All ER 481.

A new call for tenders was initiated on the basis of a User Requirements Specification (URS) drawn up by SWW. The defendant entered into negotiations on the basis of customising a package (Custima) developed by a third party, Creative Computer Systems (CCS), in which it held a 30 per cent stake. The Custima package would require to be customised to meet the user's requirements. The extent of customisation required was at the heart of the subsequent legal dispute. In his findings of fact, the judge held that:

> In my view the problem started here. Although SWW never agreed with ICL or CCSL any specification other than in conformity with the URS, ICL proceeded on the basis that in the end it would be able to persuade SWW that it did not need to provide what was specified in the URS.[56]

Essentially, it would appear, the supplier was very keen to obtain the contract, not least because with the existence of a considerable number of privatised utilities, it saw prospects of a lucrative market in selling further versions of the system. The customer's specifications were seen as being unnecessarily rigorous and it was hoped that it could be persuaded to accept a more realistic approach, one which would involve significantly less work in customising the Custima software.

Following extensive discussions, a contract was awarded to ICL in September 1994, with the completed system being scheduled for delivery on 31 October 1995. The contract was costed at some £3.6 million. Expert evidence before the court was of the view that the timetable was a tight one. Progress was poor, with several deadlines for delivery of component parts being missed. Even though a delay in completion until the end of March 1996 was agreed between the parties, by early in that month it was clear that the timetable would not be met and the customer served notice terminating the contract. An action was brought seeking recovery of sums paid under the contract plus compensation for additional losses. The claims were based on allegations both of misrepresentation and of breach of contract. These contentions were rejected by the supplier, who argued that its entry into the contract had followed misrepresentations from the customer regarding the amount of work that would be required in order to customise the software to suit its needs. It was also contended that exclusion clauses in the contract served to limit the extent of its liability.

In the event, the customer succeeded on all counts. A key factor in the failure of the contract was identified as lying in the lack of a properly structured agreement between ICL and CCS. The need for what was described as a 'seamless relationship' between these parties had been identified as critical by the customer. In its absence, there could be no guarantee that the effort required to customise the software would be forthcoming. It was argued on behalf of ICL that there could be no representation as, at the time relevant statements were made, there had been the intention to conclude such a contract. The judge disagreed, holding that there was no evidence to support such an assertion. Records of discussions between ICL and CCS indicated clearly that the latter would not have been willing to enter into a contract on the basis of the arrangements

---

[56] *South West Water Services Ltd v International Computers Ltd* [1999] Masons CLR 400 at 402.

proposed by ICL. Even if the representation had originally been made in the belief it was warranted, there was ample evidence to show that ICL must have been aware before the conclusion of the contract that it did not continue to be valid.

In respect of ICL's claim that the customer had misled them as to the amount of work required, the judge was not able to accept that the evidence supported this. In any event, it was clear that:

> Not only were ICL not misled but ICL were in fact the experts whose duty it was to evaluate the project and use their skill, with the assistance from (CCS) in making proposals as to how the project was to be carried out.[57]

Whilst this falls short of imposing duties to advise, counsel, or warn customers regarding the merits and suitability of their wares, it does suggest that suppliers cannot, as was indicated in this case, remain silent concerning what are considered to be unrealistic expectations on the part of the customer in the belief that it could subsequently be persuaded to adopt a more realistic view as to its requirements.

The Monday software package

In *SAM Business Systems Ltd v Hedley & Co*,[58] the claimant supplied the defendants, a small firm of stockbrokers, with a software package called Interset. The software was intended to replace an existing system called ANTAR, which it was feared (perhaps wrongly) was not 'year 2000 compliant'. Following some negotiations, the contract was signed in October 1999 and it was estimated that a period of twelve weeks would be required to install the software and transfer the defendant's processing operations from its old system.

In pre-contractual negotiations, the customer alleged, the sellers stated that the system would cost no more than £180,000, with a money-back guarantee in the event it failed to work in a satisfactory manner. Although no particular figures were specified in any of the contractual documents, the case proceeded on the basis that this was the appropriate figure relating to the supply and installation of the software and some items of associated hardware. The licence for supply and use of the software was costed at £116,000. Half of this sum was to be paid at the time the contract was entered into, with two further payments to be made when the software was installed and finally when it had been accepted. Under the terms of the contract, the customer was given a period of 30 days to test the software to ensure conformity with specification. In the event that defects were discovered, these were to be reported. If they were not rectified within 90 days, the customer would have the option to reject the software and obtain a refund of all sums paid. This, it was stated, represented the full extent of the supplier's liability.

The migration to the new system proved an unhappy experience for all concerned. The salient facts will be considered in more detail below but in February 2001, some

---

[57] Ibid.
[58] [2002] EWHC 2733 (TCC), [2003] 1 All ER (Comm) 465.

seventeen months later, the defendants decided to abandon their efforts to make the new system work and had decided instead to outsource their processing operations to another company. By this stage, the defendants had paid a total of £183,000, reflecting payments in respect of the licence, the purchase of some items of hardware, and a sum of approximately £14,000 in respect of a separate maintenance contract. The final licence instalment had not been paid. Further negotiations took place between the parties, but in June 2001, the claimant commenced proceedings claiming some £310,000 partly in respect of the outstanding licence fee but principally for what was described as 'post-installation maintenance'. A total of 785 hours of work was alleged to have been expended in this manner. The defendant counterclaimed, seeking nearly £790,000, reflecting a total refund of all sums paid for Interset, plus damages reflecting 'increased cost of working, write-offs, fines and additional charges, mitigation costs, and loss of profits'.

As has been typical in cases involving liability for software, the judgment can be split into two components concerning the questions of whether the software supplied complied with contractual and legal requirements relating to quality and, in the event that the answer to this question was in the negative, whether clauses limiting or excluding the supplier's liability complied with the requirements of unfair contract terms legislation. In respect of the quality requirements, the court accepted that terms must be implied into the contract to the effect that the software would be developed and installed with 'all professional skill and care' and that it would be 'reasonably fit' for the purposes required by the customer and, more specifically, would perform in such a way as to allow the customer to meet its own obligations as required by the Financial Services Authority.[59]

From the early stages, the attempts to introduce Interset proved difficult and doubtless frustrating for both parties. The judgment charts a familiar if depressing path through the detritus of a failed commercial relationship lasting for some eighteen months. The software was supplied timeously but errors continually manifested themselves, to the extent that the defendant was warned by the financial services regulator for failing to comply with its requirements regarding record keeping and accounting and was also fined by the Inland Revenue for late payment of Stamp Duty taxes arising from transactions. Although the suppliers acknowledged that there were some bugs in the software which required to be corrected, it was also argued that the defendant's staff were largely to blame for failures. The system did mark a substantial change from the defendant's existing package which operated under the DOS operating system, making use solely of keystrokes for command and control purposes. Interset operated under Microsoft Windows and provided the now ubiquitous graphical user interface. As was concluded by the judge:

> what was being presented to Hedleys was a system with a very high degree of automation, a system that was going to be operable by ordinary people, and not technically qualified people.[60]

---

[59] *SAM Business Systems Ltd v Hedley & Co* [2002] EWHC 2733 (TCC), [2003] 1 All ER (Comm) 465 at [50].
[60] Ibid., at [21].

This was to be a matter of some importance, as one of the claimant's chief arguments was to the effect that the system had been installed and was working effectively in a considerable number of other business environments. A prime cause of any failure to operate in a satisfactory manner for the defendants was allegedly 'because the staff at Hedley's were not trained for the work or were otherwise incompetent'. Although it was acknowledged that the staff's IT knowledge was limited and somewhat dated to the extent that they were not familiar with the use of a mouse,[61] it was accepted that they were committed to attempting to make the new system work. It was the supplier's responsibility to provide training and blame for failures in this respect was placed upon the trainer supplied by them, whose evidence left the judge rather unimpressed. She, he commented, 'gave her evidence in a curiously deadpan manner. Perhaps it was due to nervousness, but if she taught in that manner I can understand that she might have difficulty in communicating computer skills.' [62]

The fact that Interset was used successfully elsewhere was considered to be a matter of limited significance:

> I am no more impressed by it than if I were told by a garage that there were 1,000 other cars of the same type as the one I had bought where there was no complaint of the defect that I was complaining of so why should I be complaining of a defect? We have all heard of Monday cars, so maybe this was a Monday software programme.[63]

Given that it is received wisdom that all copies of software are identical, this is at first sight a rather puzzling comment. Certainly, there should be few if any instances of what can be classed as production defects in copies of software. Linked with the issue of training, however, indication can be seen of some of the complex interactions which impact upon the user's ability to use software effectively. Many of the applications of Interset software were in larger organisations. At the time of the case, the evidence was that only one other stockbroking firm was using the system and in general it appears that most users had staff with greater IT skills than those possessed by the defendant's.

A litany of complaints is reported in the judgment[64] and the claimant expended very significant amounts of staff time in seeking either to rectify problems or establish work round procedures whereby operators could avoid undesirable results. The decision of the Court of Appeal in the case of *Saphena v Allied Collection Agencies*[65] was cited as authority for the proposition 'that in a bespoke system bugs were inevitable'. The later decision of the Court in the case of *St Albans District Council v ICL* was also referred to, Lord Justice Nourse here ruling that:

> Parties who respectively agree to supply and acquire a system recognising that it is still in the course of development cannot be taken, merely by virtue of that recognition, to

---

[61] Ibid., at [5].
[62] [2002] EWHC 2733 (TCC) at [83].
[63] *SAM Business Systems Ltd v Hedley & Co* [2002] EWHC 2733 (TCC), [2003] 1 All ER (Comm) 465 at [103].
[64] Ibid., (Comm) 465.
[65] [1995] FSR 616.

intend that the supplier shall be at liberty to supply software which cannot perform the function expected of it at the stage of the development at which it is supplied.[66]

The systems involved in both *Saphena*[67] and *St Albans*[68] were referred to as 'bespoke' systems and therefore distinguishable from the customised system supplied to the present defendant. This is perhaps putting matters too strongly. In *Saphena*, the supplier's business was described as consisting of providing 'hardware obtained from others, and software comprising some standard items and others specially written'. In *St Albans*, the tax collection system at issue had also been supplied to a number of other local authorities. Where a better distinction perhaps lay was in the state of development of the system. In *St Albans*, the software was being developed in parallel with the enactment of the legislation establishing the tax which it was designed to help collect. Upgrades and revisions were continually being supplied to the users and, indeed, the fluid nature of the software posed serious problems in trying to replicate and explain the nature of the error which gave rise to the litigation. Interset, however, had been promoted as a 'developed system'. Such a system, it was held, should not have any bugs in it. This is perhaps a counsel of perfection but the judge did accept that if defects were speedily rectified without cost to the customer there may well be no liability on the part of the supplier. This seems an eminently correct ruling, although as was recognised in the judgment:

> SAM, like some others in the computer industry seem to be set in the mindset that when there is a 'bug' the customer must pay for putting it right. Bugs in computer programmes are still inevitable, but they are defects and it is the supplier who has the responsibility for putting them right at the supplier's expense.[69]

In line with these arguments, the sums claimed by the claimant in respect of the time and effort incurred in seeking to modify the software was rejected. The defendant was held to have been entitled to take the view that the software contract had not been completed in a satisfactory manner and the claimant's claim for additional payments was rejected. However, from its perspective, it was unfortunately also necessary to consider the effectiveness of the claimant's exclusion clauses, which effectively limited its liability to providing a refund of sums paid in the situation that the customer followed the contractual procedures regarding rejection. As will be discussed below, the defendant failed in this task, rendering victory in respect of the claim of defectiveness pyrrhic.

Exclusion or limitation of liability

In the previous sections, consideration was given to the nature and extent of the liabilities which may arise pursuant to the production, supply, and use of software. Although

---

[66] [1996] 4 All ER 481 at 487.

[67] *Saphena Computing v Allied Collection Agencies Ltd* [1995] FSR 616.

[68] *St Albans District Council v ICL* [1996] 4 All ER 481 at 487.

[69] *SAM Business Systems v Hedley* [2002] EWHC 2733 (TCC) at [19].

the argument that software should be treated in the same manner as any other product is a weighty one, it must also be conceded that software producers may be exposed to a greater degree of risk than their more traditional counterparts. First, if one copy of a software product exhibits defects, it must be extremely likely that all copies will be so tainted. With manufactured products generally, most defects are introduced at the production stage and affect only a portion of the products in question. A finding that one copy of a software package is unmerchantable might, by way of contrast, leave its producer liable to every purchaser. A further problem is that many losses resulting from software defects will be economic in nature. Such losses may not only be extensive but are also extremely difficult to quantify and, accordingly, to insure against. A spreadsheet program, for example, may be used for domestic accounting purposes, where the degree of financial exposure in the event of error may be minimal, or in the course of preparing a multi-million pound construction contract, where any error might threaten the financial viability of a contracting party.

Few would argue that the state of the law relating to software liability is satisfactory. Uncertainty feeds upon uncertainty and perception appears more significant than reality. The producer's fear that it may be exposed to crippling legal actions has resulted in an almost universal practice of seeking to exclude some and place limits on the extent of their liabilities in respect of other forms of loss resulting from the operation (or non-operation) of their software. The validity of such clauses[70] has been at issue in most of the disputes which have reached the courts.

An initial point to note is that in order to be effective, a clause must be incorporated into the contract. The rules relating to this are to be found in common law rather than statute, and require that reasonable steps be taken to bring the existence of the clause to the notice of the other contracting party. This may be accomplished in a number of ways, with a major factor being whether the software is supplied pursuant to a written contract signed by both parties. In such cases, there will generally be little doubt that the exclusion clause forms part of the contract, and discussion will focus on the effect of the provisions of the Unfair Contract Terms Act 1977 and the Unfair Terms in Consumer Contracts Regulations 1994.[71]

More difficult issues arise when software (typically standard) is supplied through less structured channels. Such software is typically supplied subject to what is generally referred to as a 'shrink-wrap licence'. The term appears to date from early forms of consumer software, mainly computer games. These were typically supplied on an audio cassette, with the terms of a very basic licence printed on the cellophane wrapping of the cassette. Today, licences tend to be printed on substantial booklets (often making separate provisions to accommodate the legal requirements of a range of countries in which the software is sold) included inside packaging. The validity of these is subject to some debate.

---

[70] In this section, the term 'exclusion clause' will be used to refer, both to clauses which seek to exclude and to those which limit the extent of liability. Most terms under discussion fall into the latter category.

[71] SI 1994/3159.

Enforceability of shrink-wrap licences

Many contracts, of course, are made other than by means of a signed document; a typical example might relate to the purchase of a piece of standard software from a shop. In this situation, the legal requirement will be that reasonable steps should be taken to bring the existence of any contractual provisions to the notice of the other party prior to the conclusion of the agreement.[72] It is not required that he or she should be aware of all of the details or of the legal implications arising from the contract. An example can be taken from a railway ticket. The ticket will contain reference to the carrier's conditions of carriage but will not itself contain details of these. The presence on the ticket of a notice referring the customer to the conditions will suffice to incorporate them into the contract. Returning to the software context, the display of a clause on the outside of the packaging (or perhaps on a notice displayed in the seller's premises) will serve to give the customer notice of its existence. It is increasingly the case that software is supplied over the Internet. The practice has implications in respect of a number of areas of the law, not least, as will be discussed below, in the field of taxation. From a licensing perspective, use of the Internet may simplify the supplier's task of establishing customer awareness of and agreement to the licence terms. It is a simple matter to cause either a set of the terms or at least reference to their existence to be displayed, with the customer required to 'click' on a button marked 'I accept' before the transaction can proceed.

Assuming that the terms of the licence—including its provisions restricting liability—become incorporated into the contract, attention must again turn to the effect of the Unfair Contract Terms Act 1977 and the Unfair Terms in Consumer Contracts Regulations 1999.[73] To date, all litigation concerned with the effectiveness of exclusion or limitation clauses in software contracts has occurred in the context of commercial transactions. The increasing use of software within the home must increase the importance of the consumer sector and initially, therefore, consideration will be given to the potential application of the legislation in this regard.

Consumer contracts

Somewhat confusingly, different definitions of the term 'consumer' are found in the Unfair Contract Terms Act 1977 and 1999 regulations.[74] The Act provides that a person deals as a consumer if:

(a) he neither makes the contract in the course of a business nor holds himself out as doing so; and

(b) the other party does make the contract in the course of a business.[75]

---

[72] See *Thornton v Shoe Lane Parking Ltd* [1971] 2 QB 163, where the display of exclusion clauses inside a car park was held to be ineffective, the contract having been concluded at the point when the customer entered into the premises.

[73] SI 1999/2083.

[74] Ibid.

[75] Section 12(1).

Additionally, where goods are supplied under the contract, these must be of a kind ordinarily used for private use or consumption. It would seem that computer games must satisfy this requirement. Although the status of other forms of software, such as word processing or accounting packages or Internet access software, may at one stage have been debatable, it would seem that they are now sufficiently widely used to be classed as consumer products. This issue may not arise under the regulations, which make no reference to the nature of goods, requiring only that they be obtained for non-business purposes.[76]

In respect of statutory requirements relating to title, description, or quality, the Unfair Contract Terms Act 1977 provides that exclusion or limitation will not be permitted.[77] In the case of consumer contracts falling under the ambit of the Sale of Goods Act 1979, the prohibition is even more extensive. Here, the Consumer Transactions (Restrictions on Statements) Order 1976[78] provides that any attempt at restriction or exclusion will constitute a criminal offence. An offence will also be committed when any form of guarantee is offered other than those provided for in the Sale of Goods Act 1979, unless it is made clear that this is offered in addition to, rather than in substitution for, the consumer's rights under the legislation. It appears common practice amongst the suppliers of computer games to display notices restricting the buyer's rights to the supply of a replacement game in the event that the original is defective. In the event that the contract is regarded as one involving the sale or supply of goods, the display of such notices will render the supplier involved liable to criminal prosecution.

In terms of their scope, the 1994 regulations are broader,[79] applying to any term in a non-negotiated contract for goods or services other than those defining the main subject-matter or relating to the adequacy of the price. Such terms will not be binding on the consumer if they are determined to be unfair. An unfair term is one which:

> ...contrary to the requirements of good faith causes a significant imbalance in the parties' rights and obligations under the contract to the imbalance of the consumer.[80]

This is a somewhat nebulous criterion. Schedule 2 to the regulations contains an 'indicative and non-exclusive list of the terms which might be considered unfair'. These include clauses purporting to limit the legal rights of consumers in the event of unsatisfactory performance. A further illustration stigmatises clauses:

> ...making an agreement binding on the consumer whereas provision of services by the supplier or seller is subject to a condition whose realisation depends on his own will alone.

It might be that this provision could be invoked in the event that a software producer seeks to link a right to use software to the acceptance of restrictive terms within a licence.

[76] Section 2.
[77] Section 6.
[78] SI 1976/1813.
[79] SI 1994/3159.
[80] Unfair Contract Terms Act 1977, s 4(1).

A further aspect of the 1999 regulations[81] may be of considerable significance. Although many forms of exclusion clause have long been regarded as of dubious quality, the difficulties facing individual litigants have prevented these being challenged before the courts. The regulations establish a role for the Director General of Fair Trading providing that the Director is to consider any complaint that a contract term is unfair and may then seek an injunction preventing the continued use of the term (or any similar term) in consumer contracts.[82]

Non-consumer contracts

In the case of non-consumer contracts for supply of goods, as well as any contracts where standard form contracts are used, limitation or exclusion clauses will be valid only in so far as they satisfy the statutory requirement of reasonableness.[83] The Unfair Contract Terms Act 1977 lists a number of factors that are to be taken into account in deciding any such question.[84] These include the strength of the parties' respective bargaining positions, the practice of the trade or profession involved, and whether the customer was given the option of contracting on terms which did not seek to exclude liability.

The term 'standard form contract' is not defined in the Unfair Contract Terms Act 1977. In the Scottish case of *McCrone v Boots Farm Sales,*[85] it was held that a standard form contract existed where a party invariably sought to do business on terms which did not differ to any material extent. It was immaterial whether these were reduced to writing or were, at least in part, agreed orally. Such an approach has been upheld in subsequent cases, with the courts being willing to overlook minor variations where it can be shown that a party will generally do business only on the basis of a substantially identical set of terms and conditions.

The definition of standard form contracts in a software context was considered in the case of *Salvage Association v CAP Financial Services Ltd.*[86] At issue here was a contract for the computerisation of the plaintiff's accounting system. The project proved unsuccessful, and, after a number of broken completion dates, the plaintiff terminated its agreement with the defendant and sought damages. Much of the dispute centred on the applicability and enforceability of clauses limiting the defendant's liability in the event of breach of contract. In respect of the question of whether the clauses were to be classed as standard form contracts, Thayne Forbes J analysed the history of the contract, pointing to the fact that extensive negotiations had taken place between the parties prior to its conclusion. Although the terms of the agreement 'closely followed CAP's standard terms of contract', this fact was not to be taken to mean that

---

[81] SI 1999/2083.

[82] Regulation 10.

[83] Section 8.

[84] Section 11 for England and Wales, s 24 for Scotland, and Sch. 2 applying throughout the United Kingdom.

[85] 1981 SLT 103.

[86] (9 July 1993, unreported), CA. The case is reported at first instance at [1995] FSR 654.

the contract was one of a standard form. Six factors were identified as relevant to the determination:

(i)   the degree to which the 'standard terms' are considered by the other party as part of the process of agreeing the terms of the contract;

(ii) the degree to which the 'standard terms' are imposed on the other party by the party putting them forward;

(iii) the relative bargaining power of the parties;

(iv) the degree to which the party putting forward the 'standard terms' is prepared to entertain negotiations with regard to the terms of the contract generally and the 'standard terms' in particular;

(v)   the extent and nature of any agreed alterations to the 'standard terms' made as a result of the negotiations between the parties; and

(vi) the extent and duration of the negotiations.

Applying these criteria he concluded that:

> In this case SA had considered the various drafts of the contract that had been sent by CAP and had taken legal and other advice on all the proposed terms in order to decide what alterations it wished to make. To the extent that SA sought changes and additions to the draft terms, CAP largely agreed them. I am satisfied that the terms of the second contract were not imposed on SA by CAP, but were fully negotiable between parties of equal bargaining power and that CAP was prepared to engage in a meaningful process of negotiation with SA as to those terms. The process of negotiation between the parties took place over a considerable period of time.

The contract was not, therefore, a standard form contract, although, as will be discussed below, its terms were struck down on the basis that they constituted an unreasonable attempt to evade liability for negligence.

A different conclusion was reached in *St Albans District Council v ICL*.[87] Here, the Council published a call for tenders, negotiated—albeit fairly incompetently—with a number of potential suppliers, engaged in further negotiations with ICL and concluded a contract, one clause of which stated that it was subject to ICL's standard terms and conditions. As was stated by Nourse LJ in the Court of Appeal:

> Scott Baker J [the judge at first instance] dealt with this question as one of fact, finding that the defendant's general conditions remained effectively untouched in the negotiations and that the plaintiffs accordingly dealt on the defendant's written standard terms for the purposes of s 3(1) (see [1995] FSR 686 at 706). I respectfully agree with him.

A similar decision was reached in *South West Water v ICL*.[88] Once again, the customer had initially argued that the agreement should be made on the basis of its own

---

[87] [1996] 4 All ER 481.
[88] [1999] Masons CLR 400.

standard terms and conditions. The defendant countered by submitting a contract governing a previous agreement between the parties. This was subject to some negotiation, but it was agreed that the limitation clauses in the contract were taken from ICL's standard terms. Considering the nature of the agreement, Toulmin J made reference to the leading textbook, *Chitty on Contracts*. This stated that:

> Since in any event, no two contracts are likely to be completely identical, but will at least differ as to subject-matter and price, the question arises whether variations or omissions from or additions to standard terms thereby render them 'non-standard' and they do not whether all the terms become standard terms.[89]

Referring to the decision in *St Albans*[90] described above, it was held that the contract was a standard form contract.

In some respects, the conclusion may be seen as a surprising one. A water authority is a substantial party and the decision makes several references to the fact that discussions between the parties were extensive. Evidence from ICL concerning one meeting was to the effect that:

> It was a take it or leave it session. They [SWW] were very hard negotiators but we took the decision to proceed as it was too good a long term opportunity to walk away from.

Perhaps the most significant factor was the fact that the contract signed between the parties was silent on what was described as the 'very obvious circumstance' of what should happen in the event of a total failure to deliver a workable system. The judge concluded:

> The reason it was not covered is because the parties used a standard ICL contract which was only slightly adapted. Those standard ICL terms were not appropriate where substantial development work was required to adapt the basic system, as in this case.[91]

The requirement of reasonableness

In determining whether clauses limiting or excluding liability can be considered fair and reasonable, the Unfair Contract Terms Act 1977 provides initially that regard is to be had to 'the circumstances which were or ought reasonably to have been, known to or in the contemplation of the parties when the contract was made'.[92] It provides further that account is to be taken of:

(a) the resources which he could expect to be available to him for the purpose of meeting the liability should it arise; and

(b) how far it was open to him to cover himself by insurance.

---

[89] J. Chitty, Chitty on Contracts 27th edn (London, 1994), para. 14–056.
[90] *St Albans District Council v ICL* [1996] 4 All ER 481.
[91] *South West Water v ICL* [1999] Masons CLR 400.
[92] Section 11.

Schedule 2 to the Act continues to provide a set of 'Guidelines' to be taken into account. These include:

- The strength of the parties' respective bargaining positions.
- The general practice of a particular trade or profession.
- Whether the goods are made, processed or adapted to the special order of the customer.

In determining the question of the reasonableness of the limitation clauses, particular reference was made to the statutory reference to the resources likely to be available to the party seeking to rely on the clause, and how far it was open to him to cover himself by insurance. In the case of *Photo Production Ltd v Securicor Transport Ltd*, Lord Wilberforce stated with reference to the Unfair Contract Terms Act 1977:

> ...in commercial matters generally, when the parties are not of unequal bargaining power, and when risks are normally borne by insurance, not only is the case for judicial intervention undemonstrated, but there is everything to be said, and this seems to have been Parliament's intention, for leaving the parties free to apportion the risks as they think fit and for respecting their decisions.[93]

In *Salvage Association v CAP Financial Services Ltd*,[94] it was accepted that the parties were of equal bargaining power. There had been genuine negotiations and the plaintiff had at all relevant times the realistic option of giving its business to another producer. A number of factors, however, operated to justify a finding that the limitation clause was unfair. First reference was made to the discrepancy between the contractual limit of £25,000 and the defendant's general acceptance of liability up to £1 million. Additionally, whilst the losses claimed by the plaintiff were covered under an insurance policy taken out by the defendant, albeit one which was subject to a £500,000 excess, it was accepted by the court that the plaintiff would have been unable to obtain insurance cover against losses of the kind incurred at other than a prohibitive price.

The decision of the Court of Appeal in *St Albans District Council v ICL*[95] provides further evidence of a judicial willingness to scrutinise the terms of contracts entered into by large organisations. Following the introduction of the Community Charge legislation, the plaintiff, in common with all other local authorities, was under considerable pressure to introduce new computer systems capable of coping with the administrative demands of the new tax. After an initial call for tenders, the choice of supplier was effectively between the defendant and IBM. Assessing various elements of the competing bids, including the terms and conditions associated with each, the decision was made to accept the defendant's tender and:

> Immediately commence negotiations with ICL to ensure the best possible deal can be secured for the authority.

---

[93] [1980] AC 827 at 843.
[94] (9 July 1993, unreported), CA.
[95] *St Albans District Council v ICL* [1996] 4 All ER 481.

The negotiations do not appear to have been conducted by the Council with great expertise. Following submission of a draft contract based upon a Council official's previous employment with London Transport, everything proceeded on the basis of ICL's standard terms and conditions (again, out of date in respect of the level of liability accepted). As the deadline for the introduction of the new tax approached, the Council was under some pressure to conclude the agreement. When concerns were raised concerning the limitation on liability clause, the defendant's response was to indicate that unless the contract was concluded by the following Monday, there could be no guarantee that the system would be delivered in time for the introduction of the tax, a consequence which could have dire financial consequences for the authority. A letter from the defendant stated:

> With regard to ICL's contractual terms and conditions...our offer is based on these standard terms and conditions, and given the tight time-scale, I would advise you to make use of them.
>
> These standard ICL conditions are accepted by over 250 local authorities, and in no way detracts from the business partnerships.[96]

The plaintiff promptly signed the contract. Given these circumstances, it is not surprising that the court held that the contract was a standard form contract and that it did not satisfy the statutory criterion of reasonableness. In reaching this decision, the Court of Appeal approved the judgment of Scott Baker J at first instance, where he identified as determining factors, the points that:

(1) the parties were of unequal bargaining power;

(2) the defendants have not justified the figure of £100,000, which was small, both in relation to the potential risk and the actual loss;

(3) the defendants were insured; and

(4) the practical consequences.

> I make the following observations on the fourth point, which follows on in a sense from the third. On whom is it better that a loss of this size should fall, a local authority or an international computer company. The latter is well able to insure (and in this case was insured) and pass on the premium cost to the customers. If the loss is to fall the other way it will ultimately be borne by the local population either by increased taxation or reduced services. I do not think it unreasonable that he who stands to make the profit (ICL) should carry the risk.[97]

The decisions of the Court of Appeal in the cases of *St Albans District Council v ICL*[98] and *South West Water v ICL*[99] cast significant doubt on the effectiveness of contractual provisions whereby software suppliers sought to limit the extent of their liabilities in

---

[96] *St Albans District Council v ICL* [1995] FSR 686 at 695.
[97] Ibid., at 711.
[98] [1995] FSR 686 at 711.
[99] [1999] Masons CLR 400.

the event that software failed to operate in a proper manner. A further decision of the court in the case of *Watford Electronics Ltd v Sanderson CFL Ltd*[100] may signal a less interventionist policy on the part of the judiciary. Albeit of less precedential value, the decision of the High Court in *SAM Business Systems Ltd v Hedley & Co*,[101] discussed above, also provides useful guidance concerning the application of the statutory criteria.

In *Watford Electronics v Sanderson CFL Ltd*,[102] the supplier, Sanderson, undertook to provide an integrated software system to control all aspects of the customer's business. Unfortunately, the project was not completed to the satisfaction of the customer and legal proceedings were initiated seeking damages of some £5.5 million. At trial, the judge found that the supplier was in breach of its obligations to supply a system of reasonable quality. The supplier's conditions of contract limited its liability to the cost of any defective goods supplied. The bulk of the customer's claim related to losses of profit resulting from the failure of the system to operate in a satisfactory manner. The trial judge ruled that this clause was invalid under the provisions of the Unfair Contract Terms Act 1977, which provide that exclusion clauses found in standard form contracts will be valid only in so far as they can be considered fair and reasonable. The present clause, it was held, could not be so regarded.

The Court of Appeal took a different view. The customer, it was held, was an experienced and established business. There had been extensive negotiations between the parties. It was noted that the customer used a very similar form of exclusion clause in contracts with its own customers. The conclusion reached was that:

> Where experienced businessmen representing substantial companies of equal bargaining power negotiate an agreement, they may be taken to have had regard to the matters known to them. They should, in my view be taken to be the best judge of the commercial fairness of the agreement which they have made; including the fairness of each of the terms in that agreement. They should be taken to be the best judge on the question whether the terms of the agreement are reasonable.[103]

The exclusion clause was therefore upheld and the supplier's appeal was upheld.

Although the judgments in the present case[104] do not refer to the decisions in *St Albans*[105] and *South West Water*,[106] the tone does differ markedly. It may be noted that especially in the *St Albans* case, negotiations between the parties appear to have been conducted in a rather ineffective manner. Owing to an error, indeed, the contract limited liability to a sum less than that which the supplier would normally have accepted. External factors also placed the customer under considerable pressure to conclude

---

100 [2001] EWCA Civ 317, [2001] 1 All ER (Comm) 696.

101 [2002] EWHC 2733 (TCC), [2003] 1 All ER (Comm) 465.

102 [2001] EWCA Civ 317, [2001] 1 All ER (Comm) 696.

103 *Watford Electronics Ltd v Sanderson CFL Ltd* [2001] EWCA Civ 317, [2001] 1 All ER (Comm) 696 at [55]–[56].

104 *Watford Electronics Ltd v Sanderson CFL Ltd* [2001] EWCA Civ 317, [2001] 1 All ER (Comm) 696.

105 *St Albans District Council v ICL* [1995] FSR 686 at 695.

106 *South West Water v ICL* [1999] Masons CLR 400.

the agreement. It may be that in these circumstances, the present court would also have declared the exclusion clause to be unfair. *Watford v Sanderson* does indicate, however, that where it appears that genuine negotiations have taken place and where it is clear that the customer has freely determined to enter into a contract in awareness of the nature and significance of exclusion clauses, the courts will be slow to interfere.

A similar approach was taken by the High Court in the case of *SAM Business Systems Ltd v Hedley & Co*[107] discussed above. Here, the contract provided in part that the customer would have a period of 30 days following installation in which to test the software and report defects. It was only if defects continued for more than 90 days from the date of installation that the contract provided for the customer's right to initiate proceedings for rejection. This, effectively obtaining a refund of the purchase price, was stated to be the sole remedy available to the customer. The customer in the present case had suffered a significant loss of business and whilst the computer system cost around £185,000, they sought damages of almost £800,000. The supplier sought to rely upon the contractual limitation provisions but the customer contended that these were not fair and reasonable.

Given that the terms were part of the supplier's written terms of business there was little doubt that the Unfair Contract Terms Act 1977 should apply. The judgment gives extensive and helpful consideration to the extent to which the various criteria identified as components of the requirement of reasonableness may be relevant in cases such as the present. A key factor to be taken into account was whether it would have been feasible for the customer to have obtained similar software without the accompaniment of exclusion clauses. The evidence before the court was to the effect that '[t]he only way to get the software they needed was by contracting on terms that made rigorous exclusions of liability because those were the terms on which all suppliers were contracting'.[108] The fact that similar terms were commonplace in the field is a relevant factor in determining issues of reasonableness.

Ultimately, considering the contract as a whole, the judge concluded that its terms were fair and reasonable. The customer was buying under constraints of time as the year 2000 was fast approaching and its existing system was not capable of coping with the change to the third millennium as required by its sector regulator, the Financial Services Authority. To a considerable extent, it was accepted, the customer was the cause of its own misfortunes. Whilst an attempt totally to exclude liability would have been considered unreasonable, in the circumstances of the case, the judge concluded:

> Not forgetting my duty to look at each term individually, it is important to look at each in relation to the whole contract. Before contract, SAM says, 'We think our system is marvellous and will do everything you need, but if you are not satisfied you can ask for your money back'....Having regard to the enormous potential liabilities, that seems

---

[107] [2002] EWHC 2733 (TCC), [2003] 1 All ER (Comm) 465.
[108] *SAM Business Systems Ltd v Hedley & Co* [2002] EWHC 2733 (TCC), [2003] 1 All ER (Comm) 465 at [70].

to me to be a reasonable arrangement in the circumstances existing between the two parties.[109]

The end result of the litigation might be considered as a draw. The suppliers were not able to recover additional costs incurred in seeking to place the software into a satisfactory state and the customers were similarly unsuccessful in securing reimbursement of losses caused through the failure of the software to operate in a satisfactory manner.

Conclusions

In the early days of software, it was commonplace for suppliers to seek totally to exclude all liabilities relating to their products. A 1993 version of the standard licence used by a major software producer stated that:

LIMITED WARRANTY AND DISCLAIMER OF LIABILITY

THE SOFTWARE AND ACCOMPANYING WRITTEN MATERIALS (INCLUDING INSTRUCTIONS FOR USE) ARE PROVIDED 'AS IS' WITHOUT WARRANTY OF ANY KIND. FURTHER, (Producer) DOES NOT WARRANT, GUARANTEE OR MAKE ANY REPRESENTATIONS REGARDING THE USE OF, OR THE RESULTS OF USE, OF THE SOFTWARE OR WRITTEN MATERIALS IN TERMS OF CORRECTNESS, ACCURACY, RELIABILITY, CURRENTNESS, OR OTHERWISE. THE ENTIRE RISK AS TO THE RESULTS AND PERFORMANCE OF THE SOFTWARE IS ASSUMED BY YOU. IF THE SOFTWARE OR WRITTEN MATERIALS ARE DEFECTIVE YOU, AND NOT (Producer) OR ITS DEALERS, DISTRIBUTORS, AGENTS OR EMPLOYEES, ASSUME THE ENTIRE COST OF ALL NECESSARY SERVICING, REPAIR OR CORRECTION.

THE ABOVE IS THE ONLY WARRANTY OF ANY KIND, EITHER EXPRESS OR IMPLIED, INCLUDING BUT NOT LIMITED TO THE IMPLIED WARRANTIES OF MERCHANTABILITY AND FITNESS FOR A PARTICULAR PURPOSE, THAT IS MADE BY (Producer) ON THIS...PRODUCT.

The world has moved on and more recent versions are somewhat more 'generous', guaranteeing that the software will perform 'substantially in accordance with the accompanying Product Manual(s) for a period of 90 days'. In general, as was indicated at the outset of the chapter, clauses excluding liability have largely been replaced by those seeking to limit the extent of liability. In a number of cases, it has been accepted that it is easier and more cost-effective for a software producer to obtain insurance cover in respect of claims which might be made by customers, than it is for customers to obtain cover against more speculative risks associated with the failure of an automation project intended to bring future gains in efficiency and productivity. There may be cases where exclusion clauses may be upheld, but the range of these may be diminishing. In *South West Water v ICL*, in rejecting the defendant's attempts to

---

[109] Ibid., at [71]–[72].

limit liability to a partial refund in the case of a total failure of the project, it was held that:

> In some cases such a clause might be reasonable to reflect the balance of risk in a developing project, but there is no evidence that this is the case here.[110]

Given the vital role played by software in the modern world, it must be right that issues of liability should be assessed by the standards and criteria applied to industrial products rather than to those of a niche market within the services sector. Whilst the cases of *Watford Electronics Ltd v Sanderson CFL Ltd*[111] and *SAM v Hedley*[112] produce results which are more favourable to the producer than was the case in the ICL cases, the emphasis remains on the criterion of fairness. Especially in situations in which its functioning is critical to the survival of the customer's business it is not unreasonable that every effort should be made to ensure both that the software itself is suitable and that arrangements—in the form of contractual safeguards or the acquisition of insurance cover—are in place to guard against the risk of failure. *Caveat emptor* has not returned to business contracts but neither is a supplier expected to act as nanny to its customers.

Suggestions for further reading

'Software Contracts after St Albans', *Comms. L.* 1(5) (1996), pp. 190–92.

'Excluding and Limiting Liability in IT Contracts', *I.H.L.* 136(Dec/Jan)(2005/06), pp. 38–41.

'How Exclusion Clauses and UCTA Apply to Software and Systems Supply Contracts', *C.L.S.R.* 19(1) (2003), pp. 11–19.

'The Nature of Software and Standard Terms', *C.T.L.R.* 3(1) (1997), pp. 5–7.

---

[110] [1999] Masons CLR 400.
[111] [2001] EWCA CIV 317.
[112] *SAM Business Systems Ltd v Hedley & Co* [2002] EWHC 2733 (TCC), [2003] 1 ALl ER (Comm) 465.

26

Non-contractual liability

Introduction

Chapter 25 has considered some of the issues which may arise between parties who contract for the production, supply, and use of software products. The all-pervasive nature of software applications means that the effects of any failure may not be limited to contracting parties. A pedestrian may be knocked down by a car whose software-controlled brakes have failed or a passenger may be on a plane whose fly-by-wire computer system malfunctions. In the first of these situations, the pedestrian will have no contract with anyone, whilst in the second, the passenger's contract will be with the airline and subject to the limits on liability contained in the Warsaw Convention. There will be no contractual relationship with the plane's producer. In such events, the focus of attention switches to the topic of non-contractual liability. In this chapter, attention will be paid first to the tort of negligence. Next, consideration will be given to the possible implications of the system of strict product liability introduced under the Consumer Protection Act 1987.

Tortious liability

A number of features can be identified as prerequisites for a successful claim in tort:

1. a duty of care must be owed to the claimant by the defending party;
2. there must be a breach of that duty;
3. loss must result from that breach;
4. the loss must not be too remote a consequence of the breach; and
5. the loss must be of a nature which is accepted as giving rise to a claim for compensation.

Brief consideration will now be given to each of these elements and as to the significance which they possess in the software field.

Duty of care

The starting point in the law of tort is the requirement that a duty be owed between the parties. In the United Kingdom, the scope of such duties is defined by reference to the neighbour principle. Under this, everyone owes a duty of care towards his or her neighbour. As defined by Lord Atkins in the seminal case of *Donoghue v Stevenson*, the word 'neighbour' encompasses those:

> ...persons who are so closely and directly affected by my act that I ought reasonably to have them in contemplation as being so affected when I am directing my mind to the acts or omissions which are called in question.[1]

It follows from this that tortuous duties do not extend to the world at large. Indeed, it was only in 1932 that it was finally accepted that the manufacturer of a product owed any duty towards the ultimate user in the event that the latter suffered injury because of a defect in the product.[2] Within continental jurisdictions, the extent of the duty of care tends to be more widely formulated. Thus, the French and German Civil Codes provide, respectively:

> Any act whatever of man which causes damage to another obliges him by whose fault it occurred to make reparation.[3]
>
> A person who, intentionally or negligently, injures unlawfully the life, body, health, freedom, property or any other right of another person is bound to compensate him for any damage arising therefrom.[4]

The application of this rule will not generally pose problems for a party claiming against a software producer. Software is a flexible tool, however, and may be put to uses which were not expected by the producer. Cases have been cited where spreadsheet packages, intended for use in the making of financial calculations, have been used by heart surgeons in the course of major operations. In the event that a failure in the package resulted in injury or death to the patient, it might well be argued that this category of person was outwith the reasonable contemplation of the software producer.

Breach of duty

Not every act which causes loss to another will give rise to an action in tort. Save in exceptional circumstances, some element of fault must also be present. This is most frequently expressed in terms of negligence—a failure to observe that standard of care which would be observed by a reasonable person placed in the position of the defending party.

The concept of the reasonable man is a flexible one, which will be adjusted to take account of the nature of and the particular circumstances under which an action occurred. In the event, for example, that the activities of a member of a profession are called into question, the requisite standard will be that of the reasonable member of

---

[1] [1932] AC 562 at 580.
[2] See Chapter 25 regarding 'merchantable quality'.
[3] Article 1382.
[4] Article 823.

that profession. Some difficulty may be anticipated in the software field in that, given the relative novelty of the subject, professional bodies have yet to acquire the recognition and status afforded to those representing the more traditional professions such as law or medicine. This has posed problems within the United States, where the doctrine of professional malpractice requires the observance of a higher duty of care on the part of members of recognised professions. In a number of cases, the courts have refused to accept the concept of computer malpractice.[5]

Such difficulties are unlikely to arise in the United Kingdom, where a more pragmatic approach prevails. Under this, questions as to the requisite standard of care are essentially factual ones, which may be resolved through the production of expert witnesses who can speak to the level of performance that they would expect of a party in the position of the defender. Although it is not unusual for expert witnesses to come to different opinions, reports of proceedings in a number of computer-related disputes appear to demonstrate an unusually high level of divergence. In the case of *Missing Link Software v Magee*,[6] a case concerned with alleged infringement of copyright, the expert witnesses' disagreements prompted the judge to comment of one report where the expert had indicated that he had attempted to express his views in as moderate a fashion as possible:

> In the course of eight or nine pages the following expressions may be found: 'effect of misleading the court in a major way'; 'fundamental errors'; 'conclusions which are at best fanciful and in my opinion not worthy of serious consideration'; 'no grounds whatsoever for the conclusions reached'; 'no person of reasonable common sense'; 'displays an inability to read a program'; 'cannot distinguish between'; 'this is a ridiculous inference to draw'; 'an error of which even a schoolboy would be ashamed'; 'attempting to mislead the court'; 'this is another absolutely basic error'; 'paragraph 17 and 18 are of course based on the same fundamental error'; 'sheer and utter nonsense' ... One shudders to think what he might have said if he had really let himself go.

The absence of a consensus regarding even basic aspects of software development must render difficult the task of a judge in determining whether any aspect of the work might have been tainted by negligence. The sheer pace of technological development also creates substantial problems. The example of the Millennium Bug provides a relevant illustration. Certainly, it would be considered negligent today to supply software which was not capable of coping with a date in the year 2000, but the question may still arise in legal proceedings as to when a reasonable software producer should have been aware of the problem. One of the first recorded uses of the term Millennium Bug was in 1989.[7] A search of the Nexis database, which contains the full text of leading United Kingdom newspapers, indicates that the first use of the phrase 'millennium bug' occurred in early 1995.

---

[5] See *Chatlos Systems Inc v National Cash Register Corpn* 479 F Supp 738 (1979).

[6] [1989] FSR 361.

[7] Cited in P. G. Neumann, *Computer-Related Risks* (New York, 1995).

Application of the concept of negligence to software

As has been stated previously, the quest for perfect software has proved as successful as the hunt for the Loch Ness monster. Cynics might suggest that neither exist. In the real world, the producer's compliance with generally observed industry standards may be sufficient to comply with tortuous requirements. A number of formal standards do exist in the information technology field, although it may be doubted how far these may assist in the task of identifying negligent conduct. An international standard, ISO 9126, identifies six quality characteristics which might be applied in determining questions of software quality. These comprise: functionality, reliability, usability, efficiency, maintainability, and portability.

Although identification of critical qualities is of value, the standard provides no assistance in answering the legal question 'how much?' Other standards may provide more precise guidance. ISO 9127, for example, is entitled 'User documentation and cover information for consumer software packages' and provides detailed guidance regarding the information which should be supplied on the outer cover of a software package. This is considered important to enable 'potential purchasers to assess the applicability of the package to their requirements'. Items covered include the intended purpose of the software, any hardware and software requirements, any design restrictions, and information about any licence provisions. Studies suggest, however, that few producers meet this standard.[8] Given this, it may be difficult to argue that a failure to observe the standard would constitute negligence. In the Scottish case of *Kelly v Mears and Partners*,[9] a failure by an architect to follow the provisions of a British Standard Code of Practice was held not to constitute professional negligence. The terms of the Code, it was held, had no evidential value in their own right and could be relied upon only in so far as it was referred to in evidence by witnesses speaking as to the professional standard applicable to the particular case.

The standard of the reasonable man will normally be determined by reference to that generally prevailing in the trade or profession. This may not always be conclusive. A professional journal has reported an instance whereby a factory employee was killed by a robot. Safety devices were available, including an electronic beam which caused the robot to cease working if a person approached too close. The report indicated that this feature was offered at extra cost. The reason advanced as to why it was not fitted as standard was that the producer had:

> ...polled customers for their reactions. But because there have been so few problems of safety until recently, customers haven't felt the need for it. [The Producer] knows of no other robot manufacturer that includes the safety device as a standard.[10]

Without attempting to analyse the particular issues involved, the example illustrates a difficulty with leaving decisions as to the level of safety devices to members of the industry involved.

---

[8] *Personal Computer World*, April 1989, p. 2.

[9] 1983 SC 97.

[10] (1985) 10 Communication of the Association of Computing Machinery 3.

Liability for the use of information technology

A number of instances have been documented of humans being injured or even killed by coming into contact with computer-controlled products. Robots have killed factory workers, computer-controlled X-ray machines have exposed hospital patients to excessive doses of radiation, computer-controlled ambulance despatch systems have failed, causing delays in the arrival of ambulances. The list could go on and on.

Save in the most extreme case, it may be considered unlikely that a decision to use technical devices will, of itself, constitute negligence. Significant issues may concern the manner in which the technology is introduced and applied. A British Standard[11] which provides a guide to specifying user requirements for a computer-based system contains detailed guidance as to the information which users should provide to and seek from potential suppliers of computer systems. Although the dividing line between the user's and the supplier's obligations may be unclear, the standard makes it clear that a user cannot abdicate all responsibility.

A particular requirement imposed upon those responsible for computer systems must be to ensure that those responsible for using the technology are adequately trained. In the case of *The Lady Gwendolen*,[12] a ship had radar installed but the owners took no steps to ensure its proper use by the crew. A collision resulted, largely as a consequence of the crew's failure in this regard, and the owners were held liable in negligence for damage caused to the other vessel owing to their failure to secure the satisfactory use of radar. The message from this case is clear. It is not enough for an employer to install an effective information technology system. Steps must also be taken to ensure that employees are trained in its operation and, on a continuing basis, to ensure that proper procedures are followed.

Evidence of the problems that may arise in this respect can be taken from the report of the inquiry into the London Ambulance Service.[13] This inquiry was conducted following a number of well-publicised failures in a recently installed computer system controlling the despatch of ambulances. Matters subjected to critical comment in the report include the selection of a supplier with limited experience of work in the field, of the haste with which the system was introduced (which did not allow for sufficient testing of the various components), the failure to provide adequate training, and the absence of contingency plans to cope with system failures.

A further issue that may arise concerns the question of whether extensive reliance is placed on information technology products. An instance has been reported from the United States of a situation where an accountant used an established tax calculation program in the course of preparing a client's tax returns. A fault in the software meant that the client made an overpayment of $36,800. Although this sum was eventually repaid, the loss of interest amounted to some $700.[14] A similar bug has been reported in a tax package developed to assist United Kingdom taxpayers in dealing with the

---

[11] BS 6719, 1986.

[12] [1965] P 294.

[13] South West Thames Regional Health Authority (February 1993).

[14] *The Risks Digest*, available from <http://catless/ncl.ac.uk/Risks>

new self-assessment system. The package was supplied free of charge to registered users of an existing personal finance package, thereby creating problems due to the lack of consideration in the event a customer sought to claim under the law of contract. Media reports indicate that the producer has offered to refund any penalties imposed by the Inland Revenue for inaccurate returns. The indications are, however, that the bug will result in over- rather than under-payment.

In this example, the relationship between the client and the accountant would be a contractual one. The requirements as regards negligence, however, will be equivalent to those applying in the non-contractual situation. It might be argued that a failure to check the output from a computer system might constitute negligence. Against this, many aspects of life today are so complex that the use of computers provides the only cost-effective means of conducting business. The report indicates that the accounts making up the tax return in question were more than half an inch thick. In such situations, there may be little option other than to place reliance upon the computer's output. Especially where the user operates in a professional capacity, it may be argued that a failure to detect major errors in output would amount to negligence.

Liability for the failure to use information technology

If the application of information technology may expose the user to the risk of liability, so a failure to take advantage of the technology might also amount to negligence. Once again, reference to prevailing practice in the particular area of activity will furnish assistance. If use of technical aids is not commonplace, then a failure on the part of a particular defendant is unlikely to constitute negligence. However, there may be exceptions to this rule. The United States case of *The T J Hooper*[15] provides an illustration of such a situation. Here, two barges were lost in a storm at sea. The storm had been forecast and a warning broadcast on the radio. Unfortunately, the tugs towing the barges did not have radio sets installed and so the opportunity to take shelter was lost. Holding the tug owners liable for the resultant loss, it was determined that the failure to provide a radio constituted a negligent omission. Although the evidence before the court fell far short of establishing that it was common practice to install radio equipment on tugs, the particular owner was held liable, the court commenting that '[a] whole calling may have unduly lagged in the adoption of new and available devices'. To this extent, producers and others may be considered under a continuing duty to keep up to date with technical developments and to modify their standards accordingly.

As the global usage of information technology products expands, so it might be reasonable to expect that their application will become the rule rather than the exception in more and more areas of activity. It has been suggested that a failure to use computers in the course of activities such as air traffic control would amount to negligence.[16] The suppliers of a computerised legal retrieval service have suggested in publicity

---

[15] 60 F 2d 737 (1932).
[16] C. Tapper, *Computer Law* (London, 1989).

materials that a failure by a lawyer to make use of their system might constitute professional negligence. To date, these issues have not been tested in court. It may be that a distinction should be drawn between the situation where technology is used to substitute for human action, for example, where automated equipment is used to perform tasks in a factory that would require humans to be exposed to some form of danger and those, as with the examples cited above, where the technology provides assistance to humans.

In terms of legal principle, the application of information technology raises no novel issues in the field of negligence. The rapid pace of technical development may pose practical problems. As discussed in the previous section, reliance upon unstable or immature technology might be held negligent, whilst excessive delay in adopting proven technical aids might also be so regarded.

Causation

To establish liability, a claimant must establish that the breach of the duty was the proximate cause of the resulting damage. In many respects, this requirement raises factual rather than legal problems. During 1987, for example, problems were encountered with a number of medical linear accelerators being used to treat patients suffering from cancer. The operation of the machines was controlled by software. Owing to an undetected flaw in the software, if the operator inserted an unusual but possible series of commands, the machine subjected the patient to a massive overdose of radiation. A number of the patients subsequently died.[17]

Assuming that the negligence can be established in such a case, there would appear little doubt that a causal link between the operation of the equipment and the injury could be established. A more recent incident occurring in the United Kingdom raises more complex issues. Once again, it concerned equipment being used to provide radiation treatment to cancer patients. In this case, however, an operator error resulted in patients receiving up to 30 per cent less radiation than intended. Whilst an overdose of radiation will cause physical injury to the recipient, a shortfall will not of itself cause injury, but may have the effect of depriving the patient of possible benefit. A spokesman for the Department of Health was quoted as conceding that 'There is no doubt that negligence was involved.'[18] Although a £2 million settlement has recently been negotiated between the Health Authority involved and about 100 of the patients affected, a report on the incident stated that 'it was virtually impossible to say whether those who had died would have survived had it not been for the mistake'.[19] Particularly given the insidious nature of the disease, the existence of a causal link between negligence and injury would be very difficult to establish in court.

---

[17] H. Bassen, J. Silverberg, F. Houston, et al., *Computerised Medical Devices*, Proceedings of the Seventh Annual Conference of IEEE Engineering in Medicine and Biology Society (London, 1985), p. 180.

[18] *Independent*, 7 February 1992.

[19] Ibid., 22 April 1997.

A further illustration of this point can be taken from the case of *R v Poplar Coroner, ex p Thomas*.[20] The Court of Appeal reversed an order that an inquest be held into the death of a young woman. The woman had suffered from asthma throughout her life. In April 1989, she suffered a serious attack and a call was made to the ambulance service. The 999 call produced only a recorded message: 'There is no one here at present. Please hold on and we will answer your call as soon as we can.' By the time contact was made with the ambulance service and an ambulance arrived, over half an hour had elapsed and the patient was dead. A post-mortem examination and report indicated that prompt treatment would have saved the patient's life.

Under the provisions of the Coroners Act 1988, an inquest may be held only in specified circumstances, including where there is reasonable ground to suspect that death was 'unnatural'.[21] The coroner refused to hold an inquest in this case on the basis that the death was not unnatural. This view was upheld by the Court of Appeal.[22] Referring to the dicta of Lord Salmon in *Alphacell Ltd v Woodward*, to the effect that:

> ...who or what has caused a certain event to occur is essentially a practical question of fact which can best be answered by ordinary common sense rather than by abstract metaphysical theory.[23]

Dillon LJ recognised that a variety of scenarios could be postulated under which an ambulance might arrive too late to save such a patient. Included in his examples was the possibility that:

> ...a newly installed computer installed by the ambulance service to handle emergency calls more efficiently malfunctioned as newly installed computers are prone to.[24]

From the perspective of the provisions of the Coroners Act 1988, however, the illness must be regarded as the 'cause' of death. Asthma being a relatively common medical condition, the death was not, he considered, unnatural.

In many cases, the result of a failure on the part of an information technology system will be to deprive a person of some form of warning. An example might be the failure on the part of a computer-controlled fire alarm to sound when a fire occurred. In such a situation, there might well be an argument that the alarm was not of satisfactory quality or fit for its purpose, but in the event that injury or damage occurred, it would be difficult to argue that the failure of the alarm was the proximate cause.

Remoteness of damage

The test of causation is essentially a factual one. Common sense dictates, however, that some limits must be placed upon the extent of a negligent party's responsibilities.

---

20 [1993] 2 All ER 381.
21 Section 8(1).
22 *R v Poplar Coroner, ex p Thomas* [1993] QB 610.
23 [1972] 2 All ER 475 at 490.
24 *R v Poplar Coroner, ex p Thomas* [1993] QB 610 at 628.

Illustrations of the extreme consequences following the application of the 'but for' test belong in the history rather than the law books. The test of remoteness sets legal boundaries determining the forms of damage and the categories of injured party to whom an admittedly negligent party may be liable.

The relationship between the issues of causation and remoteness is close, and similar issues may arise under both headings. In the example of the delayed arrival of an ambulance, the defence to an action by a patient might be based either on the absence of a causal link or on the ground that the injury was too remote a consequence of the original negligence.

Once again, the test of reasonable foresight will come into play, with a defendant being held liable only for losses of a kind which it was reasonably foreseeable could spring from his or her negligent acts or omissions. In the event that damage of a particular kind could have been anticipated, full liability will be incurred even though the extent of the damage might not have been foreseen. The literature on computer viruses is replete with plaintive tales of students creating and disseminating viruses by way of a practical joke, only to discover that the consequences of their action were much more serious. Once the intent to cause a little harm can be established, the perpetrator will be liable for the full amount of damage, even though the scale is much greater than might have been intended or expected.

Novus actus interveniens

One factor which may serve to terminate a party's liabilities on the ground of remoteness may arise where a third party intervenes in the chain of events leading from negligent act to injury or damage. In some instances, the third party will serve merely as a conduit whose involvement will not diminish the original actor's responsibilities. A party may, for example, develop a computer virus and put infected disks into circulation. If the virus spreads, it will be through the action of third parties using the disks. In the event that the intermediary acts negligently or intentionally in propagating the virus, liability may be incurred on this basis, but it must be doubted whether this will diminish in any way the liability of the originator of the virus towards those whose computers are affected.

More complex issues arise where the involvement of the third party contributes in larger part towards the ultimate injury. Where a complex information technology system is supplied which requires a high degree of skill on the part of its users, injury to a third party resulting from the negligent operation of the system would normally be considered too remote to impose liability upon the supplier. Although there appears no authority on the point, it might be argued that the supplier would remain liable in the event that he or she should have been aware that the user would not be able to obtain staff of a sufficient level of expertise to operate the product in a reasonably safe manner. Again, a failure to supply adequate instructions for the use of the product might leave the supplier exposed to an action by an injured third party.

Compensatable loss

The final requirement for a successful claim in tort requires that the particular form of loss suffered by the claimant should be recognised at law. In principle, damages may be claimed under the law of tort in respect of any form of damage. During the 1970s and early 1980s, the distinction between contractual and tortuous liability appeared to be steadily eroded. In the case of *Junior Books v Veitchi*, Lord Roskill commented that:

> I think today the proper control lies not in asking whether the proper remedy should lie in contract or instead in tort, not in somewhat capricious judicial determination whether a particular case falls on one side of the line or the other, not in somewhat artificial distinctions between physical or economic loss when the two sometimes go together and sometimes do not (it is sometimes overlooked that virtually all damage including physical damage is in one sense financial or economic for it is compensated by an award of damages) but in the first instance in establishing the relevant principles and then in deciding whether a particular case falls within or without those principles.[25]

The effect of such an approach was at least to accept the possibility that damages might be awarded in tort in respect of defects which served to diminish the value of a product, rather than requiring that the product cause injury damage to persons or property. More recently, however, the courts have retreated substantially from such a proposition. In the case of *CBS Songs Ltd v Amstrad Consumer Electronics plc*,[26] the House of Lords considered and rejected the proposition that the manufacturer of audio equipment, in this case a hi-fi unit with two cassette decks, owed a tortuous duty of care to the owners of copyright in musical works whose interests, it was alleged, would be adversely affected in the event that users of the equipment used its facilities to make unauthorised copies of pre-recorded cassette tapes. Delivering the judgment of the court, Lord Templeman was critical of the approach in *Junior Books*[27] and the earlier case of *Anns v Merton London Borough Council*,[28] stating that since these decisions:

> ...a fashionable plaintiff alleges negligence. The pleading assumes that we are all neighbours now, Pharisees and Samaritans alike, that foreseeability is a reflection of hindsight and that for every mischance in an accident-prone world someone solvent must be liable in damages.[29]

In particular, the courts are today extremely reluctant to award compensation for economic loss.[30] The concept of economic loss is not easily or precisely defined. It may consist of a sum representing the diminished value of a product which is considered

---

25 [1983] 1 AC 520 at 545.
26 [1988] AC 1013.
27 *Junior Books v Veitchi* [1983] 1 AC 520.
28 [1978] AC 728.
29 [1988] AC 1013 at 1059.
30 See *D & F Estates v Church Comrs for England* [1989] 2 All ER 992 and *Murphy v Brentwood District Council* [1990] 2 All ER 908.

to be defective, or it may represent lost profits resulting from an inability to perform what would otherwise be a profitable activity. An example might be found in the case of a person who negligently cuts off a factory's electricity supply, causing cessation of production. Certainly, the party will be held liable for any form of physical damage which may be caused to the factory or its assets, but will not be held responsible for the lost profits which may result from the breakdown in production. Although the case of *Junior Books*[31] remains as precedent for the proposition that economic loss might be compensated in the event that the relationship between the parties is akin to one based in contract, it must be questioned how far this approach will be followed in any future decisions.

In many instances, the arguments that have persuaded the courts to backtrack from the award of damages for economic loss outside the contractual relationship will apply with particular force to information technology. Comparatively few products operate in the safety-critical field, most being concerned with more mundane tasks where the consequence of a failure will be some form of economic loss. The example of the tax calculation program cited above provides an excellent illustration. Thousands of copies of such a product may be sold, they may be used in a large number of situations, and their operation may result in exposure to a great variety of risks, ranging from minor inconvenience to the substantial losses referred to in the example. In this and in many other situations it might be unreasonable to hold the producer liable. Another example cited from the United States may further evidence the point. In this, proceedings were initiated against the Lotus Corporation, alleging that a defect in their spreadsheet had resulted in a building contractor submitting a tender which was too low. The contract was awarded, only for the contractor to discover that the work could be carried out only at a loss.

This action was withdrawn before trial but the case provides some evidence of the range of situations in which a basic software product might be used and of the impossibility for the producer to anticipate the extent of potential losses. A final example might be cited from the author's own experience. Students on a postgraduate course were required to submit a sizeable number of items of assessment. The marks attained were entered into a spreadsheet program to calculate the final mark. Two different departments used two different makes of spreadsheet. When the figures were rounded up or down to the nearest whole number, the result in the case of one student was that there was a disagreement between the spreadsheets. One gave a pass mark of 50 per cent and the other a fail at 49 per cent. Analysis of the possible legal consequences of such a result might occupy most of this book. Could either of the spreadsheets be considered wrong? Should the users have been aware of this possibility? Should all marks be double-checked? Assuming the student was denied a degree because of an incorrect output, would any form of compensation be available? Fortunately for the student, and unfortunately for the legal profession, this incident ended with the higher mark being selected.

[31] *Junior Books v Veitchi* [1983] 1 AC 520.

Defences

In the event that liability can prima facie be identified under the law of tort, attention must be paid to the defences which may be available, and as to the forms of loss or damage which may be compensated. An obvious defence to any action in tort will consist of the claim that the claimant has failed to establish any of the factors outlined above adequately. Two further defences should receive specific mention.

Contributory negligence

Contributory negligence should, perhaps, be regarded as a plea in mitigation rather than as a defence per se. Under its ambit, the defender admits a degree of culpability but argues that the claimant was also partially responsible for the damage. Contributory negligence may be an appropriate plea in the event that a claim relates to the inadequacy of instructions supplied with a product. Save in the event that the instructions are simply erroneous, any loss may result from a combination of their deficiencies and the claimant's failure either to comprehend their proper message or to realise that they provided an unsafe basis for reliance and, therefore, that the product should not be used pending clarification.

Another area where contributory negligence may be relevant would be in the situation where the claimant failed to take precautions such as ensuring that back-up copies were maintained of programs or data. Dependent upon the nature of the activity and the risks involved, further measures might be required to guard against the risk of software or hardware failure. Where computers are utilised in aircraft, for example, a party could be guilty of at least contributory negligence if adequate provision were not made against the possibility of failure. In most cases, this involves the provision of two or even three independent systems, each of which can enable the plane to operate safely.

Volenti non fit injuria

The underlying basis of the doctrine of *volenti* is that acts which would otherwise give rise to legal liability will not do so in the event that they are directed against a person who has consented to accept that particular risk of injury. The application of the doctrine is most prominent in the sporting field. Under normal circumstances, the act of punching another party would undoubtedly constitute a tort (and render the perpetrator liable to criminal prosecution). A boxer, however, by agreeing to enter into a contest with another, must be taken as accepting the risk of injury. With *volenti*, however, it is important to recognise the limitations of the consent. A party will be taken to have accepted only those risks which are inherent to the sport itself. If a boxer strikes a blow outside the rules of the sport, his opponent will be entitled to raise an action in tort.

The above sporting example is an illustration of a situation where consent to a risk may be implied from the very fact of participating in an undertaking. Such situations will be rare. In the normal course of life, people are entitled to assume that their interests will not be adversely affected by the negligence of others. It may be that if a hacker secures access to a computer system only to find that, owing to a defect in the victim computer, his or her own system is damaged, *volenti* will provide a complete defence to any claim for compensation which might be raised.

Measure of damages

The purpose of an award of damages under the law of tort, in so far as is possible, is to return the injured party to the position occupied prior to the occurrence of the negligent act. This approach is to be contrasted with the position under the law of contract, where the purpose of an award of damages is to put the innocent party in the position that would have been occupied had the contract been completed. In the event, for example, that A contracts to provide B with a piece of software for £50,000, if A fails to deliver the software so that B has to obtain the product elsewhere at a cost of £100,000, this latter figure will be the appropriate amount of an award. Under the law of tort, if A negligently destroys B's software which cost £50,000 when new but will now cost £100,000 to replace, the maximum measure of damages will be £50,000. To this extent, contractual damages may be more extensive than their tortuous equivalent.

Exclusion of tortuous liability

A further aspect of this topic relates to the extent to which a party may give notice of a refusal to accept liability for losses arising in the course of a non-contractual relationship. The issues involved here are similar to those applying in the context of contractual exclusion clauses. Couched this time in terms of the tortuous duty of care, it might be argued that if a party announces an unwillingness to accept any responsibility for the fate of another, this will serve to prevent the creation or continuance of any duty of care. An illustration here might see the provision of a notice on the screen of a computer program warning users against placing reliance upon the program's output. Alternatively, the provision of a notice warning of a risk, for example, a 'beware of the dog' sign, might be seen as fulfilling a duty of care.

Under the provisions of the Unfair Contract Terms Act 1977, any attempt to exclude tortuous liability in respect of personal injury or death resulting from a negligent act will be invalid.[32] This is not to say that a claim for compensation in respect of such an occurrence will succeed. The provision of a suitable warning notice may well discharge the duty of care. What will be necessary in this case is that the notice be sufficiently brought to the attention of the other party at a stage where this party retains genuine freedom to determine whether to proceed with a particular course of action, accepting the consequential risk of loss. In the case of software, this would require that a prominent notice appear as soon as a user begins to operate the system.

---

[32] Section 2.

Product liability and software

The entry into force of the product liability provisions of the Consumer Protection Act 1987 has brought about major changes in the non-contractual liability regime in the United Kingdom. The Act, which was introduced pursuant to the requirements of an EC Directive[33] on the 'Approximation of the Laws, Regulations and Administrative Provisions of the Member States Concerning Liability for Defective Products',[34] serves principally to introduce a system of no fault liability in respect of certain forms of injury and damage.

The rationale behind the Directive[35] can be found in its Preamble, which asserts that:

> ...liability without fault on the part of the producer is the sole means of adequately solving the problem, peculiar to our age of increasing technicality, and of a fair apportionment of the risks inherent in modern production.
>
> Thus, public policy demands that the burden of accidental injuries caused by products should be placed upon the producer and be treated as a cost of production arguing that the producer can best afford and meet these costs. A further factor in this calculation lies in the relative ease with which a producer should be able to obtain insurance cover against any costs incurred in this manner.

Removing the requirement that a claimant establishes negligence effectively places a defending producer in the position of an insurer. In some respects, the Consumer Protection Act 1987 equates the non-contractual liability of a producer with the contractual liability of a supplier under the Sale of Goods Act 1979, although this is restricted to incidents of injury or damage and does not afford the consumer with any rights where the product is of poor quality. This marks a fundamental change in the common law approach, although the Directive[36] requires fewer changes in civil law-based systems, which in consumer cases have increasingly tended to impose either strict liability or apply a presumption of fault, thereby shifting the onus of proof on to the defendant. Although the doctrine of *res ipsa loquitur* permits a similar approach to be followed in the United Kingdom, this has operated only in restricted circumstances.

Scope of the legislation

Parties liable

A number of parties involved in the production or distribution chain may incur liability under the provisions of the Directive[37] and the Consumer Protection Act 1987. An

---

[33] In most respects, the Directive and the Act utilise terminology that is substantially similar. Where this is the case, specific references will be to the provisions of the Act.

[34] Directive 85/374/EEC, OJ 1985 L 210/26.

[35] Directive 85/374/EEC.

[36] Ibid.

[37] Ibid.

action may be brought against the producer of the finished product—or any persons who, by putting a name or brand mark on goods produced by a third party, hold themselves out as being the producer. Action may also be taken against the producer of any component incorporated into the product where it is claimed that that component is defective. In the case that a product is imported into the EC, the importer will be liable in the event that it proves defective.[38]

Any supplier of the product may also incur liability under the Consumer Protection Act 1987. This liability, however, will arise only in the event that it is asked by an injured consumer to identify one or more of the parties referred to in the preceding paragraph and, without reasonable excuse, fails so to do.[39] This provision is likely to be of relevance only where products are imported or carry no brand or other identification marks.

Products

The Consumer Protection Act 1987 and the Directive[40] apply in respect of products. A further EC Directive was proposed which would apply approximately equivalent provisions in respect of the liability of service providers.[41] This Directive was withdrawn for revision following the adoption of the new doctrine of subsidiarity, although the Commissions' Consumer Action Plan 1999–2001'[42] indicates the intention to bring forward a new proposal.

For the purposes of the Directive, a product is defined as:

> All movables, with the exception of primary agricultural products and game, even though incorporated into another movable or immovable…'Product' includes electricity.[43]

The Consumer Protection Act 1987 utilises different terminology, defining a product as 'any goods or electricity'.[44] Assuming the application of the Sale of Goods Act 1979 definition whereby the word 'goods' encompasses 'all personal chattels other than things in action and money',[45] the British and European definitions appear virtually identical. The question as to their application to software has, however, produced significant disagreement between the United Kingdom and the Community authorities. In a consultative document published by the United Kingdom Department of Trade and Industry concerning the introduction of legislation on this topic, it was stated:

> Special problems arise with those industries dealing with those products concerned with information such as books…and computer software. It has been suggested that

---

[38] Section 1(2).
[39] Section 2(3).
[40] Directive 85/374/EEC.
[41] COM (90) 482 final—SYN 308.
[42] COM (98) 696.
[43] Directive 85/374/EEC, Article 2.
[44] Section 1(2).
[45] Section 61(1).

it would be absurd for printers to be held liable for faithfully reproducing errors in the material provided to them that by giving bad instructions…indirectly causes injury.[46]

By contrast, Lord Cockfield, in responding to a written question in the European Parliament concerning the application of the Directive to software, stated unequivocally that:

> Under Article 2 of [the] directive…on liability for defective products[47]…the term product is defined as all movables, with the exception of primary agricultural products (not having undergone initial processing) and game, even though incorporated into another movable or into an immovable. Consequently the directive applies to software in the same way, moreover, that it applies to handicrafts and artistic products.[48]

Neither comment can be regarded as definitive of the status of software under the respective instruments. It may be that questions as to the scope of the Directive and as to the conformity of national implementing legislation will have to be determined before the European Court of Justice.

Issues of product liability concerning the operation of information technology products may arise in two respects. In the present chapter, consideration will be given to the liability that may arise where software is used to control the operation of some other product. Numerous examples could be cited—it is an unusual car or aircraft which does not possess its quota of microprocessors. Even mundane household objects such as washing machines and video recorders may be so equipped. In this situation, the question of whether the software is itself a product is of limited significance. The plane or the car or the washing machine will undoubtedly be so regarded and the issue to be discussed will be the manner in which that product functions, taking account of the role of any software.

Damage

Only limited categories of damage may be compensated. Compensation may be claimed in respect of personal injury or in respect of damage to any property which is of a kind ordinarily intended for private use or consumption and which is used for such a purpose. A *de minimis* rule applies, with the effect that the damage must be costed at a minimum of £275. Finally, the producer will incur no liability in respect of damage to the product itself or to any other product of which it constitutes a component part.[49] Thus, in the event that the software controlling the operation of a motor car's anti-lock braking system fails, causing an accident, no compensation will be payable in respect of the damage to the vehicle itself.

---

[46] Department of Trade and Industry, *Implementation of the EC Directive on Product Liability, Department of Trade and Industry* (London, 1985), para. 47.

[47] Directive 85/374/EEC.

[48] OJ 1989 C 114/42.

[49] Consumer Protection Act 1987, s 5.

The Directive provides that national legislation may impose an overall ceiling of €70 million on the liability of a producer in respect of damage arising from identical items.[50] This option was not exercised in the Consumer Protection Act 1987, so that a producer may be held liable for any amount of damage resulting from defective products.

Defectiveness

A producer will incur liability only when a product is defective. A product will so stigmatised if 'it does not provide the level of safety that persons generally are entitled to expect'.[51] In determining questions of defectiveness, account is to be taken of the manner in which the product is marketed, any normal or intended uses, and any instructions supplied to the user. Account is also to be taken of the state of the art in respect of products of that kind, both the Consumer Protection Act 1987 and Directive[52] providing that a product is not to be characterised as defective merely because a safer product subsequently becomes available.[53]

In considering the level of safety that may legitimately be sought by persons coming into contact with a product, it may be argued that they expect complete safety. Although a degree of risk may attach to almost any activity, be it a plane journey or the carving of a joint of meat, the passenger and the carver are surely entitled to expect that they will arrive safely at their intended destination. The effect of the approach adopted in the legislation would appear to be to establish a presumption of defectiveness in the event that injury or damage occurs connected with the operation of a product. The onus is then upon the producer to demonstrate that the cause was something other than a defect in the product. In the event, for example, that a cook cuts his or her hand whilst carving the meat, it is arguable that any defectiveness lies with the user rather than the product. In this context, the adequacy of any instructions supplied for the use of a product may be of considerable significance. Disregard by users of warnings concerning design limitations in a product's capabilities might result in them being regarded the author of their own misfortune in the event they suffer injury or damage.

More significant in the information technology field is the provision that the performance of a product in safety terms is to be judged against contemporary products. To illustrate this provision, we might take the example of cars designed in 1970 and 1990 being driven at the same speed. If the cars' brakes were to be applied simultaneously, one would expect the more modern design of brakes to stop the car within a shorter distance. If the difference in stopping distances marked the difference between hitting an object or stopping short, the older car would not be considered defective on this count. Given the pace of developments in information technology, this provision

---

[50] Directive 85/374/EEC, Article 16(1).
[51] Section 3(1), Article 6(1).
[52] Directive 85/374/EEC.
[53] Section 3(2), Article 6(2).

might be of considerable importance, although its application may not prove a simple matter.

The possibility of drawing comparison with the general level of performance reasonably to be expected from a product of the kind in question will apply only in respect of risks which are inherent to the activity involved, but which are extrinsic to the product itself which performs at the level that a user might reasonably expect. On this basis, it might be argued that as every computer program possesses defects, every product so controlled will be defective and that a user is entitled to expect only a defective product. This argument appears to run counter to the basic philosophy of the product liability regime. As described above, the Directive proclaims that:

> ...liability without fault on the part of the producer is the sole means of adequately solving the problem, peculiar to our age of increasing technicality, and of a fair apportionment of the risks inherent in modern production.[54]

In many areas of activity, there are statistically verifiable risks associated with product failure. An aircraft will be certified for public use, not on the basis that its components will never fail, but that it is extremely unlikely that this will occur. If it is calculated that one accident will occur per 10 million hours of flight because of some defect introduced at the design or production stage, it would not appear open to a producer to utilise the defence subsequent to an accident that its occurrence was in line with the statistical predictions.

On this basis, a defence would be available to a motor car manufacturer that the state of technical knowledge would not permit the production of a braking system capable of stopping a car travelling at 50 mph within 30ft. In the situation where the car's brakes had failed, it would not be open to the producer to claim that it was not possible to produce a braking system with a failure rate of less than 1 in 100,000 applications. In the same manner, a software producer should not be heard to argue that a product fails no more often than its competitors.

Defences

The basic defence to a claim under the product liability legislation will consist of the assertion that the product was not defective at the time it left the producer's control.[55] As indicated above, this will normally be an issue of fact. In one respect, the position of a software producer will be less tenable than is the case with more tangible products. Software will not deteriorate with the passage of time. The possibility that a user may have introduced a defect by mishandling the product will also have limited application in respect of software. To a greater extent than with other products, the state of a software-based product at the moment an accident occurs can be considered equivalent to its state at the moment that the product left the producer's control.

---

[54] Directive 85/374/EEC, Preamble.
[55] Consumer Protection Act 1987, s 4(1)(d) and Directive 85/374/EEC, Article 7(b).

Compliance with legal requirements

Additionally, it will be a defence for the producer to establish that the defect resulted from compliance with any requirement imposed by or under any enactment or with any Community obligation.[56] Effectively, this will require evidence that the producer was legally required to produce to particular specifications and that the defect lay in the specifications. Few, if any, legal requirements exist in the software field, although they are more prevalent in the area of information technology products concerning such matters as electromagnetic emissions and electrical safety. Even here, the regulations are more likely to prescribe standards—leaving the manner in which these are attained to the producer—than to prescribe particular aspects of product design.

Conformity with specification

A more relevant provision applies in the situation where a product is produced for incorporation into another product. In this instance, the legislation provides the component producer with a defence that the defect:

> ... was wholly attributable to the design of the subsequent product or to compliance by the producer of the product in question with instructions given by the producer of the subsequent product.[57]

Where a product is to incorporate software, the production of which is the responsibility of a sub-contractor, it might be that the latter will be able to use this defence where the requirements are laid down by the main producer and where any defect lies in these. A simple example might see a software company being required to develop a controlling program to work in certain temperatures, being told that it is to recognise temperatures of between –10 and +40°C. If the control system fails in temperatures of –20°C, it would appear inequitable to hold the software producer liable. The presence of the word 'wholly' in the statutory provision must limit its application. In the report of the Inquiry into the London Ambulance Service, where the system specifications were drawn up by the customer, it is stated that:

> The (specification) is very detailed and contains a high degree of precision on the way in which the system was intended to operate. It is quite prescriptive and provided little scope for additional ideas to be incorporated from prospective suppliers.[58]

Interpretative difficulties may also be anticipated in the not uncommon situation where the two parties cooperate on the production of requirements, but where the contract for the work itself sees these being 'imposed' by the main producer.

---

[56] Consumer Protection Act 1987, s 4(1)(a) and Directive 85/374/EEC, Article 7(d).
[57] Consumer Protection Act 1987, s 4(1)(f). Directive 85/374/EEC, Article 7(f) is in similar terms.
[58] South West Thames Regional Health Authority (1993), para. 3017.

Development risks

This defence represents perhaps the most controversial element of the new product liability regime. As contained in the Directive, the development risks defence allows for the producer to demonstrate that, although the product failed to provide the requisite level of safety:

> ...the state of scientific and technical knowledge at the time when he put the product into circulation was not such as to enable the existence of the defect to be discovered.[59]

The Consumer Protection Act 1987 adopts different terminology, providing that the defence will be available where:

> ...the state of scientific and technical knowledge at the relevant time was not such that a producer of products of the same description as the product in question might be expected to have discovered the defect if it had existed in his products while they were under his control.[60]

By substituting the phrase 'might be expected to have discovered' for the original 'enable the existence of the defect to be discovered', the United Kingdom legislation might be seen as extending the scope of the defence. This was the view of the Commission, which initiated legal proceedings against the United Kingdom authorities, alleging that the change in terminology constituted a failure to implement the provisions of the Directive[61] fully, having the effect of 'transforming the strict or no-fault liability introduced by Article 1 of the Directive into liability founded on negligence on the part of the producer'.[62] This claim was rejected by the Court of Justice in the case of *European Commission v United Kingdom*.[63] The Directive's requirements relating to the defence, it was held, were:

> ...not specifically directed at the practices and safety standards in use in the industrial sector in which the product is operating, but, unreservedly, at the state of the scientific and technical knowledge, including the most advanced level of such knowledge, at the time when the product in question was put into circulation.
>
> Second, the clause providing for the defence in question does not contemplate the state of knowledge of which the producer in question actually or subjectively was or could have been appraised, but the objective state of scientific and technical knowledge of which the producer is presumed to have been informed.[64]

The only additional feature which might limit the producer's exposure would be whether knowledge of risks might be accessible to the producer. The Advocate General in his opinion cited the example of a Manchurian researcher discovering information

---

[59] Directive 85/374/EEC, Article 7(e).
[60] Section 4(1)(e).
[61] Directive 85/374/EEC.
[62] [1997] All ER (EC) 481 at 484.
[63] [1997] All ER (EC) 481.
[64] Ibid., at 494–95.

about a potential danger but where at the relevant time, the information was published only in an obscure Chinese journal.

The United Kingdom provision, it was held, also referred to objective standards. The Commission's criticisms, it was ruled:

> ... selectively stresses particular terms used in s 4(1)(e) [of the Consumer Protection Act 1987] without demonstrating that the general legal context of the provision at issue fails effectively to secure full application of the directive [Directive 85/374/EEC].[65]

The decision of the court provides useful guidance on the interpretation of the Directive.[66] It is perhaps surprising that in the ten years in which the legislation has been in force, not a single case relating to the product liability regime has reached the High Court. Given the absence of any case law on the application of the defence—indeed, no cases have been reported under any of the product liability provisions of the Consumer Protection Act 1987—any comment must be speculative. For a variety of reasons, it is suggested, the defence should have little application in respect of software defects.

Accepting that the Court of Justice's interpretation will be followed in the United Kingdom, it may further be noted that the defence refers to a particular type of defect rather than to its occurrence in a particular product. Thus, the defence will have no application in the event of failures of quality control. A producer's method of ensuring that mass-produced goods adhere to their design specifications can never be absolute, for 'the possibility remains of a rogue product and of an undiscoverable defect arising in this way'.[67] Such a producer will, knowingly, but without negligence, put into circulation defective products. The individual defects would, however, have been susceptible to discovery and the defence does not apply to defects that were foreseeable but undiscoverable in the current state of knowledge governing the principles of quality control.

Assuming that the defence will have no application in respect of the frailties of quality control systems, when may it apply? Two categories of defect might be anticipated. First, those which result from some property or characteristic of the product which was not foreseen at the time of production. An example might be found in the case of drugs whose side effects might only become apparent when they are prescribed in conjunction with other drugs, or where they are used for a long period of time. A second situation arises where the defect is foreseeable but the claim is that the technology does not permit the elimination of risk. This might typically relate to failures in a quality control system, where it could be claimed that economic considerations rendered the complete elimination of defects impracticable.

Most software defects will come within the first of the above categories. A producer must know that any software produced will possess defects. Whatever procedures

---

[65] *European Commission v United Kingdom* [1997] All ER (EC) 481 at 495.

[66] Directive 85/374/EEC.

[67] C. Newdick, 'The Development Risks Defence of the Consumer Protection Act', *Cambridge Law Journal* 47 (1988) p. 455 at 469.

and tools are used to create and validate the program, 100 per cent accuracy cannot be guaranteed. Whilst it might, of course, be argued that a drug manufacturer must realise that there is a very high probability that any drug will prompt adverse side effects in some patients, the two situations are not precisely comparable. In particular, given that software is purely a creation of the human intellect, any defects are the product of human error. Although the production of modern drugs may require a vast application of human skill and knowledge, the base building blocks are natural products. To this extent, defects are the manifestation of existing physical properties.

The onus is on the producer to establish the development risks defence. In practical terms, it would be virtually impossible to establish that nowhere had there been a warning as to possible defect. Additionally, consideration will have to be given to the weight to be attached to any piece of evidence. Scientific and technical opinions may be conflicting and contradictory. In the recent controversy concerning the supply of contaminated blood products to haemophiliacs, resulting in large numbers of persons contracting the AIDS virus, it was alleged that a scientific paper warning of the risks was rejected for publication in a scientific journal. It was further alleged that had the paper been published, screening for the virus might have been introduced and the haemophiliacs safeguarded. The case illustrates two aspects of the problems which may face the courts. First, would such a paper be regarded as forming part of the corpus of available scientific knowledge; second, as the reason for its non-publication presumably lay in a difference of opinion between experts as to the validity and relevance of the information, could a producer be expected to rely on it, or be held liable for failing so to do?

In civil cases, issues are decided on the basis of the balance of probabilities. The approach for a producer must be to produce expert witnesses who will testify to the fact that the danger was not foreseeable. As seen earlier, it will be a rare event for them to agree and the court will be faced with the task of determining which opinion it should accept.

It must be likely that software defects will fall into the second category. In most cases, the consequences of a defect will be foreseeable, the producer's argument being that current validation and verification techniques are incapable of ensuring the identification and eradication of all defects in software. Given the intangible nature of software, a producer would be unable to detect and extract defective products from the production line.

In the past, inevitable deficiencies in a quality control process have not been held to excuse the producer. In the case of *Smedleys Ltd v Breed*,[68] the House of Lords rejected an appeal by a food producer and retailer against conviction under the Food and Drugs Act 1955. Although the terminology of the 1955 Act is not precisely comparable with that of the Consumer Protection Act 1987, the issues and principles involved are sufficiently similar to justify consideration of this decision.

---

[68] [1974] AC 839.

The genesis of this case lay in the presence of a green caterpillar in a can of peas. This unadvertised ingredient proved unwelcome to the purchaser, a Mrs Voss, although it was asserted that:

> This innocent insect, thus deprived of its natural destiny, was in fact harmless, since, prior to its entry into the tin, it had been subjected to a cooking process of 22 minutes duration at 250° Fahrenheit, and, had she cared to do so, Mrs Voss could have consumed the caterpillar without injury to herself, and even, perhaps, with benefit.[69]

Under the provisions of the Food and Drugs Act 1955, a defence would be available where the presence of a foreign body was an 'unavoidable consequence of the process of collection or preparation'.[70] Evidence was led as to the firm's quality control procedures. These consisted of a mixture of mechanical checks and human inspections. The efficiency of these might be gauged from the fact that only four complaints had been received relating to an annual production of some 3.5 million cans. This statistically impressive performance availed the firm not at all. It was stated that the caterpillar could have been discovered had the inspection been targeted in its particular direction. This was considered to be the critical issue and even though it would not have been economically feasible or commercially practicable to have conducted more extensive tests, the defence was not available.[71]

The analogy with software production is clear, even though it might be argued that the software production process is not comparable with that of canning peas. Application of the principles laid down in *Smedleys*[72] will, it is submitted, render the development risks defence of little utility to software producers. Even in the event that this precedent might not be considered in point, a further argument can be advanced against the application of the defence. Software is the creation of the human intellect. It represents the ideas and aspirations of its creator. To this extent, any defects are introduced by the software developer. This position is to be contrasted with more tangible products. Although considerable amounts of human ingenuity may be involved in the development of, for example, a new drug and a cocktail of ingredients of staggering complexity may be created, the ingredients are natural substances and, although the drug may display undesired side effects, these arise from natural causes. Although the producer might be stigmatised for failing to anticipate dangers, he or she cannot be said to have created them. With software, the producer is put in the position of creator. The act of creation involves responsibility. In such a circumstance, it is submitted, the producer cannot disclaim knowledge of his or her creature's properties.

---

[69] *Smedleys Ltd v Breed* [1974] AC 839 at 845, per Lord Hailsham.

[70] Section 3(3).

[71] *Smedleys Ltd v Breed* [1974] AC 839. A similar reasoning is found in the decision of the French Court of Cassation in a case involving the supply of contaminated blood for transfusion purposes. Although the defects were considered to be undetectable, the development risk was held to be applicable only in cases where some undiscoverable external factor caused the damage. Cited in the Commission Green Paper, *Liability for Defective Products* COM (1999) 396 final, p. 23.

[72] *Smedleys Ltd v Breed* [1974] AC 839.

Conclusions

To date, there has been almost no litigation concerned directly with the non-contractual liability of software producers or suppliers. It seems unlikely that this can continue. Whilst the requirement that a claimant establish negligence may be a barrier to claims based in negligence, there appears steadily increasing recognition that software is to be regarded as a product and hence will be subject to the product liability regime. Although the limitation to situations where software causes injury or damage to non-commercial property is a significant one, the ever-expanding range of software applications must make a similar expansion in litigation a not unreasonable prospect.

Suggestions for further reading

'Product Liability, Computer Software and Insurance Issues: The St Albans and Salvage Association Cases', *C.L. & P.* 10(5) 1994, pp. 167–72.

27

Defamation and the Internet

Introduction

The notion of freedom of expression is widely recognised as a fundamental human right, the European Convention on Human Rights providing, for example, that:

1. Everyone has the right to freedom of expression. This right shall include freedom to hold opinions and to receive and impart information and ideas without interference by public authority and regardless of frontiers.[1]

As with other rights, however, the right cannot be absolute. The Convention goes on to provide that:

2. The exercise of these freedoms, since it carries with it duties and responsibilities, may be subject to such formalities, conditions, restrictions or penalties as are prescribed by law and are necessary in a democratic society, in the interests of national security, territorial integrity or public safety, for the prevention of disorder or crime, for the protection of health or morals, for the protection of the reputation or rights of others, for preventing the disclosure of information received in confidence, or for maintaining the authority and impartiality of the judiciary.

Prohibitions against the publication of pornographic or obscene materials constitute an example of a case where restrictions and penalties might be justified on the ground of the protection of morals. The law relating to defamation constitutes a further example relating to the 'protection of the rights or reputations of others'. As with national rules relating to obscenity, considerable variations exist between states. In the United States, for example, comments made concerning public figures will attract liability only if it can be shown that they were motivated by malice. This is a very difficult hurdle for any litigant to overcome. Although United Kingdom law recognises that certain forms of communication should benefit from a similar form of protection, as a general rule, no distinction is drawn between public figures and private individuals. A consequence is that statements which might be made with impunity in the United States could attract legal sanctions if published in the United Kingdom. Differences

---

[1] Article 10.

also exist between the United Kingdom and many continental legal systems. In the United Kingdom, defamation is almost entirely a matter for the civil courts, whereas in countries such as Germany it is primarily a criminal matter. Again, countries such as France offer protection under the law of privacy in the event that information about an individual's private life is brought into the public domain.

Given the ease with which material may be published on the Internet and the range of dissemination which can readily be achieved, it is little cause for surprise that issues relating to the law of defamation have assumed considerable significance. Whilst in the early days of the Internet the response of users faced with the presence of unwelcome comments or allegations was to publish a forthright rebuttal and response, increasingly today the response is to turn to the legal system and seek a remedy under the law of defamation.

A number of significant issues arise in the attempt to apply the law of defamation to Internet-related behaviour. Whilst there is seldom doubt that a party who makes a defamatory allegation is liable to legal proceedings, the reality has often been, especially in jurisdictions such as those in the United Kingdom where the legal response takes the form primarily of an award of financial compensation, that there has often been the issue of the individual concerned having limited financial assets. The tendency for those aggrieved by a publication has been to take action against some third party whose financial strength is likely to be greater than that of the individual responsible. As will be described below, the application of general principles of vicarious liability has meant that employers may be liable for the words of their employees uttered in the course of their employment. Traditionally, newspapers and broadcasting corporations have also incurred substantial exposure to the risk of legal proceedings in respect of comments made in their columns or programmes. Given that the possibility for a considerable degree of editorial control generally exists, this is not generally contentious in itself. In the emergence of the Internet, most users acquire access to its facilities through the medium of an ISP. This party may well provide facilities for hosting web pages. As will be discussed, the question has arisen as to what extent an ISP will be classed as equivalent to traditional media publishers and broadcasters for the purposes of the law of defamation.

In addition to issues of substantive law, the global reach of the Internet poses significant jurisdictional challenges. In the era of the printed word, the vast majority of a newspaper's circulation would be restricted to its country and jurisdiction of publication.[2] Similarly, most television and radio broadcasts have been received only in one national territory—although satellite broadcasting is changing this situation. With the Internet, the place of publication becomes a matter of little practical significance so that it is as easy for a United Kingdom-based browser to view the web version of the *New York Times* as its London equivalent. Questions of where and when a defamatory comment is published have assumed considerable importance.

---

[2] The existence of separate legal systems in Scotland and England has posed some difficulties in the past in respect of the law of defamation.

The nature of defamation

The term 'defamation' tends to be used as a generic descriptor for actions in which it is alleged that the making of untrue and unwarranted comments about an individual have tended to lower that person's standing in the eyes of right-thinking members of society. The question of what sorts of comments would produce this effect is not easy to answer and will vary with changing social attitudes. Until the Second World War, it was not considered defamatory to accuse someone of being anti-Semitic. The term 'computer hacker' was originally used to describe someone who was particularly skilled in operating computers and finding solutions to problems. In this context, the phrase could not be considered defamatory. Today, of course, the generally accepted meaning has changed and the accusation that someone is a computer hacker might have legal consequences.

In English law, a distinction exists between libel and slander. The law of libel applies to comments which are recorded in some permanent form—in print or on tape, whilst slander is reserved for comments which are more transient in nature. In general, the law of libel operates on a stricter basis than that of slander, based in part on the assessment that statements which are recorded are likely to be more damaging to the subject than those which are not. Developments in recording and broadcasting technology have served to blur both the distinction between libel and slander and the rationale for distinct treatment. A statement on a live television broadcast might be heard by tens of millions of viewers and be far more damaging to the reputation of the subject than would be the case with a letter published in a local newspaper. In the case of broadcasting, the Defamation Act 1952 provided that the law of libel was to apply in respect of any statements made.

In the case of email and the contents of the Internet and WWW, it seems beyond question that there is a sufficient degree of recording to ensure that the law of libel will apply. Some doubt remains, perhaps, concerning the status of services such as chat rooms, where the atmosphere at least is closer to a conversational forum and where no permanent record is maintained. In cases of slander a defence is available, commonly referred to as 'vulgar abuse'. The essence is that statements were made in the heat of an argument. The essence of the defence is that words, albeit defamatory in content, were neither intended as such nor would be so regarded by anyone listening to the exchange. Such a defence might seem appropriate in relation to many postings to Internet newsgroups, where the concept of the flame war is well established. Anyone perusing computer newsgroups will be aware that forthright expression is often the order of the day and that 'flame wars' in which discussion is reduced to a level of personal abuse, are not uncommon. One newsgroup, 'alt.flame', even specialises in this topic. Although the existence of a culture encouraging robust and blunt debate cannot affect the determination of whether a message is defamatory, there may be an element of consent on the part of those participating in such fora. With newsgroups, although there would seem no doubt that postings are written and the range of dissemination is comparable (perhaps even wider) than that associated with the written word, the attitudes and practices coupled with the speed of communication are perhaps more akin to the spoken word.

Communication

In order to be actionable, it is necessary that a statement be communicated to at least one person other than the subject. The range of dissemination need not be wide. A letter or email to a third party will suffice, as would posting a comment on a public noticeboard. Indeed, in terms of impact on an individual, a letter to an employer making false and defamatory comments might have far more serious consequences than a communication accessible to a wider audience. The Internet provides a superbly effective communications medium. Email permits cheap and swift communications of messages between individuals, whilst newsgroups allow anyone to express views on almost any topic under the sun and the WWW permits individuals to establish themselves as electronic publishers. Given the volume and variety of traffic carried by the Internet, it would be a source of considerable surprise were its contents to be free of defamatory comments. The essence of defamation is that a statement is published which is both inaccurate and likely to have the effect of lowering the standing of its subject in the eyes of right-thinking members of society.

Who is liable for defamatory comments?

Liability of the poster

There is no doubt that a person making a defamatory comment will incur liability. It has, for example, been reported that a student has been warned by the office of a government minister that postings to a politics newsgroup were considered to be defamatory, although no legal proceedings followed.[3] In addition to cases concerning the liability of service operators, which will be discussed below, in the United States, a journalist has reportedly faced a legal bill in excess of $25,000 after settling a libel suit resulting from a posting which he made on the Internet.[4]

Although it may be stated that the poster of a defamatory message runs the risk of legal action, the task of identifying the party responsible may not be an easy one. Even if a message appears to originate from a particular individual, it may be necessary to establish that it is genuine. In the United States case of *Stratton Oakmont v Prodigy*,[5] a message appeared to have been sent from a particular user's account. The user, however, denied that the message had been sent by him or from his equipment. In the particular case, the issue was not of great significance as the action proceeded against the service provider, who, it appears, had always been the major target of the litigation. In other cases, it may be necessary for a claimant to establish that a message was sent

---

[3] *The Times*, 3 July 1995.
[4] *The Quill*, October 1994.
[5] (1995) 195 NY Misc LEXIS 229.

by the party whose identifiers appear. It appears that it is possible for a user's identity to be impersonated. Instances have been reported of forged email messages purporting to have originated from the White House. Another technical facility which may complicate any legal proceedings is the use of anonymous remailing services. These services, which may be based anywhere in the world, accept messages from users, strip out the details of the original poster and forward them to the addressee, with no indication of the identity of the original poster. Such a technique makes it impossible to identify the author without the cooperation of the operator of the remailing service. Such cooperation may not readily be forthcoming, and considerable controversy surrounded attempts by the Church of Scientology to discover the identity of a user who posted documents relating to the organisation, allegedly in breach of copyright. On this occasion, the remailing service involved was based in Finland.[6]

Even in the event that a service provider does not actively refuse to cooperate with a complainant, legal complexities may arise. The decision of the Court of Appeal in the case of *Totalise v Motley Fool Ltd*[7] raises a number of interesting issues concerning the interaction between the requirements of data protection and other elements of law. Interactive Investor operated a business providing financial information to individual investors. The information was made available via a website. Included on the website was a bulleting board facility allowing users to post views and comments.

In order to access the website, users had to register and indicate acceptance of the operator's terms and conditions. These contained a data protection notice to the effect that the provider was:

> registered under the Data Protection Act 1998. All personal information you supply to us will be treated in accordance with that Act. We will collect and use your personal information in order to operate, enhance and provide to you the Information Services you request.
>
> We will not pass your personal information on to any other person except to our Service Providers, where it is necessary, to enable us to provide you with the Information Services you request from us.

One user, operating under the pseudonym 'Zeddust' posted comments which were defamatory of the claimant company. The claimant company complained to Interactive, who removed the posting and suspended the user. Totalise then requested provision of information identifying the poster in order that it might initiate proceedings for defamation. This was refused by Interactive, who stated that the supply of personal data would place it in breach of its terms and conditions and also of the requirements of the Data Protection Act 1998.

Totalise instituted proceedings seeking a court order requiring disclosure of the data. This was granted by a High Court judge, who also made an order holding Interactive liable for the costs incurred by Totalise. An appeal was made on the issue of costs, the key question being whether Interactive had acted unreasonably in refusing

---

[6] *Independent*, 4 March 1995.
[7] [2001] EWCA Civ 1897, [2002] 1 WLR 1233.

to hand over the data without subjecting Totalise to the expense of obtaining a court order (costs were assessed at just under £5,000).[8]

The Court of Appeal held that the behaviour was not unreasonable. The issues involved, it was ruled, were complex, especially with the addition of the Human Rights Act 1998 to the United Kingdom statute book. A balance had to be struck between the interests of the claimant in being able to secure a remedy and the right of the individual to respect for private life. Such a task was one for the courts and, it was held:

> It is difficult to see how the court can carry out this task if what it is refereeing is a contest between two parties, neither of whom is the person most concerned, the data subject; one of whom is the data subject's prospective antagonist; and the other of whom knows the data subject's identity, has undertaken to keep it confidential so far as the law permits, and would like to get out of the cross-fire as rapidly and as cheaply as possible. However the website operator can, where appropriate, tell the user what is going on and to offer to pass on in writing to the claimant and the court any worthwhile reason the user wants to put forward for not having his or her identity disclosed. Further, the Court could require that to be done before making an order. Doing so will enable the court to do what is required of it with slightly more confidence that it is respecting the law laid down in more than one statute by Parliament and doing no injustice to a third party, in particular not violating his convention rights.[9]

It is important to keep in mind that there was no appeal against the initial ruling that in this case the identifying data should be handed over to the claimant. The decision, therefore, gives no sort of green light for the posting of defamatory comments under the shield of anonymity. It does, however, provide welcome recognition of the fact that privacy issues are important and are not to be discarded lightly in the face of competing claims.

Employer's liability

As more and more companies make use of email as a method of communication between staff, so there will be increasing exposure to action on the basis of vicarious liability in respect of the use or misuse made of the communications network. In 1997, the Norwich Union insurance company reached a settlement in a libel action brought by a health insurance company, Western Provident Association. Under the terms of the agreement, Norwich Union agreed to pay £450,000 in damages and costs in respect of libellous messages concerning the association's financial stability which had been contained in email messages exchanged between members of the Norwich Union's staff.[10]

The fact that a settlement was reached prior to trial means that the case is of no value as a legal precedent. The lesson for those engaging in email discussions is obvious: that although communications may be approached as a form of conversation, everything is recorded almost without limit of time and can be retrieved at a later date. A similar example of this phenomenon can be seen in the discovery of internal Microsoft

---

[8] *Totalise v Motley Fool Ltd* [2001] EWCA Civ 1897, [2002] 1 WLR 1233.
[9] Ibid., at [26].
[10] *The Times*, 18 July 1997.

emails during the legal investigations into their commercial practices conducted by the United States Department of Justice. One significant factor limiting the extent of liability for defamatory communications made by employees may be that the vicarious liability applies only in respect of acts committed in the course of employment. In the Norwich Union case, the communications were clearly work-related but it is unlikely that an employer would be held liable in the event, for example, that employees used email facilities to exchange defamatory comments on subjects unconnected with work. To minimise the risks of liability, it would be advisable for employers to indicate clearly in contracts of employment or staff handbooks what uses may or may not be made of electronic communications.

Faced with concern at their potential liabilities for misuse of electronic communications, it is commonplace for employers to monitor use of the facilities. In the United States, a number of actions have been reported of corporations being sued 'for millions of dollars' by employees alleging that fellow workers have been engaging in some form of electronic harassment involving the posting of abusive or offensive messages.[11]

Faced with such exposure, employers may well be tempted to use packages to monitor email communications within the workplace. One such package, it is reported:

> ...system may be programmed to suit the offensiveness threshold of each particular firm. Thus it might be that a message between two secretaries that contained the words 'sex' or 'black'—or something profane—would immediately appear on their boss's computer screen for inspection.[12]

Under present United Kingdom law, it would appear that use of such a system would not be unlawful. Although the provisions of the Interception of Communications Act 1985 will govern the interception of email messages passing through a public telecommunications network, this statute does not apply to private networks. In the case of *Halford v United Kingdom*,[13] however, the European Court of Human Rights held that the Convention's requirements relating to protection of privacy had been breached where telephone calls made from work premises by a senior police officer had been 'bugged' on the authority of her Chief Constable. Argument on behalf of the United Kingdom to the effect that the telephones in question belonged to the employer, in this case the government, did not sway the court. It would appear that any monitoring of email might be challenged on this basis, although it is not clear whether the giving of notice to employees that phone calls or email messages might be monitored would remove their 'reasonable expectation' of privacy in their communications.

Liability of ISPs

With the exception of the issue of whether a defence should be available for those who post defamatory messages in the heat of a flame war, there can be little dispute that the

---

[11] *Independent*, 20 July 1997.
[12] Ibid.
[13] [1997] IRLR 471.

author of such a posting should face the legal consequences. More controversial is the question of how far the operators of an online service should incur liabilities akin to those of traditional publishers in respect of messages appearing on their systems.

The first United Kingdom case to reach the stage of High Court proceedings was that of *Godfrey v Demon*.[14] Although the case was settled prior to a full trial, preliminary hearings have raised a number of interesting and potentially significant issues concerned with the extent of an Internet Service Provider's liability for defamatory postings carried on its services.

The plaintiff, Dr Laurence Godfrey, was a United Kingdom-based lecturer in computer science, mathematics, and physics. He appeared to be a keen poster to Usenet, with reference being made in the court proceedings to a posting record of more than 3,000 messages. A number of Dr Godfrey's postings, it was suggested by the defendant at a later stage in proceedings, were intended to provoke a violent response from other posters. As was stated in the judgment:

> The words complained of were posted to a newsgroup. Newsgroup users have come to abide by an informal code of conduct known as 'netiquette', which is intended to introduce an element of restraint and moderation with regard to the content of postings. Those who persist in breaching netiquette are almost invariably exposed to irate (and sometimes offensive or aggressive) postings from aggrieved users: this practice is known as 'flaming'. As a regular newsgroup user, it is to be inferred that the Plaintiff would at all material times have known of the foregoing facts and matters.[15]

Rather than perpetuating a flame war, Dr Godfrey had, on at least seven occasions, instituted proceedings against both posters and ISPs alleging that comments defamed him. The defence alleged that:

> ...the Plaintiff has cynically pursued the tactic of posting deliberately provocative, offensive, obnoxious and frequently puerile comments about other countries, their citizens and cultures; and has done so with a view to provoking others to trade insults which he can then claim are defamatory and seek to use as the basis for bringing vexatious libel actions against them and against access or service providers such as the Defendant.[16]

The conduct at issue in the *Demon* case[17] was slightly different. A message purporting to come from Dr Godfrey had appeared in the Newsgroup 'soc.culture.thai'. The message was a forgery, and in its tone and content was described by the judge as being 'squalid, obscene and defamatory of the plaintiff'. The basis for the defamation would lie in the argument that the plaintiff's standing in the eyes of right-thinking members of society would be damaged if it was thought that he held the views attributed to him in the email. The defendant, Demon, is a well-known ISP. Messages in 'soc.culture.

---

[14] [1999] EMLR 542.
[15] *Godfrey v Demon* 1999 WL 33285490 at para. 7.
[16] Ibid.
[17] *Godfrey v Demon* [1999] EMLR 542.

thai' could be accessed by its subscribers, the postings being held on Demon's servers for around fourteen days.

The posting at issue, which originated in the United States, appeared in the newsgroup on 13 January 1997. On 17 January, Dr Godfrey faxed the defendant's managing director with the demand that the posting be removed from Demon's servers. It was accepted by both sides that this could have been done. Although Demon acknowledged that the fax had been received, it appeared that it never reached its managing director's desk and the message remained on its site until routinely deleted after a fortnight. The plaintiff subsequently brought proceedings seeking damages in respect of the damage to his reputation caused by the defendant's actions. The defendant denied liability on two grounds. First, it was argued, its conduct was covered by the defence of innocent dissemination established under the Defamation Act 1996. Second, it was denied that there had been any publication of the comment by it. The plaintiff brought action before Moreland J in the High Court, seeking as a preliminary step to strike out these defences as invalid.[18]

The Defamation Act 1996 was enacted in an attempt to update the law relating to defamation. It followed a study conducted by the Law Commission which recommended the introduction of a new defence of 'innocent dissemination'. The Act accordingly provides that:

1. In defamation proceedings a person has a defence if he shows that—

    (a) he was not the author, editor or publisher of the statement complained of;

    (b) he took reasonable care in relation to its publication; and

    (c) he did not know, and had no reason to believe, that what he did caused or contributed to the publication of a defamatory statement.[19]

It is further provided that:

In determining for the purposes of this section of whether a person took reasonable care, or had reason to believe that what he did caused or contributed to the publication of a defamatory statement, regard shall be had to—

(a) the extent of his responsibility for the content of the statement or the decision to publish it;

(b) the nature or circumstances of the publication; and

(c) the previous conduct or character of the author, editor or publisher.

The section proceeds to define the terms 'author', 'editor' and 'publisher'. It is important to note that these definitions apply only for the purposes of the section. A publisher is defined as:

...a commercial publisher, that is, a person whose business is issuing material to the public, or a section of the public, who issues material containing the statement in the course of that business.[20]

---

[18] Ibid.
[19] Section 1.
[20] Defamation Act 1996, s 1(2).

It is further provided that for the purposes of the section a person will not be classed as an author, editor, or publisher if the involvement with the work is 'only' in specified capacities. The relevant categories relate to involvement:

(a) in printing, producing, distributing or selling printed material containing the statement;

(b) in processing, making copies of, distributing or selling any electronic medium in or on which the statement is recorded, or in operating or providing any equipment, system or service by means of which the statement is retrieved, copied, distributed or made available in electronic form; or

(c) as the operator or provider of access to a communications system by means of which the statement is transmitted or made available, by a person over whom he had no effective control.[21]

It was held by Moreland J that Demon was not to be considered as acting as a publisher in respect of the postings and therefore satisfied the first requirement of the defence.[22] The provisions, however, were cumulative, with Demon also being required to demonstrate that they had taken reasonable care and were unaware of the fact that their actions had caused the publication of a defamatory comment. From the Recital of the facts presented above, it is clear that these elements constituted a much more substantial hurdle, and it is perhaps not surprising that the court held that the defence could not be sustained. The defamation action related only to the period after 17 January 1997, when the plaintiff's fax arrived and, as the defendant had taken no action to examine the matter, it was not in a position to demonstrate that reasonable care had been taken.

The judge's finding[23] appears in line with the provisions of the Defamation Act 1996 and with the Law Commission's recommendation. In its Consultation Paper, the Law Commission had suggested:

> The defence of innocent dissemination has never provided an absolute immunity for distributors, however mechanical their contribution. It does not protect those who knew that the material they were handling was defamatory, or who ought to have known of its nature. Those safeguards are preserved, so that the defence is not available to a defendant who knew that his act involved or contributed to publication defamatory of the plaintiff. It is available only if, having taken all reasonable care, the defendant had no reason to suspect that his act had that effect.[24]

The fact that a faxed message of complaint attracted no response of any sort makes it difficult to see how Demon could have availed themselves of the defence of innocent dissemination. The more interesting and controversial question might relate to what

---

[21] Section 1(3).

[22] *Godfrey v Demon* [1999] EMLR 542.

[23] Ibid.

[24] Law Commission, 'Reforming Defamation Law and Procedure', (1995), para. 2.4.

could have been expected of the defendants if their administrative procedures had been more effective. It is clear from the calendar of events described above that the case concerned a period of about ten days. There would have been limited opportunity for the defendant to undertake in-depth inquiries. As noted above, the offending message entered the Internet via a United States-based ISP. Without the active cooperation of this party, there may well have been little that the defendant could do to verify the true identity of the sender: even with cooperation, with the proliferation of ISPs offering free access to the Internet with a minimum of registration procedures which could themselves be falsified with minimal effort. Given the timescale and the technical constraints identified, it would appear that an ISP in receipt of a complaint regarding a posting would have little choice other than between doing nothing and removing the posting from its servers. The first action obviously carries the risk of an action for defamation, but the automatic removal of messages upon receipt of a complaint is something which carries its own problems and dangers.

It would appear that following the decision, a number of ISPs have adopted a policy of automatically withdrawing access to material in respect of which any form of complaint has been received. One case reported by the Campaign Against Censorship of the Internet appeared to go even further:

> Outcast magazine hadn't even done anything wrong: the solicitors alleged that Outcast might commit a libel at some unspecified time in the future, and that if they did, they would hold Netbenefit responsible. The ISP demanded a lawyer's guarantee against any such future wrongdoing, and when Outcast was unable to provide it within 3 hours, deleted the entire web site.[25]

To an extent, the nature of the Internet may provide such organisations with a means of self-help. The Campaign Against Internet Censorship found its site evicted from its United Kingdom-based ISP following a complaint from Dr Godfrey regarding its account of the Demon litigation. It is, however, a comparatively simple matter for an organisation put in such a position to find an alternative ISP; in the case of the Campaign Against Internet Censorship, one based in the United States.

Although Demon was not classed as a publisher for the purpose of the defence of innocent dissemination, the definitions discussed above apply only to this defence. The issue also arose of whether Demon might be classed as a publisher under the general law of defamation. Once again, the court found against the company.[26] Reference was made to a number of authorities, the most relevant being the case of *Byrne v Deane*,[27] where the directors of a golf club were held liable as publishers in respect of a defamatory message placed by a third party on a noticeboard in the club. Here, the court held that:

> It is said that as a general proposition where the act of the person alleged to have published a libel has not been any positive act, but has merely been the refraining from

[25] <http://test.liberty.org.uk/cacib/>
[26] *Godfrey v Demon* [1999] EMLR 542.
[27] [1937] 1 KB 818.

doing some act, he cannot be guilty of publication. I am quite unable to accept any such general proposition. It may very well be that in some circumstances a person, by refraining from removing or obliterating the defamatory matter, is not committing any publication at all. In other circumstances he may be doing so. The test it appears to me is this: having regard to all the facts of the case[,] is the proper inference that by not removing the defamatory matter the defendant really made himself responsible for its continued presence in the place where it had been put?[28]

In the present case, the conclusion was reached that:

In my judgment the Defendants, whenever they transmit and whenever there is transmitted from the storage of their news server a defamatory posting, publish that posting to any subscriber to their ISP who accesses the newsgroup containing that posting. Thus every time one of the Defendants' customers accesses ['soc.culture.thai'] and sees that posting defamatory of the Plaintiff there is a publication to that customer.

I do not accept [the] argument that the Defendants were merely owners of an electronic device through which postings were transmitted. The Defendants chose to store 'soc.culture.thai' postings within their computer. Such postings could be accessed on that newsgroup. The Defendants could obliterate and indeed did so about a fortnight after receipt.[29]

Following the striking out of its defence in March 1999, it is difficult to identify what ground Demon might have had for opposing the plaintiff's claim. The case did return to the court in the following month, when Demon sought leave to introduce evidence of the defendant's activities on the Internet which, it was claimed, demonstrated a history of postings whose nature appeared calculated to produce an intemperate response. Although permission was granted, this material could only have been relevant to the assessment of damages. It would also appear that at least some of the allegations made were unsubstantiated. In the event, a settlement was reached shortly before the case was scheduled to proceed to trial in Spring 2000. The terms of the settlement saw Demon making a payment to the plaintiff of some £250,000. Although this headline figure attracted a great deal of publicity, less publicised was the fact that all bar £15,000 represented the plaintiff's legal costs.

ISPs and the Electronic Commerce Directive

Although it has not been the subject of litigation, provisions of the European Directive on Electronic Commerce[30] may provide some protection for ISPs. It provides in Article 12 that:

1. Where an Information Society service is provided that consists of the transmission in a communication network of information provided by the recipient of the service, or

---

[28] [1937] 1 KB 818 at 837.

[29] *Godfrey v Demon* [1999] EMLR 542 at 550.

[30] Directive 2000/31/EC.

the provision of access to a communication network, Member States shall provide in their legislation that the provider of such a service shall not be liable, otherwise than under a prohibitory injunction, for the information transmitted, on condition that the provider:

(a) does not initiate the transmission;

(b) does not select the receiver of the transmission; and

(c) does not select or modify the information contained in the transmission.

2. The acts of transmission and of provision of access referred to in paragraph 1 include the automatic, intermediate and transient storage of the information transmitted in so far as this takes place for the sole purpose of carrying out the transmission in the communication network, and provided that the information is not stored for any period longer than is reasonably necessary for the transmission.

Article 15 provides further that:

Member States shall not impose a general obligation on providers, when providing the services covered by Articles 12 to 14, to monitor the information which they transmit or store, nor a general obligation actively to seek facts or circumstances indicating illegal activity.

Implementing these provisions, the Electronic Commerce (EC Directive) Regulations 2002[31] provide that:

19. Where an information society service is provided which consists of the storage of information provided by a recipient of the service, the service provider (if he otherwise would) shall not be liable for damages or for any other pecuniary remedy or for any criminal sanction as a result of that storage where—

(a) the service provider—

(i) does not have actual knowledge of unlawful activity or information and, where a claim for damages is made, is not aware of facts or circumstances from which it would have been apparent to the service provider that the activity or information was unlawful; or

(ii) upon obtaining such knowledge or awareness, acts expeditiously to remove or to disable access to the information, and

(b) the recipient of the service was not acting under the authority or the control of the service provider.

The scope of protection extended under the provision is somewhat uncertain. In a scoping report on the law of defamation published in 2002,[32] the Law Commission comment:

There has been some debate on how far this test differs from the test under section 1 of the Defamation Act 1996. One view is that article 14 [of Directive 2000/31/EC] mirrors

[31] SI 2002/2013.
[32] CP5 (Special) Scoping Study No. 2.

section 1 by providing that once an ISP is aware that material is defamatory and fails to act, the protection is lost. The other view is that it may provide wider protection: it is not enough for the ISP merely to know that the material is defamatory. They would also need to know that it was 'illegal' (or at least be aware of facts and circumstances from which the illegal activity was apparent). On this basis, the ISP would need to know that the material was not only defamatory but also libellous (i.e. that the potential defences of justification, fair comment or privilege were not available).[33]

The Commission's conclusion was to the effect that:

> In order to resolve this question, one needs to ask what constitutes an 'unlawful activity' in defamation law. Under current English law, it is *prima facie* unlawful to publish a defamatory statement that refers to the claimant (though in some circumstances it may be open to a defendant to prove a defence, such as truth). On this basis, it would seem that an ISP has 'actual knowledge of unlawful activity' as soon as they become aware that a publication has taken place that would make reasonable people think less well of a third party. The provider does not need to be aware that the material is false.[34]

It seems doubtful that the Electronic Commerce Directive[35] and the Regulations[36] significantly clarify the previously uncertain state of the law and, as indicated above, it appears that most ISPs adopt a 'safety first' policy whereby information is withdrawn. Whilst understandable, such a response and situation is not desirable and clarification of this area of the law would be beneficial.

Single or multiple publications?

With many traditional works, ascertaining the date of publication is a relatively straightforward matter. Different factors may apply in the case of online resources, as was at issue in the case of *Loutchansky v Times Newspapers Ltd*.[37] Here, the claimant sued the defendant newspaper in respect of a number of stories which suggested that he was linked to organised crime in Russia. In common with most other newspapers *The Times* publishes an 'online' edition with the added capability for readers to search an archive of previous editions. The stories relating to Mr Loutchansky appeared on the online edition.

Actions for defamation require to be commenced within one year of the publication of the material complained of.[38] The action relating to the online publication was not raised within a year of the initial publication but it was argued on behalf of the claimant that publication in the context of an online work occurred anew each time the material was accessed by a reader. This argument was accepted by the trial judge and endorsed by the Court of Appeal. By way of contrast, the courts in the United States

---

[33] At para. 2.18.
[34] Para. 2.22.
[35] Directive 2000/31/EC.
[36] SI 2002/2013.
[37] [2001] EWCA Civ 1805, [2002] QB 783.
[38] Limitation Act 1980, s 4A.

apply what is referred to as the 'single publication' rule. The basis of this was explained in the case of *Ogden v Association of the United States Army*:

> it is the prevailing American doctrine that the publication of a book, periodical or newspaper containing defamatory matter gives rise to but one cause of action for libel, which accrues at the time of the original publication, and that the statute of limitations runs from that date. It is no longer the law that every sale or delivery of a copy of the publication creates a new cause of action.[39]

Counsel for the newspaper did not seek to argue that its case was sustainable under the established United Kingdom position but sought to persuade the Court of Appeal that it should adopt the single publication rule on the basis that the emergence of the Internet and the wide and long-lasting possibilities for accessing material raised the possibility of an excessive degree of liability for defamatory material. The ongoing nature of the liability, which would begin again whenever someone downloaded material, would, it was claimed, render meaningless the provisions of the Limitations Act 1980,[40] which require that legal proceedings be brought within a year from the date of publication. The availability of Internet-based databases of the contents of newspapers and magazines, it was argued, provided a valuable social function and the law of defamation should evolve to meet the needs of the Internet age. Reference was made to the European Convention of Human Rights, which in Article 8 guarantees the right to freedom of expression. The presence of a perpetual threat of defamatory actions would, it was argued, deter exercise of the right to an unreasonable extent.[41]

The Court of Appeal was not convinced, whilst accepting the argument that the maintenance of archives performed a valuable role, this was a relatively insignificant aspect of the right of freedom of expression:

> Archive material is stale news and its publication cannot rank in importance with the dissemination of contemporary material. Nor do we believe that the law of defamation need inhibit the responsible maintenance of archives. Where it is known that archive material is or may be defamatory, the attachment of an appropriate notice warning against treating it as the truth will normally remove any sting from the material.

It is certainly difficult to defend the deliberate retention on a database of material which is known to be defamatory. The situation is more complex where its status is unclear, especially, perhaps, in a situation where a challenge is made to the accuracy of a report several years after the date of original publication.

The defendants' argument for an evolutionary change in the nature of defamatory liability received rather perfunctory treatment, the court concluding to the effect that:

> The change in the law of defamation for which the appellants contend is a radical one. In our judgment they have failed to make out their case that such a change is required.[42]

---

[39] (1959) 177 Supp. 498 at 502.

[40] Section 4A.

[41] [2001] EWCA Civ 1805 at [71].

[42] *Loutchansky v Times Newspapers Ltd* [2001] EWCA Civ 1805, [2002] QB 783 at [74]–[76].

Further and more extensive discussion regarding the desirability of adopting a 'single publication' rule took place in the Australian case of *Dow Jones & Co Inc v Gutnick*.[43] Here, a story had appeared in the appellant's journal and website which was allegedly defamatory of the defendant. Proceedings were raised in the Australian courts. The appellants sought to have these struck out on the basis that publication had occurred when the material was loaded onto its servers in New Jersey in the United States. The Australian courts, it argued, were not therefore, the most appropriate forum for the action.

Once again, the defendant sought to persuade the court to change traditional practice. The argument was addressed with some sympathy by Mr Justice Kirby. In the course of a judgment which is replete with useful information and comment regarding the impact of the Internet on legal rules he stated that:

> The idea that this Court should solve the present problem by reference to judicial remarks in England in a case, decided more than a hundred and fifty years ago, involving the conduct of the manservant of a Duke, despatched to procure a back issue of a newspaper of minuscule circulation, is not immediately appealing to me. The genius of the common law derives from its capacity to adapt the principles of past decisions, by analogical reasoning, to the resolution of entirely new and unforeseen problems. When the new problem is as novel, complex and global as that presented by the Internet in this appeal, a greater sense of legal imagination may be required than is ordinarily called for. Yet the question remains whether it can be provided, conformably with established law and with the limited functions of a court under the Australian constitution to develop and re-express the law.[44]

Although he recognised that trenchant criticisms could be made of the existing state of the law he concluded, in line with the remainder of the High Court of Australia, that change of the nature and extent required was properly a matter for the legislature rather than the courts. Echoing comments of the Canadian Supreme Court in the case of *R v Stewart*,[45] he concluded:

> It would exceed the judicial function to re-express the common law on such a subject in such ways. This is a subject of law reform requiring the evaluation of many interests and considerations that a court could not be sure to cover.[46]

Conclusions

The English law of defamation is generally regarded as being considerably stricter than that applying in most other jurisdictions. Assuming the necessary connection with the jurisdiction can be established by a claimant, the general rule applied by the courts

---

43 [2002] HCA 56, Aus HC.
44 *Dow Jones & Co Inc v Gutnick* [2002] HCA 56 at 92.
45 50 DLR (4th) 1.
46 [2002] HCA 56 at 138.

to jurisdictional issues was described by Lord Goff in the case of *Spiliada Maritime Corpn v Consulex Ltd*,[47] in the following terms:

> The basic principle is that a stay will only be granted on the ground of *forum non conveniens* where the court is satisfied that there is some other available forum, having competent jurisdiction, which is the appropriate forum for the trial of the action, i.e. in which the case may be tried more suitably for the interests of all the parties and the ends of justice.

Although there will often be considerable practical difficulties in pursuing and enforcing an action against a foreign-based party, the suggestion has been made by one lawyer that:

> Plaintiffs will be able to choose countries with repressive libel laws, like Britain. Anyone with an international reputation will sue here, because, relatively speaking, it's like falling off a log.[48]

Pending reform of the United Kingdom's defamation laws, this may indeed be the case but, as with so many aspects of the topic, we are once again brought to the realisation that national boundaries may be of little effect in the era of the global information infrastructure. As always, however, there may be a significant gap between an individual considering himself or herself to be the victim of defamation finding a claimant-friendly jurisdiction and securing enforcement of any award made in other jurisdictions. It may be considered unlikely, for example, that a United States court would enforce an award of damages made against a United States citizen by an English court in respect of a defamatory comment posted on the Internet from the United States. In the case of *Telnikoff v Matusevitch*,[49] the claimant had obtained an award of damages in the English courts following publication of a newspaper article deemed to be defamatory. He took action to enforce the award in the United States, only for the Court of Appeals for the District of Columbia to rule that the 'cause of action on which the judgment is based is repugnant to the public policy of the State' and it refused to order its enforcement.

Suggestions for further reading

'The Internet: Some Important Legal Issues',
   C.T.L.R. 1(2) (1995), pp. 35–7.

[47] [1987] AC 460 at 476.
[48] *Guardian*, 25 April 1995.
[49] 702 A 2d 230 (1997).

Index